Tool-Based Requirement Traceability between Requirement and Design Artifacts

T0188840

Bernhard Turban

Tool-Based Requirement Traceability between Requirement and Design Artifacts

Foreword by Prof. Dr. Christian Wolff

Bernhard Turban
Nabburg, Germany

Turban, Bernhard: Tool-Based Requirements Traceability between Requirement and Design Artifacts for Safety-Critical Systems
Zugl.: Regensburg, Univ., Diss., 2011

This work was accepted as a Ph. D. dissertation thesis by the Faculty of Languages, Literature and Cultural Studies of the University of Regensburg in 2011.

D 355

ISBN 978-3-8348-2473-8　　　　　　ISBN 978-3-8348-2474-5 (eBook)
DOI 10.1007/978-3-8348-2474-5

The Deutsche Nationalbibliothek lists this publication in the Deutsche Nationalbibliografie; detailed bibliographic data are available in the Internet at http://dnb.d-nb.de.

Library of Congress Control Number: 2013933878

Springer Vieweg
© Springer Fachmedien Wiesbaden 2013

Printed on acid-free paper

Springer Vieweg is a brand of Springer DE.
Springer DE is part of Springer Science+Business Media.
www.springer-vieweg.de

While the discerning layman understands that
in the design of large constructions,
a new town or an airport, the problems are overwhelming,
he probably does not realise so clearly
that there are problems just as pressing
and difficult for the designer
in the design of almost any trivial product.
A bad town will do more harm than a bad toothbrush
but the designer of either will experience his job
as the necessity to make a series of decisions
between alternative courses of action,
each affecting the decisions which come after it;
and if no life hangs on the outcome
of the series of decisions about the toothbrush,
the livelihood of several people does.
David Pye [Py78; p.75]

Foreword

What is the way design decisions are made in Software design and implementation? What is the relationship between a software artifact and customer requirements? What are the reasons, what is the rationale for a specific technical solution? How should design decisions be documented? These are only some of the questions which Bernhard Turban tackles in his dissertation on *Tool-Based Requirements Traceability*.

One of the major merits of this book is the successful bridging from design theories to practical tool design for embedded real-time software: Bernhard Turban actually puts design theory to work, in a way from which software designers and engineers may directly benefit. At the same time, this effort is firmly rooted in current software engineering standards like SPICE (Software Process Improvement and Capability Determination, ISO/IEC 15 504).

Tackling the documentation needs for software design decisions by implementing a tool using a specific algorithm or forwarding these decisions shows the authors inventiveness: For a problem many software engineers are constantly confronted with, this solution provides an innovative solution. At the same time, this approach generates traceability-relevant information.

In addition, the author does not only present a plausible and functional algorithm for documenting design decisions across different levels of the development process, he also realizes a complex interactive interface tool which seamlessly adds to the functionality of modeling tools. Based on this work, a commercial software development tool was created.

This work was developed not in an academic context, but in an industrial setting within a group of software engineers working in the domain of automotive embedded real-time systems. Thus, the author can draw all examples for his work from immediate observations in the development projects he was working on. This adds to the credibility of the work presented here, and I am sure that both academia as well as industrial software design can learn a good deal lot from Bernhard Turban's work.

With the complexity of software projects still rising, the demand for better documentation and traceability will grow beyond typical fields like the engineering of embedded systems. Therefore, it is to be hoped for that many software projects will benefit from Bernhard Turban's theoretical approach towards design decisions as well as from the tool solutions he has created.

Prof. Dr. Christian Wolff

Acknowledgements

This work would not have been accomplished without the support of so many people. I would like to thank them all for their support.

University of Regensburg
To begin with, I would like to thank my supervisors at the University of Regensburg Professor Dr. Christian Wolff and Professor Dr. Rainer Hammwöhner for their constant support. I specially thank them for giving me the chance to write this thesis.

University of Applied Sciences in Regensburg
Particularly, I would like to thank Professor Dr. Athanassios Tsakpinis from the University of Applied Sciences Regensburg and director of the Competence Center for Software Engineering. Without his very significant support the results described here might not have been accomplishable.

I further want to thank Professor Dr. Markus Kucera and Professor Dr. Bernhard Kulla for their advice and support.

Former Micron Electronic Devices AG
Further, I would like to thank Peter Schiekofer and Jörg Aschenbrenner for giving me a chance to perform my doctor's thesis with the Micron Electronic Devices AG and specially thank them for their open-mindedness to the vague ideas I first sketched to them seeing the innovative potential within the ideas.

Mercedes Benz technology (MBtech)
At the MBtech Group, I would like to thank Dr. Nico Hartmann for giving the R2A-project a home, after the integration of Micron Electronic Devices AG.

The PROVEtech:R2A development team
I also would like to thank the R2A development team for their good work and enthusiasm.

My Editors
I also want to thank Florian Weiss and my brother Andreas Turban for cross-reading my thesis. Futher, I especially want to thank Anita Wilke from Springer Fachmedien Wiesbaden GmbH for helping me bringing this thesis to a book.

Family and Friends
Last but not least, I would like to especially thank my parents, grandparents and all my friends for their patience and encouragements in difficult situations.

Bernhard Turban

Abstract

Developing *safety-critical systems* imposes special demands for ensuring quality and reliability of the developed systems. Process standards such as SPICE (ISO15504) or CMMI have been developed to ensure high quality processes, leading to the development of high quality systems. Central principles of these standards are demands for *requirements traceability*. *Traceability* means comprehensible documentation of all origins and later influences of a requirement throughout the complete development endeavor. Among other uses ascribed, the *traceability* concept tries to ensure that every requirement is adequately considered in development and that if changes on the requirement are needed, *impacts* of these changes can be adequately estimated and consistently implemented later on. Even though the *traceability* concept seems promising in theory, it faces substantial problems in practice. One problem is that despite the needed efforts, the perceived benefits for developers are often low because the quality of captured *traceability* information is often coarse grained, does not prove helpful in the situational context, or has already degraded.

This thesis tries to show that *traceability* between requirements and design is an especially difficult problem. To analyze the problem context, the thesis at first analyzes theories, in which the problem is cross-cutting. These are *embedded systems development, systems engineering, software engineering, requirements engineering* and *management, design* theory and *process standards* for *safety-critical systems*.

This analysis mainly identifies a twofold gap between the requirements and the design domain. Obviously a tooling gap exists because different tools are used for the requirements and design domain. However, more important, between requirement descriptions and designs a substantial inherent gap exists because design is a creative decision process of designers often guided by *intuition* and *tacit knowledge* thus difficult to trace by current *traceability* concepts. To prove this argumentation, the author analyzes four design theories (*symbolic information processing* (Simon), *wicked problems* (Rittel), *reflective practice* (Schön) and *patterns* (Alexander)). As a solution to the gap problem, the thesis introduces a tool-based *traceability* method that supports designers in their thinking, avoids disturbing designers in their intuitive phases of creativity, allows establishing *traceability* nearly as a *by-product*, provides *early benefit* to designers, improves collaboration between designers and extends usual *traceability* concepts by two *integrated decision models* allowing further decision information (*rationale*) to be documented. The *decision models* also allow deriving new design internal

"requirements" (*design constraints* and *budgeted resource constraints*) as consequences. In this way, it is possible to clearly distinguish real *requirements* originating from customers from 'requirements' arising from internal decision processes during design leading to the definition of a '*requiremental items taxonomy*'. As the thesis further shows, these concepts also prove to be helpful to avoid
unnecessary redundancies in the *artifact process models* of SPICE (ISO15504) or
CMMI, where different requirement (*system requirements, hardware requirements* and *software requirements*) and design artifacts (*system design, hardware
design* and *software design*) are considered in their interplay. Last but not least,
mechanisms for *graphical impact analysis, consistency management* and *supplier
management* complete the approach.

Through funding of the support program IUK-Bayern, the results presented
here could be integrated into a commercial tool solution called PROVEtech:R2A,
now offered by the MBtech Group as a decisive means to significantly improve
requirement-based design processes with improved support to achieve real benefit from the *traceability* concept.

Contents

Foreword VII

Acknowledgements IX

Abstract XI

Contents XIII

    List of Figures XIX
    List of Tables XXIII
    Abbreviations XXV

Introduction 1

    Introduction to the Topic 1
    Context of this Thesis Project 4
    General Remarks on this Thesis 7
        Registered Trademarks 7
        Argumentation 7
        Citations 8
    General Structure of this Thesis 9

I. General Context and Theories 11

    I.1 The *Model* Concept 13
    I.2 Embedded Systems Development 16
        I.2.1 Definition and Context 16
        I.2.2 Characteristics 16
        I.2.3 Embedded Development in the Automotive Domain 19
    I.3 Software Engineering (SE) 24
    I.4 Systems Engineering (SysEng) 26
    I.5 Requirements Engineering and Management 31
        I.5.1 The Term 'Requirement' 34
        I.5.2 Phases, Artifacts and Techniques in *REM* 40
        I.5.3 Requirements Management 43
        I.5.4 Models in REM 44

I.5.5 Separation between Requirements and Design 48
I.5.6 The Role and Nature of Requirement Change........................ 49
I.5.7 Traceability in the Context of Requirements Management 55
     I.5.7.1 Traceability in Different Aspects of Development
             Activities... 57
     I.5.7.2 Traceability as an Issue of Quality 61
     I.5.7.3 The Potential Uses of Traceability 62
I.5.8 Deficiencies of Today's REM Practices................................ 64

I.6 Design in Systems and Software Development........................ 65
I.6.1 Different Design Phases in SysEng and SE.......................... 66
     I.6.1.1 System Design 67
     I.6.1.2 Software Architecture 67
     I.6.1.3 Detailed Design... 70
I.6.2 General Theories about Design 70
     I.6.2.1 Design as Symbolic Information Processing 71
     I.6.2.2 Design as Wicked Problems.. 84
     I.6.2.3 Design as Situated Action 89
     I.6.2.4 Design as a Language of Patterns 94
I.6.3 Comparison of General Design Theories 103
I.6.4 Dependency between Design Models and Code 105
I.6.5 Architecture Documentation... 107
I.6.6 Design in the Automotive Domain 110
     I.6.6.1 Modeling Methods and Tools Used in Automotive
             Design...111
     I.6.6.2 Integrating other Organizations into a Design 115

I.7 Quality Standards for *Safety-Critical* Development Processes....116
I.7.1 SPICE (ISO 15504)...119
     I.7.1.1 The Process Reference Model of SPICE 120
     I.7.1.2 The Measurement Framework 121
     I.7.1.3 The Process Assessment Model (PAM) 122
I.7.2 Requirements, Design and Traceability in the Context of
       SPICE... 124
     I.7.2.1 ENG.1: Requirements Elicitation 124
     I.7.2.2 ENG.2: System Requirements Analysis 126
     I.7.2.3 ENG.3: System Architectural Design........................ 130
     I.7.2.4 ENG.4: Software Requirements Analysis 132
     I.7.2.5 ENG.5: Software Design.. 133
     I.7.2.6 ENG.6: Software Construction................................. 134
     I.7.2.7 SUP.10: Change Management................................... 135

I.7.3 Traceability in SPICE 137
    I.7.3.1 Intersect: Dangers of Prescriptive Process Models ... 138
    I.7.3.2 The Nature of the ENG-Processes, *Traceability*, and
             its Implications 142
I.7.4 Automotive SPICE **148**
I.7.5 Safety Engineering: IEC 61508, ISO 26262 151
I.8 Feedback from Embedded Practice 153

II. Rationale Management and Traceability in Detailed Discussion 159

**II.9 Rationale Management in Systems and Software
       Engineering 159**
    II.9.1 Characterization Criteria for Rationale Approaches 162
        II.9.1.1 Representation 162
        II.9.1.2 Basic Rationale Processes 163
        II.9.1.3 Descriptive versus Prescriptive Approaches 164
        II.9.1.4 Intrusiveness 164
    II.9.2 Rationale Management Systems (RMS) 165
    II.9.3 Overview of Different Rationale Approaches 166
        II.9.3.1 Schemas for Argumentation 166
        II.9.3.2 Approaches beyond Argumentation 173
        II.9.3.3 Alternative Categorization 175
    II.9.4 Why Rationale Management Could not yet Succeed
            in Practice 177
        II.9.4.1 Cognitive Limitations 178
        II.9.4.2 Rationale Capture Limitations as Central Challenge
                  in Rationale Management 179
        II.9.4.3 Retrieval Limitations 186
        II.9.4.4 Usage Limitations 186
        II.9.4.5 Synopsis of Rationale Limitations
                  Concerning Alternative Design Theories 187
    II.9.5   The Role of Rationale in System and Software Design ... 188
II.10 Requirements Traceability 192
    II.10.1 Overview 192
    II.10.2 Traceability and Consistency Gaps between Artifacts 194
    II.10.3 Impact Analysis and Traceability 197
    II.10.4 Core Dimensions for Characterization 201
        II.10.4.1 Purpose 202

II.10.4.2 Conceptual Trace Model 204
II.10.4.3 Process 229
II.10.4.4 Tools 234
II.10.5 Traceability and its Benefit Problem 242
II.10.6 Traceability between Requirements and Design 245
II.10.6.1 Theoretic Research Results 245
II.10.6.2 Tool Couplings between REM- and Design
Tools in Practice 248
II.10.7 Traceability between Requirements, Design and Code 254
II.10.8 Rationale Management and Traceability 257

III. PROVEtech:R2A – A Tool for Dedicated Requirements Traceability 259

III.11 Research Goals 261

III.12 Accompanying Case Study 265

III.13 Closing the Tool Gap 268

III.14 Closing the Gap between Requirements and Design 271

III.15 Abstraction Layers and Abstraction Nodes 272

III.16 Models Crossing Tool-Barriers 280
III.16.1 Insertion: Coupling Different *REM-* and *Modeling
Tools* 280
III.16.2 Integrating Several *Modeling Tools* in a Single Model 281

III.17 Basic Support Features of R2A 284
III.17.1 Support for Collaborative Design Tasks 284
III.17.2 The Notes Mechanism 285
III.17.3 Extensibility: XML-Reporting and User Tagging 286
III.17.4 Unique Identifier Support for any Item in R2A 287
III.17.5 Evolutionary *Traceability* – Recording History and
Baselines 287
III.17.6 The Properties Dialog 288

III.18 Requirements and Requirements *Traceability* 290
III.18.1 Managing Requirement Sources 290
III.18.2 Establishing Requirements Traceability 293
III.18.2.1 *Traceability* Operations in R2A 296
III.18.2.2 The Requirement Influence Scope (RIS) 299
III.18.2.3 Representing Requirement Contextual Data 302
III.18.2.4 The Requirement Dribble Process (RDP) 304
III.18.2.5 Overview over Navigation and Handling of
Requirements Aspects in R2A 311

III.19 Taxonomy of Requiremental Items..**313**

III.20 Support for Capturing Decisions...**316**

    III.20.1 Relation to Approaches of Rationale Management..........319

    III.20.2 Effects on the Traceability Model 322

    III.20.3 Example How to Tame the Development Process Model
             of SPICE 324

    III.20.4 Implementation of the Decision Model in R2A 326

    III.20.5 Additional Support of the Decision Model for Designers 337

           III.20.5.1 Patterns..338

           III.20.5.2 Ensuring Adequate Realization of Design and
                      Decisions...339

           III.20.5.3 Support for Architecture Evaluation 339

III.21 Resource Allocation as a Special Decision Making Case **341**

    III.21.1 *Budgeted Resource Constraints* as further
           Requiremental Items..343

    III.21.2 Advantages for Collaboration and Sharing Project
           Knowledge 345

           III.21.2.1 Within Project Refinement..............................345

           III.21.2.2 Communicating Information across
                      Organizational Boundaries..............................346

           III.21.2.3 Change Management.......................................347

           III.21.2.4 Different Views on the Same Problem 348

    III.21.3 Representing Budgeted Resource Constraints in SysML. 349

    III.21.4 Combining both *Decision Models*...................................351

III.22 Managing Changes and Consistency..**352**

    III.22.1 Usage of Traces – Managing *Requiremental* Changes.....353

           III.22.1.1 Selective Tracing: Impact Analysis 353

           III.22.1.2 Interactive Tracing: The *Model Browser*..........357

           III.22.1.3 Non-Guided Tracing: Additional Features
                      for Fast Look-Up..358

    III.22.2 Consistency Maintenance of Requirements, *Traceability*
           and Design...359

III.23 Aspects of Embedding R2A in a Process Environment..........**362**

    III.23.1 Avoiding Redundancies in *Supplier Management* 363

    III.23.2 *Traceability* over Several Artifact Models without
           Redundancies 365

    III.23.3 Decoupled Development of Requirement and Design
           Artifacts...368

III.24 Overall Architecture of R2A 370
    III.24.1 General Architecture 370
    III.24.2 The *Meta-Model* 372
    III.24.3 Further Interfaces 376

IV. Synopsis 379

IV.25 Summary of the Achieved Research Results 379

IV.26 Perspectives for Further Research 385

IV.27 Conclusions 392

Bibliography 395

Index 435

List of Figures

Figure 1-1   Properties of original and model [LL07; p.6 (*)].......................14

Figure 4-1   The view of *systems engineering* processes of Hood et al.
[HWF+08; p.29]..30

Figure 5-1   Functional and nonfunctional requirements [HR02; p.86 ff]......37

Figure 5-2   The Requirements Engineering framework defined by Pohl
[Po08; p.39 (*)]...41

Figure 5-3   The view of Hood et al. [HWF+08] logically derived by the
author...44

Figure 5-4   Overview over different *traceability* terms oriented on Brcina
[Br07a; p.4]..58

Figure 5-5   The three dimensions of the *RE framework*
[Po93; p.284], [Po08; p.42]...61

Figure 6-1   The design problem space according to Goel [Go99; fig.1].......93

Figure 7-1   Processes defined in ISO/IEC 15504-5 basing on
ISO/IEC 12207...123

Figure 7-2   The example in current practice of the SPICE process model..143

Figure 7-3   The altered example above with less redundancies..................146

Figure 7-4   Summary of traceability BPs in A-SPICE [ASPICE08a;
Annex E]...149

Figure 9-1   IBIS schema example outlining a discussion..........................168

Figure 9-2   QOC schema as interpreted by [HHL+06; p.413]....................169

Figure 10-1   A requirements specification with attributes in IBM Rational
DOORS..207

Figure 10-2   Efficiency gains, process orientation and tool support
[Eb08; p.290]...235

Figure 10-3   Traceability tool couplings via surrogate modules...................250

Figure 10-4   Requirements fan-out effect according to Alderidge [Al03].....253

Figure 12-1   Example *use case* of the case study...................................265

Figure 12-2   Requirements specification for the case study in IBM
Rational DOORS..266

Figure 12-3   Example *SW design* for the *requirements specification*
in fig. 12-2..267

Figure 13-1   R2A in combination with a *design tool* (Sparx Systems
Enterprise Architect)...268

Figure 13-2   Logical structure of the R2A tool approach...........................270

Figure 15-1   Hierarchical decomposition of a system shown as
                 abstraction tree.. 273
Figure 15-2   Detailed content and structure of an *abstraction node*
                 (SubSystem1).. 274
Figure 15-3   Example of a UML project repository in Enterprise Architect. 276
Figure 15-4   With the *AN* tree view and the tab "Views and Description" ... 279
Figure 16-1   Different modeling tools integrated into one *design model*
                 via R2A.. 283
Figure 17-1   The properties dialog in R2A 289
Figure 18-1   Managing different requirement sources in R2A..................... 291
Figure 18-2   *Requirements source document* synchronized with IBM
                 Rational DOORS 291
Figure 18-3   Ways of establishing *requirements traceability* via *drag-
                 and-drop* in R2A.. 298
Figure 18-4   Requirements and the *requirement influence scope*.................. 300
Figure 18-5   Showing requirements in the design situational context of
                 an *AN* 303
Figure 18-6   Overview of how the requirements-related features are
                 integrated into R2A concerning navigation and handling......... 312
Figure 19-1   *Requiremental items*, *requirements* and *design constraints*
                 taxonomy 314
Figure 20-1   Interactions between nonfunctional, functional requirements
                 and architectural decisions [PDK+02]...................................... 317
Figure 20-2   Documented decisions build the connection between
                 requirements, *design elements* and resulting *design
                 constraints* 318
Figure 20-3   The newly emerged and more detailed *traceability*
                 information scheme... 323
Figure 20-4   The example of SPICE conforming design processes in
                 the new way 325
Figure 20-5   Decision dialog in R2A 326
Figure 20-6   R2A's visualization of the decision taken above 328
Figure 20-7   *Architectural influence factors assessment* with R2A's
                 decision model... 333
Figure 20-8   Consequences of the *architectural influence factors
                 assessment* of fig. 20-7 334
Figure 21-1   *Requiremental items taxonomy* with *budgeted resource
                 constraints* 343
Figure 21-2   Resource allocation example with *budgeted resource
                 constraints* 344

Figure 21-3   Sub budgeting of the Light_hdl module 346
Figure 21-4   Tabular view with corresponding abstraction hierarchies. 348
Figure 21-5   Tabular view with assignment inconsistency (selected line) 349
Figure 21-6   Representation of the same information as fig. 21-4 but
                in SysML view 350
Figure 21-7   Example for combining both decision models together 352
Figure 22-1   Two examples for visualizing *impact* on the *abstraction
                nodes hierarchy* 354
Figure 22-2   *Impact analysis dialog* and R2A's main window with an
                impact set taking *decisions* into account 356
Figure 22-3   The *model browser* in R2A 358
Figure 22-4   Life-cycle of a *requiremental item* and its color coding
                in R2A 361
Figure 23-1   Process chain of an integrated *design model* for *system, HW*
                and *SW design* 366
Figure 23-2   Process chain of multi-layered requirements and design
                artifacts 367
Figure 23-3   Consistent integration of changes (Δ) beyond version
                barriers 369
Figure 24-1   High-level *architecture* of R2A 372
Figure 24-2   The *meta-model* of R2A 374

List of Tables

Table 7.1   Maturity Levels and their Process Attributes
(cf.[HDH+06; p.16]) 122

Table 9.1   Alternative categorization of rationale approaches
[OM07; p.16] 176

Table 9.2   Relation to design theories and rationale in design
according to [HA06a; p.77] 187

Table 10.1   Prioritization of stakeholders and usage purposes concerning
traceability between requirement and design artifacts 203

Table 10.2   Characteristics of low-end and high-end traceability users
[RJ01; p.65] 225

Table 10.3   Kinds of traceability tools according to [GF94] and
[Kn01b; p.57] 236

Table 20.1   Example of an architectural influence factors assessment 332

Table 21.1   Example resource estimation of RAM consumption in
design 342

Abbreviations

The following lists the most common abbreviations used in this thesis over several chapters:

AIS	Actual Impact Set
AN	Abstraction Node – a concept of R2A (cf. ch. III.15)
ANH	Abstraction Nodes Hierarchy – a concept of R2A (cf. ch. III.15)
A-SPICE	Automotive SPICE (cf. ch. I.7.4)
BRC	Budgeted Resource Constraint – a concept of R2A (cf. ch. III.21)
CCB	Change Control Board
CMMI	Capability Maturity Model integrated (cf. ch. I.7)
COTS	Commercial Off The Shelf
CRS	Customer Requirements Specification
CTM	Conceptual Traceability Model
CusSysDes	The Customer's System Design
DC	A Design Contraint as a concept of R2A (part III)
DEC	A conflict based Decision a concept of R2A (part III)
DOD	United States Department of Defense
DRL	Decision Representation Language an RatMan approach (cf. ch. II.9)
DXL	DOORS eXtension Language
ECU	Embedded Control Unit
EEPROM	Electrically Erasable Programmable Read Only Memory
EIS	Estimated Impact Set
FR	Functional Requirement
GUI	Graphical User Interface
GUID	General Unique IDentifier
HMI	Human Machine Interface

HIS	Hersteller Initiative Software – Standardization Board of German Automotive OEMs (cf. ch. I.7)
HW	Hardware
HW_RS	Hardware Requirements Specification
IBIS	Issue Based Information System an RatMan (cf. ch. II.9) approach (see also gIBIS)
IDE	Integrated Development Environment
ISO	International Standards Organization
MF	Measurement Framework (see SPICE)
NFR	Nonfunctional Requirement
OCL	Object Contraint Language
PAM	Process Assessment Model (see SPICE)
PRM	Process Reference Model (see SPICE)
QOC	Questions, Options, Criteria an *RatMan* approach (cf. ch. II.9)
R2A	PROVEtech:R2A – The tool environment resulting from this research (part III)
RatMan	Rationale Management (cf. ch. II.9)
RDP	Requirements Dribble Process a heuristic supported by R2A (part III)
REM	Requirements Engineering and Management
REQ	Requirement from the customer as a concept of R2A (part III)
RI	Requiremental Item a concept of R2A (part III)
RIF	Requirement Interchange Format
RIS	Requirement Influence Scope a concept of R2A in connection with the RDP (part III)
ROM	Read Only Memory
RUP	Rational Unified Process
RE	Requirements Engineering
RM	Requirements Management
REM	Requirement Engineering and Management
RMS	Rationale Management System

RSD	Requirement Source Document as a concept of R2A (part III)
RTF	Rich Text Format
SE	Software Engineering
SEI	Software Engineering Institute (SEI) of the Carnegie Mellon University in Pittsburg
SIL	Safety Integrity Level as described in IEC 61508
SIS	Starting Impact Set
SPICE	Software Process Improvement Capability dEtermination (ISO 15504), (cf. ch. I.7)
SysEng	Systems Engineering (ch. I.4)
SYS_RS	System Requirements Specification
SuppRS	Supplier Requirements Specifications
SW	Software
SW_RS	Software Requirements Specification
SysML	System Modeling Language
TQM	Total Quality Management (cf. ch. I.7)
UML	Unified Modeling Language

Introduction

Nothing is more powerful in the world than an idea whose time has come.
Victor Hugo (*)

Introduction to the Topic

Usually, systems developed by humans are not developed for their own sake of existence. Instead, these systems shall help to achieve certain human goals or purposes. Goals or purposes, however, are often very abstract and vague in the same way as the usage situations of these systems are manifold and complex. Correspondingly, a more precise definition of what a system must exactly perform is needed. This leads to the need for defining the exact requirements of a system. Then, such a system must just be designed and constructed to fulfill the defined requirements.

Concerning the development of software-based systems, development experiences of the last decades have been rather disenchanting. Often, five out of six development projects are considered as rather unsuccessful [BMH+98; p.3], [St95], [St01], [Eb05; p.23ff]. One major issue identified through the years is that the developed systems often do not achieve the goals and purposes they were intended for, or if they fulfill them, the resulting system's development project significantly has exceeded planned budget and (resp. or) effort [St95], [St01].

Research on the causes for these problems is ongoing. Among others, three issues can be identified as root causes (cf. ch. I.5): Unclear requirements, often changing requirements and inadequate processes for handling.

One approach to solve the first problem is to spend extra effort on identifying and defining clear and adequate requirements upfront. Today, a whole set of artifacts, heuristics, practices and processes around the topic requirements are available summarized under the theory of *requirements engineering* (*RE*). However, development experiences have shown that even though extra focus and effort is spent upfront on the definition of requirements, changing requirements are still more the norm than the exception. As ch. I.5.6 shows, reasons are manifold.

In the author's opinion, at least two essential causes for the requirements change problem exist:

1. Software (SW) and SW-based systems are abstract and thus essentially difficult to define comprehensively.

2. In addition, SW-based systems themselves with their intercorrelations with other systems and their embedding into processes infer a significant complexity leading to the problem that not all cases and eventualities can be considered beforehand.

These causes – among others described in ch. I.5.6 – significantly challenge the paradigm that the extensive specification and analysis of requirements upfront will tame the requirements change problem. They might rather be a good leverage to mitigate the problem, but changing requirements will still remain a decisive factor for projects. *RE*-theory also seems to have acknowledged this fact in the way that it more and more emphasizes the aspect that requirements must also be adequately managed (see ch. I.5.3). Thus, the author rather prefers to speak of *requirements engineering and management* (*REM*).

In *REM* theory, *requirements traceability* (in the following simply called *traceability*) is considered as central means to manage requirement changes. *Traceability* means "comprehensible documentation of requirements, decisions and their interdependencies to all produced information resp. artifacts from project start to project end" ([RS02; p.407 (*)]). Through recorded *traceability* information, *impact analysis* of changes is possible allowing estimating the *impact* of suggested requirement changes. This information allows project stakeholders to decide, whether the benefits of a requirement change outweigh its costs, thus avoiding disadvantageous changes. Once it is decided to perform a change, *traceability* helps to consistently propagate the change to all *impacted* locations in a project. Thus, consistently inferring the change into the project prevents dangers of forgetting to change affected locations leading to defects or even fatal consequences. In this way, the *traceability* concept is a promising means to improve *REM* and especially change management processes, thus avoiding inconsistencies – introduced during inevitably applied changes – leading to failures in the system, thus leading to significantly improved quality of developed systems.
Even though the *traceability* concept is already known for over 20 years and it always has seemed very promising to be a significant value gain in a project, it is still not very widely spread in development practice except for development projects under certain circumstances. As ch. II.10.5 tries to outline, this seems to

be the case, because it suffers from a general problem of efficiency and of low direct benefit perceived by the project members intended to capture the *traceability* information.

The quality of developed systems generally is a decisive factor. On the other side, ensuring quality involves significant efforts and costs. Even though quality must not necessarily be seen as a cost factor, but should rather be seen as a factor of investment, only finite resources can be spent for quality in order to ensure economic success. For once, this appeals to ensuring a high degree of effectiveness on quality assurance methods in general. For the other, demands for quality may differ concerning the purpose of the system. As an example, it may be an acceptable risk for PC-based SW systems that some minor bugs or other minor flaws remain undiscovered in a delivered system, because applying an update on a PC is acceptable as long as the number of updates is acceptable to the users and it is easy to apply the updates. Concerning embedded systems steering a technical equipment, it is much more difficult to perform SW-updates, as this in most cases implies a product recall to apply the new software update. Besides high costs, this is rather not acceptable for the users and often involves significant image losses for the involved companies. Beyond that, so called *safety-critical systems* exist, where a malfunction can lead to significant damages to values or even impose hazards for persons' health or lives In these cases, even minimal probabilities of failures involving injury or death of persons must be best possibly eliminated

Another important means to ensure good product quality is to employ good development processes. In the context of embedded projects and especially for *safety-critical* embedded projects, significant efforts have been undertaken to standardize the processes with their decisive characteristics to be performed in order to achieve high quality outcomes. Ch. I.7 describes these efforts and the demands for these processes. In these process standards, a demand crosscutting through all engineering processes is the demand for *traceability* of every requirement to the influences it imposes on every artifact developed in any engineering process.

The implementation of these demands in practice, however, often makes apparent that these demands themselves are difficult to implement and if they are implemented it is highly questionable whether the effort and resources spent really bring significant benefit to development projects. Instead, *traceability* demands are often rather performed to correspond to the standards' demands.

In this thesis, the author tries to identify several core reasons for these problems. Besides the *benefit problem* mentioned above, an essential problem is that different tools are used for different processes. This, however, implies that the *traceability* concept must somehow cross these tool gaps in order to connect the information within the different tools. In the author's opinion, this actually is one essential cause for the *benefit problem*, as crossing these gaps generally requires higher efforts, decreases accuracy and significantly increases potentials for inconsistencies.

Unfortunately, the author considers one problem as even more essential: This problem origins from the fact that requirements describe a *problem space* that must be transformed into a solution. This transformation process is usually referred to as design. Usual *traceability* models rather assume that these connections between requirements and design artifacts are rather linear semantic allowing to trace these connections.

The author, however, believes that a semantic gap exists between the *problem space* described by requirements and the solution found. This gap exists, because design is a complex task of performing sequences of complex design decisions leading to the solution. There, the connections being rather nonlinear make it very difficult to record valuable *traceability* information.

As a way to address these problems identified, this thesis also introduces a tool environment called PROVEtech:R2A (R2A) to support *requirements traceability* to design with specific focus on diminishing both mentioned gaps. In this way, the author also hopes to diminish the benefit gap to a degree that collecting *traceability* information provides direct benefit for the designers thus hoping to really achieve the promises of the *traceability* concept.

Context of this Thesis Project

In order to provide a better understanding to the reader how the research results described in this thesis have emerged, this chapter provides a short overview about the history of this research project.

First ideas to some core problems and features addressed by R2A arose as a consequence of the direct development experiences of the author in an automotive ECU development project for lights steering with SPICE level two processes. At that time, the Micron Electronic Devices AG (MEDAG) and the Competence Center for Software Engineering (CC-SE) at the University of Applied Sciences Regensburg have begun a collaboration with the goal to improve the connection of theoretic research with industrial practice.

In the development project, from 2004 to 2005 the author worked as representative of the CC-SE at MEDAG where the author was at first responsible for introducing *REM*-processes with the *REM-tool* IBM Rational DOORS[1] to be newly introduced into the company's project practice. During further development, the author was responsible for module design and implementation. In this way, the author was also responsible for maintaining the *requirements traceability* to the module design directly experiencing the shortcomings and problems involved.

These experiences have lead to the idea about a tool environment, where designers should directly benefit from gathered *traceability* information by making the influences of requirements on design directly visible to designers (basic ideas of ch. III.13, ch. III.15 and ch. III.18.2.2) and by improving the collaboration of all involved designers (basic ideas of ch. III.18.2.4).

In 2005 the identified key concepts have then been formulated in a theoretic outline with an extended theoretical case study being reviewed by representatives from MEDAG and CC-SE. The concepts proved promising. As the concepts also base on extensive user interaction, where usability is a key factor for success, the project made contact to the Institute for Media, Information and Cultural Studies at the University of Regensburg, where usability is one major research topic.

The three organizations have decided to form a partnership to realize the project. For this goal, the partners decided to develop a prototype tool evaluating the theoretical results by practical feedback and to apply for financial aid at the IUK[2]-program of the Bavarian Ministry of Economic Development.

During the application phase in 2006, the prototype tool implementation has been developed and has been continuously assessed by design practitioners of the partners to achieve immediate feedback of implemented features.

With these granted financial aids, a two years project for six persons could be realized to transfer the achieved theoretical and prototypical research results into a solution relevant for practice. The project has been performed from Feb. 2007 to Feb. 2009 leading to the commercial tool PROVEtech:R2A as it is discussed in this part. Because the tool's features have been considered as very innovative, where good usability at complex user interactions is essential, and because most core features have been extensively analyzed upfront by theoretical discussion and the prototype, the project members decided to develop the project using the evolutionary prototyping concept from agile development methods. Evolutionary prototyping means that the project started with a prototype where all identified features were successively integrated into the prototype so that the prototype

---

[1]   At that time called Telelogic DOORS
[2]   The IUK program (In German: Information Und Kommunikation (Information and Communication)) is a research funding program to support transferring newest research results into commercial solutions applicable in practice.

successively evolves to the final product. In this way, new features could at first be realized via a prototype implementation. These features then could be introduced to design practitioners to acquire direct feedback on the prototypical implementation. This feedback could then be used to improve and *refactor* the implementation to fully integrate it into the project's program base. Concerning the tool's architectural design, therefore, only an *architectural skeleton* has been developed sketching the core concepts of the tool environment and leaving details of the architecture open for change.

This proceeding may, at first, seem to contradict principles discussed in this thesis about *REM*, but, as discussed in ch. I.5.6 and ch. I.6.2.2, prototype-based requirement evaluation is a common practice to address the problem that highly innovative projects face a high volatility of requirements.

During the project in the midst of 2008, the MEDAG has been taken over by the MBtech Group GmbH & Co. KGaA (in the further simply called MBtech) a subsidiary company of the Daimler AG specialized on engineering services. The concepts and ideas of the project convinced the MBtech of the innovative potentials of the tool leading to a continued endeavor to develop the results to a commercial solution. In this way, the developed tool has been named PROVEtech:R2A[3] (called R2A in the following) and has been integrated into the PROVEtech tool family.

Currently, R2A is offered as commercial solution of the MBtech to address the *traceability* problems described in this thesis. It is continuously maintained and improved through a half-year release cycle. In this way, the project described here also is an example of how theoretic research results can be successfully brought into commercial project practice.

---

[3]   R2A stands for Requirements 2 Architecture. Further information on PROVEtech:R2A can be found at the company homepage: http://www.mbtech-group.com/eu-en/electronics_solutions/tools_equipment/provetechr2a_traceability_management/traceability_management.html (Access: 2010/09).

General Remarks on this Thesis

Before stepping into the thesis, the reader should note some general remarks.

Registered Trademarks

The reader of this thesis should note that some mentioned techniques and tools referred to in this thesis are registered trademarks or under protection of copyright laws.

Argumentation

The thesis introduced here is not an empirical study, but rather a theoretical work. The work can be considered somewhere between *systems engineering* and *software engineering* theory. As a matter of fact, many of the mentioned theories and 'facts' presented in this thesis have no irrevocable evidence but are to a certain degree a 'fact' of experience, interpretation and believe. When the author collected these 'facts' from different sources, dangers of misinterpretation or selective interpretation by the author cannot be excluded. Facts found in a research paper cannot always be seen on their own. Often, these 'facts' are embedded in a certain context (e.g., a special research theory or project). Now, taking conclusions from these 'facts' should be done with a certain care. To address this problem, the author often considered not only to cite the pure 'fact' concluded somewhere, but also tried to outline the context where these 'facts' have arisen and he also tried to provide available possible alternative interpretations by other authors, or theories to allow the reader to derive his (her) own conclusions about the evidence and how cogent the author's argumentation is. As a matter of fact, however, most theories are not compatible or consistent to each other. Correspondingly, a technique to outline the context of some argumentation may also result in some inconsistency or contradictory statements. The reader should consider these inconsistencies or contradictions as phenomenon of the manifold complexity that research theories produce in their connection to each other and the limited capabilities of humans to completely cope with these complexities. Besides, the author generally doubts the potential existence of one grand unified theory about systems and software development. Rather the author considers inconsistencies and contradictions as spring of new knowledge in research.

For some of the encountered inconsistencies and contradictions the author developed suggestions or assumptions born from the author's own experience and thinking. To highlight these suggestions or assumptions, where the author could not find adequate proof derived from 'facts' basing on evidence, the author uses terms like 'the author feels', 'the author thinks', 'in the author's eyes' and 'the author believes', where these terms have an increasing weight of evidence possibility ascribed by the author.

Citations

During the work on this thesis, the author has developed a slightly individual citation practice. First of all, it is to mention that the author experienced some citation practices of other authors as unsatisfactory to really follow some argumentation. One problem, e.g., often is that some authors simply refer to an extensive text (e.g., a complete book) as an evidence for a single argument. Really retrieving the original statement is then very difficult. The author tried to make the evidence of his thoughts more explicit by referring to the exact page or at least to a collection of pages, when the evidence was rather a synthesis of several paragraphs than just a statement. Only if some more general theoretic discussion has been performed, where the whole book, or article has to be considered the author cited the source without reference to pages.

Furthermore, the author thinks that an evidence found in several sources has a higher potential to be true than originating from a single source. Correspondingly, the author also tried to mention all sources he encountered within a certain argumentation to indicate the potential evidence of the argumentation to the reader.

During writing the thesis, the author often stepped over some wordings of other authors providing a very concise or precise formulation of an argumentation, where any rewording or changes could only lower the quality of the statement or infer a falsification of the original meaning. Correspondingly, in these cases the author decided to cite these wordings verbatim to preserve the conciseness or preciseness of the argumentation for the reader.

Citing verbatim, however, invoked a further problem about quotation marks. The author used the following rules. For verbatim quoting of some other author's argumentation the author has used double quotation marks ("..."). If quotation marks were used in some verbatim quoted text, these quotation marks have been transformed to single quotations marks ('...'). In some cases, the author wanted to refer to a certain jargon-like term generally used by developers or the research community associated with a discussed topic or to refer to a term having a doubt-ful connotation[4]. In these cases, the author also used single quotation marks ('...').

It is also to mention that the author is a German native speaker. In many cas-es, it happened that the author has read German publications with interesting passages to cite. Sometimes, even some books originally published in English have been only available in German translation. This leads to the fact that some citations were translated by the author. Any translation, however, imposes the risk of – hopefully only slightly – changing the meaning of the citation. Therefore, the author decided to mark any citation translated by himself with an asterisk sur-rounded in brackets ('(*)') indicating the translation by the author to the reader.

General Structure of this Thesis

This thesis is dissected into four parts. Part I tries to outline the connections of this research to other general research topics that must be considered for a tool dealing with *traceability* concerns in the context of processes for *safety-critical* projects. Afterwards, part II discusses the main research topics of interest for this thesis. These are *rationale management* and *requirements traceability*. In part III, the problems surfaced in part I and II are picked up again to outline how these problems can be solved by the innovative concepts of PROVEtech:R2A. Last but not least, part IV provides a synthesis of the results achieved and an outlook, where new ideas about further possible research are outlined.

---

[4] Above, e.g., the author used the connotation 'facts' to indicate that 'facts' in research are not necessarily absolute facts but are often bound to a certain paradigm. If such an paradigm is replaced by a new research paradigm, a considerable portion of 'facts' pre-viously believed as true becomes invalid, obsolete or at least doubtful (e.g., cf. [Fe86]).

I. General Context and Theories

He who loves practice without theory is like the sailor who boards ship
without a rudder and compass and never knows where he may cast.
Leonardo da Vinci

This part shall provide the fundamental understanding of most core concepts involved in the construct of ideas leading to this thesis and its results. Consequently, the following chapters provide an overview over the major research fields having influence on the outcome of this thesis. If employed, *requirements traceability* can be seen as a crosscutting concern of all development activities. Correspondingly these chapters strive a considerable set of very different general research disciplines.

Stepping into any research topic of considerable depth often implies a steep entry curve for any reader being non-expert of the research domain. One of the problems is that topics arc often manifold interconnected making it difficult to find a good start. The author has tried to flatten the entry curve by starting with chapters with lower entry barriers. These are the chapters that are more independent of the other chapters. With the understanding and argumentation collected in the first more independent chapters, the further chapters build on the previous chapters and then have lower entry barriers.

In this thesis, the model concept is an essential foundation, since different types of models are referred to in different theories. Correspondingly, this part starts with a general discussion on the model concept and related terms needed at later discussions (ch. I.1). This is followed in ch. I.2 by a general discussion about developing embedded systems in general. A certain category of embedded systems, called *safety-critical embedded systems*, demand special concerns about quality, because malfunctions in these systems can involve significant fatal consequences. Correspondingly, special standards for development processes (ch. I.7) have evolved to ensure quality of the developed systems. One central demand are especially rigid demands for *requirements traceability*. As results of this thesis arose in the context of companies involved in the automotive domain, a special ch. I.2.3, discusses specific peculiarities of the automotive domain. Even though the concepts of the developed R2A tool in principle can be applied to any development project, some of the features provide special help in embedded projects of the automotive domain. This is, e.g., the case for the special improvements of *supplier management* (see ch. III.23.1), as the automotive domain is a domain with very extensive and deep chains of suppliers.

Ch. I.3 and ch. I.4 then provide general introductions into the theories of software engineering and systems engineering. Both theories' concepts are an integral part of current development process standards such as the quality standards applied for *safety-critical embedded systems* (ch. I.7).

In ch. I.5, current *requirements engineering* and *management* (*REM*) theory is discussed. The *traceability* concept is a nascent of this theory. Correspondingly, the sub ch. I.5.7 also discusses the *traceability* concept in the context of *REM*-theory and explains concepts needed in the following chapters of this part. An extensive discussion of the *traceability* concept is then performed in ch. II.10 of part II.

Concerning the transition from requirements to design, the author considers this an especially difficult *traceability* problem, because this transition is a transition from the *problem space* description (requirements) to the *solution space* description (design) implying a considerable semantic gap between both. Therefore, this thesis lies a special focus on this topic. Ch. I.6 outlines design with its concepts and theories that are important to understand the problems of *traceability* concerning this transition. Instead of concentrating on a specific modeling paradigm or method related to software or systems engineering, this chapter rather tries to outline several general theories about design that describe the role of design and how design emerges from designers' thinking.

After the previous chapters have outlined fundamental concepts of different general theories building the theoretical groundwork of this thesis, ch. I.7 describes process standards to be fulfilled by organizations developing *safety-critical* embedded systems. Due to its extent and complexity, the outlined process standards cannot be described in full depth. Instead, after a general overview is provided, the engineering processes concerning requirements and design with their *traceability* demands are described in detail. In this way, the author derives important demands, which the tool-approach described in part III must fulfill in order to conform to the standards.

Last but not least, ch. I.8 refers to findings from practice of embedded engineering that should be kept in mind considering a practice-oriented solution for *traceability* in the context of design.

I.1 The *Model* Concept

> *We can only make a model of a fact in the world we live in,*
> *i.e. the model must be essentially related to the world we live in*
> *and what's more, independently of whether it's true or false.*
> Ludwig Wittgenstein (*)

"Models are a fundamental concept of our world's handling. All scientists and engineers use and create models to prove universal evidences for and to find more detailed information on their speculations. Often models mark intermediate step on the road to new artifacts as bridges, cars and mobile telephones. In Software Engineering the importance of models is even higher, because they not even represent the intermediate steps, but the endpoints of our work: a specification but also a program is a model" [LL07; p.3 (*)].

Stachowiak [St73] found several general properties that models have in common with each other (the following statements are taken from [LL07; p.5-6] and [BR07b; p.4]):

- A *purpose* (or purposes),
- A reference to the original, also called *mapping characteristic*[5] [LL07; p.5],
- Abstraction of certain qualities of the original, also called *shortening characteristic*[6]: A diversity of relationships can exist between model and original emerging by the model's usage purposes [BR07b; p.4],
- A *pragmatic characteristic*: "Under certain conditions or problems, models can supplement the original" [LL07; p.6 (*)];

Fig. 1-1 shows the connections between original and its model according to [LL07; p.6] and [St73]. Together three kinds of properties can be distinguished:

- *Essential properties* (also called non-neglected) are the properties of the original considered in the model.
- *Preterated properties* (also called neglected) are properties of the original not considered in the model.
- *Abundant properties* are properties in the model, not present in the original. These properties emerge from the nature of the model[7] (Simon [Si06; p.113] calls this the implicit logic of the sign system).

---

[5] In German: Abbildungsmerkmal
[6] In German: Verkürzungsmerkmal
[7] Considering the photo of a person, preterated properties of the person would be its weight, name, type, whereas the quality of the photo paper or the photo's format would be abundant properties (cf. [LL07; p.6]).

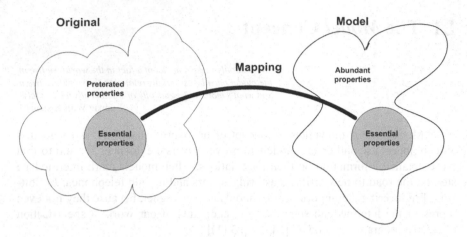

Figure 1-1 Properties of original and model [LL07; p.6 (*)]

These properties distinctions lead to two fundamental problems that should always be considered when working with models:

1. Due to the *preterated properties*, "models are always a 'simplification, a kind of idealization' of the aspects to be modeled. ... We choose for our model these characteristics of the reality that we consider essential for our purpose. In complex situations ... this act of already distinguishing the essential from the non-essential must be at least partially an act of judgment, often of political or cultural judgments. And this act must then necessarily base on the intuitive thinking model of the model constructor" [We76; p.202 (*)].

2. On the other hand, *abundant model properties* can lead to erroneous conclusions about the original. "The implicit logic of the sign system resp. symbols, representations, languages, texts, formulas, etc., are in general different to the represented phenomena or items; If both are mixed up, the danger arises that peculiarities of the observation method (resp. the observers) and its results are considered instead of the observed fact" [Si06; 113 (*)].

Generally, two different model types exist according to [LL07; p.5] (also cf. [St73], [Mo04; p.64f]):

*   *Descriptive models* describe already existing connections or systems.
*   *Prescriptive models* are manuals for the construction of, e.g., systems.

In the context described here, both types of models occur. Thus, e.g., a SW documentation is a *descriptive model*, whereas a model as basis for model based code generation represents a *prescriptive* one. Following these interpretations, a

SW design model can be first a *prescriptive model* determining the structure of the code to develop. After coding has been finished, however the model would become *descriptive*. Later in ch. I.7, it is shown that a similar connection may exist in the area of *process models* and that users of *process models* should be aware of possible misinterpretations sparked by an inadvertent transformation of *descriptive process models* into *prescriptive process models*.

Due to these possible interpretation ambiguities where the real character of a model is not absolutely clear, Schefe [Sch99; p.132] asks for abandoning meaning from the model concept in *software engineering* except its clear meaning emerges from the usage context [Sch99; p.134] (see also [Mo04; p.65]). In fact, as the discussion in ch. I.7.3.1 shows, these dangers of interpretation and unconscious shift of meaning can happen.

The main purpose of a model is the communication of ideas and concepts [Mo04; p.171]. Correspondingly, attention must be paid for conclusiveness of the modeled ideas. In this context, it seems legitimate to speak of a certain aesthetics models should have [Kr95; p.43]. Ch. I.6.1.2 again discusses model esthetics in connection with *SW architectures*.

Concerning system and software development, models have some special characteristics. In more complex development processes, at least two kinds of models must be considered ([De04], [Br07a]):

- A model[8] for the targeted system.
- A model for the development project's processes.

This thesis deals with both kinds. In the context of design (but also a bit in *requirement engineering*) the first mentioned model kind is essential. When process standards as SPICE (see ch. I.7) or process related concepts such as *traceability* are discussed, the second kind is equally essential.

Often, strict *formal* semantics are also observed as an obstacle to designers ([Sch83], [HA06a]). As further discussed in ch. I.6.2.3 and ch. II.9.4.2, this is especially the case in earlier phases of design, or when designers encounter significantly complex situations where no solution covering all aspects can be found at once. In this context, some designers (cf. [AMR06], [Kr95; p.49], [Go99], [Go95]) emphasize that especially sketching is important because it produces ambiguity, a widening of the problem scope and general uncertainty about the final solution as nourishment for designers' creativity to bring up new solution ideas (see ch. I.6.2.3).

---

[8]   In most practice, not one model but several models exist. This is the case, because different models with different semantics are often employed at different levels of abstraction. Perhaps it is better to say that it should be the goal to have a model of the system.

I.2 Embedded Systems Development

Grey, dear friend, is all theory and green is the golden tree of live.
J. W. v. Goethe (*)

Most of the topics and interrelations discussed in this thesis are not really limited to the embedded systems development market, but the special conditions of the embedded area force a much stronger need for employing some of the later described concepts and techniques. Therefore, before beginning with other more specific topics a short introduction into this very complex field shall be given.

I.2.1 Definition and Context

Embedded systems – or better *embedded control units* (ECUs) – are computer based systems embedded into a bigger surrounding technical (total) system (automobiles, airplanes, power plants, consumer electronics etc.) often also referred as the context of an ECU. In most cases, ECUs perform complex control, regulation, observation and data processing activities on physical-mechanical components with decisive impact on functionality and performance of the complete system (cf. [Sch05], [Ge05; p.5]).

ECUs itself mostly work very integrated into the complete system so that users are usually not really aware of the ECUs itself, but the bigger processes or technical components are somehow controlled by humans [Ge05; p.5]. Nonetheless due to its broad range of employment from very small systems as RFID[9] chips to normal day-life devices (CD-players or washing machines) to high technology devices (air planes or computer tomographs), over 90 percent of electronic components are embedded systems. This means that of 8.3 billion produced processors in 2002, 8.15 billion were used for embedded systems whereas only 150 millions of processors were part of ordinary computers [Sch05; p.2]. Due to the diversity of usages for embedded systems, the embedded market is still one of the fastest growing markets [Sch05; p.2].

I.2.2 Characteristics

The fact of being embedded in a higher technical system leads to a set of characteristics different to ordinary computers [Sch05; p.3ff], [Ge05; p.5f].

---

[9]   Radio Frequency Identification

An ECU's primary source of interaction is not humans but the surrounding processes or technical components. Humans indirectly influence ECUs by controlling the processes and devices they are integrated, but, primarily, ECUs retrieve input by sensors and perform output by actuators integrated into the surrounding system. Accordingly to the special purposes ECUs often fulfill, the ECUs in most cases have specialized hardware (HW) specifically designed for efficiently fulfilling their purposes.

Since the surrounding system mostly is an electronic, physical-mechanical, chemical or biological device or process, developing ECUs has a strong need for interdisciplinary development efforts such as *systems engineering* discussed in ch. I.4.

Ordinary computer systems can be described as *interactive* systems. This means, the computer system actively determines the interaction process with the environment. Whenever an *interactive* system needs input for further processing the system prompts the user for input and proactively synchronizes with the environment.

ECUs on the contrary react more on the settings and changes of the environment. They are therefore called *reactive* systems. This difference has significant influence on their behavioral determinism. Interactive systems can be more seen as non-deterministic (e.g., interactive systems decide on their own how to schedule different tasks), whereas ECUs have well defined input and reaction relations with mostly strict temporal interdependencies derived from the needs of their surroundings. Three implications can be deduced from this fact:

- At first, Scholz emphasizes that "the different characteristics of both system types must be considered when adequate techniques, methods or tools are developed" [Sch05; p.4 (*)].
- Secondly, *SW designs* of *reactive systems* can heavily rely on the very well defined and researched concept of *state machines*. Since *state machines* are deterministic and have a complete *formal* semantics (other to, e.g., the semantics of activity diagrams in UML), they can be properly used for *formal requirements specification*, their early simulation, verification and complete code generation providing very positive effects on complexity handling [Ma08a; p.19] (see also [MB05]).
- Unfortunately, the temporal interdependencies force ECUs to obey timing limits. In this context, ECUs are often referred as *real time* systems. *Real time systems* can be distinct between systems that must obey their timing rules at any time (so called hard real time) and systems that should obey their timing rules as good as possible with exceptions allowed (so called soft real time) [Do04; p.3], [Sch05; p.4].

Another not yet explicitly mentioned demand for ECUs is their functional correctness. Different to programs running on ordinary computer systems, errors in already delivered ECUs cannot be easily fixed by users installing updates. Instead, expensive product recalls are necessary to fix those problems.

In many application contexts, such as medical equipment, space, aviation, nuclear power plants, production lines or automotive, system malfunctions and other defects can cause more severe consequences such as threats to life or physical condition. Such systems are called *safety-critical*. Constructing *safety-critical* systems demands enforced efforts on avoiding or at least diminishing the probability of malfunctions, other defects, or fatal consequences. Two factors are the central means to achieve this goal:

1. Explicit consideration in the design of these systems (e.g., providing redundant system parts).
2. Employing development processes ensuring high quality of the resulting system.

Concerning the first point, it is to say that this thesis speaks about design, but more on a higher *meta-level* and therefore point one will not be directly[10] in the focus of this thesis. The second point, however, is directly addressed in this thesis, as *requirements traceability* is seen as an important foundation to achieve those high quality development processes.

A fundamental principle of these processes is that their potential to ensure high quality outcomes must be controlled in an objective way. This is achieved by a set of standards such as the ISO 15504[11] (SPICE) defining necessary characteristics that development processes for *safety-critical* systems must fulfill. Correspondingly, the solution proposed here must obey the criteria demanded by those process standards. Ch. I.7 provides a description of these standards with the demanded criteria that are important to this thesis.

Differently to normal PC applications, ECUs are designed for a specific purpose. To optimize costs, the principle of HW/SW Co-design[12] is used, where HW and SW are designed in parallel with high interdependencies between each other to only fulfill its specific purpose. Especially for applications with high volumes, the so called mass market, the costs per part are decisive. Therefore

---

[10] Indirectly it well touches this issue in the sense that design for *safety-critical* issues involves decisions to be taken that impose significant consequences on the design outcome. As communication and documentation of decisions and their consequences is one of the special concerns of this thesis, this topic is indirectly connected and this connection is show in part III as real-world example of decision-making in embedded projects.

[11] Software Process Improvement Capability dEtermination (SPICE).

[12] For more information on this topic cf. [ME01].

extreme optimization of HW costs has highest priority often leading to highly specialized SW. This kind of SW has to deal with very tight resource restrictions leading to a significantly higher complexity to be handled in the SW development activities.

I.2.3 Embedded Development in the Automotive Domain[13]

> *Technical complexity of electronics and software in the automotive industry is similar complex as avionics and aerospace. Today, cars are the mass production product with the strongest cross-linking of separate computers at the smallest space. Meanwhile, more than 90 % of all functions are realized with support of software. The quality of a car is substantially determined through the quality of electronics and software. For this reason, software quality has become a central competitive factor.*
> [HDH+06; p.267-268 (*)]

"Modern premium automobiles contain by now up to 100 ECUs, with increasing tendency accompanied by approx. 3 kilometres of cable and approx. 2000 plug connectors. In these ECUs, SW with more than 600 000 lines of code regulates numerous functions and their cooperation. ... In this way, the value creation changes significantly in Automotive construction. 90% of the innovation in cars are driven by electronic components, thereof 80% software" [Sch05; p.12f (*)].

At present as in the near future, the proportion of software (SW) and SW-based ECUs in everyday products increases exponentially [Br06], (also cf. [CFG+05], [KCF+04], [HDH+06; p.267]) and this increase is accompanied by a growth of development complexity. Correspondingly, developing these SW-based ECUs meanwhile has a central strategic importance for the automotive industry.

The automotive domain has some special conditions imposing special challenges for embedded systems engineering. Generally, the following special challenges can be identified playing significant key-roles in automotive embedded development (cf. [Br06], [Gr05], [KM06], [SZ06; p.20], [Sch05; p.5]):

1. *Safety-criticality*: As mentioned in the chapter before, cars involve several *safety-related* issues. These issues must be significantly addresses as described in the chapter above.

2. *Costs*: As cars are mass-market products with high unit volumes, costs play a decisive role. Thus, proportional manufacturing costs dominate the price. In this way, ECUs' costs are also under strong pressure. The proportional manu-

---

[13] Parts of this chapter base on [TWT+08].

facturing costs of ECUs are mainly dominated by HW costs. This leads to highly cost-optimized HW with minimal HW resources concerning memory calculation power, and other components. Correspondingly, software must often be fitted to handle these, often leading to higher complexity and unnatural solutions in the software design [SZ06; p.20], [Sch05; p.5].

3. *Quality*: Buying a car involves significant costs for the customer. In consequence, cars are intended for long product life-cycles of about 25 years [SZ06; p.20]. Correspondingly, cars must provide a high overall quality, especially if they are premium products.

4. *Hard or at least weak timing restrictions*[14]: Reasons can be physical requirements for exact timing (e.g., when controlling motor injection), extremely cost optimized HW where strong resource restrictions lead to strong demands for timing; or *safety-related* issues (e.g., exact timing of inflating airbags during crash situations).

5. *Strong cross-linking of ECU systems*: Increasing cross-linking of vehicle functional features leads to increasing cross-linking of ECUs[15]. Such features are typically realized by a collaboration of several ECUs, leading to higher interdependencies between ECUs. ECUs in automotive development are usually an integrated system consisting of HW, SW and mechanical components [MHD+07; p.91]. In most cases not one ECU handles a certain function in a car, but several ECUs in interplay with each other realize a certain function. Thus, the different ECUs can communicate with each other using communication protocols such as Controller Area Network (CAN), Local Interconnect Network (LIN), Media Oriented System Transport (MOST) or Flexray. In summary, the interconnected ECUs can be seen as distributed systems with distributed control logic and changing control hierarchies [Ge05; p.5].

6. *High demands on inter-organizational collaboration*: The development of a strongly cross-linked car system can only take place in collaboration with the car manufacturers (Original Equipment Manufacturers (OEM)) and heterogeneous chains of suppliers.

7. *High numbers of variants*: Today, the buyer of a car has the choice between hundreds of options being partly connected to each other (e.g., different motors can be combined with different gearboxes) [SZ06; p.9]. As a plus, cars

---

[14] Mostly, not all timing restrictions of hard real time systems are strict. Some functions may also have weaker or even no timing restrictions.

[15] A typical scenario might look like this: A car crash triggers crash sensors which activate several airbag ECUs and a crash management ECU (CM-ECU). The CM-ECU sends an 'Unlock_Doors' signal to all door ECUs, requests the position from the Global Positioning System-ECU and sends an automatic emergency call via a Universal Mobile Telecommunications System-ECU to local rescue organizations.

are sold to very different countries with different legislation. Car systems are designed to work as very different variants. As HW costs are a significant constraint, ECUs' *variants* also involve different HW assemblies [PS05; p.112]. In the following of this thesis, this point – although it is important – is neglected. This topic could be a topic for further research basing on the results of this thesis.

From the development viewpoint, two fundamentally different perspectives on ECUs with partly different requirements for them can be observed:

- The car manufacturers (OEMs) are engaged in how the complete car system is assembled and how its parts work together to fulfill the intended requirements of the car. From the OEM perspective, the complete system 'car' is in the focus and this system is divided into several layers of sub systems, where the individual ECUs are only some parts of a complete system 'car'. The OEM, thus, mainly cares for partitioning and mapping of the functions and other technical issues on the different ECUs as subsystems, whereas the actual development of the ECUs is performed by its suppliers[16]. Thus, for the OEM the focus lies on best possible specification of the ECUs' requirements as basis for supplier management and the later integration of the developed ECUs into a complete system car, including extensive acceptance testing [SZ06; p.19]. Thus, OEMs are more concerned with what is also called *systems engineering* (see ch. I.4) and *supplier management*.
- The suppliers must then use the OEM's specification of the ECU to design and develop a system with the software. This involves *systems engineering*, but also *hardware*[17] and *software engineering* activities. In some cases, several suppliers must cooperate to develop one ECU together. In these cases also one supplier must manage the other suppliers.

At first, this implies that frictionless information exchange between all project members is a critical success factor and requirement documents are the cornerstones of this collaboration, since they are the central interfaces between organizational units of a project. In addition, the strong cross-linkings of ECUs may even urge partners to employ compatible development processes. A good step toward this goal are process standards and maturity models like SPICE (Software Process Improvement and Capability dEtermination, [HDH+06]), its

---

[16]   In some cases, however, also the OEM develops ECUs. This is, e.g., the case for highly innovative or research based systems.

[17]   In this thesis, the HW engineering domain is someway neglected, but it is assumed that the principles developed here for *traceability* and design can be equally applied to HW engineering. Further, the tool approach shown in part III should be equally able to integrate with a HW engineering tool.

new domain specific adoption Automotive SPICE (cf. [HDH+06]], [MHD+07]), or CMMI (Capability Maturity Model Integration, cf. [Kn06]). These standards are also important for addressing *safety-critical* issues that must also be addressed by additional *safety* mechanisms in ECUs (e.g., *fail safe modes*, HW and SW redundancies) and increasing complexity put additional stress on the quality of development processes [BHM01]. Secondly, this implies that the worlds of the OEMs and the suppliers are in some way different and not completely comparable. Thus, problems may be different in both branches[18].

However, also the OEMs experience a paradigm shift towards intensified model-based development efforts [CFG+05], [KCF+04]. Conrad et al. [CFG+05] – interpreted by the author – describe that this model based shift consists of three cornerstones:

- Usage of enhanced *requirements engineering* and *management* techniques. An experience report of Heumesser and Houdek [HH04] – from formerly Daimler Chrysler – mentions *requirements specifications* for the electronics of the whole system 'car' to contain about 20 000 pages, in which the *requirements specifications* for the single ECUs contain 200 to 600 pages. These high numbers of requirements must be adequately handled. Additionally, these requirements form a contractual basis for all further development activities performed with suppliers (CFG+05; p.5], [RS07; p.481f]).
- Design and implementation are more and more dominated by the continuous usage of models. "Hereby, the functionality appears in different subsequent model representations" [CFG+05; p.5 (*)].
- Both core activities will be accompanied by *verification* and *validation* procedures to assure correctness and reliability of the developed components.

All these points show that automotive development is more and more coined by flipping interactions between *requirements specifications* and *design models* at different levels of abstraction interacting with each other. This, in combination with the heterogeneous scattered development of complex, intertwined customer and supplier relationships press for the need to ensure consistency between these manifold different artifacts developed in the course of a car development endeavor. In theory, *requirements traceability* is seen as a distinct means for ensuring consistency between artifacts. Sparked from these findings, two major research goals of this thesis are *requirements traceability* in context with heterogeneous *design models* and issues of supplier management in order to ensure consistency

---

[18] Unfortunately, the author sometimes feels that literature about automotive embedded systems development often neglects this differentiation. In the past, one difference has been that OEMs mainly concentrated on the textual specification view, whereas suppliers were also forced to translate these specifications into *design models* and code.

between the complex and heterogeneous interdependencies arising out of automotive development projects.

Last but not least to mention, automotive ECUs development can be divided into four different sub domains [SZ06; p.6, p.18f], [CFG+05; p.4]:

- *Powertrain* deals about control of the motor(s) and gearing.
- *Chassis* deals about wheels, steering, breaks, etc., but also concerns persons' *safety* systems such as ABS or ESP[19].
- *Body* deals about electrical control of doors, lights, mirrors, wipers, seats, heating and climate control. Here are also included passive *safety* systems such as airbags.
- *Telematics*[20] and *Infotainment* provide multi-media applications such as radio, CD, DVD, telephone, route navigation, video etc. to the passengers. An essential part here is the *human machine interface* and possible interconnectivity with devices not being original equipment of the car (e.g., cell phones, MP3-players, car-to-car-communication, etc.).

The domains *Powertrain*, *Chassis* and *Body* are comparable to each other [CFG+05], whereas the *Telematics* domain significantly differs from them. The first three deal with controlling and steering of mostly physical process involved with the usage of a car. Correspondingly, these domains rather deal with complex calculations and complex steering functions, where relatively low amounts of data are processed (often only a few bits indicating states of sensors and actors). These systems often have hard real-time constraints, often involve *safety-critical* issues and face the pressure for extremely cost-optimized HW. Concerning development techniques, the programming language C and the real-time operating system standard OSEK-OS[21] are employed.

In the *Telematics* environment, complexity is imposed by human interaction, high amounts of data, high demands for data processing (comparable to PC-based systems), data bandwidth, and soft real-time constraints. Correspondingly, higher programming languages such as C++ or Java are used and more sophisticated operating systems – with, however, only soft real-time support – such as Microsoft Windows (Embedded) CE, Linux etc. are used. Altogether, this domain is more minted by issues of classical computer science. As these systems directly

---

[19] Antilock Braking System and Electronic Stability Control
[20] The term Telematic is a made-up word deriving from a combination of Telecommunication and Informatik (German expression for Computer Science) [MEK03; p.1].
[21] OSEK/VDX ("Offene Systeme und deren Schnittstellen für die Elektronik im Kraftfahrzeug / Vehicle Distributed eXecutive") is an industrial standardization board. The board has defined the operating system standard OSEK-OS being a standard definition for the real-time operating system used in the automotive industry.

influence user experience in comparison to the other domains, where the ECUs are more integrated into a merely technical aspect, these systems also generally have weaker resource restrictions if this favors better user experiences (e.g., by a better *human machine interface* (*HMI*)) or additional values (e.g., by offering higher value components for bandwidth).

Concerning this thesis, all four domains generally are of equal interest, since *traceability* most probably will be an issue in all four development domains. However, as the first three domains have significant harder restrictions for timing and other resources, these restrictions may be important for considerations in this thesis. Thus, these domains with the hard restrictions are considered in the examples and case studies of this thesis (see, e.g., ch. III.12).

Altogether, it can be said that the automotive domain is very heterogeneous with very different used techniques and technologies. However, all of them must be concerned with high quality processes leading to high quality outcomes. In this context, *requirements traceability* will play a decisive key role as it improves consistency between work-products being essential for the high distribution of development tasks over heterogeneous chains of suppliers.

I.3 Software Engineering (SE)

The whole trouble comes from the fact that there is so much tinkering with software.
It is not made in a clean fabrication process, which it should be.
What we need is software engineering.
F.L. Bauer

The term *software engineering* (*SE*) was first coined in 1968 by Friedrich L. Bauer during a conference of the NATO (North Atlantic Treaty Organization) science committee [Ja08; p.1] as reaction on experiences that, despite gigantic efforts, some SW projects could not be completed satisfactorily [LL07; p.46].

The central idea behind this concept is the application of engineering to software (SW). According to Sommerville, "*software engineering* is a technical discipline that deals with all aspects of software development, from the early phases of system specification to maintenance of the system, after it has been commissioned" [So01; p.22 (*)].

The IEEE Standard glossary of Software Engineering Terminology [IEEE610] defines *SE* as:

1. "The application of a systematic, disciplined, quantifiable approach to the development, operation, and maintenance of software; that is, the application of engineering to software. "

2. "The study of approaches as in (1)".

Ludewig and Lichter [LL07; p.47] indicate that this definition is in a way problematic and idealistic[22], as engineers "more often rely on experience and intuition than often admitted" [LL07; p.47 (*)] and propose the following value-free definition [LL07; p.47] (see also Jackson on what he calls radical design in software-intensive systems [Ja08; p.21]):

"SE is any activity concerned with creating or changing SW, where goals are beyond the SW" [LL07; p.47 (*)]. This means for Ludewig and Lichter, *SE* is involved anywhere, where SW is developed.

In this thesis, the following SE topics are addressed:
1. *SW development process models* (ch. I.7),
2. *Requirements engineering* and *management* (ch. I.5),
3. *SW design* (ch. I.6).

SW development *process models* provide a process road map for transforming user needs into a SW product. A SW process can be described as "a set of activities and thus interrelated results leading to the development of a SW product" [So01; p.55 (*)]. The process chain involves transforming user needs into SW requirements that are again transformed into a design. Then, the design is implemented in code. Several quality assurance methods – as testing or code inspections – accompany these processes [IEEE610]. Today, most *process models* are iterative incremental which means that the process chain mentioned above is iterated several times with new user feedback (changed or new requirements) gathered from the previous developed version [MBP+04; p.425].

The main goal of a structured model is to find and establish clearly defined processes and process interdependencies for the different development tasks ensuring structured and reproducible process results. This thesis also deals with how high quality SW and systems can be achieved using development *process models* and standards (see ch. I.7).

Requirements specification and *analysis* phases are concerned with the questions of 'what the user needs' and 'what the SW has to do' (what exactly shall the SW do?). Thus, *requirements specifications* are often described as the 'what description'. In recent years, a more or less independent field of research has evolved called *requirements engineering*. This thesis has one of its groundings in this area. Therefore, this topic is deeper discussed in ch. I.5. Historical experi-

---

[22] In fact, other organizations as the software craftsmanship movement ([Mc01], http://www.softwarecraftsmanship.org/main/about (Access: 2009/08)) challenge the paradigm of systematic engineering in software development, but emphasize a view of software development as a craftsmanship, where "engineering skills and scientific understanding are required to write good code software ... in combination with a pragmatic attitude and a sense of quality".

ence, however, has shown that describing requirements proves to be very difficult and even the best *requirements specification* efforts could not avoid significant requirement changes during development progress. As a result, *SE* theory has acknowledged that requirements and their changes must be adequately managed. *Requirements traceability* as discussed in this thesis can be considered as an activity of *requirements management*.

After the requirements have described the *problem space*, software design deals with finding an adequate solution out of the set of possible different solution alternatives (*solution space*). The design phase has the goal to sketch a possible solution and assess its consequences in order to find out, whether the solution is sustainable for the problem. Design mainly with about making general decisions about the structure of a solution that is then implemented into code.

I.4 Systems Engineering (SysEng)

Systems engineering is about creating effective solutions to problems,
and managing the technical complexity of the resulting developments.
At the outset, it is a creative activity, defining the requirements
and the product to be built.
Then the emphasis switches again, to the integration and verification,
before delivering the system to the customer.
[SBJ+98; p.7-8]

In most embedded projects, "it is crucial to consider not only the software aspects, but also the system aspects" [Do04; p.29]. Since the first introduction of the term *systems engineering* (*SysEng*) by Goode and Machol [GM57], *SysEng* has evolved to a key success factor for developing large scale complex systems, because it "deals with all aspects of developing and enhancing complex systems" [So07; p.34 (*)] and its function "is to guide the engineering of complex systems" [KS03, p.3].

The IEEE describes *SysEng* as "an interdisciplinary collaborative approach to derive, evolve, and verify a life-cycle balanced system solution which satisfies customer expectations and meets public acceptability" [IEEE1220; p.12]. Correspondingly, Douglass [Do04; p.29] defines *SysEng* as "the definition, specification, and high-level *architecture* of a system that is to be realized with multiple disciplines, typically including electrical, mechanical, software and possibly chemical engineering".

As the name *SysEng* and all these definitions mention, the term *system* plays a decisive key role. Several slightly different definitions exist:

- According to the IEEE 610, a system can be described as "a collection of components organized to accomplish a specific function or set of functions" [IEEE610; p.73]. This indicates that a system is composed of components with common goals.
- However, Müller defines a systems as "a set of elements being connected to each other by relationships and having to pursuit a certain goal together" [Mu00; p.48 (*)]. This indicates that a system is composed of components coupled by *relationships* with each other (IEEE 610 weakly indicates this by using the term 'organized'; cf. also [So01; p.36ff], [MHD+07; p.41]).
- Weilkiens defines a system as "a collection of system components aiming to fulfill a shared goal. A component can be of software, hardware, mechanics" [We06; p.10 (*)], or of any other engineering domain. This indicates that a system can be composed of components from different engineering domains interacting together.
- However, other definitions go beyond this view: "A system is an integrated composite of people, products, and processes that provide a capability to satisfy a stated need or objective" [DAU01; p.7]. In this definition a system is not just consisting of components (static view), but can also involve humans[23] and its processes (dynamic view).
- Geisberger[24] also emphasizes that "a system as a whole has system boundaries and a context" [Ge05; p.196 (*)]. This implies also a difference between the system and its environment (elements not part of the system) and indeed defining the system's context is a central task in *SysEng* [So01; p.38] leading to the definition of Hatley et al. of *system* as "an organized set of components that interact with each other and its surrounding in order to provide a significant benefit to humans" [HHP03; p.16].
- Last, but not least, the IEC 61508 defines systems as "a set of elements which interact according to a design, where an element of a system can be another system, called a subsystem, which may be a controlling system or a controlled system and may include hardware, software and human interaction" [IEC61508; part 4; p.25], (also cf. [MHD+07; p.41]).

---

[23] Or, as Hatley et al. put it [HHP03; p.17 (*)]: "Hardware and software without humans is not capable of anything ... When we specify systems, we must view the whole system – its software, all hardware-technologies, the role of the humans and the question, how humans can benefit from it".

[24] The interested reader may be invited to read Geisberger's extended comment on the term *system* describing its origins from biological and *sociological systems theory* and *cybernetics* [Ge05; p.196].

In summary, several – more or less complete – definitions of what a system is exist. Generally a system may have the following characteristics:
1. A *system* is composed of several *components*.
2. These components can again be further decomposable systems (so called *sub systems*). This gives way to that *SysEng* can also deal with developing cascades of systems built up by *sub systems*, called *systems of systems engineering* [Ja09].
3. A system has a surrounding context (i.e. environment) it interacts with. A part of this context and its interactions can be humans.
4. The system's components have *relationships* with each other and with the context. Different kinds of *relationships* exist, such as 'interaction', 'composition' or 'other dependencies'.
5. Different *components* can deal with different engineering disciplines. In the automotive domain, for example, systems often involve HW, software and mechanics [MHD+07; p.41], but components can also involve other disciplines such as chemistry, nuclear physics, biology, etc..
6. A system may not only be composed of static aspects as components, but also humans or processes may be aspects of a system.

SysEng is concerned with regarding the system over his complete life-cycle from its early ideas to its disposal [We06; p.2], [DAU01; p.3]. In reference to the International Council on Systems Engineering[25] (INCOSE) [TBI04], Weilkiens describes the focus of *SysEng* as the concentration "on the definition and documentation of system requirements in the early development phase, the preparation of a *system design*, and the verification of the system as to compliance with the requirements, taking the overall problem into account: operation, time, text, creation, cost and planning, training and support, and disposal" [We07; p.8].

SysEng thus emphasizes a holistic view [We06; p.2] on a system to be developed: "Detached from specific detailed knowledge, the requirements and structure of a system, the whole life-cycle from the idea to its disposal are planned to develop a system that meets the demands of all involved stakeholders" [We06; p.2 (*)]. As mentioned above developing complex systems can include several different engineering disciplines. *SysEng* deals with coordinating those disciplines and their tradeoffs with each other[26]. Therefore, Weilkiens also speaks

---

[25]   INCOSE can be described as the most important international society concerned with *SysEng*.

[26]   [We06; p.9] provides an example where all involved disciplines produce best possible solutions, but lacking interactions make integration impossible. This shows that making compromises between the disciplines and their solutions is an essential part of *SysEng*.

of *SysEng* as a kind of *meta-discipline* [We06; p.11], [We07; p.8]. To achieve this, *SysEng* is split into two significant sub disciplines [DAU01; p.3]:

1. The technical aspect system engineers work in also referred to as *technical knowledge domain.*
2. The *systems engineering management.*

This means *SysEng* defines a general engineering and management approach dealing with developing systems [DAU01] [Sa92], where three concepts form the cornerstones of interdisciplinary coordination:

- Definition and management of the requirements concerned with the system as a whole [TBI04]. According to Geisberger, *requirements engineering,* therefore, is the key phase (i.e., task) of *SysEng* [Ge05; p.2].
- Proper identification and definition of interfaces between the methods of different disciplines [We06; p.9].
- Proper product and project management that coordinates and moderates all interdisciplinary efforts [We06; p.9].

In the view of Stevens et al., *SysEng* deals with "coping with risk and complexity" [SBJ+98; p.9]. In this way, *SysEng* for once mainly deals with defining the requirements and thus the system to be built. The implementation of these definitions is then left over to the individual engineering disciplines of the system's components. *SysEng* encompasses these implementation activities with reviews and testing at the *components'* boundaries to ensure proper matching *Interfaces.* Finally, *SysEng* has to address significant issues of integrating the *components* into the system and verifying the assembled system [SBJ+98; p.7-8].

From a similar viewpoint, Weilkiens identifies *project management, requirements analysis, requirements management, requirements definition, system design, system verification, system integration,* and *risk management* as tasks included into a *SysEng* effort [We06; p.12], [We07; p.9].

Thus, according to Sage and Rouse, *SysEng* "is the management technology that controls a total system life-cycle process, which involves and which results in the definition, development, and deployment of a system that is of high quality, trustworthy, and cost effective in meeting user needs" [SR09; p.3].

This thesis also is concerned to a certain degree with interactions of processes and corresponding process standards. Accordingly, *SysEng* must also be taken into account. In the course of the thesis, the reader may also notice that the topic of this thesis is even more related to *SysEng* than maybe originally expected, since requirements and *requirements traceability* are the core interface for a close integration of *SysEng* and *SE* activities. Sommerville points out that "system development is an older discipline than *software engineering.* Since over 100 years, people have designed and built complex industrial systems like aircrafts and chemical factories. However, the share of software-based systems has increased and techniques of *SE*-like modeling of *use cases* and *configuration management* are used in system development processes" [So07; p.34 (*)].

Vice versa, it is to state that *SE* also is increasingly influenced by the *SysEng* discipline, as SW often is developed for ECUs and thus it is very seldom an entity of its own, but is employed in an higher level system environment. Evidence for this claim can be found in *SE* books also mentioning *SysEng* (e.g., Sommerville provides an extra chapter [So07; chapter 2]) or standards on SW development processes as ISO 12207 [ISO12207] or SPICE [ISO15504] embedding the SW development processes into higher level *SysEng* processes (e.g., processes ENG.2, ENG.3 in SPICE).

In his analysis of the future about *SE* and *SysEng* processes, Boehm [Bo05] points out his view that the separation between *SE* and *SysEng* has been an artificial one rather manifested by historic development than real needs of development. Correspondingly, Boehm forecasts that in the future *SE* and *SysEng* will grow together to one integrated theory and one block of activities in practice.

Currently, a second slightly different notion of *SysEng* seems to evolve originating more from engineering practice. Here, Hood et al. [HWF+08] could get a good catch of this opinion in their book's title "Requirements Management – The interface Between Requirements Development and All Other Systems Engineering Processes". In this point of view, *SysEng* is either considered as a kind of synonym for *requirements engineering* in connection with a certain management level above a normal SE project. This notion can be seen in the following fig. 4-1 taken from [HWF+08; p.29]. It shows all '*SysEng* disciplines' from the perspective of Hood et al.. Hood et al. now propagate that *requirements management* (see fig. 5-3 in ch. I.5.3) interconnects these disciplines with each other.

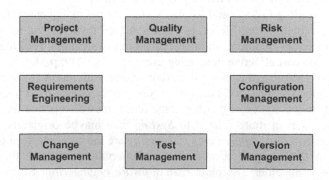

Figure 4-1 The view of *systems engineering* processes of Hood et al. [HWF+08; p.29]

The author can share this notion as he also sees a certain potential for *requirements management* to be a decisive interface connecting the 'management' activities with the *requirements engineering* activities (information on this notion is also described in ch. I.5.3). From the *SysEng* perspective, however, the author thinks this view neglects the originally emphasized dimension of design taking place in *SysEng* processes and reduces *SysEng* to a 'little advanced version of *requirements engineering* and *management*'. The similar notion is found by Douglass [Do04; p.37-38] (and also seems to be present at Geisberger [Ge05]), when describing the ROPES[27] *process model* subordinating the *SysEng* activities to the analysis activities as a kind of extension to requirement analysis. However, it is doubtful, whether a '*system design*' is just some kind of 'analysis'.

This only reflects the dimension of *SysEng* management but neglects the dimension of a technical knowledge domain that has to consider different engineering disciplines and their correlations. Thus, a good *system design* will acknowledge the special needs, strength and weaknesses of each involved engineering discipline so that the different parts from the different disciplines can frictionless cooperate to fulfill the systems tasks, whereas a weak *system design* might neglect some characteristics of an engineering discipline resulting in a system with collaboration problems between the different parts.

I.5 Requirements Engineering and Management

> *I believe the hard part of building software to be the specification, design, and testing of this conceptual construct, not the labor of representing it and testing the fidelity of the representation. We still make syntax errors, to be sure; but they are fuzz compared to conceptual errors in most systems. If this is true, building software will always be hard. There is inherently no silver bullet.*
> [Br87]

"The key to every successful software project is its ability to meet the needs of its intended customer" [BCM+08; p.139]. Or as Endres and Rombach call it Glass' law [ER03; p.16 (*)]: "Requirement deficiencies are the prime source of project failures".

---

[27] Rapid Object-oriented Process for Embedded Systems – a kind of adaption of the RUP (Rational Unified Process) *process model* [Kr99] for embedded systems development.

Thus, "in the 1970's, customer needs were documented in a customer requirements specification" [HWF+08; p.39 (*)], but the process "did not have a fancy name, it was just engineering" [HWF+08; p.39 (*)]. Starting with the "IEEE International Symposium on Requirements Engineering" in 1993, an independent discipline called *requirements engineering* (*RE*) started to evolve [PD04].

Pohl [Po08; p.43 (*)] gives a very concrete definition of *RE*: "*RE* is a cooperative, iterative, incremental process with the goal to assure that:

1. All relevant requirements are known and understood in the necessary degree of detail.
2. The involved stakeholders gather a sufficient agreement about the known requirements.
3. All requirements are specified conforming to documentation, i.e. specification, instructions".

The basic idea behind *RE* is that the requirements state the needs of the future users of a system or SW[28] therefore requirements form the basis (key driver) for all development efforts. Experience has shown that requirements are not easy to gather, because most systems are developed for people not involved in systems or SW development. This means *RE* deals with bridging the user worlds (domains[29]) and their vocabulary to the world and vocabulary of the developers.

On a second behalf, a system also has its own life cycle. All phases of the life cycle can also raise[30] requirements on the system.

Summing it all up, *RE* activities involve a lot of different people which must be brought together in an optimal communication process. As Ebert states in the preface of [Eb05], the *RE* theories therefore include at least "experiences in system techniques, psychology[31], business administration, marketing, product management, project management and computer science" and its application has "less technical aspects and much more 'political' and psychological aspects than usually admitted" [Eb05; p.10 (*)].

Rupp lists seven central problems and risks addressed by *RE* and thus encountered by improper *RE* [RS02; p.19ff]:

*   Unclear visions on the goals of the system due to different types of stakeholders with different usage characteristics,

---

[28]   In the further, only the term system is used, but SW is also implied by this term.

[29]   Mostly, there is not one type of user but several user types connected to several usage domains.

[30]   For example, the maintenance phase is unavoidable and requires that the developed system fulfills requirements for good maintainability.

[31]   On the importance of psychology in *RE* see [Ru02]

- High complexity of the task to solve,
- Communication problems due to different languages (vocabulary) of different stakeholders,
- Continuously changing goals and requirements (often referred to as 'scope creep' or 'requirements creep'),
- Poor quality of requirements due to ambiguity, redundancies, contradictions or imprecise information,
- Unnecessary or unspecified features[32]
- Imprecise project planning and tracking due to imprecise requirements;

The aspects mentioned above only mention one aspect of the problem. The core problem closely connected with the problem of bringing very different stakeholder perspectives together is the problem of inevitable requirement change during the whole project progress, where "changing requirements is one of the most significant motivations for software change" [JL05; p.120]. A diversity of reasons for requirement changes exists (see the following sub ch. I.5.6), but one of the key reasons surely is that bringing all different user perspectives together will always lead to compromises and inconsistencies not discoverable at early stages. This leads to the need that requirements and their changes must be appropriately managed. Consequently, this aspect is called *requirements management* (*RM*) (see ch. I.5.3, cf. also [Eb05; p.18ff]: "Contents of Requirement Management").

The user should note that, in the English speaking community, the term *requirements engineering* (*RE*) stands for both aspects described here (cf. [Eb05;

---

[32] Also often referred as gold-plating [RR99; p.275]. The most usual source of gold-plating are 'ideas' of developers they just implemented without feedback from the customer. Unnecessary features increase development costs and complexity of the SW.

Evaluations show that 45% of system features are not used (cf. [[Yo03; p.45]). An also important role in avoiding gold-plating may play *rationale management* (see ch. II.9). Haynes [Ha06b; p.66] describes a survey on the usage of *rationale* in an U.S. military application project, where of 74 discrete features only 19 rendered to be "important or of high *impact*".

However, two other factors must be considered. First of all, the SW product must also allow possibilities for the developers to bring in their creativity. Thus, the ideas of the developers must be considered. A good tactic is to manage developer ideas as change requests that can be discussed with the customer ([RS02; p.23]). Secondly, as Rupp et al. point out, in certain situations (e.g., when the product aims at a market leading position), [RS07; p.113f] excellent products must also grasp unknown customer wishes as enthusiasm factors (In German: Begeisterungsfaktoren). This indicates that gold-plating can also be useful in certain situations as long as it is some conscious, controlled process.

p.VII]), but the author agrees with other authors ([Eb05], [RS02], [HWF+08]) that the aspect of managing requirements should be emphasized in the term[33].

Thus, in the following, the author will speak generally of *requirements engineering* and *management* (*REM*) and he will only use the term *RE* if he directly refers to aspects of *requirements engineering,* and *requirements management* (*RM*) when directly referring to aspects of *RM*.

As some indications show, *REM* seems to emancipate as a separate discipline apart from *computer science* theory. This is especially true in the embedded domain, where *REM* must be an interdisciplinary approach to integrated aspects of *mechanical engineering, electronics engineering* and *computer science* [Ge05] containing also significant overlaps with the *SysEng* discipline. Humans and the handling of requirement information are a central issue of *REM*. In this aspect, *REM* seems also to be a promising field for information science, because certain parts of *REM* theory like *user interface design* already have a strong focus in *information science*.

Last but not least, it should be mentioned that not all developed systems are necessarily driven by requirements [HHP03; p.33]. As an example, the consumer market is rather driven by market changes resulting in extended requirement changes. *Requirements analysis* and other *REM* techniques, however, can also prove helpful in these areas (see also [BCM+08; p.139]).

I.5.1 The Term 'Requirement'

> *There are two things success in every respect rests upon.*
> *The one is that purpose and object of the task are correctly determined.*
> *The other, however, consists in finding the actions leading to this final object.*
> Aristotle (*)

Before different concepts of *REM* are introduced, the term requirement and its characteristics shall be defined. The IEEE Standard Glossary of Software Engineering Terminology defines a requirement as [IEEE610; p.62]:
1. "A condition or capability needed by a user to solve a problem or achieve an objective".
2. "A condition or capability that must be met or possessed by a system or system component to satisfy a contract, standard, specification, or other formally imposed documents."

---

[33] A quite good summary about the historical development of the terms Requirements Engineering, Requirements Management and the historical causes for the confusing usage of the different terms is provided by [HWF+08; p.39-41].

3. "A documented representation of a condition or capability as in (1) or (2)".

Geisberger [Ge05; p.2] defines the term very similar, but instead of the term user she uses instead of user the term stakeholder giving the definition a wider scope. This notion is more accurate, because also stakeholders exist being not the users of the system[34], and these stakeholders also raise requirements. Hatley et al. [HHP03; p.29ff] provide a collection of other possible sources for requirements. Among these a lot of different stakeholders exist:

- The customer: the person or organization ordering and paying the system development.
- Users: any person really using the system.
- Managers: managers in house of the developing party. These people are mostly concerned about cost optimization and, e.g., reuse.

It is to emphasize that requirements do not alone arise from the customer, but among others the following sources of requirements exist: the users[35], managers of the developing company, industrial standards, the development process and many other.

Current *REM* theory distinguishes two fundamental types of requirements:

- *Functional requirements* (*FR*),
- *Nonfunctional requirements* (*NFR*), also referred to as quality attributes [BCK03], [Bo00b];

A *FR* is concerned with a functional aspect of a system. The scope of a *FR* generally is very specific. Thus, *FRs* are mostly very concrete, Its Implementation can be directly localized in code, and testing the SW for its fulfillment is relatively simple.

NFRs are requirements "not specifically concerned with the functionality of the system" [KS98]. They specify a quality property and / or constraint of a product [Eb05; p.298]. In his comment in [RS07; p.259f (*)], Hruschka points out that he would rather prefer the term "required constraint", since he defines *NFRs* as "everything constraining the freedom of the designer in fulfilling the functional requirements". Mostly, *NFRs* refer to a so called quality attribute as, e.g., performance, usability, scalability or maintainability[36] (see [RS07; p.272]).

The scope of a *NFR* mostly is very general referring to the system to be built as a whole. Therefore, *NFRs* are significantly more difficult to specify, implement

---

[34] For example, the stakeholders paying for a system are seldom the users of a system.

[35] The users (people using the system/SW) are mostly different to the customer (person or company ordering and paying for a system/SW).

[36] These are also called the "ilities" [Fi98]. However, also some more detailed differentiations exist in literature. The interested reader may look at [CY04], [RS07; p.256], [Eb06; p.98f].

and to test than *FRs* (for more specific information see [CNY+99], [CY04], [RS07; p.259]). In practice, *FRs* are often identified and specified in a relative fast fashion [Mo04; p.336], whereas *NFRs* are often neglected, even though they have a decisive influence on the overall success of a project [Mo04; p.337]. Often, projects miss important goals if one or even several important *NFRs* have been neglected[37] ([RS07; p.259f], [RS02; p.264], [Mo04; p.337]).

In [HR02; p.86 ff], Hruschka and Rupp provide a good overview of the different kinds of *FRs* and *NFRs* encountered in a project (see fig. 5-1). The interesting part of this view is that *NFRs* are not just limited to the real requirements of a system, but it is also acknowledged that the environmental settings pose important constraints on a project. These constraints can be the future usage environment of the system – often referred to as the context of the system –, but also organizational aspects, as demands on used development processes or management related context of the project in the organization, are important key success

---

[37] A colleague of the author working at a different company was once hired to perform system archeology on a system developed by a near shoring contractual project where the original system supplier refused any further maintenance support on the system. The reason was that the developed system turned out to be very slow and not maintainable. Even though the system was intended to run on one computer, the designers of the system chose to use CORBA (Common Object Request Broker Architecture) as a communication middle ware to connect all different components of the system. In this way, the designers probably thought to achieve an open architecture flexible to later changes. As, however, the system just was intended to run on one computer, the communication middle ware proved to be an overhead causing low performance. Additionally, the flexibility of decoupled components lead to the effect at the developing company that the different project developers used their favorite programming language for their components to develop leading to a mixture of different programming languages used for the different components. This finally resulted in a system not being maintainable. By addressing on the one side *NFRs* about flexibility and maintainability through the decision to use CORBA, the drawbacks on the performance *NFRs* were neglected. Finally, the flexibility achieved by the decision for CORBA inadvertently lead to developers disregarding the maintainability *NFRs* by individually choosing their programming language at will. As a result, the company lost the project and the customer. The customer in need for the system was forced to spend significant extra money to find out all aspects about the system in order to start a new endeavor for developing a running system. Ironically, due to the high losses of the failing project, management decided to save money in the new project by assigning a far-shoring company to develop the new system, even though the near-shoring approach disclosed significant communication problems and significant loss of control over the project. In retrospect, it might have been a far better and less expensive idea to directly hire a few well-paid, but also well-trained near-by developers with short communication paths and a significantly better control of the project by the customer.

factors for a project. These aspects should not be neglected as important sources for *NFRs*.

As mentioned above, it is especially important to not oversee some important *NFRs*, since they often determine the success of a project. Rupp et al. provide here the valuable expression of quality scopes: "A quality scope defines a limited set of defined quality characteristics" [RS02; p.270 (*)]. Such quality scopes are – among others – standards such as [ISO9126] or [ISO25000], the *'Volere Template'* propagated by the Robertsons [RR99] or the FURPS[38] model developed by Grady and Caswell at Hewlett Packard [GC87; p.159] or *'Planguage'* [Gi05], (see also [Em10]). These scopes have the advantage of providing structured listings of quality aspects that can be used as check lists for systematically perusing them, thus identifying and specifying (not forgetting) any important *NFR*.

Besides finding, properly specifying, implementing and testing all relevant *NFRs* is crucial for project success [RS02; p.264]. Since *NFRs* do not represent concrete functionality, *NFRs* are often minted by malleable terms and weak criteria [Mo04; p.352] especially difficult to handle, often leading to intangibly specified and thus untestable *NFRs*[39].

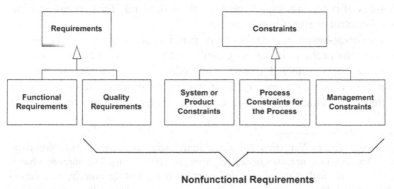

Nonfunctional Requirements

Figure 5-1 Functional and nonfunctional requirements [HR02; p.86 ff]

---

[38] Functionality Usability Reliability, Performance Supportability. Later evolved to FURPS+ ([Gr92]), where '+' reminds that additional requirements as design, implementation, interface and physical constraints must be considered. FURPS+ is widely used in the IT industry (e.g., by the Rational Unified Process (RUP), (cf. [Kr03], [Kr99; p.142])). Eeles [Ee05] describes how FURPS+ is used by IBM in context of the RUP.

[39] Therefore, significant parts of literature to *REM* are concerned with handling *NFRs*. A good starting point for research information is found in [CY04].

Generally, in order to achieve testable requirements, *REM* theory propagates that for each requirement also the verification criteria should be equally specified. If then no concrete verification criteria can be found for a requirement, strong indications exist that a requirement is not testable and thus realization of the requirement is not sure [RS02; p.71ff, p.293-336]. Process standards as described in ch. I.7, thus, also explicitly demand that testability of any requirement must be ensured by specifying verification criteria.

To tackle these problems, Rupp et al. propose using an approach they call IVENA[40] [RS07; p.459], [RS02; p.271ff]. IVENA describes the idea that *NFRs* with their verification criteria being considered as very accurate in a project are collected in a structured data system, where developers of a new project can systematically search for and retrieve propositions for specified *NFRs* and their verification criteria for a project. A further possible cognate heuristic may provide the application of *requirement patterns* [RS02; p.337-385] (concerning *patterns* see ch. I.6.2.4). *Requirement patterns* intend to give support for identifying and documenting recurring requirement problems. The *pattern* structure includes requirements and its verification criteria. An interesting application of a *requirement pattern*, e.g., might be addressing the *NFR* 'access control' as *pattern*, as it has high degrees of recurring requirements such as demands for user authentication, password control or rights management.

Both experience-based approaches may provide an interesting leverage to improve tackling the problem in the long run[41], but they are no help for concrete situations, where such collected expert knowledge infrastructures are not yet present. Literature about *software architectures* theory proposes handling *NFRs* that are difficult to tackle by deriving concrete scenarios[42] that are verifiable

---

[40]   In German: Integriertes Vorgehen zur Ermittlung nicht-funktionaler Anforderungen (Integrated Approach for non-functional requirements elicitation). The approach bases on collecting *NFRs* and other related information (e.g., testing criteria, test cases) specified in other (older) projects in a database repository ordered by quality topics. Now, the requirement engineer searching for a good specification of a *NFR* can research the database for suggestions used in the other projects.

[41]   It is interesting to note that both methods in some way can also be considered in the context of *rationale management* (see ch. II.9). In this context, both approaches could be seen as a way to collect information about a decision process, whose results are later reused in a new project.

[42]   As an example, an ECU in an Automotive project contains the *NFR*: "The system must have good performance.". Such an *NFR* is not testable, because it is too vague. However, the *NFR* can be used to derive the following concrete scenarios for the intended performance:

(*verification criteria* can be defined) [BCK03; p.78-95], [Bo00b; p.34ff], [PBG04; p.82ff], [Mo04; p.339, p.352].

Some *REM* theory proposes handling *NFRs* by transforming them into (expressing them through) several functional requirements [Pi04; p.99], [PKD+03]. As scenarios are closely related to the *use case* concept being a heuristic for requirement documentation (see ch. I.5.4), it is very likely that both theories mean the same at this point.

A further important point here to consider is how *FRs* and *NFRs* impose an influence on software design. In connection to *SW architecture*, Eeles [Ee05] claims the existence of '*architectural requirements*': "An *architectural requirement*, in turn, is any requirement that is architecturally significant, whether this significance be implicit or explicit". This implies at least that also requirements may exist with no relevance to the *architecture*. It turns out that the *SW architecture* is hardly dominated by *FRs*. Instead, *NFRs* impose the main influence on the *SW architecture* [BCK03; p.72f], [PBG04; p.72], whereas *FRs* are then mainly con-sidered in the detailed design or the code.

Concerning implementation, it is to note that the actual accomplishment of a requirement is better than the demand imposed by the requirement in order to guarantee it is actually fulfilled in any situation [HHP03; p.32]. This is especially the case, when it involves tackling *NFRs,* as it is more difficult to guarantee them for any situation (e.g., this is especially the case for performance requirements.).

A further aspect to be considered in the context of requirements is that requirements form the contractual basis for development [Eb05; p.18; p.268ff] (see also [BCM+08; p.139]). This issue is discussed in detail in ch. I.7.2.2.

Last, but not least to mention, in order to have a high quality *requirements specification*, *REM* theory also has formulated a set of quality criteria each requirement should fulfill. The following listing orients on Pohl [Po08; p.222 (*)], but the same (or, at least very similar demands) are listed in any book on *REM*:

- *Completeness*: A requirement is complete if it is documented according to fixed criteria (e.g., templates) and if its content does not contain any gaps in relation to itself or in relation to other requirements.
- *Traceability*: A requirement shall be traceable to its origin, its evolution (history), its realizations in the system (design, code) and its tests.
- *Correctness*: The requirement is correct if the affected stakeholders acknowledge its correctness and need to be implemented in the system.
- *Unambiguity*: A requirement must not allow any ambiguous interpretation.

(1.) "Function 1 must be performed within ... ms".
(2.) "Function 2 must be performed within ... ms".
(3.) ...

- *Understandability*: The requirement is understandable if its content is described as simple as possible.
- *Consistency*: A requirement is consistent if it does not contradict with any other requirement.
- *Testability*: It must be possible to test a system whether it correctly fulfills a requirement or not.
- *Evaluated*: The requirement's importance on the system to develop is assessed and captured.
- *Actuality*: The requirements must contain the current state of the project.
- *Atomicity*: A requirement shall only describe one issue, fact, aspect or need.

  Equally as quality requirements exist for a requirement, the following quality demands can be derived for a *requirements specification* as a whole (see above for its description of meaning) [HDH+06; p.88]:

- *Correctness*,
- *Unambiguity*,
- *Completeness*,
- *Verifiability*,
- *Consistent*,
- *Changeability*

I.5.2 Phases, Artifacts and Techniques in *REM*

The field of *REM* is relatively new and no common understanding of *REM* has already condensed. Thus, a lot of publications and proposals for processes, artifacts and techniques exist [BHJ+10]. Since all three aspects are related to each other, this chapter tries to give a short introductory overview of these correlations. However, since *REM* accompanies the whole development process and a high variety of establishments to different project situations exist, this chapter does not claim for completeness. It should further be mentioned that, due to the high variety of different project situations *REM* is employed, a full understanding of a common set of activities to be called a *REM* theory will most probably be never achieved. Vice versa, it is questionable if 'a common understanding' of *REM* is necessary or even useful, as SW projects vary in high degrees from each other (and concerning *SysEng* even a higher variety of disciplines and project are involved), where *REM* processes have significantly different appearances.

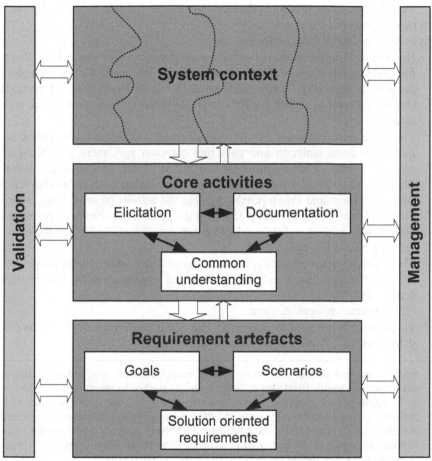

Figure 5-2 The Requirements Engineering framework defined by Pohl [Po08; p.39 (*)]

However, some authors, such as Pohl [Po08], give a valuable structure for understanding the correlations in *REM*. Pohl [Po08], e.g., has developed his so called *RE framework* [43] (see fig. 5-2).

---

[43] "The term *RE-frameworks* refers to generic models describing and structuring the requirement processes, artifacts, organizations, and roles, or combinations of these" [BHJ+10; p.6 (*)]. Birk et al. [BHJ+10] report that their working group could identify about 40 different *RE* frameworks. Their endeavors to compare these frameworks sparked the conclusion that "the landscape of *RE-frameworks* is currently still broadly

Pohl's framework [Po08] is divided into a *core* (middle block of fig. 5-2) and two *crosscutting activities*.

The *core*[44] consists of three major aspects:

- No system is self-contained but has an environment it interacts with, therefore the systems context and its interactions are important for understanding the system itself. Pohl further differentiates four different kinds of contexts (for details refer to [Po08; p.39ff; ch.5]) emphasizing the importance of considering each.

- The three core activities of *RE* consisting of *requirement elicitation*, requirement documentation and gathering common agreement (resolving all conflicts – also called requirement negotiation[45]) between all stakeholders. This part also includes the often referred requirement analysis as characterized by Gerdom and Posch [GP04; p.64] as the activity of structuring, examining and prioritizing [PR09; p.129-134] the present requirements, where the requirement analyst closely works together with the customer and the architect (see also [BGK+07; p.130]).

- The major requirement artifacts consisting of major goals, major *usage scenarios*[46] (i.e. *use cases*) and solution oriented requirements the system shall accomplish.

The *crosscutting activities* are:

- *Validation* has the goal to find errors that occur in all three core aspects (for details refer to [Po08; part V]).

---

scattered and fragmented. Correspondingly, demand for examination and structuring of this knowledge exist" [BHJ+10; p.7 (*)]. It should further be mentioned that Broy et al. in [BGK+07] try to define a so called reference model for *REM* processes most probably having a similar purpose as the *RE framework* idea. The author has decided to sketch Pohl's framework, since it provides a relatively compact overview of the correlations important to the author in this context. The reader more interested in a detailed process setup, should also refer to [BGK+07] or [BHJ+10].

[44] The author tends to name this core the actual *RE* activities. However, as mentioned, no common agreement on the terms has yet established on this field.

[45] The purpose of negotiation is to discover missing requirements, ambiguous requirements, overlapping requirements and unrealistic requirements. The result of the negotiation process is a definition of the system requirements, which are agreed on by requirements engineers and stakeholders [SS97].

[46] Ambler [Am05] recommends that requirements should at first be analyzed in breadth (the set of feature shall be explored) and then later in depth (details of the features). Ambler there also refers to a speech of Jim Johnson, chairman of the Standish Group, at the XP2002 conference (see http://martinfowler.com/articles/xp2002.html (Access: 2010/06)) claiming that up-front detailed *RE* and modeling can lead to 80% of relatively unwanted functionality, whereas only 20% of the features are often used.

- *Management* involves for Pohl all planning, steering and control activities concerned with all three core aspects [Po08; p.46] (for details see [Po08; part VI]). Due to the importance of this part in this thesis this topic is dealt with in the following ch. I.5.3.

One dimension not mentioned yet is the correlation between *REM* and the different development phases. As Pohl describes in [Po08; p.32], the former view on *REM* was phases-driven, i.e. *REM* was mainly part of early development phases involving several disadvantages leading to Jarke and Pohl's [JP94] proposal of continuous *REM* activities (as described in detail at [Po08; p.34-35]) during development activities.

Today, continuous *REM* can be called the state of the art, meaning that *REM* are accompanying activities throughout the whole development life-cycle.

I.5.3 Requirements Management

Since the main subject of this thesis is a sub part of *requirements management* (*RM*), some extra words on *RM* shall better illuminate this context. *RM* is the activity of organizing, administrating and supervising requirements during the whole development process [TKT+07; p.274].

Rupp et al. [RS02; p.15] emphasize that *RM* establishes methods that enable the handling of unmanageable numbers of requirements in complex projects. Among others, it permits parallel and worldwide distributed work on requirements.

Hood et al. define *RM* as "a set of activities which ensure that the requirements information is always up to date and can be accessed by all project staff that may benefit from it. In other words, requirements management integrates all relevant pieces of information from all the other *systems engineering* disciplines" [HWF+08; p.35 (*)].

It should be mentioned that Hood et al. imply a different but interesting perspective on *RM* [HWF+08; p.29]. As Hood et al. define *SysEng* as a set of the processes *project management*, *quality management*, *risk management*, *configuration management*, *version management*, *test management*, and *change management* (see fig. 4-1 in ch. I.4 [HWF+08; p.29]).

Now, as Hood et al. call their book "Requirements Management – The interface Between Requirements Development and All Other Systems Engineering Processes.", they imply that *RM* is the interface connecting the processes together. Thus, orienting on fig. 4-1 in ch. I.4 from [HWF+08; p.29], fig.5-3 shows Hood's view [HWF+08] as logical derived interpretation by the author. And *RM*, in fact, often uses techniques known from these mentioned management theories, but uses them in the limited focus of managing belongings of requirements (indicated by also referring *RE* in fig. 5-3).

The fact that *RM* borrows much of its techniques from the other management disciplines is not coincidental but directly derives from the fact that these are the fluent transition points to the other management disciplines in a way that these management disciplines then also make use of the results of *REM*. An example for this fact is that requirements prioritization [Po08; p.527-544], [PR09; 129-134] and conflict management [Po08; p.399-409] results performed as *RM* activities are results that directly influence *project management* and *risk management*.

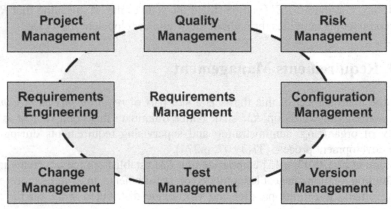

Figure 5-3 The view of Hood et al. [HWF+08] logically derived by the author.

At first glance, this now seems to be a trivial insight, but, if it must be considered that consistency between the findings of these disciplines must be ensured in order to have trustworthy results of the different disciplines. This sheds light to one of the core activities of RM: *Requirements traceability* is intended for being the central means to achieve this consistency.

I.5.4 Models in REM

REM is usually accompanied by the usage of models helping to analyze the problem situation. These models are often referred as *analysis models* (*AM*) as they support analysis of found requirements in order to discover contradictions or inconsistencies thus indicating missing requirements and thus directly supporting requirements elicitation. *Design models* are discussed separately in the chapter about design ch. I.6.

According to Sommerville [So07; p.204], user requirements should be formulated in natural language, since they need to be understood by humans being no technical experts. More detailed system requirements[47], however, can be expressed in more technical ways.

In this way, a widely used technique is to support documentation of the system specification as a collection of *system models* or *AMs*. *AMs* can be categorized as *descriptive models*, since their main goal is to describe the facts portrayed by the requirements. *AMs* can here be seen as a different view to the ordinary specified requirements. In some projects the analysis model is part of the *requirements specification* in other projects it is a separate artifact.

A special case is the so called *use case* driven approach (see [Co00]). *Use cases* describe usage scenarios of the product to develop. These *use cases* often consist of a relatively simple schematic drawing such as described by the UML[48] *use case* diagram in addition to a template based textual description of the *use case* (the UML only standardizes the *use case* diagram but formulates no concrete demands for the template). For further detailing of the *use cases* so called scenarios are modeled, where in many cases one *use case* is described by several scenarios, e.g., being modeled by UML sequence diagrams. In this way, *use cases* can be seen as a kind of hybrid between a textual requirements specification with a seamless starting point for analysis with AMs. *Use cases* provide a good means for grouping the textual requirements through their *use case* template. However, Cockburn [Co00; p.28ff] remarks that *use cases* admittedly document and structure requirements, but this is only the case for a certain portion of the requirements (Cockburn [Co00; p.28ff] estimates one third). Thus, for example, details for external interfaces, data formats, business rules, complex formulas or *NFRs* are very difficult to cover.

Originally, *use cases* have been intended to improve communication (i.e. understanding) between user domain experts of the customer not familiar with computer science and SW developers not familiar with the user domain.

Before this, computer science oriented lingo was often used where understandability, however, was difficult for none-computer science specialists. Through *use cases,* SW developers are forced to be more geared to the language

---

[47] In ch. I.7.2.2.1, the differences between *user* and *system requirements* are described and how they can be compared to the German concepts of 'Lastenheft' and 'Pflichtenheft'.

[48] Refer to Booch's first hypothesis [ER03; p.25]: "Object model reduces communication problems between analysts and users".

of the users. In this way, the language monopole as well as the critical faculties is left to the users.

Due to these advantages, a better fitting of the developed system to the real needs of the users can be achieved. Correspondingly, the technique of eliciting, structuring and documenting requirements using the *use case* concept has succeeded in nearly all development areas except for purely technical systems [RS02; p.212f]. Such a case is the automotive domain, where technical textual *requirements specifications* in combination with *formal specification models* are preferred over *use case* approaches. A cause for this may be that at automotive system development, the language barriers described above do not exist in this form, because the customers are often equally accustomed to technical description languages as the developers are.

Groß et al. [GDM+10] report an empirical evaluation result comparing *use case specification technique* with *functional specification techniques* usually used in the automotive industry. As basis for the comparison an "Automotive Door Steering Device" has been the target for specification. The authors came to the conclusion that the *use cases* approach lead to a more complete *requirements specification* as it discovered and covered more project *goals*. On the other side, the *functional specification* approach provided more specific and thus better understandable requirements for the developers.

Concerning *REM*-techniques in the automotive domain, Weber and Weisbrod [WW02; p.23] emphasize: "Although most specification activities are still document-based, a growing number of specifications require complex models, such as executable *analysis models*, *system* and *software design models*, and HMI[49] models". Thus, in these cases often more formal *domain specific languages* such as *state machines* can be used. These languages have the advantage that through their better defined semantics more explicit content and content of higher information can be specified. For example, *state charts* have the following advantages compared to pure textual descriptions [Do04; p.317f]:

- *Precision*: Due to the concrete *formal* semantics, misinterpretations are almost impossible.
- *Model generation*: Due to its deterministic and complete semantics, an executable requirements model or executable program code can be generated.
- *Verifiability*: Through its mathematical semantics, early model analysis, simulation, or model execution is possible.

In this way, such *formal* description techniques are used in combination with adequate tools (such as Matlab Simulink, Matlab Stateflow [Matlab] or ETAS ASCET [ASCET]) to analyze extensive parts of the functional requirements of an

---

[49]   Human Machine Interface

automotive system. These *AMs* can be used to simulate the behavior in early design phases as executable prototype. In later phases, these models can be used to directly generate the source code implementation. In this, way these *AMs* seamlessly also become *DMs* and the code but significantly avoid redundancies. As these techniques allow handling extended parts of the functional requirements often implying significant complexity in their interdependencies, these techniques can be a significant means to early reduce development complexity and quality risks. At the moment, however, these techniques are not capable of modeling a complete system. Thus, still significant parts of ECUs must be developed in conventional system and software development techniques. If those techniques are then used, then design activities must additionally find ways to properly integrate these parts into the complete system (see ch. I.6.6.1 for a further discussion).

Last but not least to mention, the analysis phase is generally difficult to handle, because on the one hand, the problem and its accompanied requirements should be sufficiently understood and analyzed in order to avoid disapproving surprises or inadequate designs, but on the other hand, too extensive analyzes lead to unnecessary extra efforts and extensive redundancies necessary to maintain in later development iterations. Extensive analysis can lead to what Brown et al. call *analysis paralysis*[50] [BMH+98; p.215-218], [Ec03] describing the fact that developers defer actions to be taken in order to perform more analysis coming to a point where they are stuck (see also remarks of Hatley et al. [HHP03; p.53] on criteria where and when to stop analysis and start with design). In summary, the maxim on analysis must be to model as much as it is necessary to achieve a better understanding of the system. As a result, any analysis method must take care of an adequate scalability of the method. This must also be taken into account when considering *traceability* to *AMs*.

Concerning *traceability* in general, *AMs* must also be taken into account. The solution discussed here does not directly address this issue, but it well has two indirect links:

1. The fact described above that parts of the *FRs* of automotive ECUs are described by special tools allowing early *AMs* become seamless *design models* and then code sparks the need to consider this in the design process. This especially involves that design is often performed using different modeling

---

[50] Brown et al. consider *analysis paralysis* as a management *anti pattern* [BMH+98; p.215-218] (the *anti pattern* concept is discussed in the course of *pattern design* theory ch. I.6.2.4). A slightly different explanation of *analysis paralysis* is provided by Conklin [Co06; p.8ff], who brings it in connection with *wicked problems* (see details in ch. I.6.2.2). According to him, "problem understanding can only come from creating possible solutions and considering how they might work" [Co06; p.11]. Thus, pure analysis might automatically lead to *analysis paralysis*.

tools in one project. This is described in more detail in ch. I.6. The solution discussed here to *traceability* also explicitly considers this in ch. III.16.

2. Generally, the tool and methodology developed here (see part III) should be equally possible and valuable to apply for establishing *traceability* to *AMs* if these *AMs* are modeled in a modeling tool supported by the tool[51] described here. In the following of this thesis, this is not explicitly discussed and may be part of later research.

I.5.5 Separation between Requirements and Design

SE and *REM* theory often propagate a clear separation between requirements specification and design (ch. I.6) meaning that the requirements must be formulated design independently and must not anticipate the design. This shall ensure as much freedom in design as possible (e.g., see Hatley et al. [HHP03; p.252] and avoid "inextricably mixing up requirements and design" [HHP03; p.252(*)]).

However, other research has shown that requirements cannot be defined completely design independent (see [Po08], [Nu01], [IBR+01], [PDK+02], [PKD+03; p.142], [Yo03; p.52]) demanding a "joint elicitation and specification of the problem and the structure" [PKD+03; p.142].

Young [Yo03; p.52] shows some examples why requirements seldom can be specified totally independently from the system (resp. SW) design:

- Systems are often targeted for environments already containing other systems (the *context*). These surrounding systems have influence on the design, since the system must interact with them. Young speaks here of the surrounding systems *constraining* the design of the new system.
- "For large systems, some architectural design is often necessary to identify subsystems and relationships. Identifying subsystems means that the requirements engineering process for each subsystem can go on in parallel" [Yo03; p.52].
- Reasons as budget, schedule, or quality can raise needs to reuse existing components sparking influences on the system requirements and the design.
- For systems designed in domains with strong external regulations (e.g., civil aircraft), approved standard (certified) designs may be necessary.

Young [Yo03; p.52] calls these resulting restrictions *design requirements* or *design constraints*. In ch. III.19, the author uses the term *design constraint* in a similar notion, but the author also uses the concept to clearly separate require-

---

[51] For example, if a UML tool such as the supported UML-Tool Enterprise Architect is used.

ments from the customer and 'requirements' someway arising from previously made decisions about the solution (design decisions). This approach is supported by a taxonomy of both requirement types (ch. III.19).

Pohl describes similar interactions between requirements and *system architecture*. He comes to the conclusion that stakeholders cannot specify detailed requirements without knowing the *architecture* [Po08; p.23]. As a consequence, he and Sikora sketch a *process model* [PS05; p.113-114] where different layers of requirements and design alternately interact. In [Po08; p.565-602], Pohl has further evolved the COSMOD-*RE* (sCenario and gOal based System development methOD) *process model* being a dedicated *REM process model* for developing embedded systems according to a goal and scenario-based requirement elicitation techniques [Po08; p.565]. The method explicitly addresses a HW/SW-Co-design approach by defining requirements and design alternately at different levels of abstraction. The model seems to be independent but compatible with Pohl's *RE framework* (see discussions about fig. 5-2 (p.41) and fig. 5-5 (p.61)). The alternating definition of requirement and design artifacts at different levels of abstraction rather resembles to the *process models* of SPICE or CMMI and is discussed in ch. I.7.3.2). The difference, however, lies in its dedication to *REM* and the explicit emphasis on goals and scenarios as requirement elicitation and specification techniques.

I.5.6 The Role and Nature of Requirement Change

> *Who wants the world to stay as it is, does not want it to persist.*
> Erich Fried (*)

Lientz and Swanson [LS80] performed "a very widely cited survey" ("repeated by others in different domains") [BR00; p.74] characterizing four different kinds of changes (see also [Kn01b; p.24]):

- *Adaptive*: Concerned with changes of the environment (e. g. new HW),
- *Perfective*: Concerned with changing *functional* and *non-functional requirements*,
- *Corrective*: Fixing errors. Knethen distinguishes "application faults" resulting from incorrect requirement documents and "coding faults" resulting from incorrect implementation [Kn01b; p.24],
- *Preventive*: Concerned with changing a system to prevent errors or to improve the structure of the system for future problems;

"Of these, the survey showed that around 75% of the maintenance effort was on the first two types, and error correction consumed about 21%. Many subsequent studies suggest a similar magnitude of the problem. These studies show that the incorporation of new *user requirements* is the core problem for software evolution and maintenance" [BR00; p.74].

These findings are not surprising, since "requirement changes affect all existing system representations" [JL05; p.118]. Diverse factors causing requirements change exist (see [Po08; p.550f], [So07; p.195f], [JL05; p.120], [LW99; p.338]):

- The problem(s) that the system is intended to solve changes due to changes in the project's environment (market, economic, political or technological reasons).
- During project progress, evolving deeper understanding of the problem(s) to solve leads to new or changing requirements.
- Interviewed stakeholders stating requirements often have implicit assumptions and knowledge (so called *tacit knowledge* [Po58], [Po66]; see ch. II.9.4.2). It is as essential as difficult to surface this knowledge. Due to the abstractness of SW and its behavior, this knowledge often cannot be surfaced until the stakeholders see first concrete versions of the SW not fulfilling the needs of their implicit assumptions and tacit knowledge [Po08; p.331].
- The users change their minds due to better understanding of their needs or new users entering the scene.
- The environment the system interacts with changes (e.g., new HW, new processes, new and other systems).
- A new release of the system lets users discover new needs and new usage ideas.
- Conceptual changes due to discovered none-sustainability of used architectural concepts or technologies *impact* requirements [HWF+08; p.176].
- The project's situation concerning costs respectively budget levels, resource situation (staffing) or schedules changes [HWF+08].

Leffingwell and Widrig [LW99; p.339] also refer to development-internal problems causing requirement changes:

- The developers "failed to ask the right people the right questions at the right time during the initial requirements-gathering effort" [LW99; p.339].
- The project failed to establish "a practical process to help manage changes" [LW99; p.339]. If processes try to force stable requirement 'freezes', a change backwater can lead to exploding situations between users and stakeholders causing stress and rework. On the other side, uncontrolled changes lead to chaotic, unclear project states.

Due to the high *impact* requirement changes have on all subsequent processes and artifacts, changes should be avoided, if possible. Therefore, acquiring as stable set of requirements as early as possible in the project is one of the central goals and paradigms of *REM*. A diversity of heuristics and techniques exists to deal with this issue. Hood et al. [HWF+08] list the following factors, where a structured *REM* process can reduce the risk of later requirement change:

- Forgotten requirements,
- Incorrect respectively contradictory requirements,
- Ambiguously formulated requirements leading to misunderstandings;

However, some heuristics in *REM* as "ask the right question to the right people at the right time" [JL05; p.121] often are a matter of experience, intuition and luck not controllable beforehand. Generally, another not yet exactly mentioned aspect the author wants to point out is that, unless the users see a concrete implementation of the system, talking about requirements and the intended system is always very abstract for the stakeholders and each stakeholder has a certain picture in his (her) mind (s)he can only insufficiently express[52]. As soon as a concrete solution is visible, stakeholders can often more easily express the discrepancy between the concrete solution and the picture in their head leading to the discovery of new requirements or the need for changing requirements.

Firstly, this is closely connected to the term "unknowable requirements" stated by Young [Yo03; p.49ff] expressing requirements not findable at project start (see ch. I.5.1). Secondly, it describes the importance of getting feedback from the stakeholders as early as possible in order to achieve a stable set of requirements as early as possible. Prototyping[53] is here the most frequently employed technique (see [RS02; p.121] for a detailed description of different available prototyping techniques). However, techniques as prototypes have its limitations and can only alleviate the *requirement change problem*.

"Requirements change from the point in time, when they are elicited until the system has been rendered obsolete. Changes to requirements reflect how the system must change in order to stay useful for its users and remain competitive on the market" [JL05; p.120]. Or expressed in Lehman's 'first law' of software evolution ([Le96], [LRW+97]): "A system must be continually adapted, or it will be progressively less satisfactory in its environment" [LRW+97; p.21].

---

[52] Boehm [Bo00a] calls this the IKIWISI (I'll Know It When I See It) users.

[53] This also refers to what Enders and Rombach call Boehm's first law ([ER03; p.17]): "Errors are most frequent during the requirements and design activities and are the most expensive the later they are removed." and the close connection to Boehms second law: "Prototyping (significantly) reduces requirement and design errors, especially for user interfaces".

Lehman's 'second law'[54], when a "system evolves, its complexity increases unless work is done to maintain or reduce it" [LRW+97; p.21] refers to the experience that "evolving software becomes more complex, and extra resources are needed to preserve and simplify its structure" [Ni04; p.276]. *Refactoring* theory [Fo99] can be seen as today's key answer to address this problem. Thus, changes are often initiated by requirement change [JL05; p.118], but also other sources for change exist. One of these sources, for example, may be rising complexity or design erosion sparking the need for *refactoring* to increase quality of an artifact as preparation for later change needs.

Taking both laws into account, Nierstrasz deduces that "requirements are not the only input to our development process, but that legacy artifacts also constitute an important input. Furthermore, as the artifacts evolve, requirements will also evolve in a never ending cycle … and, as complexity increases, quality will degrade and productivity will decrease" [Ni04; p.276]. Nierstrasz here implicitly also refers to two further laws of Lehman: 'Law 6' outlines that software always underlies a continuing growth of functionality (see [Le96; p.111] for a detailed description and the differences to the 'first law'), whereas 'law 7' states that evolving software faces "declining quality unless rigorously maintained and adapted to a changing operational environment" [Le96; p.111].

Changes always imply high deterioration risks of the involved artifacts [JL05; p.120]. These risks can be diminished by a controlled *change management process* [JL05; p.120]. Diverse suggestions for *change management processes* exist (see ch. I.7.2.7 for a *change management process* definition in *SPICE*). Leffingwell and Widrig [LW99; p.341-347] present a "framework for change" presenting core factors that must be considered in order to ensure a proper working *change management process* (see also comments in [JL05; p.121]):

- *Plan for change*: involves that the project's stakeholder must be acknowledge the fact that changes occur and are necessary and thus must be open for change.
- *Baseline requirements*: at certain development states, the current state of the requirements should be *baselined*. Subsequent changes can thus be compared with this 'stable version'.
- *A single channel*: ensures that no requested changes are forgotten and proper planning (including the decision whether to perform or not) has been per-

---

[54] From his research starting in 1968 till the late nineties, Lehman (cf. [Le96], [LRW+97]) identified all together eight laws that evolutionary software (he calls them E-type software) underlies. Only the important subsets for this discussion are referred here, as the other laws are difficult to discuss without the proper context leading to extended distraction away from the scope of this discussion.

formed before implementing the change. In larger projects, often a *Change Control Board* (*CCB*) [PR09; p.144f] [VSH01; p.184f, p.216] performs this action. A good description on details about a *CCB* such as how to be organized, statutes, involved stakeholders, etc. are provided by Wiegers [Wi05; p.315-327].

- *Change control system*: collects and administers change requests "allowing the stakeholders to track and assess the *impact* of changes" [JL05; p.122] (see ch. II.10.3).
- *Manage hierarchically*: shall ensure changes are introduced *top-down* avoiding that changes are introduced into code neglecting potential effects on requirements, design artifacts and tests[55].

This framework for change is more a collection of principles (heuristics) leaving open the actual change process. Different proposals of change processes (see, e.g., [Po08; p.545-560] [RS07; p.426-434], [HWF+08; p.175-191], [Kn01b; p.27-29], [So01; p.534-542], [HDH+06; p.213-219], [MHD+07; p.160-168], [Wi05; p.305-327]) exist "with varying levels of detail and explicitness" [JL05; p.122]. In most cases, however, details on how to perform these processes in practice are mostly left out [JL05; p.118]. Here, the *requirement change management process* of Wiegers [Wi05; p.305-327] is an exception as it provides checklists [Wi05; p.322-323] for developers to apply directly in practice.

The concrete implementation of a process should always underlie the specific individual project situations (see [HWF+08; p.190], because project individual factors in most cases influence the change management process)[56]. Later, ch.

---

[55] Knethen [Kn01b; p.24] makes here a different distinction. She claims that perfective changes and corrective changes concerning "application faults" should be introduced top-down, since affecting the whole system. Whereas coding faults should be introduced bottom-up starting with the artifact the fault was detected and ending with the artifact being the source of the fault. The author tends to the opinion that different kinds of changes may include different strategies. Knethen's proposal leaves open the question what to perform with adaptive changes and preventive changes. The author thinks, adaptive changes are equally requirement related as perfective changes and should be introduced top-down, whereas preventive changes may be more a matter of design or coding and should be introduced at the abstraction level they have their first occurrence (e.g., a simple if in the code ensuring robustness to further changes is very low, whereas framework-like *patterns* (ch. I.6.2.4) for a component to ease later changes is more an issue of design).

[56] Of course, such a process should be accompanied by a certain set of constraints and orders from the strategic organization (e.g., company guidelines) the project is embedded in. Moreover, also process standards as SPICE and Automotive SPICE (see ch. I.7) outline a change management process (SUP.10, see ch. I.7.2.7) with a set of constraints for the implementation of a SPICE conforming change management process.

I.7.2.7 highlights the essential demands of the development process standard ISO15504 for a change management process.

An essential foundation of any change management process is the need to estimate the *impact* of a change. *Impact analysis* theory tries to provide the essential principles necessary for a structured approach on change *impact estimation* (ch. II.10.3). As ch. II.10.3 shows, *requirements traceability* is a central means for most *impact analysis* concepts.

Practice, however, shows that changes seldom have the small *impact* they are initially believed to have [Wi05; p.305], [JL05; p.117]. A study by Lindvall and Sandahl [LS98] suggests that the *impact* of most changes is underestimated by a factor of three.

Boehm and Turner indicate that change also is connected to a *pareto distribution* [Pa1897] meaning that 20% of the changes drive 80% of the costs as they have "the most system-wide *impact*" [BT04; p.219].

In the experience of Reißing, up to 80% of change effort is caused by correcting wrong design decisions [Re02; p.1] (also cf. [Mo04; p.90]). Lehman [Le96; p.110] emphasizes that many of the unpredictabilities about changes are related to what he has called the *"software uncertainty principle"* [Le89] describing the fact that assumptions upon which design decisions depend on can be implicit or explicit to developers, but both kinds can get invalid due to changes.

In the author's opinion, the connection between these statements lays in the fact that design decisions are usually taken with pending uncertainty of incomplete requirements. Later, new requirements and requirement changes cause significant numbers of design decisions to get invalid[57]. Thus, changes often cause the adaption of significant aspects of design decisions taken before. When these decisions have a far reaching influence (e.g., system wide scope), change effort and risks are correspondingly higher leading to the *pareto* observation of Boehm and Turner [BT04; p.219]. As a consequence, the author is convinced that *impact estimations* must find a way to adequately include decision information in order to achieve better results. This, again, is especially important for tackling the decisions involved in the 20% causing 80% of the effort.

However, estimating the possible *impact* of a change is not the only crucial point. Once the decision has been made to perform a change, the change must also be introduced consistently into all affected artifacts. This can be called *consistency management* (cf. [BCM+08; p.121f]). Here again, the identified *impacts*

---

[57] In the author's experience, design decisions often do not get directly invalid by one change. It is rather a creeping erosion caused by several changes. Correspondingly, the author finds the term architectural erosion used in some design literature very to the point.

through *impact analysis* guides the way to ensuring that no affected part is forgotten.

Another aspect to consider is that requirement change can be foreseen to a certain degree. Knethen [Kn01b; p.40], e.g., proposes that the change probability of a requirement can be estimated and documented beforehand (also cf. ch. II.10.4.2.1). With this information at hand, designers could design extra flexibility mechanisms for parts influenced by requirements with high change probability. In the author's opinion, such strategies are usually done *informally* by designers during design, because designers often try to keep parts flexible, where their intuition tells them to expect later changes.

In summary, requirement change is a matter of fact and will not be avoidable (ch. I.5.6). Further, the rapidity of change has continuously increased [BT04; p.149] and, thus, probabilities of further growing requirement changes are very high. One factor in this consideration is that the role of software has changed over the years. In the early times, software was used to automate activities (e.g., type writing by word processing) or replace other solutions (e.g., mechanical steering of motors by electronic steering), because software provided certain advantages. In these cases, the scope of these software solutions was relatively well-defined by the solution to replace [Po08; p.32].

Additionally, it is to mention that these replaced solutions often provided concrete real world user experience, whereas software often provides very abstract experiences to users[58]. In opposition to this, most today's projects aim to create innovation basing on earlier created software [Po08; p.32]. In these cases, definitive knowledge about the needed outcome of a solution is exorbitantly more vague leading to significantly increasing rates of requirements changes.

I.5.7 Traceability in the Context of Requirements Management

The IEEE Standard Glossary of Software Engineering Terminology (cf. [IEEE–610; p.78]) defines *traceability* by the following two definitions:
1. "The degree to which a relationship can be established between two or more products of the development process, especially products having a predeces-

---

[58] For example, a mechanical steering device can be opened and its mechanics can be analyzed in a very definitive way, but a SW based ECU replacing the mechanical steering is very difficult to analyze in an equally definitive way. Gerlich and Gerlich [GG05; p.91] describe that SW in comparison to HW, where problem are discovered relatively easily, rather has a characteristic of a gas or chemical.

sor-successor or master-subordinate relationship to one another; for example, the degree to which the requirements and design of a given software component match. See also: consistency".

2. "The degree to which each element in a software development establishes its reason for existing; for example, the degree to which each element in a bubble chart references the requirement that it satisfies".

The earliest provided definition the author could find is made by the IEEE830-1984 ([IEEE830-84][59]): "A software requirements specification is traceable, if (i) the origin of each of its requirements is clear and if (ii) it facilitates the referencing of each requirement in future development or enhancement documentation".

Currently, the definition of Gotel and Finkelstein "has become the common definition of *requirements traceability*" [Pi04; p.92]: "*Requirements traceability* refers to the ability to describe and follow the life of a requirement, in both a forwards and backwards direction (i.e., from its origins, through its development and specification, to its subsequent deployment and use, and through all periods of on-going refinement and iteration in any of these phases)" [GF94].

In other words, the basic idea behind *requirements traceability* is to describe and track a requirement from its first occurrence (its origin) to all further considered points (design, code, tests) [Pi04; p.92].

Reading this outline of *traceability* concept, the ingenuous reader may grasp a feeling that *traceability* is very intangible and rightful concerns about the usefulness may arise.

In fact, *traceability* mainly gathers its right for existence by two factors:

1. Consistency gaps arise between different artifacts ([Lin94], [Kn01b], [Eb05; p.138f]). *Traceability* information can be seen as bridge between these gaps.

2. The inevitable fact of *requirement change*.

Point one refers to the problem that different artifacts are not completely consistent to each other. Chapter II.10.2 explains this in more detail.

As already described in ch. I.5.6 above, the second point concerns with the problem that *requirement change* is inevitable, but possible to handle if properly managed. In the authors view, the key issue about proper *requirement change management* deals with identifying the actual *impact* of a change as accurate and as early as possible. Such attempts are called *impact analysis* (*IA*) and are described in detail in ch. II.10.3. When a *change management process* such as described in ch. I.5.6 is used, *IA*s provide the necessary information for estimating

---

[59] Now replaced by [IEEE830-98] – a good description of the standard is provided by [Sch00; p.89-101].

the effort of the change. If the decision was positive for implementing a change, the *IA* supports the developers in consistently implementing the change[60].

I.5.7.1 Traceability in Different Aspects of Development Activities

Traceability can involve different aspects of development activities. For a better distinction of these aspects, different terms related to the considered aspects exist. The following description will outline these different aspects and explain the terms used in relation to these aspects.

At first to mention, Gotel and Finkelstein [GF94] defined the terms *pre-* and *post-requirements specification* (*Pre-RS* and *Post-RS*) *traceability*:

- "*Pre-RS traceability* refers to those aspects of a requirement's life prior to its inclusion in the *requirements specification*" [GF94; p.1] (see also [Pi04; p.93]).
- "*Post-RS traceability* refers to those aspects of a requirement's life that result from inclusion in the *requirements specification*" [GF94; p.1] (see also [Pi04; p.93]).

Pre-RS is useful, because it preserves the original origin of the requirement. In case a change of a requirement comes to discussion, the project members know which documents or stakeholders they should consult before deciding to change the requirement.

Post-RS is useful to get the direct implementations (e.g., design, or code files) or tests of the requirement. This can be the starting point for an *impact analysis*.

The terms *forward* and *backward traceability* are closely related to this. They describe the direction of the established *traceability* (cf. [GF94], [GF95], [Wi95], [Pi04]):

- *Forward traceability:* means following the traces in direction to later artifacts (as, e.g., from the requirements to design or test artifacts).
- *Backward traceability:* means following the traces in direction to earlier artifacts (e.g., from the requirements to its source (a person, customer requirement, institution, law, standard, meeting protocol, etc.)).

---

[60] In other words: Not overseeing (resp. forgetting) an *impacted* location. As Boehm has already pointed out in the early 80ies [Bo82; p.40], problems discovered in late development phases (e.g., during testing phase) are significantly more expensive to fix and, thus, finding and fixing all *impacted* changes at the beginning is crucial to project success.

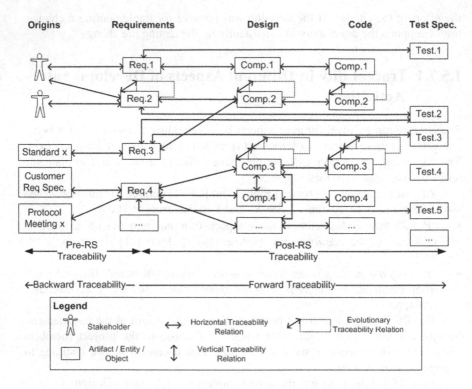

Figure 5-4 Overview over different *traceability* terms oriented on Brcina [Br07a; p.4]

Forward traceability is useful when an *impact analysis* (see ch. II.10.3) of a proposed change is made, since it helps to find all *impacts* of the change.

Backward traceability again refers to the basic reason for the existence of the item in the development process. In case of an *impact analysis* for a proposed change, going back to all reasons for existence of an item helps to ensure the change conforms to all its needs, which ensures consistency.

Both concepts sound similar, but they are not the same. Knethen [Kn01b; p.46] provides a good description of the differences: "*Forward* and *backward traceability* does not look at *traceability* from the perspective of a certain document in the way that *Pre-RS* and *Post-RS* do. *Forward traceability* describes tracing documentation entities to realization documentation entities on succeeding abstraction levels, whereas backward *traceability* describes tracing documentation entities to source documentation entities on preceding abstraction levels".

Forward traceability can also mean tracing a design element to its realization in code and *backward traceability* vice versa; whereas *Pre-RS* and *Post-RS traceability* are limited to the perspective of the *requirements specification* (see fig. 5-4).

In the literature, an early agreement (cf. [RE93], [GF94], [Kn01b; p.46]) has arisen that *traceability* should be *bidirectional*. In other words, *traceability* should combine both *forward* and *backward traceability* and they should be possible at the same time.

When it comes to relationships of items within an artifact or between objects in different artifacts, the terms *vertical* and *horizontal traceability* are used. Unfortunately, the terms are used by different authors with different meanings.

The following definition seems to origin from Ramesh and Edwards [RE93]. It seems to be preferred in literature (see [Li94], [Br07a], [Kn01b; p.43]):

- *Horizontal traceability* is the possibility to trace dependencies of an item to other artifacts or models.
- *Vertical traceability* is the possibility to trace dependencies of an item within one artifact or model.

Contrary to this, Bohner [Bo91] – probably orienting himself by the waterfall model – defined the meanings in the exact opposite direction to the former definitions. *Horizontal traceability* at Ramesh and Edwards is *vertical traceability* at Bohner and *vertical traceability* at Ramesh and Edwards is *horizontal traceability* at Bohner (also cf. [Kn01b; p.41-43], [Li94; p.17]). With the adoption of the process standard Automotive SPICE[61] (*A-SPICE*), this problem of confusing the terms has additionally increased, since *A-SPICE* again provides definitions of *horizontal* and *vertical traceability* with a deviating semantics to the ones introduced above (see ch. I.7.4 for details).

Due to these incompatible usages of the terms *horizontal* and *vertical traceability*, the author prefers to avoid these terms in the following. Pinheiro has avoided these terms by using the terms *inter-requirements traceability* for *traceability* relationships between requirements and *extra-requirements traceability* for relationships between requirements and other artifacts [Pi04; p.95]. These terms seem more adequate. At the moment, however, *traceability* is seen beyond the scope of requirements (e.g., there also exists *traceability* between a *design model* and its representing source code). Correspondingly, the author prefers to use the terms *intra-artifact traceability* for relationships within one artifact and *extra-artifact traceability*, instead of the misleading *horizontal* and *vertical traceability*.

---

[61] Automotive SPICE is a domain specific adaptation of the general SPICE standard. Both standards are described in detail in ch. I.7.

Traceability also has a temporal dimension, meaning requirements change during projects and thus also *traceability* relations may change. Recording and retrieving this history is also a necessity in *requirements traceability*. This aspect is called *evolutionary traceability* ([Br07a; p.4], [Po08; p.509]). For more information on *traceability* and configuration management the author recommends reading [HWF+08; p.114ff], [Kn01b; p.45], [Li94; p.20].

In connection with his *RE framework* (see also fig. 5-2 (p.41), Pohl [Po93], [Po96], [Po08; p.42ff] also provides a model describing the evolutionary trace of the *RE* process within three dimensions (see three axes in fig. 5-5):

- "The specification dimension deals with the degree of requirements understanding at a given time. ... Focusing on this dimension, the aim of *RE* is to transform the operational need into a complete system specification through an iterative process of definition and validation (e.g., analysis, trade-off-studies, prototyping)" [Po93; p.280].
- "The representation dimension copes with the different representations (*informal* and *formal* languages, graphics, sounds etc.) used for expressing knowledge about the system" [Po93; p.281].
- The agreement dimension "deals with the degree of agreement reached on a specification. At the beginning of the *RE* process each person involved has its own personal view of the system. Of course, few requirements may be shared among the team, but many requirements exist only within personal views of the people, e.g., stemming from the various roles the people have (system analyst, manager, user, developer etc.)" [Po93; p.283]. In the further project progress, a specification emerges with rising agreement between the team members.

A *RE* process in a development project starts at a certain initial stadium (initial input) and then meanders within these three dimensions, until it reaches the desired output (fig. 5-5). The *RE framework* is interesting in the context of *traceability* as *traceability* relations can be involved in any of the three dimensions.

Ch. II.10 discusses the different dimensions of the *RE framework* in connection with *traceability*.

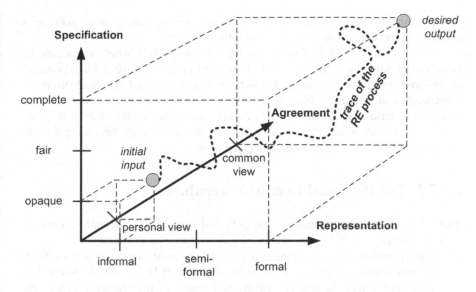

Figure 5-5 The three dimensions of the *RE framework* [Po93; p.284], [Po08; p.42]

I.5.7.2 Traceability as an Issue of Quality

Currently, due to the above outlined significant support potential[62] *traceability* can offer a project, as outlined above, *requirements traceability* is seen more and more as decisive quality issue of processes for developing *safety-critical systems*. This is also reflected by new process standards putting more and more emphasis on *requirements traceability* as seen in *SPICE, Automotive SPICE, CMMI,* and IEC61508 (cf. ch. I.7).

In many projects employing one of these standards, the customer requests the obedience of the standard as a requirement. As already discussed in ch. I.5.1, these requirements for the development process can be seen as *nonfunctional requirements*. Since this *nonfunctional requirement* also includes certain demands

---

[62]   In the following chapter, the author will show that this is in fact at first only a potential not necessarily gathered by most implementations of *traceability*.

for *requirements traceability, requirements traceability* can also be seen as a process related *nonfunctional requirement* for a project[63].

In *Automotive SPICE*, discussions have been sparked, whether *traceability* should even have the status of a separate support process (cf. ch. I.7.4). As *traceability* involves many artifacts of other engineering disciplines apart from requirements and also *traceability* between none requirement items and artifacts is already the case (e.g., *traceability* between design and code), it may be even possible that *traceability* further dissects from the *REM* scope becoming a more exceptional position as an overall management process.

I.5.7.3 The Potential Uses of Traceability

The following listing summarizes the potential uses of the *traceability* concept (also cf. [Wi05; p.332f]):

- *Impact analyses* (*IA*) of changes are one of the most important uses of *Post-RS* and *inter-requirements traceability* (see ch. II.10.3) since it determines the effects (items to change, efforts and costs) of the change on other requirements and all subsequent requirement artifacts. It has also some importance in *Pre-RS traceability* since it must become clear whether these changes (especially changes of requirements effecting of former changes of requirements) are still conforming to the original needs of the requirements' originators.
- *Pre-RS traceability* supports project planning. The relevance of a requirement and thus its prioritization is often determined by the importance of the source of the requirement. It is even possible that found requirements are considered irrelevant, because the originating stakeholder is not one of the primary target stakeholders.
- *Traceability* helps that all found requirements are adequately considered in all subsequent activities of design, code and testing[64]. Missing *traceability links* of a requirement indicate that it may be forgotten or that certain artifacts have not yet developed. In this case, *traceability* also gives important indications about the status of a project [Wi05; p.333].

---

[63]   See also [RJ01; p.59]: "*Requirements traceability* has been identified in the literature as a quality factor – a characteristic a system should possess and include as a nonfunctional requirement".

[64]   As shown in ch. I.7, this is even also concerning lower level *requirements specifications*, when *REM*-processes are performed at different levels of abstraction.

- *Traceability* helps to improve the consistency of all development artifacts by making more interdependencies explicit.
- Explicit *traceability relationships* help in later phases of maintenance, especially when the original developers are staffed into a new project and thus different developers must perform the maintenance effort [Wi05; p.333].
- In the same way, risks or detrimental effects caused by important developers leaving a company are diminished because parts of their knowledge about the connections within the project are kept in the *traceability* information [Wi05; p.333].
- The *traceability* concept also includes the evolutionary aspect of requirements helping to reproduce older development situations of the project, if needed.
- *Traceability* can be used to fulfill certain certification criteria. This is especially important in the field of *safety-critical systems*, where a certain process maturity must be proved (see ch. I.7).
- *Traceability* can be used as a proof in law suits. This fact is especially important for *safety-critical systems* to ensure that, if an accident with fatal consequences occurs the developers can prove they did not act carelessly.
- Present *traceability* information can also be an important help for *reverse engineering* or *integration* of legacy systems.
- In a similar direction, *traceability* information can also help in decisions about the *reuse* of components or systems in new projects [Wi05; p.333].
- Last but not least, *traceability* can improve *testing*. Firstly, the knowledge of which tests cover which requirements helps to avoid unnecessary redundant tests. Secondly, *traceability* can help to identify causes for problems found in tests because through the *traceability* connections between tests, requirements and design (resp. code) the probable code candidates causing the problem can be easier identified.

Since the further thesis mainly concerns itself about *traceability* to design, the specific uses of *traceability* in the context of design are now listed again (cf. [HDH+06; p.94]):

- Ensure adequate consideration of all requirements in the design(s) (and thus on the resulting system resp. SW).
- Support for assessing the *impact* of requirement changes on the design (*IA*).
- Support for consistent implementation of a requirement change at all affected places (previously identified by an *IA*).
- Support for verification procedures: It is easier to track which requirement is relevant for which SW module and thus must be considered by implementation and testing.

I.5.8 Deficiencies of Today's REM Practices

At the end of this chapter, it is to say that *REM* such as all development methodologies do not provide a "silver bullet" [Br87]. The following problems may be most critical issues of today's *REM* methodologies:

- No clear definition of "best practice" exists [BGK+07; p.131]. Thus, accepted reference models are missing [BGK+07; p.131]. Solution attempts for this shortcoming are provided by Broy and Geisberger ([BGK+07], [Ge05]), or Pohl [Po08].

- Requirements are often experienced as poorly documented, too solution oriented, incomplete, inconsistent, not implementable and not scalable [BGK+07; p.131]. In the eyes of Sousa and Castro, most development approaches lead to requirements that are specified "in a scattered and tangled fashion" [SC04; p.350]. This opinion leads them to propose using *use cases* in combination with a *NFRs framework* to systematically identify and document requirements [SC04].

- Available tools are ineffective, offer only very general concepts, are too implementation oriented, require high administrative effort and offer low sophisticated visualization [BGK+07; p.131].

- No homogeneous approaches and communication media exist between product management, research and development, marketing and distribution [BGK+07; p.131].

- Frequent and late requirement changes are unavoidable and are often – especially in sequential processes – not sufficiently handled [BGK+07; p.131].

- According to Pohl [Po08; p.32f][65], requirement elicitation has become more difficult, because today's systems are built on formerly developed systems. Traditionally, it was easier to identify the real needs of a system to be developed up-front, because the goals mainly targeted to automation or partial automation of manual processes, where the workers had concrete experiences. Thus, the processes were deeply understood. After most of these processes have been already automated, today's development goals often aim for improving already automated processes or combine them in complete innovative ways. As computerized systems hide the actual complexity and business logic from the users and only provide abstract feedback (e.g., via *human machine interface* controls), today's workers only have partial, abstract experiences of these processes. Pohl [Po08; p.32f] also explicitly references to

---

[65] The reader further interested in this topic may consult Pohl [Po08; p.32f], who mentions a few further aspects on this topic.

problems in the automotive industry, where long-running research endeavors develop new complex systems in research environments (e.g., ABS or ESP[66]) that must then be integrated into a real-life car system environment already containing other complex computer-based ECUs.

- In a similar direction, Boehm and Turner [BT04; p.149] argue that up-front specification techniques, as required by traditional *RE*, work quite well for batch, sequential, non-interactive applications of the 1960 and 1970 but have dwindling significance for applications with interactive user interfaces, because these applications involve complex, nonlinear combinations of different user interactions. In the converse argumentation, as embedded systems often do not have significant user interfaces, up-front specification may be a good means for embedded systems development. On the other side, embedded systems are often embedded into complex environments requiring significant complexity of the ECU's control mechanisms, which might also be difficult to specify up-front.

I.6 Design in Systems and Software Development

Although in many fields designers quite frequently make inventions,
designing and inventing are different in kind.
Invention is the process of discovering a principle.
Design is the process of applying that principle.
The inventor discovers a class of system – a generalisation –
and the designer prescribes a particular result,
object, and source of energy he is concerned with.
[Py78; p.21]

"Design is an activity that generates a proposed technical solution that demonstrably meets the requirements. In that process, we simulate (mentally or otherwise) what we want to make or do, before making or doing it. We iterate until we are confident that the design is adequate" [ER03; p.34].

---

[66] Antilock Braking System and Electronic Stability Control

Most[67] current state-of-the-art *SysEng* and *SE* theories assume that after the requirements specification has reached a certain quality degree and before the system (resp. *SW*) is implemented, a certain phase of design takes place.

This chapter gives a short introduction to this topic. However, design is a very complex topic and this thesis is not really concerned with a detailed design theory in the usual sense that it discusses a way how to design a specific type of system or a specific design language as the *Unified Modeling Language* (*UML*). In fact, the thesis rather aims at letting open a specific approach for design and is more interested in design at a higher *meta-level*. In this way, the author hopes to identify general principles and techniques that give way to identifying requirements a requirements-to-design-*traceability*-tool must obey in order to provide value for designers. Such an attempt seems legitimate in the view of the author, because *traceability* information and a tool aiming at *traceability* is per se a tool working at a higher *meta-level*.

Nevertheless, only analyzing a higher *meta-level* can lead to soft, blurry and unspecific talks. In this way, a certain 'grounding' shall be achieved by references to more concrete techniques or facts, where and whenever it is appropriate.

At first, this chapter will introduce different phases of design in course of applying *SysEng* and *SE*. This in mind, the next chapter shall widen the focus by introducing some very general theories (or even to be called philosophies) about design that describe important aspects of design and have led to certain trends in *SysEng* and *SE* design theory, which are observable today. At the end, the author will make a short reference to some design practices in the automotive sector in order to identify further issues that a design *traceability* solution should additionally consider to provide uses for automotive projects.

I.6.1 Different Design Phases in SysEng and SE

During development of ECUs, different design phases occur. In this context, three different phases of design are of concern:

---

[67] In fact, some agile methods such as eXtreme Programming [Be00a] seem more to propagate a kind of architecture evolving out of the development. The heuristics is to design the code [Be00a, p.57] as simple as it can fulfill all currently planned requirements (here often called stories, features or *use cases*). Since it is not sure that future requirements are really implemented, the design shall not care for these requirements. For new features really decided to implement, the old code is *refactored* [Fo99] until it also fits with the new requirements. This does not mean no design is present. It is more that the design implicitly evolves during programming – also called emergent design [St04; p.65f].

- *System design* in the context of *SysEng* (ch. I.4),
- *Software architecture* as kind of high level design of the SW during *SE*,
- *Detailed software design;*

I.6.1.1 System Design

During *SysEng* phase (ch. I.4), the *system design* (i.e., *system architecture*) cares for the general outline of the system. Douglass brings this to the point [Do04; p.37-38]: "In multidisciplinary systems development – that is, those include software, electronic, mechanics, and possible chemical aspects – the *system architecture* is constructed early and system-level requirements are mapped down onto the various aspects of the *architecture*". So, a major concern is to adequately partition the complete system into the parts concerned by several engineering disciplines (SW, HW, mechanics …), to outline the interactions and interfaces between those parts and to map (partition) the overall system requirements to the specific parts. Douglass [Do04; p.29] names the following primary activities in *SysEng*:
1. "Capturing, specifying and validating the requirements of the system as a whole",
2. "Specification of the high-level *subsystem architecture*",
3. "Definition of the subsystem interfaces and functionality",
4. "Mapping the system requirements onto the various subsystems",
5. "Decomposing the subsystems into the various disciplines – electronic, mechanical, software, and chemical – and defining the abstract interfaces between those aspects";
   Apart from the first point, the latter points can be seen as the primary activities during *system design*. "In all these activities, systems engineers are not concerned with the design of the discipline-specific aspects of the software or the electronics, but are concerned with the specification of what those design aspects must achieve and how they will collaborate" [Do04; p.29].

I.6.1.2 Software Architecture

In SW development, design is separated into the *SW architecture* and *detailed design*.
   SW architecture is the high level design of a SW performed by the architect(s). It "defines the essential structures of the software system and is the basis for the development. Thus, it can be seen as the construction plan facilitating the

development of complex and extensive SW" [DH03; p.1 (*)]. In the view of Douglass [Do04; p.38], "architectural design identifies the strategic design decisions that affect most or all of the application, including the mapping to the physical deployment model, the identification of runtime artifacts, and the concurrency model. This is typically accomplished through the application of *architectural design patterns*".

As a first definition, Bass et al. define *SW architecture* as "the structure or structures of the system, which comprise software elements, the externally visible properties of those elements, and the relationships among them" [BCK03; p.3]. Bass et al. provide three reasons for the importance of a *SW architecture* [BCK03; p.26]:

1. *"Communication between stakeholders"*: *"Software architecture* represents a common abstraction of a system that most if not all of the system's stakeholders can use as a basis for mutual understanding, negotiation, consensus and communication".

2. *Catalog of "early design decisions"*: *"Software architecture* manifests the earliest design decisions about a system, and these early bindings carry weight far out of proportion to their individual gravity with respect to the system's remaining development, its deployment, and its maintenance life. It is also the earliest point at which design decisions governing the system to be built can be analyzed".

3. *"Transferable abstraction of a system"*: *"Software architecture* constitutes a relatively small, intellectually graspable model for how a system is structured and how its elements work together, and this model is transferable across systems. In particular, it can be applied to other systems exhibiting similar quality attribute and functional requirements and can promote large-scale reuse".

The IEEE 1471 [IEEE1471] defines *SW architecture* as "the fundamental organization of a system, embodied in its components, their relationships to each other and the environment, and the principles governing its design and evolution".

Moro characterizes *SW architecture* as "the carrier of knowledge" [Mo04; p.29 (*)]. Thus, he [Mo04; p.171] considers the communication of ideas and concepts as the main task of a *design model*, where conclusiveness of the modeled ideas is especially important to consider. In this way, he follows the argumentation of Kruchten [Kr95; p.43] and others that these models must also fulfill a certain aesthetics[68].

In the view of Moro [Mo04; p.171], one significant negative influence on aesthetics is the occurrence of clones in a model. Additionally, clones are often a symptom of *copy-and-paste reuse*[69]. *Copy-and-paste reuse* involves the dangers that flaws in copied code are dispersed over all locations it has been pasted [Mo04; p.171]. Correspondingly, current *SW design* literature recommends avoiding code clones, except it is designed on purpose as redundant components for addressing *NFRs* such as reliability (e.g., *triple modular redundancy*) [TCS98]. From a more general perspective, it is to say that redundancies should be generally avoided throughout all development situations. As knowledge and understanding of a project often get unstable very quickly (see ch. I.5.6), an extensive amount of time is needed to reorganize and reformulate the documented knowledge and understanding [HT03; p.24].

The problem is now is that it is easy to duplicate the knowledge represented somewhere in specifications, processes and programs, but this invites projects to become a "maintenance nightmare – one that starts well before the application ships" [HT03; p.24].

As a consequence, the author agrees with the recommendation of Hunt and Thomas [HT03; p.24-30] to obey a principle, what they call the *DRY-principle* (Don't Repeat Yourself): "Every piece of knowledge must have a single, unambiguous, authoritative representation within a system" [HT03; p.24]. Thus, for the following ideas and concepts of this thesis, the author has always tried to follow this principle.

Fowler [Fo03] expresses a different view about *architecture*. According to him, *architecture* emerges out of design (design can here also be implicit in code and not explicitly stated via a model etc.) as a kind of shared understanding of the developers' group consensus of what is important within the design. In this way, *architecture* is a "social construct" [Fo03; p.3]. He further points out that *architecture* often addresses decisions that are difficult to change later. A system can

---

68 Bloch [Blo95; p.16] emphasizes that the "physical form or design is an unquestioned determinant of its marketplace success". Transferring this to engineering, the architect must also sell his design ideas to the implementers of her/his design. Therefore, aesthetics may have decisive influence, whether a design is abided by a project. Some specific advices for aesthetics in design documentation can be found in the chapter. Clements et al. argue in the same direction mentioning that also the presentation of ideas is important to achieve acceptance [CBB+03; p.321-323].

69 The term *copy-and-paste reuse* is taken over by the known *anti pattern* for design [BMH+98]. The *anti-pattern concept* is discussed in the course of *pattern design* theory ch. I.6.2.4.

usually be solved in different ways. Thus, multiple *architectures* lie in a system [Fo02; p.1] and the architect must decide which possible *architecture* is to be followed[70]. Over a system's lifetime its usage and purpose can change. In this way, what is important for the *architecture* may change during a system's lifetime [Fo02; p.1]. Thus, *architecture* is at last all of whatever is important concerning a system [Fo02; p.1].

I.6.1.3 Detailed Design

Detailed design is a low level design of – for instance – a module in a SW system. It "adds low-level information necessary to optimize the final system" [Do04; p.38]. The *detailed design* is performed by the developer engaged with the implementation of a module, or component. A *detailed design* for a component (module, class...) must address the following aspects (see [Do04; chapter 10; p.589-616]):

- The structuring of the contained and handled data,
- *Refactorings* within the component,
- Implementation of associations to other components,
- The set of operations defined on the data,
- Visibility of data and operations,
- Algorithms used to implement those operations,
- Strategies for error or exception handling.

I.6.2 General Theories about Design

As a study of Atwood et al. [AMW02] suggests, different notions about design exist within the design research community (cf. also [HA06a; p.74-77]). This chapter tries to outline a few fundamental design theoretic views on what design and its processes are about. The collection is oriented on Horner and Atwood [HA06a; p.74-77] that, in the author's view, reflect most characteristics of design, of which designers should be aware[71]. All these theories do not actually originate in *SE* or *SysEng* theory but originate from a broader scope on a general theory of design. It may be a matter of discussion whether these general theoretical find-

---

[70] Later in ch. I.6.2.1.2, it is shown that this decision making process is rather arbitrary.

[71] [AMW02] provides some additional views, more details and a detailed analysis of interconnections (co-citations) between the different notions, not discussed here. Thus, the author recommends the interested reader to read [AMW02] for further information.

ings can be directly transferred to *SE* and *SysEng* design, since these general theories embrace wide scopes (as e.g., design of buildings). However, as these chapters also show, each of the theories discussed here have already been transferred to *SE* or *SysEng* design theory by other researchers as this chapter will also outline (the most prominent example may be the *pattern* concept (ch. I.6.2.4)).

An aspect of design purposely neglected by the author is design theories about '*aesthetics*'. Even though Kruchten [Kr95; p.43] or Moro [Mo04; p.171] emphasize that also *SE* design has and needs its own *aesthetics*, the author thinks it may be problematic to find a common understanding of this very intangible concept within such a broad design theory. Some researchers may even object that *SW* or *systems design* should concentrate on pure functionality, or may just define *aesthetics* as a kind of attribute improving clarity in design. Indeed, the author thinks that aesthetics may have a deeper – however very intangible – *impact*. An indication of this deeper meaning may be the interpretation of the *bad smells* concept introduced by Fowler [Fo99]. A code having *bad smells* actually works; however, the developers have bad feelings about the code. Here, in the author's experience, *bad smelling* code is very often connected to bad *aesthetics*. On the other hand, Coggins pointed out that [Co90; p.1] (cited after [Bo94; p.333]) "pragmatics must take precedence over elegance, for *Nature* cannot be impressed" meaning that aesthetic-oriented design itself can also be a source of *complexity* (or, *complication*) and designers should search for simple solutions to avoid *complication* (cf. footnote 80 (p 77))

I.6.2.1 Design as Symbolic Information Processing

"Design, so construed, is the core of all professional training; it is the principal mark that distinguishes the professions from the sciences" [Si96; p.111]. Simon [Si96] is concerned with artificial worlds (somehow constructed by humans) in comparison to natural worlds. According to him, the manifestation of an artificial world is an artifact. Simon [Si96; p.3] sees that an artifact reflects an adaption to human goals or purposes that must obey natural law. Therefore in his eyes [Si96; p.111], "everyone[72] designs who devises courses of action aiming at changing existing situations into preferred ones". However, Simon appeals to a "professional responsibility" to "discover and teach a science of design, a body of intellectually tough, analytic, partly formalizable, partly empirical, teachable doctrine

---

[72] Taking this statement seriously, also developers just writing code without an explicit design do also design. Similar notions are know from the agile community, where design implicitly manifests through implementation and later refactorings.

about the design process" [Si96; p.113]. As he observed most of the up-to-then known design theories "as intellectually soft, intuitive, *informal* and cook-booky[73]" [Si96; p.112], he tried to outline general principles for a general design theory[74] ([Si96; ch.5 (p.111-138)]: "The science of design: Creating the artificial"):

- A decision theory as a logical framework for rational choice among given alternatives. Tang et al. [TJH07; p.5] – also interpreting Simon – refer to design as "a process of synthesizing through alternative solutions in the design space. Reasoning to support or reject a design solution is one of the fundamental steps in this process".
- Techniques for actually deducing which of the available alternatives is the optimum. Simon explicitly remarks here that this is not about finding the best solution, but a *"satisficing"* one [Si96; p.119], because "so called 'figures of merit' permit comparison between designs in terms of 'better' or 'worse' but seldom provide a judgment of 'best' … in the real world we do not have a choice between satisfactory and optimal solutions, for we only rarely have a method of finding the optimum" [Si96; p.119].
- "Adaption of standard logic to search for alternatives. Design solutions are sequences of actions that lead to possible worlds satisfying specified constraints" [Si96; p.124]. Possible solution worlds are seldom unique. Research should search for sufficient, not necessary, actions to fulfill goals.
- "The exploitation of parallel, or near-parallel, factorizations" [Si96; p.124] means to factorize the problem into smaller independent partial problems for easier analysis of alternatives[75].
- The allocation of resources is a twofold criterion. "First, conservation of scarce resources may be one of the criteria for a satisfactory design. Second, the design process itself involves management of the resources of the de-

---

[73] In the author's opinion, this observation is still the case as most design literature still refers to *heuristics*, *patterns* (ch. I.6.2.4) and other rules of thumb. As the next chapters about *wicked problems* (ch. I.6.2.2) and Schön's *Theory of Reflective Practice* (ch. I.6.2.3), etc. will show, this may be what design often is about. As design deals with artifacts made by and for humans, it often involves social aspects inferring high complexity not to be handled by plain analytical and transformational processes.

[74] The author has reworded and interpreted the original principles to better fit the context mentioned here. Simon's first version on the book dates from 1968. Even though the book has been updated twice, some of the mentioned techniques in the original formulation are not up to date. However, as this chapter shows, the underlying principles are still valid up to now. The interested reader may read the original source.

[75] See also thesis 15 by [GG05; p.43 (*)]: "If problems are resolved into partial problems, the solution will be found faster".

signer, so that his efforts will not be dissipated unnecessarily in following lines of inquiry that prove fruitless" [Si96; p.124f].

- "The organization of complex structures and its implication for the organization of design processes" [Si96; p.131].
- "Alternative representations for design problems" [Si96; p.134] describes the fact that problems can often be described in different ways (e.g., by different models).

These points, sketching aspects of a universal design process, lead to a set of characteristics of design. When looking at the points one to five, making decisions appears to be the central concept of design. *Rationale management (RatMan)* theory deals with managing decisions and how the underlying *rationale* of decisions made can be recorded (ch. II.9 describes details of this research field in connection with design). In the points one and two, Simon mainly addresses the fact that a decision can only be made if alternatives are present. Exploring the possible alternatives and their *impact* is a central concept in *RatMan* from start. In fact, from *RatMan* perspective, Bass et al. formulate "design as a sequence of decisions" [BCN+06; p.258]. One of the most heavily used concepts with close connections to *design rationale* in the *RatMan* sense is the usage of *patterns* [DMM+06a; p.19], but *patterns* also "constitute one of the most heavily used approaches for organizing reusable knowledge" [DMM+06a; p.19]. Today, *patterns* are organized in *pattern catalogs* as a source for search for standard problems and may thus be seen as today's most heavily used solution for addressing point three. However, the *pattern* concept may also be seen as a kind of design theory and is accordingly discussed in the following ch. I.6.2.4.

Problem factorization, as discussed in point four, is also an issue of *RatMan*. Nevertheless, these kinds of factorizations bear a close connection to point six which refers to a – in the author's believe – major concern in design. The high quantities of information involved in design lead to high complexity that must be adequately organized to enable designers keeping an overview. As the following sub chapter about complexity shows, Simon's view of design is deeply connected to this and his research helped laying ground for several connected paradigms and many concepts encountered today in systems and software design theory. Among others, *hierarchic decomposition* and the *'view'* concept may be the most influential ones.

Point seven refers to the problem of proper representation. Representation is usually performed by models. As models are only abstractions, different kinds of representations of the same facts are possible. The view concept addresses this fact, what closes the circle back to point six and the following sub chapter.

Last but not least, point five describes a third major driver of design. As one of the human-adaptable world's properties is finiteness, any design is limited by the available finite resources. The relationship between resource and design can be described as double-edged. Finite resources are involved in the production and implementation of a design and design itself cares about the finite resources involved in the described solution.

I.6.2.1.1 Complexity as a Central Force in Design

"Complexity... is the biggest factor involved in anything having to do with the software field. It is explosive, far reaching, and massive in its scope" [Gl02; p.19]. Furthermore, complexity is a significant factor deciding about success or failure of a developed system or software[76]. Therefore, as Brooks [Br87; p.11] states, "complexity of software is an essential property, not an accidental one". This means that complexity can only be mastered but cannot disappear. Correspondingly, complexity must be addressed.

Empirical experiments by Woodfield [Wo79] indicate that a massive increase of complexity happens during the transition between requirements (problem description) and design (solution description), where a "25 percent increase in problem complexity results in a 100 percent increase in programming complexity" [Wo79; p.76]. This can also be seen as a strong indication for a *pareto principle*-like [Pa1897] connection between the problem and solution domain showing "that the difficulty of solving a problem in software grows exponentially" [Gl02; p.19]. As explanatory thesis of this fact, somebody could tend to state that finding a pure solution for the functionality may encounter about 25 percent, whereas preventing and handling all sorts of potentially occurring errors and other quality criteria as flexibility or maintainability is about the other 75 percent. From the requirement engineering perspective – where errors relate somehow to quality aspects –, it could also be termed that software complexity is dealing with 25 percent *functional* and 75 percent *NFRs*, explaining the importance and focus that *REM* theory lays on dealing with *NFRs*.

Another observation is provided by Glass: "Explicit requirements explode by a factor of 50 or more into implicit (design) requirements as a software solution proceeds" [Gl02; p.19]. This expresses the observation that any solution has a certain structure. In order to ensure proper collaboration of several parts of the solution, the parts must fit into this structure[77]. These needs are the implicit requirements and they can be seen as a consequence of formerly taken decisions. The author is convinced that it will be important to also write down these re-

---

[76] "The more complex the system, the more open it is to total breakdown" [Pe86; p.153].
[77] This characteristic intuitively described here is closely connected to what is called *conceptual integrity* [PBG04; p.102ff] and is discussed in the following of this chapter.

quirements, if they are – as those – rationally explicitly available. This problem is a central part of the concept, the author has developed for *traceability* improvement and discussed in detail in ch. III.19.

In his first chapter, Booch [Bo94; p.2-24] introduces complexity as the main driver of analysis and design of SW. His argumentation reveals very close connections to Simon. He [Bo94; p.2] argues that any software but software with "very limited purpose and a very short life span", for which it is more profitable to dispose of it and replace it rather than to reusing it, is complex[78]. The "distinguishing characteristic" inherent in this kind of software is "that it is intensely difficult, if not impossible, for the individual developer to comprehend all the subtleties of its design. Stated in blunt terms, the complexity of such systems exceeds the human intellectual capacity" [Bo94; p.3]. Booch identifies four sources for SW complexity[79]:

- *The complexity of the problem domain* [Bo94; p.3-5] means that the problem to be solved involves elements of high complexity resulting in "myriads of competing, perhaps contradictory requirements". In addition, imprecise stakeholder wishes and inter-stakeholder-communication problems lead to permanent change of requirements. This topic is discussed in detail in chapter I.5.6. *REM* is today's answer to this problem.
- *The difficulty of managing the development process* [Bo94; p.5] arises due to continuing rapid growth of software program size. One cause is the fact that a fundamental task of development teams is "to engineer the illusion of simplicity" [Bo94; p.5] to shield users from the complexity of the developed systems. This, at first positive, effect has also the negative side-effect that the illusion of simplicity also drives developers to build systems based on formerly developed systems leading to exponential growth of program size and system complexity. Additionally, projects also involve growing project teams leading to higher complexity concerning communication and coordination.
- *The flexibility possible through software* [Bo94; p.6] leads to manifold possibilities how to find solutions, but it "turns out to be an incredibly seductive property" for inconsistencies forcing developers to develop most of the basics of their solutions again. "While the construction industry has uniform building codes and standards for the quality of raw materials, few such standards exist in software industry".

---

[78] According to Booch [Bo94; p.3], reactive systems (he means embedded systems) have a very rich set of behaviors. "Software systems as these tend to have a long life span, and over time, many users come to depend upon their proper functioning".

[79] The interested reader may also read Broy and Rump providing an overview on source of complexity [BR07b; p.3].

- *The problems of characterizing the behavior of discrete systems* [Bo94; p.6] refer to that software based systems are discrete systems containing large amounts of different variables. Along with the current value of each variable, the address and call stack of each process and the current state of the application is determined. Other than continuous analog systems describable by a discrete function, such software-based systems can possibly enter uncontrollable different states as "in discrete systems all external events can affect any part of the system's internal state" [Bo94; p.7]. This sparks the need for vigorous testing, but exhaustive testing proves nearly impossible, because developers have "neither the mathematical tools nor the intellectual capacity to model the complete behavior of large discrete systems" [Bo94; p.7].

I.6.2.1.2 Design Means Managing Complexity

As Simon can also be seen as "pioneer of complexity theory" [EFS98; p.23 (*)], he already emphasized the strong importance of mastering complexity in design issues. His thoughts about complexity orient themselves on findings of Miller [Mi56]. Miller's experiments (see also [Si96; p.66f]) on human cognition capabilities indicate that average humans are capable to consider around seven plus, minus two aspects at the same time. This leads Simon to argue "that people do not, and cannot, consider all possible conditions, alternatives, and constraints, and therefore cannot design an optimal course of action .... Rather than exhaustively considering design issues, people choose satisfactory solutions based on the information available" [HA06a; p.74].

Simon termed this *bounded rationality* [Si96; p.166]: "The meaning of rationality in situations where the complexity of the environment is immensely greater than the computational powers of the adaptive system." As a consequence, humans must factorize (resp. chunk) the complexity in order to cope with it (see point 4 above). In this context, Simon proposes to use *hierarchic decomposition*[80] to tame the complexity[80] of systems as "comparatively little information

---

[80] It is to mention that hierarchic decomposition (as, e.g., the analytic method) has been used long before Simon. However, it seems that Simon communicated its important function as means to tame complexity to a broader community. Today, the hierarchic structure scheme is central for the term complexity [EFS98, p.23] used as central property to characterize complexity as the following definition of Ebert shows [Eb05; p.198 (*)], [Eb08; p.282 (*)]: "A system is termed as complex, if it is linked and interwoven in diverse combinations. The term 'complex' is here understood as a characteristic of a technical system ... containing heterogeneous components, having heterogeneous relations between the components, and being able to switch into different

is lost by representing them as hierarchies" [Si96; p.207]. Leading to what Endres and Rombach call "Simon's law" [ER03; p.40]: "Hierarchical structures reduce complexity" [ER03; p.40]. Due to *bounded rationality*, Simon also discovered the principle that design usually not emerges in a kind of big-bang process but evolves from *stable intermediate forms*[81]. This means that design can rather be seen as an evolutionary process where design reaches stable states forming the basis of evolution to the next stable state.

From this perspective, Horner and Atwood describe Simon's view on design as "symbolic information processing and humans as goal-oriented information processors" [HA06a; p.74] where "design involves devising courses of action aimed at changing current situations into preferred ones" [HA06a; p.74]. Or, in other terms, "design is viewed as a process of generating and navigating through a state-space" [HA06a; p.74].

Concerning software development, Booch tried to analyze complexity. In his view [Bo94; p.7], failures to master complexity have led to the effects that are called the software crisis, but, as this state now has continued for a long time, it may be considered as the normal state. Taking account to Simon and other research results of software engineering theory, Booch [Bo94; p.10-11] derived five characteristics of complex systems being important for software design:

---

states. The complexity, thus, describes the connection, i.e., collaboration of a system and its parts as objects". In contrast to this, Ebert also provides a definition for complication [Eb05; p.199 (*)], [Eb08; p.282 (*)]: "In literature, 'complicated' is used in the sense of difficult or embroiled (corresponding to the Latin origin complicare = to fold together or to confuse). The term 'complicated' is used as summarizing characteristic of a technical system that is difficult to understand, to figure out or to handle. Thus, complication denotes the interaction of a system as object and an observer as subject. The complication is a perceived – psychological – complexity and depends from the observer. In this way, complication also includes difficulties in the understanding of graphical representations as they are often used, e.g., in the form of data flow diagrams or petri-nets, in software development for the representation of relations of different components (so-called visual complexity). Such graphical representations can well create a correlation of technical and psychological complexity. The complication of a software system depends on the previous knowledge of the observer ..., on the impression of the representation on him (her) and on the suitability of a chosen representation for a certain problem. A mastery of complexity, as already demanded by E. Dijkstra in 1972 in the course of the bestowal of the Turing Award, will only be possible if the complication is actively reduced."

[81] Close connection to this seems to have Lehman's fifth law on software evolution "Conservation of Familiarity" [Le96], [LRW+97].

1. Frequently, complex systems can be decomposed in hierarchic dependencies with interrelated subsystems. Simon argues [Si96; ch.8 (p.183-216)][82] that hierarchies and hierarchic systems can be considered as the decisive means to provide a simplifying description of complexity, even though he admits not all complex systems appear in hierarchical structures [Si96; p.191][83]. Unfortunately, such hierarchic dependencies are *nearly decomposable, where* "interactions between subsystems are weak but not negligible" [Si96; p.197]. Also to mention in this context, Simon [Si96; p.209] emphasizes that the discussed hierarchic structures contain a high degree of redundancy.

2. In contrast to most science disciplines as physics, "software may also involve elements of great complexity; however, the complexity is of fundamentally different kind" [Bo94; p.2]. Booch refers here to Brooks [Br87; p.12] speaking of *arbitrary complexity*[84]. This means that decisions concerning hierarchic decompositions or other aspects performed by designers in order to manage complexity are to a certain point arbitrary[85], because often they could also be performed according to other criteria leading to different outcomes [Bo94;

---

[82] According to [Si96; p.XIII], the chapter bases on an essay originally published in Proceedings of the American Philosophical Society, Dec 1962.

[83] As an example, he describes chemical polymers as large chains or single to each other similar or identical parts. But, he emphasizes in the same moment that this structure can be described as a hierarchy of only one present level. Interestingly, the software *architectural style pattern* 'pipes and filters' has a similar structure [BMR+00; p.54ff] and can be most probably be seen as a kind of analogy. He even goes beyond by assuming that complex systems not providing an apparent hierarchical order "may to a considerable extent escape our observation and understanding" [Si96; p.207].

[84] See also Hull et al. [HJD02; p.1] providing the following comment on *arbitrary complexity*: "The most complex systems tend to be those with software, often integrated deep inside the system's components. The complexity of such products is limited only by the imagination of those who conceive them".

[85] An interesting point is what Alexander (also cf. ch. I.6.2.4) says in its introduction to his first publication on what later became the *pattern* concept [Al64; p.1]: "Today functional problems are becoming less simple all the time. But designers rarely confess their inability to solve them. Instead, when a designer does not understand a problem clearly enough to find the order it really calls for, he falls back on some arbitrarily chosen *formal* order. The problem, because of its complexity, remains unsolved". This statement strikingly resembles to what Conklin calls taming a *wicked problem*. It may be possible that the *pattern* concept is a kind of strategy to address the *wickedness* of problems by proposing abstract standardized solution possibilities for forces within *wicked problems*. On the other hand, what is called arbitrariness may only seem arbitrary but is in fact a result of a process of *knowing in action* as proposed by Schön (ch. I.6.2.3).

p.11]. As ch. I.6.2.3 shows, parts of these decisions may even not be made by rational reflection but by intuitive *tacit knowledge*.

3. "Intra-component linkages are generally stronger than inter-component linkages" [Si96; p.204] indicates "a clear separation of concerns among the various parts of a system, making it possible to study each part in relative isolation" [Bo94; p.11].

4. "Hierarchic systems are usually composed of only a few different kinds of subsystems in various combinations and arrangements" [Si96; p.209]. Booch [Bo94; p.11] analyzes here that complex systems underlie common patterns. These patterns may involve the reuse of small components (such as cells in plants or animals), or of larger structures (such as vascular systems also found in both plants and animals) [Bo94; p.11]. This bears strong resemblance to the *pattern* concept introduced in ch. I.6.2.4.

5. In [Bo94; p.20], Booch refers to *stable intermediate forms* as "proven abstractions and mechanisms" building "a foundation upon which to build new complex systems" [Bo94; p.20]. "Complex systems generally evolve from *stable intermediate forms*" [Bo94; p.23][86], where he explicitly mentions that the usage of object-models to produce systems leads to systems basing on intermediate forms being more open for change [Bo94; p.75].

In [Bo94], Booch has proven to be a follower of Simon's design theory. As Booch also has been one of the founding fathers of the UML standard (cf. [BJL98]), the principles and conclusions derived from these findings about design as a means to handle project complexity may have imposed high influence on *SW* and *systems design* theory. Surely, other researchers may also have influenced today's *SW* and *systems design* theory in equal ways.

Altogether, today's *SW* and *systems design* theory knows – at minimum – the following fundamental principles to be obeyed by a sound *SW* and *systems design* (see [PBG04; p.102ff], [Kn01b; p.12ff], [BR07b; p.17]), each in some way connected to managing complexity:

Abstraction: "describes the generalization of facts" [Di04a; p.117 (*)]. The usage of models and different views is "the most important toolbox" for abstraction [PBG04; p.104]. Abstraction[87] helps humans to distinct unimportant facts from the important ones, but the judgment of what is important and what unim-

---

[86] In this context, Booch [Bo94; p.11] explicitly refers to findings of Gall: "A complex system that works is invariably found to have evolved from a simple system that worked. ... A complex system designed from scratch never works and cannot be patched up to make it work. You have to start over, beginning with a working simple system" [Ga86; p.65].

[87] See also [HHP03; p.51ff] and [HHP03; p.67] for good remarks about how to use hierarchies and abstractions in practice.

portant varies from the persons involved. Correspondingly, in development different models (and *views*) applied [PBG04; p.104].

Structure: "represents a relationship network between the individual elements of an entity as a whole. It includes a reduced view of the reckoned system allowing the analysis of the whole. ... At the reckoning of the system, static and dynamic structures can be differentiated" [Di04a; p.117 (*)].

Modularization: means a decomposition principle based on coupling and cohesion[88] [Di04a; p.32]. In this context, the term 'module' can be seen as "a responsibility assignment rather than a subprogram" [Pa72, p.1054], indicating that modularization is about grouping and assigning *functional requirements* to the *architecture*. Ideally, modules have a strong internal cohesion but low coupling, because designers should obey what Endres and Rombach [ER03; p.43] call Constantine's law: "A structure is stable if cohesion is strong and coupling low". Parnas [Pa72] discusses the criteria to consider in making modularization decisions and shows five different alternative aspects to decide on. Alas, the chosen modularization criterion influences what is seen as strong cohesion or coupling. Correspondingly, modularization results may differ if different modularization criteria are chosen. With a similar meaning, Simon [Si96; p.197-204] emphasizes that complex systems may be approximated by a theory of *nearly decomposable systems*. Booch [Bo94] – in reference to Brooks – speaks of *arbitrary complexity*: Design looks different when other decomposition criteria are considered as the most important. However, in practice, design may not be so arbitrary, when "Conway's law" is considered [St05; p.24] which indicates an isomorphism between organization structure and its *architectures*. According to Conway, developing organizations design systems in a way that represent copies of the organization's communication structures [Co68], [Ec04; p.113]. Today, strict modularization oriented compositional structures are also again softened by design theory about architectural aspects (e.g., *cross cutting concerns*) leading to new compositional structures [CRF+06].

Encapsulation supports the principle of *information hiding [Pa72]* to obtain higher change flexibility. The underlying assumption is that necessary changes that only effect parts being behind an encapsulating interface are easier to implement since only these internal encapsulated parts must be changed, whereas the latter system parts stay untouched. Encapsulation is a "central principle of object oriented design" [PBG04; p.104] Modularization and encapsulation could be seen as entangled twins, where "its success in making future changes easy depends on having identified a right decomposition" [Be04; p.56]. Otherwise new

---

[88] Others as Dunkel and Holitschke [DH03; p.3] call this the *coherence* principle, but
       seem to mean the same.

requirements or requirement changes "causes changes that bridge several modules" [Be04; p.56]. Consequently, refactorings of the design considering new decomposition criteria may be necessary, otherwise the software tends to decay [Be04; p.56].

Hierarchy: In complex designs, often more abstractions exist than usually manageable by designers. *Modularization* can help designers but this is often not sufficient. A solution can be to arrange abstractions into a sequence called hierarchy [PBG04; p.106]. Booch refers to two fundamental kinds of hierarchies [Bo94; p.19], [PBG04; p.107]:

- *Structure*: Describes the decomposition structure an item '*consists of*'.
- *Generalization and inheritance*: Describe inheritance hierarchies, where an item '*is a*'.

Besides these 'static' hierarchies, Marwedel refers to a *behavioral* hierarchy [Ma08a; p.13ff]. This refers to the point below about *views*. In a more generalized way, it may be the case that each possible *view* may be structured by a *hierarchy*.

View partitioning describes the fact that complex systems have manifold aspects difficult to describe from one perspective [PBG04; p.128]. Thus, systems can be described from different points of perspective called *views*, or *viewtypes*[89]. Often, different *views* involve different kinds of models. Or, described in the point above about *abstraction*: Different views consider different facts (aspects) as important and thus show different aspects. The probably most known view concept is *"4+1 View Model"* introduced by Kruchten [Kr95] building an essential part of the RUP process framework [CBB+03; p.344F]. The concept differentiates four main views (*logical, development, process* and *physical*) in association with one overlapping, comprehensive view (*scenarios*). Concerning the characteristics of *views*, Kruchten emphasizes that his concept is rather generic and independent from any tool or any modeling language [Kr95; p.43]. Further, the *views* by themselves are neither fully orthogonal nor independent from each other [Kr95; p.47]. Correspondingly, relations between views must also be considered, and in fact theories like *architecture documentation* explicitly demand for documentation of inter-view relationships (see ch. I.6.5). Inspired by Kruchten, literature has proposed several other *views*. A comprehensive overview can be found in [CBB+03; p.343-380], [PBG04; p.128-167] or [St05; p.86]. Explicitly to mention here is UML: As it is envisioned as 'unified' modeling language, it contains dif-

---

[89] A *view* is "a representation of a set of system elements and its relations to each other" [CBB+03; p.472] (see also [PBG04; p.128]), whereas a *viewtype* comprises "the element types and relation types used to describe the architecture of a software system from a particular perspective" [CBB+03; p.472].

ferent sets of diagrams addressing *structural, collaboration, behavioral, functional* and *timing* views [Do04; p.43]. From the perspective of a theoretic, *formal* modeling theory, Broy and Rumpe could categorize [BR07b; p.6] several 'essential views' that may build a kind of taxonomy for all other views identified in practice. From the practitioner's viewpoint, Bass et al. [BCK03; p.39-40] describe how architectural structures can be identified as sources for views during a design. As indicated above to *hierarchies*, it is possible that different views may follow their own hierarchic order independently from other views. Last but not least, the question arises, whether certain views may be more important over others. According to Starke's practical experiences, 60 to 80 percent of effort is spent on the structural model [St05; p.88]. In the author's view, this may indicate that indeed the structural model including *hierarchical structural decomposition* may have a certain preceding importance. This assumption – supported by the fact that historically hierarchical, structural decomposition – has been discovered and used as one of the first principles to structure models (e.g., cf. *structured analysis* and *design* [De78]). As a consequence, the tool introduced in part III relies on the hierarchical, structural decomposition principles to build a *skeletal structure* upon which other views can be related and structured. This principle helps to reduce complexity as the hierarchical, structural decomposition builds the first contact point for a designer to get into a design. Starting from this, the designer can then enrich the structure by adding further additional views on this basic structure. As a further plus, part III also shows how the hierarchical, structural decomposition will also build the basis for developing a new process heuristic allowing to establish *traceability* between requirements and design as collaborative process, orienting itself on Simon's ideas about design as a transgression of *stable intermediate forms*.

Conceptual integrity [PBG04; p.102ff] describes the idea of thorough usage of concepts and design decisions in the complete system in order to avoid extra solutions and dilution of the original concepts [PBG04; p.108]. Brooks emphasizes the importance of *conceptual integrity* as "the most important consideration in *system design*. It is better to have a system omit certain anomalous features and improvements, but to reflect one set of design ideas, than to have one that contains many good but independent and uncoordinated ideas" [Br95; p.42]. Not only growth of size, but also growth of structure increases complexity [Di04a; p.22]. Following Balzert's observation, "the stronger the shape of a structure, the lower also is its complexity" [Ba98; p.474 (*)], *conceptual integrity* shall enforce one strong structure instead of several weak structures and thus "simplicity and straightforwardness proceed from *conceptual integrity*. Every part must reflect the same philosophies and the same balancing of desiderata. Every part must even use the same techniques in syntax and analogous notions in semantics. Ease of use, then, dictates unity of design, *conceptual integrity*" [Br95; p.44]. *Conceptual integrity* can best be achieved if one chief architect is responsible for it [Br95; p.42ff], [PBG04; p.108], [Ec04; p.113]. At the end to mention, *conceptual integrity* refers to another general design heuristic about design [Ec04; p.116], [PBG04; p.116]: A design should have the goal to be as simple as possible, but not simpler.

I.6.2.1.3 Shortcomings of this View about Design

Simon's view has the advantage that it provides a sound scientific theoretical foundation about design as a means to manage complexity. Further, the principles described here cannot be called as 'cook-booky' but have a deep general meaning having deeply integrated into current systems and *SW design* theory. However, as, e.g., the next chapters show, Simon's design theory also has been heavily criticized and challenged by findings of other researchers and practitioners.

In the author's view, this may be applicable, because Simon admittedly describes the principles to apply to achieve a good design, but does not provide a satisfying answer on how to apply the principles. If he does, then Simon's answer on the 'how' is a linear step-by-step, *top-down* approach (cf. [Bu96; p.13]). However, other authors emphasize that *top-down* approaches are rather an exception [Sa05; p.276]. Empirical studies on *SW design* processes such as provided by Curtis [Cu90], [Cu92] indicate that designers rather oscillate between abstraction levels, jump through discrete system states, and develop the problem and *solution space* simultaneously (also cf. [ER03; p.60], [HHP03; p.52]). Accordingly, these findings drove Endres and Rombach to state that "the idea of a *top-down* design is an over-simplification; although it may be a good way to explain a design once it is completed" [ER03; p.60]. Hruschka and Rupp [HR02; ch.10] express the opinion that functional aspects are rather designed *bottom-up*, but nonfunctional aspects should be designed *top-down*. The author believes that this is also a simplification of a rather situation-dependent decision process.

These findings indicate – in accordance to the author's belief – that Simon's view rather comes from considering the end results that indeed may be structured by the principles described here. The following chapters will now introduce design theories that might rather provide better explanations for the genesis of a design. As it turns out, most of these theories have open space for intuition, uncertainty or fuzzyness involved as means to explore and structure the complexity of the problem and design space by humans. From this perspective, the 'cookbooky 'nature (i.e., *heuristics* or *patterns*) of design theories criticized by Simon may turn out to be an inherent property of any design's genesis.

I.6.2.2 Design as Wicked Problems

Rittel and Webber dissented from the views of Simon (cf. [Co05; p.06], [HA06a; p.75]) by introducing the term *wicked problems*[90] ([RW73], [RW84]) as "an alternative to the linear, step-by-step model of the design process being explored by many designers and design theorists" [Bu96; p.13]. In Simon's understanding, design was merely seen as a linear process of analyzing a problem, defining a solution and implementing it (cf. [Bu96; p.13], [CBV07; p.9]). "However, some critics were quick to point out two obvious points of weakness: one, the actual sequence of design thinking and decision making is not a simple linear process; and two, the problems addressed by designers do not, in actual practice, yield to any linear analysis and synthesis yet proposed" [Bu96; p.14].

Here, Rittel and Webber argued that most of the design activities address solving *wicked problems* [Bu96; p.14]. *Wicked problems* mean a "class of social system problems which are ill-formulated, where the information is confusing, where there are many clients and decision makers with conflicting values, and where the ramifications in the whole system are thoroughly confusing" ([Ch67] quoted in [Bu96; p.14]). In contrast to *"tame problems"* usually occurring in natural sciences [RW73], *wicked problems* – as including social aspects – can be characterized by ten properties [RW73; p.161-167]:

1. *"There is not definitive formulation of a wicked problem"* [RW73; p.161] indicates that an exhaustive formulation with all necessary information can only be done for a *tame problem*, whereas the understanding of *wicked problems* "depends upon one's idea for solving it. ... The reason is that every question asking for additional information depends upon the understanding of the problem – and its resolution – at that time" [RW73; p.161].

2. *"Wicked problems have no stopping rule ...*, because the process of solving the problem is identical with the process of understanding its nature, because there are no criteria for sufficient understanding and because there are no ends to the causal chains that link interacting open systems, the would-be planner can always try to do better. ... The planner terminates work on a *wicked problem*, not for reasons inherent in the 'logic' of the system. He stops for considerations that are external to the problem: he runs out of time, or money, or patience" [RW73; p.162]. This is closely related to Simon's term

---

[90]   Buchanan [Bu96; p.14] points out that the term was taken from Karl Popper, but "Rittel developed the idea in a different direction" [Bu96; p.14]. Buchanan further remarks that the first published information on Rittel's concept has been performed by Churchman [Ch67].

on *satisficing solutions*, both showing the inherent nature of finding compromises in design activities.

3. *"Solutions to wicked problems are not true-or-false, but good-or-bad"*, since "many parties are equally equipped, interested, and/or entitled to judge the solutions, although none has the power to set *formal* decision rules to determine correctness. ... Their assessments of proposed solutions are expressed as 'good' or 'bad', or, more likely, as 'better' or 'worse' or 'satisfying' or 'good enough'" [RW73; p.163].

4. *"There is no immediate and no ultimate test of a solution to a wicked problem"* is a direct consequence of point one. Any work on a *wicked problem* "will generate waves of consequences over an extended – virtually an unbounded – period of time", where following works "may yield utterly undesirable repercussions which outweigh the intended advantages or the advantages accomplished hitherto" [RW73; p.163].

5. *"Every solution to a wicked problem is a 'one-shot operation'; because there is no opportunity to learn by trial-and-error, every attempt counts significantly"*. As already indicated by point four, "every implemented solution is consequential. It leaves 'traces' that cannot be undone" [RW73; p.163].

6. *"Wicked problems do not have an enumerable (or an exhaustively describable) set of potential solutions, nor is there a well-described set of permissible operations that may be incorporated into the plan"* [RW73; p.164] directly results from the ill-defined nature of wicked problems (see point one).

7. *"Every wicked problem is essentially unique"* describes that, "despite long lists of similarities between a current problem and a previous one, there always might be an additional distinguishing property that is of overriding importance" [RW73; p.164]. Here, the close notion to software projects generally considered as an "unique undertaking" [MW03; p.24] must be mentioned in the first place and secondly the connection to Alexander's *pattern* concept (ch. I.6.2.4).

8. *"Every wicked problem can be considered to be a symptom of another problem"* [RW73; p.165]. Problems have causes. These causes can be considered as other 'higher level' problem, where the originally considered problems are mere symptoms.

9. *"The existence of a discrepancy representing a wicked problem can be explained in numerous ways. The choice of explanation determines the nature of the problem's resolution"* [RW73; p.166]. As Simon also stated that different representations (now design theory says view) exist, the chosen representation determines the found solution.

10. *"The planner has no right to be wrong"* [RW73; p.166]. Unlike the scientific community, allowing hypotheses to be falsified later, designers are "liable for the consequences of the actions they generate" [RW73; p.167].

Summing it up, "Rittel saw design problems as *wicked* in the sense that they presented fundamental difficulties that could not be overcome using either strictly scientific methods or purely automated methods" [BCM+08; p.6]. In Conklin's opinion, "Rittel's contribution is that he distinguished a new domain of problem type, as opposed to, say, a new way of solving complex problems. Problem *wickedness* is not about a higher degree of complexity, it is about a fundamentally different kind of challenge to the design process, one that makes solution secondary and problem understanding central" [CBV07; p.3]. Or, in the words of Coyne: "The radical point of Rittel and Webber's characterization of design as '*wicked problem* solving', is to instil a certain attitude and responsiveness to research questions. Questions of design do not exist as if issued from some source of eternal inquiry. Rittel and Webber suggest that certain questions can now simply go unanswered, or we may riposte with a volley of counter questions, or offer a challenge to the frame from which the problems are posed in the first place" [Co05; p.13].

Conklin [Co06; p.14-18] provides a probably more to the point reformulation of *wicked problems* characteristics:

1. "You don't understand the problem until you have developed a solution" [Co06; p.14].
2. *"Wicked problems* have no stopping rule" [Co06; p.14].
3. "Solutions to *wicked problems* are not right or wrong" [Co06; p.15].
4. "Every *wicked problem* is essentially unique and novel" [Co06; p.15].
5. "Every solution to a *wicked problem* is a 'one-shot operation'" [Co06; p.15].
6. *"Wicked problems* have no given alternative solutions" [Co06; p.15] – instead "an immense space of options" [Co06; p.18] exists that can be combined.

Wicked problems are also closely related to technical and social complexity. These three build "the 'centrifugal' fragmenting forces pulling a project apart" [Co06; p.35]. Especially social complexity is "inseparable from *problem wickedness*" as "no single stakeholder *wicked problems* exist" [CBV07; p.4]. Correspondingly, "because of social complexity, solving a *wicked problem* is fundamentally a social process. Having a few brilliant people or the latest project management technology is no longer sufficient" [Co06; p.29]. This corresponds to findings of Starke about SW development claiming that "technology alone is insufficient" [St05; p.42 (*)], because no pure technical problems exist [St05; p.42 (*)]. Rather, "they quickly grow to organizational or political difficulties" [St05; p.42 (*)].

In the author's view, Ehn [Eh88], [Eh89] has a similar notion when he describes design as a collaborative, democratic and participatory process of learning together. Ehn's view, however, origins from Wittgensteinian language games: "In a Wittgensteinian approach, focus is not on the 'correctness' of systems descriptions in design, on how well they mirror the desires in the mind of the users, or on how 'correct' they describe existing and future artifacts and their use. Systems descriptions are design artifacts, typically linguistic artifacts. The crucial question is how we use them, which role they play in the design process. ... In the language-game of design we use these artifacts as reminders and as paradigm cases for our reflections of future computer artifacts and their use. The use of design artifacts brings earlier experiences to our mind and it 'bends' our way of thinking of the past and the future. I think that this is how we should understand them as representations. And this is how they 'inform' our practice. If they are good design artifacts, they support good moves within a specific design language-game" [Eh89; p.147].

Contrasting *wicked problems*, Rittel and Webber also mentioned *tame problems*. Conklin derives from the formulation of *wicked problems* characteristics above a set of *tame problems* characteristics [Co06; p.18f]:
1. "Has a well-defined and stable problem statement" [Co06; p.18].
2. "Has a definite stopping point" [Co06; p.18].
3. "Has a solution that can be objectively evaluated as right or wrong" [Co06; p.19].
4. "Belongs to a class of similar problems that are all solved in the same similar way" [Co06; p.19].
5. "Has solutions that can be easily tried and abandoned" [Co06; p.19].
6. "Comes with a limited set of alternative solutions" [Co06; p.19].

Conklin [Co06; p.19] emphasizes that "tame does not mean simple – a *tame problem* can be technically very complex". On the other side, a problem needs not to encompass all six *wicked* characteristics to be a *wicked problem*. "Most problems have degrees of *wickedness*. ... There seems to be a natural inclination to see problems as tame, and to avoid *wicked* ones. ... The first step in coping with a *wicked problem* is to recognize its nature. There is a tendency to treat all problems as tame, perhaps because *tame problems* are easier to solve, reinforced by the lack of understanding about *wicked problem* dynamics and the tools and approach they require. There is a psychological dimension here – a shift from denial to acceptance" [Co06; p.19-20].

In other words, *wicked problems* are often approached by analyzing and taming it. Pure analysis – without designing actions – of *wicked problems* is often very limited and leads to *analysis paralysis* [BMH+98; p.215-218], [Ec03] (see also ch. I.5.4), "a Catch 22 in which we can't take action until we have more information, but we can't get more information until someone takes action" [Co06; p.20]. *Taming* a *wicked problem* means that the problem is simplified to make it more manageable rather than treating the full *wickedness* ([Co06; p.21] lists several *taming strategies*). "However, attempting to tame a *wicked problem*, while appealing in the short run, fails in the long run. The *wicked problem* simply reasserts itself, perhaps in a different guise, as if nothing had been done. Or, worse, sometimes the tame solution exacerbates the problem" [Co06; p.22-23]. Since peoples' "education and experience have prepared them to see and solve *tame problems, wicked problems* sneak up on them and create chaos" [Co06; p.36]. Coyne argues in a similar direction: "*Wickedness* is the norm. It is tame formulations of professional analysis that stand out as a deviation" [Co05; p.12].

In this context, Rittel's *wicked problems* can be seen as a pleading for extended requirements engineering. However, Rittel emphasizes that the solution must be equally considered. As shown in ch. I.5.5 also *REM* theory acknowledges that requirements cannot be defined unless parts of the solution are considered. In fact, experience shows that formulated requirements are often abstract to stakeholders as long as they don't see any concrete solution, where they then can tell the delta of their needed solution in contrast to the presented solution. Prototyping and iterative development directly address these issues. Agile methods (e.g., cf. [BT04]) with their notion to short iterative release cycles with continuous stakeholder feedback, where evolutionary prototypes stepwise turn into the productive system, can be seen as a direct addressing strategy to handle the *wicked* nature of design. In many other projects, however, such a tight integration with "informed and collaborative stakeholders" [BT04; p.95] as needed by agile projects is not feasible, or projects demand for more disciplined approaches, where the final outcome is not as vague as it might be by using the evolutionary prototype paradigm[91]. Thus, in these contexts, pressure on project progress and pressure to find solutions may press for taming a *wicked problem*. Besides, the question arises whether taming a *wicked problem* must per se be considered as wrong. In many cases, finding any feasible solution may be *satisficing* (see ch. I.6.2.1 above) for a start. This can be rather the case for technical equipment such as automobiles.

However, when a problem returns back to the agenda, because the first solution did not prove as *satisficing* enough, the deciders should reflect on, whether:

- First, the problem may be an unintentionally tamed *wicked problem*, and whether more sophisticated courses of action to elicit the problem may be more adequate. Otherwise, it may happen that considerable energy is spent

---

[91]   Examples for more disciplined approaches are the processes for *safety-critical* embedded systems discussed in ch. I.7.

on curing continuously new arising symptoms of a basically poor solution rather than finding a better solution leading to a problem 'smoldering around' in a project. Often, some stakeholders anyway have themselves intuitions about such problems they feel uncomfortable about. In this context, it may be considerable whether the *bad smells* of Fowler [Fo99] provide a certain analogy for this. Good processes may play a certain decisive role to avoid such problems as Janis [Ja72] indicates. According to him, organizations with poor processes can tend to *group-think* [Ja72] meaning that the organization quickly decides on a poor solution, and the rest of the energy is spent on relatively insignificant issues about this solution. As Janis made his observations on analyzing foreign policy making and Rittel derived parts of his experiences in social planning, it is very probable that Janis discovered the *group-think* problem in the context of decision making for *wicked problems*.

• Secondly, if a decision must be reconsidered, it will be important to know about the reasons leading to the former decisions (so called *rationale*), about the reasons now making a reconsideration of the decision necessary (also *rationale*), and the consequences arising from a reconsidered decision.

Rittels *wicked problems* idea resulted in the development of the so called *IBIS* system, which can also be seen as the initiating momentum for a research field today called *rationale management (RatMan)*. *RatMan* deals with finding concepts and techniques to support elicitation, documentation and further usage of *rationale* about a taken decision. Correspondingly, Rittel can be seen as a pioneer of *RatMan* (see very first page of [DMM+06]). Ch. II.9 describes the concepts and ideas of *RatMan* in detail.

I.6.2.3 Design as Situated Action

Schön [Sch83], [Sch87] analyzed the way competent practitioners think when they perform their actions. His theory bases on the assumption derived from the work of Polanyi [Po66] on *tacit knowledge* (see ch. II.9.4.2) describing that not all knowledge can be brought to consciousness and/or be rationally described by the knowing person[92]. Correspondingly, Schön formulates his assumption as "competent practitioners usually know more than they can say. They exhibit a kind of knowing in practice, most of which is tacit" [Sch83; p.8].
Thus, Schön differentiates two very distinct cognitive processes:

---

[92] For example, it is difficult to describe and teach a person how to ride a bicycle, since it is an unconscious process skill. The person must learn this on its own. Similar concepts are experience, intuition etc..

- "An intuitive process of skillful action" [DMM+06a; p.21], called *knowing-in-action* [Sch83; p.54] or *professional artistry* [Sch87; p.22].
- "*A* reasoned process of reflection" [DMM+06a; p.21-22], called *reflection-in-action* [Sch83; p.55].

Design is then a continuous, intertwined alternation between both processes, where both "cannot be done simultaneously, because reflection disrupts *knowing-in-action*" [DMM+06a; p.22]. In *knowing-in-action,* the practitioner applies knowledge he knows "how to carry out spontaneously"[93] [Sch83; p.54], until he experiences "surprise, puzzlement, or confusion in a situation which he finds uncertain or unique" [Sch83; p.68]. This leads to *reflection-in-action,* where he "reflects on the phenomena before him and on the prior understandings which have been implicit in his behavior. He carries out an experiment which serves to generate both a new understanding of the phenomena and the change in the situation" [Sch83; p.68]. In other words, "reflection is only productive when intuition fails to cope with some new circumstance arising" [DMM+06a; p.22]. Reflection not only applies knowledge, but creates new. In this context, "practitioners are frequently embroiled in conflicts of values, goals, purposes and interests" [Sch83; p.17] leading to these new unique circumstances.

A big part of these new and unique circumstances may be connected to the *wicked problems* concept (see ch. I.6.2.2 above) as the following statement about the relations between the clients (other stakeholders the future users) and the practitioners in a project show: Practitioners "bring to their encounter a body of understandings which they can only very partially communicate to one another and much of which they cannot describe to themselves" [Sch83; p.297].

However, as Atwood et al. analyze, "the Reflective Practitioner is not a design text in the sense that it describes a particular view of design. Rather, it presents a theory of how professionals learn" [AMW02; p.128] and − the author would say − apply knowledge. Horner and Atwood [HA06a; p.75] interpret Schön's theory about practitioners' handling of knowledge and action "as a reflective conversation with the environment", where the practitioners "reflect on what they are doing in the action present" [HA06a; p.75] (see also [AMW02; p.126]).

In the author's opinion, another interesting connection may exist between Schön's concept of *knowing-in-action* and what cognition psychology terms as *flow* [Cs90]. *Flow* describes a state of thinking "in which knowledge and experi-

---

[93] "Although we sometimes think before acting, it is also true that in much of the spontaneous behavior of skillful practice, we reveal a kind of knowing which does not stem from a prior intellectual operation.... It seems right to say that our knowing is in our action" [Sch85; p.157].

ence come together easily and knowledge workers seem to 'flow' through their highly demanding work" [HA06a; p.93].

The author risks another interpretation in connection to Simon: In often encountering situations of *bounded rationality* (see ch. I.6.2.1 above), practitioners often use intuitive *knowing-in-action* strategies to cope with, until they encounter a direct problem situation (*action present*), where the intuitively found solution breaks down (i.e. conflicts with) and a rational process of *reflection-in-action* takes over to solve the problem[94].

I.6.2.3.1 Intuitiveness versus Formality of Design Models

Theoretical computer science often demands for highly *formal* modeling approaches. *Formal* approaches are often complex in itself and require a deep understanding of the approach. In the author's view, this demand directly contradicts with the view of Schön. Further, as Shipman and Marshall [SM99a] strikingly have analyzed, users of systems supporting intellectual work often perceive *formality* as significant obstacles to their work (see ch. II.9.4.2 for a detailed description). Thus, *formal* methods may impose high entry barriers when applied in practical engineering. In the authors opinion this fact may be one explanation for the great success of UML in practical engineering, since its first versions did not rely on a strict *formalism* but proclaimed a kind of notion 'it's okay as long as it says what you wanted to say'. This freedom lowered the entry barriers for practical engineers significantly and thus supported *knowing-in-action*.

The author has also encountered this experience in his own practical work as contact person for the introduction of UML 2.0 into automotive embedded modeling of the Micron Electronic Devices AG. At first, most designers were insecure and concerned whether their design really was conforming to UML. The fear of producing non-conforming UML diagrams made designers reluctant to model diagrams, unless the designers were convinced that UML-conformance is not of primary importance, as long as the diagrams showed what the designers wanted to express and as long as they were not used as basis for code generation. This UML in a sandbox style encouraged the designers to experiment with diagrams and improved designers' experiences of UML by learning by doing.

Shamonsky [Sh03] emphasizes that Schön's findings rather indicate a strong need for sketching: "In observations of designers sketching, Schön [Sch87] found a process of negotiation between designer and sketch. The designer draws, then interprets his or her own sketch, then continues or redraws the sketch in a process

---

[94] In the *pattern* approach terminology (ch. I.6.2.4) this would be called 'resolving the forces'.

that yields a progressively more refined design" [Sh03; p.63] (see also [Sch87; p.63]).

Also experiments by [Go99] show strong evidence that design without sketching phases does not work (see also [BD03], [BGP06]). Goel [Go99], [Go95] approaches the design process by psychological studies. He identifies four core activity phases in design:
- Problem structuring (can be seen as something like the requirement phase),
- Preliminary design (sketching),
- Refinement,
- Detailed specification;

Referring to Witt et al. [WBM94], Kruchten [Kr95; p.49] states similar findings to design phases in *SE* describing four phases of design (+12 sub phases): sketching, organizing, specifying, optimizing. Aliakseyeu et al. provide an overview about sketching support in design [AMR06].

Fig. 6-1 shows Goel's findings[95] [Go99] about correlations between the phases design *problem space*, cognitive processes and representations. Between the problem statement (requirements) and the resulting design, a phase of *preliminary design* leads to the exploration of several design ideas (alternatives) [Go99; p.1]:

"Preliminary design is a classical case of creative, ill-structured problem solving. It is a phase where alternatives are generated and explored. This generation and exploration of alternatives is facilitated by the abstract nature of information being considered, a low degree of commitment to generated ideas, the coarseness of detail, and a large number of lateral transformations. A lateral transformation is one where movement is from one idea to a slightly different idea rather than a more detailed version of the same idea. Lateral transformations are necessary for the *widening of the problem space* and the exploration and development of kernel ideas.

The refinement and detailing phases are more constrained and structured. They are phases where commitments are made to a particular solution and propagated through the *problem space*. They are characterized by the concrete nature of information being considered, a high degree of commitment to gener-

---

[95]   In the author's view, these findings can be directly transferred to the topics discussed here, where the design phase "Problem Structuring" can be considered as *REM* activity and the other phases ate considered as design phases. The transition from *REM* artifacts to design then takes place during the sketching phase. This also indicates why *traceability* information between requirements and design may be more difficult to capture than most *traceability* approaches usually consider (see ch. II.10.6 for a more detailed discussion).

ated ideas, attention to detail, and a large number of vertical transformations. A vertical transformation is one where movement is from one idea to a more detailed version of the same idea. It results in a *deepening of the problem space*."

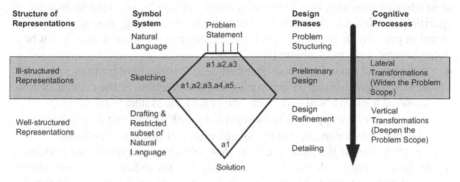

Figure 6-1 The design problem space according to Goel [Go99; fig.1]

Goel [Go99], [Go95] claims that the ill-structured nature of sketches facilitates lateral transformations (changes of alternatives, ideas) because of ambiguities, syntactical and semantic overlaps. Shamonsky emphasizes that the ambiguity beared by sketches can be seen as "nourishment for creativity", where "the designer or other designers opportunistically discover new ideas based on misinterpretations or reinterpretations of the sketch" [Sh03; p.63].

Schön reveals a similar notion, when speaking about ambiguity in design: "When design terms are ambiguous in this way, they may create confusion, but they also call attention to multiple consequences" [Sch87; p.60f].

I.6.2.3.2 The Role of Expertise in Design

Cognition research on design indicates that sketching is an essential activity for generating and refining ideas and solving problems [DGN+00]. Research results of Bilda et al. [BGP06] indicate however that sketching is not essential for expert architects to develop conceptual ideas, but "the ability to read or produce sketches appears to be the only way to develop expertise in *architecture*" [BGP06; p.587].

In the author's opinion, this corresponds to another finding of Reenskaug [Re97] possibly explaining why software developers often do not use models for analyzing and design. When training students, Reenskaug observed that the students could not model a solution *top-down* without any concrete solution experience at hand. After the first system of this type has been built, however, the students improved in modeling such a system in a *top-down* fashion. Sensitized by these finding, Reenskaug then realized that he himself encounters the same problems when approaching new kinds of systems, because he lacks the knowledge of specificly needed solution details. Accordingly, Reenskaug assumes this as an essential property of the design problem. Reenskaug proposes a three point heuristics to cope with this problem [Re97; p.6]:

- "Choose the modeling idiom that best describes the hard parts of your problem. A program-centered approach will give overview of the code; a system-centered approach will give overview of how the system works".
- "Use an iterative approach to help get both *architecture* and details right".
- "Do not over-document, but try to maximize self-documenting code".

In other words, Reenskaug claims that only domain experts can perform a model based design solution[96], whereas non domain expert developers should address the core problems by sketching a design (point one), whereas the remaining non-hard problems should addressed by self-documenting code instead of models (point three). Both together must be addressed in a continuous iterative fashion (point two)[97].

According to Paech et al., designing is a creative task that "can only be learned through experience and apprenticeship" [PKD+03; p.142]. Hazzan [Ha02] provides a general discussion of the reflective practitioner principle in connection with *SE* theory and teaching practice. He appeals for using sketching classes in a design studio[98] atmosphere, where students learn from coaches being "first-class faculty members" [Sch87; p.171].

I.6.2.4 Design as a Language of Patterns

During his research on properties of good design in buildings *architecture*, Christopher Alexander ([Al64], [AIS77], [Al79]) discovered that problems are often

---

[96] This is an indirect explanation why designers are usually referred to as experienced expert developers.

[97] Reenskaugs findings strongly resemble to important heuristics propagated by the agile development community.

[98] "Studios are typically organized around manageable projects of design, individually or collectively undertaken, more or less closely patterned on projects drawn from actual practice. They have evolved their own rituals, such as master demonstration, design review, desk crits, and design juries, all attached to a core process of learning by doing" [Sch87; p.43].

recurring in the context of different design situations. This lead Alexander to propose a concept that addresses these problems referred to as *patterns*.

Alexander realized that the average designers can only insufficiently cope with the involved growing complexity: "To match the growing complexity of problems, there is a growing body of information and specialist experience. This information is hard to handle; it is widespread, diffuse, unorganized. Moreover, not only the quantity of information itself is by now beyond the reach of single designers, but the various specialists who retail it are narrow and unfamiliar with the form-makers' peculiar problems, so that it is never clear quite how the designer should best consult them. As a result ... the average designer scans whatever information he happens on, consults a consultant now and then when faced by extra-special difficulties, and introduces this randomly selected information into forms otherwise dreamt up in the artists' studio of his mind" [Al64; p.3-4][99].

His discovery, however, was that the complexity is not completely at random but contains similar problems *recurring* in different situations. Even though – as Rittel showed – the problems are not completely the same, they contain certain similarities. Accordingly, the solutions also show certain similarities. Or, as problems contain a kind of *pattern*, the solution may also follow a kind of *pattern*: "Each *pattern* describes a problem which occurs over and over again in our environment, and then describes the core of the solution to that problem, in such a way that you can use this solution a million times over, without ever doing it the same way twice" [AIS77, p.X]. Or, as Booch puts it: "complex systems have common *patterns*. These *patterns* may involve the reuse of small components, such as the cells found in both plants and animals, or of larger structures, such as vascular systems, also found in both plants and animals" [Bo94; p.11].

In short, a *pattern* describes a commonly recurring problem and a generalized description of a core solution generally adaptable to in different shapes for the individual problems [AIS77; p.X]. Now, if a good solution for such a recurring problem is found in a specific design solution, the designer can document the general essence[100] of the problem and its solution. Such documented *patterns* can then be used as a solution alternative in similar design problem situations. When the designer then decides for applying the *pattern*, the general solution essence defines the general structure of the design, whereas the individual local conditions of the current design problem context define the individual peculiarities of

---

[99] In the author's eyes, the following statement of Alexander also reveals close connections to the Simon and Booch's views of arbitrary complexity (ch. I.6.2.1), Rittel's *wicked problems* and Schön's view.

[100] Essence emphasizes the need to describe generalized information on the problem and the solution apart from a specific problem-solution context.

the applied *pattern* in the current design context. The problem essence[101] is often referred to as conflicts or forces[102] being torn apart [Al64; p.20]. Or, as Hagge et al. put it: "The underlying notion is that *patterns* help in resolving conflicts or stress situation– which are frequently perceived as 'being torn apart by ... forces'" [HHL+06; p.412].

In general, at least four essential aspects must be treated by a *pattern* [GHJ+95; p.3f], [Do04; p.530]:

- Name of the *pattern* [GHJ+95; p.3] works as a kind of keyword that can be used as placeholder (vocabulary) to refer to the complex knowledge of the problem and solution during design talks and documentation.
- A common problem, including a common problem context describing the forces, or the conflicts to be solved [GHJ+95; p.3], [Do04; p.530].
- A general approach to a solution [Do04; p.530], or general solution essence. The structure of the *pattern*. The solution neither describes a specific design or specific implementation. It can be seen more as a generic template adaptable to different situations [GHJ+95; p.4].
- The consequences arising from the use of the *pattern* enlist either the advantages as also the disadvantages involved with the usage of the *pattern*. "Although consequences are often left unspoken, when design decisions are described, they are still of central importance for the assessment of design alternatives and for the understanding of the advantages and disadvantages of a *pattern's* application" [GHJ+95; p.4].

In the software development context, the first proposal for the adoption of Alexander's *pattern* concept to software development seems to have been made by Kent Beck and Ward Cunningham [BC87] within the Smalltalk programming community for developing user interfaces[103] [BMH+98; p.7]. Even though other publications exist [CS95], the book of Gamma et al. [GHJ+95] – often referred to as *Gang of Four (GoF)* – sparked broad resonance in the design community lead-

---

[101] See [HHL+06; p.412] for a good discussion on this.
[102] A good example is the *pattern* "A window place" [Al79; p.112] that can be summarized in the following way: "In living rooms where people want to be comfortable, a sitting area should be located close to the windows. In rooms where the sitting area is not placed near the windows, people would be caught in a conflict: they would be drawn to the chairs to sit down and relax, but at the same time they would also be drawn towards the windows where the light is. Using the *window place pattern* would resolve and prevent the stress situation" [HHL+06; p.412].
[103] See, e.g., the *model-view-controller pattern* concept

ing to the wide influence of *patterns* in today's *SE* theory. *Patterns* can thus be found and used at different levels[104] of abstraction in design and *SE* theory:

*   *Requirement patterns* can be used to support elicitation and specification of requirements in combination with their verification criteria and test cases [RS02; p.346f]. A good description about other *RE patterns* and their role in *RE* is provided by [HHL+06].
*   *Analysis patterns* support analysis of requirements and especially can provide help that important *nonfunctional requirements* are already considered during the analysis phase [Mo04; p.142], [Ha01a], [Fo97].
*   *Architectural styles*[105] define "a family of systems in terms of a *pattern* of structural organization. More specifically, an architectural style defines a vocabulary of components and connector types, and a set of constraints on how they can be combined" [SG96; p.20]. In other words, *architectural styles* describe global structuring or organization principles to be found over and over again [PBG04; p.202]. An example for an *architectural style* is the *three layer architecture* separating data storage, functional logic and user interface into three different horizontal layers [BMR+00; p.31ff].
*   *Architectural patterns* describe rules or methods to address recurring aspects of system functionality often also referred to as *crosscutting concerns* [PBG04; p.207] such as persistence, multi-threading, distribution or the *user interface* [PBG04; p.208]. In this way, *architectural patterns* do not so much emphasize the functional domain but address technical aspects [PBG04; p.208]. An example for this category is the *model-view-controller pattern* addressing the *crosscutting concern* of designing flexible and reusable *GUI*-components [BMR+00; p.125ff].
*   *Design patterns* describe solutions for recurring design problems. Whereas *architectural styles* and *architectural patterns* rather address the global perspective, *design patterns* address more local perspectives in the way that they either effect one component or the collaboration of a few components [PBG04; p.214] [BMR+00; p.222ff]. In this way, *design patterns* can be ap-

---

[104] Also cf. Buschmann et al. [BHS07, p.213ff], who admit that these categorizations also are in some way arbitrary, as *patterns* often involve more than one of the different *pattern* categories described here and thus overlaps are fluent.

[105] It is to note that Buschmann et al. [BMR+00] do not distinct architectural styles from *architectural patterns*. This separation seems to be introduced by Posch et al. [PBG04]. However, even [BMR+00] provides a kind of segmentation, because the first are referred to as *architectural patterns* bringing structure into the overall architecture, whereas the latter then refer to more detailed implementations of aspects. In this way, the author finds this distinction between *architectural styles* and *architectural patterns* plausible.

plied without having effect on the overall *architecture* of a system or software [PBG04; p.214]. Furthermore, several *design patterns* can have effect on a component in parallel.

- *Idioms* [BMR+00; p.345-358], or *implementation patterns* [Be08], in programming languages or programming practice describe special – often programming language specific – peculiarities to provide an elegant solution for a specific recurring programming problem[106]. Beck [Be08] (also cf. [BMR+00; p.348f]) further shows that *idioms* can be an elegant mean for writing self-documenting code helping to improve development communication, simplicity and thus code flexibility [Be08; p.24ff].

- *Process patterns* describe *patterns* within a process landscape. Most notably, the agile development methods community [Co95], [BDS+98], [MWS+07], [HHL+06] and the wiki community [Ma08b] have also internalized the *pattern language* concept as they can be seen as an implementation of so-called *process pattern languages* ([Co95], [MWS+07]). A good starting point for the definition and usage of agile *process patterns* are found in [BG06].

- *Anti-patterns* indicate design flaws by enumerating symptoms and their negative effects [Ak96], [BMH+98], [Mo04; p.149 ff], [Kr08]. *Anti-patterns* arise when an originally fitting solution increasingly becomes unfitting due to changes of the solution's context (e.g., changing requirements) [Mo04; p.150]. The *anti-pattern* concept allows to document symptoms in a structured way to detect recurring unfitting solutions. Therefore, *anti-patterns* are also called recognition *patterns* [Mo04; p.156]. A good description about *architectural anti-patterns* and how they happen is provided by Kruchten [Kr08].

---

[106] As an example, the '?:'operator in the programming language C allows to assign different values to a variable basing upon a condition within one line of programming. As an example for *idioms* imposed by the automotive industry can be the MISRA standard for C programming [MISRA2004]. The standard defines *idioms* to be used in order to avoid known programming pitfalls encountered in C. In MISRA conforming code, e.g., the expression 'if (x==1)' is not allowed, because an incautious programmer could have written 'if (x=1)', where in this case a value assignment would take place and the 'if' statement would never be reached (besides a construct such as 'if (x=1)' is generally forbidden in MISRA). To avoid such unintended side effects, the MISRA standard demands to use 'if (1==x)', because if the developer wrote 'if (1=x)' the C compiler would issue a compiler error, as a value assignment to a constant ('1') is not allowed. In other domains such as Linux programming, however, the *idiom* 'if (x=1)' is considered as an elegant way of programming as it combines a value assignment with an 'if' in one line and thus avoids unnecessary code.

- *Usability patterns:* Borchers [Bo01] describes *patterns* usable for human interaction design.
- *Means*: In connection with *patterns*, Paech et al. [PKD+03] define the term *means:* "*Means* are principles, techniques, or mechanisms that facilitate the achievement of certain qualities in a *SW architecture*. They are abstract *patterns* that capture a way to achieve a certain *quality requirement*, but are not concrete enough to be used directly" [PKD+03; p.144]. However, *means* may be connected with concrete *patterns* [PKD+03; p.144], because *means* are selected according to *NFRs* and lead to the identification of the correspondingly usable *patterns* [PKD+03; p.147]. Hagge et al. refer to a *RE pattern* "Organize Specification Along Project Structure" (OSAPS) [HHL+06; p.419]. *SysEng* (ch. I.4) can be seen here as the *means* to fulfill the OSAPS *pattern*.

To support convenience and clarity [AIS77; p.X], Alexander proposes to describe each *pattern* in the same format today referred to as a *pattern template*. The *pattern template* provides a *formalized skeleton* of all important points to consider and document about a *pattern*. In this way, a structured method for documenting *patterns* that are comparable to each other is enforced.

As an exemplary *pattern template*, the properties of the *GoF pattern template* [GHJ+95; p.8ff] are shortly introduced in the following (for other sources about *pattern templates* the author recommends [PBG04; p.217]):

- The *pattern's name and classification*: as indicated above the name is intended to become part of the designer's design vocabulary. Thus, the name should transport concisely and precisely the essential information of the *pattern*.
- *Purpose*: This section shall provide a brief sketch of the *pattern's* general achievement, general principles, general purpose and what general issues or problems can be addressed by the *pattern*.
- *Also known as*: Refers to possibly known different names. This is, e.g., used to refer to other authors having described the *pattern* by using a different name.
- *Motivation*: Here, a certain specific exemplary scenario describes a design problem and how the structure of the *pattern* can help to solve the problem.
- *Application*: This section describes the problem situations the *pattern* can be applied to and how the situations can be recognized by the designer.
- *Structure*: The structure part describes the general structure of the *pattern*. For this, usually a structure diagram is provided with a textual description.
- *Participants*: Participating classes and objects are discussed in this part.
- *Interactions*: The interactions between the participants are described in this section.

- *Consequences*: As described above, the application of a *pattern* can involve positive and negative consequences. This part describes all known consequences.
- *Implementation*: The implementation section describes tips, techniques and pitfalls of the *pattern* to be known in order to be able to apply it successfully. It further refers to programming language specific aspects and possible ways of implementation.
- *Example code*: Example code fragments demonstrate a possible implementation within a programming language.
- *Known usages*: This part shows where the *pattern* has already been applied in real systems giving indications where the effecting *pattern* can be studied in practice.
- *Related patterns*: The last section describes how the *pattern* is related to other *patterns*, what the differences are to other *patterns*. Further, the part describes what *patterns* harmonize with the *pattern* and what *patterns* may involve dissonant effects if applied with the *pattern*.

A single *pattern* can provide a valuable solution for a problem. Alas, design deals with a lot of problems and correspondingly several different *patterns* may be applied in a design to solve these problems. Hence, the different applied *patterns* in a design may influence or stay linked to each other. This raised the idea in Alexander that design may be expressed as a *language of patterns* [AIS77], where the different applied *patterns* and their connections to each other structure the design. These connections between *patterns* can be influential (e.g., two *design patterns* can benefit or oppose each other) and also be of a kind of hierarchical nature, where higher abstraction level *patterns* are built up by lower abstraction level *patterns* (e.g., a *design pattern* can be implemented by several *idioms* working together, and the *design pattern* can work together with other *design patterns* to implement an *architectural pattern*) [AIS77; p.XII]. This idea is considered by Gamma et al. by defining a so called *pattern catalog* including a map, where possible connections between the *patterns* are introduced for *design patterns* [GHJ+95; p.16]. However, connections to *patterns* on other levels of abstraction are not considered. The concept of collecting *patterns* in a *pattern catalog* is usual [Mo04; p.143].

Also to mention is the *Portland Pattern Repository*[107] (PPR) wiki providing a possibility to collect *patterns* of all possible different categories[108], where inter-

---

[107] See http://www.c2.com/cgi/wiki?PortlandPatternRepository (Access: 2010/03).
[108] The PPR even describes socio-political *patterns* concerned with SW-development such as 'Melting Pot', describing how immigrants can be integrated into a SW development company in order to support company growth.

connections between *patterns* at even different categories are possible to describe. According to Greenfield et al. [GSC+04; p.210-211], the *formalization* of a *pattern language* may be a step toward defining a new modeling language. In fact, some *design patterns* (such as, e.g., 'Singleton') can be expressed in repeatedly the same implementation in code; however for others this may not be always achievable in the same way. However, Rupp et al. [RS02; p.348] utter the opinion that such a detailed *pattern language* may be an unrealistic goal for the software development community. Nevertheless, it is also to mention that Alexander himself does not insist on the opinion that only one *pattern language* exists, but that each individual may develop his (her) own unique language [AIS77; p.XVI]. In this way, a *formalized pattern language* was not in the focus of Alexander and may even to a certain extent contradict the original intentions of Alexander.

Evidence exists that *patterns* may also be implicitly present in expert designers thinking [VM02], [WV03]. In the Schönian context, one advantage of *patterns* may be that they represent a set of condensed reflective structures evolved from the design community. In other words, the *pattern* design community often identifies probably knowingly (intuitively) found solutions as 'good' and then reflectively explores the exact circumstances of their 'goodness'[109] and documents this knowledge as a *pattern*. Even though such an rationalization of intuitive knowledge may tend to provide falsifications [Sch87; p.23], Alexander's "method of capturing expertise was innovative, as it made explicit many of the 'soft' attributes that were previously attainable only through years of experience" [BMH+98; p.7].

Thus, *patterns* can be seen as written-down expert knowledge about a problem area and an offering of special opportunities to transfer and acquire this knowledge [Ha01a], [RS02; p.344], [Mo04; p.139]. Hereby, "*patterns* provide clarity. *Patterns* alone by their names represent a set of *knowledge* and *meta-knowledge* building a standard language (own set of vocabulary), where issues are reduced to a handy manner by essence building and abstraction" [RS02; p.345 (*)]. Thus, the role of *patterns* can be seen similar to symbols in a language, where sheerly mentioning the *pattern name* transports complex knowledge to all persons being familiar with the *pattern*.

In this way, *patterns* are also a possible answer to the problem of complexity and rapid change in software development: "*Formalizing* knowledge is a costly process. Aiming at achieving a perfect *formalization* is perhaps not worth, because software development, as any other intensive human activity, is evolving. Therefore the focus should be on providing an easy to customize and simple to apply solutions like the framework of *patterns*" [BG06; p.389].

---

[109] In the context of *anti-patterns*, the term 'good' can be replaced by 'bad'.

As indicated in ch. I.6.2.1.3, Simon's principles may be the end results of a design process, but Simon does not provide adequate indications on how to apply the principles in the design genesis. The problem seems to be that due to the complexity of factors, which make it impossible to rationally capture all factors adequately, intuitive *knowing-in-action* and *tacit knowledge* (see Schön, ch. I.6.2.3) are often the means to structure design. Here, *patterns* help designers in the decision process by documented expert knowledge. As an example, at the beginning of a project where nearly no structure is recognizable yet, a style as the *three layer architecture* builds a guide to overcome this by building a heuristics for early decomposing the design according to general aspects most SW-systems for PCs usually have.

In summary, the following positive effects can be achieved by *patterns*:

- Novice software designers can significantly improve their design quality from start [PU99], [Mo04; p.143].
- Experienced designers can also improve their design quality but more important, can better communicate their design ideas through *patterns*, being a design vocabulary transporting complex knowledge [PU99], [Mo04; p.143].
- Generally, only very few situations exist where *patterns* are weaker in comparison to another alternative solution [PU99], [Mo04; p.144].
- Most *patterns* have very positive effects on flexibility, whereas the *impact* on maintainability stays stable if they are not misused (see below for description of possible misuses) [PU99], [Mo04; p.144].
- *Design patterns* often *influence nonfunctional requirements* in one or the other direction. In most cases, however, choosing the right *design patterns* can significantly affect positive *impacts* on *NFRs* otherwise difficult to address [PBG04; p.214].
- *Patterns* offer proven and tested solutions to problems [RS02; p.344]. However, its positive effects should be tested, before employing a *pattern*.
- Douglass proposes using a *pattern* for each *design view* (see ch. I.6.2.1) employed in a design. In this way, *conceptual integrity* shall be enforced [Do04; p.478].

If *patterns* are used in a design, its usages should be documented in order to alleviate later maintenance [M004; p.321]. This will also be especially important when the documentation is the basis for an architectural assessment. In these cases, *pattern* can be significant indicators to detect tendencies and overall quality of a design [Mo04; p.140], [Mo04; p.293], [Mo04; p.381ff].

However, *patterns* can also provide problems. Dittert [Di04b; p.37] describes her own practical experiences how the *pattern* idea can be misused (i.e. *pattern usage anti-patterns*):

- "The *pattern canon*" [Di04b; p.37 (*)] has happened, if a simple implementation would have been sufficient, but some probably somewhere in the future occurring problem could have spoiled the solution. Correspondingly, the applied *pattern* may have prevented problems, if the change case may have happened some time. On the other side, the – most probably unnecessarily – applied *pattern* has heightened the complexity.
- "*Pattern euphoria*" [Di04b; p.37 (*)] can occur, if the application of a *pattern* at first brought significant advantage and then lead to extended use of the *pattern* to increase code flexibility, until the code became unreadable and small changes induced tremendous side effects.
- "*Pattern decoration*" [Di04b; p.37 (*)] describes properly working code that is decorated with some additional *patterns*, because the implementation was easy enough, whereas no significant new value has been generated.
- "*Pattern record*" [Di04b; p.37 (*)] indicates attitudes of designers thinking that a program's quality will automatically be high, when all known *patterns* are someway employed in it.

Last but not least to mention, Alexander saw *pattern* solutions as "timeless" [Al79]. However, this timelessness refers to the method but not the *patterns* themselves. Practice in software development, for example, shows at least in the software context that *patterns* also change, during increased usage and gained experiences [Wi06]. Consequently, their documentation i.e. specification need to be changed, too [Wi06]. From this perspective, close connections between the *pattern* concept and what Simon describes as *stable intermediate forms* reveal. Maybe *patterns* are a – maybe others exist as well – kind of notation for (resp. manifestation of) *stable intermediate forms*.

I.6.3 Comparison of General Design Theories

The author does not see that the different views on design expressed here are fully contradicting. In fact, the views supplement each other at certain states.

As Rittel's view tells something about social dynamics – as artificial worlds are created by and for humans they are deeply social – in design, it explains commonly observed core phenomena as the occurrence of permanent change in the requirements and the corresponding solution. A major implication may be that designs underlie stronger forces for change than often admitted.

Heavy-weight design approaches often implicitly assume a certain stability of the solution design or demand extensively built-in flexibility mechanisms (as, e.g., extensive frameworks) in the design. However, flexibility has its price in higher complexity and thus higher effort and higher costs[110]. Correspondingly, only finite flexibility is possible. Thus, these kinds of approaches must often rely on the designers' abilities to foresee changes in order to provide corresponding flexibility mechanisms. The *wicked problems* theory strongly challenges the feasibility of this. In other words, design approaches should impose as few obstacles to changes as possible in order to address the *wicked* nature of the addressed problems that necessarily result in extended changes.

Even though Simon's positivist linear view on design may somehow be called naive, Simon provides valuable insights into the toolkit available for designers to handle the complexity imposed by the manifold of information to be considered at design. Principles as *abstraction, hierarchical design* and *views* that have evolved from his pioneering research are state of the art in any kind of design –may it be aware or ignorant of the *wicked* nature of design problems.

Schön, on the other side, uncovered that designers do not perform design in a merely objective-rational cognitive setting but are equally intertwined driven by intuition, *tacit knowledge*, experience, taste, style and maybe even wisdom. Correspondingly, the author agrees on Knuth that computer programming – as it inherently contains design even if not necessarily explicitly present – is a science and an art [Kn74].

Last but not least, the *pattern* concept addresses recurring problems in design and creates possibilities for collecting and communicating design knowledge.

All views on design sketched here have one common concern. Requirements constitute a *problem space*, whereas design constitutes a *solution space*. Between both exists a considerable semantic gap that is constantly mentally bridged by designers. This gap is the result of an irreproducible, non-deterministic and ontogenetic path of intellectual decisions created by a collaborative collective of human beings shaping an artificial – in relation with SW even abstract and virtual – environment. *Requirements traceability* aims at closing semantic gaps. However, the ordinary link concept as usually provided by *requirements traceability* refers to a linear relationship between requirements and design. As the characteristics of the design process sketched above suggest, design rather is a nonlinear complex

---

[110] "The problem with building flexible solutions is that flexibility costs. Flexible solutions are more complex than simple ones. The resulting software is more difficult to maintain in general, although it is easier to flex in the direction. ... Even there, however, you have to understand how to flex the design" [Fo99].

process. Correspondingly, the author suggests considering relationships between requirements and design as equally nonlinear[111].

In other words, design processes are creative and complex mental transfers of unique problem constellations into a sustainable solution. Correspondingly, a substantial gap between requirements and design exists that is – in to the author's belief – not really manageable by a linear linking concept as current *traceability* theory suggests[112]. A sustainable design *traceability* concept must orient itself on the designers' way of designing, not interrupt the designers' thinking, find an adequate support for decision making, be able to support design as a collaborative process and last but not least provide the necessary flexibility for changing the design.

I.6.4 Dependency between Design Models and Code

Design models in relation to source code can be either *descriptive* or *prescriptive*. When a code documentation model is generated from developed source code, the model is *descriptive*. Otherwise, when a *design model* is designed before the code, these models are *prescriptive*, because they prescribe the further outcome of the code. Usually, design is performed before the code, thus most *design models* are *prescriptive*.

Generally, design theory recommends that besides the *design models* also a *programming model* must be developed [GP04], [PBG04; p.69]. The *programming model* deals with defining the transformation regulations for transforming *design models* into code. *Design models* and the *programming models* must not be confused with each other [PBG04; p.69].

Usually, three ways for a programming model to develop code from *prescriptive* models exist:
- Manual implementation,
- Partial code generation,

---

[111] Of course, in any project a high amount of fairly linear relationships between requirements and design may exist. However, as these are relatively trivial ones, the nonlinear relationships will often be more critical to identify, if a requirement change shall be implemented consistently.

[112] Similar findings are expressed by Medvidovic et al. [MGE+03; p.202]: "Unfortunately, the large semantic gap between high-level, sometimes ambiguous requirements artifacts and the more specific architectural artifacts (e.g., modeled in a *formal* ...(architecture description language)...) often does not allow one to establish meaningful links between them". As a consequence they developed their so called CBSP approach, discussed in the ch. II.10.6 about *requirements traceability* to design.

- Complete code generation;

From the technological perspective, manual implementation is the simplest way. However, development efforts are the highest. In the long run, risks that a significant drift between *design model* and its code arises are nearly not avoidable, because *design model*s represent a redundancy to the code. Thus, maintenance must care to adapt both the model and the code. Maintenance effort will be lower, if the models are not very detailed. In fact, design theory emphasizes that models should just show the core ideas and concepts of a system, but no implementation details [GP04; p.64].

Partial code generation can be achieved by two possible ways. One way is to generate complete code for certain parts of an application. It is, e.g., possible to generate complete code representing a state machine from a state chart model. Another possible way is that certain aspects of a model can be used to automatically generate certain code outlines that must then be accomplished by manual implementation. In this way, e.g., variable names and method names in a model can be used to generate source code files with automatic generation of the variables definition and method stubs. These method stubs must then be populated by manual source code development. Both techniques allow saving effort by directly reusing modeled information for the source code. Further, later changes of a model can be directly propagated to the source code thus diminishing risks of a drift between models and source code. On the other side, this method is accompanied by the need for more sophisticated tooling. Additionally, automatically generated code can lead to lesser code efficiency (lower performance or worse resource efficiency).

Full code generation would completely solve the redundancy problem between models and its code, because the full code is generated from the model. Therefore, a drift between models and code is impossible. On the other side, very sophisticated tooling is necessary and the code efficiency may be significantly lower than the efficiency of manually or partially generated code. Additionally, models must be modeled in significantly more detail, as all instructions of the code must be somehow represented by the models or the code transformation algorithms. This means that models must also represent implementation details rather than just ideas or concepts (see, e.g., [Do04; p.589ff]), or the code transformation algorithms contain much of the complexity of the implementation details. This, however, involves the problem that the developers must either completely rely on the code transformation algorithms, or the developers must instrument the code transformation algorithms by setting complex sets of parameters and performing a certain restricted way of modeling. Both techniques involve significant intransparencies of the transformation processes that may also be an issue for *traceability* considerations. Additionally, using these tools also requires having extra expert skills of the developers in using the tools.

Last but not least, it is to mention that *requirements traceability* between *design models* and code is relatively easy to handle due to the redundancies between both. As both model and code usually use the same names for concepts being redundant to each other, the *traceability* technique of *name mapping* (cf. ch. II.10.4.2.2) solves the *traceability* problems as long as no significant drift between models and code occurs leading to a drift, where the names drift apart from each other.

I.6.5 Architecture Documentation

Besides just designing the diagrams of a model, further textual documentation must be delivered with them. Managing complexity and achieving a common understanding are core goals of any design. However, diagrams can be ambiguously interpreted by different persons. Correspondingly, the diagrams must be accompanied by a textual description. The research field *architecture documentation* (*AD*) tries to define important criteria on what must be documented about a *SW architecture* in order to be useful. As the R2A tool introduced in part III also provides certain support for design documentation, some general principles for *AD* shall be sketched[113] here. Of course, *AD* actually only cares for *SW architectures* (one of the three different designs identified in ch. I.6.1), but in the author's opinion the points discussed here are equally valid for *systems design* and up to a certain point also valid for *detailed SW design*.

At first to mention, Clements et al. [CBB+03; p.24-28] introduce seven rules any sound textual documentation should consider (also cf. [PBG04; p.124-125]):

- *Documentation should be written from the point of view of the reader, not the writer*: This ensures that the documented information can be really understood by the reader.
- *Avoid unnecessary repetition:* As discussed before in ch. I.6.1.2, redundancy should be generally avoided (*DRY-principle*).
- *Avoid ambiguity*: The information provided must be precise and should not leave open space for misleading interpretation.
- *Use a standard organization schema*: An architectural template helps to document information in a certain standard scheme for all projects. In this way, project members can easier understand new documents.

---

[113] The interested reader may read [IEEE1471], [CBB+03], [PBG04; p.121-169] or [HS06] for a deeper understanding.

- *Record rationale*: Important decisions must be documented.
- *Keep documentation current but not too current*: Documentation should be continuously kept up to date, but updates should not be performed immediately to avoid unnecessary costs.
- *Review documentation for fitness of purpose*: Documentation must be reviewed whether the documentation fulfills its goals.

Concerning *AD*, the following basic requirements must be supported [PBG04; p.126-128]:

- *Efficiency of the project must be supported*: The documentation must support the developers to efficiently and easily acquire the information needed for their current tasks.
- *Communication and common understanding of important stakeholders must be supported*: The *AD* is responsible to enable communication and common understanding of the *architecture* throughout all important stakeholders. In the following, several stakeholder needs are described.
- *Minimize risks*: The *AD* must help to reduce risks by making possible risks transparent. This means, for example, that documentation should be structured risk-oriented meaning that high-risk issues should be addressed with higher priority and extent than rather low-risk issues [PBG04; p.127]. Another important means to expose risks is structured documentation about decisions taken in order to address certain risks and how taken decisions may spark new risks.
- *Preserve the core knowledge of the designed system*: The core knowledge about a certain *architecture* should be preserved throughout the life time of a project. *AD* should therefore help to preserve this knowledge in the developing organization and assist in deriving knowledge and experiences reusable for new projects.

As point two has mentioned, *AD* also is about promoting communication and common understanding between important stakeholder groups. *AD* must at minimum support the following stakeholders with their goals [PBG04; p.127]:

- The *project manager* needs an overview of the design in order to take organizational decisions. Further, the project manager must get to know the technical risks.
- The *architect* creates the architectural documentation of the project. For this, he must capture and understand the important concepts, strategies and technologies used.
- The *software developer* realizes parts of the *architecture*. In this way, he must understand the basic principles of the overall *architecture*, the basic

context of the parts he must realize and – probably most important – detailed information on the interfaces of the parts to be realized.

An *AD* must contain the following essential points [PBG04; p.128-131], [St05; p.105], [CBB+03]:

- *All relevant views* must be documented in the *AD*. All views should be documented in the same manner by a standard organization template [CBB+03; p.317]. In [CBB+03; p.317-320], Clements et al. introduce such a template which follows seven criteria.
- As each view only describes a certain aspect of a system, the *AD* must also document the *intercorrelations, interactions and tradeoffs between the different documented views*[114].
- To achieve the efficiency requirements of *AD*, the *AD* document should include a *description of its structuring and assistance to the reader*.

Concerning the last point, Posch et al. [PBG04; p.130-131] provide the following remarks:

- The *AD* should use a hierarchic structuring. This structuring could, e.g., be the *hierarchic decomposition* structure of a system, but also other *views* may be organizable in a hierarchic ordering scheme.
- Descriptions of relationships between views should be explicitly highlighted.
- Finding and retrieving essential information must be easy. Thus, important information should be in the center of description.
- Documentation must be target-group-specific. This means that information for a specific target group should be rather located at one cohesive location than be scattered over the whole documentation.
- The documentation must support target-group-specific navigation. At least, information about target-group-specific navigation information should be provided.

Last but not least to mention, the IEEE 1471 standard [IEEE1471] defines a conceptual model for documenting *architectures* in combination with recommendations how to apply these concepts. Among other concepts, the correlations between a system, its *architecture*, its *AD* and *views* are defined. Especially interesting is the fact that the IEEE 1471 derives a view from stakeholders and their perspectives called viewpoints. From this viewpoint construct, characteristics and

---

[114] "The basic principle of documenting an architecture as a set of separate views brings a divide-and-conquer advantage to the task of documentation, but if the views were irrevocably different, with no relationship to one another, nobody would be able to understand the system as a whole. Managing how views are related is an important part of the architect's job, and documenting it is an important part of the documentation that applies beyond views" [CBB+03; p.200].

constraints for views shall be derived. As the IEEE 1471 only provides concepts and recommendations, no specific demands for modeling languages, techniques, used *design models* or *views*, or other *AD* related concepts are provided. In this way, the IEEE 1471 only defines a frame for deriving an individual *AD* approach [PBG04; p.132]. Besides the general principles for *AD* sketched here, the IEEE 1471 with its conceptual framework is not further considered in this thesis. Another standard to consider is the IEEE 1016 [IEEE1016] (also cf. [Sch00; p.112-121]) providing a "recommended practice for describing software designs" [Sch00; p.112]. The standard specifies the information content and recommended organization for a *software design description* as a representation of a software system that is used as a medium for communicating software design information [Sch00; p.112].

A comprehensive general treatment of the topic architectural documentation is provided by the book of Clements et al. [CBB+03] describing the basic principles of sound documentation and providing a fundamental terminology and method. According to Hruschka and Starke [HS06; p.56], the proposals for structuring *AD* documents in general are „brilliant" with its basic structure for documenting views. Hruschka and Starke [HS06; p.57], however, consider Clements et al. [CBB+03] as hardly suitable for a practice-oriented *AD*. In [HS06], Hruschka and Starke give an overview on other *AD* approaches. Further, they introduce a more pragmatic and practice-oriented approach on *AD* they call "arc42-template".

I.6.6 Design in the Automotive Domain

After the previous chapters have provided a rather general view on how design arises, this chapter describes the modeling methods and tools typically used in automotive development. This helps to derive some extra requirements for the R2A tool solution described in part III.

Generally, it is to mention that the tool solution described in part III is a general solution not especially dedicated for the automotive domain. In this way, this chapter can rather be considered as a kind of exemplar description of modeling approaches used in a specific engineering domain. On the other side, the automotive domain has some peculiarities that should be considered in order to provide high value for the automotive domain. At the end of this chapter, the reader will see that the features derived from these peculiarities are also useful for other domains, but they are especially useful in the automotive domain.

In the following, two peculiarities of the automotive domain are discussed:
- The usage of different heterogeneous modeling languages and tools,

- The need to integrate other organizations (e.g., suppliers) into the considerations of design;

I.6.6.1 Modeling Methods and Tools Used in Automotive Design

In the automotive domain, different modeling methods are used:
- Tools basing on UML and (resp. or) SysML,
- Automatic control engineering oriented tools,
- Tools basing on *state charts*;

I.6.6.1.1 UML and SysML

The Unified Modeling Language (UML) has established itself as worldwide standard for modeling SW [We06; p.3]. UML has also established itself in the embedded community ([Gr03], [Al03]). In automotive, it is also gaining growing usage[115], even though the other approaches mentioned here exist. UML's advantage is its high variety of different design elements and diagram types allowing to flexibly model different aspects concerning SW. Thus, UML directly supports to model different views. Although UML supports hierarchic decomposition of systems, UML does not prescribe a hierarchic order. The standard rather concentrates on defining the different diagram types with the semantics of the used elements in these diagrams. Decisions about how to arrange elements and diagrams in a model are left open to the designers. It is rather possible to use different hierarchies (e.g., it is possible to have different hierarchies for different views). This leads Broy and Rumpe to the conclusion that UML is rather pragmatic and practice-oriented without a uniform model, but has rather worked out partial aspects as views however not being consistent to each other [BR07b; p.4].

UML also provides extensibility through offering a *meta-model* and a profiling mechanism. Whereas, first versions of UML have rather concentrated on usability in practice, UML 2[116] defines an action-semantics with improved support for executable models allowing model simulation and code generation [Mo04; p.180ff]. Model simulation allows early verification of requirements, because the models can be used as a simulation prototype (see ch. I.5.6 for ad-

---

[115] A clear indication of its importance in Automotive is the fact that its notation is used in defining Automotive SW standards as, e.g., the AutoSAR standard [KF09].

[116] A detailed overview of the major changes between the first UML versions and UML2 is provided by [JRZ04].

vantages of prototypes in *REM*) to simulate the behavior of the system, before it is finally constructed thus enabling to identify missing or wrong requirements earlier [Mo04; p.177ff]. Model simulation can also help to achieve early estimations about *NFRs* related to the dynamic behavior of a system (e.g., performance, scalability) [Mo04; p.183]. Known UML-tools employed in practice for model simulation are IBM Rational Rhapsody and Artisan Realtime Studio (see also [Ge05; p.42-44], [Sa05]). However, as long as it concerns model simulation and code generation, often other tools described in the next chapters are mostly employed in the embedded domain.

For *system design* as used in *SysEng* processes, the *Systems Modeling Language* (SysML) has been developed. SysML [SYSML] is defined as standard by the Object Management Group [OMG] basing on UML 2.1.1 [We07; p.16]. SysML extends UML in certain aspects but also leaves out some aspects of UML not necessary for systems design. Besides extensions for modeling systems such as support for time-continuous modeling or block diagrams, a major extension is that SysML defines a notion for requirements together with several relationship types that describe *traceability* mapping between requirements and design. Ch. II.10.4.2.3 describes this aspect of SysML in more details.

Concerning tool support, SysML can usually be used by UML-tools extended by a SysML profile. A detailed description of the SysML standard is provided by Weilkiens [We06], [We07].

I.6.6.1.2 Automatic Control Engineering Oriented Tools

As Bauer et al. [BRS05; p.195] point out; automotive SW development has diverse connections to mechanical engineering and automatic control engineering. Accordingly, several *design tools* exist that have automatic control engineering-oriented[117] semantics.

In ECU development, the most applied tool of this kind is probably Matlab Simulink [Matlab] (see [Te01]). In the automotive domain, besides Matlab Simulink, the tool ETAS ASCET [ASCET] is also used in equal project contexts (ASCET, however, in contrary to Matlab Simulink seems to be used only in the automotive domain). Marwedel [Ma08a; p.86] describes Matlab Simulink as simulation and modeling tool basing on mathematical principles (e.g., partial differential equations). Different elementary mathematical operations as integrators, characteristic diagrams[118] or filters are symbolized by so called block libraries (cf. [BRS05; p.195]), which can be connected together via data flow model-

---

[117] German: Regelungstechnik
[118] German: Kennlinie

ing. Matlab Simulink (and equally ETAS ASCET) provides facilities to simulate the behavior of those models as prototypes for early requirement verification of complex physical or logical interdependencies between requirements (ch. I.5.4). Furthermore, these models can also be used for code generation of large parts of the application (see also [Sa05], [Ge05; p.42-44], [MB05]).

As Bauer et al. [BRS05; p.195] point out; this modeling technique emphasizes synchronous function blocks, signals, periods connected by data flow transitions. However, these models depend on a synchronous uniform time basis. Thus, problems as concurrent tasks or shared resource management are difficult to handle in those tools (see [BRS05; p.195] for details). Therefore, – as the author experienced in practice – those tools are often used for modeling certain components having complex behavior. These components are then integrated with other components in a higher level *architecture*.

I.6.6.1.3 State Charts

Most ECUs are reactive systems (see ch. I.2.2). This means the system reacts on the settings and changes of the environment. Therefore, ECUs or at least parts of it are often state based. Due to the long existence of state machine theory, it is also a well-known theory describing deterministic behavior.

The techniques usual today for modeling complex state based behavior are *state charts*[119] originally introduced by Harel in 1987 [Ha87]. The semantics of the language bases on finite deterministic state machines. More on *state charts* as modeling technique in the context of ECUs can be seen in ch. I.5.4, [Ma08a; p.18ff] or [Do04; p.317f].

Requirements describing state based behavior can be very numerous and complex and so can also become the state machines. Therefore, advantages and limitations of this method concerning early model verification for early requirement evaluation are comparable to the approaches described in the previous chapter about automatic control engineering oriented tools (see also ch. I.5.4).

---

[119] Pettit [Pe04] provides the following experiences about state charts in embedded design practice with UML: "In the author's experience, state charts are one of the most underused UML diagrams in designing embedded software system. The hierarchical state charts employed by the UML offer significant expressive power for capturing the reactive, state-dependent behavior often found in embedded systems. State charts should be constructed for each class that encapsulates state dependent behavior" [Pe04; p.4]. Ch. I.8 provides a more detailed discussion on the practical experiences of Pettit in embedded development.

Due to the possible high complexity of the *state machines*, the *state machine models* can be managed hierarchically, where states can have sub *state machines* [Ma08a; p.19], [Do04; p.317f].

The tool Matlab Stateflow is a professional *state charts* modeling tool offering the possibilities to simulate gathered *state machine models*, where the models can later be used for automatic code generation.

Besides Matlab Stateflow, also the UML-tools IBM Rational Rhapsody and Artisan Realtime Studio allow similar functions to early simulate modeled *state charts* and generate code of it. The advantage of these tools is that the state charts are integrated into an UML modeling environment.

However, Matlab Stateflow still seems the most used tool for modeling *state charts* in automotive development (see also [Sa05], [Ge05; p.42-44]).

I.6.6.1.4 Conclusions

In the automotive industry, different methods are used. *Formal* methods, as automatic control engineering and state chart tools, have their individual strength in early *formal validation* and *verification* of requirements or in modeling algorithms, where the gathered resulting models can be directly used to automatically generate code. This often helps to cover large extents of the *functional requirements*. However, automotive ECUs are complex, where extensive parts of the code do not cover *functional requirements* but rather deal with directly handling the HW or managing special problems caused by the extremely cost-optimized HW.

For these cases, UML and SysML are better suited with their rather pragmatic, but rich tool set. Moreover, UML and SysML have their focal point on architectural modeling, whereas the other *formal* methods rather concentrate on partial aspects such as state charts or algorithmic modeling.

In this way, UML and SysML can be a notational framework for the overall design of the *architecture*. For parts, however, often covering extensive parts of the *FRs*, the *formal* modeling approaches can develop partial models helping to early verify and stable these requirements with the ability to directly use the models as basis for code generation. Other parts of the system, however, are not needed for *formal* verification, because they cover *FRs* only to low extents, but rather deal about fulfilling supportive tasks (e.g., steering of HW or managing special problems). UML or SysML may then again be the better choice.

In fact, the author thinks that another form of *pareto*-kind connection might even exist (see also ch. II.10.4.2.2): 80% of the *FRs* might be covered by 20% of the code. This kind of code can often be covered by modeling tools supporting early simulation and verification of requirements with subsequent code generation. In this way, most functionality of the system can be elicited early in projects. However, for the other 80% of the code (being mostly the handler and driver layer in an automotive ECU project) dealing with behavior in error cases and steering of HW manual coding may still be the best alternative. Another way around the problem may be to have standardized COTS[120] components such as the AutoSAR [KF09] standardization endeavor aims for.

As a consequence of these facts collected in the chapters above, automotive projects often use several *design tools* in one project together. Correspondingly, a *requirements traceability* solution to include design must enable to include several *design tools* into one integrated model. Such a notion is also expressed by Grimm [Gr05]: "Current SW tools are generally dedicated to specific phases and tasks within software or systems development. Thus, there is an urgent need for continuous integrated tools in order to achieve that different developed artifacts and processes can be developed in an concerted way with optimal support of the defined modeling approach" [Gr05; p.421 (*)]. Such a solution is provided by R2A (see ch. III.16.2).

Last but not least, other tools that exist in automotive design need to be mentioned. These are, e.g., tools such as IBM Rational DOORS or Aquintos PREEvision are used by OEMs in practice to design systems of systems, where the OEM derives the *requirements specifications* for the singular ECUs to commission suppliers to develop the ECUs (see the following chapter). In research, tool environments such as AutoFOCUS [BRS05] exist especially dedicated for automotive development. In the following, these tools are not further considered as design[121] tools.

I.6.6.2 Integrating other Organizations into a Design

"In the development of complex embedded systems, often several companies work together on the development. At such an interconnected development, often partnerships are built, where mostly one supplier is engaged as the system supplier having – besides other tasks – the responsibility to coordinate the other suppli-

---

[120] Components Off The Shelf

[121] DOORS is considered as *REM-tool* but not as a means for design. In fact, DOORS as *design tool* also is very limited in the way that it rather supports a text-based design comparable to Microsoft Word, where pictures can, e.g., be created via Microsoft Visio. However, also more sophisticated addons for DOORS exist allowing to combine the textual specifications in DOORS with modeling aspects (see, e.g., http://www-01.ibm.com/software/awdtools/doors/analyst/ (Access: 2010/07)).

ers. Therefore, selection and coordination of suppliers is of special importance in embedded development.

Often, even a hierarchy of client-supplier-relationships emerges, meaning that a supplier (*second tier*) acquires further sub components of the system from his own suppliers (so called *third tier*) and coordinates the collaboration. Additionally, the customer often prescribes the supplier certain *third tier* suppliers" [HDH+06; p.65 (*)].

As this statement of Hörmann et al. indicates, complex relationships between customer and supplier exist. This makes it necessary to coordinate collaboration between organizations. This also means that often the work of different suppliers must be integrated into a working system where one of the suppliers is responsible to coordinate the others. This implies that the coordinating suppliers must define an *architecture* where the parts of the other suppliers must be integrated in. As the different suppliers also have strong interest to protect their knowledge, it is especially important to define interfaces between the different parts.

This together means that the *coordinating suppliers* must find ways to effectively communicate parts of their architectural design essential to suppliers whose delivered parts must be integrated into the *architecture*, but also avoid communicating essential knowledge to be protected. On the other side, the coordinating suppliers must also ensure that the supplied parts to be integrated really match the requirements and directives of the architectural design. The R2A tool solution introduced in part III addresses this topic through allowing the export of parts of a *design model* as direct requirements specification for a supplier (see ch. III.23.1). In this way, a direct and frictionless *supplier management* can be realized.

I.7 Quality Standards for *Safety-Critical* Development Processes

If you can't describe what you are doing as a process, you don't know what you're doing.
William Edwards Deming

According to diverse authors (e.g., [Eb05; p.23], [GG03], [HDH+06; p.50], [St01]), SW quality has been significantly improved due to concentration on SW processes and their improvement.

In the view of Hatley et al. [HHP03; p.41], attempts for SW quality improvement have their origins in a study on quality by Deming [Deming86] and the *Total Quality Management* (*TQM*) movement in the 1980ies. There, *TQM* mostly defines quality as the correspondence of a product with its requirements, what implies the following core ideas of *TQM* [HHP03; p.41-42]:

- Requirements must be defined with extreme precision.
- The fulfillment of requirements must be measurable.
- Not fulfilled requirements are an error.
- Maximizing quality, thus, means minimizing the errors.

In summary, *TQM* is completely dependent on precise definition of requirements and management of requirements [HHP03; p.42]. *TQM*, however, is more a holistic organization management theory (e.g., cf. [Ro01; p.64-67]) than a quality practice for the specific quality issues concerning software development.

Around 1986, during the SDI-project (Strategic Defense Initiative), the United States Department of Defense (DOD) encountered major problems concerning the developed software for high complexity systems [Kn06; p.1]. This sparked the DOD to perform a study in cooperation with the Software Engineering Institute (SEI) of the Carnegie Mellon University in Pittsburg. In 1989 the disclosed study came to the conclusion that only 24 % of software functionality delivered was actually usable [HDH+06; p.7]. As a consequence, the DOD mandated the SEI to develop a quality improvement model for software processes. As a result, the SEI developed the *Capability Maturity Model* [PCC+93], [PWG+93]. In the following years, the *CMM* model was about to become a major success story for process improvement for organizations far beyond the scope of the DOD [Kn06; p.1]. During the years of implementation, besides the SW *CMM*, also *CMM* models for SysEng and *product engineering* have been developed leading to the development of the *CMMI* (*CMM integrated*) standard model integrating the different models in 2001 [Kn06]. The original CMM standard has been set deprecated in 2003 [HDH+06; p.7].

The major success of CMM also sparked ambitions by the European Union to develop a similar model by the BOOTSTRAP project [SE96] finally leading to the definition of an international ISO standard for the assessment of software process quality. These ambitions finally lead to the international ISO/IEC 15504 [ISO15504] also referred to as *SPICE* (*Software Process Improvement and Capability dEtermination*[122]).

---

[122] Originally, SPICE was called Software Process Improvement and Capability Evaluation [HWF+08; p.28], [HDH+06; p.9]. As the translation into French language would have changed the semantics, Evaluation has been replaced by Determination without changing the acronym [HDH+06; p.9].

In contrast to *CMM* and *CMMI* being a proprietary model[123] of the SEI institute [BHV09; p.135], the *SPICE* model is designed as open international standard. Even though *CMMI* currently seems to have a wider pervasion in industry (it
is even widely spread in Automotive industry) [MHD+07; p.4-5], the HIS[124]
initiative has decided to use *SPICE* as their standard for auditing suppliers
[MHD+07; p.3], [HDH+06; p.4]. In the last years also an industry specific adaption of *SPICE*, called Automotive *SPICE* (*A-SPICE*), has been developed to better fit to the peculiar needs of the automotive industry.

Due to these facts, the author has decided to use the following chapters to
introduce *SPICE* as exemplar quality model highlighting the *traceability* demands of such standards. As the development team of *CMMI* aimed to be consistent and compatible to *SPICE* [Kn06; p.9], and because both *process models*
base on the ISO 12207 [ISO12207] *process model* for software development, the
identified discussion points should so far also be valid for *CMMI*[125]. In addition,
after discussing *SPICE* a small chapter will outline some minor changes concerning *traceability* demands, when *A-SPICE* is used.

Last but not least, it is to mention that also new quality standards (IEC
61508, ISO 26262) concerning *safety-related aspects* of embedded systems are
currently gaining importance in the automotive industry also imposing effects on
traceability demands. Consequently, at the end of this chapter, the demands of
these two standards are also discussed.

---

[123] Although the *CMMI* model is proprietary, it also has become a kind of de-facto standard [BHV09; p.135].

[124] "Hersteller Initiative Software" (Car Manufacturer Initiative) – A community of German automotive OEMs (http://www.automotive-his.de/ (Access 2010/02)) defining
specific stan–dards for the german automotive industry often becoming de-facto
standards for the world-wide automotive industry.

[125] It is to mention that certain differences between CMMI and SPICE exist, but these
differences should not have significant influence on the topics discussed here. For the
more interested reader, [MHD+07; p.273-283] and [BHV09] provide a detailed description on the differences between CMMI, SPICE and Automotive SPICE and how
organizations can best migrate from CMMI to SPICE or maintain both models in parallel.

I.7.1 SPICE (ISO 15504)

Today, order mostly is where there is nothing. It is a phenomenon of shortage.
Brecht (*)

SPICE is a standard for assessing the maturity (quality) of development process-es. It covers the aspects process assessments, requirements for processes and their assessment as well as guidance principles for how to employ the standard [HDH+06; p.13]. The standard itself is divided into five parts [HDH+06; p.13-14]:

1. Part I – "Concepts and Vocabulary": Offers a general introduction into the important concepts and terms of the standard.
2. Part II – "Performing an Assessment": Minimal requirements for performing an assessment in order to acquire consistent and reproducible benchmarks. Part II "is the (normative) core of the standard; the other parts have a more imperative character" [HDH+06; p.13 (*)].
3. Part III – "Guidance on performing an assessment": Guidance for interpreting the requirements imposed by Part II.
4. Part IV – "Guidance on use for process improvement and process capability determination": "Guidance for usage of process assessments within a process improvement effort or for determination of the *maturity level*" [HDH+06; p.13 (*)].
5. Part V – "An exemplar Process Assessment Model": Example of a *process assessment model* for the application of assessments according to the re-quirements imposed by part II. According to Hörmann et al. [HDH+06; p.18], this part has the most importance for practice (cf. ch. I.7.1.3).

Two further parts are still in standardization work:

- Part VI – "An exemplar system life cycle process assessment model": Exam-ple about creating an assessment model for life-cycles of human created sys-tems according to [ISO15288].
- Part VII – "Assessment of organizational maturity": Defines a framework to determine organizational maturity.

As normative part, Part II defines the following normative aspects [HDH+06; p.14]:

- Requirements for the assessment process including planning, performing, data collection, data validation, definition and validation of process attributes and reporting,
- "Requirements on roles and responsibilities" [HDH+06; p.14 (*)],
- "Requirements on the assessment inputs and outputs" [HDH+06; p.14 (*)],
- The framework for measuring the process maturity,

- The requirements for process reference and process assessment models;

SPICE is structured in three different models [HDH+06; p.17]:

1. The *process reference model (PRM)* describes a set of processes as a reference model. The processes are defined in high level terms of purpose and expected outcomes [BHV09; p.135].
2. The *measurement framework (MF)* defines the basic maturity levels, process attributes and the evaluation scale. As the name framework indicates, the *MF* just defines a measuring frame and is not alone sufficient for measuring process maturity.
3. The *process assessment model (PAM)* refers to the *MF* and is built up by one or more *PRMs*. It defines concrete criteria (so called *indicators*) for maturity evaluation. The *PAM* has two dimensions:
   - The *process dimension* defines the *indicators* for all processes of the used *PRM*.
   - The *maturity dimension* defines how to determine the *maturity level* from measured results of processes according to the *indicators*.

I.7.1.1 The Process Reference Model of SPICE

A *PRM* offers a basis for the development of an individual organization-specific *process model* describing the ideal processes to be employed in a company. In principle, it is possible to create an organization-specific *process model* without any *PRM*, but a *PRM* helps to improve the development of an organization-specific *process model* [FL02; p.9].

In the following, such an activity is called *process implementation*[126] and the performer of this activity is called *process architect*. In SPICE, the *PRM* describes a set of processes to be adapted for implementation by an organization. The processes are described with regard to their goals, practices to perform and outcomes to reach the goals. An example of a widely referred standardized *PRM* is the ISO 12207 [ISO12207] *process model* for software development.

Since SPICE itself is a very generic standard, organizations can also refer to other *PRMs* (or even other *PAMs*) [HDH+06; p.14]. As also discussed in ch. I.7.4,

---

[126] Concerning adaption of a *PRM* to an organization, also the standard IEEE 1074 [IEEE1074] provides valuable support for process architects, as it describes how activities of a *PRM* can be mapped to an organization to create an organization-specific *process model* [Sch00; p.58-79]. Especially concerning process implementation of ISO 12207, the IEEE 12207 [IEEE12207] standard gives valuable guidance how ISO 12207 may be implemented in industry practice [Sch00; p.50-58].

the automotive industry specific *SPICE* adoption, called *Automotive SPICE (A-SPICE)*, uses a slightly different *PRM*[127] specifically adapted to process concerns of automotive development [HDH+06; p.269].

Nevertheless, when a *PRM* is used deviating from ISO12207, a separate assessment must clarify whether the *process model* fulfills the requirements imposed by *SPICE*, part II [HDH+06; p.14].

I.7.1.2 The Measurement Framework

The *PAM* has the goal to assess development processes according to their maturity. *SPICE* defines in part II different *maturity levels (ML)* where each assessed process can be categorized. Altogether, part II defines 6 *MLs* [HDH+06; p.15-16]:

- Level 0 – Incomplete: The process is not established or the goals of the process are not reached.
- Level 1 – Performed: The process is established and fulfills its goals, however in an uncontrolled manner.
- Level 2 – Managed: The process is planned and its progress is tracked. Resulting work products are adequately performed, are controlled by *configuration management*, and quality is ensured through dedicated *quality management*.
- Level 3 – Established: An organization-wide standard process is established, where each project uses a tailored version of this process.
- Level 4 – Predictable: The performance of processes is continuously measured and monitored leading to a quantitative understanding of the process with improved predictability.
- Level 5 – Optimizing: Basing on the business goals of the organization, quantitative goals are derived for processes and its compliance is continuously tracked.

For each of the levels so called *process attributes (PA)* define more detailed criteria for assessment. Altogether, 9 *PAs* exist shown in table 7.1 in correspondence to their *ML*.

---

[127] Besides these two *PRMs*, Bella et al. explicitly name the ISO/IEC 15288 (for Systems Engineering life cycle processes) as fully compliant to SPICE [BHV09; p.135].

Table 7.1 Maturity Levels and their Process Attributes (cf.[HDH+06; p.16])

Maturity Level	Process Attributes
5 – Optimizing	PA 5.1 – Process Innovation PA 5.2 – Continuous Optimization
4 – Predictable	PA 4.1 – Process Measurement PA 4.2 – Process Control
3 – Established	PA 3.1 – Process Definition PA 3.2 – Process Deployment
2 – Managed	PA 2.1 – Performance Management PA 2.2 – Work Product Management
1 – Performed	PA 1.1 – Process Performance
0 – Incomplete	–

During an assessment, for each process, each *PA* can get one of the following four achievement values as evaluation scale (for details on meaning and measuring cf. [HDH+06; p.223ff]):

- N – Not achieved,
- P – Partially achieved,
- L – Largely achieved,
- F – Fully achieved;

Then, each process gets its *ML* by analyzing the achievement values. A *ML* is reached when at minimum all *PAs* of all sub *MLs* are fully achieved and all *PAs* of the *ML* are largely achieved[128] [HDH+06; p.225].

I.7.1.3 The Process Assessment Model (PAM)

The *PAM* orients itself on the processes described in the *PRM* and defines concrete *indicators* for evaluation. SPICE, part V (ISO/IEC 15504-5) illustrates an example *PAM* and thus part V is of the highest importance for process implementation in an organization as well as for process assessments in practice [HDH+06; p.18].

---

[128] For example, ML 3 is reached, if PA 1.1, PA 2.1 and PA 2.2 are fully achieved, and PA 3.1 and PA 3.2 are largely achieved.

Concerning process implementation, the *PAM* defines processes in a standardized way. This definition includes basic *indicators* (so called *base practices*) to be fulfilled at minimum in order to determine that the process is performed. Fig. 7-1 shows the standard set of processes of the standard *PAM* described in part V basing on ISO 12207. The process set is divided into 9 *process areas* with 40 *processes*. Each process is defined by a standardized structure [HDH+06; p.61]:

- *Process-ID*: A unique identifier for each process. The identifier consists of a combination of three letters and a number between 1 and 12.
- *Process name*: The name of the process.
- *Process purpose*: The purpose of the process.
- *Process outcomes*: The defined process results.
- *Base practices (BP)*: *Base practices* describe the directly relevant aspects to pay attention when performing a process.
- *Work products (WP)*: Define artifacts that can be either an *input* or *output* of a process. Each *WP* has an unique identifier and is detailed in part V., Annex B.

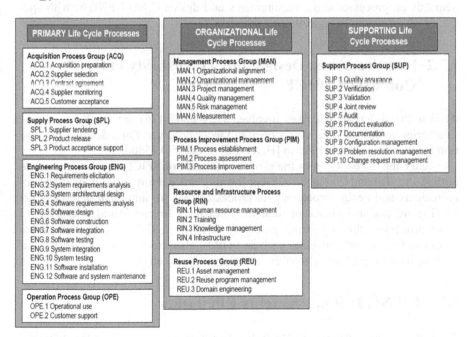

Figure 7-1 Processes defined in ISO/IEC 15504-5 basing on ISO/IEC 12207

The points one to four have been taken over from ISO 12207, whereas the latter two points are defined in ISO 15504-5. In this way, the BPs and WPs can also be seen as the basic *indicators* for reaching *ML* 1 meaning that processes fulfill their goals, but they are not really planned.

Concerning process evaluation for higher maturity levels, the individual *PAs* defined in the *measurement framework* are again further refined through the following *indicators* [HDH+06; p.222f]:

- *Generic practices* (*GP*) are generically defined activities or practices supporting the implementation of a specific *PA*. A lot of the *GPs* support *BPs* by demanding specific activities of process management. As an example, GP 2.1.2 ("Plan and monitor the performance of the process to fulfill the identified objectives.") demands to perform basic project management principles for each process.
- *Generic resources* can be applied to fulfill *GPs*.
- *Generic work products* can be used and created by *GPs*.

Corresponding to the focus of this thesis, the following discusses the *PAM*'s demands on processes about requirements and design (ENG.1-ENG.6) with special focus on needs for *requirements traceability*.

I.7.2 Requirements, Design and Traceability in the Context of SPICE

At first the different processes involved (ENG.1-ENG.6) are briefly sketched. Categories are *purpose*, *base practices* and *work products*. For a detailed description the user is invited to refer to [HDH+06] or the ISO 15504.

After the introduction to the process demands of SPICE, the author tries to outline the demands for a SPICE-conforming *traceability* environment for requirements and design processes. As processes that are important here (ENG.2-ENG.5) are not an instance of their own but must be considered in context of other processes, the contextual processes ENG.1, ENG.6 are also considered. Additionally, support processes such as SUP.10 also impose demands on *traceability* or its further usage. Therefore, SUP.10 is also sketched.

I.7.2.1 ENG.1: Requirements Elicitation

Purpose: All customer requirements for a product or service over the complete life-cycle shall be identified and collected [HDH+06; p.81-89].

Base Practices:

- BP1 "Obtain customer requirements and requests": Additionally, not only pure customer requirements and wishes must be considered. Instead often standards, guidelines, legal constraints or constraints imposed by the environment of a system to develop impose further requirements. According to Hörmann et al. [HDH+06; p.82], the number of documents to analyze and search for additional requirements can easily become several hundred leading to enormous complexity as the elicited requirements also often include inconsistencies or contradictions.
- BP2 "Understand customer expectations": Requirements must not only be elicited. Instead, customer and supplier must have a common understanding of the requirements. Practice has proofed joint reviews as helpful to gain a common understanding of the requirements.
- BP3 "Agree on requirements": All development teams involved in the project must express agreement on the *customer requirements*. This means that at least one representative of each development team must validate the requirements and determine whether a requirement is feasible[129], or not.
- BP4 "Establish customer requirements baseline": The agreed status of collected *customer requirements* must be integrated into a consistent *customer requirements specification* (*CRS*) and a baseline of the *CRS* must be established as basis for the development and to be able to track later changes.
- BP5 "Manage customer requirements changes": Starting from this first baseline all changes or extensions of the *customer requirements* must be tracked. Besides changes imposed by the customer changes can also be sparked by changes of used standards or technologies [HDH+06; p.87].
- BP6 "Establish customer query mechanism": Demands to establish procedures to notify customers and planning concerning a *requirement change request*. In practice, this is often achieved via a *change control board* (*CCB*) [PR09; p.144f], [VSH01; p.184f, p.216].

Work Products:

1. *Change control record*: See the following ch. I.7.2.7 about SUP.10: Change Management.
2. *Customer requirements specification* (*CRS*): Depending on the project, the *customer requirements* are either collected by the customer himself, or the supplier collects the requirements. In the German-speaking community the

---

[129] It is to note that SPICE does not make any claims about how to proceed with not feasible requirements [HDH+06; p.85].

CRS is usually documented by the customer[130]. Besides the usual quality demands for a requirements specification (see ch. I.5), SPICE explicitly demands that each requirement is separated and individually traceable to all origin artifacts (*backward traceability*) and all subsequent artifacts (*forward traceability*) [HDH+06; p.88 (*)].

Starting from here, it shows that SPICE imposes high demands for *traceability* as each individual requirement must be traceable to all subsequent artifacts. However, requirements elicitation lies not in the focus of this thesis. Thus, in the following it is assumed that a *CRS* is available.

I.7.2.2 ENG.2: System Requirements Analysis

Purpose: Transform the defined *customer requirements* in a set of technical system requirements building the basis for *system design*. "The *system requirements analysis* is one of the most important processes as it prepares the foundation of the complete further development work" [HDH+06; p.89 (*)]. Hörmann et al. [HDH+06; p.89] also emphasize that besides the *customer requirements* other requirements basing on other stakeholders' input should be considered. This includes that the coordination of different development areas such as HW development, software development and testing must be integrated.

Base Practices:

- BP1 "Establish *system requirements*": The *CRS* as basis must be used to identify the demanded functions and abilities of the system to be afterward documented in a *system requirements specification* (*SYS_RS*) afterward. The *SYS_RS* must be baselined and the feasibility of the identified requirements must be analyzed. Further the project solution shall be analyzed for feasibility.

- BP2 "Optimize project solution": The specification of a *SYS_RS* already predetermines a certain solution at a very high-level[131]. During determination of the *SYS_RS* also other alternative solutions must be analyzed here.

- BP3 "Analyze *system requirements*": The identified requirements are prioritized and analyzed whether they fulfill quality demands (see ch. I.5.1) and whether they imply further requirements to be elicited. Analyzing requirements often leads to identification of cross-linkings between them and new

---

[130] In the German speaking community, the *CRS* usually corresponds to what is called 'Lastenheft' (see the following chapter I.7.2.2.1).

[131] However, it is to mention that the author recommends avoiding an unnecessarily early determination of a solution and leaving the *solution space* as wide as possible.

requirements can be derived. Both kinds of dependencies must be made explicit [HDH+06; p.92].

- BP4 "Evaluate and update *system requirements*": Any proposed change on the *system requirements* must be assessed for changes on costs, deadlines, risks and technical *impacts*. It must be possible to approve or reject proposed changes and new requirements.
- BP5 "Ensure consistency": Consistency between the *CRS* and the *SYS_RS* must be ensured. Consistency is ensured by applying *traceability* between *CRS* and *SYS_RS* [HDH+06; p.93].
- BP6 "Communicate *system requirements*": System requirements must be communicated to all stakeholders somehow involved. Correspondingly, a communication mechanism must keep them up-to-date.

Work Products:
1. *Traceability record*: Artifact containing the information for backward and forward *traceability*.
2. *Interface requirements*: Define the requirements for interfaces. Interfaces are differentiated into external and internal interfaces.
3. *SYS_RS*: The *SYS_RS* contains all requirements from the customer and the newly elicited requirements from the system requirement analysis[132]. Altogether, the following aspects must be considered in the *SYS_RS* [HDH+06; p.90]:
   - *Functional requirements,*
   - Functions and abilities of the system, interfaces, system performance and timing-constraints,
   - *Nonfunctional requirements,*
   - Technical constraints (e.g., the context of the system),
   - Reuse, maintenance and product servicing,
   - Norms and standards,
   - Economic constraints (business needs, market constraints, time-to-market);

According to Hörmann et al., "the *SYS_RS* also provides an overview of the overall system and the relationships of its sub parts, especially the relationships between the system elements and the software" [HDH+06; p.96 (*)]. It is true that the *SYS_RS* already may predetermine a certain high-level solution, however, as the following intersect chapter shall outline it is also to consider to outweigh the advantage of a clear description of the characteristics of the system to be supplied and the disadvantages of imposing unnecessary restrictions of the project's *solution space.*

---

[132] Usually, also the *interface requirements* (*context*) are part of the *SYS_RS*.

I.7.2.2.1 Remarks on the German Terms 'Lastenheft' and 'Pflichtenheft'

At this point, remarks to some peculiarities of the German-speaking SE community and their interpretation of the SPICE standard seem useful. German SE tradition has developed two terms not available in the English-speaking community[133]:

- 'Lastenheft': According to Balzert, a 'Lastenheft' "contains a collection of all functional basic requirements to be fulfilled by the software product under development from the customer's viewpoint. 'Basic requirements' means a conscious concentration on the essential characteristics of a product and its description in a sufficient level of abstraction" [Ba96; p.57-58 (*)].
- 'Pflichtenheft': Whereas the 'Pflichtenheft' "contains a collection of all functional requirements that must be fulfilled by the software product under development from the customer's viewpoint. ... The 'Pflichtenheft' must be formulated in a way that it can serve as basis for a jurisdictional contract. The 'Pflichtenheft' thus represents the contractual description of the scope of delivery" [Ba96; p.104-105 (*)].

Usually, the 'Lastenheft' is written by the customer whereas the 'Pflichtenheft' is usually written by the supplier. However, the direct connections between these terms and the terms in the English-speaking community often stay vague. According to Schienmann [Sch02; p.83], the 'Lastenheft' is comparable with what the Kruchten [Kr99] calls a "vision document" in the context of the *Rational Unified Process*.

Concerning *SPICE*, the concepts of 'Lastenheft' and 'Pflichtenheft' do not exist [HDH+06; p.64], because the standard just talks about different requirements specifications, but in the German-speaking *SPICE* adoption practice, the *customer requirements specification* (ENG.1) is often equalized to the 'Lastenheft' concept, whereas the system requirements are equalized to the 'Pflichtenheft'. The author agrees that this takeover of the analogous terms is fruitful as it alleviates communication and because well-established terminology is used. On the other side, it is important to consider whether taking over may not also bring the dangers that this terminology unconsciously infers new meaning.

One example is that a 'Pflichtenheft' also has a jurisdictional dimension that is not treated by the ENG-processes but slightly touched by the acquisition processes (ACQ.1-ACQ4) in *SPICE*. In the author's eyes, this also is fruitful especially when considering the *automotive* domain because, in fact, the processes

---

[133] To make the German meaning transparent to the English speaking community, Weber and Weisbrod [WW02; p.19] provide the literal translations "demand booklet" for 'Lastenheft' and "duty booklet" for 'Pflichtenheft'.

and work products of ENG.1 and ENG.2 often mark the transgression point, where the customer's development efforts melt with the supplier's development efforts and correspondingly the legal effects of the work products must be taken into consideration.

This makes way for another point of consideration that will later lead to considerations influencing the further outcome of this thesis. In ENG.2 BP1 and BP2, the standard also speaks of a 'project solution'. According to Hörmann et al., this means the "general approach to the solution" [HDH+06; p.96 (*)] and thus does not mean a detailed description of the solution. In ch. I.7.3.20, the author describes how an insufficient separation of problem description and solution description leads to unnecessary redundancy and problems of identifying the real requirements from 'requirements' merely originating from some formerly taken design decisions[134]. Both problems impose significant problems concerning *requirements traceability* and adaption of requirement changes. This gives way to the author's plea to clearly separate real requirements from 'requirements' imposed by former *design decisions* (cf. ch. III.19 for a taxonomy of both requirement types). However, on the other side, both requirement types have their rights to exist and both are connected to each other. As a better solution of the problem, the author shows in ch. III.20 how both can be connected via a *decision model*, thus improving *traceability* and additionally improving decision documentation.

In general, it is to say that it is very important to mind here what is really necessary to describe and what can be left open. Because of the fact that the *system*

---

[134] In [WW02; p.19], Weber and Weisbrod seem to disagree with the notion that *requirements specifications* such as the *'Lastenheft'* should only contain requirements. Thus, they rather demand for the notion that these documents also have to contain architectural descriptions beyond the scope of the *problem space*. They enlist several arguments for their demand. However, this may be a kind of misconception. In the author's opinion, the arguments rather describe the following situation: When the developers at an Automotive OEM create different *'Lastenheft'*s for the different ECUs, the developers perform a design activity for the complete system car. The decisions taken at that design level, however, include that the suppliers of the different ECUs must obey the consequences of these decisions. In this way these consequences become new requirements for the different ECUs and must be included in the *'Lastenheft'*. This does not mean that the *'Lastenheft'* contains extensive design aspects, but it may rather be the relation described here. Later in ch. III.23.1, when it comes to the tool solution, it is described that a requirements specification can be created for parts of a *design model* in order to propagate all design settings of the part to a supplier. This is exactly a mechanism to solve this problem. In this way, even though part III discusses the tool with a case study from a supplier perspective, the R2A tool solution can be equally used by an Automotive OEM to design the complete system, where then *requirements specifications* can be generated as *'Lastenheft'*s for the different suppliers.

requirements specification also has a *contractual relevance*, the author recommends to also consider *contractual negotiability*[135], because if an item is integrated into the *SYS_RS*, it in principle gets contractual relevance. Correspondingly, a supplier should concentrate on describing the requirements of the customer in detail but avoid to unnecessarily restrict the project's *solution space* by, e.g., extensively describing the project solution.

In some cases, of course, requirements cannot be described without also providing some solution stipulations (cf. ch. I.5.5), but the developer(s) of a *SYS_RS* should avoid unnecessary stipulations, because if changes on those stipulations are needed, the occurring changes must then be harmonized with the customer via a *change control board* (*CCB*) [PR09; p.144f], [VSH01; p.184f, p.216].

This corresponds to the observation of Balzert emphasizing for 'Lastenheft' [Ba96; p.58] and '*Pflichtenheft*' [Ba96; p.105] that both describe the 'what' but not the 'how' on different levels of details (the '*Pflichtenheft*' is more detailed as the '*Lastenheft*'). However, it must also be noted that this does not necessarily represent a common agreement in German SE community. As for example, the DIN 69905 speaks that a '*Pflichtenheft*' contains "… the realization propositions developed by the supplier basing on the conversion of the '*Lastenheft*' supplied by the customer" [DIN69905 (*)]. In this definition, the '*Pflichtenheft*' also contains a certain 'How'; but – in the author's eyes – this view will be problematic, if it leads to premature stipulations for the solution.

I.7.2.3 ENG.3: System Architectural Design

Purpose: A *system architecture* must be developed showing how the system requirements are realized in the system. In this way, one main purpose of this process is to show how system requirements are mapped to the system elements.
Base Practices:
- BP1 "Describe *system architecture*": The *system architecture* must be created. The following aspects must be considered:
  - The realization of the system in different parts is in most cases referred to as *system elements*. Different *system elements* usually need different engineering disciplines such as, e.g., mechanical, HW, or SW engineering that must be coordinated.
  - The overall processes and operations of the system.

---

[135] Rupp et al. [RS07; p.481-510] emphasize that requirements build the contractual basis for development. A detailed discussion about contracts, contract negotiations and *REM* is provided by Rupp et al. [RS07; p.481-510].

- BP2 "Allocate *requirements*": As a main goal, all *system requirements* must be allocated to the elements of the high-level *system architecture* to ensure they are properly considered in the overall *system design*. In this way, *traceability* between *SYS_RS* and the *system architecture* shall be established. Often, however, these allocations are not possible at first because important design decisions are still lacking [HDH+06; p.99]. This again often leads to the project practice that the *traceability* information is established after the design has reached a very stable state. This again leads to the problem that *traceability* is only established after most of the connections to be recorded have already been forgotten by the designers and thus are not recorded. The R2A tool solution introduced in part III actively addresses the problem in the way that it promotes recording *traceability* information as a *by-product* of the normal design activities, thus avoiding the problem of deferred *traceability* capturing.
- BP3 "Define *interfaces*": The external and internal *interfaces* of each *system element* must be designed and documented.
- BP4 "Verify *system architecture*": It must be ensured that the *system architecture* fulfills all *stakeholder* and *system requirements*. "In practice, it is not possible to specify all factors to consider in the *SYS_RS*. Thus, a broad reconciliation is important. These reconciliations significantly contribute to reduce the risk of later needed conceptual changes" [HDH+06; p.100 (*)].
- BP5 "Evaluate alternative *system architectures*": Evaluation criteria for the *system architecture* must be defined in order to analyze possible alternative system solutions according to the criteria. The *rationale* (see ch. II.9) for the choice of the current *system architecture* must be captured. Hörmann et al. explicitly emphasize here that in practice architectural and other basic issues (which seemingly have been cleared) are often recurring back to the agenda during project progress. In these cases, it is not seldomly decided to change or perform other compromises imposing considerable changes on the *architecture* [HDH+06; p.101]. As this can infer significant risks for project success especially in late project phases, Hörmann et al. call for a thorough exploration of these basic issues accompanied by a documentation of the decisions taken where the documentation is later update with the results of later discussion [HDH+06; p.101]. This again can be seen as an explicit plea for integrating *RatMan* (ch. II.9) into design. Ch. III.20 describes how this idea is realized by the R2A tool.
- BP6 "Ensure consistency": Consistency between *SYS_RS* and *system architecture* must be ensured. Consistency is supported by establishing and maintaining *traceability* between *SYS_RS* and *system architecture*.

- BP7 "Communicate *system architecture design*": A communication mechanism for distributing the *system architecture* design and effected changes to all involved stakeholders must be employed.

Work Products:

- *System architecture design*: The *system architecture* provides a *high-level* description of all system-relevant *system elements* as well as their interdependencies and interfaces to each other [HDH+06; p.97]. It is especially important to ensure *traceability* of requirements or functions over several levels of detail [HDH+06; p.102].
- *Traceability record*: See ENG.2;
- *Verification results*: The results of the verification procedures described in BP4 must be documented. Documentation can include review protocols, filled checklists and test protocols [HDH+06; p.102].

I.7.2.4 ENG.4: Software Requirements Analysis

Purpose: This process deals with eliciting all requirements for the software parts of the system.

Base Practices:

- BP1 "Specify *software requirements*": *Software requirements* must be defined and prioritized in a *software requirements specification (SW_RS)*.
- BP2 "Determine operating environment *impact*": The interfaces between the *software requirements* and other elements of the operating environment as well as the *impacts* of the requirements on the environment must be determined.
- BP3 "Develop criteria for *software testing*": *Verification criteria* must be developed for the software requirements to ensure that the software can later be tested whether it fulfills the requirements.
- BP4 "Ensure consistency": Consistency between the *SYS_RS* (ENG.2) and the *SW_RS* must be ensured. This is achieved through establishing and maintaining *traceability* between both artifacts.
- BP5 "Evaluate and update *software requirements*": The requirements must be continuously evaluated and change needs must be identified in accordance with the customer. Changes must be introduced in a controlled way using the *change management process* (SUP.10; see ch. I.7.2.7).
- BP6 "Communicate *software requirements*": A communication mechanism for distributing requirements and effected changes to all involved stakeholders must be employed.

Work Products:
- *Traceability record*: See ENG.2;
- *Interface requirements*: See ENG.2;
- *SW_RS:* Contains all elicited *SW requirements*. The following requirement sources must be considered [HDH+06; p.108]:
  - Requirements from the customer,
  - Valid norms and standards,
  - Relationships of the different SW components to each other[136],
  - Performance characteristics, *safety* and *security* characteristics and other *NFRs*,
  - Required interfaces (the context of the SW),
  - Requirements resulting from the data base design,
  - Behavior in failure cases and failure fall back mechanisms;

Further, Hörmann et al. emphasize that ENG.4 (*software requirements analysis*) can be seen as an intermediate step between ENG.3 (*system architectural design*) and ENG.5 (*software design*). In practice, however, the transition between the three processes are mostly fluent and are rather of iterative and recursive nature [HDH+06; p.103]. This statement gives way for the author's argumentation in ch. I.7.3.20 that a separately maintained *SW_RS* mainly infers significant redundancy being detrimental to the development process. In part III, ch. III.19, ch. III.20 and ch. III.23.2, the author shows how a better suited solution for the redundancy problem may be found through employing an integrated *system(s)* and *software design* in combination with R2A's *decision model* concept (ch. III.20).

I.7.2.5 ENG.5: Software Design

Purpose: A *SW design* must be created fulfilling and being testable against all *SW requirements*.

---

[136] The author disagrees with the view of [HDH+06; p.108] in this point. In the view of the author, a *requirements specification* should best possibly only contain the *requirements* and avoid solution specifics, since otherwise a possibly negative solution may be kept in a project because the solution was specified in the *requirements specification* and thus is later considered as required by the customer. Additionally, as such information must also be specified in the *architectural description*, this information rather represents a redundancy that should be avoided (see *DRY-principle* in ch. I.6.1.2). On the other side, as shown in ch. I.5.5, *requirements* cannot be completely defined unless parts of the solution are considered. Nevertheless, the author rather suggests minimizing and avoiding parts of the solution, if possible.

Base Practices:

- BP1 "Describe s*oftware architecture*": The *SW requirements* must be transformed in a *SW architecture* design describing the *high-level* structure and the main parts of the SW. At this phase the central design decisions for SW are taken. Hörmann et al. explicitly point out that it is essential to document these decisions [HDH+06; p.110-111] (cf. also ENG.3 BP5).
- BP2 "Define interfaces": The external and internal interfaces must be defined and documented.
- BP3 "Develop detailed design": The *software architectural design* must be further refined into a detailed design for all specific software parts describing all parts to implement and test.
- BP4 "Analyze the design for testability": The design must be evaluated for correctness and testability to ensure the SW modules are testable.
- BP5 "Ensure consistency": Consistency between the *SW_RS* (ENG.4) and the *SW design* must be ensured. Consistency is supported by establishing and maintaining *traceability*.

Work Products:

- *SW architecture design*: The *SW architecture* describes the *high-level* structure of the software and the collaboration of the different sub-parts of the SW.
- *Low level SW design*: Describes the detailed design of a software unit. It contains the interfaces to other software units, algorithms, memory allocation, data structure specifications, etc..
- *Traceability record*: See ENG.2;

I.7.2.6 ENG.6: Software Construction

Purpose: The SW modules must be implemented correctly reflecting the *SW design*.

Base Practices:

- BP1 "Develop *unit verification procedures*": Procedures and criteria for unit verification must be developed and documented.
- BP2 "Develop *software units*": Source code for the software module must be implemented according to the *SW requirements* and *design*. Further, testing requirements and user documentation must be actualized.
- BP3 "Ensure consistency": Consistency between software design and its implementation must be ensured. Consistency is supported by establishing

and maintaining *traceability* between *SW_RS*, *SW design* and the *software units*.

- BP4 "Verify *software units*": The unit verification procedures developed according to BP1 must be applied to ensure that the software unit fulfills its design requirements. The results must be documented.

Work Products:

- *Unit test plan*: See ENG.8 (not further discussed here);
- *Software unit*: The source code for a software module;
- *Test incident report*: See ENG.8 (not further discussed here);
- *Test case specification*: See ENG.8 (not further discussed here);

I.7.2.7 SUP.10: Change Management

Purpose: It is to ensure that requests for change are managed, tracked and controlled.

Base Practices [HDH+06; p.214-217]:

- BP1 "Develop a change management strategy": A strategy must be developed and established to ensure that changes are: described, recorded, analyzed and maintained.
- BP2 "Record the request for change": Each *change request* must be documented and a unique identifier must be provided.
- BP3 "Record the status of *change requests*": Status indicators shall help to trace status and status changes of *change requests* and performed changes. Hörmann et al. [HDH+06; p.215] explicitly emphasize with regard to this BP that also *traceability* to the reasons for a change must be established (e.g., reference to a problem or error report).
- BP4 "Establish the dependencies and relationships to other *change requests*": *Change requests* can have dependencies. These dependencies must be made explicit.
- BP5 "Assess the *impact* of the change": Proposed changes must be assessed for effects, needed resources, risks and potential uses. Here, *traceability* builds the foundation for *impact assessments* (i.e., *impact analysis*; see ch. II.10.3).
- BP6 "Identify the verification and validation activities to be performed for implemented changes": Before a change is approved, it must also be clear how and to what extent verification and validation actions must encompass the change. Planning verification procedures for a change implies knowing the *impact* of a change (BP5) and thus also demands for *traceability*.

- BP7 "Approve changes": All proposed changes are approved[137], i.e. accepted, before they are implemented. Additionally, it must be determined for what release cycle a change must be performed.
- BP8 "Implement the change": All approved changes must be implemented. Here, consistent implementation – not forgetting an *impacted* point – is a central issue. Also *impact assessments* (BP5) and thus *traceability* play a decisive key role to fulfill this BP.
- BP9 "Review the implemented change": After implementation, all implemented changes are reviewed whether they meet the expected goals and effects.

Work Products:

- *Change management plan*: A plan determining how change requests are captured, managed, decided, implemented and tested.
- *Change request*: A *change request* usually involves the following information:
  - Description of the requested change,
  - Status of the *change request,*
  - Change initiator (with information how to contact the initiator),
  - *Impacted* systems,
  - *Impacts* on documentation,
  - Criticality of the change,
  - Wanted and planned deadline for implementation;
- *Change control record*: Documentation about a performed change to make the change traceable in the system in accordance with a specific version baseline [HDH+06; p.218]. The record includes the wanted change (e.g., as reference to the change request) and a record of all individually performed changes on system, or software components and documentation.

The R2A solution introduced in part III covers the demands of this process by the *impact analysis* features[138] (ch. II.10.3). Especially, the demands about a *change control record* are addressed by R2A's features to save results of an *impact analysis* and use such discovered *impact sets* as a checklist for implementing a change.

---

[137] Schienmann [Sch02; p.111-113] gives clear advice what criteria should be clarified positively in order to approve a change. Otherwise a change should be rejected.

[138] The process SUP.9 ("Problem Management") [HDH+06; p.202-213] is not discussed in detail in this thesis, but demands of BP5 "Assess the *impact* of the problem to determine solution" and BP10 "Track problem status" can also be fulfilled by R2A's *traceability* and *impact analysis* features (ch. II.10.3).

I.7.3 Traceability in SPICE

If you don't know where you go, it can happen that you arrive somewhere else.
Yogi Berra (*)

The processes described above impose a set of demands for *traceability*. Now, the question arises which of the *traceability* demands must be fulfilled at what *maturity level* (*ML*). According to Hörmann et al. [HDH+06; p.227-229], *ML1* also only demands that a *BP* is performed in a way that it fulfills the *purpose* of the process. This means for *ML1* the *traceability* records may not necessarily be documented. In a more detailed analysis, it would even be possible to achieve a "Largely" for *ML1* and to reach *ML1* in this way; *traceability* with deficiencies is sufficient. Not until for reaching to *ML2* needs to be reached, extended planning documentation, review protocols etc. must be provided in a documented form[139] [HDH+06; p.229]. This leads to the conclusion that at least to reach a *ML2* extended *traceability* demands as formulated above must be performed to reach at least *ML2*.

Traceability must be maintained to be traceable over several levels of details (ENG.1-ENG.6), [HDH+06; p.102]. In such a way, *traceability* must also be considered at a larger scope than implementing relationships between two artifacts. For evaluating and ensuring these goals in assessments, the assessors should pick several random samples of some items to be traceable of some process and then request the project members to identify all *backward* and *forward traceability* implications [HDH+06; p.95].

A weak point of *SPICE* is that it merely concentrates on *SysEng* and *SE* processes neglecting HW, mechanics or other engineering dimensions that can have significant influence ([MHD+07; p.4-7], [TJH07; p.3]). In the automotive domain, an important example in the following is that the pressure for developing extremely cost-optimized HW often imposes new constraints and problems for the software that must handle this HW. Here, it seems that the *CMMI* model has some additional support for HW [MHD+07; p.4-5].

Another major problem is imposed because of the high demands for documentation sparking the danger that development efforts become unnecessarily bureaucratic with potentially detrimental effects on development efforts [BT04; p.25-57]. This problem can especially be the case for the high *traceability* demands imposed by the standards. As discussed again in ch. II.10.5, the good idea

---

[139] In this context of ML2, also the Process Attribute 2.2 must be considered: "Dependencies between work products are identified and understood. Requirements for the approval of work products to be controlled are defined." The PA 2.2 additionally defines a hallmark to be fulfilled only achievable by extended *traceability*.

of *traceability* in theory may face a similar *benefit problem* in practice as the demands to capture *rationale* face it (cf. ch. II.9.4.2). In the author's opinion sparked by practical experience, developers often establish *traceability* in order to fulfill demands of some standards, but they seldom experience significant usefulness in comparison to the effort and the 'stupidity' required by most tasks to establish *traceability*. A key to solving or at least improving this dilemma may be avoiding unnecessary documentation overhead or easing *traceability* establishment efforts. Egyed et al. [EGH+07] argue that standards demand *traceability* but do not explicitly state about the appropriate level of quality of trace links. In this way, they argue that problems with *traceability* effort can be reduced by choosing a more coarse grained *traceability* model; however, in this context it is to mention that *SPICE* defines the demand for the work product *customer requirements specification* (see ENG.1) that each requirement is separated and individually traceable to all origin artifacts (*backward traceability*) and all subsequent artifacts (*forward traceability*) [HDH+06; p.88 (*)].

Correspondingly, alternative solutions like using more coarse grained *traceability* models may be difficult to employ in a *SPICE* conforming process environment. It should be noted that the author does not say 'impossible'. In fact, a promising alternative is consequent tailoring. The following chapter describes a alternative significantly reducing bureaucratic overhead with minimal impact on quality of most process landscapes.

Further it is to note that in the following of this complete thesis, only the processes ENG.2-ENG.5 are considered as they are in the focus of this thesis. Certainly, these processes are also embedded in the processes ENG.1 and ENG.6, but *traceability* connections between ENG.1 (*customer requirements*) and ENG.2 (*system requirements*) are in general managed using *REM-tools* such as IBM Rational DOORS and connections between ENG.5 (*software design*) and ENG.6 (*software implementation*) are relatively easily manageable using *name mapping* (cf. ch. II.10.4.2.2). Thus, as the following chapter tries to outline, the processes ENG.2-ENG.5 dealing with transitions between requirements and design impose the critical problem concerning *traceability*.

I.7.3.1 Intersect: Dangers of Prescriptive Process Models

It is a capital mistake to theorize before one has data.
Insensibly one begins to twist facts to suit theories, instead of theories to suit facts.
Sherlock Holmes, A Scandal in Bohemia

In the author's opinion, the proper adoption of *SPICE*, *CMMI* or other quality standards can significantly support improving process quality of SW-based products. However, as the word 'proper' in the preceding sentence indicates, the author also sees a set of risks that can even lead to results contra-productive to the originally issued goals of *SPICE* to support a process landscape leading to high quality processes and outcomes. In this sense, 'proper' does not refer to a process landscape fully conforming to *SPICE* but rather emphasizes the goal to have a process landscape leading to high quality products meeting their goals.

At first view, *SPICE* is a heavy-weight plan-driven method and "plan-driven methods need stability" [BT04; p.31], because "plan-driven methods work best, when the requirements are largely determinable in advance (including via prototyping) and remain relatively stable" [BT04; p.31]. As ch. I.5.6 has shown, chances for increasing rates of changes are very high. Thus, in order to avoid unnecessary overhead, an organization adapting the *SPICE* standard should concentrate on the problems and try to design a process landscape being open for change. Being open for change in this case mainly means to provide flexibility and to avoid unnecessary obstacles to change implementation. A promising approach avoiding unnecessary changes is to avoid redundant information because changing redundant information implies that all redundancies must be changed in concert. Otherwise inconsistencies would arise endangering the common understanding in a project, thus leading to inconsistencies in the system to be developed, leading to higher error rates to be discovered at later times in the project and finally leading to significantly higher development costs.

According to the author's opinion, a promising starting point is to look deeper into the *process model* of *SPICE*. In this context, a peculiarly problematic development exists, usually neglected by theory but in the author's opinion essential to keep in mind: When standards such as *SPICE* have been developed, formerly *descriptive process models* describing industry practice of software development have now become *prescriptive* ones. The dangers involved with this are that *preterated elements* of the description now turn to *prescriptive elements*. *SPICE* bases on the ISO/IEC 12207 *process model*. Nevertheless, this *process model* – as all models (see ch. I.1) – should be seen as idealization. Seen in the historic context, however, the question arises whether probably an unrecognized transformation has taken place. At first in SE research history, *process models* have been *descriptive models* describing development activities. The researchers created models analyzing how developers approached the development of software and the resulting models were idealized abstract descriptions of the real development steps happened. With high probability, these models contained some idealizations as the ethos of research publishing demand to consider issues such as *conceptual integrity*, clear classification and other idealizing effects. These idealizations can be compared with *abundant properties* of a model (see ch. I.1). In other words, the development model researchers described the – what they thought – *essential properties* of the development effort, neglecting the *abundant properties* accompanied by a certain simplification, i.e., idealization. Nierstrasz [Ni04; p.274] hits this mark when he claims *SE, software architecture*, etc. as being rather 'metaphoric'.

Later, these *descriptive models* now formed the basis for development models of *prescriptive* nature as CMMI or SPICE. Now, in the run of adopting these idealized *descriptive process models* to *process models* norming development activities, these *process models* have become *prescriptive models* (see ch. I.1). In this unconscious transgression, the dangerous effect could have happened that previously *abundant properties* (see ch. I.1) are now seen as *prescriptive* mandatory properties of the processes to be performed. Now, the question arises which of the *prescriptive models'* properties are really *essential* (correctly passed on) and which may be *abundant properties*. As described in ch. I.1, *abundant properties* lead to wrong conclusions. Just as well, *abundant properties* may exist in development standards deconvolving negative *impact* on the development effort. Correspondingly, the author does not necessarily appeal for abandoning these standards. A lot of these issues are related to the proper adoption of *SPICE*. *SPICE* is a very flexible and vague standard. It can be compared with the constitution of a state. A law in a constitution will never have a concrete definite character, otherwise it risks to be unfitting to several concrete problems and thus loses its general purpose of building a frame of basic agreements on values, whereupon a set of people (e.g., a nation) build its society.

In the exact same way, *SPICE* (or *CMMI*) can be seen as a frame of basic agreements on values all projects comply with. But each project develops its own rules interpreting the abstract and vague rules of the standard. An example of the flexibility of standards as *SPICE* or *CMMI* is the fact that several authors show [Pa01], [FK07], [Kn06; p.89] that the principles of agile methods as *eXtreme Programming* have the potential to reach *maturity level* 3 in *CMMI*[140]. Similarly, a project should also be able to have *SPICE*-conforming processes when the processes are not necessarily fulfilled by exact, word-for-word obedience[141] of

---

[140] As shown in the beginning of ch. I.7, *CMMI* and *SPICE* have comparable *process models* and needs for *traceability*. Thus, this claim should be – more or less – equally valid for the *SPICE* process landscape.

[141] See also the – in the author's view still valid – criticism of Curtis et al. about *process models* resulting from empirical studies: "A typical statement that we heard from participants was that, you've got to understand, this isn't the way we develop software here. This type of comment suggested that these developers held a model of how software development should occur, and they were frustrated that the conditions surrounding their project would not let them work from the model. The frequency of this comment also suggested that the model most developers envisioned accounted poorly for

the standard. Instead, especially concerning *traceability* aspects in the ENG processes, the author claims that a freer interpretation of the *SPICE* processes may help to ensure higher flexibility of the process landscape without contradicting the principal ideas of the *SPICE process model* on condition that it is accepted that *process models* may be – very valuable – metaphors for practice but provide no claim for strict obedience. This claim is further described in the following chapter, but its full implications on this research are then again highlighted in ch. III.19, ch. III.20 and ch. III.21.

At the end, however, it must also be mentioned that the *SPICE* assessors decide whether a process landscape conforms to the demands of *SPICE*. In this way, the power of the assessors and process designers may not be underestimated. If these people do not understand or share the view that different interpretations of a *SPICE* demand are possible, then the process landscape is determined as non-conforming. In this way, organizations open to deviating interpretations undergo a certain risk and should be aware that they must be prepared for watertight argumentation.

At least, even *SPICE* literature for assessors acknowledges indications that process practice can significantly deviate from the original demand of *SPICE* and thus in the author's view also indirectly concede the metaphoric nature of *process models*. As an example, [HDH+06; p.104] directly gives further reinforcement for the argumentation of the next chapter and will be discussed in detail there.

---

the environmental conditions and organizational context of software development. The participants we interviewed were uniformly motivated to do a good job, but they had to mold their development process to navigate through a maze of contingencies. These interviews provided a clearer understanding of such crucial processes as learning, technical communication, requirements negotiation, and customer interaction. These processes are poorly described in software *process models* that focus instead on how a software product evolves through a series of artifacts such as requirements, functional specifications, code, and so on. Existing software *process models* do not provide enough insight into actual development processes to guide research on software development technologies. Models that only prescribe a series of development tasks provide no help in analyzing how much new information must be learned by a project staff, how discrepant requirements should be negotiated, how design teams resolve architectural conflicts, and how these and similar factors contribute to a project's inherent uncertainty and risk" [CKI88; p.1284].

I.7.3.2 The Nature of the ENG-Processes, *Traceability*, and its Implications[142]

The SPICE *process model* concerning the requirement and design related processes (ENG.2-ENG.5) is a layer model where *problem space* descriptions (requirement view: ENG.2, ENG.4) alternate with *solution space* descriptions (designs: ENG.3, ENG.5), (cf. [Nu01], [PS05; p.113f], [Po08; p.565-602], ch. I.5.4):

- ENG.2: Derives from the *user requirements specification*[143] a general *system requirements specification* (*SYS_RS*).
- ENG.3: Uses the *SYS_RS* to create a *high-level system design* with the prior emphasis on *HW-SW-partitioning*.
- ENG.4: The *software requirements specification* (*SW_RS*) derives from ENG.2 and ENG.3.
- ENG.5: Uses the *SW_RS* for the design of the *SW architecture*.

SPICE-oriented *traceability* models require a continuous link chain between the artifacts of ENG.2, ENG.3, ENG.4 and ENG.5 to ensure the consistency of the entire model (cf. [DC04], [Kn01b]).

In the author's practical experience, a strict obedience to the *process model* described above can cause several disadvantageous problems. To outline these problems, the following example *SYS_RS* is given with three requirements causing a problem encountered by the author at practical work at the former Micron Electronic Devices AG (since June 2008 part of the MBtech Group) by one of its projects:

- Req.1: An external watchdog component must monitor the system.
- Req.2: Parametric data must be changeable by the customer during operation.
- Req.3: Parametric data must be stored on EEPROM.

In current practice, the *system design* determines that the system will include a micro controller (controller), an external watchdog component and an external EEPROM (cf. fig. 7-2).

The *HW requirements specification* (*HW_RS*) is derived from the *SYS_RS* and *system design*. It again contains *Req.1* and *Req.3* linking back (fig. 7-2: bold blue arrows) to the *SYS_RS*. The detailed *HW design* determines that watchdog and EEPROM will share the connection pins to the controller by an SPI[144] communication interface, because other connected components have already used up

---

[142] The following chapter bases on [TKT+07].
[143] I.e., *customer requirements specification*
[144] Serial Peripheral Interface Bus

all remaining pins of the controller. Req.1 gets linked to the watchdog symbol and Req.3 to the EEPROM symbol in the *HW design*. The *SW_RS* contains Req.1, Req.2 and Req.3 linking back to the *SYS_RS*.

During *SW design*, the architect discovers the potential resource conflict in the shared usage of one SPI for EEPROM and watchdog. Since driving the EEPROM is very time intensive and triggering the watchdog is very time critical, the architect rates this combination as risk, but changes of the HW are rejected due to higher costs. The solution for this conflict, the EEPROM and watchdog drivers must be "artificially" coupled to implement a cooperative handshake[145] solution (fig. 7-2: association between EEPROM driver and Watchdog driver marked with „!!!").

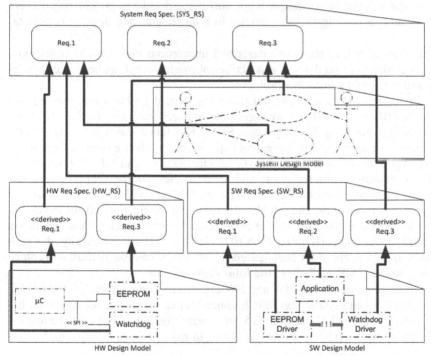

Figure 7-2 The example in current practice of the SPICE process model

---

[145] When triggering of the watchdog is needed soon, the SW module responsible for triggering the watchdog requests the SPI-bus resource from the EEPROM SW module, which handles preempting its task in a secure state and then notifies the watchdog SW module that the SPI-bus is now available to trigger the watchdog.

The solution implies that the planned original standard drivers of a supplier must be adapted internally. In the further progress of the project, these adaptions caused extra efforts not traceable to its background.

In the long run of the project, the following disadvantageous effects have been discovered:

- Redundancies needed significant extra effort to be maintained up-to-date.
- Despite all efforts, sometimes redundancies have been forgotten to maintain. This effected in small drifts between the system, HW and SW views leading to communication problems between the different developer groups.
- As sometimes requirements cannot be reasonably explained without referring to the solution, also design more and more details crept into requirement documents leading to redundancies in requirements and design documentation.
- Problems such as the above described interactions between *HW design* and its implications on the SW as described above have still not been plainly elicited yet, leading to further problems.

In summary, this example illustrates the central problem that the requirements in *HW_RS* and *SW_RS* are copies of the requirements in the *SYS_RS*, leading to high redundancy. In many cases, SW or HW functionality is already clearly demanded for in the user requirements specification. Thus a clear separation of those requirements must be taken over into the *SYS_RS* and *SW_RS* respectively *HW_RS*, causing additional effort and redundancies. As the chapter above has shown, this clear separation between System, HW and SW can also be seen as a more or less metaphoric one (cf. [Ni04]) providing orientation aid for the developers as *process models* do. However, in practical terms, such a clear separation is mostly not viable ([HDH+06; p.104], [PS05; p.114]). Especially the pro-claimed *specification of SW requirements*[146] should be cautiously dealt with, since a really separate *SW_RS*[147] faces the following problems:

- Often, requirements on HW and SW are strongly interwoven (cf. [HDH+06; p.104]). Even literature on SPICE concedes that in practice the traversals between ENG.3, ENG.4 and ENG.5 are mostly floating and of iterative and recursive nature [HDH+06; p.103]. Thus, in most projects no separate *SW_RS*

---

[146] If the concept of a separate SW *requirements specification* is consequently followed, then also a HW requirements specification should be maintained. However, as mentioned before, SPICE has the weakness that it does not adequately address HW aspects.

[147] Boehm [Bo05] points out that the separation between Systems and SW engineering has been a historical and artificial one.

is maintained, but *functional requirements* are collected on the level of SYS_RS^{148} (ENG.2) [HDH+06; p.104].

- In many cases, SW functionality is already clearly demanded in the *customer requirements specification* (ENG.1). Thus, if applying such a clear separation, those requirements must be taken over into the SYS_RS (ENG.2) and SW_RS (ENG.4), causing additional efforts and redundancies.

- Other requirement types exist not attributable to either HW or SW (e.g., project management, quality management, mechanical construction). Alternatively, in current requirements management tools like IBM Rational DOORS®, a *HW-SW-partitioning* of requirements is also viable using an attribute (proposed values: 'System', 'HW', 'SW', 'construction', 'management').

- Generally, linking of different artifacts is a time consuming, unproductive and errorprone administrative work[149] that should be minimized (see details in ch. II.10.5).

As a way out, the author proposes orienting on more pragmatic views of the agility scene (e.g., cf. [BT04]) and to concentrate merely on *one* dependable, consistent requirement artifact[150] to store all *contractually relevant*[151] requirements as one common view i.e. interface to synchronize the views of all stakeholders in the project. This artifact can be called the SYS_RS. The artifacts HW_RS and SW_RS can be indirectly derived from the SYS_RS by maintaining an attribute marking a requirement as important for HW and SW. Starting from this

---

[148] See remarks of [HDH+06; p.104 (*)] to ENG.4, BP.1 ("Specify the SW_RS"): "In many projects, no separate *software requirements specification* is maintained, but *functional requirements* are described in one single document at the level of *system requirements* (e.g., a *'Pflichtenheft'*). The underlying reasons are that system functionality is often mainly determined by software, but it cannot be reasonable separated from hardware functionality. The *requirements* of this *base practice* are completely fulfilled if it can be proved that the *functional* and *nonfunctional requirements* are unambiguously specified and are adequate to the range of functions" [HDH+06; p.104 (*)].

[149] "As systems evolve, it becomes increasingly ineffective to maintain *traceability* information. RT (*requirements traceability*) in practice often suffers from the enormous effort and complexity of creating and maintaining traces. It also suffers from incomplete trace information" [EG04; p.55].

[150] This corresponds to the *DRY-principle (don't repeat yourself)* in [HT03; p.24] also more elaborately described in ch. I.6.1.2.

[151] Contractually obligatory means here to clearly distinguish between requirements originating from the customer and 'requirements arising internally within the project' (see also ch. I.7.2.2.1). The real meaning of this statement can only be described later in ch. III.19. Roughly speaking, the idea is to distinguish between requirements from the customer (requirements) and requirements arising within design phases (*design constraints*).

common view on requirements, all further design artifacts (*system design, HW design* and *SW design*) are derived.

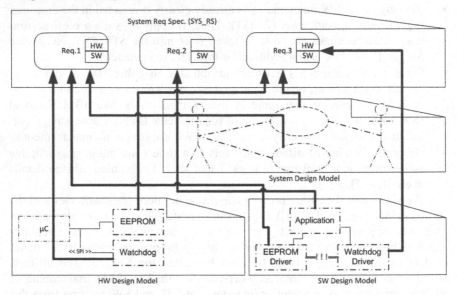

Figure 7-3 The altered example above with less redundancies

Fig. 7-3 shows how the example above (see fig. 7-2) looks like if these principles are applied. The *system design* is done similarly to the example above (fig. 7-2). Additionally, the *SYS_RS* contains an attribute that allows SW-HW partitioning. Req.1 and Req.3 are marked as relevant for HW and SW, Req.2 only for SW. Correspondingly, the *HW_RS* is not directly applied, since the relevant HW requirements are marked in the *SYS_RS*. Apart from that, the *HW design* is done similarly to the previous chapter and linked to the Req.1 and Req.3 in the *SYS_RS*. In the same way as the *HW_RS*, the *SW_RS* is not applied, since the relevant *SW requirements* are marked in the *SYS_RS*. The *SW design* will be developed from the *SYS_RS* and the *system design model*.

As a comparison between fig. 7-2 and fig. 7-3 shows, redundancies are significantly reduced and thus unnecessary project complexity[152] is avoided. In

---

[152] As Diederichs [Di04a] shows, unnecessary complexity in processes is one of the major sources for partial or complete failures of project endeavors. Correspondingly, reducing unnecessary complexity is one of the best leverages to avoid project failures.

[HDH+06; p.104] it is indicated that such an approach as adaption to the SPICE *process model* is spread in industrial practice (also see footnote 148 (p.145)).

In this way, this concept also gives tribute to Boehm's predictions about the future of *SysEng* and *SE* processes [Bo05]. According to Boehm the separation between *SysEng* and *SE* was an artificial one driven by historical development. For the future, he predicts a growing together of both disciplines. In fact, this trend becomes evident in the emphasis of SysEng processes in SW development standards as the ISO 12207 ([ISO12207]) or SPICE (ISO / IEC 15504) and also in the SysML [SYSML] standard being an extension of UML as support for *SysEng*. Further indications speaking for the latter approach are comments provided by Hood et al. [HWF+08; p.195] claiming that process thinking must get away from the document view and turn more toward an information view.

However, the solution sketched here does not yet provide any help for covering the problem concerning watchdog and EEPROM. This points to a gap between the adaption following the latter example and an intention of the original intentions of the SPICE *process model*: Design activities concerning one design artifact (in this example *HW design*) can have serious implications for other requirement or design artifacts (in this example *SW design*). This fact is partially considered in the *process model* of SPICE: *System design* has high *impact* on its *SW design* by raising new "requirements" in addition to the original requirements of the stakeholders. Thus, the idea behind a *SW_RS* is to collect the SW-related requirements from the *SYS_RS* and to derive new requirements from the *system design*. On the other side, especially concerning the automotive sector, *SW design* often must be subordinated under constraints of extremely cost-optimized HW components. At the moment, SPICE completely neglects these critical connections between HW and SW.

A dedicated goal of this thesis is to find a way out of the dilemma that current project practice either has to decide between the dangers of extensive redundancies or lacking means to make intercorrelations between different design phases that spark new 'requirements' for other designs explicit. As ch. III.19 and ch. III.20 (especially ch. III.20.3) will describe, the dilemma could be solved in integrating a *decision model* directly within design processes and the evolving *traceability* information. This follows the basic idea that design decisions taken at a certain design situation can imply influence upon other parts of design by sparking new 'requirements' for these parts. Additionally, this decision model approach has further significant advantages as it provides explicit coverage for another important demand of SPICE: Several *BPs* (e.g., ENG.3 BP5 ([HDH+06; p.101]), ENG.5 BP1 ([HDH+06; p.110-111])) explicitly demand that important

design decisions must be evaluated and documented[153]. This can be easily fulfilled using the *decision model* described in ch. III.19 and ch. III.20. Additionally,
this also provides an important connection hook to Rittel's design theory (ch.
I.6.2.2) and what is now called *RatMan* (ch. I.6.2.2 and ch. II.9).

Following the saying "no rule without an exception", at least two cases are
dedicated exceptions which should be dealt with on their own and therefore will
not be part of the discussion of ch. III.19 and ch. III.20. They will be discussed
later in connection to ch. III.23:

- *Complex systems (System of systems)*: If complex systems can be divided
  into relatively independent subsystems (with exactly definable interfaces),
  then the subsystem specifications should be separated.
- For development parts delegated to subcontractors the interface and context
  of these must be deeply analyzed and defined.

I.7.4 Automotive SPICE

Starting in 2001, the Automotive Special Interest Group (A-SIG) is working on
an industry specific adaption of *SPICE*, called *Automotive SPICE* (*A-SPICE*)
[ASPICE08a], [ASPICE08b], [AutomotiveSPICE], [MHD+07; p.3ff]. Since
2007 all members of the HIS (see beginning of ch. I.70) have decided to prefer *A-
SPICE* for supplier assessments, making *A-SPICE* to a de-facto standard in the
automotive industry [HDH+06; p.267ff].

A-SPICE has its own definition of a *process reference model* (*PRM*) and a
process assessment model (*PAM*) [HDH+06; p.267] slightly deviating[154] from the
original *PRM* and *PAM* of *SPICE* [HDH+06; p.267ff]. Even though some *base
practices* have been slightly adapted to the peculiarities of automotive embedded
engineering, concerning the ENG and SUP processes discussed here, the changes

---

[153] In *CMMI* the *generic practice* "Decision Analysis and Resolution" must be fulfilled to
reach up to *maturity level* 4 [Kn06; p.54].

[154] The following *SPICE* processes are left out by *A-SPICE* [HDH+06; p.269],
[MHD+07; p.7]: MAN.1, MAN.2, MAN.4, ENG.11, ENG.12, SUP.3, SUP.5, SUP.6
(product evaluation), ACQ.1, ACQ.5, RIN.1-4, OPE.1-2, SPL.3, PIM.1-2, REU.1 and
REU.3. Instead five new acquisition processes have been defined: ACQ.11 ("Technical
Requirements"), ACQ.12 ("Legal and administrative requirements"), ACQ.13 ("Project requirements"), ACQ.14 ("Request for Proposals"), ACQ.15 ("Supplier qualifica-
tion"). Further, it is to note that the HIS (see beginning of ch. I.07) has defined a subset of the *A-SPICE process model* called HIS-Scope. The HIS-Scope defines the minimum of processes to be assessed by each assessment of a HIS member.

made are not significant concerning this thesis except for the new demands on *traceability* discussed below.

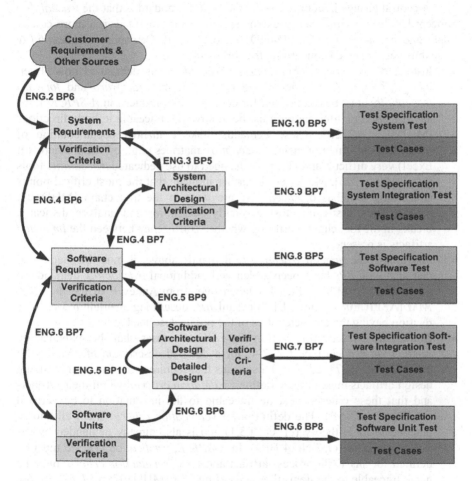

Figure 7-4 Summary of traceability BPs in A-SPICE [ASPICE08a; Annex E]

A major improvement from the embedded engineering perspective is that the key concepts of the engineering processes now also explicitly include mechanical and HW aspects, and these aspects are handled analogously to the handling for software aspects described above. This means that mechanical and HW requirements are derived from the *SYS_RS* and that then these requirements must be mapped onto the mechanical and *HW design* [ASPICE08a; Annex D], [MHD+07; p.15].

A central change in comparison to the *SPICE* standard is that the *traceability* concept has been "significantly extended and thereby defined in a more consequent and consistent manner" [MHD+07; p.222 (*)]. Demands for *traceability* have thus been changed concerning the following aspects:

- Instead of *traceability*, *bidirectional traceability* is demanded now. Even though, it was already demanded by SPICE that *backward* and *forward traceability* must be established for certain work products, in *A-SPICE*, now, any *traceability* information must be in any way traceable in both directions [MHD+07; p.222ff]. These demands make a manual documentation of *traceability* information using *traceability* matrices (e.g., by using Microsoft Excel) very difficult and press for the need to use dedicated *traceability* tools [MHD+07; p.225]. Müller et al. further indicate that the most critical points concerning tool based *traceability* are gaps in the tool chain [MHD+07; p.225]. Thus, assessors must explicitly search for and analyze dedicated breaks in the tool chain, verifying whether consistency between the *impacted* artifacts is present.

- Subsuming the general *traceability* demands above, it must be mentioned that also new *BPs* have been added with additional *traceability* demands to the original of SPICE. Fig. 7-4 taken over from Annex E of the *A-SPICE PAM* [ASPICE08a; Annex E] shows all *BPs* describing a certain *traceability* relation having the characteristics of the points described above.

- Additionally, *traceability* within the ENG processes shall be extended by *verification criteria* (see fig. 7-4; for a detailed description cf. [MHD+07; p.47, 53, 59, 66, 74, 225ff]). This means that requirements and their realizing design artifacts must already define *verification criteria* within their artifacts and that these criteria must be traceable to the information to be verified [MHD+07; p.225ff]. The definition of *verification criteria* is a well-known practice in *REM* theory (cf. ch. I.5.1) and is also already demanded by the SPICE standard (cf. ENG.4 BP3). In *A-SPICE*, *verification criteria* must be defined for any ENG process artifact and these *verification criteria* must be made traceable to the items they are defined for [MHD+07; p.47, 53, 59, 66, 74, 225ff].

- At the moment, the A-SIG also seems to discuss whether *traceability* should become an individual SUP-process as *problem management* etc. have become, but no definitive decision about this issue has yet been made [MHD+07; p.222ff]. The summary on *traceability* demands as referred to in fig. 7-4 may be the basis for such a process to be defined.

- *Horizontal* and *vertical traceability*: Even though the current standard version does not officially employ this terminology, Müller et al. [MHD+07; p.222] point out that at the A-SIG debate seems going on about whether to include the terms *horizontal* and *vertical traceability* in the future *traceability* process description. Obviously orienting on the *V-cycle process model* [DHM98], the *A-SPICE* standard's definition of *horizontal* and *vertical traceability* has its own notion completely different to the notions[155] described in ch. I.5.7.1: *Horizontal traceability* is illustrated as relationships in horizontal direction in fig. 7-4 (e.g., ENG.10 BP5), whereas *vertical traceability* refers to the vertical direction (e.g., ENG.2 BP6) [MHD+07; p.222]. In [MHD+07; p.225], Müller et al. emphasize that these definitions have the advantage that the aspects realization (*vertical traceability*) in other artifacts and test coverage (*horizontal traceability*) can be distinguished. As described in ch. I.5.7.1, the author, however, considers the ambiguous usage of the terms as alarming and rather prefers to avoid these terms. Besides, the author also considers the obvious preference on the *V-cycle process model* as problematic, because such standards usually should be as generic as possible and should not drive organizations toward a specific implementation of their processes as this orientation on the *V-cycle process model* suggests.

At the moment, *traceability* generally seems to be a trend topic in the automotive industry and changes of industrial practice in the next years are very likely.

Even though it is mentioned above that the ENG processes do not contain changes significant for the outcome of this thesis, one other exception exists: With ENG.5 BP5 "Define goals for resource consumption" the *A-SPICE* standard requests that resource consumption for each software module is explicitly planned and tracked [MHD+07; p.64]. In ch. III.21, it is shown how this demand can be fulfilled in a way that these 'resource consumption goals' are even integrated into a larger *traceability* structure showing new perspectives beyond the usual demands of the *A-SPICE* standard.

I.7.5 Safety Engineering: IEC 61508, ISO 26262

In the automotive industry, more and more ECUs have influence on *safety-related* functions, where malfunctions can lead to significant dangers of injury or death

---

[155] Müller et al. [MHD+07; p.222] also emphasize that CMMI has a different notion equal to the notion of Bohner [Bo91] (see ch. I.5.7.1).

of humans. Correspondingly, questions about the so-called functional *safety* of ECUs are becoming increasingly important.

The IEC 61508[156] "*Functional safety* of electrical/electronic/programmable electronic *safety-related systems* (E/E/PES)" [IEC61508] describes a standard for conception, planning, development, realization, launching, maintenance, modification, shutdown and deinstallation of systems containing *safety-critical* E/E/PES components, whose breakdowns impose significant risk for humans and the environment [LPP10; p.8ff].

The standard demands that a system possibly implying risks for humans or the environment must be assessed for the probability that these risks become reality. This includes that the individual components of the system are analyzed for potential malfunctions leading to *safety* hazards. If significant risks can be identified in those components or the system, then these parts or the complete system are classified as *safety-related*. Hereby a malfunction or a combination of malfunctions can lead to *safety* risks. The rating of the *safety*-relevance orients on fixed upper bounds of probabilities leading to a *safety* hazard. Corresponding to these probabilities each *safety-related* component can be classified into four different *safety integrity levels* (*SIL*) determining the actions to be taken in order to reduce hazard entry probabilities (see, e.g., [MHD+07; p.286] showing a risk probability graph for determining a corresponding *SIL* for a component).

The IEC 61508 can be seen as a basic norm helping to define industry sector specific implementations [MHD+07; p.285]. Such an implementation[157] for the automotive industry is provided by a new standard ISO 26262 ("Road vehicles – *Functional safety*"). The ISO 26262 [ISO26262] is a norm draft of the automotive industry for *safety* of electronic road vehicles derived from IEC61508 [LPP10; p.9]. The *SIL* levels are called *automotive safety integrity levels* (*ASIL*) but have the same meaning. The difference is that they are classified by grades from A (*SIL 1=ASIL A*) to D (*SIL 4 = ASIL D*).

Benediktsson et al. [BHM01] empirically proved that to fulfill *SIL1* or *SIL2* minimum *SPICE maturity level 2* (*ML*) is essential. For higher *SILs* (*SIL3* and *SIL4*), the study indicates the need for higher *MLs*. Concerning *A-SPICE*, Mueller et al. emphasize that "reaching ML2 in the processes of the HIS-scope is a necessary (but not sufficient) premise to develop *safety-critical* software (*SIL1* or higher)" [MHD+07; p.288 (*)]. Beyond this (for *SIL2*, *SIL3* or *SIL4*), no specific practice of *A-SPICE* is mappable, because SPICE standards only demand

---

[156] Also known as EN 61508, DIN EN 61508 and VDE 0803.

[157] Other industrial sector implementations are for example: IEC 61511 (process industry), IEC 61513 (nuclear power plants), DO-178B (aviation), or EN 50129 (railway). See [LPP10; p.9] for an overview of standards derived from IEC 61508.

'what' has to be performed, whereas IEC 61508 (and ISO 26262) additionally imposes certain demands 'how' activities have to be performed [MHD+07; p.288]. This leads to the conclusion that *traceability* demands must be fulfilled whenever a *safety-related* function has been identified in a system to be developed.

I.8 Feedback from Embedded Practice

In theory there is no difference between theory and practice. In practice there is.
Yogi Berra

After the theoretical terrain, an adequate *traceability* between requirements and design solution should consider, has been outlined, the following chapter discusses some feedback from practice that should help in the considerations.

Pettit [Pe04] describes a series of lessons learned "derived from several different embedded software development efforts observed by the author during the period of 2000-2004" [Pe04; p.1]. The projects[158] involve "large-scale embedded software often with real-time requirements and often with a high degree of concurrent processing" [Pe04; p.2]. As modeling standard, UML 1.4 without any further profile or real time extensions or special case tool has been applied. Thus, the presented lessons learned reflect Pettit's experiences with the basic features of a modeling language as UML not requiring the presence of specialized modeling features or other sophisticated tool sets [Pe04; p.1-2]. The described experience divides into lessons about processes and lessons about modeling (design).

Lessons about the processes are:

- A well-defined process is as important as any modeling itself. Pettit distinctively emphasizes the difference between a well-defined development process and a general process framework such as SPICE. Many projects go for the latter, ignoring the individual project implications. "While these frameworks are a good starting point, it is crucial for each project to capture the specific process flows, activities, and milestones that will be employed for

---

[158] Even though, the referred projects seem to involve the aerospace domain (This is not explicitly mentioned in the article, however Pettit's organization is called "The Aerospace Corporation") that may not necessarily match with other domains as Automotive and the reference to UML mentioned before, the author believes that the findings of Pettit are fundamental and abstract enough to also match with other engineering domains and other modeling paradigms. The reader may decide on his (her) own whether the author's claim is correct.

their projects. This is nominally accomplished through the creation of a software development plan that documents not only the framework being applied, but the specific process steps applied for the project" [Pe04; p.2].

- Simply adopting new process technologies does not reduce the development effort. At first, mostly higher efforts due to learning phases must be considered. Concerning the adoption of UML techniques, the most positive experience is that not necessarily the projects' overall development effort has changed, but the effort has rather shifted to up-front requirement definition and problem analysis. If these up-front activities have been performed soundly, efforts for *detailed design* and implementation have reduced at least marginally. However, it has been observed that projects with a solid analysis model and *SW architecture* have reduced maintenance efforts including efforts for adding new features in future adaptions [Pe04; p.2].

- "One of the most immediate benefits observed from adopting a *use case* driven UML design is the improved visibility to stakeholders. Through applying this highly visual modeling, software engineers are able to more readily communicate with systems engineers and even to the end customer" [Pe04; p.2]. In this way, confidence in the developed features and understanding of requirements in early development phases could be increased. Additionally, the usage of a standard language like UML helped developers to get easier up to speed in new projects, because the standardized modeling constructs lowered the learning curve for understanding concepts within the new project [Pe04; p.2].

- "The lack of thorough *requirements traceability* is one of the most common and critical problem areas observed in current object oriented development efforts. Often, requirements are traced to the *use cases* for a particular system or subsystem, but are not propagated to the individual design elements. When requirements are not completely traced to the specific design elements (e.g., classes, messages, state charts, etc.), there is a tendency to lose focus as to the specific responsibility of the classes being designed. This can lead to costly changes late in the life cycle and can also lead to incorrect or missing functionality in the delivered system. Additionally, gaps in *requirements traceability* complicate the testing and verification process, especially at the unit or white-box level" [Pe04; p.2].

- Prototyping is a heavily used technique for exploring unknown parts of a system. This is especially important in embedded development in order to gain insights and confidence in the employed HW. However, "extreme care" [Pe04; p.3] should be taken about decisions how to integrate backlashes of the gathered results. "Specifically, care should be taken to appropriately update the software design based on the results of the prototype" [Pe04; p.2-3].

Pettit has observed that drifts between design and the implementation are one major driver for later maintenance and upgrade efforts and problems of the developed software [Pe04; p.2-3].

Subsuming point one in the context of process standards such as SPICE, the crux about it is how to adequately adapt a process framework to a specific project. The usual answer of such process frameworks is employing a process tailoring concept [HDH+06; p.245], [BT04; p.36f]. The author believes that this is an issue not yet completely solved issue as the discussion between more disciplined or more agile processes is also in open discourse (see, e.g., [BT04]). Findings of projects practice are disillusioning in the sense that process tailoring is often not performed, because process framework definitions are so complicated that accountable project members do not dare to perform significant tailoring in fear of being blamed for negative consequences discovered later [BT04; p.152] driving Boehm and Turner to the recommendation to build methods up rather than to tailor them down [BT04; p.152]. The point tangents this thesis by the question how far tools and processes are connected and influence each other. As shown in ch. I.7.3.2 and later in part III (ch. III.20.3), tools such as R2A introduced in part III may also have the potential to infer a different interpretation of artifact connections that allow process standards to be tailored in a different way in order to avoid problems such as unnecessary redundancies between artifacts. The second and third point refer to experiences that are generally encountered, when extended *REM* practices are used. Besides the technique of *use cases*, other *requirements specification* techniques exist and it is probable that stakeholders' understanding may be improved if a structured method for elicitation and structuring requirements is used, which is understandable for the stakeholders (e.g., reflects their vocabulary and understanding) and is somehow standardized so that it must be learned just once. *Use cases* fulfill these criteria to a very high degree, what explains their high preference in projects. Point four directly describes the core problem this thesis works on. It claims for a fine-grained and detailed *traceability* solution. Last but not least, point five addresses the issues of how to explore the *solution space* (the possible design alternatives) and how to integrate knowledge achieved outside the standard development information flow. Further, the problem of view drift (here the drift of the model and the code) is mentioned. As described in ch. I.6.6.1, these problems can be avoided by specialized *design tools* allowing early functional prototyping with automatic code generation.

Concerning the modeling, the following lessons are described:

1. "Capturing interfaces to external devices is a critical element in the design of embedded software systems" [Pe04; p.3]. Two kinds of interfaces shall be considered. The context of the embedded device involves all devices and users that interact with the system. Therefore, a context analysis (a good de-

scription of possible context analysis methods with UML is provided by [HR02]) is essential for identifying all involved interfaces. Secondly, an embedded SW must interact with the HW. Often the HW interface knowledge is encapsulated in some kind of controller class. However, to improve flexibility each interface should be encapsulated by its own controller class.

2. Often an imbalance between static and dynamic models exists, whereby static aspects are mostly preferred. "This practice results in an unbalanced design that, while providing a good data model, may not completely capture the behavioral aspects of events and messages that are prevalent in embedded software systems. Without adequately capturing this dynamic behavior, it is difficult to assess whether the final design will completely satisfy the functional or performance requirements of an embedded system" [Pe04; p.3-4].

3. Often dynamic interactions are modeled using sequence charts. However, a sequence chart often only shows one scenario of interactions, whereas the overall interaction context is neglected. UML also provides communication diagrams. "By utilizing both forms of UML interaction diagrams, engineers can achieve a more complete description of both the sequence of events within a scenario and of the behavior across a set of scenarios" [Pe04; p.4].

4. Identification of concurrency situations is essential in embedded systems design, if more than one concurrent thread is employed. Often concurrency situations are described in a different diagram, whereas UML language features are neglected. "This leads to a disconnect between the as-built software and the UML design artifacts" [Pe04; p.4].

5. In the experience of Pettit, state charts are the most underused means for capturing the reactive, state-dependent behavior often found in embedded systems. Especially, hierarchical state charts prove helpful to tame complex behavior [Pe04; p.4].

Point one discusses that defining the context of a system is an essential task (see ch. I.4 and ch. I.5.2). In the second notion, Pettit emphasizes that access to HW components from SW shall be encapsulated by controller classes. Even though not directly discussed in this thesis, in automotive ECU design so-called 'driver' modules perform this encapsulation for HW components of the micro controller, and 'handler' modules encapsulate knowledge of the control paths of a specific functionality at the printed circuit board. The accompanying case study of part III (cf. ch. III.12) uses the encapsulation principles of drivers and handlers.

Point two discusses that there should also be a suitable possibility to get the connections between the static and the dynamic behavior. Usually, this is performed through the *view* concept. The *traceability* solution discussed in part III also provides a way to adequately model connections between different views. This can help to document connections between the static and dynamic aspects.

Points three and four are rather problems to be addressed by modeling and are therefore not further discussed in this thesis.

Point five gives further prove for the argumentation provided in ch. I.6.6.1.

II. Rationale Management and Traceability in Detailed Discussion

> *The more you plan in details, the more you are struck by coincidence.*
> Peter Rühmkorf (*)

After the last part described the different major topics this thesis is related to, this part now discusses the two central research topics in detail. These topics are *rationale management (RatMan)* and *requirements traceability*. In ch. II.9, *RatMan* is discussed as major research field on how information about important design decisions can be successfully captured in order to ensure that information important for change management and long-term collaborative is conserved.

Ch. II.10 then discusses the current state of research on *requirements traceability*. At first, this discussion is made from a general perspective. At the end, ch. II.10.6 discusses *traceability* research in the special context of the transition from requirements to design being in the focus of this thesis.

II.9 Rationale Management in Systems and Software Engineering

> *The wise man never takes a step too long for his leg.*
> African saying

Making decisions is the basis of all development activities. *Rationale* describes "the justification behind decisions" [DMM+06a; p.1]. In other words, "the term *rationale* denotes the reasoning underlying the creation and use of artifacts. *Rationale* research seeks ways of aiding decision-makers by creating explicit records of this reasoning. Most other types of research on decision-making, by contrast, seek to create *formal*, computational methods for deriving decisions. *Rationale* research primarily deals with *informal* and *semi-formal*, verbal reasoning; but it does not ignore *formal* reasoning and computation, both because humans sometimes use these in reasoning about decisions and because they can augment human reasoning" [BCM+08; p.3].

The general goal of *rationale management (RatMan)* and its research efforts can be described as "to use *rationale* to improve the processes of creating artifacts of various kinds, including physical artifacts such as buildings, cities ... as well as cognitive artifacts such as software and government policy" [BCM+08; p.5]. To achieve these goals, the following aspects are in general considered by methods and supporting tools developed by *rationale* research (cf. [BCM+08; p.5]):

- Elicitation of important and useful *rationale* from different sources. Mostly these sources of *rationale* are stakeholders involved in the decision process (often called the *rationale bearers)*.
- Recording useful *rationale*,
- Structuring and indexing the recorded *rationale* for *retrieval*,
- *Rationale retrieval*, when it is needed or useful,
- Imparting *rationale* to all stakeholders if it is needed or useful,
- Handling of the *rationale* by stakeholders;

Historically, *rationale* research was given birth by the Rittel's design [RW73] theory about *wicked problems* [RW84] (see ch. I.6.2.2) and thus focused on design processes [DMM+06a; p.1]. Correspondingly, most literature on *rationale* uses the term *design rationale*. However, as "*rationale* models are used during all activities of development, including requirements engineering, architectural design, implementation, testing and system deployment" [DMM+06a; p.1], Dutoit et al. [DMM+06a; p.1] propose using the term *software engineering rationale* to emphasize that *rationale* occurs during all phases of software development and is not necessarily limited to design contexts. In principle, the author agrees with this extended context, but as this thesis also considers *SysEng* approaches, an even wider scope is needed. In particular, the term *software engineering rationale* again provides strict limitations to software related contexts only, whereas the former term *design rationale* also includes non-software related design activities as, e.g., *social planning*. In the context of this thesis, *rationale* is only discussed in the context of design. Correspondingly, the term *design rationale* would seem adequate for this thesis, but to avoid both limitations, the author just uses the term *rationale*.

Burge et al. [BCM+08; p.17-19] enlist the potential benefits of including *rationale* into software engineering processes (these results are of either value in *SysEng*). The author will enlist all main points. For the points important to this thesis, the sub points are also listed:

- Support for *requirements engineering* can involve identification and explanation of requirements. Here, *rationale* can help requirement engineers with decision making through improving underlying reasoning. Additionally, decisions with their reasoning are recorded thus helping to assess *impacts* of changes.
- Support for *design and implementation*: On one side, *rationale* can provide *traceability* of between requirements and design decisions and vice versa. On

the other side, *rationale* can help designers to make better decisions through improving communication and underlying reasoning (e.g., by providing *rationale* behind *patterns* (cf. ch. I.6.2.4)). Recorded decisions and their reasoning further help with change assessments.

- Supporting *software maintenance* by helping maintainers to understand the *rationale* for requirements, design or implementation decisions.
- *Project management* is supported because *rationale* helps to communicate decisions to management. As a plus, performed *RatMan* during project management can help to make better decisions.
- Supporting *use* by providing *rationale* explaining the functioning of complex systems.
- *Collaborative working in groups* can be supported by "using *rationale* as a vehicle for communication amongst different kinds of experts and stakeholders" [BCM+08; p.18], because different points of view between stakeholders can be elicited and the decision making process is made transparent. Additionally, decisions can be better communicated. In this way, conflicts between decisions taken by different groups can be surfaced. Besides improved transparency and exposition of conflicts, also "areas of agreement" [BCM+08; p.18] can be revealed helping to achieve group consensus.
- *Change* is supported. On one side, change need can be detected because *rationale* denotes information about assumptions and consequences. If captured assumptions become invalid or unforeseen consequences become apparent, need for change will be indicated. On the other side, changes can be better handled because dependencies among decisions and other elements can become apparent helping to identify *impacts* of changes (*impact analysis*). Further, *rationale* can contain evaluations on decision alternatives giving decisive supportive information for redesign decisions.
- *Software reuse* is eased, because *rationale* can provide explanations why software components are designed and implemented the way they are.
- *Knowledge transfer* is supported because *rationale* helps to learn from successes, failures and ideas of former projects. Also, *rationale* helps to perform design validation assessments. Such collected knowledge can be transformed to reusable knowledge for training and education or help researchers for on research on real-world project practice.

In the context of this thesis, *rationale* is important in the context of *REM* and *design*. In fact, literature for both research fields recommends the capturing and use of *rationale*[159]. This begins at early design decisions already at the *require-*

---

[159] As examples for *REM* theory with extensive focus on *traceability*, [RJ01] or [Ge05; p.6] can be mentioned.

ment elicitation phase, which is especially important to define system interfaces (context of the system) [Ge05; p.6].

Especially for *safety-critical* systems, "*rationale* may facilitate the *safety analysis* of the design" [DMM+06a; p.38] and thus provide significant support for *safety-critical* processes (cf. ch. I.7.5). But, surely, not every topic can be extensively discussed in a project: "If large, complex design and development projects are to be completed within their inherent resource constraints, not every decision and relevant factor can be deliberated, and the challenge becomes one of defining an acceptable level of ambiguity rather than eliminating it altogether. That said, this ambiguity poses a significant challenge to providing comprehensive explanations." [Ha06b; p.62].

In other words, "the complete *rationale* for even a small system is impossible to represent; consequently, developers are faced with selecting which *rationale* to represent" [DMM+06a; p.2].

II.9.1 Characterization Criteria for Rationale Approaches

Before sketching several *rationale* approaches, some general characterization criteria shall be discussed. Several categories characterizing *rationale* approaches exist (cf. [DMM+06a]):
- *Representation*,
- *Process implementation*,
- *Descriptive* versus *prescriptive approaches*,
- *Intrusiveness*;

II.9.1.1 Representation

Captured *rationale* must be somehow represented. "Although *formality* is typically a continuum, not a set of categories with thresholds" [Le97; p.81], Lee [Le97; p.81-82] distinguishes three kinds of representation:
- *Informal* representation uses unstructured forms such as natural language, audio or video recordings or raw drawings to *capture rationale*. *Informal capturing* can be created easily; however, further computer-based processing is difficult due to lacking in *formal* structure.
- *Semi-formal* representation only partially relies on a *formal* structure analyzable by computers. The *formal* structure builds a *scaffold* or *skeleton* of element types and relationships, whereon the *rationale* can be mapped on and thus structured. The content of the elements and relationships, however, re-

mains *informal*. During *rationale capturing* (e.g., during meetings), a certain *formal* structure can be helpful for structuring discussions (similar to check lists) or suggesting what information is expected. Thus, *semi-formal* representations may even reduce overhead or complexity in discussions and prevent topic digresses.

- *Formal* representation only includes *formally* defined items and their relationships, which allow a computer-based system to perform *formal* operations on. "The creation of *rationale* thus becomes a matter of creating a knowledge base in some *formal* language". The type of *formal* representation depends on the types of operations intended to be performed on the gathered information.

In *semi-formal* and *formal* representations, the *rationale* is "divided into chunks that are assigned to certain properties and/or relationships" [DMM+06a; p.2], where "by far, the most common way" [DMM+06a; p.2] is the usage of a *conceptual rationale schema* representing the items, properties and relationships to be captured and represented. Other ways are either to link *rationale* chunks to elements of the discussed artifact, or to relate *rationale* chunks to process descriptions about the usage of the discussed artifact [DMM+06a; p.2], [BCM+08; p.29f].

Lee [Le97; p.82] emphasizes that the more *formalization rationale* has, the more services can be provided by a computer-based system. However, *formalizing* knowledge is complex and costly. A way to reduce complexity and costs is to *formalize* incrementally. In this way it would be possible to first *capture rationale informally*, then transform it to a *semi-formal representation* and – if needed – transform it further to *formal representations* [Le97; p.82].

II.9.1.2 Basic Rationale Processes

Rationale approaches can be characterized by how they provide basic *rationale processes*. Three basic processes must be considered [DMM+06a; p.4]

- *Capturing rationale* describes how *rationale* can be elicited and recorded. Different possibilities exist. Either the *rationale bearer* itself, or *rationale* specialists document it, or it is extracted from communication recordings of project participants, or it is captured as a side-effect by the use of another design-support software [DMM+06a; p.5].
- *Formalizing rationale* describes processes of *rationale* transformation into the desired representation, as, e.g., a *rationale schema*. "Traditionally, capturing and *formalizing rationale* were combined in a single operation. In recent years, however, alternative approaches separate the *formalizing* of *ra-*

tionale from its *capture*" [DMM+06a; p.5]. Either the *rationale* is *formalized* by the *rationale bearers*, or trained *rationale formalizers*, or some software provides support to partially or completely *formalize* the *rationale*.

- *Providing access to rationale* deals with how recorded *rationale* can be communicated to or retrieved by users: "The most common approach to accessing ...(*rationale*)... is through use of a system that lets users browse a hyperdocument containing the *rationale*" [DMM+06a; p.5]. Other techniques are *information retrieval*, or *knowledge based systems* alerting users about possibly important *rationale*.

II.9.1.3 Descriptive versus Prescriptive Approaches

Another common way of categorizing *rationale* approaches is through distinction between *descriptive* and *prescriptive* approaches [DMM+06a; p.5]:

- *Descriptive approaches* purely concentrate on describing the thinking of designers involved into the decision process. They do not try to influence or change the way of reasoning of designers, but the recorded *rationale* information may influence other development processes as implementation, maintenance or later design decisions to be made. Further, they support recovering *rationale* about older decisions, which would have been forgotten otherwise and support in passing on information to other development team members or new team members. Lee [Le97; p.80] calls this the *documentation perspective*.
- *Prescriptive approaches*, on the other side, aim at improving design processes via improving reasoning or altering thinking of designers during the decision process [DMM+06a; p.5], [BCM+08; p.160]. To achieve this, they prescribe to follow a certain structure for discussing and/or capturing the *rationale* information. Lee [Le97; p.80] calls this the *argumentation perspective*.

II.9.1.4 Intrusiveness

A further differentiation criterion for *rationale* approaches is the characterization of their *intrusiveness*. "This includes not only how *intrusive* they are, but in what respects they *intrude*. Thus, an approach might be highly *non-intrusive* during *capture* of ...(*rationale*)... but relatively *intrusive* during *retrieval* and display of *rationale*. Measures of *intrusiveness* can include the degree to which a ...*rationale*... approach dictates the way design is done as well as the amount of extra effort required to use the approach" [DMM+06a; p.6]. The tolerable extent of *intrusiveness* may also be different concerning the *capture, formalization* and access processes. According to Dutoit et al. [DMM+06a; p.6], most *rationale* approaches are highly *intrusive* concerning *rationale capture*, because they intervene into the design process through enforcing designers to *rationale elicitation* as by the usage of a *rationale schema*.

During the past two decades, less *intrusive* approaches for *rationale capture* and *formalization* have been aspired by researchers [DMM+06a; p.6], because *intrusiveness* is seen by many researchers as central obstacle to success of *rationale capture* in practice [DMM+06a; p.6]. *Prescriptive approaches* are not necessarily the more *intrusive* approaches. However, *descriptive approaches* can ease the use of less *intrusive* techniques to *capture rationale* [DMM+06a; p.6].

II.9.2 Rationale Management Systems (RMS)

The concept of a *rationale management system* (*RMS*) denotes a system that makes capturing and accessing of *rationale* possible. *RMS* may offer the following potential benefits [DMM+06a; p.2]:

- Support for project management by providing valuable information about decisions;
- Improvement of *dependency management* as, for example, *traceability* dealt with in this thesis;
- Generally providing greater design support;
- Support of development team collaboration;
- Supporting later users of design;
- Allowing better and more detailed documentation;
- Requirement engineering support;
- Support of design reuse;
- Support for learning about and evaluating design;

Typically, the following *RatMan* tasks involve an *RMS* [DMM+06a; p.36ff]:

- Identifying the kind of *rationale* need involves *rationale* goal definition, measurement and identification. Typically this is not part of the *RMS* itself but defines the kind of needed *RMS*.
- *Rationale capture* concerned with *rationale* acquisition and how *rationale* can be further developed (i.e., detailed).
- *Rationale usage* deals with distribution (i.e., communication), *retrieval*, use, and long-term preservation of *rationale*.

"Recent research tends to combine these systems with other forms of design support systems" [DMM+06a; p.36]. The tool discussed in part III also combines mechanisms to capture *rationale* with mechanisms to capture *traceability* information in an integrated design environment in order to improve information on the performed design.

II.9.3 Overview of Different Rationale Approaches

II.9.3.1 Schemas for Argumentation

At the time Rittel and Webber have carved out the *wicked* nature of design problems (see ch. I.6.6.2), Kunz and Rittel developed the *Issue-Based Information System* (*IBIS*) approach [KR70] as "a way of modeling argumentation" [DMM+06a; p.7]. In Rittel's eyes [Ri72], *wicked problems* could only be addressed by an argumentative approach surfacing the pros and cons of different positions. *IBIS* relies on a fixed *conceptual documentation schema* helping to elicit different positions on an issue [BCM+08; p.6]. Four different elements build the *schema*:

- *Issues*: The analyzed topic; "Issues have the form of questions" [KR70; p.4].
- *Positions*: "The origin of issues are controversial statements" [KR70; p.4]. *Position* elements represent these controversial statements.
- *Arguments*: Either support or contradict a *position*,
- *Resolutions*: The resolutions deduced from the discussion;

Fig 9-1 shows an outline of a discussion structured in the *IBIS schema*[160] elements, represented by the author's thoughts about the usefulness of *rationale* approaches. Between the elements different relationships "forming networks between the items of the 'issue bank'" [KR70; p.4] are possible [DMM+06a; p.8].

---

[160] The *IBIS schema* has a resembling connection to Toulmin's *model of argumentation* [To58]. The *model of argumentation* consists of a layout of six interconnected elements helping to analyze an argument [To58]: A *claim* is an issue or argument that must be proved through the argumentation. *Grounds* describe data or hard facts reinforcing a *claim*. *Warrant* describes the connections between the *claim* and the *grounds*, thus legitimizing the *claim*. If a *warrant* alone is insufficient, a *backing* verifies a *warrant*. *Qualifiers* are expressions of certainty (e.g., definitively, surely) or affirmation (e.g., most, always or sometimes) for the *claim*. Last but not least, a *rebuttal* describes possible limitations or refutations on an element. Toulmin considers the first three items (*claim, grounds* and *warrant*) as essential to any argument, whereas the other (*backing, qualifier* and *rebuttal*) can be possibly omitted.

Rittel himself mainly targeted *IBIS* for promoting debate on issues of many very differing points of view (*wicked problems*), whereas he considered noncontroversial design questions as trivial issues not to be dealt with *IBIS* [DMM+06a; p.8]. In the following decades, Rittel applied *IBIS* to social and political planning in the United Nations, the European Community and West Germany (cf. [DMM+06a; p.7]), whereas other researchers discovered its use in general design questions (cf. [Mc78], [Mc79]).

Originally, the approach based on pen and paper. In the 1980ies Conklin recognized the *wicked problem* theory as potentially fruitful for understanding the crucial difficulties discovered in the course of ongoing software design practice. Consequentially, Conklin developed the tool gIBIS [CB88], where the *IBIS schema* can be expressed as graphical hypertext argumentation maps. Streitz et al. [SHT89], [SHH+92] introduced a tool called SEPIA as a hypermedia system environment for collaborative editing of argumentation [Sch07; p.226]. SEPIA uses a modification of the IBIS method [SHH+92; p.15].

From the beginning on, *IBIS* has been "from the outset both *prescriptive* and *intrusive*, as were almost all of his *IBIS* projects. Other researchers, however, have sought much less *intrusive* ways of using *IBIS*" [DMM+06a; p.8], (see also [IR97]).

The *rationale* research field developed from the pioneering work of Rittel and Kunz. During the research that followed, a diversity of approaches has been developed. Burge et al. give a good orientation aid by stating that roughly all approaches can be differentiated between either variations on *IBIS* or as "fundamental alternatives" [BCM+08; p.5]. In the following of this chapter the most important[161] variations are shortly described. Later in part III of this thesis, the author describes an approach helping to combine *traceability* and *rationale* information. This approach can be combined with *IBIS* or any of the following approaches as a kind of documentation template for *rationale*. However, its main concern lies more in alleviating the fundamental difficulties that documentation and management of *rationale* faces in *SE* practice. These issues are part of the next following chapters.

Procedural Hierarchy of Issues (*PHI*) [Mc78], [Mc79] is an extension of *IBIS* whose "main innovation is to show that frequently the decision on one issue depends on the decisions made on others" [BCM+08; p.8]. As a central concept, *PHI* provides a *subissue* relationship. An issue can only be resolved by the resolution of its sub issues. In this way a hierarchy of issues evolves, where the root issue represents the whole project. JANUS [FMM89], [FLM+96] and PHIDIAS [MBO+92] are a tool implementations of PHI.

---

[161] The listing itself orients on [DMM+06a] and [BCM+08].

Issue: How can *rationale* be included into processes to ensure significant support in development?

Position 1: *Rationale* must be collected for any decision.

Arguments on Position 1:

    For: The process of collecting *rationale* for decisions ensure that decisions are made on rational facts and not on unconscious implicit criteria.

    Arguments on this argument:

    For: The noted down facts must be formulated and thus acquire a certain degree of rationality.

    Against: Generally not all criteria of a decision may be rationally expressible. This may lead to negligence of these 'fuzzy' criteria.

    Against: The extensive number of decisions makes it impossible to collect *rationale* for any decision.

Position 2: *Rationale* must only be collected for the most important decisions.

    For: The important decisions matter most. This approach ensures that at least that the most important decisions are appropriately discussed and considered.

    For: Documentation effort is limited to a manageable amount.

    Against: Separating the important decisions from the less important ones is a decision process with a certain degree of arbitrary subjectivity. Correspondingly, important de- cisions may be forgotten.

Position 3: Documenting *rationale* is not useful at all.

    For: A lot of documentation must be produced resulting in extended extra effort and diminished project documentation overview.

    For: The *rationale bearers* often do not receive adequate benefit.

    For: Research on the process of making design decision surfaced that *rationale capturing* often interrupts the designers in their thinking.

    Against: Unreflected decisions are more likely to be wrong decisions.

    Against: A high number of wrong decisions can cause complete project failure.

    Against: Even one wrong decision with far-reaching consequences can risk complete project failure.

Resolution: Position 2 represents a capable, promising compromise and should be employed.

Figure 9-1 IBIS schema example outlining a discussion.

Inspired by *IBIS*, McLean et al. [MYB+91] proposed a method for design space analysis, called *Question, Options and Criteria (QOC)*. The approach is independent from *IBIS* but has resembling characteristics. McLean et al. saw *QOC* as support in the context of Schön's *reflection-in-action* design phase [MYB+91; p.216]. Fig. 9-2 shows the *QOC schema* as interpreted by Hagge et al. [HHL+06; p.413]. As *IBIS* does, *QOC* approaches *rationale* issues by design *questions* (cf. [BCM+08; p.305]). *Questions* can be addressed by several *options* providing possible alternative solutions [NS06; p.212]. Vice versa, *options* can also be a consequence of several *questions*. "Criteria as the basis for evaluating *options*" [MYB+91; p.234] represent the desirable properties and requirements of the artifact to be designed. Additionally, *arguments* provide further means to assess and justify *questions*, *options* and *criteria*.

QOC's notation has a *semi-formal* structure [MYB+91; p.219] meaning that the concept items (*question*, *option*, *criterion* and *argument*) and their relations build a *formal* structure, whereas the actual content within any of the concept items is *informal* and unrestricted. Thus, McLean at al. considered *QOC* representations as "effective communication vehicles, because they are simple enough to be understood by a variety of people, they are flexible enough to represent a variety of issues from a variety of viewpoints, and they are explicit enough to expose assumptions that can be challenged by others" [MYB+91; p.219]. Thus, *QOC* is mainly a *descriptive approach*, but requiring designers to perform a thorough description of the design space, makes *QOC intrusive*.

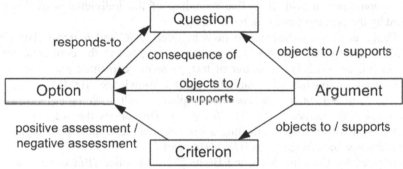

Figure 9-2 QOC schema as interpreted by [HHL+06; p.413]

According to McLean et al. [MYB+91], *IBIS* rather is restricted to capturing *rationale* "on the fly", thus recording the historical development of *rationale* during the process. *QOC*, though, is more interested in the logical representation of the design space. Thus, it can also be retrospectively restructured [NS06; p.212]. In the context of *REM*, Nguyen and Swatman [NS06] show that *IBIS* and *QOC* can complement each other and propose an approach in which both methods are used in different situations:

- *IBIS* provides possibilities to record an "ad-hoc" [NS06; p.222] *rationale* as it "describes the on-going evolutionary development of requirement" [NS06;

p.223] (the history of the decision process) and thus captures *"how"* the requirements develop over time" [NS06; p.223].

- *QOC*, on the other side, provides the possibilities for a "post-hoc" [NS06; p.223] conversion of the *IBIS rationale* to perform "a holistic examination of the *problem space"* [NS06; p.224] finding insights *"why"* a requirement model takes a certain form it does" [NS06; p.224].

Buckingham Shum et al. [BSS+06] analyze *gIBIS* and *QOC* after 15 years of employment. As a result of the experiences with both approaches with the "particular flavor of ... creating graphical argumentation maps for design deliberations" [BSS+06; p.111], they developed a tool called Compendium [Compendium]. Detailed information on design processes and the use of Compendium can be found in [Co06] and [BSS+06]. Compendium supports modeling graphical maps of argumentation in a hypermedia environment meaning that Compendium is a collaborative system, where the graphical maps can be enriched with other media such as textual documentation, audio and video recordings of design meetings in combination with time line recording of the individual activities performed by the participants of such a meeting.

Hagge et al. show interconnections between *QOC* and *patterns* [HHL+06; p.413]. In their view, the *QOC schema* can be mapped to the core concepts of *patterns* (cf. ch. I.6.2.4). As matter of fact, *patterns* "constitute one of the most heavily used approaches for organizing reusable knowledge" [DMM+06a; p.19], where the *"pattern* concept has *rationale* explicitly built in, though this *rationale* is relatively unstructured" [DMM+06a; p.19]. This opens the way to another research area within *RatMan* dealing about *rationale* as a means for organizing *organizational knowledge bases* [DMM+06; part 4].

Inspired by Conklin, Potts and Bruns [PB88] applied *IBIS* to *software design*. They extended the *IBIS schema* by including *"intermediate artifacts"* (models, documents, prototypes and other design artifacts) representing the designed software. This idea was enhanced by Lee and Lai ([Le90a], [LL91], [LL96]) by developing the *Decision Representation Language (DRL)* accompanied by a tool called Sybil ([Le90b], [LL96]), a knowledge-based hypertext system. *DRL* includes the following main elements [DMM+06; p.12]:

- *Decision problems* are the issues to be decided (cf. *questions* in *QOC*; *issues* in *IBIS*).
- *Alternatives* have very similar meaning to *options* in *QOC*.
- *Goals* corresponds to *criterion* in *QOC*. *Alternatives* can be related to goals by an *achieves* relationship similar to *positive assessment* in *QOC*.
- *Claims* can be made about *achieves* relationships, thus analyzing *alternatives* (comparable to *arguments* in *QOC*). *Claims* can have *support* or *deny* relationships to other *claims (*see similar relationships in *QOC* and *IBIS*).

- *Groups* group objects (*decision problems, alternatives, goals ...*). The *member* attribute of a *group* describes the grouping criterion. Any relation can link to *groups* in the same way as to single objects.

As striking similarities to *IBIS* and *QOC* exist, *DRL* also provides some new aspects [DMM+06; p.12]:

- *Claims* can have *presupposes* relations between each other.

- Each *Claim* has the properties *evaluation, plausibility* and *degree*, where the *evaluation* property derives its value from the other two values describing the likelihood for a *claim* to be true (*plausibility*) and the degree to which it is true (*degree*).

- Further, *DRL* allows hierarchies of *goal-subgoal* dependencies. As well as it allows hierarchies of *decision-subdecision* dependencies corresponding to the *subissue* relationship in *PHI*.

In order to suit it better to *SE* processes, Burge and Brown [BB04], [BB06] have developed *RATSpeak* as an extension of *DRL*. Besides the *DRL* concepts, the *RATSpeak schema* uses new element types and provides an argument ontology tailored for *SE* [BB06; p.280], [BCM+08; p.305]:

- *Requirements* include *FRs* and *NFRs*. *Requirements* can be modeled within the *RATSpeak schema*, or they can be included as references to a *requirements specification* document.

- *Questions* describe questions to be answered in order to find an answer to the *decision problem*. "*Questions* augment the argumentation by specifying the source of the information used to make the decision (the procedure, program or person)" [BB06; p.280].

- *Assumptions* are similar to *claims*, but for *assumptions* it is not definitively clear whether they are true and whether they will continue to persist in the future.

- *Argument ontology* describes a hierarchy of common argument types tailored for the software development domain serving as *claims* that can be used in the system (e.g., development costs, portability). The entries build a basic vocabulary used for inferencing. Each entry has a default importance that can be changed by associated *claims* [BB06; p.281]. *RATSpeak* handles *NFRs* as parts of the *argument ontology*.

- *Background knowledge* can be seen as a container for all modeled *tradeoffs* and *co-occurrence* relationships between different arguments in the *argument ontology*. The container is used to check the gathered *rationale* for any violations with these relationships.

Burge and Brown also have developed a tool implementation of RATSpeak called SEURAT (Software Engineering Using RATionale). SEURAT integrates directly into the Eclipse-IDE[162] environment, because Burge and Brown assume that "the developers are more likely to be willing to record their *rationale* if they do not need to start an additional tool to do so" [BB06; p.284].

SEURAT, however, is a prototypical tool environment with the goal to evaluate the potential uses of *rationale* mainly from the maintenance perspective. Accordingly, *rationale capture* was not in the focus of the SEURAT environment BB06; p.284]. In this way, SEURAT does not address what the author considers as main obstacle for practical use (see ch. II.9.4.20; cf. also [DMM+06a; p.33], [DMM–+06a; p.39]).

The Sysiphus tool developed by Dutoit and Paech [DP02] has "a similar short-term incentive strategy" [OM07; p.14] by allowing the combination of *rationale* and *use case* specifications in a collaborative modeling environment.

According to Dutoit et al., "*DRL* appears to be more *prescriptive* than *QOC*, though less *prescriptive* than *IBIS*" [DMM+06; p.12]. Further, Dutoit et al. [DMM+06; p.13] express the supposition that *DRL* can be seen as a super-set of *QOC*, because all *QOC* features are somehow represented in *DRL*, though *DRL* also provides new features. In comparison with *IBIS*, *QOC* and *DRL* can be considered as more expressive as they provide more fine-grained models for argumentation about artifact features [DMM+06; p.13]. On the other hand, *QOC* and *DRL* are more limited to artifact features as topic, whereas *IBIS* addresses any design topic [DMM+06; p.13]. However, Dutoit et al. further point out that schemes of *IBIS*, *QOC* and *DRL* only have such few significant differences that the differences more appear as possible extension features for the other approaches. "This suggests that it might be both possible and useful to combine the three schemes" [DMM+06; p.14], in similar ways as it is proposed by Nguyen and Swatman [NS06] for *IBIS* and *QOC* [NS06].

REM "is ill-structured, complex and rather domain specific" [NS06; p.213] and can thus be "described as '*wicked*' in Rittel's terms" [NS06; p.213]. Correspondingly, several approaches exist to support argumentation and *rationale capture* during *REM* processes. Here to mention are *contribution structures* [GF94] that support modeling of stakeholders and their relationships, WinWin ([BEK+98], [BK06], [WinWin]) as a support for negotiating requirements with different stakeholders and REMAP providing an *IBIS*-like argumentation model integrated in an *REM-tool* environment. In [MR07], the authors develop a tool suite to connect different tools via a *traceability* framework with dedicated support for group decision and negotiation. The approaches mentioned here are also connected to *requirements traceability*. Correspondingly, they are also discussed in the following ch. II.10. For a deeper discussion on *rationale* as a means for

---

[162] See www.eclipse.org (Access: 2010/06).

REM processes, the author recommends reading [BCM+08; ch. 11], or Nguyen and Swatman [NS06] providing insights how *rationale* approaches may promote and support creativity in *REM* processes.

Pena-Mora and Vadhavkar [PV96] describe the *Design Recommendation and Intent Model* (*DRIM*) method with the tool *DRIMER*. *DRIM* is a *rationale* description language similar to *DRL* [DMM+06a; p.34] with the purpose to describe *design rationale* concerning the usage of *patterns* in a system. *DRIMER* allows documenting *rationale* concerning the design of software using *DRIM*. This *rationale* can then be used to extract *patterns* in a *pattern catalog* with included *DRIM* descriptions. *DRIMER* then allows searching in the *pattern catalog* where the *DRIM* model can help to find matching *patterns* for a specific design problem (see also [OM07; p.14], [BB06; p.275], [DMM+06a; p.34]).

Concerning tool support, "most tools supporting argumentation-based approaches are hypertext-based systems that connect all pieces of information through hyperlinks, e.g., gIBIS [CB88], SYBIL ([Le90b], [LL91], [LL96]), and the recently developed Compendium [Co06]" [OM07; p.14].

II.9.3.2 Approaches beyond Argumentation

Some *rationale* researches suggest that *rationale* is not just about argumentation. The following chapter will outline some alternatives.

A different possibility to structure *rationale* is using the structure of the artifact that *rationale* is created for [BCM+08; p.12]. Approaches of Reeves and Shipman [RS92] or Domeshek and Kolodner [DK96] use this strategy to combine *design models* of physical artifacts with textual descriptions of *rationale*. In software development, Schneider [Sch06] proposes a similar system to link textual *rationale* to source code. As it integrates into the Eclipse IDE, SEURAT [BB06] also can be seen in this category even though it is *argumentation schema-based*. SEURAT can also directly link to artifacts, showing that *argumentation schemas* and *artifact structure schemas* can be combined. The *rationale* support of the tool described in part III also allows combining both methods in order to take effects of their strengths. In their synopsis on the current state of *rationale* research, Burge et al. claim that integrating a rational tool into an artifact-centered decision-making is essential for being successful [BCM+08; p.245].

In Gruber and Russel's view [GR96a], *argumentative schemas* do not cover all *rationale* designers' needs, because the *schemas* prejudge which information is relevant and thus collected. They claim that no advanced collection can foresee all later information needs and thus a lot of later important *rationale*, which would have been important later on, is lost. Instead of forcing designers to elicit and document *rationale* in highly detailed models, it might be better to collect engineering data and models that can help to later deduce *rationale* according to the real information need (cf. also [BCM+08; p.13], [DMM+06a; p.15]). Gruber's and Russel's arguments inspired a set of other approaches:

- Myers et al. [MZG99] try to record *rationale* through automated collection of data in a *none-intrusive* manner (see also [Do05]). Their *Rationale Construction Framework* (*RCF*) tried to enhance a *Computer Aided Design* (*CAD*) tool with a monitoring module for recording the designer's behavior, then a *rationale* generation module tries to infer the *design history (the what)* and *design intent* (*the why*) (also cf. [BCM+08; p.56-57]).

- Haumer et al. [HPW+99] present an approach to extend *traceability* information with information on decisions by integrating videos or other media (see [TJH07; p.4]).

- Schneider [Sch06] outlines on the one side a prototypical tool for collaborative project risks assessment called CoRiskPT. The tool includes an attached chat system, where discussions on the single risks are recorded to be used as later *rationale*. A second tool called FOCUS, allows recording audio, video and computer screen information together and thus records meeting discussions. The tool integrates into the Eclipse-IDE in order to link the recorded *rationale* to source code.

Several approaches [MZG99], [HPW+99], [Sch06] combine Gruber and Russel's paradigm [GR96a] with the paradigm to orient on artifact structures. The *rationale* approach of the R2A tool (part III) can be seen in this tradition as it on the one side highly relies on artifact structure of *systems* and *software design*. Then again, the R2A tool – similar to Myers et al. [MZG99] – records the *history* of taken actions in combination with other information (e.g., author and timestamp of a change) about any item present in R2A via a configuration management component. This can be used by the users to infer *rationale* information in the sense of Russel and Gruber.

Lewis et al. [LRB96] describe the experience that design is not about solving one problem after another. Often design must solve a *suite of problems* at the same time. Correspondingly, Lewis et al. propose an approach allowing such suites to be defined and design alternatives to be assessed on how good they affect solving the problem suite (cf. also [DMM+06a; p.15], [BCM+08; p.12-13]).

Not all *rationale* is raised by designers; instead, other stakeholders are involved [BCM+08; p.156]. In the context of user interface design, Carroll and Rosson [CR92], [CR98] developed the *Scenario-Claims Analysis* approach where software system features are evaluated by possible, hypothetical software usage scenarios with focus on user goals. The approach mainly bases on three concepts:

- *System features,*
- *User goals* evaluating the *system features,*
- Evaluation results of user that can either be positive or negative in respect to their goals;

The approach includes no deeper argumentation on the evaluation results, thus it does not represent the decision making process or alternatives evaluation. A deeper discussion of *Scenario-Claims Analysis* can be found in [BCM+08; p.11-12, p.158-159, p.227] or [DMM+06a; p.15].

Other approaches use techniques of *artificial intelligence* such as *Case-Based Reasoning* (*CBR*) to develop *Case-Based Design Aids* (*CBDA*) for support and documentation of *rationale* on human decision processes. Here to mention is the pioneering work of Kolodner sparking tools such as ARCHIE CBDA [Ko93] and DesignMuse [DK96] for architectural design of buildings. Burge et al. provide an overview of current approaches using *artificial intelligence* [BCM+08; p.61-66].

II.9.3.3 Alternative Categorization

Ocampo and Münch [OM07; p.16] provide an alternative categorization with the following categories:

- *Support for debate, i.e. argumentation.* Approaches and tools of this category focus on collaboratively debating *wicked problems.* Important functionalities are *rationale capture, management* and *visualization. Rationale visualization* is typically achieved via graphical browsers connecting the *rationale* pieces. Through linking mechanism also information outside of the tool environment can be referenced.
- *Support for editing work and rationale documentation:* Within this category, approaches and tools provide *rationale* as important additional information, but their main features concentrate on the original tasks the users aim to perform. The front-end of the tools are specializing in the original tasks, where possibilities to *capture, visualize* and *retrieve rationale* to the current original task to perform are offered.
- *Support for integrated editing work and debate i.e. argumentation:* These approaches and tools address encountered problems in the *rationale* field concerning costs, *intrusiveness*, and benefit by seamless integration of their *rationale* support into other collaborative tasks. These tools concentrate on easy switching between tasks, on capturing their *rationale* and on visual integration of *rationale* information into the other tasks' information, where the tasks and their *rationale* are seen as a whole.

Using these categorizations, they provide a table segmenting *rationale* approaches into different categories and contrasting approaches[163] with their corresponding tool support mechanisms (table 9.1).

Table 9.1 Alternative categorization of rationale approaches [OM07; p.16]

Approach	Tool / Prototype Support
Category 1	
IBIS [KR70]	gIBIS [CB88], Compendium [Compendium]
Design Space Analysis (*QOC*) [MYB+91]	Compendium [Compendium]
Decision Representation Language (*DRL*) [Le90a]	SYBIL [Le90b]
Inquiry Cylce (Potts et al.) [PB88]	Active Hypertext Prototype [PT93]
Category 2	
Contribution Structures (Gotel and Finkelstein) [GF95]	Contribution Manager Prototype [GF95]
Como-Kit [DKM96]	Como-Kit System [DKM96]
Agile Process Mining [WRW+05]	ADEPT [RD98], CBRFlow [WWB04]
Category 3	
Hierarchy of Issues (*PHI*) [Mc78]	JANUS [FLM+96], PHIDIAS [MBO+92]
REMAP (Ramesh and Dhar) [RD92]	REMAP System [RD92]
SEURAT (Burge and Brown) [BB04], [BB06]	SEURAT System [BB04], [BB06]
Sysiphus (Dutoit and Paech) [DP02]	Sysiphus [DP02]
WinWin (Boehm et al.) [BEK+98]	WinWin Negotiation Tool [WinWin]
DRIMER [PV96]	SHARED-DRIMS [PV96]
C-ReCS (Klein) [Kl97]	C-ReCS-System [Kl97]

Ocampo and Münch [OM07] introduce an approach with a prototype tool called REMIS (Rationale-driven Evolution and Management Information Sys-

---

[163] Some of the referred approaches (Como-Kit, Agile Process Mining, C-ReCS) are not further mentioned, but taken over from the categorization in [OM07] as additional information for the reader interested in further research.

tem). The tool approach is an environment for supporting development of a *pro-cess model* (e.g., to develop an organization specific *process model* from the demands of the SPICE standard). The environment shall support *rationale* collection and usage for process designers during activities of designing or changing processes [OM07]. The gathered information can be stored together in a – what the authors call – "*process model* evolution repository" [OM07; p.12]. Ocampo and Münch do not provide a direct answer to what category their approach belongs to. The author tends to category 2, even though they seem to be concerned about costs and *intrusiveness* [OM07].

Concerning the tool approach introduced in part III, the author also tends to classify it as category 2 approach because the tool in the first instance concentrates on improving design processes and *traceability* between requirements and design. On the other side, the author acknowledges the importance of providing further information on taken decisions in design and tries to actively diminish potential barriers to that. Further the *decision model* is directly integrated into *traceability* information and design processes. From this perspective, the R2A tool approach also has tendencies to category 3.

II.9.4 Why Rationale Management Could not yet Succeed in Practice

A lot of effort has been put into identifying the opportunities the usage of *rationale* can provide. However, in the end, these opportunities will only become reality if the approaches for capturing and further usage of *rationale* can be successfully integrated into the conventional design processes in practice [BCM+08; p.155].

Currently, *rationale* approaches have not yet encountered a breakthrough in real-world design practice. Successful usage examples of *rationale* approaches in real-world settings exist, but these examples mostly resulted from special circumstances as, e.g., having a '*rationale* usage champion' or professional documenters at hand [CB96], [BCM+08; p.235]. In most projects, such fortunate conjunctures cannot be expected [DMM+06a; p.20]. Typically in these 'normal' projects, the documentation effort is left to the persons participating in the decision-making process (mostly the designers) with the effect that documenting *rationale* has been largely neglected [BCM+08; p.235].

Concerning the reasons, Horner and Atwood [HA06a] could identify four categories of barriers for successful *rationale* usage in practice:
- *Cognitive limitations,*
- *Capture limitations,*
- *Retrieval limitations,*
- *Usage limitations*;

In the following these barriers are discussed. Currently, the capture limitations are seen as the central obstacle to successful *rationale* approaches. Consequently, this topic will have a more detailed focus.

II.9.4.1 Cognitive Limitations

Humans only have a limited capacity to process and handle information at the same time [Mi56]. From this point, Simon developed the idea that the designer's rationality is bounded and not all alternatives can be considered, implying that designers find rather *satisfactory* than optimal solutions ([Si96], ch. I.6.2.1). As first implication, it is to state that *captured rationale* will necessarily be incomplete [HA06a; p.78]. Thus, any decision can impose unintended consequences [Te96]. *Rationale* may help to ensure extensive explorations of the design space in order to minimize detrimental risks of unintended consequences. However, any *rationale* will be incomplete.

A possible improvement might be to have systems where similar problems can be identified from other projects providing new insights into possibly overseen consequences or problems. Research on this topic is related to *rationale* as a *body of knowledge* (see [DMM+06; part IV]) and especially the *pattern* movement can be seen as the most successful area slightly pointing in this direction, but systems really addressing this issue might need to provide mechanisms for comparing projects with each other as well as such systems must have a *rationale* base as *body of knowledge* large enough for comparing problems.

A second problem encountered is that extensive explorations of the *design space* produce high amounts of additional documentation significantly leveraging project complexity. This problem is enforced by the fact that most systems are designed in team collaboration. Thereby, problems arise in integrating diverse perspectives, maintaining *conceptual integrity* [HA06a; p.79] (also cf. ch. I.6.2.1) and communicating concepts to all team members involved. Horner and Atwood explicitly mention that these situations require *rationale* systems "to help designers think about the right issues" [HA06a; p.79]. This has a close connection to what Moro [Mo04; p.310-330] discusses as *neuralgic points* of a project, where he proposes identifying, documenting and continuously tracking *neuralgic points*. Moro proposes the following approached for identification of *neuralgic points*:

- Risk assessments [Mo04; p.324] of the used technologies.
- Risk assessments of requirements [Mo04; p.326] where especially *NFRs* are in the focus.
- Deriving dominating discussion topics from the project diary or discussion protocols [Mo04; p.328].

Different designers often have different views on problems and their solutions. Concerning diverging views of designers about design alternatives, "reflecting on the *why* aspect of design can help to identify better solutions" [HA06a; p.79], but as long as solution ideas are still formulated, it might often be better to consider *what* other alternatives are possible rather than *why* each alternative might be appropriate [HA06a; p.79].

Organizations can tend to *group-think* [Ja72], i.e., in organizations with poor processes, often a poor solution is decided quickly, whereas the rest of the energy is spent on relatively insignificant issues. Thus, *rationale* approaches must find ways to spark discussions about the important issues in decision-making. *Rationale* tools, on the other side, should spark reflection in a way to encourage and enhance good design practices, but they should not expect or press for changing poor practices [HA06a; p.79]. This matches with Schneider's advice: "Encourage, but do not insist on further *rationale management*" [Sch06; p.100] meaning that *rationale capture* and *usage* itself cannot be prescribed but only be encouraged.

II.9.4.2   Rationale Capture Limitations as Central Challenge in Rationale Management

As Burge et al. emphasize, "the biggest challenge facing the use of *rationale* in real-world projects is the *rationale capture problem*" [BCM+08; p.55], because "it is extremely difficult to *capture rationale* in a real-world setting" [BCM+08; p.55]. Or, as Dutoit et al. put it: "In fact, so little …(*rationale*).. has been captured to date that has been relatively little opportunity to investigate the problem of …(*rationale*).. access in real-world settings" [DMM+06a; p.20]. Consequently, the author will in the following concentrate on the *capture problem* as the central obstacle to successful *RatMan* in practice [DMM+06a; p.20], [BCM+08; p.305]. In other words, even though its importance is widely acknowledged, *rationale* currently does not face a breakthrough, because people in project practice neglect to capture it.

Traditionally, the capture problem involved three aspects in one [BCM+08; p.262]:

- *Elicitation* of *rationale* from decision makers,
- *Structuring* the *elicited rationale* according to a given *schema*,
- *Recording* (documentation) of the *elicited rationale* in structured form;

   Some newer approaches try to cope with the capture problem by separating the aspects from each other. Especially structuring and documentation of *rationale* seem to impose high problems, as they are often highly labor intensive [BCM+08; p.262]. The following enumerates several reasons *rationale* research has collected as possible explanations for the capture problem and shows potential ideas how to ameliorate the problem in practice. In the author's opinion, two ideas seem to be very promising:

- *Automated capturing* of casual information arising as *by-product* of design processes (e.g., the change history of items) that allows inferring (resp. deducing) *rationale* later, when it is needed and, when the real information need is known (see, e.g., [GR96a]).
- Concentrate on light-weight *capturing* of *rationale* during decision processes and deferring structuring and detailed documentation (i.e. recording) to later phases.

   First to mention is *intrusiveness* in the sense that it leads to extensive work for *capturing rationale* (see ch. II.9.1.4). Most *rationale* approaches require structuring *elicited rationale* through a *schema* demanding significant extra work. These *rationale* representation structures can also be inappropriate in a way that they only inadequately consider information needs of the targeted design domain or that they simply do not cover all varying kinds *rationale* expresses itself. More comprehensive representations allow capturing more *rationale*, however, they also can significantly divert cognitive effort from the design process and – as described in the following paragraphs of this chapter – can intrude as detrimental effects into the designer's thinking. Flexible notations such as free text impose high difficulties for *retrieval* (e.g., indexing) and its later usefulness. Techniques such as automated recording of meeting conversations are less *intrusive*, but this information is then difficult for *retrieval* as well as they are also very likely to capture lower amounts of *rationale* (also cf. [DMM+06a; p.6, p.20], [HA06a; p.80-81]).

   Political and legal factors can make developers reluctant to documenting, what could later be seen as a mistake. Especially they might fear potential liability if a recorded decision may later become responsible for a catastrophic failure of the designed system [CB96], [BB06; p.274].

   Also, designers may want to make themselves irreplaceable by other designers or to justify their expert status, thus using information hiding strategies. This point also involves concerns about privacy and security playing a decisive role. Recorded *rationale* might touch competitive advantages of a company, which might not be opportune to be documented (e.g., if companies work together), [HA06a; p.82].

Design itself is an intense, time-consuming activity. As a result, an explanation can be that designers simply lack time and resources for additionally *eliciting* and *capturing rationale* as many of the *rationale* approaches demand [DMM+06a; p.20]. Often, many decisions are made in *informal* situations such as design meetings or during conversations at breaks, where *rationale capturing* is hardly possible [SA96].

Another explanation may be that the original designers are able to effectively reconstruct *rationale* from other past designs data than *rationale* recordings [DMM+06a; p.18]. Therefore, these designers may consider *capturing rationale* as not necessarily important enough to spend resources on.

This point has a close interaction with what is called Grudin's principle ([Gr87], [Gr88], [Gr96b]). In his "seminal work" [Sch06; p.97] about collaborative work and benefit, Grudin ([Gr87], [Gr88], [Gr96b]) discovered that collaborative systems tend to fail, if the persons performing the work are not the beneficiaries of this work. Or as Endres and Rombach put it [ER03; p.60]: "Group members usually prefer fairness and justice over altruistic appeals". The persons providing *rationale* on a decision (also referred to as *rationale bearers*) often also remember later the background of a decision. In this context, they do not have much benefit from documenting *rationale*. This is especially the case for *descriptive approaches* as they just document *rationale*, whereas *prescriptive approaches* may provide benefits to the *rationale bearers* due to their guidance on what to consider during decision making, but either *prescriptive approaches* did not succeed better in practice [DMM+06a; p.21]. Directly rewarding knowledge sharing is also difficult, because it would involve "creating tangible rewards for intangible ideas" [HA06a; p.81]. Other alternative ways around the problem are the ideas of Gruber and Russel [GR96a] to automatically collect data thus disburdening the designers or the idea of Schneider [Sch06] proposing to disburden the experienced *rationale bearers* of their communication/documentation work by deferring the documentation work to the inexperienced *rationale seekers*. Schneider's ideas are discussed in detail after the following paragraph.

Rationale approaches may also create a deeper lying *intrusiveness* onto design. Referring to Schön's *Theory of Reflective Practice* (ch. I.6.2.3), Fischer et al. [FLM+96] argue that the *rationale* approaches are disrupting designers' thinking when designers in their intuitive *knowing-in-action* phase are forced to rationally argue about their doing. In this case, designers would be forced to transform unconscious *tacit knowledge* [Po66] ("knowledge users employ without being conscious of its use" ([SM99a; p.341]) into conscious, rationally justifiable knowledge[164]. Such transformation processes are *intrusive* during *knowing-in-action* design phase and can lead to a degradation of design quality [FLM+96], [DMM+06a; p.21]. In summary, the following negative effects can be spotted [FLM+96], [DMM+06a; p.21]:

- One effect can be that intuitive knowledge is omitted in preference to conscious knowledge falsifying the results [FLM+96], [DMM+06a; p.21].

- Another effect can be that designers are interrupted in their *flow* of thinking [Cs90] endangering motivation and slowing down design work [Sch06; p.94]. "During the *flow* state, knowledge workers are typically not willing to switch tasks and take care for *rationale*" [HA06a; p.93].

- As an effect, "designers may not be willing to spend the energy to articulate their thoughts", when "designers focus should be on solving problems and not on capturing their decisions" [HA06a; p.80].

- Incompletely *captured rationale* can also impose negative consequences on the design process. Such a case can, e.g., occur during a design review, where the reviewers inference a wrong understanding of a design decision basing on incomplete *rationale* [HA06a; p.82].

As a more radical position, Shipman and Marshall argue that the *formality* itself imposed by much approaches imposes a big obstacle as people are seldom thinking in *formal* terms [SM99a]. According to them, *formalisms* impose the following fundamental problems:

- *Cognitive overhead*, as the users must learn the *formal* language. Even though practitioners use *formal* languages in electrical engineering and computer science, they "seldom use more generic *formal* languages, such as production rules or frames, for non-computational tasks" [SM99a; p.340], because "users often must engage in activities that might not ordinarily be part of their tasks: breaking information into chunks, characterizing content with a name or keywords, categorizing information, or specifying how pieces of information are related" [SM99a; p.334].

- *Tacit knowledge* [Po66] as discussed above.

- *Formality* enforces *premature structure* where people must commit themselves to structuring information often before they often know their later information need. This leads later to problems in again retrieving the now really needed information [SM99a; p.343].

---

[164] Haynes provides strong indications that design significantly involves *tacit knowledge*: "Analysis of full-text meeting transcripts suggests that design options sometimes emerge almost mystically from design discussions. It was sometimes difficult to see the chain of reasoning that led to a particular design option being proposed and then being either accepted or rejected" [Ha06b; p.62].

- Further, people simply "aren't always able to chunk intertwined ideas" [SM99a; p.338] and "people seldom agree on how information can be classified and related in this general scheme" [SM99a; p.338].
- The premature and *prescriptive* natures of *formal* approaches also increase probabilities for *group-think* [Ja72] effects (see chapter before).
- "There is always information that falls between the cracks, no matter how well thought out the *formal* representation is" [SM99a; p.338].
- Finally, different people often have different tasks. *Formal* structures must then represent all peoples' different views. In these cases, "the prospect of negotiating how information is encoded in a fixed representation is at best difficult" [SM99a; p.342][165].

However, in order to have any computer support, information must somehow be *formalized*; Shipman and Marshall also show ways how to ameliorate the problems imposed by *formalisms* [SM99a; p.344ff]:

- Any design for a system supporting intellectual knowledge work must identify the central tasks and their essentials needs for *formalization*.
- The cost and benefit trade-offs must be analyzed for any feature requiring further *formalization*.
- Incremental *formalization* strategies can rely on gradual *formalization* and restructuring of information, thus alleviating capture of information by delaying the overhead imposed by *formal* structuring to later times or other users. Nevertheless, incremental *formalization* techniques are only effective if they do not overwhelm the users with too many requests to infer structure [SM99a; p.345], (cf. also [SM99b], [HA06a; p.76]).
- Otherwise, more automated approaches should be considered. In these cases, structure must be automatically inferred through recognition heuristics for

---

[165] "An analogy can be drawn between collaborative *formalization* and writing a legal document for multiple parties who have different goals. The best one can hope for in either case is a result sufficiently vague that it can be interpreted in an acceptable way to all the participants; ambiguity and imprecision are used in a productive way" [SM99; p.342].

"textual, spatial[166], temporal, or other patterns" [SM99a; p.345]. As it tends to more falsely inferred structures, automatically inferred information should not be treated alike user inferred structure or at least be marked differently.

- Acceptance of *formalisms* can also be improved by training users to "learn and understand the expected use of the *formalisms* through training or through facilitation" [SM99a; p.346]. In some cases, also the developers of the *formalisms* may intervene temporarily to spark the learning process.

Summing up the difficulties described above, leads Schneider to formulate what he calls the *"rationale paradox"* [Sch06; p.93]: "When most *rationale* is created, chances to capture it are lowest" [Sch06; p.93].

The paradox describes the problem that *rationale* occurs when key decisions are made. During such decision-making processes (e.g., meetings), the participants are very attentive. Thus, the *rationale* is considered important and 'evident' when it is created, and nobody can really imagine how it ever may be forgotten; but it will be forgotten, because decisions base on earlier decisions and new decisions overlay the old *rationale*. Pressure for fast progresses in projects hinders documentation as well as extensive *rationale capture intrudes* detrimental effects in *knowing-in-action design* phases.

Due to all these problems, Schneider proposes the *"Rationale as a By-Product"* [Sch06; p.94] paradigm. The paradigm consists of two *goals* [Sch06; p.94]:

- *"Capture rationale* during specific tasks within software projects".
- "Be as little *intrusive* as possible to the *bearer* of the *rationale*".

As Beck [Be00b] could describe an approach by a list of interconnected principles [Sch06; p.95], Schneider also defined a set of principles to reach both goals described above [Sch06; p.95]:

1. "Focus on the project task in which *rationale* is surfacing".
2. *"Capture rationale* during that task (not as a separate activity)".
3. "Put as little extra burden as possible on the *bearer* of the *rationale* (but maybe on other people)".

---

[166] An example of spatial inferred structure is provided by the VIKI system [MSC94] a hypertext environment allowing the user to spatially arrange symbol representing textual parts. The system infers interconnections between the text parts according to their spatial arrangement to each other. This means, the system derives an interconnection between texts when the user has spatially arranged the texts nearby, and vice versa infers that texts are not connected, or opposing when they are spatially arranged far away from each other. In *SW design* activities a resembling grouping mechanism can be observed sometimes. Thus, e.g., the *three layer architectural pattern* also operates with spatial grouping in the form that items concerned with the topics persistence, data model, and user interface are spatially grouped together to three layers.

4. "Focus on recording during the original activity, defer indexing, structuring etc. to a follow-up activity carried out by others".
5. "Use a computer for recording and for capturing additional task-specific information for structuring".
6. "Analyze recordings, search for patterns".
7. "Encourage, but do not insist on further *rationale management*".

Principle 1 and 2 emphasize that *rationale* solutions should not be something stand-alone, but ask for *rationale* support being integrated into the really performed design task[167] without imposing significant *intrusion* (principle 3). Effort for the required structuring and other tedious tasks must be deferred from the *rationale bearers* towards the profiting *rationale seekers* (principle 4). Principles 5 and 6 demand for computer support and higher-level automation (if possible). Finally, principle 7 emphasizes that people cannot be forced but well encouraged, to record and use *rationale*.

In the author's view, Schneider's paradigm provides several good ideas on how the *rationale capture problem* can be ameliorated in a way that *rationale* approaches bring benefit for practice. Accordingly, R2A's *rationale* extension to *design traceability* developed by the author (cf. ch. III.19 to ch. III.21) tries to incorporate Schneider's principles, as far as possible.

Last but not least, an also possible explanation for the *rationale capture problem* could be that current *rationale* approaches just concentrate on collecting the wrong information. As introduced in ch. II.9.3.2, some approaches indicate that the design information to be captured may be more than the argumentation or designer's reasoning. Dutoit et al. point out "There are enough dissenters from the argumentative view of ...(*rationale*)... to leave room to doubt that we are capturing the right information. Nevertheless, there is little evidence to date that differences in information recorded have made any difference to the success of ...(*rationale*)...*capture* in practice" [DMM+06a; p.22].

In this category also the phenomenon can be accounted that *rationale* may also be communicated through omission [HA06a; p.81]. As an example, a project manager could ask the design team whether somebody has experience with a certain technology. In such a situation project members usually communicate their inexperience by not responding. Similar situations occur when people stay tacit disagreeing with a certain decision, but they do not want to appear confrontational.

At the end, it must also be mentioned that Burge et al. express that software engineering approaches especially for *safety-related* applications are changing

---

[167] Dutoit et al. emphasize that *rationale* approaches have been most successful if they have been adapted to a specific activity, or specific goals [DMM+06a; p.18].

toward favoring *rationale capture*. Through process standards such as SPICE or CMMI, demands for rigorous definition, monitoring and adaption of the software development process are induced demanding structured and reproducible decision processes. However, Burge et al. are not sure whether these changes are enough to spark the final breakthrough for the *rationale capture problem* [BCM+08; p.262-263].

II.9.4.3 Retrieval Limitations

Between initial *rationale bearers* and later *rationale seekers* different notions of *relevance* may exist. According to Wilson [Wi73], relevance is determined by the situational context and concerns of the information seeker independent from truth [Wi73; p.462]. Thus, besides the temporal gap between the *rationale bearers* and *seekers*, a situational gap of context and concerns may exist with detrimental effects on the usefulness of recorded *rationale* [HA06a; p.83]. The ideas of Gruber and Russel [GR96a] can also be seen as actively addressing the relevance problem.

Besides relevance, *retrieval* imposes technological needs such as the need for indexing, playing a decisive role. Efficient *rationale retrieval* techniques might require a certain *formalization* of *rationale* information. As discussed in ch. II.9.1.4, *rationale formalization* imposes significant *intrusiveness* and burden onto the documenter. An alternative solution is the idea to shift the *formalization* burden to the *rationale* beneficiaries [Gr96b], [Sch06], but this works only if the beneficiaries experience the burden as not too strenuous. Otherwise, the whole endeavor may be jeopardized [HA06a; p.84]. Further, another alternative is to use the artifact structure as *formal* structure for *rationale retrieval* (see ch. II.9.3.2). This is also what the *decision models* in this thesis (see ch. III.20 and ch. III.21) use.

II.9.4.4 Usage Limitations

Following Rittel's assumption about *wickedness* of problems, most design problems have a certain *uniqueness*. Thus, *rationale* about a problem has only limited value for other problems. It can be helpful to evaluate how *rationale* is connected with a problem in order to support solving future problems, but design is often highly interrelated. Thus, *rationale* can weave connections between several problems that can even build an area of conflict. As a further type of connection, taken decisions impose new consequences on other problems, where recorded *ra-*

tionale about the decision may also include a description of these consequences, thus also being *rationale* for the other problems. Accordingly, Horner and Atwood emphasize that designers must consider the "holistic affects" of problems, their *rationale* and solutions [HA06a; p.84]. Due to the complex nature of design, measuring effectiveness of *rationale* approaches proves to be extremely difficult. One problem faced here is that recording *rationale* and its further usage may involve a significant temporal gap. Thus, designers recording or documenting *rationale* may not immediately be able to know what information will later prove to be useful and what not [HA06a; p.85].

II.9.4.5 Synopsis of Rationale Limitations Concerning Alternative Design Theories

Table 9.2 Relation to design theories and rationale in design according to [HA06a; p.77]

Design Theory	Support	Barriers
Simon – Symbolic information processing (ch. I.6.2.1)	*Rationale* can help to focus cognitive energy and provides opportunities to view the considerations during design to reviewers or other developers.	Additional information increases the complexity of a design problem. Designers may also be reluctant to *capture rationale*, because the decision may be criticized in later phases by other persons having more information at hand than the initial designers. These persons may analyze the taken decisions with the new information and would probably come to a different view on the problem.
Rittel – *Wicked problems* (ch. I.6.2.2)	*Rationale* supports structured discussions and integrates different peoples' perspectives.	The *wicked* nature of design problems limits the possibilities of using the *rationale* at a different time or a different project.
Schön – Situated action (ch. I.6.2.3)	*Rationale* can support designers in reflecting on decisions during the *reflection-in-action* phase and show the decision influences on later encountered problems. Furthermore, incremental *formalization*	Using *rationale* as basis for identifying solutions could result in less reflection in the design process through distracting cognitive resources away from solution finding. *Intrusive rationale capture* methods (cf. ch. II.9.1.4) can influence the designers' reflection capabilities in disadvantageous ways or even hinder the de-

	could support later *reflection-in-action* and communication	signers in finding good solutions.
Alexander Patterns (ch. I.6.2.4)	– *Rationale* provides mechanisms to understand the problem context. Especially the forces may be better analyzed that help to find the best fitting *pattern*.	Because of the rapid advances in software design, few stable *design patterns* may exist (see Simon's concept of *stable intermediate forms*).

In ch. I.6, the author has outlined a few fundamental design theoretic views on what design and its processes are about. In the context of *design rationale*, Horner and Atwood [HA06a; p.77] have collected an overview of the potential support and barriers of *rationale* management enlisted in table 9.2.

II.9.5   The Role of Rationale in System and Software Design

The ultimate goal in documenting architectural decisions is to alleviate a major problem in the field: architectural knowledge vaporization.
[HAZ07; p.39]

Design can be seen "as a sequence of decisions" [BCN+06; p.258] and therefore the importance of decisions in design has been widely acknowledged. In the view of Booch [Bo94; p.63, p.167], design decisions get apparent through the *modeling language* used. However, newer research rather sees that decisions cannot be explicitly derived from the *design models* and merely exists as *tacit knowledge* [HAZ07; p.39].

Besides attempts to recover assumptions and *rationale* from design artifacts [RLV06], capturing decisions' *rationale* in the *system* and *SW architecture* has received high attention in recent research (cf. [CBB+03], [BCK03], [PBG04], [Ha06], [BCN+06], [HAZ07], [TA05], [TJH07], [AKL+07a], [AKL+07b], [LK-08], [ALK09]), because a growing recognition exists that decisions may be "the fundamental construct in engineering design" [WC01; p.1], [Kr04; p.54]. *Architectural decisions* are made early and have a far reaching scope of influence [BCN+06; p.256]. Additionally, "much of design work is done through evolutionary redesign, thus long-term collaboration is essential" [DMM+06a; p.86], because the implications of decisions usually cannot be overseen in their entirety during taking the decision, which make later adaptions and reassessments of the decision necessary [BCN+06; p.258].

Due to these facts, also process standards such as *SPICE* (ch. I.7) acknowledge that important decisions about *system* and *SW architecture* must be carefully explored and documented [HDH+06; p.101]. In *CMMI*, even an explicit *Decision Analysis and Resolution* (*DAR*) process area has been defined [BCM+08; p.262] "to evaluate 'high risk' decisions" [BCM+08; p.263].

A main purpose of *system* and *SW architectures* is to find handling strategies for *NFRs* [BCK03; p.72f], [PBG04; p.72], (see also ch. I.5.1). Correspondingly, Chung et al. [CNY+00] developed a *NFR framework* with an approach where *NFRs* explicitly drive the software design process that creates the design and its *rationale*. Tradeoffs and synergies of *NFRs* can be modeled in a graph. The graph can then be used to qualitatively propagate the *impact* of these decisions into *design models* (see also [BB06; p.275]).

In architectural practice, decision documentation is considered in the context of balancing concurring and conflicting factors through making compromises, where decisions about the foundation of technical solutions must be taken in insecure situations due to lacking fundamental information [HS06; p.53]. Approaches and standards (e.g., IEEE 1471 [IEEE1471]) demand to include these decisions in *architecture documentation*. As dedicated practice-oriented tooling is usually missing [BCN+06; p.265], several available approaches provide templates for structured decision documentation using text authoring or spreadsheet applications ([BCK03], [BCN+06], [Bo00b], [CBB+03], [HNS00], [HS06], [PBG04], [TA05]).

Posch et al. [PBG04; p.79] have analyzed the views of Bass, Clements et al. [CBB+03], [BCK03], Bosch [Bo00b] and Hofmeister et al. [HNS00]. As a consequence, they have derived an approach for systematically assessing influence factors[168] for an *architecture* beforehand in order to identify and document the most important influence factors and the strategies how to address them in concert with the other influence factors. Ch. III.20.4 shows how an adaption of this *influence factors assessment* can be integrated in the R2A tool approach proposed here (part III) in order to improve *traceability*, derivation of consequences, *impact analysis*, and *consistent change implementation*.

In [BCN+06], Bass and Clements propose to extend their decision documentation template by a causal graph allowing decisions to be ordered in a temporal,

---

[168] *NFRs* as addressed by Chung et al. [CNY+00] are here considered as one important type of influence factor, but also other influence factors exist, such as effects on stakeholders, available resources, costs, strategic considerations beyond the individual project etc..

causal dimension. Decisions are displayed as nodes linked together according to their causal dependencies. Lee and Kruchten [LK08] show different forms of possible decision visualization. Besides the temporal, causal dimension they call *Decision Chronology Visualization*, they identified the following possible views:

- *Tabular listing* enlists decisions in a table to provide a better overview of the decisions.
- *Decision structure visualization* shows the structure of a decision to increase the decision's understanding.
- *Decision impact visualization* makes the influences of decisions on design transparent.

Ch. III.20.4 also shows that most of these views are fulfilled by the tool described in part III.

In [Eb08; p.332], Ebert argues that software development follows the *pareto principle* [Pa1897]. In his conclusion, 20% of the implemented functionality cause high usage value, high potentials for failures and resource consumption. As a consequence, he recommends marking parts of the application in order to indicate high complexity or shape problematic constellations as early as possible (he recommends to start within the analysis phase) to ease further planning. Such a marking often has influence on very important decisions (in design such aspects are often important) and thus provide important *rationale*. A similar case is the proposal of Knethen to include an attribute characterizing the change probability [Kn01b; p.40].

Tang et al. [TJH07] show how UML-based design can be extended via an UML-profile for capturing decisions. Decision elements (class elements having the stereotype <<decision>>) can be linked to any other element present in a UML model. This offers the opportunity that any UML environment offering support for UML-profiles can be easily extended with a decision documentation mechanism, where decision information can be integrated seamlessly into a UML *design model*. On the other side, decisions modeled in usual design diagrams rise complexity of the diagrams, causing clutter. If the decisions are modeled in extra diagrams (as different *views*), they raise the amount of present diagrams in the modeling repository, thus rising complexity and clutter in the repository. Another possibility is not to model the decisions, but to use the UML's *meta-model* as structure only. In this case, other mechanisms must be found how decision information is linked to related elements and how they are visualized. Thus, the author prefers to avoid raising complexity of modeling languages by including decision models but rather prefers to provide augmented information that can be faded out on demand as it is provided by the tool in part III.

Jansen and Bosch [JB05] see decisions mainly as a means to select a solution from several possible solutions and to deal with the tradeoffs of a solution.

Once a decision is taken, its results are the major driver for architectural modifications.

To capture *architectural decision* information, they propose a *conceptual decision model* containing the following elements:

- *Design rules* describe general rules on how parts of a design (e.g., design elements) must be designed in order to realize a sustainable solution. Any potential solution can have one or several *design rules*.

- *Design constraints* "define limitations or constraints on the further design of one or more architectural entities" [JB05; p.4]. These constraints must be obeyed in order to ensure that the potential solution can solve its addressed problem.

- *Pros* describe the benefit(s) and *impacts* on requirements that can be expected if the solution is employed.

- *Cons* describe the drawbacks on the solution, because the negative effects are equally important as positive.

- *Consequences* elements describe the expected consequences of the decision's solution on the *architecture* and thus provide extra *rationale* behind the pros and cons of the selected solution.

For translating the conceptual decision model into practice, Jansen and Bosch propose an *architecture modeling* environment called "Archium", where the conceptual decision model is integrated into a *meta-model* for *architecture modeling*. The environment can contain a log (stack) of possible solutions, where the individual decisions can be mapped on to deal with the tradeoffs. The conceptual decision model of Jansen and Bosch should be fully compatible to the decision model introduced in ch. III.20.

Pointing in a similar direction to [JB05], Kruchten [Kr04] describes a general ontology of architectural design decisions. He identifies three kinds of decisions, eight fundamental properties a decision can be characterized by, eleven different relationship types a decision can have to *architecture* and how decisions may have connections to other artifacts. The question whether the approach described here matches with this general ontology is left open in this research as well as discussions about how *rationale* and decision approaches are generally connected to a general view on architectural knowledge as, e.g., discussed by Avgeriou et al. [AKL+07a], [AKL+07b], [ALK09].

Another research field also concerned about decision making in design processes are *decision trees*[169] known from *operations research*. Their focus lies not directly on documenting a decision process but on providing support for optimiz-

---

[169] At http://www.smartdxl.com/content/?page_id=144 (Access 2009/10), an implementation of decision tree modeling in IBM Rational DOORS DXL is provided.

ing the decision outcome. Different decision alternatives with their consequences can be modeled in a tree in combination with probabilities about the achievable results. A problem, however, is that decision trees require comprehensive knowledge about the concrete decision situation (e.g., all consequences and their probabilities), limiting their use to rather very *tame problems*. Noppen et al. [NBA08] acknowledge this problem and introduce a decision process for designer situations with imperfect decision situations by combining requirements and design issues with a *decision tree* model, allowing fuzzy probabilistic estimations of probabilities. Thus, Noppen et al. hope to support decision optimization. In this way, *decision trees* could also be chosen as a *schema* or an additional means for documenting *rationale*.

As this chapter has shown, manifold approaches for supporting *rationale documentation* in *systems* and *software design* exist. The tool approach introduced in part III uses an approach to integrate *rationale* and *requirement traceability* approaches together in order to improve design processes in system and software design (cf. ch. III.19, III.20 and III.21).

II.10 Requirements Traceability

Despite the importance of traceability, there is surprisingly little written about it.
[KS98]

After ch. I.5.7 has given a quick overview of *traceability* to support an initial understanding for describing the other chapters of part I, this chapter will now go into detail.

II.10.1 Overview

Rupp describes the meaning of *traceability* as the "comprehensible documentation of requirements, decisions and their interdependencies to all produced information (resp. artifacts) from project start to project end" [RS02; p.407 (*)].
Pinheiro points out two further considerable points about *traceability* [Pi04; p.92]:
- *Traceability* means "the ability to capture the traces we want to follow".
- "*Traces* should be viewed as naturally produced occurrences".

Point one means that most likely not all traces of requirements may be captured and (resp. or) followed due to the high number of possible traces. Therefore, at a certain point a decision must be taken which traces are followed.

The idea about the second point indicates that the traces are not artificially made up by something or someone but "are naturally produced as a result of activities, actions, decisions and events happening during software development" [Pi00; p.2]. This idea is near to the view of Lindvall who sees *traceability* as the means to bridge consistency gaps (see ch. II.10.2).

This leads to the definition provided by Pinheiro [Pi04; p.93]: "*Requirements traceability* refers to the ability to define, capture, and follow the traces left by requirements on other elements of the software development environment and the traces left by those elements on requirements".

Following this definition, any tracing model contains three major aspects [Pi00; p.3f]:
- *Trace definition*: As not all possible traces can be maintained, the traces to maintain should be defined beforehand.
- *Trace production*: Defined traces must be recorded somehow. As the following ch. II.10.2 shows, traces are a means to cross consistency gaps between artifacts. Correspondingly, most traces cannot be recorded automatically and must therefore be produced manually. *Trace production* is especially essential to consider as it may be *intrusive* to the other development activities (cf. II.10.5). In the author's opinion, also maintenance of already captured traces is equally essential as otherwise artifacts and involved traces continuously degrade.
- *Trace extraction*: In order to be useful, once recorded traces must be extracted. Trace extraction depends *on trace definition* and *trace production* in the sense that only once produced traces can be extracted.

Pinheiro also points out that "the software development environment involves not only the technical, but also the social aspects of software development" as "people, policies, decisions, and even less tangible things like goals and concepts" [Pi04; p.93].

II.10.2 Traceability and Consistency Gaps between Artifacts

Between artifacts (or respectively models) of different development processes emerging from structural interruptions[170] – semantic gaps ([Li94], [Kn01b; p.45], [Eb05; p.138f]) – endanger a project's consistency and thus the common understanding of its stakeholders. *Traceability* relations between and within artifacts help to diminish occurring semantic gaps[171]. In development projects without *traceability*, these gaps are mentally bridged by the minds of the developers leading to the known problems when developers leave projects or new team members are added. Recording and retrieving *traceability* information shall support the developers in mentally bridging those gaps[172]. As an example for this mental help, the *traceability* heuristic exists that each requirement must have at least one reference to the design (and resp. or code), otherwise the requirement is regarded as 'not considered' in the design.

Correspondingly, Finkelstein [Fi91] argues here that the *traceability* problems arise from the *informality* of most system development processes. According to Lindvall [Li94; p.15], applying *formal* methods can also help to diminish the semantic gaps to an extent making *traceability* irrelevant. In the best case, the usage of *formal* specification languages with automated code generation – also called model driven development – would allow different models of different abstraction levels and different views to be seamlessly connected to each other [Li94; p.15] (also cf. [Kn01b; p.45]). On the other hand, Sommerville emphasizes that *formal* methods are seldom used in practice, because the entry barriers are high [So07]. As ch. II.9.4.2 shows in reference to Shipman and Marshall [SM99a], the usage of *formal* methods can also involve fundamental drawbacks. As an example, *formal* approaches are accompanied by the dangers that *informal*

---

[170] Examples for these inconsistencies are different levels of abstraction or different viewpoints within an abstraction.

[171] As discussed in ch. II.10.6, besides dedicated *traceability* relationships several other kinds of relationships (e.g., „depend on", part of", „refine") exist in a design being usually modeled in a *design model*. Several *traceability* methods also include these relationships for *impact analysis* (ch. II.10.3), but can also lead to unwanted overestimation of the *impact* (so called *requirements fan-out effect* [Al03]; cf. ch.II.10.6.21 for a detailed description).

[172] *Traceability* "focuses on how to trace between models to understand the system structure and to understand the implications of a certain requirement" [Li94; p.20].

information is reduced[173] to fit a *formal* structure falsifying the information and spoiling the *traceability* needs [Pi04; p.101].

Pinheiro further points out that "*informality* is needed to deal with the fundamentally unstructured way in which information is gathered and used. ... Therefore, what should be made traceable is in many cases inherently *informal*, e.g., natural language statements, interview's transcripts, and images" [Pi04; p.101] (also cf. [Go96], [Pi00]). On the other hand, a certain *formality* is needed, when tracing approaches shall be automated [Pi04; p.100].

Discussing *traceability* experiences in development practice, Ebert [Eb05; p.138 f] emphasizes that the transitions from requirements and *analysis models* (*AM*) to solutions involve a structural break, which is especially problematic. Requirements and *AMs* (ch. I.5.4) can have a completely different character than the structure of the design solutions due to different languages used. A possibility to avoid the gap is using languages that can integrate all processes from *requirements specification* to analysis, design and implementation in one language. Usually, these languages must support strong restrictions on its problem focus to further use the generated models as far reaching and consistent as possible. As a consequence, Ebert here refers to domain specific languages as a solution to this problem [Eb05; p.139]. Other similar but less ambitious attempts can be seen in UML, where *analysis* and *design modeling* are supported through a uniform language and in such a way minimize the semantic gaps between both worlds[174] [Kn01b; p.45]. With the new SysML standard [SYSML], UML is extended to promote a unified language for *systems analysis, systems design, software analysis* and *design*.

---

[173] A good example is provided by [Ja08; p.6]: "In a *non-formal* world there are several obstacles to reliability in *formal* reasoning. To make our reasoning useful we must begin by establishing a correspondence between the *formal* terms we intend to use and the physical phenomena they denote. Here there is an immediate difficulty. In a system to control road traffic, we may decide to reason about pedestrians and their use of the controlled crossings provided for them: for example, to base some design decisions on the maximum and minimum time taken to cross the road. But, what, exactly is a 'pedestrian'? A child in a pedal car? A cyclist pushing a bicycle with an attached trailer? A user of a motorized invalid carriage? Whatever alphabet of *formal* terms – for example, of predicates, events, and entities – we choose, there will be some hard cases in the problem world for which we cannot easily decide whether or not they are properly denoted by a particular *formal* term".

[174] An exactly opposite opinion is expressed by Hatley et al. [HHP03; p.252]. In their opinion, object-oriented methods (such as UML) have the weakness that they indissolubly mix up requirements and design.

UML can also be used for model-driven development. "Model-driven design holds the promise of improving application development significantly by capturing design steps in explicit model transformations" [AIE07]. Through this way, model transformations can lead to the generation of source code and thus consistency can reach to source code. In the context of embedded systems, examples of *formal* specification languages can be seen in [PS05; p.120]. However, most up to date existing languages are very limited, need a very proper application and often concentrate on partial aspects [Sa05; p.276ff]. In the context of the automotive domain, not UML-tools, but the tools Matlab Simulink resp. Stateflow and ETAS ASCET are the most heavily used tools concerning model driven development with automated code generation (also cf. ch. I.6.6.1), but these techniques are fully comparable in the context of the topic addressed here.

Additionally, the usage of model driven development imposes a new problem concerning consistency and *traceability* [AIE07]: In most cases, these transformations do not only depend on the model to be transformed, but the transformation process is steered by parameter settings and transformation procedures. This means, requirements can also be implemented by setting parameters or choosing specific model transformation procedures over other procedures. Ergo, consistency not only depends on the models but also by these parameter choices. In these cases these elements should also underlie *traceability* needs [AIE07].

Additionally, Wieringa [Wi98] shows that design principles such as hierarchical decomposition are used according to different criteria at different levels of design. Wieringa [Wi98; p.6] concludes that "a seamless transition between different levels, as is claimed by many object-oriented methodologists" should not be expected, and because isomorphic design structures cannot be expected at the different levels, explicit manual links to maintain *traceability* across levels are necessary.

Consequently, *formal* methods without *semantic gaps* between processes are not very likely (yet) to replace today's often coarse, *informal* and incomplete processes and artifacts. Therefore, *traceability* is a means to cope with problems arising from the imperfect world of development and a *traceability* to design solution must support a solution for bridging these inhomogeneous processes and artifacts.

In the view of Chang and Lu [CL09], the gap problem exists, because current design approaches only consider the abstraction hierarchies dimension as criterion for decomposition. In this way, functional dependencies (e.g., between two requirements) are created by accident. Chang and Lu [CL09] suggest to use a new design paradigm developed by Suh [Su01] called „*axiomatic design*". In this paradigm, a *domain dimension* is introduced as second dimension. The paradigm origins from physical engineering and Chang and Lu [CL09] try to transfer it to

SE design theory. In their case study, Chang and Lu come to the conclusion that through *axiomatic design* "the reasoning of each step of the design process and the mapping through the requirements, abstractions, realizations and technological choices are clearly described" [CL09; p.17]. Currently, the described *axiomatic design* paradigm seems to be at an early stage of research, at which its real value for practice has not yet come clear. Even though the examples provided in [CL09] indicate that *axiomatic design* may have some strength, the author preserves certain doubts that *axiomatic design* can close the semantic gap.

At the end, manual *traceability* and designers' minds may prove as the only really dependable means for bridging the gap.

II.10.3 Impact Analysis and Traceability

The ability to perform correct *impact analysis* of changes is often referred to as the most important motivation for establishing *requirements traceability*. Traditionally, as Jönsson and Lindvall point out [JL05], the idea about *requirements traceability* originates from the *impact analysis* research domain being one of several techniques to support *impact analysis*. *"Impact analysis (IA)* is the activity of identifying what to modify to accomplish a change, or of identifying the potential consequences of a change" [AB93; p.292].

Research on *IA* traditionally origins[175] from research about software maintenance. Thus, most research is only loosely connected with software development itself. Over time, *requirements traceability* has become an issue of *REM* during normal development. Consequently, Jönsson and Lindvall argue that, as *requirements traceability* more and more became an issue of requirement engineering and thus of the development processes itself, *IA* should be seen analogously.

However, the topic *IA* often is only mentioned as one way to use *traceability* information. Interpreting Jönsson and Lindvall, the author believes that two historically based misconceptions may exist:

- *IA*s have already been performed by developers long time before the name existed, since "the need ... to determine what to change in order to implement requirement changes has always been present" [JL05; p.122]. However, for the original developers knowing their code, assessing the code change is less difficult than for others. Software maintenance is often performed by other often less skilled and experienced people than the original developers [Kn01b; p.2]. Accordingly, *IA*s were seen as a more urgent issue for software maintenance, neglecting its usefulness and *informal* (unconscious) usage in

---

[175] [Ha72] is often referred to as the first paper on *impact analysis* [JL05; p.122-123].

normal development processes. As the systems to develop grow, the needed documentation grows and the rates of changes grow, also the need for conscious *IA* support grows.

- *Requirements traceability* may have originated as a sub part strategy of *IA*. However, the *requirements traceability* concept proved its usefulness in scopes beyond *IA* (see ch. I.5.7.3). Thus, the independence is reasonable. However, the topic 'gains versus costs' of *traceability* cannot be discussed without considering the needs of *IAs*. The author often has the feeling that *traceability* is established for the sake of conforming to the demands of some process standard, but the recorded *traceability* information is seldom really considered when practitioners think about changes. They rather prefer their *informal* methods. Correspondingly, the problem of how to get real gains out of *traceability* should be sharply considered. In this context, effective *IA* is a central issue.

In the following the author will outline the *IA* concept. It shall furthermore be mentioned that the author does not see *traceability* based *IA* as a core problem. Valuable *IAs* depend on the correctness and usefulness of the analyzed information. The value of *traceability* based *IA* depends on the accurateness and a sufficient level of detail of the *traceability* information. However, capturing this high quality *traceability* information and maintaining its high quality in an efficient way, may be the more important problem (see ch. II.10.5). Otherwise, values gained by *traceability* may not outweigh the costs.

Two types of *IAs* are distinguished ([BA96], [Kn01b; p.3], [JL05]):

1. *Dependency analysis*: extracts detailed dependency relations between program entities from source code (e.g., the usage of a variable).
2. *Traceability analysis*: analyzes relationships that "have been identified during development among all types of" artifacts [JL05; p.119].

This distinction seems to be a bit artificial. Since *dependency analysis* can also be seen as a special subset of *traceability analysis*. However, *dependency analysis* is probably the most employed type of *traceability analysis* since it is possibly used by any programmer who needs to employ a change.

Jönsson and Lindvall argue that the difference consists in the level of detail, and in fact Knethen provides in [Kn01b; p.42-43] a more evident distinction oriented on the level of abstraction (a detailed description of this can be found in chapter II.10.4.2.2):

- *Dependency analysis* of source code,
- *Design description techniques,*
- *Requirements traceability tools;*

In the author's opinion, these kinds of distinctions are some kind of historical due to formerly independent areas of research. Currently, these areas and their understanding grow together to build a more complete view (see ch. I.7), where all these dependencies are seen as a subset of *traceability*.

In the experience of Jönsson and Lindvall [JL05; p.118], *IA* "is an integral part of every phase in software development". In some sense, *IA* might have been performed long time before the term was known and it may have been performed in a very uncontrolled and inefficient way [JL05; p.122], since the need for SW practitioners to determine the effects of a change may have been present as long as the need for change has existed.

Bohner and Arnold [BA96] further describe (see also [JL05; p.119]) different sets of *impact* (in the following called *impact sets* (*IS*)):

- The *system set* is the set of all items in the project. This set is the super set of all other sets.
- The *starting impact set* (*SIS*): represents the item initially considered as affected. This is the input for an *IA*, whereat the *SIS* is the starting point to identify further connected items also *impacted*.
- The *estimated impact set* (*EIS*) represents the items estimated to be affected when the *IA* is finished.
- The *actual impact set* (*AIS*) consists of the items really affected once the change has been implemented. "In the best case scenario, *EIS* and *AIS* are exactly the same, meaning the estimation was perfect" ([JL05; p.119]).

As described in ch. I.7.2.7, the *IA* concept is part of a *change management process*[176] and required by process standards such as *SPICE*. Knethen [Kn01b; p.36] describes a generic *IA* process orienting on the process description of Bohner and Arnold [BA96]. *IA* is important in two phases of the change management process:

- When a change is requested, the *IA* helps to identify all effects as a support for making a decision whether to apply or not to apply a change. In this phase the changes are predicted as *EIS*.
- Once the decision has been taken to apply the change, the *IA* results can be used to orient oneself on them for consistent implementation of the change. The actual change determines *AIS*. The *AIS* can then be used to compare the *EIS* in order to improve later *impact estimation*. Knethen [Kn01b; p.53-55] indicates how *impact* effectiveness, completeness, correctness, and efficiency can be assessed.

An *IA* should address the issues required effort, time, money and available resources [JL05; p.122]. Leffingwell and Widrig enlist the following aspects that must be especially considered in a change assessment [LW99; p.379]:

---

[176] Schienmann [Sch02; p.111-113] also provides a good description for a *change management process*.

- "The *impact* of the change on the cost and functionality of the system",
- *Impact* on external stakeholders not well represented in the project (e.g., other project contractors, component suppliers etc.),
- The potentials to destabilize the system;

Besides the *impact sets*, two other kinds of information can help to predict a change's *impact* [JL05; p.119]:

- The dependencies between affected items;
- Knowledge about the propagation of the changes between the affected items;

The first point clearly is an issue of *traceability*, the second is "often expressed in terms of rules or algorithms" [JL05; p.120]. If the second point is neglected, the – what Versteegen et al. [VSH01; p.83]call – *dominoes effect* can occur: At first, a requested change seemed to be rather harmless, but during implementation new effects on other project parts are incessantly identified leading to design erosion and instabilities of the developed system.

Changes are usually distinguished by *primary* and *secondary change* [JL05; p.120]. *Primary change* also called *direct impact* refers to the items (artifacts) directly identified by the *change impact assessment*. *Secondary change* also called *indirect impact* expresses in two effects [JL05; p.120]:

1. "*Side effects* are unintended behavior resulting from the modifications needed to implement the change. *Side effects* affect the stability and function of the system and must be avoided" [JL05; p.120].
2. *Ripple effects* are effects occurring when small changes are employed to a system, imposing affects to many other parts of the system [AB93; p.292]. "*Ripple effects* cannot be avoided, since they are the consequence of the system's structure and implementation. They must, however, be identified and accounted for when the change is implemented"[JL05; p.120]. If *ripple effects* are not effectively addressed, the *dominoes effect* mentioned above [VSH01; p.83] can be the consequence.

To identify possible *impacts*, several strategies for *IA*s exist [JL05; p.124-130]:

- *Automatable strategies or techniques* "usually rely on algorithmic methods to identify change propagation and *indirect impacts*" [JL05; p.125]. However, the prerequisite of any automated technique are highly structured (e.g., *formal* specifications [JL05; p.125]. The following possible strategies exist:
  - *Traceability*, as discussed in this chapter.
  - Other *dependency analysis* techniques such as extracting dependencies from source code (see [Kn01b; p.40] for an overview) or *design models* (e.g., [BLO+06]).
  - *Program slicing* (e.g., [We79], [We84], [GL91]) divides the source code in the *decomposition slice* containing the change's location, and a *complementary slice*. At first, the *decomposition slice*'s scope is as narrow as

possible. Then, when further dependencies are identified, the scope of the *decomposition slice* is widened. Programmers use slicing implicitly during debugging [We82]. *Program slicing* can orient itself on analyzing static code information (so called *static program slicing*) or also try to find out dynamic relationships within code (so called *dynamic program slicing* [KR98]). Between those two extremes also hybrid methods are possible as *conditioned slicing* [GB08]. Also methods for architectural slicing exist [Zh98].

* *Manual strategies* involve consulting available project documentation, or interviewing knowledgeable developers. Burge et al. [BCM+08; p.120f] show how information collected through *RatMan* approaches can be connected to improve *IAs*.

"The complexity of the *change management process* makes it necessary to use some sort of tool support" [JL05; p.137]. According to Jäälinoja's opinion, *IAs* in practice are typically performed manually due to weak tool support [Ja04; p.37]. Automating *IA* is typically difficult, "because it is mainly based on human experience" [JL05; p.120] and "human analysis is still required to interpret the nature of the *impact* and assess its significance" [Kn01b; p.53].

Wiegers [Wi05; p.322-323] emphasizes that *IA* quality can be significantly improved by using checklists and defined procedures to discover possible implications. The *IA* results must be typically reported from a developer to a *CCB*. A standard reporting template can ensure that the *CCB* receives and easily recognizes all needed information to make a decision [Ja04; p.37].

II.10.4 Core Dimensions for Characterization

Knethen characterizes [Kn01b; p.37] (also cf. [PKD+03]) *traceability* approaches by four core dimensions:
* The *purpose,*
* The *conceptual trace model* (or what Ramesh and Jarke call *traceability reference model*),
* The *process,*
* Used *tools;*

The author also sees these dimensions as a valuable structure for ordering approaches. Therefore, the following chapter will discuss these dimensions orienting itself on Knethen with additional information from other sources. Since the main interest of this thesis lies on *traceability* from requirements to design artifacts, this category will be emphasized.

II.10.4.1 Purpose

Different *traceability* approaches may pursue different purposes. In projects, different stakeholders have to fulfill different needs and tasks. Accordingly, the different stakeholders may have their "own view on *traceability*" [Kn01b; p.37]. Correspondingly, the *conceptual trace model* will be highly influenced by the purpose.

Knethen [Kn01b; p.38-39] extracted from literature a variety of different stakeholders and their main purposes:

- *Customers* want to ensure that all stated requirements are adequately fulfilled, the project duties are done and changes can be made transparent.
- *Project planners* mainly need to perform *IA*s to adapt their plans to changes.
- *Project managers* want to control project progress. *Traceability* information can be used to match requirements to *use cases* or design modules often forming the basis for staffing. *Traceability* to tests can provide information on which requirements are currently fulfilled (tests have passed) and which not.
- *Requirements engineers* want to ensure correctness and consistency of the requirements. *Traceability* to the requirements origin helps to consider all aspects involved in a later requirement change.
- *Designers* want to understand interdependencies between requirements, between requirements and design and between design elements. Additionally, they are interested in *IA*s for implementing changes in their designs
- *Verifiers* want to ensure all requirements to be allocated both to design, resp. code, and to verification procedures. This shall also prevent over-engineering, i.e., unneeded (unspecified) features.
- *Validators* want to establish testing procedures proving that the system fulfills all stated requirements. Correspondingly, *traceability* between requirements and their developed test cases indicating full test coverage of the requirements is their main concern.
- *Maintainers* want to use *traceability* for assessing the *impacts* of new changes to perform.

In the author's eyes, Knethen has forgotten to mention the following other important stakeholders, as they are not necessarily the same persons as the designers:

- *Implementers* or coders are interested in the requirements that must be realized by the components they are assigned to for implementation.

Any purpose, however, is constrained by a fundamental rule [SWG+08; p.217 (*)]: "*Traceability* is only of use if its traces are up to date and correct. If developers have no trust in the correctness of the traces, they will not use the gathered information. ... On the other hand wrong or patchy traces lead to wrong results in *IAs* or to gaps in the test coverage".

Table 10.1 Prioritization of stakeholders and usage purposes concerning traceability between requirement and design artifacts

Priority	Stakeholder	Rationale
High	Designers, Implementers, Maintainers	Will directly work with the requirement and design artifacts. As they will also be directly engaged in establishing and maintaining the *traceability* information, they will have concerns about effort and usability of the approach.
Medium	Requirement Engineers	Requirements should be stated independently from the solutions. However, as ch. I.5.5 indicates this is not always viable in practice.
Medium, Low	Project Planners	Might – as the customer, project managers and verifiers – be more interested in statistical data. On the other hand, (s)he might also adapt his (her) plans on the allocation of requirements to design[177].
Low	Validators	Testing activities should usually orient themselves on the requirements not on the design (cf. [Ja04; p.32], [Iv99; p.373]). However, when module testing is concerned, the tester should know the exact requirements allocated to the module to perform well shaped module tests for early error discovery before SW integration.
Low	Customers, Project Managers and Verifiers	As they are concerned with overall management, they are expected to be more interested in statistical *meta information* (e.g.: "how many requirements of all requirements are currently considered in the design?").

Correspondingly, when a purpose is considered to be supported by a *traceability* approach, the following two criteria are inevitably to be considered as well [SWG+08; p.217 (*)]:

- "The effort for establishing and maintaining traces must be – sustainably feasible – by the project".

---

[177] According to Conway's law from 1968: "The structure of an organization and its architecture are isomorphic." This means that architectures, organizations and systems influence each other (see [St05; p.24], [Eb05; p.11]).

- The establishment of *traceability* provides a concrete gain in the project.

As often encountered in *REM*, it seems that not all stakeholder needs can be equally fulfilled. Therefore, a prioritization of the stakeholders and their derived needs must be made. Table 10.1 shows a prioritization of the stakeholders and purposes reflecting the author's appraisal of the *traceability between requirements and design problem*. The R2A tool approach introduced in part III follows this prioritization. The first column shows the priority values (as one of "High", "Medium", "Low"). Column two enlists stakeholders as taken from the above listing. The last column provides the *rationale* behind the prioritization decision.

II.10.4.2 Conceptual Trace Model

Pinheiro [Pi04; p.92] points out that too many possible traces exist. This underlines the importance to decide which traces should be documented and used. He recommends using what he calls a *traceability model*. For trace definition, such a *traceability* model should [Pi04; p.110]:
- Define few basic types,
- Allow specification of user-definable traces,
- Allow the use of richer representations of traceable objects such as hypermedia objects (videos, recordings, and images (see *nonfunctional traces*, ch. II.10.4.2.20);

A similar notion is expressed by Knethen ([Kn01b]), who uses the term *conceptual trace model* (*CTM*) to describe the entities (items) and relationships that shall be considered in a *traceability* approach to fulfill the corresponding stakeholder needs.

Following Knethen [Kn01b: p.38] a *CTM* consists of two major elements:
- Entities,
- Relationships;

II.10.4.2.1 Entities

Entities describe the elements, i.e., artifacts taken into account of a *CTM*. As Knethen [Kn01b; p.39] – similarly to Pinheiro [Pi04; p.92] – points out, the purpose of the tracing approach mainly determines what entities are to be considered.

Entities can be described by three characteristics [Kn01b; p.39]:
- The kind of entities taken into account,

- The granularity,
- The attributes;

a) Kinds of Entities

Concerning the kind of entities to be taken into account, only few hints are provided in literature. Lindvall [Li94; p.19] emphasizes that basically two kinds of artifacts (work products) exist (also cf. [Kn01b; p.39]):

- *Temporary work products,*
- *Permanent work products*;

In contrast to *permanent work products, temporary work products* "are not intended to be saved and maintained in the future" [Li94; p.19]. Lindvall recommends including only *permanent work products* into the set of artifacts for which *traceability* shall be maintained. Indeed, it is doubtful that *temporary work products* have a life-span long enough to make sense for *traceability*. However, the author thinks that an exception of this obvious thought may be what is called *model transformations* [KM05], [AIE07], where *intermediate models* can occur. As an example, the UML provides mechanisms to automatically transform *platform independent models* to *platform specific models*, which are the further basis of code generation. Such *intermediate models* must also transform the *traceability* information from its original model to the end model. Now, if the *intermediate model* is only a *temporary work product*, it must also be considered by the *traceability* process.

The author is not sure whether or not some of the strategies describing automatable *traceability* through model transformation indirectly rely on *traceability* to *temporary work products* as a strategy (algorithms) to bridge the gap. In these cases, the strategy has an enormous influence on the resulting *traceability* information from the start product to the end product of *model transformation(s)*. Thus, analyzing a *traceability model* by taking the temporary *intermediate models* into account can make sense to verify that the *model transformations* fulfill the requirements for the specific *traceability* need between transformation source and the transformation outcome.

Pfleeger and Bohner [PB90] refer to a *traceability model* considering requirements, analysis, design and code. Ramesh and Edwards [RE93] argue to include requirements, specifications and implementation into *traceability* considerations. Other very concrete ideas about entities taken into account in *traceability* considerations are provided by process standards as *SPICE* (or *CMMI*). Apart from that, the author agrees with Knethen that the entity kinds to be considered for tracing depend on the purpose [Kn01b; p.39].

b) Granularity
Granularity refers to the level of detail (granularity) the entities are considered in a *traceability* approach. Lindvall speaks here of "different levels of *traceability*" [Li94; p.18]. "The most coarse level is the ability to trace from one document to another .... The most fine-grain level would be to be able to trace every single statement" [Li94; p.18]. Undetailed *traceability* between documents may be sufficient to coordinate development team members [De99], [RUP+90], but for specific *IA*s more detailed information is needed. An example of very detailed approaches for *IA* are *dependency analyses* of source code [KP02; p.6], [Kn01b; p.40]. These are described in the course of ch. II.10.3. As Knethen [Kn01b; p.40] points out, the level of detail is mostly guided by the needs of the purpose to be followed [Kn01b; p.40]. However, the question about the costs and values of a specific level of *traceability* [RE93][178] is most probably the main concern in making a decision for or against a specific level. This is directly connected what Egyed et al. call the two fundamental problems of *traceability* [EGH+07; p.115]:
- "Finding the right level of trace quality with finite budget",
- "Increasing the quality of trace links comes at an increasingly steep price";

Lindvall [Li94; p.19] further argues that granularity is connected to "the *problem of comprehension* – which models should be included in a *traceability* model for a certain system?" This is very similar to what is discussed above about kinds of entities. Consequently, both topics can be considered as closely connected.

As ch. I.7 shows, *traceability* demands for *safety-related* development processes rather require a very fine-grained granularity of *traceability* information (every requirement must be individually traced) and require to take any available artifact of the engineering processes into account. Correspondingly, significantly steep prices for *traceability* issues in *safety-related* development projects can be expected.

c) Attributes of Entity
This concept describes possibilities to add attribute information to entities. Current state of the art *REM-tools* and a lot of *design tools* as, e.g., UML-tools allow possibilities to add further information (so called attributes) to entities. In the *REM* context, attributes are usually used to collect *meta data* (as, e.g., the author, time stamp of last change, responsible developer [Tv99; p.372], responsible test-

---

[178] "It may be unnecessary or even undesirable, considering the overhead involved in maintaining *traceability*, to maintain linkage between every requirement and every output created during the systems design process" [RE93].

er, release …) or other development process related data (e.g., priority seen by customer [Tv99; p.372], status of the requirement in the development process).

Attribute information can be used as *traceability* information. As an example, fig. 10-1 shows an excerpt taken from the *REM-tool* IBM Rational DOORS with the attributes 'ID', 'Origin', 'Priority', 'State' and 'Scope'. Concerning *traceability*, these attributes have the following meaning:

- 'ID': Assigns a unique identifier to each requirement. The unique identifier is an essential concept in any *REM-tool* to allow textual references to a requirement (e.g., in a *traceability matrix*) as the identifier never changes, whereas the requirement text does. In fig. 10-1, another kind of possible textual reference is indicated in attribute 'Origin' of 'Requirement1', where a textual reference to an item with identifier 'CRS_1' is set referring to a requirement in the *customer requirements specification*.
- 'Origin': Allows a textual reference to the origin(s) of a requirement for *backward traceability*. This allows referring to origins not represented in IBM Rational DOORS (If a requirement can refer to a origin also present in IBM Rational DOORS, a link relation can be set).
- 'Priority': Marks the priority of a requirement being often an important *rationale* for decisions. For example, 'Requirement3' in fig. 10-1 is marked with priority 'NiceToHave' being most probably an important *rationale* to decide for rejecting (not implementing) it in the project.
- 'State': Shows the current state of the requirement in the project.
- 'Scope': Refers to the expected scope where the requirement must be implemented. 'Requirement1', e.g., seems to have a general system wide scope meaning that it influences HW, SW and probably other engineering domains that must work together on system-level to fulfill the requirement. In this way, this can be seen as the first step towards *forward traceability*.

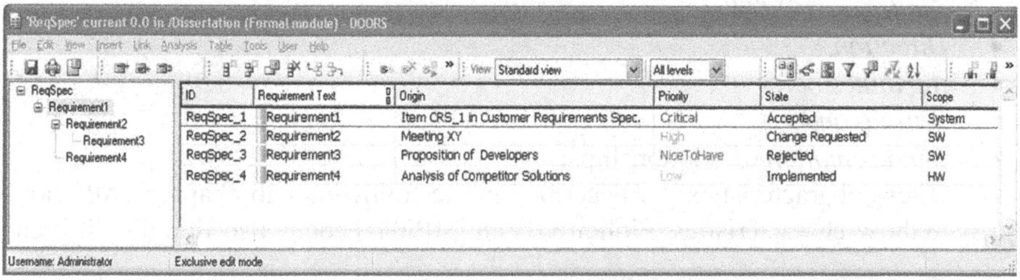

Figure 10-1 A requirements specification with attributes in IBM Rational DOORS

Paech and Knethen [KP02; p.6] argue that such attribute information is per se *traceability* information as it usually relates information to other information. The author is not sure whether this is correct for all attributes, but for some it is correct. Knethen and Paech [KP02; p.6-7] list a set of attributes that can be seen as *traceability* information.

Rupp et al. provide a detailed discussion about attributes and document structuring in *REM* practice [RS07; p.381-393]. In practice, it is necessary "to tailor the right set of attributes so that the effort to define and maintain them is balanced by the benefits of better process control and specification reuse" [WW02; p.18].

Some of the possible attributes can also have directing effects to subsequent design processes such as Knethen's proposal [Kn01b; p.40] to use an attribute describing change probability for each requirement. Such an attribute can have *impact* on design decisions taken, because such an attribute helps to identify the stability of a requirement and the stability of a requirement can impose direct influence on design. Gerdom and Posch [GP04], e.g., argue that significant costs can be avoided, when designers concentrate on modeling only parts considered stable rather than a complete *architecture*[179]. As another possible strategy, requirements identified with high change probability can be addressed by handling strategies for flexibility such as encapsulation or *patterns* to minimize *impacts* if the case of change happens.

II.10.4.2.2 Relationships

Traceability mainly relies on relationships. The type and kinds of relationships to be established and maintained differ. Knethen could distinguish the following characteristics of relationships and their connected approaches:

* *Kind,*
* *Direction,*
* *Attributes,*
* *Setting, and*
* *Representation* of relationships;

These characteristics are described in the following sub chapters. Additionally to these characteristics, Pinheiro ([Pi00], [Pi04]) could also find the differen-

---

[179] Gerdom and Posch [GP04] call this modeling an *architectural skeleton*. This principle seems rather to be a principle originating from the agile community, because the author heard similar claims proposed by Ivar Jacobson at his key note speech on requirements and agile development at the Requirement Engineering Conference (REconf) in Munich 2009.

tiation characteristic between *functional* and *nonfunctional traces* discussed in the last sub chapter.

a) Kind

This describes the kinds or types of relationships in a *CTM*. Knethen [Kn01b; p.39], [KP02; p.8] distinguishes "three general kinds":

- Relationships between documentation entities on the *same abstraction*[180],
- Relationships between documentation entities at *different abstractions*,
- Relationships between documentation entities of *different versions* of a software product;

Before discussing different kinds of relationships, the author should note that relationships are not necessarily distributed in a uniform way. Instead, as an industrial survey [CSL+01] on requirements interdependencies in SW product release planning indicates, relations between requirements can be very inhomogeneously distributed. They rather follow a kind of *pareto*-like relation [Pa1897]:

- "20% of the requirements are responsible for 75% of the interdependencies" [CSL+01; p.84].
- 20% of the requirements are singular (with no significant interdependencies) [CSL+01; p.88].
- The study also suggests that interdependencies differ according to the project setting. As an example, customer oriented projects consider more feature-oriented interdependencies, whereas market driven development projects rather orient themselves on more abstract values [CSL+01; p.84].

These findings could have significant influence on considerations about new research approaches to *traceability*. In the author's opinion, even connections to the author's *pareto* presumption described in ch. I.6.6.1.4 may exist. These 20% are responsible for extensive portions of complexity (due to the 75% of interdependencies). Now, e.g., if it would be possible to tackle these requirements through tool methods for early prototypical requirement evaluation with later automated code generation (see ch. I. 6.6.1.2 and ch. I. 6.6.1.3), extensive portions of complexity could be tackled this way. At the moment, however, these two points are just suggestions of the author. Further research would be needed to find out whether these suggestions may have some substance and could be interesting as a new leverage for the *traceability* problem.

---

[180] In Knethen's terminology, abstraction means different artifacts in different engineering processes. For example, systems requirements, systems design, SW requirements and SW architecture are four different abstractions for her. Later in part III, when the author introduces his tool approach, abstraction can also mean a different abstraction level within one artifact.

Relationships on the Same Abstraction
Knethen [Kn01b; p.41], [KP02; p.8] distinguishes two kinds of relationships:
* *Representation*,
* *Dependency*;

Representation Relationships
Representation relationships connect together documentation entities representing the same information but providing different *views* (or *viewpoints*) on it.

In the requirements domain, different stakeholders have different perspectives on a system [GF95]. Ergo, *requirements specifications* may contain different *views* on a system. This is represented by the representation axis of Pohl's *RE framework* (see ch. I.5.7.1). An aspect is then to avoid or handle inconsistencies. Here, different answers are given from the translation into *formal* logic [FGH+94] to heuristics in conflict recognition and handling [LDL98], or to *meta-model* approaches [NJJ+96], [Kn01b].

In the design domain, the *view* concept is very essential [Kr95] (see ch. I.6.2.1.2). Here, a vast set of approaches exist in research to support *view* handling in modeling environments. Endeavors exist [BR07b] to embed the *view* concept into a *formal* definition of modeling description language to avoid inconsistencies. In design practice, above all the UML language [UML] (starting with Kruchten [Kr95] the UML specifically included *view* support in its language) provides support for modeling representation relationships between diagrams (resp. *views*) via defined relations in the *meta-model*. These relationships can be further detailed (restricted) by constraints formulated as constraints via the *object constraint language* (*OCL*), which is part of the UML standard. Basing on these relations other tools and approaches offer support for managing consistency problems and *IAs* [BLO+06].

Dependency Relations
Dependency relations describe relationships "between two documentation entities that depend on each other and represent different logical entities on an abstraction" [KP02; p.10]. Approaches exist on different abstraction levels, or – better to say – artifact types:
* *Requirement* or other *specification* (e.g., this technique is also very valuable to administer testing specifications) *artifacts* are typically handled with *REM-tools* such as IBM Rational DOORS or in *traceability* research environments as PRO-ART [PDJ94], [Po99] or TOOR [PG96], [Pi96], [Pi00]. "Dependent documentation entities are linked manually or automatically and maintained and represented by the tool."[KP02; p.11]. Knethen and Paech emphasize here that commercial tools do not provide guidance on how such

traces shall be established and maintained. The author thinks this is good since such tools should allow the projects as much freedom as possible to adapt them to their needs. It is more an issue for the processes to define project specific rules. Process standards as SPICE provide here concrete demands and guidance.

- *Design description techniques* make use of the modularization principle (see ch. I.6.2.1.2) decomposing a system into sub elements interacting together to fulfill the purposes of the system. Correspondingly, manifold dependencies between those elements exist and describing those dependencies is an essential part of design. Rigorous decoupling through definition of capable interfaces helps to decouple the elements ensuring independent development of the elements.

- Model-based *RE* approaches try to establish *traceability* in a similar fashion as *design description techniques*. Research projects such as QUASAR [PSS04], (also see [Ge05; p.171]) or the approach introduced by Geisberger [Ge05] have developed model-based *RE* approaches for embedded systems engineering. An overview of other comparable approaches is provided in [Ge05; p.167-185].

- For code artifacts, source code *dependency analysis* tools provide support for automated identification of dependency information between data, control and components [BA96]. One of the usable methods is program slicing [KP02; p.10] as described in ch. II.10.3. These approaches are limited to source code level not taking dependencies on other abstractions into account [Kn01b; p.42], [KP02; p.10].

Relationships between Abstractions
Two kinds of relationships between traceable elements on different abstractions can be identified [Kn01b; p.43], [KP02; p.12]:
- *Within-level refinement,*
- *Between-level refinement;*

Within-Level Refinement
Within-level refinement means relationships between entities at different abstraction levels within one artifact level (e.g., in *system requirements*). Several approaches exist [KP02; p.12]:
- Hierarchically structuring the identified goals of a system [LDL98] allows defining sub goals to contribute to a higher goal.
- Decomposition of requirements describes the practice of *deriving* sub requirements from higher level requirements forming a *requirement hierarchy* [Ki98], [Pi04]. Kirkman [Ki98] identifies this as an essential heuristic in

REM. Usually, these relationships are captured by the usage of *REM-* or *traceability* tools such as IBM Rational DOORS. Fig. 10-1 above shows an excerpt from IBM Rational DOORS, where the four requirements are also part of a decomposition structure indicated by the tree view component at the left. According to Pinheiro [Pi04; p.91], it must be considered that several requirements are derivable from one origin, a requirement can have several origins, a requirement can be the deriving source for several requirements, and a derived requirement can also collapse several predecessor requirements.

- *Hierarchical refinement* of models is offered by a lot of modeling languages. It allows designers to refine and decompose elements by sub elements. All modeling tools discussed in ch. I.6 support *hierarchical refinement*. The tool approach presented here (see part III) relies on this principle for establishing the requirement to design *traceability*.

- The *Queinsian In-Order-To Rule*[181] [RS07; p.417] is a heuristics from *RE* practice helping to identify the real nature of connections between a formerly known requirement (in the former called old requirement) and a new arising requirement if both requirements have nearly similar semantics. It helps to determine whether the new requirement must replace the old one (old and new requirement are in a *historic versioning relationship*), or whether the new requirement is a refinement of the old requirement (old and new requirement are in a *hierarchic decomposition dependency*).

Between-Level Refinement

Between-level refinement describes relationships between entities on different artifact levels (e.g., between system requirements and *system design*). The following approaches exist:

- The *specification axis* in Pohl's *RE framework* (see ch. I.5.7.1) represents this dimension [KP02; p.14].

- Development approaches themselves influence how *traceability* is established. As development processes often focus on different artifact levels and their corresponding artifacts, they have special influence on *between-level refinement traceability*. Several approaches provide certain characteristics:
  - Pre-object-oriented development methods as *structured analysis* and *design (SA/SD)* [De78] propagate strict separation of the *problem* (requirements) and the *solution* (design) *space*. Hatley et al. [HHP03; p.252] emphasize this as strength since it prevents uncontrolled intermixing of both areas, which poses a threat to object-oriented methods.

---

[181] In German: "Queins'sche UmZu-Regel"

However, the semantic gap between the *problem* and *solution space* is very large, thus the need for explicit *traceability* information is higher and especially difficult to establish [Kn01b; p.45], [KP02; p.14].

- Object-oriented development (OO) approaches as, e.g., the UML [UML] have a smaller *semantic gap* between analysis and design. Thus, the need for explicit *traceability* is not as needed and easier to establish. Often *traceability* is implicitly present.

- *Four variable model (FVM)* as introduced by Parnas [Pa85] propagates a design process with strict separation between input processing, the internal core functions and the output processing and relations between them. The *FVM* allows separating the system from the environment by the distinction of four variables: monitored and controlled environment variables, data read from sensors and data written to actors. These four variables can be set into *formal* dependencies. As embedded systems often relate input signals from sensors to output signals for actors, the *FVM* is especially suitable for embedded systems design and is used in embedded design practice [Fa95], [HHP03; p.56ff], [HJL96]. Knethen shows in [Kn01b; p.44] that in embedded systems design the input and output processing variables are mainly in the focus of systems analysis and design, whereas the internal core functions are usually allocated to software analysis and design. Ergo, the *FVM* relations are of the type discussed here. The *FVM* can be used as an extension to *SA/SD* [HHP03; p.56ff] as well as to OO approaches [Kn01b]. In the course of the QUASAR project [PSS04] (see also [Ge05; p.171]), Knethen developed her requirement to design *traceability* approach, whose foundations base on concepts of UML and the *FVM* (see ch. II.10.6 for details).

- The *SPICE process model* defines artifact levels and how relations between the corresponding artifacts of the levels are connected.

- Relationships defined in *requirements traceability* methods for *product line engineering* [RTM02], [BP06] can be seen as *between-level refinement traceability relationships*.

- *REM-* or *traceability* tool environments allow linking between different artifact levels. The environment introduced in part III explicitly addresses this issue concerning transitions between requirements and design.

In practice, the following approaches are used (see also [KP02; p.14]):

- *Dependency links* between two elements indicating that one element derives its justification from the other element. Knethen and Paech call this 'applicability links' [KP02; p.14]. A similar dependency is given by the R2A approach described part III where consequences of decisions can be modeled

that spark new *design constraints* (ch. III.20). From the perspective discussed here, the *decisions* justify the *design constraints*.
- Links between requirements and models:
  - Relations between textual requirements and its origins in other documents.
  - Links between textual requirements and analysis models, such as *use cases* and other analysis diagrams (ch. I.5.4).
  - Links between requirements and *design models*. Further relations can propagate the requirements to detailed design elements as software components and to source code.
- Links between requirements, test specifications, test cases, test logs and (resp. or) error listings [Tv99; p.373]. According to Jäälinoja [Ja04; p.32], these connections are so essential that this kind of linking should always be established. The author recommends conferring [Ja04; p.31-33] and [WW03; p.20-21] for concrete hints about this issue in the embedded domain.
- Links between issue tracking items (bug reports and change requests) and affected entities [Tv99; p.373]. *Application life-cycle management* tool suites like MKS [MKS] offer dedicated support for these actions in practice (see ch. II.10.4.4.4).

Relationships between Different Versions

Hamilton and Beeby [HB91] see an important task of *traceability* to "discover the history of every feature of a system" to ensure proper *impact* identifications when requirements change. This has a twofold meaning. One is to trace the history of the documents and can be seen as "an extension to what usually is called version control, namely to trace all previous versions of a particular documentation entity to recover its development history" [KP02; p.15]. These relations are usually called historical links [RUP+90] or *evolutionary traceability* [Po96], [Pi04]. A second, more enhanced meaning is described by the *RatMan* approaches. As these approaches record the *rationale* behind decisions and changes, they provide important information about the historical evolution of project artifacts. Without this information only the "how" of the evolution is recorded, but the "why" is in the best case covered somewhere in the brains of the developers and in the worst case simply forgotten. *RatMan* and *traceability* is described in detail in the later ch. II.10.8.

The following approaches consider *evolutionary traceability* with respect to recording artifact history:
- The *agreement axis* in Pohl's *RE framework* (see ch. I.5.7.1) describes this [KP02; p.16].

- Ramamoorthy et al. [RUP+90] introduce the *Evolution Support Environment* (*ESE*) system that can be described as a version control system enhanced by support for *traceability* relationships. Besides the history links (trace to an item's change history), *ESE* supports hierarchy links (trace to the hierarchical structure an item is embedded in) and development links (trace how an item is produced and used in the development project) [RUP+90; p.1230], (cf. also [Li94; p.20]).

- Leite and Oliveira describe a system where *configuration management* concepts are used to control the evolution of the individual requirements [LO95].

  The following approaches are found in practice:

- Several *REM* and *traceability* tool environments as, e.g., IBM Rational DOORS provide *configuration management* mechanisms to record the history of items and their traces. The approach discussed in part III provides a similar mechanism. Also tools as MKS [MKS] originating from the *configuration* and *change management* domain have developed new approaches to address evolution and *traceability*. This is discussed in the following chapter about *traceability* tool support.

- The already above described *Queinsian In-Order-To Rule* [RS07; p.417 (*)] can be seen as a practice-oriented heuristics to decide whether to version or refine a requirement.

b) Direction

Refers to the direction *traceability* is established or used in. Terms used here are *PRE-RS, POST-RS, backward* or *forward traceability* as discussed in ch. I.5.7.1. Early agreement exists that *traceability* should be *bidirectional* (see ch I.5.7.1). Standards as *A-SPICE* (see ch. I.7.4) oblige to use *bidirectional traceability models*.

A lot of approaches can be characterized by their *traceability* direction or orientation within a *process model*. *CTMs* for *PRE-RS* are, for example, the *contribution structures* model by Gotel and Finkelstein [GF95], [GF96] or the *RE framework* of Pohl [Po93], [Po99], (see ch. I.5.7.1). In the *POST-RS* direction, approaches exist for design (ch. II.10.6), code (ch. II.10.7), and testing [Tv99; p.373]. The COSMOD-*RE* model by Pohl [Po08; p.565ff] is a model combining a *PRE-RS* and a *POST-RS* approach in parallel.

c) Relationship Attributes

Just as documentation entities, relationships can also be enhanced by attributes. Examples for valuable attributes for relationships are status, creation date, creating author.

Relationship attributes can also support *IAs* and change implementation. Knethen and Paech describe here a "weighting attribute", which enables to distinguish more important from less important relationships, thus helping to tell the more important *impacts* apart from the less important (*side*) *impacts*[182] [KP02; p.18].

Such an attribute can also be used to record *rationale* behind a link, however, with very limited support for extensive documentation of *rationale*. *Rationale* in context of *traceability* is discussed in ch. II.9.

As an example, the *REM-tool* IBM Rational DOORS supports creation and management of relationship attributes. Thus, this technique is available for practice.

The R2A tool approach introduced in part III uses relationship attributes to automatically capture information about the current status, author, and editing time of each relationship, where especially the status information is a central concept to implement a *consistency management* mechanism (see ch. III.22.2).

d) Setting (i.e. Traceability Establishment)

This part discusses how *traceability* is established. Pinheiro calls this *trace production* and stresses out that this issue has high importance, when considering the applicability of a *CTM* in practice [Pi04; p.105] (this is discussed in ch. II.10.5). Generally, two fundamentally different ways are available [Li94; p.19]:

- *Implicit relationships*,
- *Explicit relationships*;

Implicit Relationships

Implicit relationships arise as a *by-product* of other processes. Knethen and Paech characterize implicit relationships as "links that do not require manual setting" [Kn01b; p.47], [KP02; p.18]. This means these relationships can be surfaced using automatable approaches.

When analyzing different literature ([Li94; p.19], [LW99], [Sm99c]), Knethen and Paech ([Kn01b; p.47], [KP02; p.18]) were able to identify the following manifestations of implicit relationships:

---

[182] A good example of this method in practice is known by the author in test management. Requirements are often tested by several test cases. Links between a requirement and its verifying test cases can be enhanced by an attribute that indicates how much each test case accounts for fulfilling a requirement. This degree of fulfillment attribute can have a per cent scale. In this way, e.g., a requirement can have a link with 80% to a TestCase1 and two links with 10% to a TestCase2 and a TestCase3. A positive test result for TestCase1, but negative for TestCase2 and TestCase3, would indicate that a requirement is fulfilled by 80 per cent.

- *Name mapping* (also called *name tracing* or *name referencing*) denotes the possibility to retrieve *traceability* information from names and abbreviations. It assumes that names and abbreviations used in different traceable entities (i.e., artifacts) designate the same items or facts. *Name mapping* is especially promising when artifacts have a high degree of *formality*, because *formality* ensures proper naming at all relevant locations. Source code has a high degree of *formality* since compilers must be able to process it. Correspondingly, names in source code are always identical, otherwise compiler errors occur. This makes source code to an optimal candidate for *name mapping*. Today's code development tools such as Eclipse or Microsoft Visual Studio offer support for analyzing references (so called *dependency analysis*) and it is highly probable the most heavily used technique applied for performing *IAs* in practice. *Design models* are models of portions of source code. Thus, they should contain the same names as in code. Ergo, *name mapping* can also be an effective strategy for tracing dependencies between code and *design models*. In the context of SPICE in practice, Hörmann et al. [HDH+06; p.94] especially recommend *name mapping* as a good strategy for fulfilling *traceability* demands between design and code artifacts. Exact name matching, however, will only be ensured if code is generated for design through *formal* automatic transformation processes (*automatic code generation*). In manual coding processes, processes must be established to avoid drifts between *design models* and code. Specially change processes must ensure that changes are properly performed in both artifacts, otherwise names can vary between design and code leading to lost name mappings and thus to lost *traceability* links. *Name mapping* can also be applied in rather document-oriented environments such as in *requirements specifications*. However, in this case similar processes for ensuring consistent naming throughout the considered artifacts must be applied. Fortunately, another heuristic significantly reinforces *name mapping* in the requirements field in an implicit way: It is very important to achieve a common understanding of the project between all different stakeholders. This can only be achieved if the project develops a common vocabulary for its used terms. Therefore, in the field of *requirements specification*, using precise terminology and establishing adequate terminology management is a central principle and thus *name mapping* is a very promising heuristic for *requirements specifications*.
- *Relationships given by structure* refer to retrieved *traceability* information by capitalizing structures emerging as effect of development methods. In object-oriented methods, a class contains private data, attributes and operations, building structures of implicit relationships usable for tracing. In *REM* practice, the heuristic of deriving more specific low-level requirements from

higher-level requirements and documenting these dependencies in a hierarchical child parent relation is widely employed [LW99]. From its first description by Nelsen [Ne90] as so-called *top-down structured analysis* and first experiences with tool support [Li94; p.25], it is supported by many *REM-tools* such as IBM Rational DOORS, which organize requirements and their dependencies by a hierarchical specification tree. In the SysML [SYSML] a *<<derive>>-relationship* between requirements is defined with analogous semantics.

- *Relationships given by modeling paradigm* refer to implicit relationships resulting from the usage of certain modeling languages, tools or techniques [LW99]. An example of this is the diverse possibilities to specify relationships in UML.

- *Dynamic relationships between code components* refer to techniques for identifying relationships occurring in code during execution. Here, *dependency analysis* methods as *dynamic program slicing* [KR98] (see [GB08] for an overview on program slicing techniques) can provide valuable support.

Explicit Relationships

Explicit representation [Kn01b; p.48-49] refer to linkages manually documented by the developers. "Explicit relationships came from external considerations supplied by the developers. So, for example, the linkage, or relationship, between a textual requirement and a *use case* that describes the requirement is determined solely by the decision of the developers that such a relationship has meaning. There are no intrinsic relationships between the documentation entities; only external decisions can establish the relationships" [Kn01b; p.48]. Explicit relationships can be used for all kinds of relationships. However, if implicit relationships are present, it should be carefully considered whether explicit relationships shall be established with the same meaning, because this creates redundant information. Any redundant information is a source of inconsistency and needs further maintenance when changes occur. Thus, it is rather preferable to extract the information from the implicit relationships. Similar findings are expressed by Pinheiro [Pi04; p.110] stating to use as much automation as possible.

In practice, the following methods are relevant:

- Simple documentation tools as Microsoft Word or Excel allow mechanisms as hyperlinks or creating mapping tables (so called *traceability matrices* as described below).

- *REM-tools* as IBM Rational DOORS allow manual linking between entities. In some tools this is possible via *drag-and-drop*.

- Modeling tools allow systems to be described by elements, diagrams and their relations. As an example, the UML tool Sparx Systems Enterprise Architect offers several ways of linking elements with diagrams, elements with elements and also hyperlinks to external documents are possible. However, the kinds of relationships also depend on the modeling techniques (e.g., *functional decomposition* produces relations different from *object-oriented decomposition*).

- Some specification languages as RSL [Al77] or PSDL [SHB91] exist, allowing references to be specified to requirements but are "not primarily intended for requirements tracing" [Pi04; p.108].

Automatable Versus Manual Approaches[183]

Research on *traceability* has proposed various approaches for establishing or retrieving *traceability* dependencies. Rochimah et al. present evaluation results of about 100 publications to current state-of-the-art *traceability* approaches concerned with SW evolution [RWA07]. Research has shown that manual creation and maintenance of *traceability* relations requires enormous effort and includes substantial complexity [EG04], [GF94], [RJ01] (see ch. II.10.5). The study of Rochimah et al. further shows that current research on *traceability* focuses on automatic or at least semi-automatic *traceability* link generation [RWA07; table 4]. Some automation approaches still depend on manually established links that are then enriched by supporting automation mechanisms while others are fully automated.

The author has analyzed the scope of automation of these approaches and can identify two major areas of automation:

1. Finding interdependencies between different requirements artifacts (e.g., textual documents, *use case* descriptions, feature-models or analysis models (ch. I.5.4)) concerned with requirements.
2. Finding interdependencies between design and code artifacts.

Only the approach suggested by Spanoudakis [Sp02], [SZP04] tries to establish automated *trace links* from requirements to models, focusing on analysis models, though. It is striking that current automated *link* generation approaches do not concentrate on establishing *links* between the requirements world and the design world. The author believes that this can be explained by the *name mapping* (cf. ch. II.10.4.2.2) phenomenon: Instead of creating explicit links between items, the same names are used [MHD+07; p.224]. If no automatic code generation is available for a *design tool* and code must be typed manually, *traceability* must also be established between design and code. As design is (and should be) a more abstract view on the problem modeled, *traceability* can also be established by naming corresponding elements in design and code identically. This is an

---

[183] This chapter bases in parts on [TKT+09].

explicit heuristic. In addition, another heuristic significantly reinforces this effect in an implicit way: It is very important to achieve a common understanding of the project for all different stakeholders. This can only be achieved if the project develops a common vocabulary for its used terms. Therefore, in the field of requirements specification, using precise terminology and establishing adequate terminology management is a central principle. However, these approaches provide no guarantee to identify all interdependencies yet, as name mismatches or other effects still can happen. Attempts try to ameliorate this problem by using requirement ontologies as a common representation of mutual understanding of the semantics of words in the requirements sentences, to establish automatable *traceability links* [ASP09].

Other approaches provide a semi-automation such as identification of *traceability* information from manually documented relationships during modeling activities [TN97], [TM00], [Eg03], extending links with notification mechanisms to automatically propagate change notes to other affected items [CCC03],[Sa06], or identifying dependency info.

[ANR+06] and [GG07] provide an overview of the most recent advances in technologies to automate *traceability* in the context of model-driven development. In summary, the author could not identify any significant automation attempts to bridge the gap between requirements and design. This matches with the author's observation that the transition between requirements and design involves a significant structural and *semantic gap*[184], where automation inevitably is very difficult (cf. ch. II.10.2).

Thus, automatable approaches may not be suitable to cross significant semantic gaps and therefore automation may in practice only become a supportive alleviation for still manual *traceability* processes. Correspondingly, the author agrees with Egyed et al. that "while some automation exists, capturing traces remains a largely manual process" [EGH+07; p.115]. As a result, the approach described in part III mainly concentrates on improving manual *traceability* strategies.

In the R2A solution (part III), the concept of the so-called *requirement influence scope* (see ch. III.18.2.2) involves that requirements assigned to a high-level element in design are inherited to lower-level design elements. This can be seen as a kind of *traceability* automation.

---

[184] Research of Gruenbacher, Egyed and Medvidovic [GEM01], [GEM03], [MGE+03] even suggest that this involves such a large semantic gap that it is even impossible to employ a meaningful link concept between both (see ch. II.10.6).

e) Representation of Relationships

Relationships must be presented to the users according to their *traceability* needs. Wieringa [Wi95] could identify three different ways for representation:

- *Traceability matrices*: "A matrix that records the relationship between two or more products of the development process; for example a matrix that records the relationship between the requirements and the design of a given software component" [IEEE610; p.78]. One artifact's documentation entities (e.g., the requirements) are enlisted horizontally as columns and the other artifact's entities (e.g., the entities of a design) are enlisted vertically as rows. Relations are then expressed as symbols in the intersecting cells (cf. [So07; p.197].
- *Cross references:* Relationships between entities are represented as references similar to hyperlinks in hypertext languages as HTML. These 'trace links' allow navigation between the entities.
- *Graphical models*: Entities and their relationships are represented in some graphical way. The method described here (part III) also provides graphical preparations of the gathered relationships. Marcus et al. [MXP05; p.57] provide an opinion about why and when graphical visualizations may provide superior support than the methods mentioned above.

REM-*tools* often rely on one or more of the ways of representation mentioned above. As an example, IBM Rational DOORS uses a cross references approach as a main editing approach. These *cross references* can also be transformed and viewed as a *traceability matrix*. As IBM Rational DOORS offers a scripting extension mechanism via the DOORS eXtension Language (DXL), some companies also have extended the standard IBM Rational DOORS environment via more graphical preparations[185] of the collected data.

f) Functional and Nonfunctional Traces

Pinheiro [Pi00], [Pi04] identifies two fundamentally different types of traces:

- *Functional traces*,
- *Nonfunctional traces*;

Functional traces are related to functional aspects. As they describe mappings between entities, they have a precise – narrow – semantic. Pinheiro argues that these traces occur naturally when well-defined models and notations are used. In this case, the traces can be directly "derived from the syntactic and semantic connections prescribed by the models or notations" [Pi04; p.96]. In other words, if precise models are used, *functional traces* can be directly derived from the relationships occurring in the models.

---

[185] See http://www.smartdxl.com/content/?page_id=144 (Access: 2009/10).

Pinheiro lists some model types and their meaning in the context of *functional traces* [Pi04; p.97]:

- *Analysis models* (ch. I.5.4) relate entities from the *REM* phase (interviews and transcriptions, documents and the extracted requirements).
- *Design models* (ch. I.6) relate entities used in the design phase (classes, diagrams, attributes, and methods). These mappings tend to be more structured.
- *Process models* (ch. I.7) relate objects of the development process (tools, activities, artifacts and people).
- *Organizational models* (organizational structures, people, goals, activities, and resources) include environment and social issues.

Pinheiro emphasizes that models may also overlap meaning that representations of the same entities may be present in several models. Identifying those overlapping representation is a good starting point to identify mappings between models.

On the other side, *nonfunctional traces* relate to goals, reasons, intentions, purpose, context of the intended system, decisions, and other intangible concepts[186]. According to Pinheiro, also *nonfunctional requirements* can be seen among these intangible concepts and correspondingly most traces involving *nonfunctional requirements* are *nonfunctional* [Pi04; p.98].

Functional traces enforce appropriate registration and extraction, promote uniform understanding, allow automation of the *traceability* processes, and allow procedures to verify consistency and correctness [Pi04; p.100].

A common way to handle *nonfunctional traces* is to reexpress them as *functional* ones that can be verified [Pi04; p.99] (also cf. [WW03; p.21]) in an analogous way as *nonfunctional requirements* can be often expressed by several more tangible *functional requirements* [JL05; p.130], [PKD+03; p.145].

In part III, the author shows how this can be expressed in design by a *requirement influence scope* concept (cf. ch. III.18.2.2) and a process heuristic ensuring that the *influence scope* is as local as possible (cf. ch. III.18.2.4).

A reformulation of *nonfunctional traces* into *functional ones* can especially promote uniform understanding, because *non-functional traces* leave open space for differences in interpretation leading to potential errors or deviations between

---

[186] "However, not all needs for tracing may be encompassed by using methods and techniques. Certainly not, when what is sought refers to the very use of them. For example, the answer to what data-flow is input to process X in a certain data-flow diagram involves only elements from the method itself, while asking why a particular process in the same diagram is described in the way it is can only be answered with recourse to a *meta model*, where the use of the model can be assessed. In this case the referential involves a wider context that may include the social environment in which the development is carried out" [Pi00; p.4].

the intended *traceability* information to be captured and the really captured *traceability* information.

However, such transformations involve dangers of significant losses of important information. To counter these dangers, "traceable objects should allow the use of hyper-media objects like videos, recordings, and images together with mechanisms for inspecting these kinds of objects" [Pi04; p.104] to record and regather real-world observations. The relationships between those hyper-media objects and parts of *formal traces* are called extended *traceability* [HPW+99], (see also [Pi04; p.104]). In the tool solution discussed in part III, a step towards *nonfunctional tracing* is done by the *decision models* described in ch. III.20 and ch. III.21. The *decision model* allows capturing *non-functional traces* into a *semi-formal skeleton* of *functional traces* that can be accompanied by a further textual description, where *non-functional aspects* can be described. This mechanism could also be extended. Not only a textual description, but also other hyper-media objects can be added.

Another strategy to deal with *nonfunctional traces* is, e.g., providing direct modeling support as shown by Graham [Gr03], who uses the profile extension for UML (UML Profile for Schedulability, Performance, and Time [Do04, ch. 4]) to model *nonfunctional* performance constraints directly in the *design model*. According to Pinheiro [Pi04; p.99], *nonfunctional aspects* can thus be *functionally captured* by using some model, but this leads again to a loss of much of the *non-functionality*.

Thus, Pinheiro [Pi04; p.110] concludes that the major obstacles to realizing *traceability* are organizational and not technical (see ch. II.10.5). "The *informal* aspects of tracing and the nonfunctional nature of some traces explain most difficulties" [Pi04; p.110].

II.10.4.2.3 Examples of Conceptual Trace Models

As an example for a defined *CTM*, Knethen refers to the proposals of Ramesh and Jarke [RJ01], who term their concept as *traceability reference model*. In the course of a three-year empirical study analyzing the handling of *traceability* information in a broad variety of usage contexts, Ramesh and Jarke [RJ01] were able to analyze the *traceability* behavior in practice of 30 target groups from 26 organizations in 11 business units. The following results produced interesting insights into growing unstructured complexity when *traceability* has been employed [RJ01]:

- Organizations as the U.S. Department of Defense spend 4% of its IT development costs for *traceability* without achieving adequate value. The authors ascribe these findings not at last to a planless realization of *traceability* linkages.

- "A broad variety of *traceability* strategies is practiced in industry and the existing models are too simple and/or too rigid to deal with this variety" [RJ01; p.59].

- In the involved organizations and literature, the analysis of *traceability* models surfaced the usage of 18 different link types at 21 different object types (artifacts or parts of artifacts).

- Concerning the employment of *traceability*, the user groups could be segmented into *low end* and *high end* users. With growing experience the tendency to use richer *traceability* models towards *high end* exists (cf. also [Ra98]). Typical needs of *low end* users are technical problems (e.g., what are interconnections between requirements) representable by *functional traces*, whereas high end users are more interested in managerial issues (decisions etc.) rather manageable by *nonfunctional tracing* [Pi04; p.100] (cf. also [Br07a], [RJ01]). Table 10.2 shows the differencing characteristics between both user types according to [RJ01; p.65] in detail.

- Ramesh and Jarke [RJ01] further point out that different *traceability* link types exist (also cf. [Br07a]): *product-related* (e.g., *dependency* and *satisfaction*) and *process-related* (c.g., *evolution* or *rationale*). However, for the decision to realize a link type, very detailed cost-benefit analyses are employed. These findings directly match with Pinheiro's differentiation between *functional* (corresponds to *product-related*) and *nonfunctional tracing* (corresponds to *process-related*).

According to Ramesh and Jarke, these findings show that establishing *traceability* is accompanied by an evolutionary learning curve tending to richer *traceability* models, in which each organization traverses rather planless phases of *traceability* (simply put, 'playing around with *traceability*') and in which a more structured and planned methodology develops tending to richer (*high-level*) *traceability* models.

In this point, the author disagrees to a certain extent to the findings of Ramesh and Jarke. When analyzing the focus groups of the study [RJ01; p.64], a broad variety of branches are taken into account including automotive industry. However, the automotive industry may have different business settings in comparison to other named branches such as avionics, military or governmental administration and telecommunications. In these branches, SW development costs are an integral part cost of development, in which often specialized pieces with low quantities but high demands for quality (especially *safety*) are demanded (see ch. I.2.3, ch. I.7.5). This allows companies to have higher software development budgets. In the automotive industry, high piece numbers often lead to HW piece costs as the main driver of costs. In this business, SW development costs are often calculated as side costs leading to tight budgets and strong cost pressures[187]. This means, establishing new *traceability* features leading to richer *traceability* models even faces stronger concerns about development costs. In this setting, a development to much richer *traceability* models will only take place if pressure is imposed[188], or if new *traceability* methods allow significant advantages with potential to cost reductions. In other words, the author believes that *traceability* is not employed in equal ways throughout all different industries. Instead, different constraints within the different industries lead to different forms of employed *traceability* models in practice.

Table 10.2 Characteristics of low-end and high-end traceability users [RJ01; p.65]

Characteristics	Low-end traceability users	High-end traceability users
Number of organizations identified in the study.	Nine	Seventeen
Typical number of participants	Fifty-four	Eighty-four
Typical complexity of system	About 1000 requirements	About 10,000 requirements
Traceability experience level	Zero to two years	Five to ten years
User definition of *traceability*	Documents transformation of requirements to design	Increases the probability of producing a system that meets all customer requirements and will be easy to maintain.
Main application of *traceability*	Requirements decomposition Requirements allocation Compliance verification Change control	Full coverage of life cycle Including user and customer, captures discussion issues, decisions and *rationale* Capturing traces across product and process dimensions

---

[187] This is especially true for the Automotive suppliers industry branch. In that way, the author is not even sure whether automotive OEMs and suppliers have comparable development settings.

[188] In the last years, such a case has taken place in which several OEMs have decided to demand SPICE based development processes from suppliers thus significantly leveraging *traceability* concepts in the automotive supplier industry.

As a consequence of their findings described above, Ramesh and Jarke [RJ01] searched for ways to lower the steep and more or less planless learning curves of most companies for *traceability* establishment in practice. As a solution, they propose the usage of so-called *traceability reference models (TRM)* [RJ01], this means, the usage of prototypical adaptable linkage models of the particular problem domain – also possible to term *traceability* framework. "Reference models are therefore an abstraction of best practice, condensed from numerous case studies over an extended period of time, followed by more case studies to refine and evaluate the proposed reference model" [RJ01; p.58]. Corresponding to the identified user types and their interview results, Ramesh and Jarke could condense a *low-end* and a *high-end traceability reference model*, the corresponding user types use.

The *low-end traceability model* is segmented in four artifact types. *Requirements* are hierarchically managed via *derive* relationships representing requirement decomposition (see ch. II.10.4.2.2). *Verification procedures* are developed to verify the implementation of requirements. *Requirements* are *satisfied* by a *system* on which the *verification procedures* are *performed* to ensure that the system fulfills the requirements. The *system* can be segmented into *subsystems* or *components* via *depend-on* relationships. The *system interfaces* with other *external systems*.

In contrast, the *high-end traceability model* is segmented into four sub models:

- The *Requirements Management Model* describes the documentation and management of the found requirements.
- The *Rationale and Decision Model* deals with comprehensible documentation of requirements or architectural related decisions.
- The *Requirements to Design Model* manages comprehensible mapping of requirements to design.
- The *Test and Verification Model* cares about mapping of requirements with test scenarios as verification of requirement fulfillment.

The *Requirements Management Model*, deals about requirement elicitation, specification (documentation) and management of the found requirements. The *Test and Verification Model* shows how *compliance verification procedures* are related to *process mandates, different testing techniques, deviations reporting, requirements*, and the *system*. Both topics are not further discussed as they are not in the center of this thesis. The interested user may consult [RJ01].

The *Rationale and Decision Model* orients itself on REMAP [RD92] (ch. II.10.8). It describes the connections between *decisions, rationale, assumptions, arguments, alternatives*, and *issues or conflicts* together taking effect on other *objects* (such as *requirements, system, components*, or *design*). As ch. II.10.8 describes, the model can be seen as a combination of *IBIS* with *REM* activities.

The *Requirements to Design Model* describes the connections between *requirements* and *design*. *Design creates*, or *defines* the *system* with its *subsystems* and *components* being structured by *depend-on* and *part-of* relationships, where *part-of* explicitly refers now to a kind of abstraction hierarchy concept. The *system* also *depends-on external systems* and *uses resources*. Inside, the *system* performs *functions addressed* (described) by *requirements*. As in the *low-end traceability model*, *requirements* are *allocated to* the *system*, *subsystems* and *components*, which *satisfy* the requirements. Additionally, the *requirements drive* the *design*, but also *change requests modify* the *design* and *mandates* describe *general policies* to be applied on *design*.

The *TRM*[189] in [RJ01] can be seen as a prototypical generic relationships model (or *traceability* scheme) for *traceability* issues, in which relevant parts can be used individually according to the *traceability* need. The *TRM* can also be seen as a kind of *meta-model* of possible *traceability* relationships and gives support for clear interpretation of the relationships.

One merit of the *TRM* is to emphasize aspects about design often neglected in *traceability* considerations, such as resource restrictions, external systems, change requests or mandates. Concerning implementation of the *TRM*, the article assumes a complete realization by using a *REM-tool*. Thus, the aspects of connecting the requirements artifacts with the design artifacts, when different tools are used (as it is usually the case), are only handled by an abstract, symbolic way, because design is only described as defining representation of the system, and requirements just *drive* the design.

As Pinheiro [Pi04] and Brcina [Br07a; p.5] indicate, the *high-end traceability model* of Ramesh and Jarke stronger supports *nonfunctional traces*. This is, for example, the case at the emphasis of *RatMan* support as important means to improve *traceability* information. However, the model is treated as a more or less separate and loosely coupled aspect. In the author's believe, *RatMan* support should be more closely integrated into the design process in order to support *rationale capture* as a *by-product* thus overcoming significant *benefit problems* (see ch. II.10.5).

Apart from [RJ01], other authors also describe rudiments for a *CTM*:

- Analyzing the problems connected with *traceability*, Gotel and Finkelstein draw the conclusion that *Pre-RS traceability* is one of the most crucial issues [GF94]. As a consequence, they developed a *CTM* called *contribution structures* for describing the origins of requirements [GF95].
- Hatley et al. [HHP03; p.33-41] provide a *requirement meta-model* for embedded development practice. The model explicitly emphasizes *non-*

---

[189] See also the remark of [Pi04; p.109].

functional aspects important in embedded systems (as for example timing constraints) and their relationships to other requirements. Further, the model is detailed by discussions about relations between requirements and *architectures* [HHP03; p.169-175]. In this way, the *requirement meta model* can also be seen as a *traceability* model or at least give indications about possible *traceability* relationships in embedded practice (see especially the *meta-model diagram* [HHP03; p.35]).

- SysML defines several relationship types to relate requirements with other items: *<<DeriveReqt>>* (=annotates a *derive* relationship between requirements), *<<Satisfy>>* (=describes that a requirement is satisfied by an item), *<<Verify>>* (=describes that a test verifies a requirement), *<<Refine>>* (=describes how a model element or set of elements refine a requirement), *<<Trace>>* (=general purpose relationship between a requirement and any item), *<<Copy>>* (indicates that an item is a copy of another), [SV08].

- Knethen [Kn01a], [Kn01b] develops a *formal meta-model* for a modeling approach to document *requirements traceability* in design artifacts as a *by-product* of the usual modeling activities.

- Leffingwell and Widrig [LW99; p.338] provide a *CTM* for managing requirements in a mainly software-driven development practice.

- Pohl's dependency model [Po99], [Po08; p.505-526], (see also ch. I.5.7.1, [MXP05]) tries to provide a systematic outline of different *traceability* types. It identifies five general *traceability* type categories with nineteen different dependency link types:

  - *Conditions* describe conditional connections such as *constraints* and *preconditions*.

  - *Content* describes whether contents are *similar* to each other, are the result of a *compare*-operation between contents, contradict each other, or *conflict* with each other.

  - *Documentation* describes connections between documents such as *example_for*, *test_case_for*, *purpose*, *responsible_for*, *background*, *comment* relationships.

  - *Abstraction* describes connections between items of the kinds *classification*, *aggregation* or *generalization*.

  - *Evolution* describes evolutionary types such as *replaces*, *satisfies*, *bases_on*, *formalizes* and *refines*.

- Wieringa [Wi98] could also identify 31 different link types possible to use to coherently connect requirement documents, design artifacts, and other documentation.

Pinheiro [Pi04; p.107] provides an overview on further proposals for *CTMs* in the context of design languages such as UML. He [Pi04; p.109] further expresses the idea that other reference models concerning *REM* as provided by [GGJ+00] and [Ge05] may be a good starting point for discussing *traceability* issues, even though they are not specifically intended for *traceability*.

Kelleher proposes making *CTMs* more flexible by using the *pattern* concept. Such a *traceability pattern* describes "best practices, good *traceability* designs and captures successful work experiences" [Ke05; p.52]. He could differentiate two different *traceability pattern* types:

- *Generative Traceability Patterns* describe characteristics of a *CTM* to be used as a *meta-model* for *traceability* establishment.
- *Traceability Engineering Patterns* "help exchange *traceability* experience or knowledge and provide rules for generating successful *traceability* practices" [Ke05; p.52].

As demonstration examples for the effectiveness of his idea, Kelleher describes three *patterns* (*Traceability Plan Pattern*, *Traceability Strategy Pattern*, and *Product Compliance Pattern*) and sketches a *traceability pattern* tool environment.

II.10.4.3 Process

In order to ensure usefulness of *traceability* information, defined processes should accompany any activities concerned with establishment, usage and maintenance of *traceability* information. Pinheiro [Pi04; p.107] calls this "*traceability methods*".

Defined processes are especially important when the number of requirements grows [Ja04; p.39], [RJ01]. Factors influencing the decisions about the right processes are "number of requirements, the system lifetime, organizational maturity, the development team size, type of the development system and specific customer requirements" [Ja04; p.39]. Smaller teams can manage requirements and their changes with rather unstructured *traceability processes*, whereas larger teams must more rely on *formal traceability policies* [Ja04; p.39].

Process standards as *SPICE* and *CMMI* also define explicit demands for *traceability* processes that must be considered. *Ch. I.7 enlists* the aspects to consider for this thesis. Another description of *traceability* methods is found in [Yu94]. Concerning goals, processes should consider ensuring the following aspects:

- A uniform and appropriate level of granularity of *traceability* information should be achieved [DP98], [Kn01b; p.57].

- Useful support for *IA*s [HDH+06; p.94], (see ch. II.10.3).
- Avoid consistency gaps [HDH+06; p.94].
- Allow *coverage analyses* whether all requirements are sufficiently considered in all further processes [HDH+06; p.94].
- Support of *verification procedures* [HDH+06; p.94].

Typically, the following processes are important for valuable *traceability* information [Pi04; p.103ff], [Kn01b; p.49ff], [KP02; p.21f]:

- *Define the entities and relationships to be traced,*
- *Capture traces,*
- *Extract and represent traces,*
- *Maintain traces;*

II.10.4.3.1 Define the Entities and Relationships to Be Traced

At first, an organization must define what entities and what traces are needed. Pinheiro calls this the *trace definition phase* [Pi04; p.103]. In order to achieve efficient and valuable *traceability*, Weber and Weisbrod call this the real challenge about *traceability* [WW03; p.22]. The discussion about *CTMs* in the chapters above provides an overview of the entities and traces that can be considered.

As differences in interpretation are a source for errors, definitions of entities and traces should promote a uniform understanding [Pi04; p.104]. Concerning trace definition, a *CTM* should consider the following aspects [Pi04; p.110]:

1. *Define a few basic types* as a manageable set of the most important information.
2. *Allow the specification of user-definable traces* to allow easy adaption to user or project specific needs.
3. *Allow the use of rich representations of traceable objects* as, e.g., representation by multimedia content to support *nonfunctional tracing*.

Knethen [Kn01b; p.40] emphasizes that a precise general definition of the types and kinds of *traceability* relationships to be maintained is currently missing (cf. also [RJ01], [RE93]). The semantics rather strongly depends on the usage purpose [Kn01b; p.40].

In the author's view, this may be normal because *traceability* approaches are not useful per se, but have a considerably strong pressure to provide benefit ch. II.10.5). Besides, a large variety of possible traces exist. Thus, rather use-driven approaches may be better to maintain and more specific than general approaches.

Pinheiro further emphasizes that the description of the traces by a *CTM* "should resemble the ways traces occur in the real world" [Pi04; p.104]. Otherwise, if a mismatch between the traces defined in a *CTM* and the traces really captured exists, dangers will arise that on one side things are captured that have not been there and then again things may be retrieved that never happened [Pi04; p.104]. Concerning the tool introduced in part III, the author has considered this problem by developing a process heuristic helping designers to capture traces resembling designers' thinking and proceeding (see ch. III.18.2.4).

Further, the authors thinks that *CTMs* must also consider what Ebert calls the "life-cycle of a requirement" meaning that requirements become valid, may change several times and may also become invalid [Eb08; p.260]. Correspondingly, R2A (see part III) also supports a mechanism to consistently maintain *traceability* information according to the requirement's life-cycle (see ch. III.22.2).

II.10.4.3.2 Capture the Traces

This aspect deals with processes concerned with the establishment of traces; also called trace production [Pi04; p.104]. Such processes must address the questions when an identified information is captured, how, and by whom [KP02; p.21]. In some cases, *traceability* establishment may be automatable. A discussion of this is provided in ch. II.10.4.2.20 above.

Referring to [Pi96], Knethen and Paech [KP02; p.21] describe two ways traces can be captured:

*   *Off-line*: describes approaches that demand trace capturing as separate activity of the actual development activity. This kind of approach can be performed manually, or automatically. *Dependency analysis* approaches that automatically extract trace information from source code are an example of automated off-line trace capturing.
*   *On-line*: describes ways of capturing *traceability* information while performing a development activity. This is why most of these approaches are automated ones, but also manual approaches can support these ways. This is supported by the approach described in part III.

Pinheiro explicitly emphasizes that a *CTM* must consider trace capture processes [Pi04; p.104], because first of all, only these traces are captured being recognized before, but – even more important – trace capturing may be the crux deciding about success or failure of *traceability*. In ch. II.10.5, the author explains that trace capturing faces a significant *benefit problem* and it may directly interfere with the developers' actual development activities [KP02; p.21], [AR05]. *Traceability* approaches may only succeed if they solve these problems.

Dömges and Pohl emphasize that *off-line approaches* (Dömges and Pohl call these approaches *trace reconstruction* [DP98; p.58]) tend to traces that "are typically incomplete and idealized in order to meet certain expectations" [DP98; p.58]. As a solution for this problem, Knethen and Paech [KP02; p.26], [Kn01a], [Kn01b] propose recording *traceability* information on-*line* as a *by-product* [KP02; p.26] of normal development activities. Pinheiro emphasizes that many functional traces could be captured as a *by-product* [Pi04; p.108]. Accordingly, the approach introduced in part III supports a manual *traceability* establishment approach that tries as much as possible to support *traceability* generation as a *by-product* of designers' normal design activities.

As an additional problem of solutions such as the solution described in part III, capturing *traceability* faces special difficulties when tool boundaries must be bridged. Weber and Weisbrod experienced tool couplings as often immature [WW02; p.23]. As a solution to avoid negative effects of tool couplings, they recommend minimizing linking between two tools to be bridged and propose using methodological approaches as design guidelines to reduce interconnections and thus linking efforts [WW02; p.23]. A detailed discussion on tool couplings is provided in the following chapter about *traceability* tools.

II.10.4.3.3 Extract and Represent Traces

This process aspect deals about extracting and representing specific information from the set of gathered information, so that the information need is fulfilled in an optimal way. In other words, the processes must answer "how to extract and represent what information is needed by whom to fulfill what purpose" [KP02; p.22].

Different and flexible ways for *trace extraction* should be possible. In Pinheiro's eyes, three different modes should have appropriate support by *trace extraction* mechanisms [Pi04; p.105]:

- *Selective tracing* shall allow to "restrict the tracing to certain selected *patterns*" of entities and relations. In this way, only certain specific classes of entities and relations could be considered. More sophisticated approaches could also include contextual information (as for example the development phase) as selection criterion.
- *Interactive tracing* means to allow an interactive browsing mechanism to navigate backward and forward in the model.
- *Non-guided tracing* shall allow the user to arbitrarily step from entity to entity analyzing contents as demanded. This shall ensure convenient tracing when little information on what or how to trace is available.

In [PG96], Pinheiro and Goguen show how all three modes can be realized with the *traceability* tool TOOR (discussed in the following chapter about tools).

Extracted information must be represented in a fashion supporting the tracing process. "It should effectively help to fulfill the need that triggered the tracing" [Pi04; p.106].

Further, the extraction procedure and the information representation should be intuitive in order to be regarded as useful and efficient. Otherwise, "it may be simpler to go around and to informally ask people" [Pi04; p.106] about any relevant information (see also [SS07]).

Summoning up *trace extraction*, a *traceability* approach should support the following criteria [Pi04; p.110]:
- Provide different and flexible ways for extracting information,
- Extraction should be context sensitive,
- Extraction procedures should get the information needed to satisfy tracing needs;

In ch. III.22.1, the author shows how the considerations about *trace extraction* are realized in the tool solution described in part III.

II.10.4.3.4 Maintain Traces

"*Traceability* is a great feature, but the real challenge is deciding which traces to maintain" [WW02; p.22]. Once captured, traces must be continuously maintained in order to keep its validity. Process definitions must define when traces must be maintained, how, and by whom. The process activities are similar to the trace capturing processes. Especially for maintaining *traceability* information, suitable tool support is essential (see next ch. II.10.4.4) when high numbers of relations are involved. Instead, less sophisticated solutions basing on spreadsheets and *traceability* matrices tend to be hard to change [LW99; p.340].

Ch. III.22.2 describes how the trace maintenance and general artifact consistency can be improved by the tool solution introduced in part III.

II.10.4.3.5 Processes and the Traceability Environment Circularity Problem

Concerning *traceability* environments and their processes, Pinheiro [Pi04; p.101ff] could identify a circularity problem: On the one hand, only primarily registered traces are considered, on the other hand, only traces can be registered that have been perceived before.

The problem discloses when considering the way *traceability* usually is installed and used:

1. At first, a *CTM* defining the potential traces is built up in the definition phase.
2. During the capturing phase, the traces are perceived and captured in the environment.
3. Later, a real need for information about the traces surfaces.
4. During the extraction phase, *retrieval* mechanisms of the environment shall help to gather the needed information out of the traces.

Now, the drawback on this is that information collection must be prepared and executed before the real information needs are exactly known. Correspondingly, situations occur that the collected information misses the real needs or it is incomplete at last.

Trying to avoid this gap by collecting as much traces as acquirable leads to high efforts spent on collection and maintenance of data with questionable value for the project. In the end, this leads to negative impacts endangering any value of *traceability*.

Another opportunity to avoid the problem would be to defer *traceability* capturing to a later point in time, when the real information need has already surfaced. However, up-to-now, almost all tracing concepts demand for information capture beforehand [Pi04; p.102]. Some automatic procedure may delay information capturing to a later point of time, but the types of information to be gathered must still be known beforehand in order to develop adequate algorithms or mechanisms.

A way to avoid this may be to make the recreation of the original situations when the trace capturing took place possible. This can be achieved by including multimedia support that can, for example, record meeting discussions about decisions [HPW+99]. Another possibility is to find ways to avoid the need for explicit links. For this, methods for *knowledge discovery* and *pattern mining* [ESS02], or *information retrieval* techniques [ACC+02] have been proposed.

In many cases, however, the only opportunity may be to reiterate the steps mentioned above several times to evolve the *traceability* models and processes according to newly gathered experiences.

II.10.4.4 Tools

Based on numbers provided by a survey of the London School of Economics analyzing about 100 companies in Europe and USA, Ebert [Eb08; p.290] provides a good schema showing the connections between efficiency, processes and tools (see fig. 10-2). This shows that proper processes can have a significant influence on efficiency but in connection with the right tools the influence is even higher. Also tool support alone without process support only provides minor advantages leading to the view of Ebert "before thinking about ... tools, ... (an organization) should cope with ... (its) processes" [Eb08; p.292 (*)].

What Ebert wants to express is that a tool alone does not guarantee proper usage. Instead, good processes provide higher efficiency potential, but good processes in combination with good tools reveal synergistic effects significantly leveraging the project quality and efficiency.

But, Weber and Weisbrod observed, when engineers request improved tool support, great opportunities exist for also improving processes and practices as a *by-product* [WW02; p.22]. Besides, employing new tools generally leads to more work and learning processes at the beginning, when processes also must be adapted to a certain point to fit to the tools.

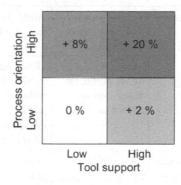

Figure 10-2 Efficiency gains, process orientation and tool support [Eb08; p.290]

Correspondingly, in the author's opinion, processes and tools should be adapted in the following way:
1. At first, the important aspects of processes must be identified and defined first.
2. Then, it should be tried to bring these 'process cornerstones' into practice. In this phase, tool support is not decisive. It rather deals with implementing prototypical processes to acquire feedback from practice whether the intended processes are capable to fulfill the intentions.
3. In the meantime, adequate tool support should be evaluated. If such support could be found, the corresponding tool should be integrated into the process environment.

4. Now, a phase of learning in practice can surface the interactions between processes and tools. Thus iterative[190] improvement of the processes and its tool support must ensure proper integration of both.

The R2A tool discussed in part III also tries to identify certain process cornerstones that are implemented in the tool, but also tried to ensure freedom for adaption of the processes and the tool environment. Weber and Weisbrod emphasize, however, that a poor tool solution can also discredit well defined processes and vice versa. Correspondingly, the application of *REM-tools* in concert with processes "provide an opportunity and a risk in *RE* process improvement" [WW02; p.23].

Table 10.3 Kinds of traceability tools according to [GF94] and [Kn01b; p.57]

	General-purpose tools (e.g., spreadsheets)	Special-purpose tools (e.g., tool couplings)	Workbenches (e.g., *REM-tools*)	Environments (e.g., CASE-tools)
Strengths	- Adaptive - Sufficient for small projects	- Tight *traceability* for particular requirements-related activities	- Fine-grained relationships within *REM* phases. - Additional *REM* checks	- Provide ongoing *traceability* - Flexible
Deficiencies	- Initial configuration costs intensive - Most only electronic version of paper - Poor control and integration	- Restricted - Poor integration, and information management	- Poorly integrated - Distracting - Tool dictation	- *Traceability* typically coarse-grained - Tightness of *traceability* varies - Flexibility counter-balanced by poorer *traceability*

Dömges and Pohl [DP98], (cf. also [KP02; p.23]) provide an evaluation about the adaption of *traceability* environments to project-specific needs. They were able to identify three key *requirements traceability tool* support must fulfill:

---

[190] Dömges and Pohl state a similar view in emphasizing the constant need for iterative, i.e., continuous improvement of *traceability* practice: "It is essential to establish and continuously improve organizational knowledge about project-specific trace definitions" [DP98; p.61].

1. In order to reduce the capture effort, the environment must provide good integration into the process environment.
2. Further, the *traceability* mechanisms must adapt to the usage situation, meaning the tasks to perform for establishing, maintaining, and using *traceability* information must not interfere with the original tasks to perform.
3. Last but not least, a tool must support organizational knowledge creation, what means that the created information must be propagated to any involved stakeholder and long-term collaboration must be taken into account.

Concerning tool support for *traceability*, Knethen [Kn01b; p.57] provides an overview on tools summarizing a survey performed by Gotel and Finkelstein [GF94] shown in table 10.3. It compares four types of tools:

- *General-purpose tools* are general tools used for common – non-requirement specific – usage purposes. In this category spreadsheet applications are often used for manually documenting *traceability matrices* (see ch. II.10.4.2.2).
- *Special-purpose tools* are tools developed for special requirement related activities as, e.g., to document information gathered for requirement elicitation.
- *Workbenches* try to offer a complete integrated set of functionality to support *REM*. "They are typically centered around a database management system, and have tools to document, parse, organize, edit, interlink, change, and manage requirements" [GF94; p.95].
- *Environments* try to offer integrated tool chains to support all development phases of a project. These tools are also called *application life-cycle management (ALM)* solutions.

In today's commercial tool market, these four categories still have actuality, as the following chapters show.

Additionally, Rupp et al. [RS07; p.399] identify a fifth category:

- *Mutants* are tools originally designed for other purposes but now also used for *traceability* purposes.

The following chapters describe these categories in more detail and provide some typical tools for the different categories. As the number of tools market in research and commercial use is very vast, only a small but rather representative portion of the available tools is described. Any other tools not mentioned here should be mappable in some of the categories described here.

II.10.4.4.1 General-Purpose Tools

In many projects, general-purpose tools, such as spreadsheets or text documentation programs, are still used [PR09; p.155] in small projects for documenting *traceability matrices* [Pi04; p.107]. However, problems as circuitous capturing, difficult maintenance of changing traces, difficult *trace extraction* (especially concerning *bidirectional traceability*) are major drawbacks. However, the generality of spreadsheet tools sparks new usage concepts as, for example, the tool Vector eASEE [Eb08; p.289-327] uses the spreadsheet application Microsoft Excel® as basis for an *ALM*-based *traceability* support (see the sub chapter about *ALM* solutions).

II.10.4.4.2 Workbenches (REM-Tools)

Workbenches are what the author in the chapters before called *REM-tools* such as IBM Rational DOORS. Evaluating reasons for the SW project success for several years the Standish Group's Chaos report of 2001 comes to the conclusion that *REM-tools* "seem to have the biggest impact on the success of a project" [St01; p.10], thus recommending the usage of an adequate *REM-tool* as top priority need of any SW development project [St01; p.10].

Rupp et al. provide an extended discussion about help and use of *REM-tools* and how to introduce a tool in project practice [RS07; p.395-408]. A vast number of different solutions exist. The International Council on Systems Engineering (INCOSE) provides a comparative survey[191] of current state-of-the-art *REM-tools*. Other information can be found in the iX study on current industry practice and available tools for *REM* [HMC+07], [Eb08; p.289-327], [RS07; p.395-408], or [DP98]. Lang and Duggan [LD01] list the basic functionality a *REM-tool* must support. Rupp et al. [RS02; p.420] provide a summary of minimum requirements and helpful optional requirements a valuable *REM-tool* solution should provide.

According to Weber and Weisbrod, *REM-tools* "are the number one instrument for leveraging *RE* practices – which means they still must be improved" [WW02; p.23]. To spark further improvements they enlist a set of deficiencies *REM-tools* should improve:

- The tools should offer "basic workflow support, such a powerful filter and view capabilities and sophisticated view management" [WW02; p.23].
- Such tools must be easily adaptable via a standard programming language to support quick adaption to project or company specific needs. The authors express here special concern that the *REM-tools* must provide possibilities options for external access to enable easy adaption of integration with other tools.

Traceability is usually established via links or *traceability* matrices, or a combination of both. Some also support features for automated *traceability* estab-

---

[191] http://www.incose.org/ProductsPubs/products/rmsurvey.aspx; (Access: 2009/10).

lishment. As it is the market leading tool for requirements management in technical development (especially in the automotive industry) [Mu06b], IBM Rational DOORS is discussed as a representative for all commercial *REM-tools* in this thesis. IBM Rational DOORS supports the following kinds of *traceability*:

- *Evolutionary traceability* is supported by *history* and *baselining mechanisms*.
- Through a linking mechanism, any items present in IBM Rational DOORS can be linked with each other. Thus, *intra-* as well as *between-artifact traceability* is supported. The established *links* can be alternatively represented as a *traceability matrix* or as *graphical visualization*. However, in the author's practical experience, both alternative representations are of limited value as they get increasingly confusing with growing numbers of traceable items.
- IBM Rational DOORS supports assigning attributes (resp. properties) to any traceable item. It further supports attributing of *traceability links*, thus allowing different semantics of *traceability links* to be modeled and gathering *meta-information* on *traceability* relationships. However, no dedicated *meta-model* support is provided. The attribute information can be used to create powerful filter and view capabilities as requested by Weber and Weisbrod [WW02; p.23].
- IBM Rational DOORS has no specific support for any *REM* process, whereas other tools exist with dedicated support specific processes. As an example, the tools IBM Rational RequisitePro or IrQA offer dedicated support for *use case* driven development.
- Last but not least, IBM Rational DOORS provides with the DOORS Extension Language (DXL) a scripting mechanism to support quick adaption to project or company specific needs also allowing access from outside as requested by Weber and Weisbrod [WW02; p.23].

However, traceability workbench tools such as IBM Rational DOORS have a significant disadvantage:

- IBM Rational DOORS has its strength in text-based artifacts meaning that text-based artifacts can be split into single traceable items that can be related to each other. Even though some extensions such as DOORS Modeler exist, IBM Rational DOORS has only weak support for model-based engineering methods Other *REM-tools* may provide a slightly better modeling orientation[192], but the discussion in ch. II.10.6 shows that coupling design with the requirements domain is generally difficult.

---

[192] For example, IBM Rational Reqtify, Borland Caliber RM or IRQA rather support requirement management methods basing on a *use case* concept similar to UML.

II.10.4.4.3 Special-Purpose Tools

Special-purpose tools describe tools that only support a certain aspect of *traceability*. The following lists some of the wide variety:

- *Tool couplings* have gained rising interest in the recent years. Especially concerning *safety-critical* embedded development an urgent need for continuous tool support has been identified [Gr05; p.421], [Br06; p.37]. Correspondingly, special tool couplings as support for *traceability* may be the most encountered *special-purpose tools*.
- *RatMan support*: As discussed in ch. II.10.8, combining *traceability* and *RatMan* approaches are promising, because both have supporting effects. Correspondingly, several tool support exists in research (see [HWA+07] and ch. II.10.8).
- Support for requirements elicitation such as *contribution structures* [GF94] allowing modeling stakeholders and their relationships or the WinWin approach ([BEK+98], [BK06], [WinWin]) supporting requirement negotiation between stakeholders.
- Support for *variation* and *product line management* [Si98], or also referred to as feature models ([BP06], [RPP04], [RTM02]) provides an extension of REMAP (see ch. II.10.8) for *product line engineering*.
- Marcus et al. [MXP05] show a prototypical tool TraceViz that integrates into the Eclipse IDEs and supports *traceability* visualizations basing on *traceability* information collected by other tools.
- *Event-Based Traceability*: Cleland-Huang et al. [CCC03] extend the ordinary link concept by a publish-subscribe mechanism. When an item is changed an automated notification event mechanism propagates change messages to all linked items thus supporting *consistency maintenance*. Their tool approach bases on IBM Rational DOORS.
- Han [Ha00], [Ha01b], [WH02] introduces the tool approach TRAM (Tool for Requirements and Architecture Management) for *system requirements* and *system architecture management* with dedicated focus on *traceability* and *rationale documentation*. The approach relies on a documentation template that can be integrated into *REM-tool* environments such as IBM Rational DOORS, but also a standalone solution exists basing on HTML or XML. The approach also has implemented a model to document decisions on *system requirements* or *system architecture*.
- As reliable exchange of requirements information between OEMs and suppliers is an essential concern in automotive industry, the HIS (see ch. I.7) has defined the *Requirement Interchange Format (RIF)* standard file format to

ensure reliable exchange of requirements between different *REM-tools*. *RIF* also allows exchanging *traceability* link information.

II.10.4.4.4 Application Lifecycle Management (ALM) Environments

Above all, large projects need to dynamically reference information created and maintained in a variety of tools and platforms [Ra98; p.43]. *Application life-cycle management (ALM)* solutions offer integrated tool chains to support all development phases of a project. In this way, produced development results in one integrated tool shall be usable in any other tool where these results are needed. Correspondingly, *traceability* is a basic feature of *ALM* solutions. Thus, in principle, *traceability* can be established between any items managed in an *ALM* solution via establishing links, but, in practice, due to the high amount of items possible to trace, establishing *traceability* is often difficult. Further, due to the very general character of *ALM* solutions, *traceability* is one of a diversity of aspects covered leading to no support by specific *traceability* functions and no specific *traceability* processes. Thus, in *ALM* solutions establishment and usage of *traceability* often prove cumbersome.

Known commercial *ALM* tools are IBM Jazz, Vector eASEE, Microsoft Visual Studio Team Server, MKS, or Siemens PLM Teamcenter.

The Ophelia[193] research project ("Open Platform and Methodologies for Development Tools Integration in a Distributed Environment") is a European project for developing the theoretical basis to integrate development tools into an integrated process chain. The attempt's goal is to define an *architecture* to couple tools as a bus system along the development life cycle. This allows linking objects of different development tools together to support *traceability*. Additionally, *traceability* information can be coupled with a notification messaging system allowing users to register for event notifications on events such as object changes. Such notifications can then be used to automatically trigger further change management mechanisms.

Mohan and Ramesh [MR07] introduce a tool-suite to integrate different tools in a *traceability* model with a collaborative environment. One major idea is to combine *knowledge fragments* (*design elements*, *requirements* and *rationale*) stored in different tools within an integrated *knowledge map*. Through the collaborative environment, group decision and negotiation shall be improved on basis of the *knowledge map*.

---

[193] See, e.g., http://entwickler.de/zonen/portale/psecom,id,101,online,624,.html (Access: 2010/09).

II.10.4.4.5 Mutants

Rupp et al. also refer to another tool type called 'mutants' [RS07; p.399]. These are tools developed for a different purpose but now also used for fulfilling tracing demands. Such a solution is, for example, the UML-tool Enterprise Architect also providing internal mechanisms to specify requirements and relate them to UML elements and diagrams. However, Enterprise Architect is not an *REM-tool* and thus lacks many features usually provided by a valuable *REM-tool* solution.

II.10.5 Traceability and its Benefit Problem

The production of traces and capture are very important aspects for the *traceability* models and a model may be just too complex to be efficiently used [Pi04; p.99]. A study [BSA07] assessing the reasoning behind decisions for using *traceability* in development practice indicates that *traceability* is not very often used in project practice except in projects with *safety-critical* background or when certain development standards (see ch. I.7) are employed.

In practical employment, *traceability* often faces difficulties to be implemented in an economically justifiable fashion [HDH+06; p.93], [Cl06; p.2], [LLY+08; p.102] .

Ambler[194] [Am05] describes the handling of requirements from the agile perspective. Concerning *traceability*, he admits its value when regulatory objectives as regulations in *safety-critical* environments are concerned. However, he advises against unreflected usage in situations where it purely seems to be a good idea. As main concern, he mentions the high efforts needed and refers to two critical points he has observed at companies with *traceability* culture:

1. High efforts for *traceability*: *Traceability* organizations often tend to update artifacts on a regular basis in order to keep consistency. This leads to high documentation maintenance costs. Ambler rather recommends following the best practice "Only update if it hurts". Nuseibeh et al. [NER00] point out that even resolving all inconsistencies can have significant negative effects because resolving inconsistencies often implies "resolving fundamental conflicts or making important design decisions. In such cases, immediate resolution is not the best option. ... Sometimes the effort to fix an inconsistency is significantly greater than the risk that the inconsistency will have any ad-

---

[194] Ambler has a strong notion for the agile development movement; however some of his criticisms have a certain legitimation.

verse consequences." [NER00; p.26]. In these cases, even ignoring the inconsistency may be a proper option.

2. Tendency of high degrees of redundancy: Secondly, *traceability* cultures tend to store the same or nearly the same information on several places. This arising redundancy will lead to extra change effort and inconsistencies unless all redundant information spots are correctly updated. *Traceability* can help to find all redundant spots. However, *traceability* is here more a cure for the symptoms, whereas avoiding redundant information avoids the cause and the extra efforts needed for *traceability* and updating of information. Therefore avoiding redundant information should have higher priority than allowing redundancies that are traceable to each other. In describing practical experiences concerning maintainability of requirement artifacts, Ebert also recommends avoiding redundancies [Eb98; p.183].

"*Requirements traceability* is a work intensive task that can only be achieved when the organization supports it" [Wi05; p.332 (*)]. Gotel and Finkelstein [GF94] diagnose that *traceability* problems primarily arise as consequence of communication breakdowns between developers under strong strains of time additionally hampered by lacking tool support and experiences of lacking benefit (cf. also [Cl06; p.2]). As in current practice *traceability* is usually established manually [Cl06; p.2], [LLY+08; p.102], these processes are time consuming, arduous, error prone, and hard to maintain [Li94; p.21], [Cl06; p.2], [LLY+08; p.102]. The following influence factors can be identified:

- *Granularity or level of detail*: At one side current *traceability* tools and procedure often lead to coarse-grained granularity of traced items and thus to coarse *IAs* [KP02; p.14], [BA96]. "Tracing at a low level of granularity supports a much more precise form of *traceability* but can create an excessive amount of work" [Cl06; p.2]. Dömges and Pohl show that too detailed traces can lead to clutter hampering understanding and maintenance. A way to reduce *traceability* costs is to perform lean *traceability* [EGH+07], [Cl06; p.2]. However, as shown in ch. II.10.6.2, *safety-critical* systems development demands for fine-granular linking.

- *Automation*: According to Egyed et al., "while some automation exists, capturing traces remains a largely manual process" [EGH+07; p.115] and such links degrade over time and must be continuously maintained. Correspondingly, if the degree of automation could be increased, efforts for capturing and maintaining *traceability* could be reduced.

- *Understanding and intention*: Further, the type of usage of the link information must be considered: Egyed et al. [EGH+07] distinguish between short-term utilization (are all requirements considered?) and long-term utilization (assessing a particular change years later). Short-term utilization is more or less covered by the simple link concept usually applied by today's *traceability* understanding, whereas for mid- and long-term utilization of more complex relations additional information such as decisions and their *rationale* must be considered. According to Pinheiro [Pi04; p.101ff], the problem is more general: It is on the one side impossible to record all possible traces. On the other side, the traces must be established, before later the actual trace need is known. Thus, it is highly possible that the wrong traces are recorded.

- *Pre-defined structures*: A way out of this problem is to use *pre-defined structures* such as proposed by Ramesh and Jarke [RJ01], but this can lead to unnecessary bureaucracy [Pi04; p.99], whereas establishing *traceability* is a "very dynamic activity guided by necessity and not by pre-defined structure" [Pi04; p.99].

- *Formality*: *Formality* is needed because it simplifies the tracing process, allows precise semantics, and eases automation [Pi04; p.100]. On the other side, *informality* is needed because most information is inherently *informal* (e.g., natural language) [Pi04; p.101]. A simplification of *informal* traces to a *formal* structure is problematic as shown in ch. II.9.4.2.

- *Intrusiveness* (cf. ch. II.9.1.4): Trace establishment may interfere directly with the actual development activities [Pi00; p.3], [KP02; p.21], [AR05]. "It may impose an overload on people carrying out these activities. The less *intrusive* the trace production, the efficient and accurate the use of the tracing model is" [Pi00; p.3].

- *Grudin's principle* ([Gr87], [Gr88], [Gr96b], ch. II.9.4.2): According to [AR05] and [BSA07; p.307], *traceability* is poorly recorded because of lacking direct perceived benefit. This matches with Ebert's observation that "developers often live in a 'shadow world', where processes and tools are only used pro forma because management wants them to" [Eb08; p.333 (*)]. In the context of *safety-critical* development standards, *traceability* may also often be performed in order to fulfill assessment needs instead of real project needs.

- *Links* degrade over time and must be continuously maintained [EGH+07; p.115].

"As *traceability* is legally required in many *safety-critical* software systems, the question is 'what is the right amount of *traceability*?' and 'what kind of *traceability* can be used to achieve the desired results in a cost-effective way?' Organizations trying to improve their ability to manage change effectively must ask very similar questions." [Cl06; p.3].

According to Pinheiro's opinion, the following points must be considered for improving *traceability* benefit [Pi04; p.110]:

- As much automation as possible should be used.
- The persons recording *traceability* information must understand how this information might be used in the future.
- *Traceability* information must be recorded as close to its occurrence as possible [Pi04; p.104].

Dömges and Pohl [DP98] further emphasize that *traceability* should evolve as a side-effect of the daily development activities and not cause extra bureaucracy.

Links can already degrade during the process activity they have occurred. Especially during design performed decisions are often adapted again, when the design proceeds. In practice, to avoid extra effort for *traceability* maintenance resulting from later design decision corrections, *traceability* is often recorded after the design process has been performed (see also comments to ENG.3 BP.2 in ch. I.7.2.3). However, at that time many of the correlations are already forgotten. Thus, Wiegers emphasizes that *traceability* must be recorded as a *by-product* during the activities and not afterwards [Wi05; p.333].

Accordingly, to address the *benefit problem*, the tool solution described in part III especially aims to provide a method allowing designers to capture the *traceability* information as a *by-product* with as less extra effort as possible not disturbing the designers at their actual tasks.

II.10.6 Traceability between Requirements and Design

Traceability helps to know how and why requirements are satisfied by system development products, because "*traceability* gives essential assistance in understanding the relationships that exist within and across software requirements, design, and implementation" [Pa97; p.364]. Ch. II.10 shows that the current *traceability* concept goes beyond this view as it includes other aspects as requirement elicitation or testing. However, the main topic of this thesis, described in part III, exactly matches the goal Palmer ascribes to *traceability*. The following chapter within this general chapter about *traceability* will summarize the fundamental issues and approaches research on *requirements traceability* to design has collected in the recent years.

II.10.6.1 Theoretic Research Results

Boerstler and Janning [BJ91], [BJ92] use *traceability* information for designers to automatically derive *design* from *analysis artifacts* (see also [Kn01b; p.39],

[KP02; p.04]). As design depends on analysis, parts of the design could be generated automatically via transformation processes basing on *traceability* (also cf. [Li94; p.14], [KP02; p.04]). Such approaches assume close connections between analysis and design artifacts as it is assumed by UML, but this may only be the case for certain aspects of design such as the data model. As described in ch. I.5.4, such approaches are used in practice as, e.g., in the automotive domain, Matlab or ETAS ASCET are used to analyze the requirements of certain functional parts as an *analysis model* that can then be transformed into a *design model* and code with applied automatic *code generation*. At certain circumstances, however, design of the remaining parts must then take special care to integrate these transformed parts thus leading to design of needed mechanisms for integration. The tool solution described in part III tries to take this into account by offering a framework to integrate several tools in one integrated design (ch. III.16.2).

Other approaches try to better integrate requirements-related concerns into the modeling languages[195]. Ambriola and Gervasi [AG98] present a visual design language, where *NFRs* can be directly represented in design diagrams. Graham [Gr03] tries to show how to better integrate *NFRs* in UML-based designs.

Cleland-Huang et al. [CSB+05], [CS03], [Cl05] propose to use a *goal graph* for modeling *NFRs* with their interdependencies. Later, when a change on a functional *design model* is performed a probabilistic *information retrieval* algorithm tries to automatically identify affected *NFRs*. The modeled goal graph then can help to identify tradeoffs with other *NFRs*. As discussed in the chapter before, automatic approaches have not yet succeeded in practice. Therefore, they are neglected in part III. In [HKL09], a goal driven approach to relate *NFRs* to *patterns* is introduced resembling the *goal graph* approach of Cleland-Huang et al..

Orienting on Dömges and Pohl's [DP98] proposal that *traceability* shall be established as a *by-product* [Kn01b; p.50], Knethen [Kn01a], [Kn01b], [Kn02] describes an UML-based design approach for embedded real-time systems having the goal that *traceability* directly emerges from design activities by employing a *formal* modeling approach. The approach itself bases on a *meta-model* extension combining UML with the *four variable model* (*FVM*) (see ch. II.10.4.2.2) in connection with the QUASAR project [PSS04].

Knethen aims at long-term collaboration as she tries to improve maintenance efforts by *traceability*, because former studies indicated that 40-75% of total software costs are maintenance effort [Kn01b; p.2], A special concern of Knethen is to improve *impact estimations* by support of *fine-grained traceability linking models* [Kn01b; p.4].

---

[195] The interested reader may consult Galvao and Goknil [GG07] for an overview on *traceability* solutions for *model driven development*.

From this point of view, the *meta-model* extension of Knethen in combination with the right modeling techniques allows designing systems in a way that *traceability* is recorded as a *by-product* of the modeling results, thus addressing the *traceability* problem. To ensure that the captured information is valuable for *IA*s, an empirical study on the effectiveness of *IA*s was performed on modeling results of Knethen's approach. The approach, however, has the following weaknesses:

1. The approach must be combined with a certain theoretical development process approach for embedded systems [KM00] that is derived from the *FVM*.
2. The created *meta-model* is very *formal*, complex[196] and difficult to understand.
3. As shown in ch. II.9.4.2, *formal* approaches are difficult to handle and may interrupt designers' thinking.
4. The *traceability benefit problem* (ch. II.10.5) is neglected because the approach does not consider the extra efforts developers must spend on applying the *formal* approach in the right manner to establish valuable *traceability*.
5. As discussed in ch. II.10.2, Wieringa [Wi98] shows that design at different design levels can follow different criteria for decomposition. Thus, semantic gaps arise only bridgeable by explicit manual linking.

As a consequence, Wieringa [Wi98] could also identify 31 different possible link types to coherently link requirement documents, design artifacts and other documentation. The study of Ramesh and Jarke [RJ01] also indicates that experienced *traceability* users tend to much richer *traceability* link models and could identify 17 different link types in connection with requirements and design. When analyzing both, some link types can be seen as emerging from the structure of a *design model* (such as 'part_of', 'depend_on' and 'perform'). These link types are usually expressed in the design diagrams and relatively easy to identify by designers. Approaches exist making these relations better suitable for *IA* (e.g., [BLO+06]). Nevertheless, these studies also indicate that significantly more different link relationship types may exist between requirements and design. However, the study of Ramesh and Jarke [RJ01] included several domains (such as military, space craft and aircraft), where development costs are not that much of a factor as in the automotive mass consumer market (see ch. I.2.3). As the study does not differentiate *traceability* practices according to different development domains, the author believes that these more complex[197] link type models might

---

[196] In the author's opinion, the approach rather infers further *complication* in the modeling process than helping to reduce *complication* (see footnote 80 (p. 77)).

[197] Some relationships might also rather infer unnecessary *complication* (see footnote 80 (p. 77)).

also result from development processes with less pressure on process efficiency. Vice versa, the automotive domain may have stronger pressure to address the *traceability benefit problems* described above (ch. II.10.5). Correspondingly, this thesis at first concentrates on addressing the *traceability benefit problems* in providing direct benefit for developers. Thus, the thesis concentrates on ensuring that the most important *traceability* relationships can be established in a way promoting benefit to developers and accurateness. In this way, – hopefully – the promises of the *traceability* concept can be redeemed. Research questions, whether these links should be further differentiated into different more sophisticated relationship types, are rather neglected.

Research of Gruenbacher, Egyed and Medvidovic [GEM01], [GEM03], [MGE+03] came to the conclusion that "the large semantic gap between high-level, sometimes ambiguous requirements artifacts and the more specific architectural artifacts often does not allow one to establish meaningful links between them" [MGE+03; p.202]. Consequentially, they developed an intermediate model approach they call Component, Bus, System, Property (CBSP) model connector. It is developed as a bridge between *requirements* and *architecture* with the goal "to facilitate the consistent transformation of a system's requirements into its implementation" [MGE+03; p.213]. CBSP contains a *meta-model*, where CBSP elements are related to requirements and derived from *architecture model elements*. The semantic allows specifying CBSP elements that resemble requirements but do not directly represent an *architecture*. They rather help to identify architectural components, properties, relations, and styles leading to an *architecture*. In this way, the CBSP elements can also be seen as an extended link concept allowing evolutionary consistency [GEM03; p.251], because the CBSP model also can be seen as a means to *capture rationale* about the decision process. "CBSP is a tool-aided, but highly human-intensive technique" [MGE+03; p.202].

The author considers this solution as rather disadvantageous because the solution introduces a new artifact (the *intermediate model*) significantly raising new redundancies and complication (see footnote 80 (p.77)). As an alternative solution to the gap problem, the R2A solution provides a *decision model* approach (ch. III.19 and ch. III.20) that promises to be more light-weight and easier to use for designers and thus might have better chances to succeed in practice.

II.10.6.2 Tool Couplings between REM- and Design Tools in Practice

Capturing *traceability* faces special difficulties, when tool boundaries must be bridged, but tool couplings are inevitable when different valuable development tools shall be used in combination. As the solution discussed here is a kind of tool coupling, the following will provide a further discussion of tool couplings concerning the transition of requirements to *design models*. Weber and Weisbrod [WW02; p.23] describe experiences made with tool couplings in the context of *requirements specifications* and *models*. They emphasize that "a growing number of specifications require complex models" what "requires engineers to develop a specification using two or more tools: a tool for textual specifications and one or more tools for model-oriented analysis and design" [WW02; p.23].

Correspondingly, tool-couplings shall bridge the tool gaps to ensure *traceability* and consistency between the artifacts. According to Weber and Weisbrod, "most tool couplings – which usually originate in a specific project and were designed and paid for by a specific customer – are insufficiently mature for serious development project use" [WW02; p.23]. Consequently, several of their projects started by using such tool couplings, "but later dropped them, even when doing so would clearly require considerable manual effort or significant process problems" [WW02; p.23]. They identified the following shortcomings:

- *Speed:* "In an average project, the number of linked objects can easily grow to several thousand, which results in unacceptably slow coupling speed (when calculating changes, for example)" [WW02; p.23].
- *Integrated document generation:* "Existing tool couplings don't support this feature, whether the documents are short status reports or lengthy documentation that satisfies a standardized structure. Although a few tools are dedicated to integrated document generation, they exist only in specific vendors' tools suites and are largely useless outside of them" [WW02; p.23].
- *User interface:* "Tool couplings usually create redundant editors for managing cross-tool information (typically one for each tool involved)" [WW02; p.23].
- *Automation:* "In most tools, the automation level is low, there is no active administrative support, and users must initiate synchronization. Also, there is no active support for indicating problems" [WW02; p.23].

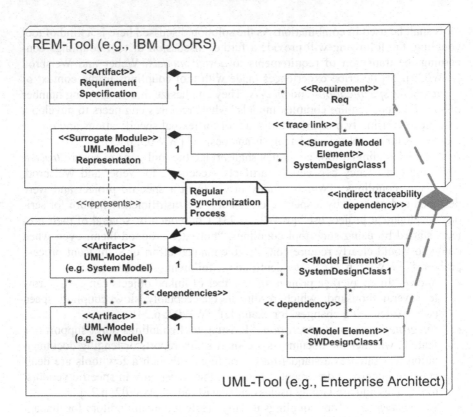

Figure 10-3 Traceability tool couplings via surrogate modules

Concerning tool couplings with modeling tools, at first so-called *surrogate module* approaches were used. Fig. 10-3 following paragraph sketches these approaches. Models with all containing model elements are exported from the modeling tool and imported into the *REM-tool* (e.g., IBM Rational DOORS) as a so called surrogate module. There, the linking between the requirements and the model elements' representations in the surrogate module are performed in the *REM-tool*. To ensure consistency, a regular synchronization process (as a rule during the night) between the model surrogate representation in the *REM-tool* and the modeling tool must be performed [Ha99]. In this way, *traceability* is established indirectly and the relationships must be established after the design process. The model elements must first be designed to be afterward imported into the surrogate module, where then the *traceability* links are generated. This indirect mechanism also makes *IA*s difficult.

Due to these problems, current commercial tool solutions such as IBM Rational Tau [TAU], Artisan RT Studio [ARTISAN], IBM Rational Rhapsody [RHAP–SODY] rely on a solution of Geensoft Reqtify [REQTIFY]. This solution offers a framework, where different tools can be integrated. Reqtify is more a kind of information broker, because Reqtify does not directly care for *traceability* establishment, but only cares for exchanging tool information and its visualization.

Through Reqtify, *traceability* is established in the following way:

- Requirements can be obtained by a requirement source such as a *REM-tool*.
- These requirements can then be propagated to a modeling tool as requirement target. The modeling tool coupling must care for taking over the requirements.
- The requirements must then be assigned in the modeling tool and thus the modeling tool must care for how the *traceability* information is produced. This information is then also saved in the modeling tool. The Reqtify framework then uses this information to visualize the *traceability* information for *IA*s.

Reqtify has the following advantages:

- Reqtify offers a high number of coupled tools.
- Reqtify also provides mechanisms to integrate tools such as MS Word or Excel allowing to integrating other information from light-weighted tools.
- Reqtify allows making visual *IA*s of relationships between different tools.

Reqtify has the following disadvantages:

- The *traceability* information is not stored and managed by Reqtify, but the different connected tools must find a way to store the information. In this way the *traceability* information is scattered across the several tools, making management of the information difficult.
- This also makes *evolutionary traceability* difficult as no integrated history *and configuration management* mechanisms are provided.
- Reqtify only provides a technical solution as an information broker for making linkings between objects of different tools possible. However, no dedicated process support is offered. Instead, the tools receiving the requirements information and where the *traceability* information shall be gathered must care about how this is realized. In the author's view, this is the most critical weakness because efficient *traceability* establishment must orient on the way traces occur. Thus, the design processes must be taken into account.
- One major shortcoming arising from neglecting design processes is that usual tracing approaches assume that requirements and the resulting design

are in a kind of linear relationship with each other. However, as shown in the ch. I.6.2.2, and ch. II.9, the author questions this assumption (for details see ch. III.20). Accordingly, an adequate *traceability* solution for design might need more than just linear linking but, e.g., possibilities to bridge *semantic gaps* through documented decisions.

In the context of UML modeling tools, the Reqtify approach is accompanied by the new SysML standard [SYSML]. SysML is an extension of UML to integrate SysEng activities (modeling of systems and allocation of requirements onto the system model), whereas UML formerly has merely concentrated on SE-activities. A central improvement of SysML in comparison to UML is the definition of a *'Requirements Diagram'* explicitly allowing modeling requirements and their interdependencies. For modeling *requirements traceability*[198] different relationships are possible (*<<DeriveReqt>>*, *<<Satisfy>>*, etc.; cf. ch. II.10.4.2.3 for details), [SV08], [HGK+09] that have a similar meaning as *traceability* links. Several UML-tools such as IBM Rational Tau [TAU], Artisan RT Studio [ARTISAN], IBM Rational Rhapsody [RHAPSODY] have dedicated SysML support and reveal endeavors to use the requirement relationships modeled via SysML as *traceability* information in combination with Reqtify. Other UML-Tools such as Enterprise Architect provide an UML-profile for modeling SysML (cf. also [HGK+09]).

A model based graphical support in establishing *requirements traceability* to model artifacts as it is intended by SysML may by all means be desirable. However as research results described later in ch. III.21.3 indicate, these approaches may be restricted by the fact that extensive requirement collections[199] may not be suitable for a universal graphical representation. Instead, the real value of SysML may be to provide *meta-model* concepts for trace links[200] (cf. also [HGK+09]).

---

[198] See also [KS06] for an approach basing on UML's *use case* concept with similar notions.

[199] In the automotive domain, e.g., [HH04] mentions about 200 to 600 pages of a *requirements specification* for one ECU system.

[200] Other similar approaches such as the following exist: Letelier [Le02] introduces a *traceability* model basing on UML and its extension mechanisms. The approach is comparable to the traces of SysML described here but provides more fine-grained differentiating relationship types with richer *meta-information* of these relationships. Due to the rather *semi-formal* character of UML's semantic, Chanda et al. [CKS+09] try to find a more *formal* semantic basing on UML allowing *traceability* and consistency verification. Kelleher and Simonsson show another extension of UML 2.0 to achieve a *traceability* concept where requirement elements can be mapped on *design elements*. Briand et al. [BLO+06] introduce an approach to enable *impact analysis* through a *dependency analysis* in UML models.

Hove et al. [HGK+09] describe a *change management process* with rules for *impact analysis* to analyze SysML models.

Weber and Weisbrod generally experienced tool couplings as often immature [WW02; p.23]. As a solution to avoid necessary tool couplings, they recommend minimizing the linking between two tools to be bridged and propose to using methodological approaches as design guidelines to reduce interconnections and thus linking efforts [WW02; p.23].

Pointing toward a similar direction as Weber and Weisbrod, [Ha99] emphasizes that with *traceability* establishment between the *REM-tool* and the UML-tool Artisan RT by means of a tool coupling, the problem of uncontrolled 'proliferation' of relationships arises. Therefore, the linking via the tool coupling should at best be minimized by only linking to some basic elements of a model as starting point (in [Ha99] these basic elements are part of an *analysis model*). Starting from these basic elements, further *traceability* information shall then be handled by model relationships between the basic model elements and other model elements. Now, when an *IA* is performed on a potential requirement change, the relationships handled over the tool coupling in combination with the other relationships identifiable in the modeling environment shall determine the *impact* [Ha99]. In terms of *IA* (see ch. II.10.3), this approach actually combines a coarse-grained *traceability* approach with a *dependency analysis* approach.

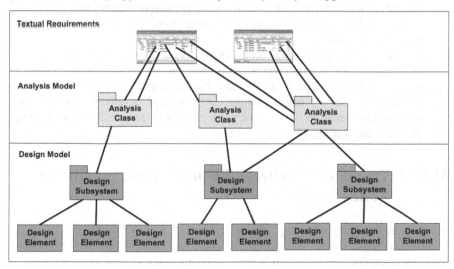

Figure 10-4 Requirements fan-out effect according to Alderidge [Al03]

Several experience reports from industrial practice (cf. [Al03], [Pe04], [Kn01a], [Kn01b]), however, emphasize the need of more fine-granular linking models:

1. Alderidge [Al03] directly refers on the process proposed by [Ha99]. He observes the so called *fan-out* effect [Al03] leading to the negative side-effect of overestimating the *impact* of requirement changes. The *fan-out effect* occurs because no direct *traceability* links to the design elements are used. Fig. 10-4 shows an example where the requirements are only directly mapped to *use cases*, whereas connections to the basic design elements are indirectly handled as *dependency analysis* via other model relationships between an analysis model and other design subsystems. A model typically has manifold relationships with different meaning. Correspondingly, a lot of dependencies can be identified, thus leading to the *fan-out effect*. As a solution, Alderidge [Al03] proposes using a more fine-grained linking model, in which the *use cases* are not used as a basis for linking, but breaking down the linking into more fine-grained *use case* steps. This solution, however, seems more to be a cure of the symptoms. In the author's opinion, the *fan-out effect* can only be avoided if fine-grained *traceability* linking is performed throughout the entire solution.

2. Also Knethen [Kn01a], [Kn01b] tries to improve the correctness of *IA*s, but via the option to model different *traceability* relationship types (similarly as SysML defines different relationship types), thus making the linking model more fine-granular.

3. Similar to Alderidge [Al03], Pettit [Pe04] reports from direct practical project experiences that *traceability* relationships are only maintained for the most high-level elements (in his case mostly *use cases*), but then not followed down to the actual design elements and diagrams (classes, state charts). This leads to the tendency that the actual responsibilities of design elements are lost (cf. ch. I.8).

II.10.7 Traceability between Requirements, Design and Code

Already in the early nineties, Tilbury [Ti89] and Kelley [Ke90] described the complexity *requirements traceability* to code can bear, because "the mapping from requirements to code often is many-to-many. This means that a requirement could be implemented by several chunks of code and that a chunk of code could implement several requirements. This is a fundamental *traceability* problem – i.e. there is no natural one-to-one mapping from requirements to code" [Li94; p.22].

Design is commonly seen as the bridge between requirements and the code, in which case it is a kind of model (or collection of models) of the code. Correspondingly, the findings of Tilbury and Kelley should be equally valid for *traceability* to design. This is normally seen in process (ch. I.7) and *traceability* theory (Knethen [Kn01b; p.46] shows in [Kn01b; fig.3.7] a one to one mapping between design and code), but taking the model characteristic of design into account (see ch. I.1) two deviations may exist:

- *Preterated characteristics* of the code are not part of the design. Correspondingly, relations between *preterated characteristics* and requirements would not have any corresponding relationship in design.
- Whereas *abundant properties* of the design might also have relations to requirements not really present in code. This seems not very plausible at first glance, but the author knows at least one certain situation, where this is of importance. A certain set of requirements may demand a special way of modeling specific aspects of systems (e.g., strict performance requirements may demand a performance analysis model). In this situation, the current requirements build the *rationale* for a specific view modeled in design.

The only complete solution of the problem would be complete code generation out of the *design model* accompanied by a process documenting all *rationale*, why the design is how it is. At the moment, this is not possible in most practical projects.

As an alternative, due to the close connection between code and design, *traceability* between design and code can also be handled via *name mapping* (cf. ch. II.10.4.2.2). Through *name mapping*, effort for linking can be avoided. This, however, involves that the two problems described above exist, so that not all possible *traceability* information may be recordable. As it is anyway very likely that all possible *traceability* information may never be recordable (cf. [Pi04; p.92]), the author considers these problems as an acceptable risk.

But as through *name mapping* no direct relationships are established allowing *IA*, a mechanism for *information retrieval*[201] must be established to retrieve all locations, where the name is used. In the context of *traceability* between design and code, this implies that the *information retrieval* mechanism must at minimum include the information from the used design and coding tools.

For this, Cleland-Huang et al. [CSD+05] have introduced the term *dynamic requirements traceability* and provide an overview of possibilities to improve accuracy of *information retrieval* techniques possible for *traceability* situations.

---

[201] *Information retrieval* can be counted to the automatable approaches discussed in ch. II.10.4.2.2).

Antoniol et al. [ACC+02] describe a tool support to partly automate *IA*s between source code and other textual documentation entities (requirement documents, design documents or code documentation). The approach bases on *information retrieval* techniques indexing code and documentation. Indirectly, the method bases on the *name mapping* assumption (cf. ch. II.10.4.2.2) as identifiers are parsed at both sides and matched together using different techniques. Maletic et al. [MMM+03] discuss a similar approach (same kinds of artifacts) but more from the perspective of artifact evolution. In their perspective, information quality of automatically acquired links continuously degrades. Thus, information quality must be continuously maintained through *link conformance analysis* (links must be regularly assessed whether they still conform to and validly express their original meaning) and inconsistencies management. In fact, Maletic et al. address the weakest point of the *name mapping* concept already discussed in ch. I.6.4 and ch. II.10.4.2.2. This is the danger that significant drifts between artifacts can occur over time if no adequate consistency management will be established.

Some authors also consider the *information retrieval* approach promising to cover the complete artifact chain from requirements to source code. Li et al. [LLY+08] present an approach for *traceability* and *dependency evaluation* basing on an approach for automatically identifying candidate traces from requirements to other artifacts by using *information retrieval* techniques. In the opinion of Li et al. [LLY+08; p.101], these other artifacts, for which their approach could provide valuable support, seem to be source code, UML-models and test cases. However, currently the approach seems only to be tested for source code [LLY+08; p.106]. The approach mainly bases on tracing names and their synonyms between requirement texts and source code. In [DLL09], the source code approach is improved by a heuristic for adding comments in source code. Settimi et al. [SCB+04] introduce and compare two *information retrieval* techniques for automatically generating links between requirements, code, and UML models. They come to the conclusion "that current *retrieval* methods may not provide an adequate replacement strategy for explicit *traceability* links such as those defined in a *traceability matrix*" [SCB+04; p.54]. On the other side, they mention that automated *information retrieval* approaches involve significantly less effort than manual approaches. In this way, Settimi et al. see potential to use them in projects, in which rather costs in comparison to accuracy are an important factor.

As expressed in ch. II.10.4.2.2 and other parts, the author has certain doubts that such approaches prove to be very accurate, when *traceability* between requirement artifacts and solution artifacts (design or code) is concerned, because the significant gap between the problem and solution description must be bridged (also cf. ch. I.6.4). The low effort costs of once established automated approaches may, however, have potential as an additional technique to identify potential relationships between artifacts otherwise overseen or neglected by developers during manual *traceability* establishment. Concerning artifacts having high correlating structures such as design and code, however, *information retrieval* basing on name mapping has high potential. This potential is especially higher because code is a *formal* language enforcing correct naming (the compiler will not accept misspelled or synonymous names in the code), and design as a model of the code usually uses the same names. As already mentioned above, however, the danger of drifts between design and code can occur over time. Therefore, generally, a better solution would be to automatically generate the code from the *design model* as it automatically creates the *name mapping* and prevents later drifts between the artifacts. But, as ch. I.6.4 and ch. I.6.6.1 show, automatic code generation often is only partially or even not at all available. In these cases, *name mapping* may be the best means for ensuring *traceability* between design and code.

As this chapter has shown and in the author's view, the problem of *traceability* between design and source code is solved to a high degree, whereas the real difficulties still lie in the transition from requirements to design. Correspondingly, in the following of this thesis, *traceability* between design and code (or between requirements and code) is not further discussed.

II.10.8 Rationale Management and Traceability

The possible supporting influences of *RatMan* and *traceability* have been discovered in the early nineties. Conklin [Co89] claimed that by providing *design rationale*, the systems maintainability is increased. As *traceability* has also been seen as mean to improve systems maintainability, Ramesh and Dhar [RD92] proposed a *traceability* model and tool approach called REMAP (REpresentation and MAintenance of Process knowledge) combining *IBIS* with *REM* activities. In REMAP, *traceable objects* (requirements, or design elements) can have four connections to the *decision model*:

- *Rationale* is *'based_on'* traceable objects.
- *Assumptions 'depend_on'* traceable objects.
- *Decisions 'affect'* traceable objects.
- *Traceable objects 'generate'* issues or *conflicts*.

According to Ramesh and Jarke [RJ01; p.59] the results of REMAP have sparked development of several commercial *REM-tools*. [RTM02] shows an extension of REMAP for *product line engineering*. In [RJ01], the REMAP *rationale model* is integrated into a general *traceability model* (see ch. II.10.4.2).

Lindvall could surface the concrete connection between *RatMan* and *traceability*. According to him, *traceability* records the traces "between models to understand the system structure and to understand the implications of a certain requirement" [Li94; p.20], whereas *rationale* is the means to collect the knowledge about the process where the traces occur [Li94; p.20].

Hull et al. [HJD02; p.143-152] introduce a practice-oriented approach they call *rich traceability*. The rich *traceability* concept bases on the extension of the *satisfy links* via *satisfaction arguments* that provide *rationale* for why the *satisfy links* exist. The *schema* can be extended by logical 'AND' and 'OR' relationships, where n-ary satisfaction dependencies arise between different items reflecting the reasoning of the developers. Hull et al. show the effectiveness of their approach in modeling satisfaction dependencies between a *user requirements specification* (approx. corresponds to a 'Lastenheft'; see ch. I.7.2.2.1) and a *system require-ments specification* (approx. corresponds to a 'Pflichtenheft'; see ch. I.7.2.2.1), but the authors emphasize that the *rich traceability* concept can be used for any *traceability relationship* in principle. The examples shown in [HJD02; p.143-152] are modeled in IBM Rational DOORS.

Dömges and Pohl [DP98; p.56] list the following possible improvements, when *capturing rationale* and *traceability* are combined:
1. Understanding between stakeholders and thus acceptance of the system to develop is improved because requirements can be justified.
2. *Change management* is improved because previously rejected solutions and the reasons for their rejection are accessible and thus risks of neglecting important aspects are reduced.

For Dömges and Pohl [DP98; p.56], however, *rationale* means not only *ra-tionale* in the sense of argumentation but generally also decisions, alternatives or underlying assumptions.

Lindvall [Li94; p.20] could also evoke that *RatMan* and *traceability* also share similar problem areas about *input, representation*, and *retrieval*. In fact, as ch. II.10.5 shows, *RatMan* also shares general problems regarding the *benefit* of the *information bearers*.

Nevertheless, the author is convinced, if both can be recorded in *non-intrusive* ways merely as a supporting *by-product* of normal design activities, and both are supportive to each other, both concepts will have good chances to provide early direct *benefit* even for the *information bearers*. In this way, both may then unfold the positive effects, which are usually ascribed to them by *SysEng* and *SE theory*, then outweighing the costs encountered in practice.

III. PROVEtech:R2A – A Tool for Dedicated Requirements Traceability

A fool with a tool is still a fool
- unknown

This part describes the *traceability* tool solution PROVEtech:R2A (R2A) especially dedicated to cross the substantial gap between the requirements (i.e. *problem space*) and the design solutions (i.e. *solution space*).

The author is convinced that a successful development of SW based systems is not alone guaranteed by strict compliance to SE processes someway developed in theory, but it is at least in the same way (or maybe even higher) influenced by both the real unique constellations of projects (so called practice) and by soft factors as humans and their communications (e.g., cf. [Mu06a]).

Correspondingly, the solution proposed here tries to account for all three factors. The next chapter (ch. III.11) outlines this in more detail deriving the goals of the tool approach described here. To better illustrate the mechanisms and findings of research about R2A, the author has tried to use an accompanying case study whose basic characteristics are described in ch. III.12.

As derived in ch. III.11, two fundamental gaps must be addressed by the R2A approach. Concerning the first merely tool related gap, ch. III.13 shows how R2A intends to address this gap. In the author's opinion, the transition between requirements and design generally is difficult, because designers perform a significant mental transfer process from the requirements to the resulting solution design leading to a substantial gap between both. This second gap is the core problem. Correspondingly, ch. III.14 describes R2A's principal ideas to ameliorate the problem.

From ch. III.15 to ch. III.21 different mechanisms of R2A are introduced helping to better overcome the second gap. To achieve this goal two major strategies are employed.

The first strategy is to better support designers on documenting design information and providing means for capturing *traceability* information as a mere *by-product* of normal design activities. Ch. III.15 to ch. III.17 describe mechanisms to generally improve the design processes without yet considering the *requiremental* dimension. Basing on these mechanisms, ch. III.18 shows then how a more requirement-centered design process (see *requirement dribble process* ch. III.18.2.4) can be employed where traceability information is rather established and information on basic design decisions is rather captured as a *by-*

product of the design activities. This first strategy part from ch. III.15 to ch. III.18 can be considered as a whole complete in itself topic where the design theory of Simon (cf. ch. I.6.2.1) dominating in the design theory about SysEng and SE is set into context with traceability needs usually expressed by *process standards* for *safety-critical* processes. These two aspects are then also combined with findings of Schön's design theory about design as situated action (cf. I.6.2.3). So far, however, the design theories considered yet rather represent a view on design assuming that the development of a design is rather a linear process of step to step actions transforming information into a design at the end. The design theories about wicked problems (see ch. I.6.2.2) and patterns (see. ch. I.6.2.4) rather suggest that the design process is not such a linear process but rather a complex nonlinear process driven by complex design decisions. In the author's opinion, design is both – in some situation design is rather a linear process of step by step transformation of information into a design, however in other situations complex decisions must be taken where the design rather emerges out in a nonlinear fashion. To cover these nonlinear aspects of design, *decision models* have been developed allowing the documentation of *rationale* behind complex decisions. These *decision models* are tightly integrated into the traceability information and the design process building a tightly woven network supporting all four design theories described in ch. I.6.2 by a unique integrated way. This second major strategy to address the second gap is treated in ch. III.19, ch. III.20 and ch. III.21.

After the ch. III.15 to ch. III.21 describe the core innovational ideas how to address the two-fold gap between requirements and design domain, ch. III.22 then shows how *traceability* information once gathered can be used in R2A for *impact analyses* and *requirement change propagation* in order to ensure consistency.

Ch. III.23 then discusses issues about embedding R2A and the R2A design processes into a higher level process environment. This starts with a description, how R2A can be used to improve supplier management. The sub chapters following then describe how this mechanism can also be used to reduce redundancies when different artifact models are crossed in a development project and how this may help to have a decoupled development of different requirement and design artifacts.

The core of R2A's innovations can be considered in the orientation on its mechanisms. Correspondingly, R2A has been designed in a way to provide an optimal support for the mechanisms. Last but not least, ch. III.24 provides an overview of the *architecture* and *meta-model* of R2A that realize the mechanisms.

III.11 Research Goals

The biggest problem of system development has always been the confusion of requirements and de-
sign.
Hatley et al. [HHP03; p.27 (*)]

Concerning *traceability*, the transition from requirements to design has been identified as one of the most critical issues as it includes a twofold structural gap:

- At first, requirement activities and design activities are usually performed in different tool environments. Correspondingly, the transition usually implies to cross a tool gap.
- More important, requirement activities deal with exploring the *problem space* and design activities deal with exploring the *solution space*. Thus a substantial conceptual gap exists between requirements and design.

A useful solution must try to bridge both gaps. The first gap seems more to be a technical issue of how to couple two tools into an integrated environment. However, as mentioned in ch. I.6 projects often use a combination of multiple *design tools* for design. Thus, an adequate solution for automotive purposes must also consider a way to couple several *design tools* in an integrated way. The next chapter will discuss the issue from the merely technical coupling perspective, but questions remain whether this gap also involves incompatible methods due to different task performed in *REM* or design.

This leads to the second mentioned gap about requirements and design discussed in ch. II.10.2. Today's *traceability* models, as seen by theory or process standards as SPICE, assume that requirements and its realizing design are connected by simple linear relationships mappable by a simple *traceability linking* schema. In reality, however, a considerable gap between requirements and design arises from the design process as it represents a creative and complex mental transfer process of a unique problem constellation into a sustainable solution that is per se difficult to reproduce. During design, designers make decisions. This gap is mentally bridged by designers by taking design decisions. Each decision involves consequences and *constrains* the *solution space* until the *solution space* (hopefully) converges to a solution fulfilling the requirements.

From the author's perspective, the second point is the rather neuralgic issue. The author even considers that point one actually is just a symptom for the deeper underlying problem described in point two, because tools were at first developed around the two core topics requirements and design having a higher cohesion[202].

Now, the question arises what exactly may be the cause for the second point. Considering the problems that *RatMan* solutions have with succeeding in practice, Dutoit et al. [DMM+06a; p.7] emphasize that *rationale* documentation *schemes* usually differ from the way a *rationale bearer* would structure *rationale* intuitively, thus creating "a *cognitive dissonance* that adds to the cognitive overhead that designers must cope with" [DMM+06a; p.7].

In the author's opinion, this also is exactly the issue for a *traceability* solution to address in order to help to bridge the gap. When a *traceability* solution helps designers to easily[203] capture *traceability* information as a *by-product* without imposing significant *cognitive dissonance* and bringing early benefit to designers, it is more likely to achieve better *traceability* information actually useful for projects. In this way, the promises of the *traceability* concept may be achievable.

Ch. I.6 has described four different theoretical views on design. All these views describe different – in the author's view essential – characteristics of design and its processes. However, current systems and *SW design* theories rather concentrate on design structural aspects as provided by the theories of Simon (ch. I.6.2.1) and the *pattern* theory of Alexander (ch. I.6.2.4), neglecting other – admittedly more ambiguous – theories about designers' thinking and decision making (cf. ch. I.6.2.2 and ch. I.6.2.3). The author considers improving support on designers' thinking in order to avoid *cognitive dissonance* as the *neuralgic point*. In R2A, this shall be achieved by a requirement centered modeling: Supported by a suitable methodology and a newly developed tool, the necessary work for establishing *traceability* to design shall be intuitive for designers and support their normal design work in a way that *traceability* occurs as a *by-product* of the usual design process. To achieve this, also the design theories about designers' thinking and decision making are significantly considered in the concepts of R2A.

One dedicated goal for the research was to find a tool solution whose usage in practice really brings early benefit (ch. II.10.5). As Moro [Mo04; p.26 (*)] points out in reference to modeling: "The primary decision criterion about what modeling technique or level of detail is used always is the benefit for the architect". In the author's eyes, this is correspondingly true for design *traceability*. The

---

[202] In terms of software theory, it may be said that the topics requirements and design have within each other a significantly higher cohesion within each other leading to the development of tools within their specific topics. Later, it was then discovered that coupling both may be a good idea.

[203] In this context, 'easily' means 'does not infer further *complication*' or even 'helps to reduce *complication*' (see footnote 80 (p. 77)).

benefit for the development team members must be in the center of *traceability* approaches. Otherwise, *traceability* usage will fail due to *Grudin's principle*. A symptom connected to this problem is the problem that *traceability* establishment is often performed later after design has reached a relatively stable state (see ch. I.7.2.3, comment on BP.2 and ch. II.10.5). In this way, the development team especially avoids effort for *traceability* establishment when design must be changed; however, paying the price that a lot of relevant *traceability* information is lost. Correspondingly, a major goal is to lower the burdens for *traceability* establishment and raise benefit for designers to an extent that designers rather establish *traceability* as a *by-product*.

As *traceability* is mainly established by hand [EGH+07], it is often very cost intensive and bureaucratic with little use for the development team [RJ01], [EGH+07]. The author disagrees with the idea to lower *traceability* effort by using coarser *traceability* to abstract high-level design elements (see, e.g., [EGH+07]), because feedback from practice [Pe04], [Al03] indicates the need for detailed *traceability* even at lower-level design elements, but the author agrees that *traceability* efforts must be lowered and benefits for the bearers of *traceability* information must be significantly raised. Otherwise, *traceability* will always face the *benefit problems* as all collaborative systems do in danger of failing due to *Grudin's principle* [Gr96b] (cf. also ch. II.9.4.2).

R2A offers several characteristics contributing to lowering the effort of establishing *traceability* and raising benefits for the *traceability bearers*:

- *Traceability* can be easily and fast established via *drag-and-drop* and other simple operations, by which multiple requirements can be selected in parallel to perform the operations.
- The operations adapt to how designers think and perform their design steps so that the designers can establish *traceability* information as a side-effect[204]. The same principles guide the operations that are possible to document decisions.
- All important information for a designer's situation is adequately presented in-time to support the designer's cognitive flow. Especially in-time information that is easily comprehensible supports designers in their phases of intuitive *knowing-in-action* (Schneider) by preventing that important aspects are missed. In the same way, the in-time information supports designers in their *thinking-in-action* phases of rational thinking, because the facts that are considered are directly presented. One of the most important information to

---

[204] As already stated in ch. II.10.5, Dömges and Pohl [DP98] emphasize that *traceability* should evolve as a side-effect of the daily development activities and not cause extra bureaucracy.

mention here are requirement information and recorded *traceability* information accompanied with information about important decisions.

- Connected to the points above, the author is convinced that a tool solution for practice should be as easy to use as possible. Theoretic research often bears theoretically sound (often in connection with strict *formality*), but complex and formal solutions (e.g., cf. Knethen's solution via *meta-models* [Kn01b]). However, in practice, developers often do not have the time to work into such complex solutions but rather prefer solutions with low entry barriers and a possibility for 'learning by doing'. This point is closely connected with the discussion about *formality* in development methods (see ch. II.9.4.2). The author tried to address these problems by providing an easy to understand, basic *skeleton* of *formal* concepts in R2A. R2A then allows enriching this *formal skeleton* with further *informal* information[205] at nearly any location.

- R2A provides a collaborative environment where all created information is automatically shared with other designers, who can immediately use and extend the information to evolve their further design.

- Operations for recording *traceability* information provide possibilities for designers to delegate requirements to other designers, who can immediately analyze and further process the requirements. In case of problems, possibilities to reissue the requirements back to the delegating designer accompanied by a note about the problem support the designers to communicate with each other.

- Short communication paths between developers and designers responsible for the model are often the decisive factor to ensure flexibility in identifying and handling necessary and reasonable model changes [Mo04; p.25]. Since all the steps of design work above are recorded, the communication actions between the designers can also happen asynchronously. This improves situations in which important designers are absent, because the other designers can delegate information (e.g., requirements or notes) to the absent designers through R2A. The absent designers are then able to consider this information and take actions after they have returned back.

---

[205] At minimum *informal* notes can be added on any item present in R2A (see ch. III.17.2), but also other mechanisms exist at specific locations to add *informal* descriptions, etc..

III.12 Accompanying Case Study

Every module ... is characterized by its knowledge of a design decision which it hides from all others.
Its interface is chosen to reveal as little as possible about its inner workings.
Parnas [Pa72; p.1056]

In the following chapters, R2A and its features are described. To explain these features, a practice-oriented case study shows how the features interact with each other to support a good design process. Here, the basic characteristics of the case study are introduced. Later, extra chapters show the case study outcome with the features described.

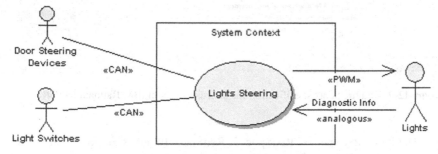

Figure 12-1 Example *use case* of the case study

    The case study starts with an example *use case* (fig. 12-1) for a lights steering device in an automotive context: At first, the system retrieves different signals from the *controller area network* (CAN) bus. Then, the lights steering task determines whether some lights must be activated or deactivated. Finally, the lights are steered via *pulse-width modulation* (PWM) and diagnostic information is retrieved via analog feedback, which must be analyzed.

    Fig. 12-2 shows an example *requirements specification* for the case study in IBM Rational DOORS. The requirements ReqSpec_2 to ReqSpec_6 are functional requirements describing the *use case* of fig. 12-1. It is here important to mention that requirement ReqSpec_2 is a special case as it also describes the context of the system. In this way, according to the view of Hruschka and Rupp [HR02; p.86ff] (see fig. 5-1 in ch. I.5.1), it can also be seen as a *system constraint* and thus as *nonfunctional requirement*. In practice, often requirements exist not clearly identifiable as being of one specific type.

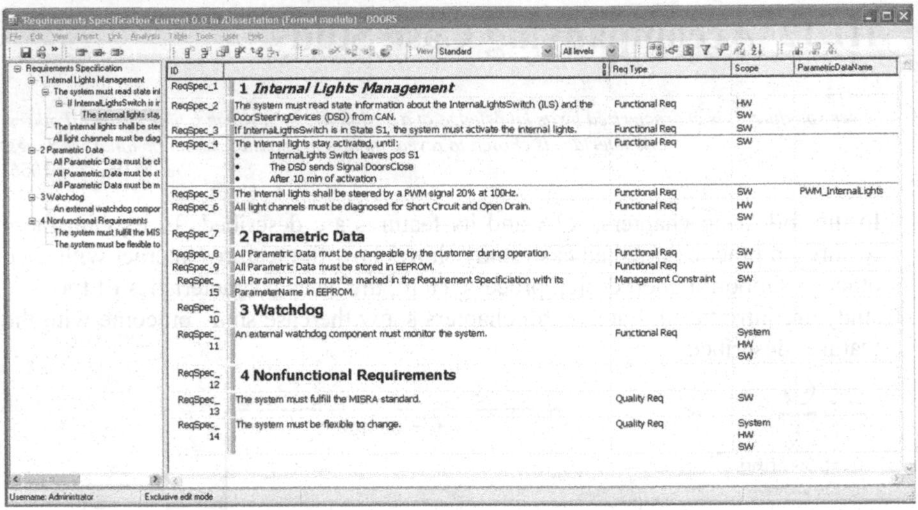

Figure 12-2 Requirements specification for the case study in IBM Rational DOORS

The items ReqSpec_1, ReqSpec_7, ReqSpec_10 and ReqSpec_12 are no requirements but just headings structuring the *requirements specification* text, whereas ReqSpec_13 and ReqSpec_14 are clearly *nonfunctional quality requirements*, and ReqSpec_15 is a *nonfunctional management constraint*.

The corresponding ECU's *SW design* outcome is shown in fig. 12-3. A high level SW architect[206] has partitioned the SW into three subsystems (the three packages *LightsManagement*, *Communications*, and *Drivers*). For each subsystem a subsystem designer determines their sub components[207].

---

[206] The term high-level does not impose any specific role such as *system designer*. High-level and lower lever are rather seen in relativity to the current design task. Design activities take place in different levels of abstraction. A high-level architect is involved in designing at a high level of abstraction, e.g., determining the overall structure of an architecture, whereas for other parts of the design – e.g., for a component – a designer at a lower level of abstraction will work.

[207] This example illustrates aspects of collaboration. In a real project of this size, only one designer could most probably cope with it. But in larger projects with complex application domains, a separation into several layers of design liability is common. In the automotive industry, a current trend exists to merge several previously independent devices into one powerful multifunctional device (cf. [Br06]).

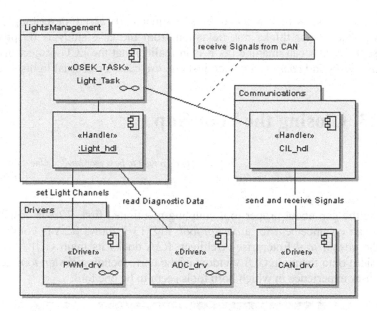

Figure 12-3 Example *SW design* for the *requirements specification* in fig. 12-2

The following project decisions have been made:

- The lights management contains an active process *Light_Task* with a complex state machine. An underlying light handler *Light_hdl* knows how to manage the underlying drivers according to the light signals to set. Both components are being developed in-house.
- The drivers (*PWM_drv*, *ADC_drv* and *CAN_drv*) are supplied by different subcontractors. Code size, performance and other parameters are highly dependent on their individual configuration. Therefore, a subcontractor manager shall monitor each driver for these parameters.
- The CIL_hdl (CIL=*CAN Interaction Layer*) depends on the types of signals relevant for the device. These settings are defined by the customer (OEM) because it affects communication.

This example case study has been chosen being as easy and clear as possible to illustrate the concepts of R2A. However, its easiness turned out to be a disadvantage for illustrating complex decision situations in ch. III.20.4. Correspondingly, in ch. III.20.4, the author deviates from the case study by referring to some further requirements and components not mentioned here in the case study. This decision situation is then again referred to in ch. III.22.1.1 describing *impact analysis*. The author thinks this deviation from the case study is no problem, because the reader can imagine (as it is in reality) that the ECU-project involves more *use cases* and *components* than just one *use case* for internal lights steering.

III.13 Closing the Tool Gap

How does a project get to be a year late? ... One day at a time.
[Br95; p.153]

To close the gap about proper tool coupling mentioned first, R2A is designed to work as an enhancement for a *design tool*. Fig. 13-1 shows R2A in combination with the *design tool* Enterprise Architect. R2A docks its main GUI[208] window (right side) onto the main GUI window of the corresponding *design tool* generating an user experience in which both tools seem to be one tool.

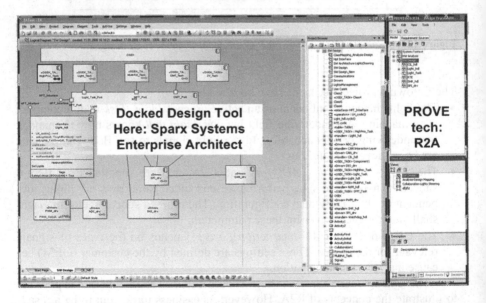

Figure 13-1 R2A in combination with a *design tool* (Sparx Systems Enterprise Architect)

---

[208] Graphical User Interface

From the logical architecture viewpoint (see fig. 13-2), R2A can be seen as an interlayer between an *REM-tool* providing the requirements and a supported *design tool*.

First of all, the requirements are imported from the *REM-tool* as direct representations (so called *'surrogate requirements'*) into R2A. Later, these representations can be synchronized with the requirement changes in the *REM-tool* by a regular controlled synchronization process. This is described in detail in ch. III.18.1.

All relationships relevant for *traceability* and *IA*s are consistently modeled and stored in R2A. Currently, the following relationships are considered:

- *Satisfy* relationships between requirements and *design model elements* (*'req model dependency'*).
- *Hierarchic* relationships between *design model elements* (*'refinement dependency'*).
- Other relationships between *design model elements* (*'between model dependency'*).

All other not *traceability*-relevant relationships occurring in design activities are not considered in R2A but must be covered by the features of the used *design tools*.

This structure provides the following advantages in comparison to other methods:

- The *traceability* relationships between requirements and design are managed directly, whereas only some distinct model relationships (the *refinement* and *between model dependency* mentioned above) are taken into account for *IA*s. This prevents the *requirements fan-out effect* (cf. [Al03] and ch. II.10.6.2) during *IA*s.
- The synchronization between the requirements in the *REM-tool* and the surrogate representations can be performed at specific points in time and thus requirement changes between the old requirement version, present as surrogate representation and the new version in the *REM-tool* can be tracked in R2A to support a consistent change of the design to fit to the requirement changes (cf. ch. III.22).
- Besides, the surrogate representations concept allows that change works on the requirements baseline for the next release is decoupled from the requirements baseline for the current release. In this way, requirements engineers can already work on the requirements specification for the next release, whereas designers can design the system according to the requirements specification baseline of the current release in parallel. Details on this are provided in ch. III.23.3.

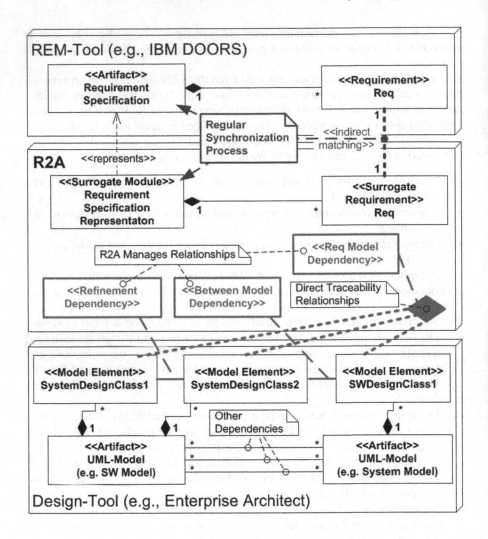

Figure 13-2 Logical structure of the R2A tool approach

III.14 Closing the Gap between Requirements and Design

Technology evolves from the primitive over the complicated to the simple.
Antoine de Saint-Exupéry

Besides the structural advantages mentioned above helping to close gap one, the R2A approach shall go beyond closing the first gap. It shall also change the way how designers treat requirements and design by establishing an intuitive process that allows to establishing *traceability* information between requirements and design as a *by-product* of the usual design activities.

According to the experiences of Moro [Mo04; p.351], it makes no sense to consider a *design model* without also considering the corresponding *requirements specification* or *software architecture documentation*. Following this finding, the author considers these items as a threefold unity. Correspondingly, R2A tries to find a solution in which all three aspects can be considered in an integrated way during design activities. The following chapters deal with the different features that try to provide a solution to better address this structural gap.

In a lot of cases, design is the result of a collaborative work between several designers working together to find a solution for fulfilling the requirements. Correspondingly, several designers must work in parallel on the same model and they must be able to easily share information. Thus, ch. III.18.2.4 shows how establishing *traceability* as part of a design process can be used as an essential means to organize collaboration and sharing contemporary requirement information between designers, working together to find a solution for all requirements. Finding good solutions essentially involves making design decisions in a collaborative manner and information about decisions must be propagated as soon as possible to all stakeholders affected by the decision. As a consequence, a design solution should also support a collaborative decision process as *rationale management systems* do.

III.15 Abstraction Layers and Abstraction Nodes

There are a lot of advantages of hierarchically organized systems and sub systems. ...
If we work on a certain level of abstraction, we will be able to concentrate on this level without
having to go into detail too fastly.
[HHP03; p.52 (*)]

Following the design theory of Simon (see ch. I.6.2.1), design deals with managing complexity. Central concepts for managing complexity are *abstraction hierarchies* (also called *hierarchic decomposition*) and posing different *views* on *design aspects*.

To simplify the understanding and the structure of the design, R2A emphasizes the *hierarchical abstraction structure view* (*hierarchical decomposition*) as nodes in an *abstraction tree*. Fig. 15-1 shows an example of such a hierarchical decomposition. In the further of this document, such a node is called *abstraction node* (*AN*), whereas the tree is called *abstraction nodes hierarchy* (*ANH*). An *AN* is formed out of two aspects. On the one side, it represents a *design element* usable as a symbol in diagrams. On the other side, an *AN* contains a diagram showing its internal structure composed of new *design elements* and thus a new *AN* in a more detailed abstraction level. In this way, detailing relationships (*refinement dependencies*) arise between an *AN* and its sub *AN*, in which the diagram of an *AN* contains the *design elements* (symbols) of the *AN* it is built of (composed) of.

Concerning this issue, it must be mentioned that all *ANs* at one level in the hierarchy represent one level of abstraction (or detail) in the design. This is called an *abstraction layer* (*AL*) in the further. In other words, an *AL* builds a comprehensive view on a system at a certain level of abstraction[209]. With increasing depth of an *AL*, the design gets more specific.

An *AN* is more than a node in an abstraction tree. *ANs* build the central starting point to connect to further design related information. Below, fig. 15-2 shows the conceptual characteristics of an *AN* in R2A on the basis of an example *AN* "SubSystem1" enriched with further information.

---

[209] $AL = \sum AN_{at\_one\_hierarchial\_level}$ – this is similar to refinements of data flows in *structured analysis* (*SA*) [De78].

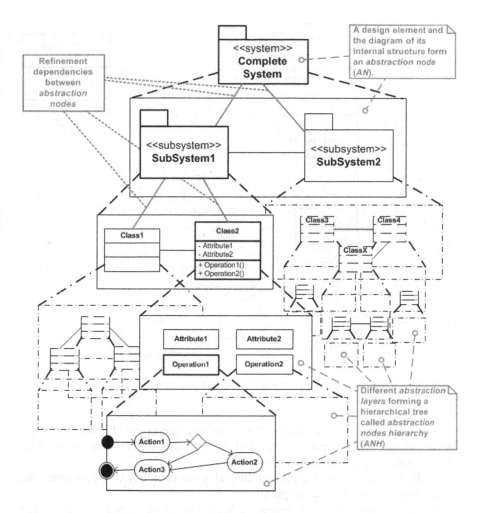

Figure 15-1 Hierarchical decomposition of a system shown as abstraction tree

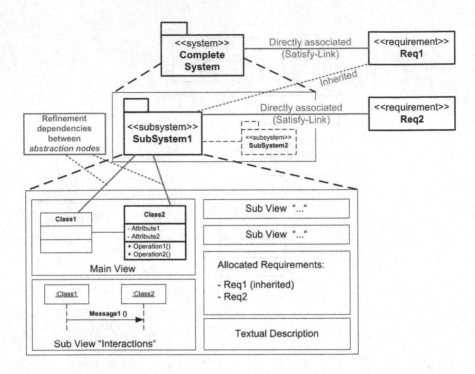

Figure 15-2 Detailed content and structure of an *abstraction node* (SubSystem1)

The goal is to present as much relevant information as possible for an *AN* and its realization. Consequently, one idea of R2A is using the *AN* concept to represent the following information to designers:

- Each *AN* consists of a representation element (symbol) that represents the abstraction node in other diagrams.
- Each *AN* has one central diagram ('Main View') as main entry point. The diagram represents a decomposition view showing how the *AN* is decomposed by sub *AN*s, in which the *design elements* of the sub *AN*s are shown in the diagram.
- Other views or diagrams can be attached to an *AN* as further views ('Sub view') to allow detailed modeling of other important aspects (e.g., dynamic behavior, concurring processes, complex behavior).
- Diagrams without further explanation can be misinterpreted. Consequently, a design must be accompanied by textual descriptions. R2A supports adding a

textual description as a rich text document for each *AN* ('Textual Description'). This allows the designers to document each *AN* separately.

- Requirements can be linked to *AN*s to indicated that the *AN* satisfies the requirements. Requirements associated to an *AN* of a higher *abstraction level* get inherited by *AN*s of lower *abstraction levels*. All these connections of an *AN* with requirements can be shown to the designers ('Allocated requirements'). The details about requirements and *AN*s are described in the following ch. III.18.

- As described in ch. II.9, important aspects about taken design decisions should be documented. The *AN* concept makes all decisions connected to structure building of the design leading to the *AN*s automatically visible to the designers. Additionally, through the history function described in ch. III.17.5, the decision history is collected. This is close to ideas of Gruber and Russel [GR96a] (see ch. II.9.4.2) to automatically capture side information on processes providing *rationale* in a way that allows to inferring *rationale* later when it is needed.

The first two points have a strong analogy to the concept of different abstractions in *structured analysis* and *design (SA/SD)* [De78]. Currently, the concepts of *SA/SD* have mostly been ousted by the concepts of UML.

Concerning the design language UML, a central concept is the usage of different *views* on a system under development. UML as well as UML-tools usually do not impose any demands on the definition or usage of views and their relationships. Instead all views are treated with the same priority. In UML-tools like Enterprise Architect, all elements present in a design are stored in one project repository browser. Fig. 15-3 shows an example of a project repository browser as it is provided by the UML-tool Enterprise Architect. A project repository containing all elements of a design is important for a project to have an overview of the available elements of a design. Besides the rich tool set, the relative freedom of not imposing demands for a structured approach has probably contributed to the vast success of UML in the development community. This egalitarian treatment of all design concepts, however, also makes it difficult to understand the design and the relationships between the different *views*[210] (resp. *diagrams*).

---

[210] Broy and Rumpe [BR07b] speak of incondite consistency between the different model views in UML (see also ch. I.6.6.1).

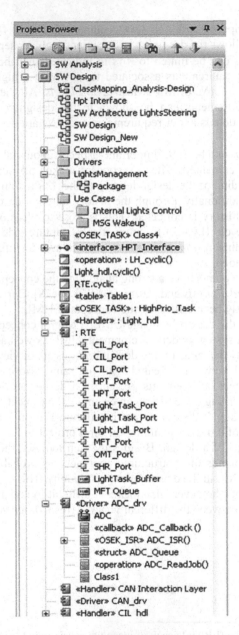

Figure 15-3 Example of a UML project repository in Enterprise Architect

This is where R2A with its *AN* concept can help designers to master complexity as it extracts and visualizes the most important structural information of a design repository. At first, R2A breaks down the information contained in a project repository into the abstraction hierarchy described in the points one and two resulting in the main view connecting the strength of the *SA/SD* concept with the strength of UML. In the next step, described in point three, each of the *AN*s in the *ANH* can contain further diagrams as further views fulfilling the concepts of view partitioning as inspired by Simon's design theory (ch. I.6.2.1). To master design complexity for designers, this structure provides an easy way to mentally structure a model with specific navigation support in two ways:

1. As main view, the *ANH* allows the designers to order the design into a structure easy to overview for a designer. This can be seen as navigation into the vertical of the *design model*.
2. To each node in the *ANH*, further associated *views* can be seen as a parallel *view* on other aspects of an *AN*. This can be seen as navigation into the horizontal of the *design model*.

Resembling accordance express the remarks from Hatley et al. [HHP03; p.47] that, if several models for a system shall be created, these models must be organized in a way orienting themselves on the relationships between the models and the system. They use the metaphor "scaffold" [HHP03; p.47]. From this perspective, R2A imposes a kind of scaffold to structure a design. Other modeling approaches as Matlab or ETAS ASCET do not provide different views but only have one view showing the *abstraction hierarchy* (corresponds to the *ANH*) of the design. As R2A's only required assumption about design is that an abstraction hierarchy is present, these design methods are fully compatible to R2A except for the only difference that these modeling approaches do not provide modeling of further *views*.

Nevertheless, the *AN*s concept has one major drawback: The *ANH* is a redundancy to the *design elements* hierarchy modeled in the modeling tools. This means that this information must be modeled twice and later changes must also be maintained twice – once in the modeling tool and once in R2A. Mechanisms to manage this redundancy should offer relief for these situations and explicitly prevent information drift between the redundant information. R2A offers three mechanisms:

1. As basic mechanism, a wizard helps the designers with combining *design elements* in a modeling tool to *AN*s in the *ANH*.
2. For better convenience, it is also possible to perform *drag-and-drop* operations dragging *design elements* from a modeling tool to R2A. If R2A can recover enough information about the *design elements* to fit them directly into the *ANH*, the elements will be directly added (as mentioned above, UML-

tools do not provide as clear hierarchy dependencies as tools such as Matlab or ETAS ASCET do). Otherwise, the wizard mentioned in point one opens, containing all automatically retrievable information, to which the designer only has to add the missing information which could not be automatically retrieved.

3. An automatic synchronization mechanism explicitly helps to resynchronize the *design elements* and their hierarchy in the modeling tool with the *ANH* in R2A. Before really synchronizing, the mechanism analyzes both structures and displays a synchronization wizard, where the differences and proposals for potential changes to overcome the differences are shown. Using the wizard, the designer can analyze the proposed changes for correctness or adapt the proposed changes in order to perform the changes according to the designer's intention. After the designer has approved the changes highlighted by the wizard, the synchronization mechanism applies them. The mechanism is explicitly helpful, when changes in a modeling tool shall be adapted to an already existing *ANH*, but the mechanism can also be applied to create an *ANH* from scratch using the *design elements*' abstraction hierarchy in the modeling tool. However, experience has shown that this mechanism only works frictionless for tools with a definite hierarchy (such as Matlab or ETAS ASCET), whereas for modeling tools in which the hierarchy cannot be determined definitely (e.g., UML-tools), the synchronization wizard often identifies unintended changes due to false-positive or misleading interpretations of the automatic synchronization mechanism. It is possible in the wizard to correct all these unintended changes and turn them into intended changes, but this can become cumbersome for designers. In these cases, using the two mechanisms mentioned first to create the *ANH* and then using the synchronization mechanism to synchronize later adaptations on the hierarchy may be the better alternative.

A design scaffold also is a central concern for design documentation purposes (cf. [IEEE1471], [GP04], [CBB+03] and [Ha06]). Design documentation aims at documenting design to communicate it to persons not directly involved with the design or even non project members. Besides the documentation of *design elements* and their relations documented in diagrams arising out of design, also the relations between the diagrams must be documented. This is implicitly fulfilled by R2A's scaffold (i.e. skeleton) structuring the relations between diagrams. Beyond these points, design documentation also demands a textual description of the design. Textual documentation is supported in R2A by the possibility to add a textual description to each *AN*, as described in point four of the listing about information possible to add to an *AN* (see p.274 in this ch. III.15). To ensure a certain quality of the textual design description, documentation templates can be defined and used for the documents. Last but not least, design documentation literature also demands for documenting other important information as assigned requirements and important decisions. As these points are also part of R2A, R2A is a valuable support for design documentation.

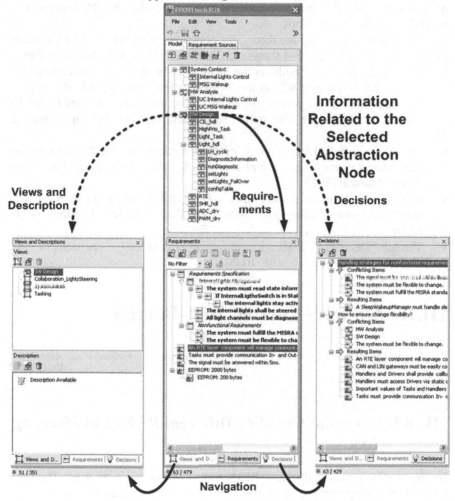

Figure 15-4 With the *AN* tree view and the tab "Views and Description"

A further point to mention here is the fact that for modeling an ECU, often several different models are used, where even several different modeling tools may be used in parallel. To reduce design complexity within such a heterogeneous model environment, R2A also provides mechanisms to manage different models and their relations in an integrated manner using the *AN* concept. Ch. III.16.2 describes this in detail.

Now, after elucidating the theory, the concrete realization of the *AN* concept in R2A is described. Fig. 15-4 shows a *design model* in R2A. In the upper part, a tree view contains all *AN*s building the hierarchical composition structure as the main view. When the user selects an *AN* in the tree view, the *AN*'s main view diagram is selected in the *design tool* and all other information related to the *AN* is shown in the lower part. This part is segmented into three tab pages (see fig. 15-4):

- The tab "Views and Description" contains a control to add diagrams as *further related views* to an *AN* and a control to add a description to an *AN* in *rich text format (RTF)*.
- The tab "Requirements" contains a control that helps to maintain *requirements traceability* information with *AN*s. This is further described in ch. III.18.
- The tab "Decisions" deals with relating important design decisions to *AN*s. This is further described in ch. III.20.

III.16 Models Crossing Tool-Barriers

Couplings between textual specification and modeling tools are immature and seldom used.
[WW02; p.22]

III.16.1 Insertion: Coupling Different *REM-* and *Modeling Tools*

In engineering practice, different *REM-* and *modeling tools* are used. The tool-based methodology proposed by the R2A project is very general and could be used by all kinds of systems or *SW design* projects. Thus, R2A is designed to be open for different kinds of *REM-* and *modeling tools* to provide flexibility in the usage of *REM-* and *modeling tools* in order to allow the usage of the best-suited tool support for a project.

To ensure this flexibility with minimal effort at maximal benefit, R2A is designed according to concepts of *software product line design* [PBG04; p.259-298]. A *software product line* is "a set of software-based systems sharing a conjoint, controlled set of product characteristics, orienting itself on the specific needs of a specific domain and being developed on the basis of a collective pool of software artifacts" [PBG04; p.262 (*)].

Here, the focus is to adapt R2A and its processes as a common development approach to fit with different *REM-* and *modeling tool* environments. In this way, R2A is not a classical *product line*, but is merely a tool framework allowing different *REM-* and *modeling tools* to be coupled. However, *product line* design differentiates a system into the invariable *product line core* and its *variation points*. The invariable core contains the constant characteristics of the systems, whereas the *variation points* define the differing characteristics of the systems [PBG04; p.276]. R2A could be differentiated in the invariant *core* of concepts described in this thesis and the *variation points* of different tool couplings to embed R2A into an integrated tool chain. Correspondingly, the *REM-* and *modeling tool couplings* have been identified as *variation points*. For each identified *variation point*, adequate strategies and design concepts to handle the variation must be found. A common problem at *product line development* is that the *product line core* is in constant danger of creeping erosion. This means that the variations along the boundaries between the *core* and a *variation point* always demand variations at parts of the *core* leading to a growing extent of the *variation point*, whereas the invariable *core's* extent shrinks (erodes) with passing time in a *product line* project.

To address creeping erosion in R2A, the main strategy for both *variation points* was to ensure strong encapsulation between *R2A's core* and its *variation points*. This is accomplished by the usage of concepts and *patterns* such as the *interface* concept, *proxy*, *observer* and *abstract factory pattern* (cf. ch. I.6.2.4).

III.16.2 Integrating Several *Modeling Tools* in a Single Model

As described in ch. I.6.6.1, often several *design tools* are used simultaneously in an automotive embedded project, due to different strengths of the different tools. Correspondingly, R2A supports to handle several *design tools* in one integrated model[211].

---

[211] See also Medvidovic et al. [MGE+03; p.199]: "While individual models help to clarify certain system aspects, the large number and heterogeneity of models may ultimately

Fig. 16-1 shows an example of such a model basing on the accompanying case study about internal lights control. The model starts with the *AN* "SW Design" that refers to the high-level design diagram of the software. This diagram is modeled in a UML-tool (in the example Sparx Systems Enterprise Architect). In the diagram, several *design elements* are shown, among them the elements "CIL_hdl", "Light_hdl" and "Light_Task". These elements become further *AN*s in R2A.

Due to the different roles and characteristics of the *AN*s, different modeling tools are used to model the diagrams showing the internal design structure of the individual *AN*s:

- The "Light_Task" contains a complex state machine. In order to tame the complexity, the state machine can be modeled, early simulated and then be converted to code via Matlab Stateflow. Thus, the diagram of the "Light_Task" *AN* refers to a Matlab model diagram.

- The "Light_hdl" maps abstract signal definitions used in the "Light_Task" to concrete signals according to the used HW and manages HW diagnosis functions. This involves complex algorithms that are sketched best via UML activity diagrams and then manually implemented in C. Therefore, the "Light_hdl" *AN* is also modeled best in a UML-Tool.

- The "CIL_hdl" (CAN Interaction Layer Handler) cares about managing different signals sent or retrieved via CAN. The signals are usually described in a so-called CAN matrix. A CAN matrix is often described in Microsoft Excel or a dedicated CAN configuration tool. Correspondingly, R2A could[212] refer to this application and the corresponding CAN matrix file.

Once an R2A-model is setup, where the *AN*s with their diagrams are realized in the different modeling tools, the designers can use R2A to navigate in the inte-

---

hamper the ability of stakeholders to communicate about a system. A major reason for this is the discontinuity of information across different models". As a solution, Medvidovic et al. [MGE+03] propose using a model connector concept, where relationships between models can be modeled. This model connector concept rather seems to be an extended link concept (link with different assignable properties) and seems not to be in significant practical application. Nevertheless, the model connector concept may be significantly more flexible than the functionality of R2A. On the other side, the model connector concept leaves open how these connections may be adequately visualized to provide an overview for designers. In this aspect, R2A's concept provides a clear structure, well-known to designers.

[212] Currently, R2A does not support to include Excel or any other application for managing *CAN matrices*, but it will be possible similar to the support for a UML-tool or Matlab, if a coupling of the tool with R2A is implemented. In this way, this indicates a possibly promising extension of R2A's current state of development.

grated model built up from the parts modeled in the different modeling tools. For example, when a designer selects "SW Design" or the "Light_hdl" *AN,* R2A will dock to the UML-tool and show the corresponding diagram. In the case of the "Light_Task", R2A will dock to Matlab and shows the corresponding Matlab diagram, and so on.

If a modeling tool is not available (e.g., the designer does not have a license for the corresponding tool), R2A provides a model viewer mode, where R2A shows a snapshot of the model as bitmap taken by R2A the last time a designer worked with the corresponding modeling tool. In this way, R2A provides one integrated *design model* to the designers even though different tools are used. The *AN* concept once again proves its value as the integrative scaffold.

In most cases, design is a collaborative task, where several designers must work together. Following the example above, it is very likely that the "SW Design" *AN* and its connected information is designed by a SW architect, whereas the details of the individual sub *AN*s ("Light_Task", "Light_hdl" and "CIL_hdl") are designed by developers being specifically responsible for their component (so-called component designers or module designers). Thus, immediate information sharing between the designers is essential. Such cases are especially important in the context of sharing information about requirements, *requirements traceability* and decisions.

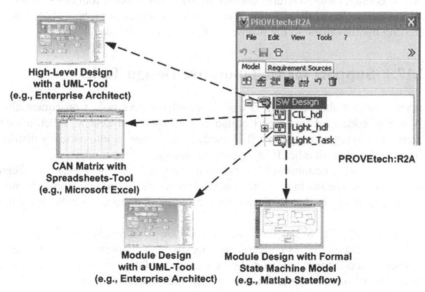

Figure 16-1 Different modeling tools integrated into one *design model* via R2A

As the following chapters describe, the *AN* concept plays the key role in connecting those information with the modeling information in a collaborative way. A possible scenario can be that the software architect makes the decision that a certain requirement must be handled by the "Light_Task". The software architect can document this decision by assigning the requirement to the "Light_Task" *AN*. R2A then immediately notifies the component designer of the "Light_Task" about the newly assigned requirement, and the component designer can immediately use the information to adapt his component design.

Details to these options are presented in the following chapter. In this context, the reader should note that all statements about information propagation between *AN*s also imply that it is possible to cross the information beyond modeling tool boundaries by the integrated model concept described here.

III.17 Basic Support Features of R2A

Design is the most demanding activity within the development cycle.
[ER03; p.34]

R2A also contains some features that are well-known in other tool environments, but the combination of these features with the innovative concepts of R2A brings interesting bonus values. In the following these features are sketched.

III.17.1 Support for Collaborative Design Tasks

As already stated above, design is usually a collaborative task. Consequentially, R2A is also construed to support collaborative aspects of design. When a user performs and saves a change in a R2A model, the change is automatically distributed and updated in all other R2A instances connected to the model.

For improving communication between users, a notes mechanism has been realized in R2A. Details to the notes mechanism are described in the next chapter. One big advantage is that it allows asynchronous communication between the users.

Later in ch. III.18.2.4, the process heuristic *requirement dribble process (RDP)* is introduced that extends the collaborative mechanisms described here to a heuristic to collaboratively find the best design solution for requirements and simultaneously documenting the *traceability* information with a history of the decision-making process leading to the solution.

III.17.2 The Notes Mechanism

Design is a collaborative task, where information sharing is essential for project success. Thus, a notes mechanism[213] provides decisive means to improve communication, i.e., reconciliation between the project members. Concerning communication, three factors must be considered:

- At first, good design lives from good (i.e. creative) ideas. Unfortunately, often creative ideas emerge from a designer's mind for particular aspects of the design, for which no specific structure around the idea has shaped yet. This means a good idea may not be immediately integrated into the current *stable intermediate form* of the design. This point appears to be closely connected to what is discussed in the course of Schön's theory (ch. I.6.2.3) about sketching as an essential activity in design. According to Goel ([Go99], [Go95]), sketching occurs at the beginning of design. Sketches often shape ideas in a kind of ill-structured nature. A notes mechanism provides a flexible, easy to use and fast way for sketching and documenting such ideas.

- R2A allows attaching these notes to any item present in R2A. This enables designers to notify other designers about their ideas. As an example, it often occurs that a designer has a good idea about the solution for a specific requirement, but it is not clear yet what part of the system will handle the requirement. In this case, the designer can attach a note to the requirement and easily sketch the idea in the note text. At a later time, the requirement gets assigned to an *AN* that shall provide the solution for the requirement. Often, a different designer will be responsible for finding the solution to this specific *AN*. In this case, this designer now can open the note attached to the requirement and retrieve a hint about the idea of the other designer how to solve the problem imposed by the requirement at best. Obviously, the example shows that the notes mechanism[214] is a means for communication between the designers inferring the advantage of enabling indirect, asynchronous communication[215] between the designers at their collaborative work.

- Additionally to sketching ideas, designers sometimes also identify interconnections between parts of their design and requirements that are difficult to express in normal design documentation. For these cases, R2A's notes-

---

[213] See fig. 17-1 (p.289) for a description of the user interface implementation in R2A

[214] Here, in combination with the *requirements traceability* mechanisms described in ch. III.18.

[215] For detailed information on implementation, advantages, and disadvantages of synchronous and asynchronous team communication mechanisms in collaborative environments refer to [GK07; p.103-114].

mechanism also allows attaching several items to one note helping designers to document these interconnections (and perhaps also sketching an idea how these interconnections may influence the further design).

- Another source of communication problems between designers are often interdependencies between the designers' work. For example, it is possible that a designer cannot design a solution for a requirement because another designer has not yet designed a solution for another part of the design (e.g., another *AN*), on which the solution of this requirement bases. In this case, the notes mechanism allows the designer of the requirement to apply a note on the requirement and the *AN* not yet fulfilling the necessary design. In this note, the designer can sketch what the other *AN* misses so that he cannot find a design solution for his design problem. Through this, the designer of the other *AN* retrieves then the information that he must find a design solution for the specific problem the other designer's work depends on.

As a side-effect, such notes also provide valuable information when later changes on the design must be maintained at later phases. In this way, notes also provide weak support for *traceability*. However, it must be mentioned here that a few chapters later a significantly stronger support for *traceability* with slightly overlapping possibilities is introduced. This mechanism deals with describing design decisions for problems and their consequences in a traceable way. It is highly possible that some notes sketching ideas about a problem, later become a documented decision.

III.17.3 Extensibility: XML-Reporting and User Tagging

No ever so big tool development effort can anticipate all user needs. This is especially true for all usages of once gathered information. To provide additional flexibility all gathered model information of R2A can be exported to XML and developers can add individual user tags in free text form. This allows organizations to reuse the R2A information in other tools or to develop own special purpose tools using the information for their specific needs.

Experiences with pilot users of R2A revealed that this is especially important for extended information analysis and specific reporting to management. Through the user tags[216] it is possible to add additional *meta-information* on R2A items which is often important to steer information analysis and reporting.

---

[216] See fig. 17-1 (p. 289) for information on how *user tagging* is integrated in R2A's user interface

For the future, the currently discovered reporting needs can be further integrated into R2A as a standard reporting concept, however the mechanisms described here further allow users to quickly check out and adapt new promising uses[217] of the gathered R2A information.

III.17.4 Unique Identifier Support for any Item in R2A

Any item created in R2A automatically receives a unique identifier. As described in ch. II.10.4.2.1, the unique identifier concept is essential to allow textual references as linking is not always possible. In this way, items can also be textually referenced in other development tools, where no direct connection exists. Thus, e.g., in the case of R2A any item in R2A can be referenced in a textual change proposal issued in a *change management* tool by simply writing the unique identifier of the R2A-item in the change proposal's text. To ensure that R2A's identifiers are unique R2A uses the GUID[218]-mechanism provided by the Microsoft Windows operating system.

III.17.5 Evolutionary *Traceability* – Recording History and Baselines

As ch. II.10 has exposed, *traceability* also involves recording the evolution history in project development. This means that all operations performed in R2A must be comprehensible in retrospect. Correspondingly, R2A provides a *history mechanism* to record the history of every operation performed in R2A accompanied by information about the performing user and a time-stamp of the time when the operation has been performed. This history information can be regathered any time by the users if needed (see fig. 17-1 (p. 289)).

---

[217] One issue regularly showing up at discussions with potential users is the idea to integrate the information with project planning information to measure accuracy of project planning and getting a deeper insight about the real status of a project.

[218] GUID stands for General Unique IDentifier and is a well-tested mechanism in Windows ensuring that each generated GUID is world-wide unique (e.g., Microsoft Windows heavily relies on the mechanism to ensure that system internal interfaces or services have a unique identifier).

R2A's history mechanism also provides a possibility for users to save a certain status of the model as a fixed version baseline[219]. Any baseline can be any time reopened in a *baseline viewer* to analyze the status of the design at a certain point in time. Additionally to all information gathered in R2A at that time, such a baseline also records snapshots of all diagrams modeled in the connected *design tools*. Thus, when a baseline is opened in the baseline viewer, also the state of all modeled diagrams at that time can be viewed and analyzed. This is especially helpful to provide an overview over a certain baseline state when more than one modeling tool is used in a model.

III.17.6 The Properties Dialog

For any item present in R2A, a properties dialog shows its properties, evolution history and attached notes. Fig. 17-1 shows the properties dialog of the *AN* "SW Design". On the left, the properties of the item are shown. This dialog varies corresponding to the item type because each item type has different properties. E.g., a requirement mainly has the requirement text as properties, whereas an *AN* type has the properties shown in fig. 17-1. Only the last property "User Tags" is an exception because this property is shown for any R2A item as it enables the user tagging mechanism described in ch. III.17.3.

Through the tab button "History", the user can navigate to the history tab shown in the middle of fig. 17-1. The history tab is segmented in an upper part showing different version entries of the item (here two). In the part below, the differences of versions selected in the upper part are highlighted (cf. ch. III.17.5).

Via the "Notes" tab shown at the right side, the user can add notes to the item according to the notes mechanism described in ch. III.17.2. This tab is divided into three sections. The lower right section contains an overview of all notes attached to the item. In the upper section, the selected note's text can be viewed or edited. All items to which the note is attached are displayed in the lower right section. To attach the note to other items, the designer can *drag-and-drop* the items in the lower right control.

---

[219] "A baseline is a configuration assembled and verified that it is considered as stable and works as referring point for further development. A release is a baseline defined for delivery to the customer" [LL07; p.521].

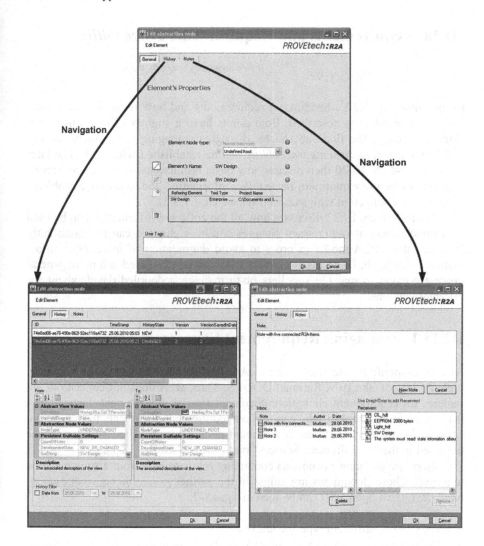

Figure 17-1 The properties dialog in R2A

III.18 Requirements and Requirements *Traceability*

If the language is not right, the spoken is not the meant.
Confucius (*)

In the following, R2A's handling of requirements and how *requirements traceability* is established is described. Both points have a slightly different meaning. Correspondingly, the first sub chapter discusses managing requirement sources and how basic *requirements traceability* can be established with R2A. The later ch. III.19 and ch. III.20 then discuss how basic *requirements traceability* can be extended to improve quality of *traceability* information and to improve problems of SPICE in connection with *traceability* (see ch. I.7.3.2).

Afterward, ch. III.22 discusses how all the collected information can be used to predict effects of requirement changes and how changes can be consistently inferred into a R2A model in order to avoid degradation of *traceability* information. Finally, ch. III.23 discusses how R2A can be integrated in a more general process context to manage suppliers or to manage decoupled development for different versions.

III.18.1 Managing Requirement Sources

At first, it should be mentioned that R2A is not intended for the usage as a complete *REM-tool* like IBM Rational DOORS. Thus, R2A does not concentrate on features for requirement elicitation, documentation or management. Instead R2A is assumed to be a broker, who can retrieve requirement documents from different sources. In this way, different requirement documents and their sources can be managed in the "Requirement Sources" part of R2A (see fig. 18-1).

Here the different documents containing requirements from a source can be managed. These documents are called in the further *requirements source document (RSD)*. An open *RSD* can be seen in fig. 18-2.

Currently two[220] different types of *RSD* exist:
- Documents originating from an *REM-tool* (*requirements specification* items),
- Sources that can be manually managed to allow documenting information otherwise neglected;

---

[220] Actually, the figure also contains the items "Decisions", "Design Constraints" and "Resource Constraints". These items are not *RSDs* in the sense discussed here. These documents are rather containers for all items discussed in ch. III.19, ch. III.20, and ch. III.21.

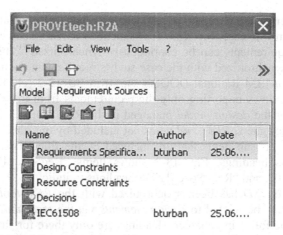

Figure 18-1 Managing different requirement sources in R2A

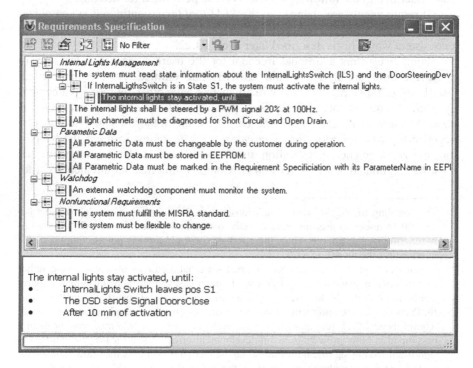

Figure 18-2 *Requirements source document* synchronized with IBM Rational DOORS

Point one refers to requirement documents that are edited and managed in an *REM-tool*. In this case, the *REM-tool* functions as data source from where the available requirements can be continuously synchronized[221]. Fig. 18-2 shows a *RSD* being synchronized with the case study's requirement document managed in the *REM-tool* IBM Rational DOORS shown in fig. 12-2 (ch. III.12). A filtering mechanism allows importing only the requirements from the *REM-tool* that are important for the *design model* managed in the R2A project. For better orientation of the designers, *REM-tool* items not included by the filter criterion but containing items as sub items that are included by the filter criterion are imported into R2A as headings. Fig. 18-2 shows items "ReqSpec_1", "ReqSpec_7", "ReqSpec_10", and "Req–Spec_12" as headings in italic.

Once an *RSD* has been synchronized with the *REM-tool*, the present requirements can be related to *design elements* via the *traceability* operations described in the following chapter. Headings are only there for structuring the document and have no further meaning. This means, none of the *traceability* operations described in the following chapters can be performed for headings.

If requirements are changed in the *REM-tool* then, continuous synchronization procedures allow the requirement changes to be introduced into the design in a consistent way. This is described later in ch. III.22.

Point two offers additional freedom for the users as easy and fast way to document information that would otherwise be omitted. As Hörmann et al. [HDH+06; p.93] emphasize, many requirements have other sources (e.g., company-internal requirements deriving from product politics or the product *architecture*). As outlined by ch. I.7.3.2 and ch. III.19, the author demands to consider negotiability as a criterion for *requirements specifications*. In the author's opinion, the requirements specification should only contain the requirements that must be negotiated with the customer. Company-internal requirements[222] (not

---

[221] The coupling of *REM-tools* is much looser than the coupling of modeling tools because R2A docks its user interface directly to a modeling tool, whereas *REM-tools* only function as data source. Thus, the interface for *REM-tools* is not as complex as the interface for the modeling tools.

[222] The probably most often occurring company-internal requirements are what the author calls internal management requirements. In most cases, internal management requirements might probably deal with ensuring cost efficiency and ensuring monetary benefit. Parts of these requirements have *impact* on design. For example, management can require using COTS (components off the shelf) components or components originally developed in other projects to avoid development effort. A significant problem for design often having significant influence on the design outcome is then how to integrate these components with the other parts of the design. Including such requirements in an extra requirement document helps to separate real requirements from the customer

originating from the customer) could thus be stored in a second requirements specification, or in more pragmatic processes, just be documented in a manually managed *RSD*, or derived from former design decisions (discussed later in ch. III.19 and ch. III.20).

Another scenario to consider here is that *requirements specifications* often refer to industry standards to be fulfilled. In this case, often the requirements imposed by the standard are not directly referenced in the *requirements specification* because these requirements are fixed. Now, the feature to manually write down requirements would allow defining a requirement source referring to the standard (e.g., IEC 61508 in fig. 18-1). In this document, the designers can now note down requirements for the design derived from the IEC 61508 standard.

A manually managed *RSD* looks like and is treated in the same way as a synchronized *RSD* shown in fig. 18-2, except that its containing requirements can be edited in R2A. The handling of the requirements described in the following is also the same as for synchronized requirements.

As described in ch. II.10.4.2.2, requirements can be managed via decomposition hierarchies and decomposition hierarchies are the state-of-the-art management technique offered by *REM-tool*. Correspondingly, *RSDs* originating from *REM-tools* take over the decomposition hierarchy in the *REM-tool*. Fig. 18-2, e.g., shows the requirements in a hierarchic tree directly taken over from the hierarchic decomposition in the IBM Rational DOORS document shown in the left column of fig. 12-2 (ch. III.12). In manually managed *RSDs*, the users can manually arrange the requirements' hierarchic decomposition in R2A.

III.18.2 Establishing Requirements Traceability

Before going into R2A's support for *traceability* establishment, some preliminary considerations shall lead to a better understanding of the ideas.

First of all to mention, different *traceability* models have identified different relationship types between requirements and design. As discussed in ch. II.10.4.2.3, e.g., SysML differentiates between *<<DeriveReqt>>*, *<<Satisfy>>*, *<<Verify>>*, *<<Refine>>*, *<<Trace>>*, and *<<Copy>>* relationship types [SV08], Ramesh and Jarke [RJ01] identify four different relations '*allocated to*', '*satisfy*', '*drive*' and '*addressed by*' in their *high-end traceability model*, other re-

---

from requirements originating somewhere in the developing organization. This already reflects an idea further discussed in ch. III.19 that requirements must be separated according to their negotiability. Surely, requirements originating within the developing organization are easier negotiable within the developing organization than requirements originating from the customer building the contractual basis of the development.

search as, e.g., [Wi98] even surfaced more relationship types. The probably most usual link type is the *'satisfy'* type, indicating that a requirement related to a *design element* is satisfied by the *design element*. In fact, the author believes that, e.g., the three types of SysML are only a little more special variation of the *'satisfy'* link type, as it is the same case for the *'allocated to'* [223] and *'addressed by'* [224] *link types* in the *high-end traceability model* of Ramesh and Jarke[225] [RJ01].

In the context of this research, the question of the relationship type has been left open as research concentrated on an efficient way to establish significant *requirements traceability* providing support for helpful *IA*s. In the author's practical experience, the question whether a relationship has been recorded and thus an *IA* identifies a possible *impact* has higher priority than the correct kind of a relationship, because relationships identified by an *IA* will still be interpreted by the developers leading to the exclusion of false-positive relationships, whereas relationships not found may just never come to the minds of the interpreting developers. In this way, R2A leaves the question about a particular kind of relationship open by using the term a requirement is *assigned to* a *design element* which equally corresponds to a *satisfy-link* type. Later, if usage of R2A in practice proves the necessity to further differentiate different kinds of recorded relationships, the R2A approach can be easily enhanced by a feature to provide more specific relationship type information.

Following Simon's design theory (ch. I.6.2.1), the design process is a continuous decision process, where a lot of the decisions are performed on the basis of the requirements. R2A directly supports this decision-making, because R2A directly shows these requirements to the designers that are important in the design situational context.

Another issue to consider is that continuous *refactoring* of the design structure is necessary due to bounded rationality, arbitrary complexity and Berry's findings about the need to restructure modularization [Be04; p.56], (see ch.

---

[223] Definition of *'allocated to'*: "REQUIREMENTS are ALLOCATED to COMPONENTS that are supposed to satisfy them" [RJ01; p.73].

[224] Definition of addressed by': "Several focus groups mentioned that it was important to identify the FUNCTIONS PERFORMED BY COMPONENTS. These FUNCTIONS are typically traced to the functional REQUIREMENTS explicitly identified in requirements documents." [RJ01; p.74].

[225] The *'drive'* relationship only expresses that requirements drive the design ("REQUIREMENTS DRIVE DESIGN, that are often BASED ON MANDATES such as STANDARDS or POLICIES or METHODS that govern the system development activity" [RJ01; p.73]). Correspondingly, the author is not even sure whether this is really intended as a link type by Ramesh and Jarke. Instead, the author considers the *'drive'* relationship as a conceptual metaphor for the design process.

I.6.2.1.2). Accordingly, it must also be possible to easily *refactor traceability structures*. Today's current state-of-the-art methods of relating requirements are not very flexible for changing requirements assignments. As an effect, designers often perform their design process first to such an extent that the design has shaped to a relatively fixed state and then establish *traceability* information.

This has the effect that the requirements are the basis for a lot of performed decisions, but on the other side the connections between requirements and design are documented afterwards. In this way, a lot of information on certain decisions is lost[226]. As described in ch. II.10.4.3.1, capturing and description of traces should orient themselves on the way the traces occur in the real world. Otherwise, a mismatch between reality and the actually captured information occurs significantly diminishing the quality of captured information [Pi04; p.104]. In R2A, all these issues are achieved by the *requirement dribble process* heuristic described in ch. III.18.2.4.

Taking into account Schön's *Theory of Reflective Practice* (ch. I.6.2.3), most design decisions are taken in an intuitive, non-reflective state of *knowing-in-action*. Former experiences and *tacit knowledge* (see ch. II.9.4.2) are important factors in this state. In this phase, tools must not interrupt the cognitive flow of the designers (see Schön; ch. I.6.2.3). Since R2A's *traceability* concept bases on the *ANH* concept, the R2A's *traceability* operations do not produce a *cognitive dissonance* for designers, thus establishing *traceability* as a *by-product* should not impose significant barriers for designers even in their *knowing-in-action* phases.

In summary, the real value of gathered *traceability* information mainly depends on the following criteria (see ch. II.10):

- Most *traceability* information must be recorded manually. Thus, the efficiency of how *traceability* can be established is crucial. This means that the effort for *traceability* must be outweighed by the reduced efforts and the higher quality, reached through improved *IA* and change processes.

- Accurateness of the *traceability* information is decisive. Approaches that establish *traceability* after the design process involve the danger that certain *traceability* information is not recorded. Thus, *traceability* should be established as a *by-product*.

- Besides efficiency itself, it is a central issue that the process does not interfere with the designers' way of thinking.

---

[226] For details see for details ch. I.7.2.3 description to ENG.3 BP.2, where it is described that allocations of requirements to design are often not possible at first because important design decisions are missing.

- On the other side, designers must perceive enough benefit for themselves because otherwise they will only record insufficient *traceability* information. One benefit can be the improved communication and collaboration between designers as, e.g., R2A offers with the *requirement dribble process* heuristic (cf. ch. I.18.2.4).
- As, e.g., ch. II.10.6.2 outlines, *traceability* information should be detailed (go deep into a *design model*) to achieve good results. It should rather be recorded directly than derived from other information such as relationships within a *design model* with other purpose because the manifold meanings of these non-*traceability*-specific relationships rather lead to a *requirements fan out effect* during IAs (ch. II.10.6.2).

To ensure these criteria and thus to ensure that the recorded *traceability* information brings a real practical benefit to projects, R2A is designed to be embedded into a process specifically addressing these issues. The following sub chapters illustrate the core concepts employed to achieve this. However, the real implementation of such a process in practice requires substantially flexible processes due to the complex connections involved in design processes. Thus, a dedicated goal of this documented research also was to find the optimal, necessary process set for these criteria, where additionally maximal flexibility to adopt processes to project specific needs is possible. In other words, the process sketched here is proposed as a possible way to use R2A, but the offered operations used in a process can also be used to perform different design processes.

Last but not least to mention, this chapter only shows mechanisms for general improvements for rudimentary *traceability* as demanded in today's *traceability* theory and process standards (e.g., SPICE). Then, in the next ch. III.20 and ch. III.21, this rudimentary *traceability* information is extended by decision models allowing much richer *traceability* information taking more complex design decisions into account to be recorded.

III.18.2.1 *Traceability* Operations in R2A

In order to prevent disturbing designers during their *knowing-in-action* cognitive phase, but nonetheless to help to document *traceability* information, R2A aims to lower the burden for documenting the traces as soon as they occur. In this way *traceability* more or less emerges as a *by-product* of the design process.

To address this point, the R2A's *traceability* approach has five key characteristics:

1. The approach takes advantage of the *AN* concept basing on the abstraction hierarchies principle strongly resembling the designers' way of thinking (cf.

ch. III.15). An approach basing on this principle, thus easily fits into the cognitive processes of the designers. If an approach does not really match with the designers' way of thinking, the designers will have to bridge the cognitive gap between their thinking and the thinking required by the approach. This would significantly disturb the designers in their *knowing-in-action* phase and therefore would increase the usage barriers for the approach.

2. Design involves processing of an extended amount of information leading to the extended complexity to be managed during design. Following Simon's theory (ch. I.6.2.1), the *abstraction hierarchies* principle addresses taming the complexity of the information produced during design. Another complexity source to be tamed in the design process is the multitude of requirements influencing the design. R2A here provides a simple answer: Only show what is relevant in the design situational context. Again referring to point one, the *AN* concept is used to set up the situational context. Fig. 18-3 shows a design situation in R2A, where the designer has selected the *AN* "SW Design". Beneath the *AN* tree view, now the tab "Requirements" is opened showing the requirements assigned to the *AN* "SW Design". In ch. III.18, the used mechanisms, and *GUI* controls with its representation features are discussed.

3. Recording *traceability* information when the traces occur but not disturbing the designers, involves that *traceability* information must be maintained in an easy and fast manner. R2A achieves this by offering an establishment of *traceability* information via *drag-and-drop* operations. As illustrated by the arrows in fig. 18-3, principally three different *traceability*-relevant *drag-and-drop* operations are possible. Via possible *multi-selection* of items in R2A, all *drag-and-drop* operations can be performed for several requirements at the same time, making the *traceability* establishment process more effective. Again, the *AN* concept appears as useful for providing central orientation to all three *drag-and-drop* operations. Operation "1.)" allows assigning requirements from the requirement source document (described in the chapter above) to any *AN* in the *AN* tree view, whereas operation "2.)" allows assigning the requirements to the currently selected *AN*. As also described above, design must also allow easy *refactoring*. In this course of action, other components than previously intended may become responsible for a requirement. Thus, requirement assignment must be changed from the formerly responsible component to the now responsible component. To easily make this possible, operation "3.)" allows reassigning requirements from the currently selected *AN* to any other *AN*. In the course of *refactoring*, it can also be evident that a requirement may just also have influence on another *design element*, but the element shall still be handled by the currently selected *AN*. In this

    case, the operation "3.)" accompanied by pressing the 'CTRL'-key just allows copying the assignment information to the other *AN*, but the assignment information of the currently selected *AN* stays untouched.

4.   Requirements can significantly differ in its influence on design. *RE* theory refers to this notion by distinguishing *FRs* from *NFRs*. R2A provides a concept to characterize the influence scope of requirements in a more fine-grained manner. Again, the *AN* concept builds the basis for this concept further described in ch. III.18.2.2.

5.   Last but not least, Simon described the phenomenon that design usually evolves from one *stable intermediate form* to another (ch. I.6.2.1). This means design usually not emerges in a kind of big-bang process but more in an evolutionary process, where design reaches stable states forming the basis of evolution to the next stable state. The R2A approach takes this into account by proposing a process heuristic called the *requirement dribble process* described in ch. III.18.2.4.

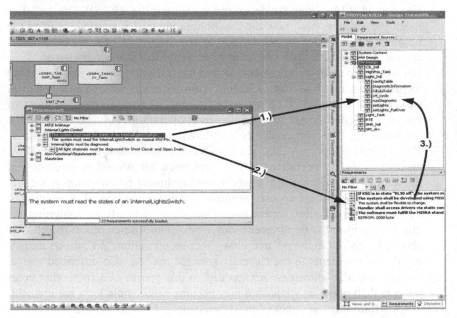

Figure 18-3 Ways of establishing *requirements traceability* via *drag-and-drop* in R2A.

In opposition to the *knowing-in-action* cognitive state, Schön has discovered that designers also switch to a cognitive state he termed *reflection-in-action*. Designers usually switch to this state when they step into a problem they cannot handle by their usual tool-set of internalized everyday problem solving experiences and knowledge. In this state, concrete rationally gauged decisions on a usually very difficult problem. In the author's view, such problems can be seen as what Rittel's design theory terms as *wicked problems* and the decisions taken to solve these problems often have drastic impact on the further outcome of the design. Correspondingly, here is the point where decision documentation and *RatMan* concepts can provide significant support to record this information. As ch. III.20 will further outline, this collected information also has strong importance for *traceability*.

III.18.2.2 The Requirement Influence Scope (RIS)

As shortly discussed in ch. I.6.2.1, strictly modularization-oriented compositional structures are again softened by design theories about architectural aspects, *cross cutting concerns* [CRF+06] or *nonfunctional requirements*. What this actually expresses is the phenomenon that not all requirements can be tamed by confining them in one module. Instead some requirements are fulfilled as a consequence of collaboration between several modules, by *architectural aspects, architectural styles, patterns* or other techniques acting on a wider scope than a single module. In order to provide meaningful *traceability*, these situations must be taken into consideration. For these situations the author will use the term *requirement influence scope (RIS)*.

Due to the *knowing-in-action* cognitive phase, an easy way to define and manage a requirement's *influence scope to design* should be possible.

Again, the *AN*s concept provides a valuable aid: If a requirement is assigned to an *AN*, all sub *AN*s beneath inherit the responsibility for the requirement. The idea behind this can be described that all *AN*s at the lower level must work together or at least share some common concern together to fulfill the requirement.

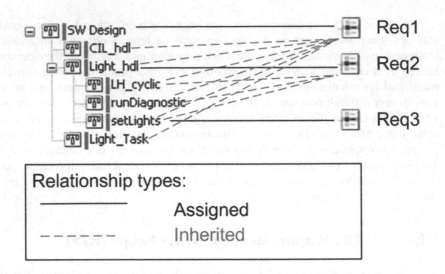

Figure 18-4 Requirements and the *requirement influence scope*

Fig. 18-4 shows an example[227]. Requirement "Req1" is assigned to the *AN* "SW Design". Its concern is then inherited by all sub *AN*s of the model, whereas requirement "Req2" is assigned to the "Light_hdl" module as a whole. This means all methods and contained data in the "Light_hdl" module must work together to fulfill "Req2". A very local requirement is then again seen by "Req3", whose influence scope only reaches to the method "setLights" within the "Light_hdl" module.

In this way, a requirement's *RIS* contains the *AN*s it is directly assigned to and the child *AN*s inheriting the responsibility. Inherited requirements of an *AN* are shown in the "Requirements" tab (cf. fig. 15-4 in ch. III.15) like all other requirements but with a gray colored requirement text.

The *RIS* has strong connection to the differentiation of *functional and non-functional requirements* in *REM* theory as *NFRs* per se have a higher influence

---

[227] Another striking analogy to this concept can be found considering a hierarchy of a company organization. If a requirement (or here rather to say issue) concerns the Chief Executing Officer of the company (corresponds to the "SW Design" *AN* on top of the design hierarchy), the issue will most likely become a concern of all other employees, whereas an issue concerning an employee at the lowest hierarchy level will be just a concern of this employee.

scope than *functional requirements*. However, the concepts are not the same. *NFRs* defining quality characteristics will most likely have the same influence scope as "Req1" meaning the whole software is responsible for fulfilling the issue. For other *NFRs* as, e.g., the demand for a user access rights management, the designers may find a realization that does not have such a high influence scope. As an example, it could be possible to define a *three layers architecture* ([BMR+00; p.31ff], ch. I.6.2.4), where the user access management – except for the graphical user interface dialog to assign rights – is handled in the data storage layer.

This example also points to three other aspects that must be considered:

- The lower the *RIS* of a requirement is in a design, the lower will be the *impact* of a requirement change to the design. Thus, designers should try to minimize the *RIS* of requirements in order to minimize the *impact* of the requirement. This topic will be a central goal in the next chapter discussing the *requirement dribble process* heuristic.

- On the other side, the *RIS* highlights requirements with high influence on a design, as they will stay at a very high level of abstraction being inherited by a lot of requirements. This is what Obbink et al. [OKK+02] term *architecturally significant requirements*[228] *(ASR)* and what most probably imposes close connection to requirements imposing *neuralgic points* in the view of Moro [Mo04; p.326] (also cf. ch. II.9.4.1). In most cases, *NFRs* will be most of the *ASRs* (but also *FRs* could be *ASRs*) staying at the very high level *INs*.

- The *RIS* of a requirement can be influenced by the designers' decisions. As ch. I.5.1 and ch. II.10.4.2.2 indicate, a promising strategy to tame *NFRs* is to refine them into several *FRs* (cf. [PKD+03; p.145], [Pi04; p.99], [Mo04; p.339]). Often, these *FRs* then might have a lower *RIS* than the *NFR* would have had. In this way, a *NFR's* higher *RIS* is reexpressed through several *FRs* with a lower *RIS*. Such a step is a decision process. Due to the importance of *NFRs* concerning the general outcome of design (cf. ch. II.9.5), a dedicated support for documenting such decisions can prove very helpful. Ch. III.20 will discuss the decision problem and how R2A provides support to tame nonfunctional aspects with high *RIS* to a lower influence scope in a traceable way.

---

[228] "A requirement upon a software system which influences its architecture" [OKK+02; p.53].

III.18.2.3 Representing Requirement Contextual Data

As mentioned in the chapters above, R2A helps designers to cope with the complexity imposed by the high numbers of requirements by providing only requirement information relevant in the design situational context.

When the user selects an *AN*, the control shown in fig. 18-5 will show all requirements relevant for the selected *AN*. Directly assigned requirements are displayed in normal black text color. Inherited requirements are displayed in gray text color.

Fig. 18-5 also highlights two buttons for the operations *"dribble-up"* and *"dribble-down"* essential for the *requirement dribble process* described in the following chapter. Both buttons allow changing the requirement assignment in orientation to the *AN*-hierarchy. A requirement assigned to an *AN* can be moved up to the *AN*'s parent *AN* via the *dribble-up* operation. This means to change the realization of a requirement to a higher abstraction level implying that the *RIS* of the requirement is widened. Vice versa, a *dribble-down* operation allows delegating the realization of a requirement down from the currently assigned *AN* to one or more of its child *AN*s (the user can choose any combination of the child *AN*s). This corresponds to a narrowing of the influence scope of the requirement. In this way, a requirement becomes more local instead of global. Accordingly, this can also be termed as the localization of a requirement. Often, design is performed by several designers working together. In such constellations, it is often the case that one designer works on a higher *AL* and the other designer works on the lower *AL*. *Dribble-down* and *dribble-up* operations thus also traverse working boundaries. In this way also a collaborative information exchange between the designers takes place.

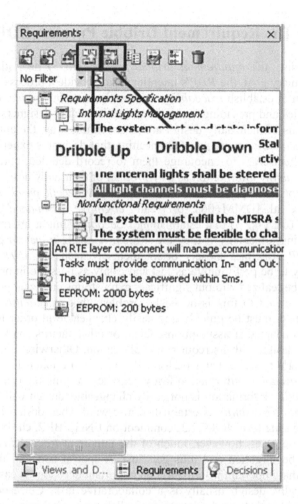

Figure 18-5 Showing requirements in the design situational context of an *AN*

III.18.2.4 The Requirement Dribble Process (RDP)

In the following, the *requirement dribble process (RDP)* heuristic[229] is introduced. As primary goal, the *RDP's* intention is to provide a process for designers allowing them to establish *traceability* information as a *by-product* of their daily design activities and providing immediate benefits for the designers when taking the next actions of their daily design activities. In that way, the author hopes to solve the *traceability benefit problem* meaning that designers experience enough benefits for themselves to encourage them to record detailed, correct and thus valuable *traceability* information as a *by-product* of their daily design activities.

One major leverage to reduce the *traceability benefit problem* is to avoid what Dutoit et al. [DMM+06a; p.7] call *"cognitive dissonance"*, meaning in Schön's view (ch. I.6.2.3) that establishing *traceability* might interrupt designers in their thinking, especially if they are in their *knowing-in-action* phase. Therefore, the *RDP* principles closely orient themselves on the *ANH* concept (ch. III.15) and try to be performable as fast and easily as possible in order to ensure that they can be realized without significant extra strains on developers.

Closely related to this issue is the problem that *traceability* information, once established, must be quickly and easily changeable in order to ensure that design is also adapted if assumptions, facts, or other factors spark the need for changing the design with its requirement allocation. Otherwise, either important design refactorings are just not performed due to more extensive effort, or *requirements traceability* information fastly degrades. A symptom often observed is that if *traceability* information is not easily changeable, design will be performed beforehand and *traceability* is established afterward when design has reached a relative stable state (see ch. I.7.2.3; comment on ENG.3 BP.2, ch. II.10.5, and ch. III.11). In these cases, however, much of the important *traceability* information may already be forgotten and thus gets lost. A special concern in this context especially is that important information on important decisions is easily lost.

Additionally, design usually is a collaborative task. Correspondingly, the heuristic provides dedicated support for collaborative information sharing between designers at different levels of abstraction.

Several ideas form the central pillars of *RDP*:

---

[229] The term heuristic emphasizes that it is more a guiding principle, where deviations are possible. However, the author is convinced that in principle most of the SW-based design processes – even in those design processes, where design is only present implicitly in code – follow this principle to the one or other extent. The so called *bottom-up* processes can be seen as the only big exception, but later it is shown that *bottom-up* processes are also merely compatible.

- The *abstraction nodes* concept,
- The concept of *stable intermediate forms* as developed by Simon (cf. ch. I.6.2.1 and ch. III.18.2),
- The *requirement influence scope* (*RIS*) concept;

III.18.2.4.1 Description of the RDP

The name '*RDP*' derives from a metaphorical analogy to rain water dribbling onto a mountain. In a similar way, the *RDP* heuristics allows design with its corresponding *AN*s to emerge in a requirement-driven way by letting requirements 'dribble' through the *ANH* tree. The basic idea is that requirements are not necessarily directly assigned to the *AN* that will finally be responsible in the future. Instead, a process is possible, where the optimal solution for a requirement is found in the course of the process heuristic. At first, this means that a requirement can be added to an *AN* at a very abstract *abstraction level* (*AL*), e.g., the highest *AN* of a model. According to the *requirement influence scope* (*RIS*) concept, this first of all implies that a large extent of the design would be responsible for fulfilling a requirement. In this constellation, later changes of the requirement would have far reaching consequences (*impact*). Thus, to avoid requirement changes having enormous consequences, all further design decisions shall act upon a maxim to reduce the *RIS* of any requirement to a level as local as possible. Keeping this in mind during design, the designer of an *AN* analyzes the assigned requirements and tries to find solutions which allow delegating the requirements to an *AN* at a lower level of abstraction via *dribble-down* operations. In this lower abstraction level with the lower *RIS*, the designer responsible for the corresponding *AN* again tries to find a solution allowing him to delegate the requirement to an *AN* to lower *AL*s, thus again lowering the *RIS*. This happens as long as a requirement cannot be realized by *AN*s of a lower *AL* in an expedient way. In this case, the requirement now either comes to rest at this *AN* and its sub *AN*s inherit the requirement as obligation to work together to fulfill the requirement's needs, or the requirement can be split[230] up to be fulfilled by several sub *AN*s of the lower abstraction.

---

[230] A split operation, however, should be omitted if possible. The general goal should be to perform "*dribble-down*"-operations of requirements into disjoint paths, so that most of the requirements will only take one way to *dribble down* into the design; but sometimes a split up may be not avoidable. If not avoidable, such a split up should occur at an *AL* as low as possible in order to avoid a *requirement-fan-out* as described in ch. II.10.6.2 leading to a high *RIS*.

In some cases, the designer of an *AN* could discover that an assigned requirement cannot be adequately fulfilled by the *AN*. For example, this can happen because the designer having delegated the requirement from a higher level *AN* to the current *AN* has not been aware of some facts (resp. problems). In this case, the designer of the current *AN* can again redelegate the requirement to its parent *AN* at the higher abstraction level by a *dribble-up* operation. Such a situation occurs when the requirement cannot really be fulfilled by the selected *AN*. Thus, the *dribble-up* operation will correct the mistake. Often, however, it could also be a communication problem when several designers work together at different *AL*s. Such a case can happen when the designer of the higher *AL* assigns a requirement to the *AN* of the lower *AL* but forgets to regard some other aspect influencing the potency of the *AN* to fulfill the requirement. For example, it can be the case that the AN is missing access to an information of another component necessary to fulfill the requirement. Here, R2A allows the designer of the lower *AN* to redelegate the requirement to the designer of the higher *AL* via a *dribble-up* operation accompanied by a note describing why the requirement cannot be fulfilled by the lower *AN* in the current setting.

This note information additionally helps the designer of the higher *AL* to regard the forgotten aspect and – if possible – to solve the problem. For example, by designing a solution that allows the *AL* to access the needed information. Afterward, the designer of the higher-level *AN* can again assign the requirement to the lower-level *AN* via a new *dribble-down* operation.

During the *RDP*, *dribble-down* and *dribble-up* operations can be performed by all designers involved in the design forming a collaborative form of information sharing. At the end, the *RDP* design process heuristic should converge to a design where all requirements are considered in pursuing the goal that each requirement has a *RIS* as low as possible, which leads to a design where changes on a requirement – hopefully – has minimal *impact*.

A significant advantage of the *RDP* is that the heuristic always preserves the exact current state of a design. Often, requirements important for an *AN* are scattered over several locations in a requirement document. Therefore in current practice, the designer of an *AN* often must analyze the complete requirements specification to identify all requirements important to the *AN*. In this way, every designer must nearly analyze the complete requirements specification to identify the requirements important for him. With the *RDP* approach, a list of the requirements concerning an *AN* is directly provided by R2A and thus, designers do not need to analyze the complete requirements specification but can directly benefit from works other designers have performed. Additionally, the *RDP* heuristic also promotes that a current snapshot of the current design status is available supporting the designers to take their next design steps and decisions, thus also promoting that *requirements traceability* is performed as a *by-product* of the design effort and not afterward.

III.18.2.4.2 A RDP Case Study

To explain the heuristic the reader must consider the accompanying case study introduced in ch. III.12. At first, it is assumed that only the *requirements specification* as shown in fig. 12-2 (ch. III.12) is present and no design has taken place. Thus, a high level software architect (in the further called architect) starts the design from scratch.

At the beginning of the project, the architect starts the process by creating an empty diagram intended as the *high-level architecture* overview and adds this diagram to R2A as the first *AN* (in the further called high-level *AN*) in the *abstraction hierarchy tree*. When analyzing the requirements, the architect decides to care for the "Internal Lights Management" use case. He assigns the requirements of the *use case* to the high-level *AN*. This means the high-level *architecture* is now responsible for the requirements of the *use case*. From this first *stable intermediate form*, the designer can now analyze the *use case* requirements and take further actions. Requirement ReqSpec_2 implies that the system has a CAN connection. Correspondingly, the design needs a CAN_drv driver to control the CAN-HW in the ECU and a CIL_hdl mapping signals from CAN to signals within the software. Thus, the designer creates both *design elements* in the modeling tool, adds both elements to the high-level *architecture* diagram (see fig 12-2 (ch. III.12)), adds the *design elements* to R2A as new *AN*s located beneath the high-level *AN* and then performs a *dribble-down* operation relating ReqSpec_2 to the CIL_hdl, thus localizing ReqSpec_2 to the CIL_hdl.

In a similar way, the architect analyzes requirement ReqSpec_3 and ReqSpec_4 and determines that he needs a Light_Task component. Correspondingly, the designer creates the *Light_Task* component in the *design tool* and adds it to R2A's *ANH*. Now, the designer can delegate ReqSpec_3 and ReqSpec_4 to the Light_Task component via *dribble-down* operation. In this way, the architect roughly analyzes the diversity of the requirements and decides the modularizations, attributes, etc. important from the architectural viewpoint.

Following the current example, the architect identifies the following modules and their important roles:

- Light_Task: is responsible for the evaluation and propagation of the light requests received from outside (e.g., via CAN). The Light_Task can involve a complex state machine.

- Light_hdl: is responsible for translating logical light function requests into the different control of light channels provided by the HW. Further, the Light_hdl is responsible for error diagnosis functionality on the controlled HW light channels and the further processing of measured diagnostic information. To achieve this, the Light_hdl also is responsible for timing the diagnosis functionality as diagnostic measurements must be exactly timed to retrieve valid values.
- PWM_drv: is responsible for realizing demanded pulse widening modulation (PWM) to control the light intensity of the controlled lights.
- ADC: controls the analog-digital converter component within the microcontroller needed to convert analogous feedback currents of the steered lights into digital measurement values for diagnosis on the controlled HW light channels.

As the architect anyhow roughly analyzes the requirements and makes his design decisions on the bases of these, the architect can already assign the requirements to the identified and modeled *design elements*. In this way, he also implicitly documents the basic information on the decision leading to the *design element* as well as to its responsibilities and thus creates *traceability* information as a mere *by-product*.

In the next step, the module designers of the modules (usually, for each module an individual module designer exists) care for realizing the assigned requirements in the specific modules. Thus, at the abstraction level of the module, every module designer starts to analyze the present requirements in detail to identify and model the necessary sub-components, data, and operations. For each identified item the designer adds an *AN* in the abstraction nodes tree and assigns the requirements for the *AN* via a *dribble-down* operation. In this way, the designer automatically documents the basis of his design decision for the corresponding *AN*.

At the level of these newly created *ANs*, the requirements are very likely analyzed in more detail than it happened at the higher-level *ANs*. Correspondingly, the module designers will also encounter contradictions and incompletenesses in the entire design. As an example, the module designer of the Light_hdl module might recognize that, in order to be able to perform the analysis of diagnostic data according to the requirements (indicated by ReqSpec_6), he needs further – not yet considered – information currently only available to the Light_Task. As the solution of the problem is outside of his decision-making authority, he must submit the issue to the designer responsible for the design of the interaction between Light_Task and Light_hdl. In this case here, this is the SW-architect. For this, in a non-R2A project, the module designer of the Light_hdl would now need to have a talk with the architect about the problem, in which both must use a synchronous communication mechanism.

However, in several cases the architect may be busy, or distributed to another location, or just absent. In all these cases, constant dangers exist that the issue gets somewhere stuck or forgotten. Using R2A, the module designer is able to redelegate the requirements back to the higher *AL* by performing a *dribble-up* operation. To provide further information on the issue, the module designer can add a note on the requirements describing the problem. The architect then is notified about these requirements again at his *AL*, can read the attached note to understand the problem, and then take decisive action whether the requirements should be fulfilled by a functionality to exchange the needed information between Light-Task and Light_hdl or an alternative strategy such as remodularization (the needed information is relocated into the Light_hdl) is used.

Through this way, asynchronous communication between the designers is possible, where no problems are forgotten, and decisions are implicitly documented in addition.

In the further project progress, the module designer can then refine the design of the module. In case the code is generated automatically, the software developer can then directly implement the realization of the module according to the design and the assigned requirements. Also, in this case, the implementer directly has all necessary requirements for the module at hand and is able to use the *dribble-up* mechanism in any case he discovers problems he cannot solve at his level of authorization.

III.18.2.4.3 Bottom-Up Design Processes within RDP

The *RDP* seems to be a method particularly fitting to *top-down* design processes. However, as discussed in ch. I.6.2.1.3, pure *top-down* design processes are rather an exception. In many cases, design evolves in rather *non-linear* decision processes. The other extreme to *top-down* design is pure *bottom-up* design. Most design processes will be a mixture somewhere between both (see, e.g., [HR02; ch.10]).

As mentioned before, the *RDP* is just a process heuristic. R2A's features provide flexibility to implement different processes. To support *bottom-up* design processes, the following process setting is conceivable:

- The designers created *design elements* in the used modeling tool, add the *elements* to R2A as *ANs* (via the wizard or *drag-and-drop*; see ch. III.15) and assign the requirements the *design element* is intended to fulfill.

- If the hierarchy later changes (e.g., a parent is added to the *design elements*), the *ANH* synchronization mechanism can easily reconstruct the new *ANH*. The requirements assignment stays untouched.
- When the *ANH* grows, the *dribble-down* and *dribble-up* operations also provide valuable support for changing requirement assignment and thus implicitly the *RDP* principles are again at work.

III.18.2.4.4 RDP Summary

The *RDP* approach offers significant advantages to other known *traceability* methods addressing *traceability* between requirements and design:

- The linking between requirements and model elements emerges indirectly as a *by-product* since the assignment of the requirements always resembles the current state of decision about a requirement (*stable intermediate form*). Later in ch. III.20 and ch. III.21, the author describes other kinds of decisions also addressed by R2A through dedicated decision models. Also products related to these *decision models* (*design constraints* and *budgeted resource constraints*; see ch. III.19 and ch. III.21) can again be treated by the *RDP*.
- In parallel, through the detailed recording of all steps taken to achieve a design, detailed documentation of the decision-making of a design is enabled allowing easier reconstruction of the original ideas behind individual design decisions in the case changes are needed.
- Also, the designer has an immediate overview of the remaining, not yet treated requirements at an *AN*, because the already treated requirements have been delegated – and thus disappeared – to one or several sub *AN*s. Later, in ch. III.22, the principle mentioned here is even extended by a mechanism for ensuring consistency.
- Normally, several developers work on a *design model*. Via R2A, the delegation of responsibilities between the developers can be achieved by interplay of the *AN*s with the *RDP* concept, building a *scaffold* (i.e. *skeleton*) for collaborative information interchange.
- Through the support of a dedicated process for assignment and care of a requirement, it is ensured that each requirement is adequately considered in the design process: If new requirements are assigned to an *AN* from a higher-level parent *AN,* these requirements get highlighted in the *AN* by a different color. Now, the designer of the *AN* must try, to find an adequate solution for the newly assigned requirements. If the designer of this *AN* is again able to delegate these requirements to a sub *AN* of the design, then these requirements 'dribble down' one level deeper to a sub *AN* and the problem is solved for the

corresponding *AN*. However, if the designer is not able to clearly delegate these requirements to any sub *AN*, then the *requirements* sticks to this *AN* and are inherited to all lower level sub *AN*s (marked 'gray') indicating that all *AN*s together must deal with fulfilling these requirements. But if the designer responsible for the *AN* realizes that these newly assigned requirements cannot be fulfilled in the current state of design, the designer is able to repel these requirements back to the higher-level *AN* (its origin) accompanied with a corresponding note. In this case, the designer of the higher-level *AN* must care for a solution under consideration of the created notes.

- Effective communication between the designers is alleviated since the approach relies on mechanisms supporting asynchronous communication via the assigned requirements and notes. Thus, less synchronous consultation between the designers is needed.

- The documentation of views in design with their textual descriptions and all important decision information is essential for *architecture documentation* (*AD*), (cf. [Ha06], [CBB+03]). Thus, R2A also supports generating reports from all recorded information to fulfill *AD* needs. In this way, also information gathered through the *RDP* heuristic completes information needs for *AD*.

- When the design process is thought beyond the scope of mind discussed now, a similar mechanism for other information to dribble through the designed system in a similar fashion could be helpful. Thus, e.g., a design decision (see fig. 20-2 (see ch. III.20)) in a high *AL* often restricts the *solution space* in the lower *AL*s. If these so-called *design constraints* are formulated once, they can dribble through the system in the same fashion. In order to allow high adaptability to project specific needs, other item categories may be individually definable by additional information for each project.

III.18.2.5 Overview over Navigation and Handling of Requirements Aspects in R2A

Fig. 18-6 shows an overview how features described in the chapter above are integrated into R2A concerning navigation and handling. At the left part, the model with the *ANH* tree as described in fig. 15-4 (see ch. III.15) is shown. Via selecting the "Requirement Sources" tab (1.), the control for managing all *requirement source documents (RSD)* is displayed (see fig. 18-1 (see ch. III.18.1)).

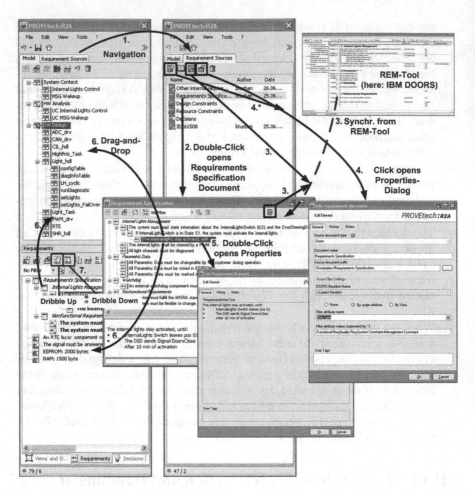

Figure 18-6 Overview of how the requirements-related features are integrated into R2A concerning navigation and handling

A double-click (2.) on a document opens the *RSD's* content window displaying the requirements of the *RSD* (see fig. 18-2 (see ch. III.18.1)). In fig. 18-6 the content of the *RSD* "Requirements Specification" is shown.

A left-click on the properties-button (4.) opens the properties dialog for the *RSD*. When the new-button (4.*) is clicked, a new, empty properties dialog is opened leading to the creation of a new *RSD* if the 'ok'-button of the properties dialog is clicked. Fig. 18-6 shows the properties dialog of the *RSD* "Requirements Specification". As the properties show, this *RSD* is configured to refer to a requirements document managed in the *REM-tool* IBM Rational DOORS.

Through the synchronization buttons (3.), a synchronization mechanism can be invoked to synchronize the requirements contained in the *REM-tool* (symbolized by the upper right window in fig. 18-6) to the *RSD*. The synchronization mechanism can be continuously invoked to synchronize changes performed in the *REM-tool* to R2A's *RSD*, keeping it up to date. Ch. III.22.2 shows how this mechanism can be used to consistently infer requirement changes into a R2A design. Requirements being synchronized from an *REM-tool* cannot be edited in R2A.

In the properties dialog, a *RSD* can also be set to status 'Free Edit'. In this case, freely editable new requirements can be created in the *RSD's* content window.

In an *RSD's* content window, the requirements are displayed in the hierarchical decomposition structure. A double-click (5.) on a requirement opens the properties dialog of the requirement.

Via *drag-and-drop* operations (6.), *traceability* can be established to the *ANs* (also cf. fig. 18-3 (in ch. III.18.2.1)). These in combination with the *dribble-up* and *dribble-down* operations (7.) form the basis for the requirement dribble process heuristic (ch. III.18.2.4).

III.19 Taxonomy of Requiremental Items[231]

> *Each definition of a system layer yields some of the requirements for the subjacent layer.*
> Hatley et al. [HHP03; p.52 (*)]

The SPICE *process model* (described in ch. I.7.2) is a layered *process model*, in which *problem space descriptions* (requirement view: ENG.2, ENG.4) alternate with *solution space* descriptions (designs: ENG.3, ENG.5) at different levels of abstraction (cf. ch. I.7.3.2 for detailed exemplification).

Ch. I.7.3.2 has outlined the problems of this layered *process model* concerning *traceability*. Two major problems were discovered:

* High redundancies between the requirement artifacts lead to higher efforts for *traceability* and consistency management (see fig. 7-2 (see ch. I.7.3.2)).

---

[231] Significant parts of this chapter are taken from [TKT+07] and [TTW07].

Additionally, despite all consistency management efforts, drifts between the different requirement artifacts' redundancies are often not avoidable.

- Between the different artifacts (especially, when also the HW dimension is considered) other correlations are not adequately manageable (see fig. 7-2 (see ch. I.7.3.2) and fig. 7-3 (see ch. I.7.3.2)).

The first problem with redundancy could already be solved to a great extent by a process artifact model described in fig. 7-3 (see ch. I.7.3.2). One prerequisite, however, is to acknowledge that *process models* such as SPICE are to a certain degree rather a metaphor providing space for interpretation than a law to be obeyed word for word. In the author's opinion, this degree of freedom is present in SPICE, because SPICE itself emphasizes that the *process model* is only an example *process model* and other *process models* are possible to be defined as long as they conform to the original metaphoric ideas of the SPICE standard[232].

Now, the solution shown in fig. 7-3 (see ch. I.7.3.2) still neglects one central metaphoric idea of the layered *process model* that is covered by R2A via the concepts described in this chapter, ch. III.20 and ch. III.23.2: *System design* has high *impact* on its *SW design* by raising new "requirements" in addition to the pristine requirements of the stakeholders. For example, in the automotive sector, *SW design* must be subordinated under constraints of extremely cost-optimized HW components. At the moment, SPICE neglects these critical connections between HW and SW but at least acknowledges this connection concerning *system design* (see ch. I.7.2.4).

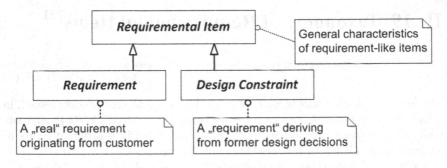

Figure 19-1 *Requiremental items, requirements* and *design constraints* taxonomy

---

[232] It is, however, more difficult for an organization to prove conformance to these metaphoric ideas for a different *process model* than for a *process model* just taking over the ISO/IEC 12207 *process model* used in the SPICE standard. Thus, most SPICE implementations in practice just use this *process model*.

However, one issue in SW requirements which might benefit from more intensive discussion is their negotiability. "Real requirements" are forming the contractual basis between the stakeholders – particularly with the customer. Occurring changes must be harmonized with the customer via a *change control board* *(CCB)* [PR09; p.144f], [VSH01; p.184f, p.216]. Whereas, for "requirements" to be changed with the origin of the definitions of the design, it is possible to search for a project-internal solution first, before escalating the issue to a *CCB* is considered.

Thus, both kinds of requirements should be strictly separated in their notion[233]. The author uses the following taxonomy (fig.19-1):

- *Requirements* are directly allocated to the *SYS_RS* since they concern the legal agreement between customer and contractor.
- 'Requirements' derived from requirements or designs are called *design constraints (DC)*.
- *Requirements* and *design constraints* have similar qualities and structure. Thus, we use the term *requiremental[234] item (RI)* for both items.

Generally, requirements have to refer to their origin (cf. description to IEEE 830-1984 in ch. I.5.7). This relation should apply to all *RIs*. The origin of *DCs* lies in previously made design decisions solving the conflicts/forces between *RIs* and/or architectural items, constraining the broader, more abstract *solution space* to a more concrete one. The *decision model* connected with the *DCs* is discussed in the following ch. III.20.

Observations leading to the *DC* concept are not new. Leffingwell and Widrig define constraint as "a restriction on the degree of freedom" the developer has "in providing a solution" [LW99; p.55]. *DCs* also resemble to what the IEEE 610 defines as *design requirements* ("A requirement that specifies or constrains the design of a system or system component" [IEEE610; p.26]) or *implementation requirements* ("A requirement that specifies or constrains the design of a system or system component" [IEEE610; p.39]).

The *DC* concept directly corresponds to observations of Hatley et al. that design decisions[235] generate new requirements for sub system components [HHP03; p.18]. These new requirements are a result of former design and should be con-

---

[233] This directly corresponds to the view of Pieper in [RS02; p.33-35] demanding a clear separation between requirements from the customer and internal requirements in the project.

[234] The artificial word '*requiremental*' has been introduced by the author as a term for describing superordinate characteristics of '*real*' requirements, *design constraints* and *budgeted resource constraints* (see ch. III.21).

[235] See also Ebert's remarks that decisions constrain the *solution space* [Eb05; p.14].

sidered in a development process [HHP03; p.31]. In general, these 'requirements' are more numerous than the original requirements [HHP03; p.32]. This matches with Glass's note on complexity that "explicit requirements explode by a factor of 50 or more into implicit (design) requirements as a software solution proceeds" [Gl02; p.19], (also cf. ch. I.6.2.1.1).

Lehman's *principle of SW uncertainty* describes that assumptions on which design decisions depend can be implicit or explicit to developers, but both kinds can get invalid due to changes [Le89]. Requirements can be seen as a kind of assumptions (however, also other kinds of assumptions may exist). In this case and in the face of high volatility rates, changes on explicit assumptions are much easier to handle than implicit assumptions. Via the *DC* concept it is possible to make these implicit assumptions more explicit, thus potentially improving *IA* and consistent implementation of changes.

III.20 Support for Capturing Decisions[236]

A further complication is that the requirements of a software system often change during its development, largely because the very existence of a software development project alters the rules of the problem.
[Bo94; p.4]

Most current state-of-the-art *traceability* models assume that *traceability* between requirements and design can be expressed by a simple bidirectional linking concept, where each requirement is related to the *design elements*. The link concept can surely be helpful to cover relatively easy situations. However, *traceability* literature ([Kn01a], [Kn01b], [PDK+02], [Pe04], [RJ01], [Al03]) provides strong indications that the influence of requirements on design processes – and vice versa – is only insufficiently modeled by bidirectional linkages.

Paech et al. [PDK+02] indicate that these relationships can be of a far more complex nature (cf. fig. 20-1). By restraining the *solution space, non-functional requirements (NFR)* restrain *functional requirements (FR)* and *architectural decisions (AD)*. On the other hand, *NFRs* are realized by *FRs* and *ADs*, whereas *FRs* are realized and restrained by *ADs*.

---

[236] Significant parts of this chapter are taken from [TKT+07] and [TTW07].

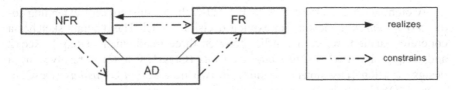

Figure 20-1 Interactions between nonfunctional, functional requirements and architectural decisions [PDK+02]

The simple linking concept indirectly assumes that requirements and design are mostly interconnected by linear relationships. As the author tried to elicit in part II and ch. I.6 of the thesis, the transitions from requirements to design is often nonlinear[237] but more a creative mental transfer process of a problem description (requirements) to a solution, where the taken decisions build the foundation of these transitions (also cf. [TKT+07]). The path from the requirements to its realizing design can be described as a sequence of decisions constraining the *solution space*. This circumstance induces that design does not only depend on its requirements to be fulfilled, but it depends to a higher extent from the decisions taken before. Now, this observation leads to the following two points to consider:

- Decisions and their effects must be communicated to other designers, developers and testers within the project. As ch. II.9 shows, approaches for decision documentation exist. In practice however, if any decision documentation is done, the information will be documented in some design documents (as, e.g., propose by Clements, Bass et al. in connection with *SW architecture documentation* [BCN+06], [CBB+03]). By such an unstructured way, problems can then arise then, when this information must be propagated to other stakeholders or even is to be processed in the further by other stakeholders.
- Later requirement changes not only influence the design but can also lead to the need to reassess formerly taken decisions and – if necessary – to revise them leading to new *impacts* on the design.

These considerations suggest the inclusion of a decision model in the *traceability* information helping to document the origin of new *design constraints* in a

---

[237] Also interesting in this connection is what Kruchten says about the design process he proposes associated with his *"4+1 View Model" architecture* approach: "Finally, this is not a linear, deterministic process leading to an optimal process view; it requires a few iterations to reach an acceptable compromise. There are numerous other ways to proceed" [Kr95; p.48]. As a consequence the question arises, why the traces of such a process should be linear.

lightweight and need-oriented way. Fig. 20-2 shows this concept extending to-day's *traceability* models by an explicit decision model. The diagram sketches a concrete situation, where a conflict between three requirements (Req_1, Req_2 and Req_3) and two *design model elements* (Class1, Class2) is resolved by a design decision (Decision1), resulting in two new *design contraints* (DesConstraint1, DesConstraint2).

The conventional scheme of relating requirements to realizing model elements is extended by a dialog allowing the capture of documented decisions. In this dialog, elements of the requirement model and the *design model* which are conflicting, i.e., causing a problem, can be chosen. Equally, diagrams describing aspects of the conflicting situation shall be attached as additional information (<<*documenting diagrams*>>).

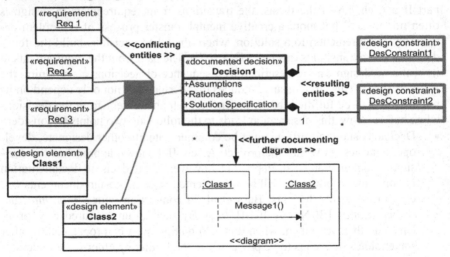

Figure 20-2 Documented decisions build the connection between *requirements*, *design elements* and resulting *design constraints*

Furthermore, the decision can be specified on demand via a text component. The text component accepts unstructured text, but – when needed – can give adequate templates to support the decision documentation. A possible way to structure – the user should choose these freely – is given in fig. 20-2 with the decision's attributes *assumptions, rationales* and *solution specification*.

III.20.1 Relation to Approaches of Rationale Management

The *decision model* presented here is strongly connected to *RatMan* (see ch. II.9), since both deal with decisions during SE processes. In classical *RatMan*, the focus lies on documenting, recovering, further usage and reuse of justifications (= *rationale*) behind design decisions. *RatMan* mainly targets on the information about the 'Why' of design decisions in order to alleviate the knowledge transfer of decision makers to other involved stakeholders.

However, existing approaches could not succeed in practice [DMM+06a], even though documenting design decisions is regularly called for in literature (cf. [IEEE1471], [CBB+03], [BCN+06], [Ri06], [PBG04], [GP04], [Bo94]) and practitioners acknowledge the importance of this type of documentation [TAG+05]. Diverse causes for this negligence have been identified, but the problem of *capturing* the *rationale* seems to be the main obstacle (cf. [DMM+06a], [HA06a]):

1. Most approaches are highly *intrusive* (bothersome and interfering) to the design process with extra effort for capturing (ch. II.9.1.4, ch. II.9.4.2, [Gr96b], [HA06a]).
2. The approaches tend to have negative impact on the decision process, since not all (aspects of) decisions can be rationally justified but arise from intuitive considerations (Schön's *"Theory of Reflective Practice"* [Sch83] adopted by Fischer et al. [FLM+96], [DMM+06a]) basing on diffuse experiences (e.g., *tacit knowledge* [Po66]; also cf. [DMM+06a], [ILA06a], [SM99a]).
3. Decisions must be made despite of unclear circumstances and it is impossible to include all relevant information (*bounded rationality* [Si96], [HA06a]). Thus satisfactory solutions must be found although problem knowledge is clearly limited [LF06].
4. *Grudin's principle* [Gr96b] suggests that collaborative systems fail if the invested value is not returned to the information bearers (ch. II.9.4.2, [DMM+06a], [Sch06]).

The problem mentioned in point one implies that *not all* decisions can be treated exhaustively in any case. For example, Clements, Bass et al. only refer to the documentation of the most important decisions ([CBB+03], [BCN+06]). Booch [Bo94] gives another lead by dividing decisions[238] into *strategic* (i.e., with striking *impact* on *architecture*, mostly made on the early stage of a project) and *tactical* (i.e., locally limited *impact* on the *architecture*).

---

[238] Also cf. Canfora et al. [CCL00] distinguishing maintenance *rationale* into two parts: *Rationale* in the large (*rationale* for higher-level decisions) and *rationale* in the small (*rationale* for implementing a change and testing).

In this context, strategic decisions must/should be thought through carefully and should –if possible– be made on explicit *rationale* grounding. For this relatively small fraction, the investment in more intensive analyzes is highly valuable, as discussed by most approaches on rational management ([RJ01], [CBB+03], [BCN+06], [TA05]). These issues may be analyzed in a *prescriptive schema* as *IBIS* [KR70], or the *Rationale Model* of Ramesh and Jarke [RJ01], or REMAP [RD92], or Clements and Bass [CBB+03], [BCN+06]. R2A's decision model (see fig. 20-2) supports this by additionally allowing defining a project individual template for the textual description component of the decision (in fig. 20-2 shortly sketched by the bullets *"Assumptions"*, *"Rationales"* and *"Solution Specification"*).

On the other hand, Booch [Bo94] also demands that *tactical* decisions should be documented. At that time, Booch thought both kinds would disclose themselves by applying adequate modeling. Today's experiences show that such modeling just documents the *how* but not the *why* of decisions. In this context, Dutoit et al. [DMM+06a; p.39] provide the heuristic to concentrate on documenting decisions that are not obvious or *impact* other decisions. Referring back to Booch's view, it can be said that modeling captures a certain part of the decisions and the R2A decision mechanisms help to document the not obvious and especially influential decisions.

In the author's opinion, the developers should at least get the possibility to document decisions on demand, but considering aspects mentioned in point 2 and 3, the *intrusion* on the development process must be minimized ([Sch06], [HA06a], [DMM+06a], [SM99a]).

Keeping this in mind, a key goal of this decision model approach is to lower the barriers to making design decisions explicit as much as possible: Therefore, this decision model mechanism offers to designers a simple, *semi-formal model* as a *skeletal structure* to easily add basic information[239]. For this, the proposed decision model provides a minimal notational framework to identify the conflicting elements (*requiremental* and *design*) and to derive the resulting consequences as *DCs*. Thus, the conflicting elements define the area of conflict with the counteracting forces, automatically documenting the basic *rationale* behind a decision as a *by-product*.

In that case, however, the model is minimalistic and of a purely *descriptive* nature. Any further users of such minimalistically documented decisions must at first derive the actual knowledge about the decision on their own. But at least the fact that the context (the conflicting items and the results of the decision as *DCs*) is present for each decision provides evidence to later users: They can infer that a

---

[239] In this way, the approach resembles to the *QOC* approach (see ch. II.9).

decision has been made consciously and first clues are given for recovering the *rationale* (cf. [RLV06]). Further, this modeling of consequences pays tribute[240] to Horner and Atwood's claim that designers must consider the "holistic affects" of problems, their *rationale* and solutions [HA06a; p.84], (also cf. ch. II.9.1.4 and ch. II.9.4.2).

In that way, not all decisions can be reconstructed. Since the tool discussed here shall also automatically record such *meta-data* like the author(s) of a decision, the later users of a decision (*rationale seekers*) can consult the author(s) about unclear aspects. Additionally to tool usage, a *process rule* shall prescribe that the *rationale seekers* must document the results of this *decision recovery* in the decision's textual description to further improve the decision's documentation.

This procedure –inspired by Schneider ([Sch06; p.97]: "Put as little extra burden as possible on the *bearer* of *rationale*") – helps to cope with the problem in point four (see above), because by deferring the documentation work to the inexperienced *rationale seekers*, the experienced *know-how bearers* are significantly disburdened from communication resp. documentation work. As a positive side-effect, the transferred knowledge is consolidated in the *rationale seeker* during his documentation work.

On the other side, only unclear decisions will go through this further *rationale* request and documentation process. Therefore, the approach indirectly minimizes the documentation overhead by orienting itself on the selective information need of the further *rationale seekers*.

Van der Ven et al. express the observation that design decisions spark these new requirements, which then also must be satisfied by an *architecture* [VJN+06; p.340]. Van der Ven et al. [VJN+06] therefore also propagate to capture information about design decisions, because this helps to address central problems in design [VJN+06; p.332, p.341]:

* *"Design decisions are cross cutting and intertwined"* [VJN+06; p.341]: Many design decisions affect multiple parts of a design. As usual design processes do not explicitly represent design decisions, this knowledge is often fragmented across various parts. The designer himself knows these connections at first but always is in danger to forget it. Also Dutoit et al. [DMM+06; p.86] emphasize that much of design is done through evolutionary redesign and therefore long-term collaboration is essential. An adequate design decision representation can help to preserve the knowledge about the intercon-

---

[240] Even though, this tribute is far from being holistic, the *decision model* approach described here is a first try to establish *rationale* in practice. If the *decision model* concept proves to be sustainably successful in design practice, the model can be enhanced by modeling further more holistic connections.

nections. Later, designers can again be made aware of such cross-cutting and intertwined connections. If then some of the interconnections are no longer desirable (e.g., due to newly discovered facts), the structure can be refactored more easily.

- *"Design rules and constraints are violated"* [VJN+06; p.341]: "During design evolution, designers can easily violate design rules and constraints arising from previous decisions" [VJN+06; p.332]. Such violations are usually the source of architectural drift. Through an adequate design decision representation, designers can be made aware of design rules and constraints imposed by former decisions. In this way, architectural drift can be avoided better.

- *"Obsolete design decisions are not removed"* [VJN+06; p.341]: During evolution of design, some previously taken decisions become obsolete. Recorded information about decisions helps to "predict the *impact* of the decision and the effort required for removal" [VJN+06; p.341].

The *DC* and *decision model concept* proposed here has potential to alleviate these issues. Thus, concerning *RatMan*, R2A tries to balance and connect *descriptive* pragmatism and structured *prescriptive* methodologies. *RatMan* is not R2A's central issue, but this chapter shows that *requirements traceability* and *RatMan* are very closely related to each other and complement one another.

A further general problem of *RatMan* not yet discussed here is the *retrieval* of documented decisions. Horner and Atwood [HA06a] argue that fixed schemes –in contrast to unstructured text– offer better possibilities for indexing according to *retrieval*. The following chapter shows how the *retrieval* problem can be avoided through usage of the gathered *traceability* information of this approach.

III.20.2 Effects on the Traceability Model

The idea of including decisions into the *traceability* models has already been proposed by Ramesh with his REMAP tool [RD92]. In a later empirical study on *traceability* (see ch. II.10.4.2.3), Ramesh and Jarke ([RJ01]) detected a real need by experienced users. Therefore they include a separate *traceability* sub-model (*rationale sub-model*) for decisions, which is oriented on the former works with REMAP.

The decision model being proposed here has been inspired by the *rationale sub model*, but in the author's view Ramesh and Jarke's [RJ01] solution lacks making concrete proposals for implementation and thus, the *RM* component appears loosely connected to the other *traceability* sub models. Besides, the *ra-*

tionale sub model (orienting on REMAP) extends *IBIS* [KR70], which is a *pre-scriptive* and *intrusive* method (cf. ch. II.9.1.4, [LL00; p.202ff]).

In contrast, this decision model directly fits into the *schema* for *traceability* to design. In that way, a *semi-formal model* has evolved which provides easy handling and which has the following characteristics:

- A constellation (combination) of requirements and *design elements* leads to conflicts.
- Decisions do not directly influence dedicated design objects, but they bear *design constraints* that can be flexibly assigned to *design elements* during the project.
- All other important information for documenting a decision can be added on demand as unstructured descriptive text.
- For important strategic decisions, a template can provide *prescriptive* elements to assure these decisions have been made thoroughly.

The usage of the decision model has effects on existing *traceability* models. The *traceability* model of simple linkage described in ch. III.18 is extended to a model briefly sketched in fig. 20-3. Since *design elements* influence the decision process as well, the requirement dimension migrates to a close coupling with the design. Simple *<<satisfy>>* relationships can occur next to (as *Req.1* maps to *DesignElement1*) more complex *traceability* networks. Thus, e.g., *Req.2* only *impacts* the design by the decisions *Dec.1* and *Dec.2*.

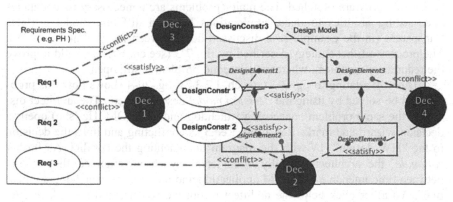

Figure 20-3 The newly emerged and more detailed *traceability* information scheme

Dec.2[241] arises from the conflict situation of *Req.3, DesignConstr.2* and *DesignElement2*, whereas *Dec.3* is only derived from requirement *Req.1* (which then corresponds to a *<<derive>>*-relationship as described in [Li94; p.33]). Consequently, *design elements* (alone without *RIs* involved) should also be able to invoke a decision (*Req1→Dec.3→DesignConstr3*). This way, chains of decision sequences can be modeled corresponding to experiences of Lewis et al. [LRB96] describing design as a *suite of problems* (ch. II.9.3.2).

With adequate tool support, these *traceability* relationships indicated in fig. 20-3 could be visualized as a *traceability* tree. A kind of browser should support:

- Detailed *IA*: Starting with a *starting impact set*, all subsequent paths would firstly be classified as *impacted*. During the following detailed check, the tool should allow to take out paths identified as none-relevant and adding paths detected as relevant (cf. ch. III.22.1).
- An adequate context for the simple *retrieval* of documented decisions. The following chapters show how R2A supports this.

III.20.3 Example How to Tame the Development Process Model of SPICE

In ch. I.7.3.2, problems of the SPICE *process model* concerning artifact handling and *traceability* are sketched. The major problems are unnecessary redundancies and lacking abilities to make implications between different model artifacts transparent (in the example case discussed here between the HW and the SW). The process artifact strategy described by fig. 7-3 (see ch. I.7.3.2) could improve the redundancy problem, whereas the second problem is still open.

Directly relating to fig. 7-3 (see ch. I.7.3.2), fig. 20-4 shows how this problem can be solved by using the *decision model* described here. The architect discovers the same problem concerning watchdog and EEPROM. He (she) opens a decision wizard and marks Req.1 and Req.3 as conflicting and links the decision to the "HW design" *AN* with the diagram documenting the conflict. As further *rationale*, the architect textually documents "synchronization conflict at SPI between time intensive EEPROM application and time critical watchdog application". A further click helps the architect to put the conflict into the risk list. As resulting *DC*, the architect sketches the cooperative handshake and links the *DC* to the EEPROM and watchdog *design elements* in the *SW design*.

---

[241] *Dec.2* is directly mapped to *DesignElement4*. This may also be possible, when no further information for understanding the decision is needed.

Our implementation follows the ideas described in the previous chapter. In the further project progress necessary changes are early detected by *IAs* (see ch. III.22.1) and the additional costs can be compared to the cost savings of the rejected HW change.

The artifacts *HW_RS* and *SW_RS*, which have not been realized, can be generated out of the model on demand by summing up all requirements related to the corresponding design (*HW design model* for the *HW_RS*, *SW design model* for the *SW_RS*). Ch. III.23.2 describes this in detail.

As it is a known problem in embedded design [Gr05; p.415], this example further shows how the *decision model* improves the design processes by making the strong influence of HW design on SW more transparent.

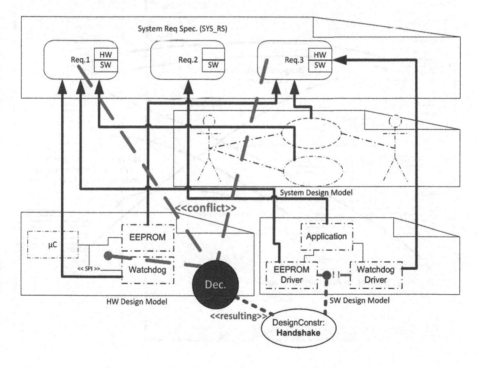

Figure 20-4 The example of SPICE conforming design processes in the new way

III.20.4 Implementation of the Decision Model in R2A

After the decision model has been theoretically discussed, this chapter will now outline how the decision model is implemented in R2A. Fig. 20-5 shows a decision modeled in R2A's decision dialog (left side). Additionally, fig. 20-5 shows possible *drag-and-drop operations* to relate information between the decision dialog and R2A's main window (right side). The modeled decision deals with how the *NFR* "ReqSpec_14: The system must be flexible to change." can be realized concerning HW and SW.

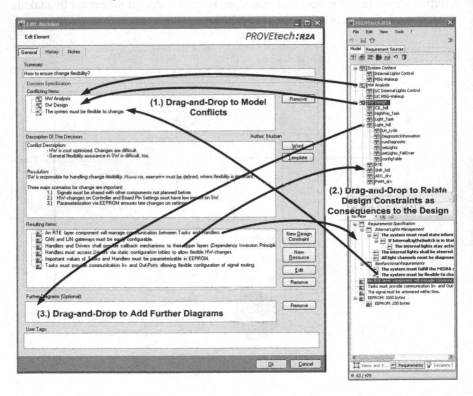

Figure 20-5 Decision dialog in R2A

The dialog implements the decision model described in fig. 20-2 (p.318), and has the following sections (see fig. 20-5):

- At the top, a summary or topic of the decision must be provided. The summary is displayed as the decision's item text in all other controls (e.g., see fig. 20-6).

- In the "Conflicting items:" section, all R2A items being in conflict with each other (and thus need to be decided about) can be added via *drag-and-drop operation* (1.). Once this decision is then saved, the items are related to the decision through <<conflicting entities>> relation described in fig. 20-2 (p.318). In the example, these items are the design *AN*s representing HW and SW in combination with ReqSpec_14.

- Further *assumptions*, *arguments*, and *rationale*, as well as any other information can be added in textual form in the "Description of the Decision" part. The approach does not prescribe any information provided here. Through the button "Word", the description can be performed using Microsoft Word, thus allowing using formatted text. The "Template" button allows loading specification templates if some more structured (*prescriptive*) *rationale* approaches shall be used. The approach does not rely on a specific *rationale* structuring method. Correspondingly, the conflicts, and results parts form a kind of *semi-formal skeleton* for structuring the *rationale*. But, for further documentation of the *rationale*, the approach does not rely on any specific style documentation as *IBIS*, *QOC*, *DRL* etc. Instead a word style documentation is possible, where a template can be prescribed that could be in any *rationale* structuring template[242]. This can be seen as an advantage, because the *rationale* documenter can choose a best-suited structuring *schema*. As Dutoit et al. emphasize [DMM+06a; p.7], schemes differing from the way the *rationale* documenter would intuitively structure it create "a *cognitive dissonance*" imposing additional cognitive strains to the documenters. Freedom of choice can here provide a decisive difference alleviating the burdens encountered at *rationale* documentation.

- To derive consequences from the decision, *DCs* can be created in section "Resulting Items". Afterward, these newly created *DCs* can be *assigned* as *RIs* to any *AN* via *drag-and-drop operations* (2.). Correspondingly, *DCs* could also be termed as 'requirements emerging from the design and decision processes'.

---

[242] It would even be possible to combine the model described here with other *rationale* capturing tools as gIBIS or Compendium.

- For further decision specification any diagrams showing important information can be added via *drag-and-drop operation* (3.) into the 'Further diagrams' section.

The decision modeled in fig. 20-5 is visualized in R2A as shown in fig. 20-6. Ch. III.22.1 and ch. III.22.2 describe how this decision structure and visualization are used to improve *IA* and *consistency management.*

The *DC* "Handlers and Drivers shall provide callback mechanisms to their upper layers (Dependency Inversion Principle)" indicates another aspect to consider. Callback mechanisms can be seen as *patterns* (or *idioms*) to decouple modules. In this way, the decision mechanism can be seen as a way to document *pattern* usage, where a designer can even prescribe the application of *patterns* for a specific situation through *decisions* and *DC*s. This is further discussed in ch. III.20.5.1.

Besides this aspect, the example also shows a situation, where a *NFR* (ReqSpec_14) is reexpressed through several more functional *DCs*. The strategy of taming *NFRs* by concrete scenarios or reexpress them by more concrete *FRs* has been already discussed in ch. I.5.1, ch. II.9.5, ch. II.10.4.2.2, and ch. III.18.2.2.

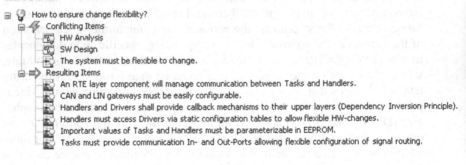

Figure 20-6 R2A's visualization of the decision taken above

Theory of *SW architecture* development has developed the so called *influence factors assessment* described in ch. II.9.5. This can be seen as a more general view on this topic in the context of design.

Table 20.1 shows an example of an *influence factors assessment* on the case study described here, orienting itself on findings of [PBG04; p.79], [CBB+03], [BCK03], [Bo00b], [HNS00], and [BCN+06]. The tabular presentation is taken over from Hofmeister et al. [HNS00]. In the first column, the factor is described, the second column discusses the priority and flexibility of the factor, the third column identifies the influences and risks that may be involved when the factor takes effect, whereas the fourth column describes handling strategies to proactively reduce negative influences and risks of the factor.

The following factors have been identified and discussed:

1. Some requests for the ECU must be responded within 5 milliseconds (ms) (*nonfunctional timing requirements*). As these requests must be fulfilled within this timing to ensure that the controlled processes work properly, the priority is high and the influence of not fulfilling the timing restrictions can lead to complete failure of the ECU. Fortunately, the timing restrictions are not completely fixed but can exceed by 0.5 ms in 5 % of the cases, but 5 ms are still difficult to achieve. Correspondingly, continuous measuring and monitoring, or schedulability analyses as provided by *rate monotonic analysis* [KRP+93] can be an adequate strategy to ensure that all timing restrictions can be fulfilled.

2. A *NFR* requires minimizing power consumption in order to reduce problematic battery work load. This issue also has high priority, but only when ignition is off. As consequence, a sleep-wake-up manager in SW must manage that the ECU goes into a sleep mode when ignition is off.

3. Current *HW design* requires reading input signals of shift registers. This issue results from internal *HW design* decisions for cost optimization and is not demanded by the customer. Correspondingly, priority is low and flexibility is high. As major drawback, the input provided by shift registers must be polled continuously. This imposes a direct risk for factor 1. This also induces a high risk for factor 2, because some of the input signals are dedicated to wake up the ECU, when it is in sleep mode (see factor 2). When shift registers are used for these pins, the ECU must wake up continuously and poll these shift registers during sleep mode, which leads to higher power consumption in sleep mode. To fulfill the wake up requirements in the current *HW design*, the *SW design* for the current SW version must provide an extra timer with a time slice of 2.5 ms for polling the shift registers (2.5 ms in order to handle requests concerned with factor 1). Nevertheless, as this again imposes high risk for factor 1, the *HW design* must be changed for the next release to employ multiplexers instead of shift registers, because multiplexers allow wake-up-able pin interrupts at the micro controller to be directly triggered, thus avoiding polling for input signals and reducing risks of not fulfilling factor 1 and 2.

4. Factor four addresses change flexibility in software as it has been discussed above in fig. 20-5. As change flexibility is rather abstract, the *NFR* is concreted by defining three concrete scenarios for change flexibility:

   a. Scenario one discusses what will happen if input signals currently measured by the environment are sent from another ECU over CAN. In this project, the scenario could be identified as low priority and is thus not further considered.

b. In scenario two a situation is addressed in which it is not quite clear whether some output signals currently sent via CAN may not also be provided via other out pins. Due to limited output pins of the micro controller, the usage of multiplexers (MUX) will then be necessary. The probability of this problem is medium and the change must be applicable within one month. Consequences would be that these output signals should be configurable by EEPROM parameters, HW must be changed, and a new SW component (MUX_hdl) handling these MUXs must be included. Negative *impacts* of the factor can be addressed by a HW reserve[243] that allows easily integrating the multiplexers on HW and an integration point to easily integrate a potential MUX_hdl to be easier integrated in SW.

c. The third scenario discusses the potential that internal SW signals within the ECU may have to be propagated to other parts of the ECU's SW. This is very likely and must be realizable within a few days, because otherwise implementation of other features needing the signals will get retarded. An extension of signal propagation imposes new efforts on the different SW tasks (processes) and may impose a risk for factor 1. To avoid these risks, an *RTE*[244] component as a decoupling layer between *tasks* and *handlers* may provide a standardized communication mechanism with configurable signal propagation through function pointers combined with asynchronous messaging mechanisms to decouple processes.

5. Factor five addresses the effects when development processes with SPICE *maturity level 2* (*ML2*) must be employed. The priority is high, because the customer demands for high quality and a scalable development process. On the other side, SPICE *ML2* demands high administrative and bureaucratic effort for documentation inducing high risks for factor six. This requires a good tool support in order to diminish unnecessary effort; but in the same way it may be acceptable to use development processes capable for SPICE *ML1*, as SPICE *ML1* also requires that all necessary processes are fulfilled; but it does not require extensive documentation.

---

[243] German: HW-Vorhalt

[244] RTE is inspired by the run-time environment (RTE) component of the AUTOSAR architecture. AUTOSAR (Automotive Open System Architecture) is a standardization en–deavor with the goal to define an open standard for automotive *SW architectures* [We07; p.18]. The design case study introduced here is not an AUTOSAR conforming design, because it would unnecessarily complicate the case study. However, the RTE concept proved a good idea to be integrated into this example about SW architectural design decisions.

6. Concerning the project resources, budget for three developers for two years is available. At first sight, this issue seems not so important, because HW part costs are at the end the dominating cost factor in the end. On the other side, risks to achieve the goal of factor 6 are significantly imposed by factor 5. This issue may at first also just seem to be a matter of planning in the sense that the project manager just performed wrong effort estimations, because he did not consider the extra effort of SPICE *ML* 2. In this sense, project staff simply must be increased; but on the other side it may also be the case that budget requirements imposed by the customer or management do not allow an increase in budget and other strategies must be taken. Generally, it is to say that factors 5 and 6 seem not to be directly connected to the design; however, as indicated by Posch et al. [PBG04; p.74f], the scope of factors to be considered should include a wider perspective in which especially organizational factors[245] should be considered. The example shown here is only a snapshot of the factor analysis at a very early state of the project, where factor 6 is in conflict with factor 5, but the effects on the *architecture* are not yet obvious. Now, in the further project progress it may become apparent that the customer insists on SPICE *ML* 2 processes and that project budget is very tight preventing to call in further developers. It may turn out at this later point, however, that two former projects are existing handling partially similar issues as the example project and parts of their SW components can be adapted to the new problem. As this promises to significantly reduce development effort and staff needs, it is then decided to reuse parts of these projects. In this case, both factors would significantly raise their influence on the design, leading to the effect that the whole character of the design may change (e.g., the design may then rather become an integrative patchwork to integrate the old components with adapter components to fulfill the new needs).

---

[245] Organizational factors such as staff size, staff skill levels, development organization, or available budget often impose significant restrictions on which solution is possible and thus significantly influence on the outcome of a design [PBG04; p.74]. Especially economic and development process contexts play an important role, because they soon become an important factor about the feasibility of an intended solution.

Table 20.1 Example of an *architectural influence factors assessment*

Factor	Priority/Flexibility	Influence/Risk	Handling Strategies
1. Response time < 5ms	HIGH; in 95% +- 0.5ms → soft deadline	K.O.-criterion	Rate Monotonic Analysis + continuous measurements of prototypes and release candidates.
2. Minimize Power Consumption	HIGH; at least when ignition is off.	ECU must go into a sleep mode.	Sleep-wake-up manager in SW.
3. Input signals over Shift Register Handler	LOW; High flexibility as not prescribed by customer	Through needed polling induced risk for 1 and 2.	Timer with t+2.5ms; HW change from shift-register to multiplexer in next release.
4. Flexibility to change	MEDIUM		
4.1 Scenario: Input signals change to CAN.	LOW; Rather low probability	-	-
4.2 Scenario: Output signal via CAN or multiplexer	MEDIUM; must be realizable within one month	Configuration parameter in EEPROM; HW change; Multiplexer handler (MUX_hdl) in SW necessary.	HW reserve; Integration point for MUX_hdl in SW.
4.3 Scenario: Internal signal processing must notify other parts of the system.	MEDIUM; very likely → must be realizable within a few days	New communication effort with other tasks → Risk for point 1.	RTE-layer with configurable function pointers and asynchronous messaging
5. SPICE *ML*2	HIGH, the customer demands for high quality, but also wants a scalable development process.	Increased administrative effort → Risk for Point 6	a) Usage of adequate tools. b) Negotiations whether SPICE *ML*1 may also be adequate. c) Adding 50 % additional developer resources
6. Project resources: Three developers for two years	LOW, costs are mainly driven by HW costs.	-	-

Following the current design theory the *influence factor assessment* example above described would be part of a design description only loosely connected to the *design model*. With the *decision model* described here, the decision can be directly integrated into the *design model* (cf. fig. 20-7).

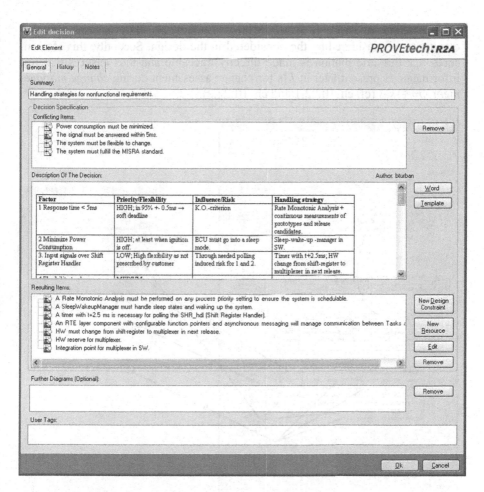

Figure 20-7 *Architectural influence factors assessment* with R2A's decision model

All *requiremental items* (*RIs*) or design related elements (*ANs*) present in R2A and being considered as influence factors can be added to the "Conflicting Items:" section. The assessment description can be documented in the "Description Of The Decision" section in an equal way as shown in table 20.1 above. The arising consequences (column "Handling Strategies" in table 20.1), can again be derived as *DCs* thus allowing directly assigning the *DCs* to the *ANs* needing to realize the consequences. At first, this helps to ensure that the designers of the corresponding *AN*s become aware of these demands and thus ensures that these demands are considered by the considered in the design. Secondly, this also ensures that this information is made directly traceable and thus ensures that this information is present later in *IA*s for change assessment during *change management processes* (cf. ch. III.22.1 and ch. III.22.2).

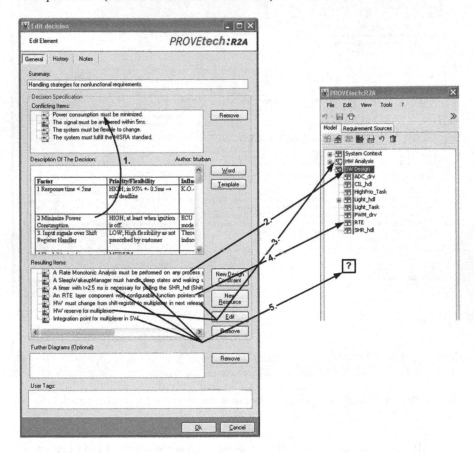

Figure 20-8 Consequences of the *architectural influence factors assessment* of fig. 20-7

Fig. 20-8 shows in more detail how the *influence factors assessment* of fig. 20-7 could impose consequences (see the different arrows) on the design and how they currently can be made explicit in R2A.

Arrow '1.' indicates a fact not yet directly discussed but possibly often occurring in design: The process of discovering *rationale* about a decision can also impose backlashes on the original sources of the decision such as the requirements involved. During the decision process of the example, the designer discovered that the requirement about minimized power consumption is only important if ignition is off, because otherwise the running motor drives the power generator generating enough energy to not strain the battery. This discovery could lead to the conclusion that the requirement itself should best be adapted to 'Power consumption must be minimized if ignition (KL15[246]) is off'. Currently, R2A does not provide dedicated support for this situation, because the situation can be managed by current state-of-the-art tooling. If, e.g., a *change management tool* with a *change proposal system* is used, the designer can initiate a change request describing the situation and the designer can directly textually refer to the decision via its unique identifier in R2A (cf. ch. III.17.4). Otherwise, if only an *REM-tool* is used, the textual reference to the decision's identifier can be added to the information about the requirement (e.g., in a comment attribute or 'Origin' attribute as described in II.10.4.2.1). However, as ch. IV.26 outlines, further perspectives of research about R2A could be supporting a dedicated integration with *change management tools.*

The first *DC* in the "Resulting Items" section demands to perform a *Rate Monotonic Analysis*. Arrow '2.' shows how this can be modeled as a nonfunctional consequence for the complete *SW design*. By assigning the *DC* to the *AN* "SW Design" via a *drag-and-drop* operation the *DC* becomes a new *nonfunctional RI* for the *SW design*. Arrow '4.' indicates a similar situation for a part of the *SW design*.

On the other side, arrow '3.' imposes consequences on the HW. As indicated in fig. 20-8, if the HW *design* is also somehow represented in the R2A *design model*, this can be performed by a *drag-and-drop* operation to the corresponding *AN* representing the HW. Currently R2A does not support a modeling tool for dedicated *HW design*, but the *product line* concept with dedicated support for integrating different modeling tools as a *variation point* should, in principle, equally allow connecting any *HW design tool.*

---

[246] In automotive terminology, ignition is coded by the term "KL15" (In German: Klemme15).

In the current state of R2A with lacking direct support of a HW modeling tool, two alternative strategies are possible to allow tighter integration of *HW design*:

- A place-holder *AN* for the HW model can be created, where all issues arising[247] from a design process performed in R2A possibly relevant for the HW can be assigned. As further described in ch. III.23.2, this place-holder *AN* can then be used in R2A to generate a *requirements specification* for HW resulting out of the design processes performed in R2A.

- In the author's experience, any embedded system or *SW design model* must integrate certain HW aspects anyway in order to model certain cross influences. As these models might need some aspects of HW in their models anyway, a certain low detailed *HW model* could be collaboratively maintained (resp. sketched) by *system designers*, *HW designers* and *SW designers* together to improve a common understanding at this core interface, in which the three domains have their significant overlap. If this *HW model* could be maintained in UML, the system and *SE* activities could seamlessly integrate the model. As a side-effect this model could also be an interface communicating effects of design processes performed in R2A to the *HW designers*. In fig. 20-8, the author indicates this idea by including an *AN* 'HW Analysis'[248].

Last but not least, arrow '5.' indicates that new *DCs* might also spark the need for modeling new *ANs* in the *design*. In fig. 20-8, for example, a *DC*[249] demands a SleepWakeupManager. This SleepWakeupManager must be modeled as a new *AN* in the design. These situations sparking new *ANs* are indicated in fig. 20-8 by a square containing a question mark. The question mark indicates that it is not yet quite exactly sure in the current design situation whether these possibly new arising *ANs* really come to existence and how they might then exactly look like, because creating any new *AN* would then be some following deci-

---

[247] These are at first *DCs* as consequences of decisions as described here in this example, but perhaps also other items in R2A as, e.g., the *budgeted resource constraint* concept introduced in the next chapter, might be relevant.

[248] The author has chosen this name, because such a model concept – in the author's opinion – rather resembles to the *SW analysis* concept as such a model might not really anticipate the *HW design* but might help to analyze certain HW parts that are of crosscutting interest for all three design domains. A real *HW design* might only make sense with a dedicated *HW design tool* allowing modeling of the HW circuits. An alternative name for such a model might be 'HW intermediate model'.

[249] The reader should note that in the situation described here actually three *DCs* might spark new *ANs*. The author has grouped the three items together to one arrow '5.' to avoid unnecessary clutter in fig. 20-8. It is very highly possible that the three items might spark the existence of three different new *ANs*.

sions of the designer, where other factors may also influence the final decisions. As described in ch. II.10.4.2.2, such consequences as indicated by arrow '5.' are connected to what Knethen and Paech [KP02; p.14] call 'applicability links' meaning that an item can derive its justification from another item. From this perspective, the decision and *DCs* concept might probably also be seen as a special form of 'applicability links'.

In [PKD+03; p.145], Paech et al. indicate that some *NFRs* can be specified via *FRs*. This is possible with the *decision model*, in which a *NFR* can spark a decision about handling strategies for the *NFRs* leading to new *DCs* as consequences[250]. Thus, it could be said that this approach is good way to cope with nonfunctional restrictions that can be split into some numerical expression as it is often the case in embedded systems.

Chung et al. [CNY+00] developed a *NFR framework*, where *NFRs* drive design creating *rationale*. The approach allows graphically modeling trade-offs and synergies between *NFRs* (also cf. ch. II.9.5). This can also be achieved by R2A's decision model, where the *NFRs* are referred to as conflicting items. Via the "Further Diagrams" section, a model graph can be modeled in the *design tool* and referred to in the decision. In a similar direction, Egyed et al. [EG04] discuss an approach, where they map *FRs* to *nonfunctional aspects* (or *software attributes*) to identify conflicting and supporting situations. This approach should be equally manageable by R2A's *decision model*.

III.20.5 Additional Support of the Decision Model for Designers[251]

In the following, additional connections and advantages of the proposed decision model in relation to design-related issues are discussed.

---

[250] As an example, a *NFRs* demanding code flexibility could be handled by a decision to employ the *visitor pattern* [GHJ+95; p.301-318] to alleviate adding new operations to the data model. As consequences, *DCs* can be derived defining that data model classes must fulfill the characteristics (operations to accept a visitor) of concrete (visited) elements, whereas operations must fulfill characteristics (operations to visit the different elements) of a visitor. This example can also be seen as an example for the claims made in the following ch. III.20.5.1 that the decision model of R2A has close connections to the *pattern* concept.

[251] Extended parts of this chapter have been published in [TKT+09; ch.5].

III.20.5.1 Patterns

"*Patterns*, as used in software engineering, constitute one of the most heavily used approaches for organizing reusable knowledge" [DMM+06a; p.19]. *Patterns* (ch. I.6.2.4) define the abstract core of a solution for a continuously recurring problem, thus allowing the solution tailored to the concrete problem to be reapplied [GHJ+95]. *Patterns* are described using a structure *template*. Even though different authors use slightly different *templates*, the description of the problem (often referred to as forces), the solution and its consequences are part of all *pattern templates*. The *decision model* discussed here can be described in terms of such a *pattern template* (see also [HAZ07; table 1]): The *conflict situation* of the *decision model* corresponds to the *problem description* part in *patterns*, whereas the description of consequences in a *pattern* description could be modeled by resulting new *DCs* in R2A's *decision model*. Due to this analogy, the author believes that this approach can provide valuable support in selecting *patterns* (e.g., the *conflict situation* of a decision can indicate the usage of a specific *pattern*). At the same time it can help knowledge engineers to identify interesting solutions as new *patterns* (for the relationship between design decisions and *patterns* also refer to [HAZ07], [PBG04; p.209]). A *pattern library* for decisions in modeling embedded systems could be the ultimate goal of such an effort.

Horner and Atwood [HA06a; p.76] characterize *patterns* (ch. I.6.2.4) as common solutions resolving conflicting tendencies. The *decision model* proclaimed here also supports analyzing conflicts and results. In the author's eyes, the decision model supports identifying matching *patterns* and identifying new *patterns* as described in [TKT+09]. In this way, the R2A has certain resemblances to the DRIMER tool [PV96] (see ch II.9.3.1).

Cleland-Huang and Schmelzer [CS03] (see also [GG07; p.315]) introduce another connected approach. Their concern is to improve *traceability* of *NFRs* to design. Due to the often global and far reaching effects of *NFRs* on design, *traceability* of *NFRs* to design is difficult to handle adequately. As a solution, they propose to use *design patterns* as an intermediary model between *NFRs* and the design. This means that *NFRs* are not directly mapped to design. Instead, *NFRs* are mapped to a *design pattern*, which then again is mapped to design. In this way, the number of *traceability* links to be manually captured is reduced. The approach then uses this information to automatically derive the relations between *NFRs* and the design through the manually captured relations.

In the author's opinion, however, this approach has the following shortcomings:

- Not all *NFRs* can be directly mapped to specific design *patterns*. Some *NFRs* may also be handled through other strategies[252].
- The approach does not consider crossinteractions between *NFRs* or other *FRs*.

    Correspondingly, ch. III.20.4 shows that R2A's mechanism may be more powerful as it also allows describing handling strategies apart from *patterns* and also allows describing crossinteractions (see, e.g., the described *influence factors assessment* in ch. III.20.4).

III.20.5.2 Ensuring Adequate Realization of Design and Decisions

As Posch et al. [PBG04; p.38] underline, architects also have to ensure that their design settings are adequately considered and realized by other designers or coders. Using this *decision model*, designers can model the consequences of a decision as *DCs* and assign the *DCs* as new "requirements" (in *R2A* terminology: *RIs*) to *design elements* that must then fulfill the *DCs*. Besides usage in further design or coding processes, the list of assigned *RIs* to a design item can also be used as basis for reviews on design and implementation of the item.

III.20.5.3 Support for Architecture Evaluation

The *R2A* approach can also provide valuable support in maintenance and *evaluating architectures* [CKK02]. Moro [Mo04; p.321] points out that the usage of patterns and other decisions must be documented for later maintenance and *architecture evaluation* issues. According to Reißing 80% of change effort is caused by wrong *architectural decisions* [Mo04; p.90]. With documented decisions and *rationale* at hand, potentially wrongly made *architectural decisions* may be easier and earlier identified in *architecture evaluation*. In this way, implementation of wrong decisions and thus later costly changes may be avoided.

When evaluating *design documentation* during design evaluation meetings, Karsenty [Ka96] found out that questions about *rationale* have been the most

---

[252] E.g., *NFR* about security may also be handled by a login and password component (prevents unauthorized access) in connection with cryptography mechanisms (prevents eavesdropping) and intensified quality assurance methods (prevents bugs susceptible for hacking).

frequent questions (approx. 50%), but only 41% of these questions could be answered (also cf. [HA06a; p.83], [BB06; p.275]).

The idea of the *decision model* is to allow *DCs* (and *budgeted resource constraints* see ch. III.21) as consequences and attaching them to sub elements also provides direct benefit for the designer himself, because he can clearly model his demands for components and in later reviews these demands can be assessed directly. Through the structure of the *decision model*, further *rationale* is already present, where designers might even have used the description text to document further *rationale*.

As already addressed in ch. II.9.4.1, a further helpful concept in this relation is the identification and tracking of *neuralgic points* in design [Mo04; p.310-330]. As Moro found out, developers are often aware of *neuralgic points* by themselves, because *neuralgic points* often recur back as issue of discussion. R2A's decision mechanism gives designers a means at hand to document new discovered *rationale* at those recurring discussions. Further, the author believes that it may also be possible to discover *neuralgic points* through the sheer amount of documentation attached to a decision. In most cases, the most extensive documentation may thus be provided to decisions touching *neuralgic points*, because the developers are often anyway aware of the *neuralgic* nature of an issue.

Other possibilities to identify *neuralgic points* through documented decisions may be to identify a metric for measuring the complexity of decisions. As a start, e.g., it may be possible to assess the number of items identified as part of the conflicting area of a decision. If this number exceeds a certain number (e.g., 15 to 20) the decision can be considered as especially complex. However, this topic should be further researched and be filled with experiences from practical usage. A further idea might be to implement a mechanism to analyze the click behavior of the designers. If certain decisions are often clicked at and further analyzed (e.g., when the properties of the decision are opened), it may indicate that this decision is more critical than decisions seldom being clicked at.

III.21 Resource Allocation as a Special Decision Making Case[253]

> *The requirements for design conflict and cannot be reconciled.*
> *All designs for devices are in some degree failures, either because they flout*
> *one or another of the requirements or because they are compromises,*
> *and compromise implies a degree of failure. ...*
> *It follows that all designs for use are arbitrary. The designer or his client*
> *has to choose in what degree and where there shall be failure.*
> [Py78; p.70]

In design activities for embedded systems an additional decision type can be identified dealing with *non-functional aspects* of limited resources such as memory resources (e.g., Read Only Memory (ROM), Random Access Memory (RAM), Electrically Erasable Programmable Read Only Memory (EEPROM)) or timing restrictions.

A core goal of embedded design is the effective administration and distribution of such resources[254] and different strategies for handling this problem exist:

1. The allocation is a more or less unconscious or uncontrolled process (i. e., no explicit strategy is established).

2. A *resource estimation* is performed as part of the design and estimations are checked and adapted at each development cycle.

3. Resource allocation is explicitly modeled in the *design model* (e.g., by using UML profiles such as the *UML Profile for Schedulability, Performance, and Timing* [Do04, ch.4] or *MARTE* [EDG+06].

With respect to collaboration in complex development teams or organizations, approaches 2 and 3 have limitations in the following aspects:

- Propagation and communication of changes to all team members involved in the change can be cumbersome.
- Minimizing redundancies as a major source of inconsistencies can result in communication errors.
- The seamless adoption and refinement of other designers' design results can be extremely difficult.

---

[253] This chapter bases mainly on [TWT+08].

[254] In fact, also Simon acknowledges *resource allocation* to be an important aspect of design [Si96; p.124-125]. Correspondingly, *resource allocation* can be considered as an important aspect of every design, but in embedded design its importance is highly more significant. When the engineering standard Automotive SPICE is applied, ENG.5 BP5 ("Define goals for resource consumption") even requests that resource consumption for each software module is explicitly planned and tracked [MHD+07; p.64].

- Sharing project knowledge in general will become more difficult.

The following example, basing on the accompanying case study (see ch. III.12), illustrates these shortcomings in more detail. The design shown in fig. 12-3 (see ch. III.12) may lead to the following estimation of RAM consumption (table 21.1) documented as a separate chapter in the design document of the high level designer.

Table 21.1 Example resource estimation of RAM consumption in design

Module	Light _Task	Light _hdl	CIL_ hdl	CAN- drv	PWM_ drv	ADC _drv	Buffer
RAM (1500 Bytes available)	600 Bytes	250 Bytes	100 Bytes	300 Bytes	100 Bytes	100 Bytes	50 Bytes

Such tables are a common format for documenting resource assignments in design documents (cf. [Mu04]). The tabular format has the main advantage that it easily gives an overview, but it has important weaknesses when collaborative aspects are considered:

- First of all, even though these assignments are typically called estimations, they should rather be treated as *RIs*. This implies that a mechanism must be in place to communicate these *RIs* on time to all interested stakeholders – especially if changes occur during project progress.
- Further, the allocation settings are estimated at a certain design stage and thus are an integral part of the design documents at this stage. Therefore, further processing of this information by other designers is difficult. In the case study, the estimations are made at the level of modules and included into the documentation of the high-level design. If the module designer of the complex *Light_Task* wants to refine the resource estimation into a more detailed estimation, a problem arises. In this case he would have to copy the information "*Light_Task == 600 Bytes*" into some document of his responsibility. This leads to unnecessary redundancy causing consistency problems when this setting changes later in the project.
- These problems are even more critical if some parts of the project are delivered by a subcontractor – as it happens to be the case in the example. In this case, all relevant requirements for the item to supply must be provided (as required by SPICE process ACQ.4 Supplier Monitoring, see [MHD+07]). In this case, the RAM estimations, since they are *RIs*, must be communicated as requirements to the supplier. This also leads to a high degree of redundancy with even worse effects if changes are not communicated.

III.21.1 *Budgeted Resource Constraints* as further *Requiremental Items*

In consideration of this problem a way to perform such resource allocation decisions in a handy fashion is needed, which also allows communication of the results for each considered *design element* throughout the entire project in an efficient way. An additional aspect here is the fact that the results of a decision act as new *RIs* on the design elements they are assigned to. As literature shows (cf. [BGT+04], [CBS+02], [FGS+01], [Do04; p.317], [Do03; p.169], [Mu04], [Gu03]), most resource allocation activities consist of numerically truncating a larger resource amount into smaller subsets –more or less in analogy with the *abstraction hierarchy* of a system's resp. software's design (see ch. III.15, fig. 21-4 resp. fig. 21-5 in ch. III.21.2.4 below). Obviously, this can be compared to the process of preparing and distributing budgets in business administration or project management area [HHS64]. Therefore, the taxonomy of *requiremental items* is enhanced by an additional type of *RI* called *budgeted resource constraint* (*BRC*) as shown in fig.21-1.

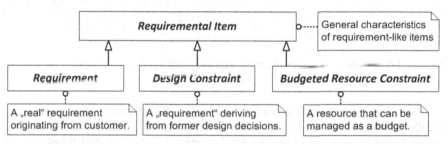

Figure 21-1 *Requiremental items taxonomy* with *budgeted resource constraints*

BRCs are similar to *design constraints (DCs)* as they represent the results of a decision making process and can be assigned as *RIs* to any *design element*.

However, there are the following differences when compared with other *RIs* (such as *DCs*):

- *BRCs* represent numerical values, whose associated *design elements* may not exceed the maximum value of the assigned *BRC*.
- A *BRC* can be subdivided into sub *BRCs*. Thus, *BRCs* at the same time represent a decision-making process as well as its results.

- As *BRCs* represent numerical values, whose sub *BRCs* divide resource amounts into smaller budgets for more detailed parts of the design, automatic consistency checks (e.g., tests for budget overruns) can avoid wrong allocations. Budget overruns may be detected at an early project stage.
- Individual *BRCs* can be added to one design item only, whereas requirements and design constraints may be added to several items.

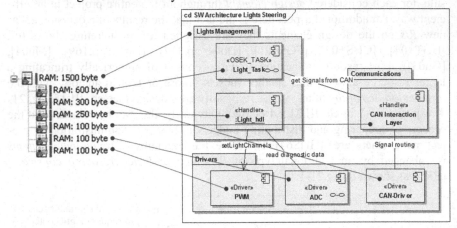

Figure 21-2 Resource allocation example with *budgeted resource constraints*

Resuming the example described above, fig. 21-2 illustrates the resource allocation problem presented using *BRCs* as implemented in R2A. The connections to the *design elements* illustrate so-called assigned to or *satisfy-link* types used in R2A to relate *RIs* to *design elements* (see description in ch. III.18.2). In R2A, all *RIs* assigned to an *AN* (thus, also *BRCs*) are displayed via the "Requirements" tab (fig. 15-4 in ch. III.15), but for better understanding they are here directly mapped on the design diagrams, where the shown elements on the diagram are *ANs* in R2A.

In this situation, the *SW architecture* is assigned to fit in a total budget of 1500 bytes of RAM. This *BRC* is subdivided into six sub *BRCs* assigned to the six modules in the *SW architecture*, thus showing a more detailed partitioning of the RAM budget.

Comparing fig. 21-2 with table 21.1 above, it can be seen that both representations have an equivalent meaning. In fact, the idea of budgets in HW and SW engineering is not new (cf. [FGS+01], [Do04; p.317], [Do03; p.169], [Mu04], [Gu03]). What this wants to point out beyond the appealing (and well-known) aspect of a more or less easy mathematical model enabling consistency checks are the advantages of the budget concept itself, when it comes to collaboration and sharing project knowledge between project members. In this sense, the budget concept is used as a means of communication during software design. The following chapters will provide more details on this.

III.21.2 Advantages for Collaboration and Sharing Project Knowledge

The following situations of this example project show the value of the *BRC concept* for the following communication situations:
- Within project refinement,
- Communicating information over organizational boundaries,
- Change management,
- Different views on the same problem;

III.21.2.1 Within Project Refinement

During the first design cycle of the Light_hdl, the Light_hdl is forecast to have a very tight RAM budget. Therefore the designer identifies several specific aspects for which he arranges budgets according to his current information and needs (see fig. 21-3):
- In normal mode, the module uses the settings in EEPROM mirrored to RAM for steering the lights. RAM consumption depends on the number of steered channels and the number of bytes needed for each channel.
- The diagnostic part supervises regular checks of the electrical current between the ECU and the connected lights to detect malfunctions as short circuit or open drain. Malfunctions lead to the deactivation of a light channel.
- In the case of severe error conditions, e.g., loss of EEPROM data, the fail over mode assures that at least essential functions like brake lights and indicators work. The code and configurations are fixed in ROM, thus no particular portion of RAM is needed.

With the type of *BRCs* proposed here, designers of sub levels can directly continue to process results produced in previous design decision processes.

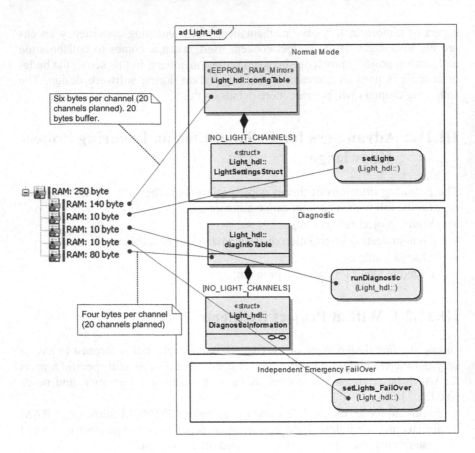

Figure 21-3 Sub budgeting of the Light_hdl module

III.21.2.2 Communicating Information across Organizational Boundaries

Information must often be provided across organizational boundaries. Such boundaries can be sub projects within the same company or between different companies. In the case study, drivers are provided by different subcontractors. This implies that all requirements for the drivers must be provided throughout all parties involved. In the author's experience, *functional aspects* are communicated in a quite complete fashion, but such *nonfunctional aspects* (e.g., restrictions on memory, timing, etc.), resulting from former design decisions, are often forgotten.

The solution described here supports exporting all types of *RIs* associated with a *design element* as a new *requirements specification* into requirements management tools like IBM Rational DOORS, which can be delivered to the subcontractor. Since *BRCs* are treated as normal *RIs*, they are directly propagated to the subcontractors via automatically generated *requirements specifications*. In later development phases, these *requirements specifications* can be continuously synchronized with the settings in the *design element*, thus ensuring proper propagation of requirements to subcontractors.

III.21.2.3 Change Management

During project progress changes occur that force designers to change decisions and assumptions. Managing those changes efficiently is essential to avoid project deviations. Two heuristics should be considered:
- Changes should be kept as local as possible to avoid unnecessary complexity.
- Changes must be implemented in a consistent way.

Our model supports handling changes of *BRCs* as local as possible. Continuing with the example, it might happen that the "runDiagnostic" function needs more than 10 bytes of RAM (see fig. 21-3 above). In this case, the designer can first try to find an internal solution for the problem (e.g., find a way to cut down on some bytes in the "diagInfoTable"). If this is not possible, the designer can escalate the problem to a higher-level designer.

In another situation, new requirements from the customer could make the creation of a new, additional module necessary. This case has effects on the design as a whole since most of the modules already present might suffer a budget cut in their *BRCs* as a consequence. R2A visualizes changed *BRCs* (in a red color coding; cf. ch. III.22.2) to alert designers of sub-layers to analyze the *impacts* on their assignments.

If the sub designer has made his changes and consistency checks (e.g., detecting budget overruns) pass, the designer can mark the change as implemented. After this, the *BRC* is shown in normal mode.

III.21.2.4 Different Views on the Same Problem

In software design theory, the idea that different aspects of SW can be modeled by different views has been proposed (cf. [Kr95]). The same can be claimed for *non-functional aspects* modeled by *BRCs*. Besides the direct allocation view (see fig. 21-2 and fig. 21-3 above), R2A supports creating an enhanced table representation. Fig. 21-4 shows this tabular lineup between *BRCs* and their allocated *design elements*. Both columns additionally show their hierarchical break down.

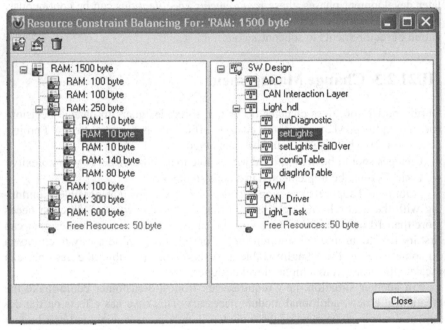

Figure 21-4 Tabular view with corresponding abstraction hierarchies.

Since the structure of the *BRCs* break down has a strong analogy with the breakdown of their associated *design elements*, design flaws of the assignment be can easily detected. Fig. 21-5 shows this situation, where a wrongly associated item disturbs the analogy, helping the designers to detect those problems easily.

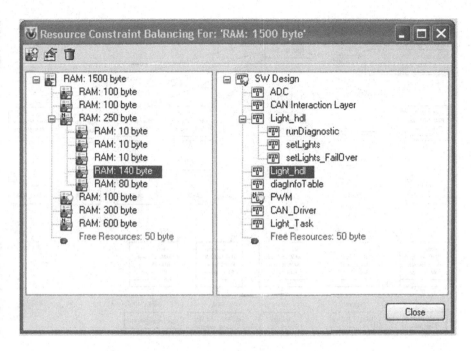

Figure 21-5 Tabular view with assignment inconsistency (selected line)

III.21.3 Representing Budgeted Resource Constraints in SysML

Another frequently used possibility of modeling resource allocations in UML[255]-design is to use UML profiles (e.g., timing constraints can be modeled in the *UML Profile for Schedulability Performance and Time* [Do04; ch. 4]).

---

[255] This statement does not refer to any specific version of UML as profiling is a general feature of UML.

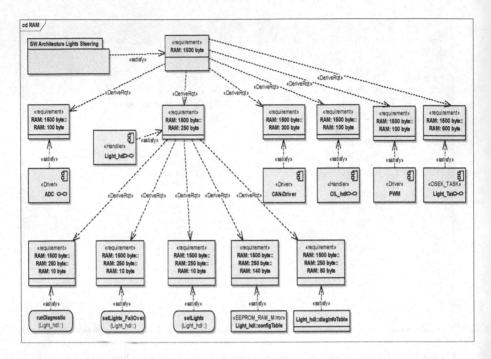

Figure 21-6 Representation of the same information as fig. 21-4 but in SysML view

In 2006, the Object Management Group (OMG) adopted an extension of UML called Systems Modeling Language (SysML; cf.[We06] and ch. I.6). SysML extends UML to improve support for Systems Engineering activities. A goal of SysML was to provide support for modeling dependencies between requirements and *design elements*.

R2A's model is compatible to SysML through the following definitions:

- *BRCs* are represented by the *<<Requirement>>* stereotype,
- Sub *BRCs* can be derived from the *<<DeriveRqt>>* relationship,
- *BRCs* are assigned to *design elements* via *<<Satisfy>>* relationships;

As a proof of this claim, R2A supports automatic generation of SysML diagrams from the *BRC*-model. Fig. 21-6 shows a SysML diagram generated from the model of the case study. However, it shows that such SysML-diagrams seem to have only limited value since they quickly can get very complex and cluttered. Thus, the real value of SysML might not be in the diagrams but the *meta model* behind it, being shown in different representations as R2A does in fig. 21-4.

Similar generation functions could be employed for timing budgets using the *UML Profile for Schedulability, Performance and Time* or the *MARTE profile* ([EDG+06]).

Except for prototypical implementation of the transformation between *BRC*-model and SysML described here, these topics have not been further pursued because R2A aims to embrace design methodologies and tools beyond the UML paradigm (as, e.g., Matlab Simulink or Stateflow).

III.21.4 Combining both *Decision Models*

As already described in [TWT+08], implementing a small change on the first decision model described in ch. III.20 allows making both decision models compatible with each other. If *BRCs* are allowed as possible results in decision model one, both models support compatible types as their major in- and out-comes (since all are *RIs* (cf. fig. 21-1)).

The following example described illustrates this in detail (see fig. 21-7). A *documented decision* "Dec1" determines the use of a specific micro-controller. This decision also determines a *BRC* "RAM:1500 byte". Through several decision steps, a sub *BRC* "RAM: 10 byte" is derived that is satisfied by the "setLights_FailOver" function in design. Both conflict with a *requirement* "Req3", resolved by a new *documented decision* "Dec2".

As the example shows, both decision models complement each other and allow modeling of more difficult decision problems.

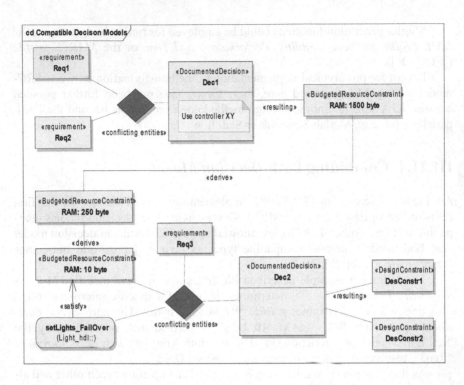

Figure 21-7 Example for combining both decision models together

III.22 Managing Changes and Consistency

Complexity is the path of growth. On the other hand, complication is the path of degradation, loss of control, evanescence of order.
Lem O. Ejiogu

Nuseibeh et al. [NER00] describe that it is not always viable resp. advisable to resolve all inconsistencies immediately. Even though resolving inconsistencies can only imply adding, changing or removing information, it more often involves balancing conflicts and taking design decisions. Correspondingly, "the choice of an inconsistency-handling strategy depends on the context and the impact it has on other aspects of the development process" [NER00; p.26].

The R2A mechanism allows keeping inconsistencies for a certain time but keeps also track of the inconsistencies so that they can be resolved later.

III.22.1 Usage of Traces – Managing *Requiremental* Changes

Ch. II.10.4.3.3 discusses the usage of traces recorded in *traceability* approaches. Pinheiro terms the usage of traces as *trace extraction*. Concerning *trace extraction* processes, Pinheiro [Pi04; p.105] describes three different tracing modes that should be supported. The following listing describes features provided by R2A to support the modes described in ch. II.10.4.3.3:

- *Selective tracing* is supported by the *impact analysis dialog*, where each element can be selectively applied to an analysis or deactivated. *IA* with the *impact analysis dialog* is described in the following sub ch. III.22.1.1.
- *Interactive tracing* is directly supported by a *model browser* described in the following second sub chapter III.22.1.2.
- *Non-guided tracing* is supported by the *model browser* as well as by other features described in the following third sub chapter III.22.1.3.

III.22.1.1 Selective Tracing: Impact Analysis[256]

As illustrated in ch. I.5.6, requirements changes occur in project practice. Thus, their consequences for the development process must be directly tracked in detail to avoid continuous drift between artifacts. For this, so-called *impact analyses* (*IA*) as described in ch. II.10.3 are the intended means for addressing these problems.

R2A offers the possibility to perform *IAs*, where *impacts* of requirements change on design can be easily made understandable for project members as well as for project outsiders (e.g., the customers) via iconographic highlighting.

Fig 22-1 shows two examples of how the *impact* results can look like during *IAs*, highlighting the *ANH* tree in R2A. The left tree shows a very local *impact* (red cross at 'Light_hdl' *AN*). Oppositional to this, the right situation shows *direct impacts* (red crosses) on the complete 'SW Design' as well as to the modules 'Light_hdl' and 'RTE'. Here, also *inherited impacts* (arrows with grey shade pointing at the bottom at 'ADC_drv', 'HighPrio_Task', and 'PWM_drv') and *indirect*

---

[256] Parts of this chapter have been published in [TKT+08].

impacts via decisions (yellow crosses at 'CIL_hdl', 'Light_Task', and 'SHR_hdl')
are visible.

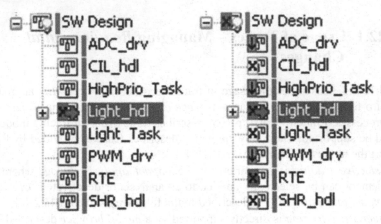

Figure 22-1 Two examples for visualizing *impact* on the *abstraction nodes hierarchy*

These opposed examples show the indisputable advantages of clear iconographic highlighting. Even though, engineering theory concentrates on reproducible results, the author is convinced that the developers' intuition (see also [LL07;
ch.2]) is more often a factor of success than usually admitted. The graphical aspect of *R2A's IA* approach supports the intuition of the developers. This means
even if no complex and detailed *IA*s are performed, the ease of just identifying a
few items will also improve the working quality. A second major improvement of
graphical *IA*s is that *impacts* of changes demanded by certain stakeholders can be
better communicated to these stakeholders, as they can also more intuitively
grasp the effects of the demanded change. Ebert emphasizes that "lots of changes
are proposed because the corresponding interest groups think that the change is
done by only changing a few lines of code or a parameter" [Eb05; p.188 (*)].

Via R2A's graphical highlighting of *impacts* such misunderstanding can be
easily cleared and thus unnecessary change efforts, where change costs do not
outweigh the change gains, are avoided.

However, development is not that easy that all effects of a change can be directly discovered. Often, changes can trigger a *dominoes effect* [VSH01; p.83] or
ripple effects (cf. ch. II.10.3). To discover these effects earlier, project members
must be able to perform more complex *IA*s because simply following the link
chain only helps to find the *primary change* but neglects to identify the *second-*

ary change often leading to the *dominoes effect*. Thus, besides the simple graphical representation, the following characteristics allow significantly more precise *IA*s:

- Often several *requirements* in combination are affected by a meaningful change. R2A allows to starting an initial *starting impact set (SIS)* with several *RIs* (*Requirements, DCs* or *BRCs*).
- The affected *RIs* often involve formerly taken decisions and consequences (as *DCs* or *BRCs*) that must be reassessed. Starting from the initial *SIS*, R2A automatically calculates direct and inherited *impacts* on *AN*s derived from the *RIS* (ch. III.18.2.2). Additionally in a next step, indirect *impacts* through modeled decisions and their consequences (*DCs* and *BRCs*) are calculated with their *impacts* on *AN*s.
- The *inherited* and *indirect impacts* are automatically calculated by R2A from the formerly gathered *traceability* information. In order to allow users to differentiate between *direct impacts* and calculated impacts, the different impact types have different iconifications.

After R2A has first calculated the impacts, R2A offers dedicated support to perform a more detailed assessment of the *IA* results:

- Automatically *calculated impact* can lead to overestimated *impacts*. For these cases, the user can again determine for all *calculated impacts*, whether they are actually real *impacts* or rather overestimated *impacts*.
- To each element in the *IS* notes can be attached, by which the user can tell the cause why an item is in the *IS*, or what has to be performed in order to implement the change *impact* on the item.
- Performed *IA*s can be saved and shared with other users. This allows already performing rough *IA*s during meetings with the customer (ideally even at the site of the customer), early sparking concrete discussions with the customer if the customer expresses a change need. In combination with the possibility mentioned above to document notes on items in the *IS*, concretely identified steps to be performed on the change or other important information can already be documented and saved. This helps to capture early *rationale* on changes to perform. In the aftermath of such a meeting the developers then can refine the captured information. Estimations on costs and duration are one of the important information possible to be added are, thus extending the sheer *IA* to a detailed effort estimation.
- Once *impacts* are identified, a decision must be taken whether a proposed change is really performed on the project (e.g., by a *change control board* (*CCB*), [PR09; p.144f], [VSH01; p.184f, p.216]). As basis of such a decision the saved detailed *IA* results can be loaded and viewed in R2A again.

- Once a change has been approved, the gathered *IA* information about the change can again be loaded in R2A, providing now a detailed road-map for the designer to perform the changes.

These described actions and information can be steered via R2A's *impact analysis dialog* shown at the left side in fig. 22-2.

Fig. 22-2 shows the complete set of information displayed in R2A during an *IA*. At the left side, the *impact analysis dialog* is shown, whereas the right side shows an excerpt of R2A's main window with the *ANH* at the top and the "Requirements" tab at the bottom.

Impact highlighting on the *ANH* has already been discussed in the context of fig. 22-1. The "Requirements" tab shows the *RIs* of the selected *AN* (here 'SW Design'), where *RIs* being in the *impact* set are correspondingly highlighted to provide the user with information about the concrete *impact* on the *AN*.

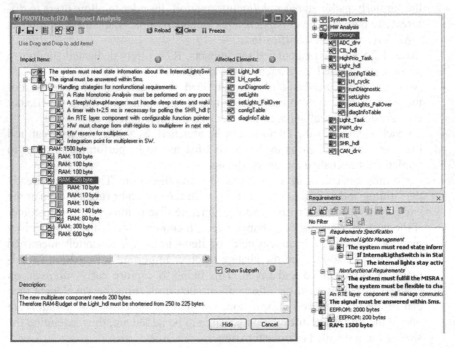

Figure 22-2 *Impact analysis dialog* and R2A's main window with an *impact set* taking *decisions* into account

The *impact analysis dialog* is divided into the left part showing the *impact* situation for *RIs* in connection with *impact* derived through decisions. The figure shows a situation of a planned change, affecting in the first instance requirement ReqSpec_2 ("The system must read ..."), requirement "The signal must be answered within 5ms" (taken from the documented decision concerning the *architectural influence factors assessment* shown in fig. 20-7 (see ch. III.20.4)) and *BRC* "RAM:1500 byte" (taken from the resource estimation described in ch. III.21 (see fig. 21-4 in ch. III.21.2.4)). All made decisions and all *DCs* or *BRCs* derived from the decisions are taken into account and shown beneath the elements identified in *SIS*. The right side shows the direct consequences on design (*ANs*) of an item selected in the left side (the complete *impact* on the *ANs* is shown in the *ANH*). Via the textual component at the bottom, notes can be edited and viewed describing additional information on the need for change of an item selected at the left side. Above, the author also mentioned that the dialog can be used as a detailed road-map to perform the changes. This is indicated in the figure by item ReqSpec_2, being checked and being highlighted via a green cross. Via this checking mechanism, changes already performed can be checked. In this way, the dialog turns into a checklist for the change to be performed showing the current status the designer is in during change implementation.

IA support is helpful to assess potential influences of changes and the captured *rationale*; during assessment it can give important guidance to how these changes must be performed. However, most probably not all *requiremental change* will run through a cycle of detailed *IA* and *CCB*. Often 'minor' changes influx into a *requirements specification* from all kinds of sources, though. For these cases the *change management mechanisms* described in ch. III.22.2 help to keep changes transparent in order to maintain changes to consistently propagate to all relevant parts of the *design models*.

III.22.1.2 Interactive Tracing: The *Model Browser*

Interactive tracing means to allow an interactive browsing mechanism to navigate backward and forward in the model.

Fig. 22-3 shows the *model browser* integrated in R2A for fulfilling *interactive tracing* needs. The *model browser* can be opened for any item present in R2A. Fig. 22-3 shows the *model browser* opened for the *NFR* "ReqSpec_14: The system must be flexible to change.". In the left part of the *model browser*, direct information on the item (e.g., the text) and several *meta-data* (e.g., author and date of the last change, version, baseline, and internal item id) are shown. At the right side, all traceable relationships to other items are shown.

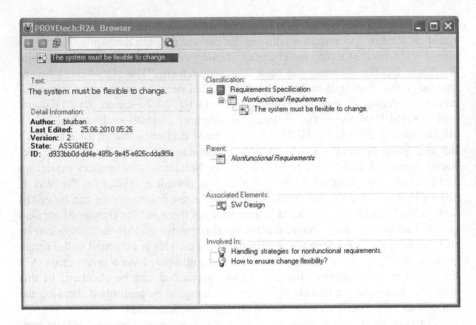

Figure 22-3 The *model browser* in R2A

There, the user can double-click on any item. Then, the *model browser* changes to this item, thus allowing navigating through the complete model present in R2A. The user can also open several *model browsers* in parallel, allowing keeping information on some items currently important to the user open; meanwhile he still can navigate further through model.

III.22.1.3   Non-Guided Tracing: Additional Features for Fast Look-Up

Non-guided tracing shall allow the user to arbitrarily step from entity to entity analyzing contents as demanded. This shall ensure convenient tracing when little information on what or how to trace is available.

Besides *IA* features and the *model browser* described in the chapters above, being also able to fulfill *non-guided tracing* needs, the following features provide possibilities for fast looking up some information:

- When the '*quick view*' option is activated, a slim version of the *model browser* automatically appears when the user works with R2A showing the currently selected item in R2A. When the user changes to the *design tool*, the *quick view* automatically disappears. In this way, the user can on one side easily gather important information on an item. On the other side, the *quick view* can be arranged in a way overlaying the *design tool* but not overlaying any other information in R2A, when the user works with R2A. But when the user works with the *design tool*, again no disturbing window of R2A hinders the designer in working with the *design tool*.

- On any *RI*, the '*locate origin*' action can be performed opening the *requirement source document* of the *RI* and selecting the *RI* in the *requirement source document*.

- In the same way as '*locate origin*' opens the corresponding *requirement source document* in R2A, the '*locate in REM-tool*' action can be performed on any *RI* originating (being synchronized) from an *REM-tool* such as IBM Rational DOORS, opening the corresponding document containing the *RI* in the *REM-tool* and selecting the *RI*.

- Vice versa, R2A also integrates a button into the *REM-tool* environment allowing a '*locate in R2A*' action, where a requirement selected in the *REM-tool* is then again shown in R2A.

- As described later in ch. III.23.1, parts of an R2A-model can be again exported into a *REM-tool* to support supplier management. Similarly to the two points above, R2A also allows navigating into such a generated document in the *REM-tool* and back.

- The '*Show related decisions*' action can be performed on any item in R2A. When performed, a window opens showing all decisions the item is involved with (either as conflicting or resulting item) in the style shown in fig. 20-6 (see ch. III.20.4).

Through the different *locate* actions, *bidirectional traceability* (see ch. I.5.7.1) is ensured, where *RIs* can be traced in the backward and forward direction.

III.22.2 Consistency Maintenance of Requirements, *Traceability* and Design[257]

In ch. II.10.4.3, establishing *traceability* has been identified as an important aspect to consider because it means significant effort to be spent. This is only one facet of the problem. A second equal problematic facet is that later changes must be efficiently and consequently inferred throughout the whole development effort

---

[257] This chapter bases on parts of [TKT+08].

in order to ensure consistency throughout the whole development project (see ch. II.10.4.3.4). Otherwise, the best *traceability* establishment processes will be in vain if the traces significantly degrade in short time. On the other side, a certain degradation of traces may be inevitable even under best support for trace maintenance.

To ensure *traceability* information is maintained best possible, obstacles for *traceability* maintenance must be as low as possible. In R2A, maintenance of *traceability* information is easy and intuitive because of the overall *drag-and-drop* support as well as operations as *dribble-up, dribble-down* and *copy*, and the concept to present only the information relevant in the given design situational context.

A main concern addressed in maintenance of *traceability* is ensuring consistency. The following now shows how R2A supports that requirement related changes are consistently inferred to design.

If a proposed *requiremental* change is decided to be performed[258], it must be possible to propagate the changes in a controlled way, ensuring a consistent implementation of the change in all artifacts. For each *RI*, R2A is able to visualize its status by using a colored status bar at the left side of each *RI* (see fig. 22-4), where each *RI* runs through the life-cycle sketched in fig. 22-4.

---

[258] The *CCB* can also decide not to perform a change. (e.g., if the effort detected via an *IA* is higher than the change's value gain).

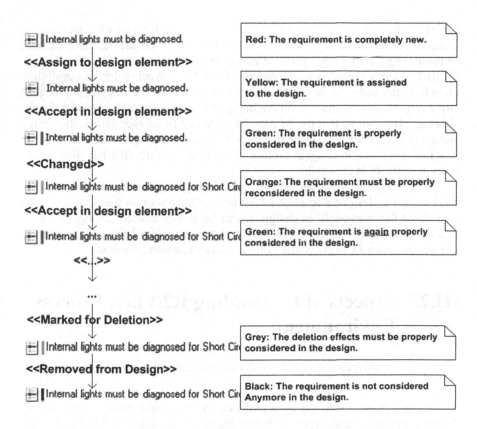

Figure 22-4 Life-cycle of a *requiremental item* and its color coding in R2A

Each *RI* not yet considered in the R2A design (status 'red') must be assigned to the design (change to status 'yellow'). Yellow means that an *RI* is considered, but it did not yet reach its final state of realization in design (see *RDP* heuristic in ch. III.18.2.4). If a designer decides that an *RI* has reached its final state of realization, the designer can perform an *accept* operation on for the *RI* at the corresponding *AN*, indicating that the designer considers the *RI* has reached the adequate location in the design. When the *RI* is *accepted* at all *ANs*[259], the *RI* auto-

---

[259] An *RI* can also be assigned to several *ANs*. Of course, it should be avoided that the realization of an *RI* is performed by several *ANs;* however in certain cases this will happen.

matically changes to status 'green' meaning that the *RI* has generally reached the adequate consideration at all parts of design it must be considered. Later changes on the *RI* (e.g., after a new synchronization of the *requirements specification*; see ch. III.18.1) may require a reassessment of the RI's current realization in design. Therefore, the status of the *RI* changes to 'orange' until the designers have performed the necessary changes on the design to again adequately consider the *RI*. This can also involve that the *RI* may be relocated to another part of the design (assigned to another *AN*). Once the *RI* is again *accepted* by the designers, at all assigned locations, it is again promoted to status 'green'. This handling recurs every time the *RI* is changed.

If an *RI* becomes obsolete during project progress, the *RI* can be *marked for deletion* by the designers (change to status 'gray'). As soon as the designers have considered the marked *RI* in design, it can be finally deleted (change to status 'black'). In this way, it is can be ensured that design settings having become obsolete can be removed, thus avoiding clutter and architectural erosion.

III.23 Aspects of Embedding R2A in a Process Environment

Getting the formula right entails knowledge, patience, foresight, and communication.
[BT04; p.99]

A tool alone is not a solution for a problem. Instead, a tool must also be embedded into a process landscape (see beginning of ch. II.10.4.4). After the chapters above described the tool R2A and how its integration supports the transition processes from requirements to design, this chapter widens the scope of considered processes in the sense that the requirement and design processes may be again embedded in a higher-level process environment, where tight integration is essential. These aspects can be that parts of a designed system are supplied by a supplier. In this case, design must be tightly integrated with *supplier management* to propagate important information to the supplier. Ch. III.23.1 describes how the information gathered during a design process with R2A can be directly used to generate a *requirements specification* for suppliers dedicated to deliver parts of the designed system (resp. SW). This helps to avoid redundancies and thus significantly improves supplier management.

Another, issue may be that several requirement and design processes may occur on different levels of abstraction, where the results on one abstraction level induce requirements and design on another level of abstraction (see ch. I.7.3.2).

Ch. III.23.2 discusses how this can be achieved best with R2A. Again, the *requirements specification* generation feature described in ch. III.23.1 also proves helpful in this case.

III.23.1 Avoiding Redundancies in *Supplier Management*

"In the development of complex embedded systems, often several companies work together on the development. At such an interconnected development, often partnerships are built, where mostly one supplier is engaged as the system supplier, having – besides other tasks – the responsibility to coordinate the other suppliers. Therefore, selection and coordination of suppliers is of special importance in embedded development. Often, even a hierarchy of client-supplier-relationships emerges, meaning that a supplier (*second tier*) acquires further sub components of the system from his own suppliers (so called *third tier*) and coordinates the collaboration. Additionally, the customer often prescribes the supplier certain *third tier-suppliers*" [HDH+06; p.65 (*)].

If a partial component of a system or software must be supplied by a supplier, a reliable and efficient *supplier management* must be installed (see ACQ.1 and ACQ.4 process in SPICE [HDH+06]).

For this, at minimum a *supplier requirements specification* (*SuppRS*) must be continuously administered. Such a partial component, however, must be included in the design of the higher-level (more abstract) component the partial component shall be integrated into[260]. In the further this design is called the *customer's system design* (*CusSysDes*).

As a main problem, high content redundancies arise between the information created during design and the writing of the *SuppRS* leading to high extra effort spent on creation, keeping the *traceability* and applying changes. Especially applying changes can be seen as a critical issue because redundancies are often accompanied by the danger that the changes are not propagated to all redundancies, leading to growing inconsistencies between the redundancies.

R2A tackles this problem by using the information about the component created in the *CusSysDes* directly to automatically create the *SuppRS*. This means that the partial component is included as *AN* in the design of the higher-level component. The requirements for the component emerge from:

---

[260] For example, a complete system, a sub system, a complete SW system, a partial SW sub system

- The previously found requirements for the higher-level component that are assigned to the partial component as requirements (*requirements* in R2A-terminology).
- The constraints for the partial component, resulting from the decision processes during design of the higher-level component (in R2A-terminology *DECs*, *DCs*, *BRCs*).
- Inherited *RIs* from parent *ANs* (see ch. III.18.2.2) as they also may be important for the component.

R2A offers the possibility to export all this information concerning an *AN* to an *REM-tool* as a new *requirements specification* artifact for the supplier. Later changes in the R2A can be synchronized into the artifact. However, a *SuppRS* usually should not just include the *requiremental* information. Instead, the context of the component to supply (embedded in the higher-level system) is important. Thus, besides this *requiremental* information mentioned above, R2A can also export the following information:

- Modeled diagrams showing how the component collaborates with the other parts of the system.
- The textual description of the component performed in R2A.

Of course, not all information created during *CusSysDes*, concerning the component of a supplier need be propagated to the supplier. In fact, often the customer must decide which information is necessary to propagate and which information must not be propagated in order to protect the customer's know how. Thus, R2A's *SuppRS* generation mechanism contains a wizard, in which it is possible for each item to set whether to propagate to the *SuppRS* or not. After the *SuppRS* is once created, the synchronization mechanism also detects later *edit changes* (i.e., changes through later editing or formatting) in the *SuppRS*. When afterwards the next synchronization with the *SuppRS* occurs, the changes in R2A and the *edit changes* performed in the *SuppRS* are equally considered. Besides allowing *edit changes* of the *SuppRS*, *R2A* mainly allows covering two other points important for the *SuppRS*:

1. The *SuppRS* as a requirement artifact read by humans also must obey the rules for a human readable document. Thus, the document must provide a continuous reading flow. In most cases, this means the raw version of the synchronized *SuppRS* must be reedited. For these reasons, also new items can be added to the *SuppRS* manually. These items are then handled outside of the R2A approach and the development team must use other mechanisms to keep these elements up to date. Besides adding new elements not managed by R2A, a *SuppRS* requirement artifact can also be restructured at will in order to improve reading by humans. This works properly when the order or hierarchy of the requirements is changed; but it involves some problems if

also the text of a requirement must be changed. In principle, changing the text of a synchronized element (e.g., to improve readability) is possible but this makes the following synchronizations more difficult to manage because then both sides to be synchronized (the R2A side and the *REM-tool* side) may have changed. In these cases, it is indicated that the designer must manually merge the texts. Thus, the author rather recommends to perform the textual change already within R2A and then again to synchronize the *SuppRS*.

2. Decisions not to propagate certain information elements to the customer may just occur during the editing phase of the *SuppRS*. In these situations, it would be very long-winded if the synchronization mechanism had to be performed again in order to select information not to propagate in the wizard. Instead, it is easier to just delete the elements in the *SuppRS*. Then the synchronization mechanism detects that these elements are deleted and will not again synchronize these elements.

Such an emerging *SuppRS* can then be used as *user requirements specification*[261] for the supplier. As the information is directly generated out of the previous design processes by R2A, the *single-source-principle* ensures that redundancies are avoided.

III.23.2 *Traceability* over Several Artifact Models without Redundancies

As discussed in ch. I.7.2.4, the topic *traceability* between requirements and design involves different artifacts at different levels of abstraction in *process models* such as SPICE. After having all pieces together now, this chapter discusses this topic from the process chain and artifacts viewpoint.

Fig. 23-1 describes the *process* and *artifact model*, when *system design, SW design* and perhaps even *HW design* are performed in one *design model*. Only a common *requirements specification* with the real requirements from the customer (corresponds to the *SYS_RS* in SPICE) are imported from a *REM-tool* and are related to the corresponding *ANs* in the *system design, SW design* and *HW design*, being responsible for fulfilling the requirements. During the design processes new 'requirements' arise in the form of *DCs* and *BRCs* from design decisions made. These 'requirements' enrich the original requirements. In this way, the *SW_RS, HW_RS* and *module requirements specifications* are all *RIs* assigned to

---

[261] In German: 'Lastenheft' (see ch. I.7.2.2.1)

the *ANs,* representing the *SW design, HW design* and *module designs* and are only metaphorically present in development.

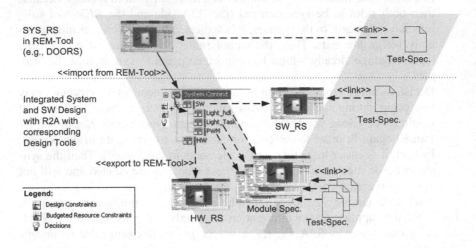

Figure 23-1 Process chain of an integrated *design model* for *system, HW* and *SW design*

However, the SPICE standard also demands that testing procedures must be performed on the corresponding *requirements specifications.* This can be achieved through R2A's feature for creating a *requirements specification* from a partial *design model* (originally intended for *supplier requirements specifications*; see ch. III.23.1). Now, these created *requirements specifications* can be used to create and link test specifications to the corresponding *requirements specifications*.

The author recommends using this *process model* because it provides optimal communication for designers, reduces redundancies to a minimum, and provides best support of R2A's *consistency management* mechanisms. As described in ch. I.7.2.4, Hörmann et al. emphasize that in practice the transition between these processes mentioned are anyway mostly fluent and are rather of iterative and recursive nature [HDH+06; p.103]. Correspondingly, this model also is closer to practice than the original SPICE *process model* is.

However, as mentioned in ch. III.19, a *process model* deviating from the original SPICE model is allowed in principle but requires higher efforts for organizations to prove that the *process model* corresponds to the original ideas of the SPICE *process model.* It may even be possible that the *process model* has lower acceptance by SPICE assessors (the power of assessors assigning negative assessment results should not be underestimated). These factors may push organizations to the decision to rather exactly follow the SPICE *process model* to avoid such problems.

Fig. 23-2 shows how such a process chain may look like when R2A is employed in an organization using the original SPICE *process model*. At start, the requirements of the customer are collected in the *SYS_RS* in the same manner as above. Via R2A in connection with a *design tool* adequate for *system design*, the *system design* is created. During *system design* as well as in the other design phases described a few lines later, new *DCs*, *BRCs* and *Decs* emerge (emphasized in fig. 23-2 by a '+'). In the *system design* artifact, a placeholder "SW" is created, collecting all relevant requirements and other items resulting from the design (*DCs, Decs* and *BRCs*) having influence on the SW. This placeholder can then be used to generate the requirements specification for the SW forming the basis for the *SW design*, again performed in R2A in connection with a *design tool* adequate for *SW design*. If needed, the same procedure can be applied to modules in the *SW design* if a dedicated *module specification* is needed (in most cases this may be especially interesting, when the realization of modules is delegated to a supplier). Through these controlled import and export actions via R2A, controlled copies emerge, whose redundancies are in most cases maintained under automation support.

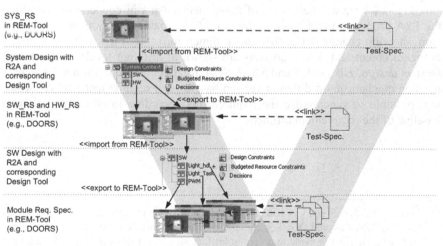

Figure 23-2 Process chain of multi-layered requirements and design artifacts

In this *process model* implementation, R2A also provides advantages of minimized redundancies because *SW_RS*, *HW_RS* and the *module requirements specifications* are generated from the *design models* made earlier with included *DCs, Decs* and *BRCs*. On the other side, *IAs* and *consistency management* become significantly more difficult because the tool barriers between artifacts in *REM-tools* and R2A must be crossed permanently. This leads to friction losses.

III.23.3 Decoupled Development of Requirement and Design Artifacts

The process chain introduced in the previous chapter still leaves one central point uncovered: Often, different artifacts are developed with a certain time-lag in parallel. Thus, after the *SYS_RS*, the *system design* is developed with a time-delay, and after the *system design* again the requirements specification and design of the SW are developed with a certain time delay. During this process, requirement changes already occur in the *SYS_RS*.

In simple link concepts, the link chain now can be paced off by an *IA*, but controlling a consistent maintenance through all artifacts proofs difficult[262].

R2A addresses this problem by an interplay of synchronization, consistency propagation (ch. III.22), and export (ch. III.23.1) mechanisms.

Fig. 23-3 shows the effects of these mechanisms in cooperation, in which the R2A process artifact chain of fig. 23-2[263] is extended by a temporal dimension, showing change deltas (horizontal dimension). From top to bottom, different requirement and design artifacts are shown at different levels of abstraction (*system design*, *HW design* and *SW design*). R2A is able to perform the synchronization mechanism on different version baselines of requirement artifacts. Thus, it is possible to synchronize the requirements according to an existing version baseline of the requirement artifact.

---

[262] Current *REM-tools* such as IBM Rational DOORS provide mechanisms to mark such links. In IBM Rational DOORS, e.g., these links are marked as 'suspect links'. However, after a baseline is made in a certain artifact all suspect links are cleared, making it unfeasible to perform baselines in a time-delayed development for a certain artifact. Moreover, the problem increases when tool gaps as the problem of an essential tool gap between *REM-* and *design tools* as exposed here are involved.

[263] The statements are analogously valid for fig. 23-1 in ch. III.23.2.

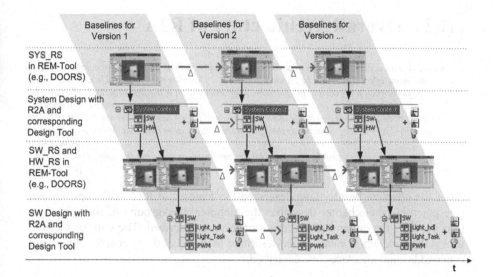

Figure 23-3 Consistent integration of changes (Δ) beyond version barriers

Through the consistency mechanism, this requirement artifact version can be propagated through the designs (with new *Decs*, *DCs* and *BRCs*) and the export mechanism then propagates this baseline version state to the requirement artifacts at lower levels of abstraction. In the meantime, the requirement changes (Δ) for the next version can already be performed, being again propagated downward to the artifacts at lower levels of abstraction within the following version baseline.

Subsuming, it is to say that R2A conducts requirement changes into controlled, consistent version pathways (gray pathways in fig. 23-3), but at the same time it allows a decoupled, further development of requirement changes for subsequent versions in parallel.

III.24 Overall Architecture of R2A

*Designers have occasionally been urged to seek for 'ideal solutions of design problems' or words to
the same effect. There can be no ideal solutions.... Design is not like that. There are, however,
occasions when it is possible to determine temporarily what is the best practicable balance between opposing requirements....
The fact that compromise is inevitable in so many kinds of design has led theorists to classify design
as a 'Problem-solving activity', as though it were nothing more than that. In is a partial and inadequate view.
Most design problems are essentially similar no matter what the subject of design is....*
[Py78; p.74f]

After the chapters before have described the features of R2A with their innovative potential, this chapter describes the technical background of the R2A solution. At first, the general *architecture* of R2A is described. The core of the R2A
tool is the *conceptual meta-model* described in the second sub chapter. Afterward,
other additional interfaces are described.

III.24.1 General Architecture

Fig. 24-1 describes the high-level *architecture* with the most important packages
and their interdependencies. The overall structure is divided into three parts:

- The *"General Reusable Libraries"* part subsumes libraries with general supportive tool (resp. utility) libraries that can also be used in other development
  projects, thus generating significant alleviations for new development projects. In the *Infrastructure* package, general solutions for *cross-cutting concerns* as error logging, threading support, or integration of unit testing, etc.
  are developed. As it provides very basic support, the *Infrastructure* library is
  used by all other packages in R2A. Basing on *Infrastructure*, the *GuiFramework* package is the equivalent of *Infrastructure* but for GUI[264] support. The
  GuiFramework provides better support for user messaging (a framework,
  where user vocabulary and messages to the user can be defined in a general
  way), encapsulates important GUI-controls to make them exchangeable and
  more stable. Further, the framework provides a general implementation of the
  model-view-controller pattern allowing easily creating new user controls with
  support of the *model-view-controller pattern*. Several other smaller reusable
  libraries addressing more special *cross-cutting aspects* exist, not explicitly
  mentioned here.

---

[264] Graphical User Interface

- The *"Product Line Core"* is the actual core of R2A. Its *architecture* follows the *three layer architecture pattern* [BMR+00; p.31ff]:
  - The *Gui* package contains all program elements directly related to the *graphical user interface*.
  - The *ProgramCore* package contains the data model and its operations of the R2A application. In *ProgramCore*, the *MetaModel* package contains the data model, whereas the *ModelController* package contains and controls operations on the data model. R2A's data model classes have detailed knowledge about their own structure. In this way this data model is more a *meta-model* about the entities represented in the R2A-model. This *meta-model* is described in the following ch. III.24.2.
  - The *Opf* package is an *object persistence framework* (*OPF*) responsible for mapping the R2A data from the *meta-model* to its representation in the database. The *OPF* also can automatically handle the *cross-cutting concerns* of *versioning* and *baselining* realizing the features described in ch. III.17.5. As the *OPF* realizes any data changes, it also contains a collaboration framework allowing other R2A instances of other developers connected to a project to be notified about data changes. These notifications then trigger the collaboration framework in the other R2A instances to update the changed model parts, thus allowing direct synchronous collaborative work between the designers.
- The *"Variation Points"* part contains the packages *RemInterface* and *MdlInterface*. *RemInterface* is the *variation point* to connect different *REM-tools*, whereas *MdlInterface* is the equivalent *variation point* to connect to different modeling tools. As both packages have equivalent responsibilities but for different tool types, the internal structure of both packages is equivalent. Both contain a general part and a tool specific implementation part. The general part shall encapsulate the tool specific part from access of the *ProgramCore* package. The general part contains an abstract interface definition each specific tool implementation must implement, a factory class that uses the *abstract factory pattern* to create a specific tool object with the implementation of the abstract interface, and objects representing items present in a connected tool. These objects (*TMdlObject* in *MdlInterface*, *TReDocumentItem* and *TReDocument* in *RemInterface*) are used to connect information of a connected tool with the data model (see ch. III.24.2).

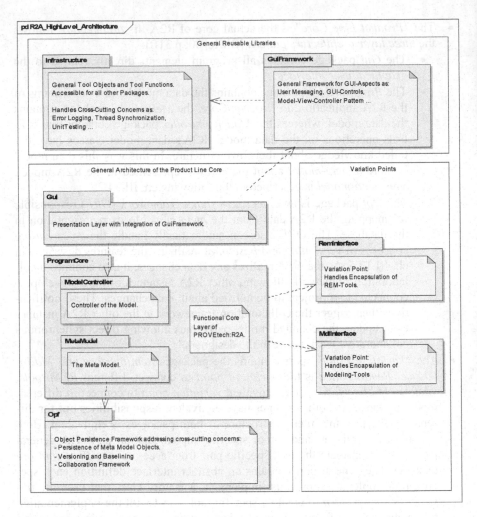

Figure 24-1 High-level *architecture* of R2A

III.24.2 The *Meta-Model*

The concepts mentioned above are embedded in R2A in a *meta-model*. The *meta-model* can be seen as the *traceability reference model* or *conceptual trace model* (ch. II.10.4.3) of the approach.

Although a certain overlapping with concepts of the *meta-model* of UML (with SysML; in the further just referred to as UML) exists, R2A's *meta-model* is not basing on an implementation of UML, because:

- The UML *meta-model* did not yet exist as a standard, when research on the *meta-model* of R2A began.
- The UML *meta-model* is substantially more complex since it is very generic and it is designed to cover all aspects and concepts of design, whereas R2A only uses some specific concepts important for design structuring, *traceability* and design documentation.
- R2A aims to be open to integrate other design modeling approaches. Thus R2A must avoid a too strong concentration on one modeling approach.
- The usage of the UML *meta-model* would demand to be conforming to UML. R2A involves research on new concepts and ways to establish *traceability* in an easy to use fashion. Strong orientation on a standard could predetermine the researcher's thinking in an unfavorable way, preventing to find a good solution. Or, probably new concepts are necessary that cannot be adequately mapped to the UML *meta-model*. Such cases of mismatch can be seen in the *DC* concept[265] or the decision model concepts.

Nevertheless, the UML and SysML concepts have been analyzed and inspired certain concepts of R2A and its *meta-model*.

Fig. 24-2 shows the R2A *meta-model* with the most important[266] classes, its properties and relationships. As a convention of the R2A-project, all type names start with a capital T as abbreviation for the word 'type'. Through this notation, inspired by the hungarian notation, types created within the R2A-project can be

---

[265] The UML has a constraint concept but with very different semantic to what is called a *design constraint* in R2A. However a certain connection between both concepts exists in the form that the UML constraint semantic can be seen as a special case of the *design constraint* semantic. As the UML constraint semantic bases on a *formal* language concept (called *Object Constraint Language (OCL)*), it is designed to describe very specific design issues in design diagrams in an annotation format. In contrast, a *design constraint* aims to describe all kinds of constraining effects of a design in natural language, thus providing significantly higher flexibility for description.

[266] The reader should note that the *meta-model* shown here is idealized to be understandable for the reader. In reality, the *meta-model* contains a few more classes, and the classes have significantly more properties and relationships. E.g., the access to TMdlObject objects (associations (5.) and (7.)) is in reality controlled through a proxy object *TToolsObjectProxy* to improve encapsulation of the *MdlInterface variation point*. This is important for the real tool implementation but is an implementation detail not necessary for understanding the fundamental concepts of the *meta-model* to be introduced in connection to this thesis.

easily differentiated from original types provided by the Microsoft C# .Net environment.

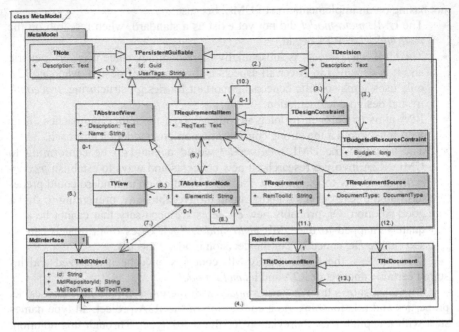

Figure 24-2 The *meta-model* of R2A

As mentioned in ch. III.16.1, R2A consists of a *core* and the two *variation points* for integrating *REM-* and *modeling tools*. In fig. 24-2, the *REM-tool variation point* is described by the *RemInterface* package and the modeling tool *variation point* by the *MdlInterface* package. The *meta-model* is located in the *core*, but information located in the connected *REM-* or *modeling tools* must be referenced through proxy objects in the *variation points*, abstracting from a specific implementation in a specific tool. In the case of the *RemInterface*, the class *TReDocument* represents a document in an *REM-tool* and *TReDocumentItem* represents an item (e.g., a requirement) within an *REM-tool's* document. *TMdlObject*, on the other side, represents any item available in a modeling tool.

Concerning the *core's meta-model*, any item inherits from *TPersistentGuifiable*. In *TPersistentGuifiable*, central characteristics necessary for any item to be part of the *meta-model* are realized.

Their characteristics are:

- *Persistence*: The item can be stored in R2A's data base through being a persistent item managed by a persistence framework (*OPF*).
- *History and baselining*: To fulfill demands of *evolutionary traceability*, the change versions' history must be recorded and it must be possible to include a version state into a baseline. Both are also accomplished by being a persistent item managed by the persistence framework.
- *Representablity in R2A's GUI*: *TPersistentGuifiable* implements all necessary characteristics for representation to be integrated into R2A's GUI concept.
- *Unique identifier* (cf. ch. III.17.4): Through the *Id* property, any item has one general unique identifier (GUID), through which the item can be referenced.
- *User tagging* (cf. ch. III.17.3): Through the *UserTags* property, any item can be tagged by users.
- *Notes* (cf. ch. III.17.2): Through association (1.), any item can be assigned to *TNote* objects representing notes. It is possible to assign several notes to an item as well as to assign several items to one note. As *TNote* is also part of the *meta-model* and inherits from *TPersistentGuifiable*, it is in principle possible to make notes of notes.
- *Being part of a conflict based decision* (cf. ch. III.20): Association (2.) represents the *conflicting* relationship in fig. 20-2 (see ch. III.20). Through this association, it is possible that any item of the *meta-model* can take part on a conflict, where a decision to solve the conflict can be modeled. This even includes notes or other decisions.

Design aspects are expressed through the concepts *TAbstractView, TAbstractionNode* and *TView*. *TAbstractView* represents general principles any view concepts in R2A have in common. The general principles are that a view has a name, can have a textual description and is expressed through a diagram in a modeling tool linked to through association (5.). *TAbstractionNode* represents the *AN* concept as described in ch. III.15. An *AN* consists of a *design element* in a modeling tool expressed through association (7.), a diagram in a modeling tool expressed through association (5.) and a description inherited by *TAbstractView*. The *ANH* concept is built up through association (8.). *TView* represents further related *views* that can be added to an *AN* (see description to fig. 15-4 (in ch. III.15)). An *AN* knows its related views through association (6.).

Requiremental aspects are expressed through the inheritance hierarchy starting from *TRequirementalItem*. This inheritance hierarchy resembles the *requiremental items taxonomy* introduced in fig. 21-1 (see ch. III.21.1), except for the fact that the inheritance hierarchy also contains *TRequirementSourceDocument*, representing requirement source documents described in. ch. III.18.1. This can be considered as a kind of artifice to create a thorough *requiremental decomposition hierarchy* in R2A. As described in ch. II.10.4.2.2 and ch. III.18.1, decomposition of requirements is a common principle in *REM*. Association (10.) from *TRe-quirementalItem* to *TRequirementalItem* is a *parent-child-relationship* used to build up requirement decomposition hierarchies. This decomposition hierarchy relationship can be used in principle for any *RI*. In fact, the hierarchy is used by requirements to reproduce the decomposition hierarchy present in *requirements specifications* from *REM-tools*, and it is used for the decomposition discussed in the course of *BRCs* sub budgeting (ch. III.21). Association (10.) is also used for *requirement source documents* (*RSDs*) to refer to the root *RIs* being at the start of the decomposition structure of a *RSD* (in fig. 18-2 (see ch. III.18.1), e.g., the *TRequirementSourceDocument* "PH" refers to the *requirements* "MSG Wakeup","Internal Lights Control", "Nonfunctional Requirements" and "HW" through association (10.)). In this way, a *RSD* is a parent of the root *RIs* in the document. This view is not wrong because a *RSD* as a container of *RIs* is itself an *RI* in the sense that the *RSD* demands that all containing *RIs* must be fulfilled. Through the *Type* property, the *TRequirementSourceDocument* specifies whether it is a free-edit document or whether it origins from a *REM-tool*. In the latter case, association (12.) refers to the corresponding document in the *REM-tool*. In a similar way, association (11.) refers *TRequirements* originating from an *REM-tool* to the original item representation in the *REM-tool*.

As *requirements traceability* to *design elements* is the core scope of R2A, *RI* must be linked to the design. This is expressed by association (9.) representing the *'assigned to'* or resp. *'satisfy'* relationship between *ANs* and *RIs* described in ch. III.18.2.

The *decision model* described in fig. 20-2 (see III.20) is realized by the class *TDecision* and its associations. As mentioned above, association (2.) represents the conflicting entities relationship. Association (3.), however, refers to the result-ing consequences derived as *TDesignConstraints* or *TBudgetedResourceCon-straints*. Association (4.) realizes references to further documenting design dia-grams in a modeling tool.

III.24.3 Further Interfaces

Additionally to the user interface, R2A has the following other interfaces:
- *REM-tool integration*: As described in ch. III.13, R2A provides a *variation point* to integrate *REM-tools* as source for requirements (ch. III.18.1) and as target to export requirements for *supplier management* (ch. III.23.1).
- *Modeling-tool integration*: R2A provides an integration interface for modeling tools as *variation point* described in ch. III.13.

- *Word interface*: For documentation of the design and design decisions, Microsoft Word is integrated into R2A. The Word documents are saved in the R2A database in *rich text format* (*RTF*) and are integrated in R2A's other information *meta model* through a *persistence framework* (e.g., the *meta model* items *TAbstractionNode*, or *TDecision* contain a *persistent* property "Description" referring to *RTF* documents editable with Word).

- *Standard report*: A standard report interface allows to generating a HTML-report of the generated model in R2A. The report includes diagrams modeled in the connected modeling-tools, thus enabling to generate extensive design documentation.

- *XML-export*: Ch. III.17.3 describes the XML-export feature allowing the complete model gathered in R2A to be exported for organizations to reuse the gathered information in other tools or to develop own special purpose tools working on the information.

- *Rule engine*: *Consistency management* is a decisive issue for ensuring quality of developed artifacts. Ch. III.22 has described the standard features for *consistency management* in R2A. However, often projects have individual characteristics influencing the consistency. To cover this, R2A provides a *rule engine*, where projects can specify individual rules for *consistency checking*. In this way, projects can ensure that the R2A model fulfills consistency criteria defined in the project. At the moment, the current *rule engine* concept implemented in R2A is only a prototypical implementation, showing a proof of concept. This point can be seen as a promising perspective for further research and improvement of the R2A concept. As an example of the possible uses of R2A's *rule engine* concept, it is possible for designers to define rules that any *design element* with a certain characteristic must obey. When the example of the decision modeled in fig. 20-6 (see ch. III.20.4) is considered, the *DC* "Handlers and Drivers shall provide callback mechanisms to their upper layers (*Dependency Inversion Principle*)." exists that must be obeyed by any handler or driver in the *SW design*. With the *rule engine*, a designer can define a rule that ensures that the *DC* is automatically assigned to any handler and driver *design element* currently present in R2A. The rule also ensures, that the *DC* is added to any *design element* with handler or driver characteristic, added later to the R2A model.

- *Special reports with the rule engine*: The reporting mechanisms can be combined with the *rule engine*. In this way, customized reports can be created in R2A for special reporting needs of a project. With the *rule engine*, scripts can be written to extract data from the data collected in an R2A-project specially prepared for the customized report. Through customized reports, e.g., it is possible to create reports about statistical data of a project to report it to management (e.g., to report how many *RIs* are not yet considered in design, partially considered in design and how many *RIs* have reached the final state in design).

IV. Synopsis

This is not the end. It is not even the beginning of the end.
But it is, perhaps, the end of the beginning.
Winston Churchill

Now, this last part finishes this thesis. At first, a short summary of the achieved results of this research project is provided. This is then followed by a prospectus of possible further questions to continue research on, either improving the current features set of R2A or more general on the research topics of this thesis. At the end, the author tries to summarize the general conclusions to draw from this thesis.

IV.25 Summary of the Achieved Research Results

To achieve anything worthy to be called quality you will have
to do a good deal more than follow a drawing or specification,
whoever made them and however carefully.
There is a good and close parallel to music.
The quality of a performance depends
on the performers as much as on the score.
The performers are said to be interpreting the score,
but in fact they are adding intention of their own
to those of the composer, recognising that no score
in practice can fully express the intentions of the composer,
that it can never be more than an indication, a sketch;
and no designer can in practice ever produce more than a sketch
even though his drawing is dimensioned in thousandths
of an inch and his specification is as long as your arm.
[Py78; p.80]

In the following the main technical innovations achieved through PROVEtech: R2A (in the further called R2A) are summarized:

- *Hierarchic decomposition* of a system (or software) is an old idea in *SE* (see *structured analysis* and *design* [De78]). In UML based design, this view is seen as one besides many others with equal rights (see, e.g., the *view* concept *"4+1 View Model"* by Kruchten [Kr95]). UML does not prefer any *view* or make relations between *views* explicit. Instead, defining *views* and their relations are left open to *architecture documentation*. However, this leads to a more difficult understanding of a designed model since all *views* and elements are mixed up in one egalitarian repository (see fig. 15-3 in ch. III.15). Besides, the heterogeneous *view* concept of UML makes UML incompatible with other modeling techniques used in embedded development such as ETAS ASCET or Matlab, which only use one *hierarchic decomposition view*. As R2A makes only one necessary assumption: that a design must be made using a *hierarchic decomposition* (in fact a claim that can be called state-of-the-art), the approach should be compatible to any other computer tool-based design approach and even to HW or *computer aided design* (*CAD*). To include such a tool, only an interface implementation for R2A's modeling tool *variation point* connecting to the corresponding tool would be necessary. Development experiences within the R2A-project have shown that this is possible within a two to three person month's development effort.

- As shown in ch. III.16.2, the mechanism of coupling modeling tools in R2A is even capable to integrate models of different modeling tools in one integrated model. In this way, all achievements described below can also be used as an embracing method to generate an integrated model, crossing tool gaps between different modeling tools. This allows using specific modeling tools together in an integrated model. In this way, it is possible to employ the specific strengths of the specific tools in one integrated model.

- As not explicitly discussed yet, but the approach for *traceability* can be equally used to establish *traceability* between requirements and an *AM*, when, e.g., a UML-tool is used to create the *AM*.

- In the approach shown here, the *hierarchic decomposition* builds the spine of the complete model because each element of the *design model* gets explicitly included into the *abstraction hierarchy tree* and is extended to a so called *abstraction node* (*AN*) having extended semantics (cf fig. 15-2 in ch. III.15). To each *AN* further diagrams can be added as additional *views*. Through this way, the orientation of the designers is alleviated as at first navigation into the *abstraction hierarchy* to the desired element can take place (vertical direction). Starting from this, also navigation along the further attached views is possible[267] (horizontal direction). However, the problem is still unsolved that some of the remaining views of a model may go *crosscutting* over different *abstraction layers* and *ANs*. At the moment, it is possible to add diagrams with such characteristics to all *ANs* touched by the view, but finding an even more consistent solution for this, is an open point for further research.

- Additionally, the *ANs* tree arisen through *hierarchic decomposition* also builds the spine for the structured approach for *requirements traceability* to design establishment. Differently to approaches, where requirements are simply added to a *design element* via direct linking, the R2A provides a complete new approach to the problem called the *requirement dribble process* (*RDP*). In this approach, developers at first do not need to know by which design solution a *requiremental item* (*RI*) will exactly be fulfilled. Instead a designer can at first assign an *RI* to *ANs*, where she roughly grasps that the *RI* may be fulfilled by. Then, when the designer's vision gets clearer about an *RI*, the designer may use the *dribble-down* and *dribble-up* actions to reallocate the *RI*. In this way, on one side Simon's idea about *stable intermediate forms* (ch. I.6.2.1) is supported, and on the other side the uncertainty and flexibility of the approach directly supports designers in their *knowing-in-action* phase.

- Through the support of a dedicated process for assigning *RIs*, it is ensured that each *RI* is adequately considered in the design process: If new *RIs* are assigned to an *AN* 'from above' (a higher-level *AN*), these *RIs* get highlighted in the *AN* by a bold font style Now, the designer of the *AN* must try to find an adequate solution for the newly assigned *RIs*. If the designer of this *AN* is again able to delegate these requirements to a sub *AN* of the design, then these *RIs* '*dribble down*' one level deeper to a sub *AN*, and the problem is solved for the corresponding *AN*. However, if the designer is not able to clearly delegate these *RIs* to any sub *AN*, then the *RIs* stick to this *AN* and are inherited to all lower-level sub *ANs* (marked 'gray' at these lower levels) indicating that all *ANs* must work together to fulfill these *RIs*. But, if the designer responsible for the *AN* realizes that these newly assigned *RIs* cannot be fulfilled in the current state of design, the designer is able to repel these *RIs* back to the higher-level *AN* (its origin) accompanied with a corresponding note. In this

---

[267] As described in the point before, the usual orientation within modeling tools is in most cases realized by a repository concept, where all items present in a model are shown (see fig. 15-3 in ch. III.15). This repository is not touched by R2A. On the contrary, R2A's *AN* concept with its representation in an *ANH* tree can be seen as a distillate of the most important information on the most important items and their relationships present in the modeling tool repository. Whereas, the *modeling tool repository* is more a dictionary containing all someway present items in a model.

case, the designer of the higher-level *AN* must take care for a solution under consideration of the created notes.

- As a dedicated goal of the *RDP*, the process set aims on principles leading to a way to find an allocation for a requirement at an *AN* at the lowest level of abstraction to ensure that a requirement is implemented as local as possible. In this way, the *impacts* of a later requirement change are also limited as local as possible.

- In the wake of this goal, the concept of the r*equirement influence scope* (*RIS*) has been developed. The concept includes that a requirement being associated to an *AN* also is propagated to the child *ANs* as "*inherited*" requirement. In this way, on one side pressure is imposed on the project team members to bring requirements to the most possible local level in the *ANH* tree. Thus, a later possible change of the requirement has only minimal *impact* (cf. ch. III.18.2.2). The *RIS* thus promotes a heuristic enforcing a design with emphasis on localization of the requirements. This heuristic is an essential part of the ideas behind the *RDP*.

- As a further plus, the history of the different requirement allocations and reallocations during the *RDP* are automatically tracked via *configuration management* features. In this way, the decision process of the designer taking the decision can be reconstructed later. This follows ideas of Gruber and Russell [GR96a] or Schneider [Sch06] to capture important information during performed action and extracting important *rationale* information later as a *by-product*.

- Some *traceability* research rather neglects the aspects about the process of *traceability* establishment (see, e.g., [Kn01a], [Kn01b]). In the author's view, however, this issue might be the central key problem of *traceability* since *traceability* faces a significant *benefit problem* (see ch. II.10.5) in a similar way as *RatMan* approaches do (ch. II.9.4.2). As a consequence, R2A's *traceability* mechanisms try to allow capturing *traceability* as a mere *by-product* of normal design activities, where designers can perceive direct benefit from recording *traceability* information. To achieve this goal, R2A at first allows capturing *traceability* by several possible *drag-and-drop* operations being performed easily and quickly as *by-product* of the decisions performed. Secondly, R2A directly shows the *RIs* assigned to each *AN*, thus directly giving designers benefit for their *traceability* work as this work is used to provide a sorted out view on the *RIs* important for the currently considered design aspect from the otherwise numerous manifold of *RIs* present in a *requirements specification*. Further, with the *RIS* and *RDP* concepts, design decisions about requirements allocation are automatically captured, following the principles of Simon's idea about *stable intermediate forms* (ch. I.6.2.1). In the author's view, the principle of *stable intermediate forms* directly reflects how designers usually develop a design out of the requirements at hand. Thus, through *RIS* and *RDP*, traces can be directly captured according to their occurrence with special emphasis on flexibility and optimal adaption into a SPICE-conforming process landscape. These concepts can also be seen as an attempt to adapt *traceability* establishment activities to the way designers are thinking, thus preventing a *cognitive dissonance* for designers. In this way, R2A tries to be less *intrusive* to designers' thinking, thus supporting designers in both, their *knowing-in-action* and *reflection-in-action* phases (see Schön, ch. I.6.2.3).

- Significant parts of the research about *traceability* concentrate on proposals to use richer *traceability* models as a kind of *conceptual trace model* (cf. ch. II.10.4.2). In the author's view, these approaches provide important points. However, it is questionable whether their *formality* is not too complex (i.e. complicated; see footnote 80 (p.77)) for activities that should best be performed as a *by-product* (see ch. II.10.5 and ch. II.9.4.2). The research attempt shown here tries to integrate good ideas from these research attempts into a complete concept. As a result, a *requiremental items taxonomy* has been developed, distinguishing real *requirements* from the customer from *RIs* (*DCs* and *BRCs*) arising as consequences from design decisions.

- This – as a further result – also has sparked the idea to enhance R2A's *traceability* concepts by an *integrated decision model* for documenting *requiremental* and design-based decisions (cf. ch. III.20). Thus, the developed *decision model* is called *integrated* because it directly integrates information about design decisions into a *traceability* concept. Again following the idea that this additional information must be rather captured as a *by-product*, the *decision model* is construed as a *semi-formal model*, where the *formalisms* build a *skeleton* to easily sketch the basic information about a decision and to add more detailed information on demand. In this way, the *decision model* on one side addresses *benefit problems* encountered for *capturing rationale* (ch. II.9.4.2) but on the other side also allows capturing deeper *rationale* information for problems of rather *wicked* nature (cf. ch. I.6.2.2). As ch. III.20.4 has outlined, the decision model is also a good means for fulfilling demands on decision documentation, imposed by research about *architecture documentation* (e.g., cf. [Ha06], [CBB+03]), and much closer integrating the thus captured information with the *design model*.

- The *decision model's* concept of modeling conflict situations and consequences resembles to the *pattern* concept expressed by Alexander (ch. I.6.2.4). In fact, as ch. III.20.5.1 shows, R2A's *decision model* can be a decisive means to document the *rationale* behind *pattern* usages to directly integrate the *pattern* concept with the *traceability* concept, to help to better include consequences of *pattern* usages with other decisions and to help to discover new *patterns*.

- As embedded design (but also other design) must often care for adequately managing *resource restrictions*, the R2A approach offers a second *decision model* to capture decisions about *resource restrictions* that can be managed as budget. The decision results are again expressed as new *RIs* assigned to *ANs*, expressing the need that an *AN* does not exceed the resource budget that was assigned to it. To cover this aspect, the *requiremental items taxonomy* has been extended by the *RI* called *BRC* expressing the budget character of the *RI* and the budgeting decision process.

- The arrangement of the *design models* in an *abstraction hierarchy tree* and the way requirements consideration in design can be handled by the *RDP*, suggest the conclusion that adequate mechanisms can help to significantly improve the flow of communication between project stakeholders. In R2A, this can be achieved by temporal decoupling (asynchronous temporal communication) of messages preventing, for example, that important information is not adequately propagated if the responsible developer is not present. Such a mechanism is intended to support goal-oriented creation of notes (cf. ch. III.17.2) for any entity present in the data model and actions performable on the entities. These notes allow sketching occurring problems with references to all affected model entities and propagating this information to concerned stakeholders.

- At the same time, these notes are included into the *history* function (cf. ch. III.17.5) in order to better enable later reconstruction of the incident's occurrence[268] (e.g., helpful during a SPICE assessment). In this context, further research attempts could enhance the mechanism described here by state-based notes (e.g., with the states: 'New', 'In work', 'Processes', or 'New solution'), or escalation paths in a consistent process-driven model.

- Additionally, all these concepts allow a high degree of flexibility to change *traceability* information again. This flexibility is also especially helpful to support *design refactorings*, where *traceability* information is also adapted correspondingly, thus preventing significant degradation of *traceability* information captured once.

- This directly segues to the next topic: *Traceability* is intended as means to manage requirement changes. Through the *graphical impact analysis* concept (see ch. III.22.1.1), R2A allows proposed requirement changes to be better predicted and helps to implement once decided requirement changes. An especially important point is to consistently infer and propagate all requirement

---

[268] Up to now, results are often only discussed and tracked orally.

changes throughout the complete model. R2A achieves this through the consistency management mechanism described in ch. III.22.2.

- In many development projects, parts of a project are delivered by a supplier. Correspondingly, *supplier management* is an important task in these projects. One of the most essential issues addressed is that the requirements for the supplied parts must be formulated in a way that the supplied parts fit together with the other designed parts of the system. R2A allows generating a *requirements specification* directly for a part of a design (an *AN* or a sub tree in the *ANH*), which can then be used as *supplier requirements specification*. In this way, all information about requirements, design and decisions performed in a R2A project relevant for a supplier of a part can be directly propagated to the supplier without unintended information loss due to tool gaps or other potential breaks in the information chain (see ch. III.23.1).

- Last but not least to mention, the mechanisms of generating *requirements specifications* for parts of a design described in ch. III.23.1 can also be used to implement a direct and seamless information propagation for situations, where a project has several requirement and design processes at different layers of abstraction as it is demanded by SPICE. Even though the author himself rather prefers an integrated design process for the different layers as it is described by fig. 23-1 in ch. III.23.2, fig. 23-2 in ch. III.23.2 shows that R2A also has the potential to improve the information flow in cases the process demands of SPICE shall be fulfilled word for word. As the ch. III.23.3 shows, R2A can even be used to achieve a temporal decoupling of the development of the different requirement and design artifacts.

IV.26 Perspectives for Further Research

It's like deja-vu, all over again.
Yogi Berra

The current research results of the R2A-project also provide perspectives for possible further research. In the following, problems or ideas are outlined that may raise interesting research questions:

- The current solution of R2A has made a significant simplification concerning the *view* concept. In R2A, *views* are merely represented by one diagram. This does not consider more complex *views*. However, in design documentation theory, a *view* often consists of a set of diagrams that must be considered together. R2A currently only considers this fact by the *ANH*. This brought the advantage that the user can more easily navigate in the model, but on the other side other *view's* being more complex than one diagram might be scattered over several *ANs* and the relationships between these diagrams may not be adequately surfaced by a model. Further research could concentrate on finding a solution, in which several diagrams could be integrated into a more complex *view* other than the *ANH view*, and where, however, the advantages of better model navigation as provided by the current R2A-solution are still present.

- In the context of the *RIS* (ch. III.18.2.2) and the *RDP* (ch. III.18.2.4), the author has only spoken from *RIs* 'assigned' to an *AN*. This leaves open space for interpretation of the concrete semantics of any relationship. In fact, different *traceability CTMs* (see ch. II.10.4.2.3) know different relationship types between *RIs* and design. The R2A-approach could be extended to allow designers to define a concrete semantics of a relationship. However, further research should then also ensure that this extension is not just leading to further complication without significant gains of value.

- In this context, a further interesting idea may be to have a relationship describing fuzziness concerning the kind of connection between an *RI* and an *AN*. Instead of 'assigned' relationships, currently describing the fact that an *AN* is directly influenced by an *RI*, there might exist relationships having notions like 'bordering' (the requirement is fulfilled nearby, thus the *RI* should be monitored whether it possibly has some influence), 'keep in mind' and 'I don't know, but might be important'. By such fuzzy relationships designers could identify connections, for which they 'feel' that there is a dependency they cannot describe rationally. This corresponds to Schön's observation that designers also work in a state of intuitive *knowing-in-action*, where they use *tacit knowledge* and thus cannot rationally explain their exact thoughts.

- Ch. III.18.2.2 describes a mechanism where the scope of a requirement is determined by the so-called *RIS*. When *RIs* are added to an *AN*, these *RIs* are automatically inherited to all child *ANs* of the *AN* in the *ANH*. In this way, developers are spurred to find the most local solutions for an *RI*. On the other side, effects of *nonfunctional RIs* can be made more transparent as than it is possible by other approaches. *Nonfunctional RIs* can be added to a very high-level *AN*, where they are inherited by large extents of *ANs*. Taming *nonfunctional RIs* is rather difficult. In the author's opinion, the *decision model* introduced in ch. III.20 proves very helpful as it allows documenting decisions about the taming strategies of *nonfunctional RIs,* allowing deriving more concrete *DCs* as decision consequences. Now, if this is thought through consequently, it may be possible that a *nonfunctional RI* is tamed by decisions, where more concrete *RIs* (*DCs* or *BRCs*) are derived. It should be considered whether a feature may be helpful to specify that a decision or several decisions together completely tame an *RI*. It must be analyzed whether it would be a logical consequence that an *RI* tamed by one or more decisions may lose its inheritance status to lower-level *ANs* (lose its *RIS*) because its influence would rather take effect through the decisions and the effects of the *RIs* resulting as consequences. Such considerations, however, must also consider that such an effect may not be realized for any decisions, but it would rather be necessary to mark certain decisions as the taming decisions of an *RI* leading to the deactivation of the *RI's RIS*. In this way, it is questionable to a certain degree whether such a feature brings significant extra value to designers or whether it just implies a further *complication* to the design (see footnote 80 (p.77)). In the case of the latter, the author would recommend leaving out the question, even though it might be slightly more logical than the current solution.

- At the moment, *consistency checking* is a rather neglected topic of this research even though rudimentary *consistency checking* can be provided by the *rule engine*. Analyses on what *consistency reporting* is necessary for users could be performed. A further problem may arise with the fact that R2A rather relies on heuristics such as the *RDP* (ch. III.18.2.4) and the *decision models*. These heuristics imply a certain *non-linearity*. As here traces cannot be followed so directly, this could make *consistency checking* more difficult. For example, usually *consistency checking* mechanisms rely on checking whether all requirements are someway associated to a *design model*. If this is the case, it is assumed that the requirement is adequately considered in the design process. The author, however, is rather skeptical towards the real expressiveness of such rather simple checks. With R2A, however, such simple checks are even not possible because the *RDP* heuristics allows assigning requirements to *design elements* not being the final destination of the requirement. Instead, the requirement assignment can change with *dribble-down* or *dribble-up* operations in order to support design decision-making. In this case, a requirement can only be seen as adequately considered after the requirement has reached its final destination. The situation can get even more complicated when a requirement is part of documented decisions. Here, e.g., the question arises whether a requirement can only be seen as adequately considered when all consequential items of all decisions involved have reached their final destination. In the author's view such a developed *consistency checking* mechanism would provide significantly more fine-grained information than current *consistency checking* approaches and thus provide even stronger expressiveness. But, because all effects of such a *consistency checking* heuristics are not yet analyzed, this point is rather an open question for further research.

- Pinheiro indicates that for capturing *nonfunctional traces, hypermedia (multimedia) systems* could provide significant support ([Pi04; p.104-105], see ch. II.10.4.2.2). The approach proposed here offers possibilities to tackle *nonfunctional traces* via the integrated *decision model* (cf. ch. III.20). It would be possible to couple the *decision model* approaches with *rationale* tools like Compendium, supporting *rationale capturing* on the fly as well as with other media objects such as tape or video recordings of meetings, in which the corresponding decisions are discussed.

- A design process is also driven by other documents such as meeting protocols, review protocols or documentation of the used COTS[269]-components. In the author's opinion, it will never be possible to integrate all documents important for development into one tool solution. Correspondingly, it should be possible to have a *hyperlink* concept to give developers the freedom to link to further documentation, someway not manageable in R2A. As projects usually use *configuration management* tools to manage versions of all documents in a project, it may be interesting to integrate R2A with configuration management systems via the standardized CVS[270]-interface.

- In *issue tracking* (i.e. *change management*) systems open issues (e.g., problems or bugs) can be managed. A direct connection of R2A to issue tracking systems could help to make influences of issues transparent, because often issues beyond requirements or requirement changes exist having influences on design decisions. The exact way of integration should be analyzed by further research. However, a starting point for integration could be to shape the integration in a similar way as the integration of *REM-tools* has been made: A continuous synchronization process cares to have all issues in an accurate state in R2A and these issues are then treated analogously to *requiremental items*. As the description to arrow '1.' of fig. 20-8 (see ch. III.20.4) describes, a better integration with change management tools might help to solve information backlashes to requirements occurring during design and especially during processes of discovering *rationale* in decision processes. However, it must be noticed that issues are slightly different to requirements because only certain issues may be interesting for design and

---

[269] Commercial Off The Shelf

[270] *Concurrent Versioning System*: This interface is an international standard for integrating configuration management systems with other environments such as programming IDEs.

should therefore be synchronized in R2A. This means a filter must distinguish the architecturally significant issues from the insignificant issues.

- *Impact analysis* (*IA*) approaches as [Ha99] propose combining a tracing approach with a kind of *dependency analysis* approach using the relationships in a model. In this way, effort to capture *traceability* information is reduced by using the model relationships present in a model. As ch. II.10.6.2 has shown, however, such approaches often lead to the so-called *fan-out* effect [Al03] because models contain manifold relationships having other purposes leading to many unnecessary traces. Correspondingly, the R2A approach rather concentrates on achieving more exact results by allowing establishing dedicated more *fine-grained traceability* information as a *by-product* of usual development effort, thus reducing efforts for *traceability*. However, on the other side, dependency information in the model can be valuable to indicate other possible *impacts* resulting from interconnections within the model. Thus, it may be possible to combine the current R2A approach with a dependency approach automatically analyzing all other relationships created in the *design model*. To avoid the *fan-out* effect, R2A's *IA* could show these *impacts* identified from *dependency analysis* with a different iconification (as it is already done for distinguishing *direct impacts* from *indirect impacts* derived from decisions or *inherited impacts* derived from the *RIS*) to distinguish them from *impacts* derived from captured *traceability* information within R2A. Further, it could be possible that this additional *dependency analysis* can be activated or deactivated for *IA*. In this way, designers could have additional support for identifying possible *impacts* from interconnections within the model but also ignore the information if they feel it is not helpful.
- Ch. II.10.2 further indicates that with *model-driven development* methods and tools a new problem arises concerning *traceability*: As code then often is generated from models, some requirements are not necessarily implemented through the models but by setting parameters or choosing specific model transformation procedures over other procedures [AIE07]. This means that *traceability* tools should also need to map requirements to parameter choices or transformation procedures of the modeling tool. Currently in R2A, *traceability* to these items could be achieved by a documented decision, where the requirements are in the conflicts section and the resulting section contains *DCs* with the chosen parameter settings or transformation procedures. Further research, however, could also try to find more adequate support by R2A for this tracing problem.
- Another research direction may be to integrate a metrics approach with R2A. Ch. III.20.5.3 indicates that architectural evaluation and identification of

neuralgic points can be supported by combining R2A with metrics. Further research could evaluate the potential of the ideas about metrics sketched in ch. III.20.5.3.

$$CEF(\text{Re}q) = \sum (AN_{direct} * Level_{AN} + coeff_{inher} * \sum ANs_{inher} + coeff_{Dec} * \sum Decs_{\text{Re}q}) \quad (26.1)$$

$$Level_{ANH} = coeff_{lvl}^{(LowestLevel - Level_{\text{Re}q})} \quad \text{where} \quad coeff_{lvl} > 1 \quad (26.2)$$

$$Avrg(CEF) = \frac{\sum (CEF(\text{Re}q))}{Count_{\text{Re}qs}} \quad (26.3)$$

- A further metric possibly interesting to evaluate could help to determine the changeability of an *RI*. As indicated by ch. III.18.2.2 and ch. III.18.2.4, a *RI* should be as local as possible. A *change effort factor* (*CEF*) metric could measure the locality of a requirement by calculating the directly assigned *ANs* in relation to the hierarchical level in the *ANH* (is it high or low in the hierarchy?), the number of *ANs* where the *RI* has been inherited to and the number of decisions the *RI* is involved in. Formula (26.1) sketches a possible measurement formula for the *CEF* metric. The formula uses a level factor[271] calculating (formula (26.2)) a factor to determine the hierarchy level dependent complexity of each directly assigned *AN*. In this way, the metric could help to estimate the effort for changing a *RI*. From a higher perspective, this metric could also be used to create a metric to evaluate an *architecture* according to the average changeability of requirements. The average changeability could be calculated by the sum over the changeability of all requirements divided through the number of requirements (e.g., formula (26.3). Here, it is to mention that the metrics as proposed here are just rough sketches. Further research could deal with how to adapt parameters (different 'coeff' variables) in the sketched formulas to achieve distinctive, meaningful results. Afterward, the metrics need to be evaluated in several practical projects to get measuring scales for the practical meaning of the measured metrics.
- As described in ch. I.7.4, *verification criteria* for design artifacts must be defined and these must be made traceable [MHD+07; p.225ff]. At the

---

[271] Through the level factor with its level coefficient, the complexity of the *design model* is taken into account because the coefficient grows exponentially with the number of abstraction levels present in a design. When, e.g., a design grows by new abstraction levels, requirements added to higher level (resp. more abstract) *abstraction levels* lead to a significantly higher CEF (assumed a corresponding adequate value for the coefficient is chosen). In this way, the author assumes that the 'Avrg(CEF)' function also grows stronger for designs having more *abstraction levels*.

moment, this can be achieved in R2A via using the notes mechanism (ch. III.17.2). Such notes are only added to the assigned R2A-items and nowhere stored centrally, which leads to an unstructured approach with no complete overview about present *verification criteria*. Further research could try to find a better solution, where easiness of usage and usability should play a central role.

- The R2A approach introduced here leaves one major field of problems concerning development of automotive systems and software untouched: Ch. I.2.3 indicates that buyers of cars can select hundreds of different options of their car individually, where also different options are connected with each other. This, however, implies that the different ECUs employed in a car can significantly vary between different cars and that in different cars individual *variants* of the ECUs must communicate with each other. As HW costs are significant constraints, different ECU variants also have different HW assemblies. Nevertheless, all different ECU *variants* and the different ECUs with their *variants* in interplay must fulfill their requirements, especially all *safety-related* issues. This together implies significant higher complexity than if all ECUs had only one fixed version. In *SysEng* and *SE* theory, management strategies for this complexity are called *variation management*. Hull et al. [HJD02; p.180-183] show that managing variation implies significant higher complexity concerning *variants*, *version management* and *change management* of requirements in connection with their *traceability* (see also [Si98], [BP06], [PR09; p.141f]) because the different *variants* must fulfill partially different requirements and the valid requirements must be – despite the *variation* – consistent to each other. In other words, *version baselines* and *change management* must in principle be performed and managed individually for each *variant* [HJD02; p.180-183]. On the other side, *variation management* issues also impose high influence on *SW architecture* and design theory (e.g., cf. [PBG04; ch. 10]), because decisions about strategies for handling the *variation* at the *variation points* ([PBG04; p.276], [Si98]; also cf. ch. III.16.1) significantly influence design[272]. As R2A also has its two major involvements in *REM* and design issues, R2A has potential to

---

[272] As an example, it must be determined whether a *variation* can be simply handled through a configuration parameter or whether the *variation* requires significantly more complex mechanisms to be integrated into design considerations (e.g., flexibility needs for a *variation point* can also lead to the decision that significant parts of the application must be created through the *abstract factory pattern* in order to allow activation of different component implementations according to the *variation* need).

improve *variation management*. However, to find suitable features, further research is needed.

IV.27 Conclusions

After you find the gold, there's still the job
of picking out your particular nuggets.
[BT04; p.147]

Now, finally, the reader has reached the end of this thesis. The author hopes that this thesis could provide valuable information to the reader so that he considered it worth, while reading it.

The main topic of interest has been *requirements traceability* between requirements and design artifacts in the development of *safety-critical systems*. As this thesis – hopefully – has shown, manifold factors must be considered, because the topic *traceability* is *cross-cutting* through research theories of *embedded systems development, systems engineering, software engineering, requirements engineering* and *management, design* theory and process standards for *safety-critical systems*. Despite all promising effects ascribed to *traceability* over the last two decades, the *traceability* concept did not broadly succeed in practice except for development organizations using process standards such as SPICE or CMMI, where, in most cases, *safety-critical systems* may be in the focus of development.

A reason may be the significantly higher effort and costs involved to make all requirements traceable throughout the complete development endeavor. Most probably, the effort and costs can only be justified, when issues of *safety* or *security* are involved. On the other side, costs will only be such a decisive factor if they are not outweighed by the benefits. This seems to be a core issue of the *traceability problem*.

Further, the thesis has shown that *requirements traceability* between requirements and design is especially *wicked* because this involves crossing a two-fold gap: First, different tools are used for *requirements specification* and design that make it necessary to bridge them. Secondly, a transition from requirements to design means a transition from a problem description to a solution description, involving a substantial, *non-linear gap* that is usually mentally bridged by designers but is difficult to cope with an ordinary link concept usually employed by *traceability* methods.

When analyzing different design theories, the author found out that design must rather be seen as a continuous decision process, where only parts of the decisions can be rationally describable by designers, but other extensive parts arise by intuitive usage of *tacit knowledge*, cook-booky *heuristics*, and creativity. As the author has tried to show, exactly this *"tacit dimension"* [Po66] may be the major obstacle for valuable *traceability* information concerning design, because it infers the *non-linearity* in the relations between requirements and design and also hinders designers to make the transition process rationally explicable.

As a consequence, the author has invented a new tool solution called PROVEtech:R2A, aiming to narrow the twofold gap between requirements and design to a degree that *traceability* endeavors bring a real benefit to development.

To achieve this, PROVEtech:R2A has been developed to allow establishing *traceability* as a *by-product* of designers' usual development activities. Through this, additional benefit shall be provided to designers as an incentive to establish valuable *traceability* information. One of these benefits is that recorded *traceability* information can be directly used to improve communication and collaboration between designers. The tool further orients itself on the view of *design as a sequence of decisions*. Correspondingly, R2A allows recording traces of the decisions made. This starts with automatically recording traces of decisions about simple requirement allocation and design structure building (e.g., see ch. III.15) and continues by providing two different *decision models* allowing designers to document *rationale* information on more complex decisions.

Besides all these considerations, one further, very important, consideration has been that such a tool must also be integrated into a process landscape compatible with *process models* for *safety-critical systems*. This thesis has shown that this is in principle the case. As a further very important plus, the thesis identified major drawbacks of these *process models*, involving unnecessary redundancy concerning process transitions from requirements to design. The author could identify the underlying core idea that also design processes spark new "requirements" as consequences from decisions taken earlier. Once having identified this idea, the author could develop a *taxonomy of requiremental items*, where requirements originating from demands of the customer could be distinguished from *design constraints* originating from taken design decisions.

As it has further turned out, the first *decision model* could be used as a means to transform processes in a way that the original ideas of the *process models* were preserved, but unnecessary redundancy could be avoided. The *decision model*, allowing modeling conflict situations of requirements and then deriving consequences as new *design constraints*, can be seen as a new major extension of current *traceability* linking concepts by a more complex *traceability* concept that allows a better bridging of the gaps in a complex design decision process, leading to the *non-linear gap* between requirements and design. As a further major plus, the four major design theories introduced in this thesis could be adequately weaved together with theories about *traceability* and *rationale management*, forming a tool set of supportive actions for designers.

Through significant research and development funding by the support program IUK-Bayern of the bavarian ministry of economics, it has been possible to develop PROVEtech:R2A to a solution now commercially available at the MBtech Group. First practical experiences at the MBtech Group are promising that the solution provides significant support for designers at their daily practical design work. In the meantime, through the coupling of the tool PROVEtech:TA (a solution of the MBtech Group for test automation) the usage context of PROVEtech:R2A has been even enlarged to a means for also bridging the gaps between a test specification and automatically executable testing code.

Bibliography

[AB93] Arnold, R.S.; Bohner, S.A: *Impact analysis – Towards a framework for comparison.* Proceedings of Conference on Software Maintenance, 1993. CSM-93, Montreal, pp.292-301, Sept. 1993.

[ACC+02] Antoniol, G.; Canfora, G.; Casazza, G.; De Lucia, A.; Merlo, E.: *Recovering traceability links between code and documentation.* IEEE Transactions on Software Engineering, Vol. 28 (10), pp.970-983, Oct 2002.

[AIE07] Almeida, J. P.; Iacob, M-E.; Eck, P.: *Requirements traceability in model-driven development: Applying model and transformation conformance.* Information Systems Frontiers, Vol. 9, Issue 4, Kluwer Academic Publishers, Hingham, MA, USA, pp.327-342, 2007.

[AG98] Ambriola, V.; Gervasi, V.: *Representing structural requirements in software architecture.* Proceedings of the IFIP TC2 WG2.4 Working Conference on Systems Implementation 2000: Languages, Methods and Tools, Berlin, pp.114-127, 1998.

[Ak96] Akroyd, M.: *AntiPatterns Session Notes.* In: Object World West. San Fransisco, 1996.

[AKL+07a] Avgeriou, P.; Kruchten, P.; Lago, P.; Grisham, P.; Perry, D.E.: *Architectural Knowledge and Rationale: Issues, Trends, Challenges.* ACM SIGSOFT Software Engineering Notes 32(4), pp.41-46, 2007.

[AKL+07b] Avgeriou, P.; Kruchten, P.; Lago, P.; Grisham, P.; Perry, D.E.: *Sharing and Reusing Architectural Knowledge – Architecture, Rationale, and Design Intent.* ICSE Companion, pp.109-110, 2007.

[ALK09] Avgeriou, P.; Lago, P.; Kruchten, P.: *Towards Using Architectural Knowledge.* ACM SIGSOFT Software Engineering Notes 34(2), pp.27-30, 2009.

[Al64] Alexander, C., *Notes on the Synthesis of Form.* Harvard University Press, Cambridge, Massachusetts. 1964.

[AIS77] Alexander, C.; Sara Ishikawa, S.; Silverstein, M.: *A Pattern Language: Towns, Buildings, Construction.* New York: Oxford University Press, 1977.

[Al77] Alford, M.W.: *A Requirements Engineering Methodology for Realtime Processing Requirements.* IEEE Transactions on Software Engineering SE-3(1), pp.60–69, 1977.

[Al79] Alexander, C.: *The Timeless Way of Building.* Oxford University Press, New York 1979.

[Al03] Allderidge, S.: *A Use Case Driven Safety Critical Programme.* INCOSE UK Spring Symposium, 2003. (Online version http://www.artisansw.com/pdflibrary–/DS&S_INCOSE_2003.pdf (Access: 2005/11)), 2003.

[Am05] Ambler, S.: *Agile Requirements Best Practises.* The Official Agile Modeling (AM) Site. (Online verion: http://www.agilemodeling.com/essays/agileRequirements–BestPractices.htm (Access: 2005/11)), 2005.

[AMR06] Aliakseyeu, D.; Martens, J.-B.; Rauterberg M.: *A computer support tool for the early stages of architectural design.* Interacting with Computers 18, pp.528–555, 2006.

[AMW02] Atwood, M.E.; McCain, K.W; Williams, J.C.: *How Does the Design Community Think About Design.* IN: Designing Interactive Systems – Proceedings of the 4th conference on Designing interactive systems: processes, practices, methods, and techniques, pp.125–132, London 2002.

[ANR+06] Aizenbud-Reshef, N.; Nolan, B. T.; Rubin, J.; Shaham-Gafni, Y.: *Model Traceability.* IBM Systems Journal; vol. 45(3), pp.515–526, 2006.

[AR05] Arkley, P.; Riddle, S: *Overcoming the Traceability Benefit Problem.* In: Proceedings of the 13th IEEE International Conference on Requirements Engineering (RE'05), 2005.

[ARTISAN] Homepage of the UML Design Tool Artisan Studio: http://www.artisansoftwaretools.com/ (Access: 2010/09).

[ASCET] Homepage of the Design Tool ETAS ASCET: http://www.etas.com/de/products/–ascet_software_products.php (Access: 2010/09).

[ASP09] Assawamekin N. Sunetnanta T. Pluempitiwiriyawej C.: *Deriving traceability relationships of multiperspective software artifacts from ontology matching.* 10th ACIS International Conference on Software Engineering, Artificial Intelligences, Networking and Parallel/Distributed Computing (SNPD), Daegu, South Korea, May 2009.

[AutomotiveSPICE] Homepage of the Automotive-SPICE Gremium: http://www.automotivespice.com (Access: 2010/05).

[ASPICE08a] Automotive Special Interest Group: *Automotive SPICE Process Assessment Model, v. 2.4,* Sept. 2008.

[ASPICE08b] Automotive Special Interest Group: *Automotive SPICE Process Reference Model, v. 4.4*, Sept. 2008.

[Ba96] Balzert, H.: *Lehrbuch der Software-Technik: Software-Entwicklung*, Spektrum Akademischer Verlag Heidelberg, Berlin, Oxford, 1996.

[BA96] Bohner, S. A.; Arnold, R.S.: *Software change impact analysis*. IEEE Computer Society Press, 1996.

[Ba98] Balzert, H.: *Lehrbuch der Software-Technik: Software Management, Software Qualitätssicherung, Unternehmensmodellierung*. Spektrum Akademischer Verlag, Heidelberg, Berlin, 1998.

[BB04] Burge, J.E.; Brown, D.C.: *An integrated approach for software design checking using rationale*. In: Gero, J (ed.): Design Computing and Cognition '04. Kluwer Academic, pp.557-576, 2004.

[BB06] Burge, J.E.; Brown, D.C.: *Rationale-Based Support for Software Maintenance*. In: [DMM+06], pp.273-296, 2006.

[BC87] Beck, K.; Cunningham, W.: *Using Pattern Languages for Object-Oriented Programs*. OOPSLA-87 Workshop on the Specification and Design for Object-Oriented Programming, 1987 (Online version: http://c2.com/doc/oopsla87.html (Access: 2009/06)), 1987.

[BCK03] Bass, L.; Clements, P.; Kazman R.: *Software Architecture in Practice*. Second Edition. Addison-Wesley, Pearson Education Inc., Boston MA, 2003.

[BCN+06] Bass, L.; Clements, P.; Nord, R.L.; Stafford, J.: *Capturing and Using Rationale for a Software Architecture*. In: [DMMP06], 2006.

[BCM+08] Burge, J.E.; Carroll, J.M.; McCall, R.; Mistrik, I.: *Rationale-Based Software Engineering*. Springer Verlag Berlin Heidelberg 2008.

[BD03] Bilda, Z.; Demirkan, H.: *An insight on designers' sketching activities in traditional versus digital media*. Design Studies Volume 24, Issue 1, pp.27-50, Jan. 2003.

[BDS+98] Beedle, M.; Devos, M.; Sharon, Y.; Schwaber, K.; Sutherland, J.: *SCRUM: An extension pattern language for hyperproductive software development* (Online version: http://hillside.net/plop/plop98/final_submissions/P49.pdf; (Access: 2009/06)), 1998.

[Be00a] Beck, K.: *Extreme Programming: Das Manifest. Muenchen*. Addison Wesley Longman Inc., 2000.

[Be00b] Beck, K.: *Extreme Programming Explained.* Addison-Wesley, Reading, MA 2000.

[Be04] Berry, D.M.: *The Inevitable Pain of Software Development: Why There Is No Silver Bullet.* In: Radical Innovations of Software and Systems Engineering in the Future, Springer Berlin / Heidelberg, pp.50-74, 2004.

[Be08] Beck, K.: *Implementation Patterns – Der Weg zu einfacherer und kostengünstigerer Programmierung.* Addison Wesley, München, Germany 2008.

[BEK+98] Boehm, B.; Egyed, A.; Kwan, J.; Port, D.; Shah, A.; Madachy, R.: *Using the WinWin spiral model: A case study.* IEEE Computer 7, pp.33–44, 1998.

[BG06] Bozheva, T.; Gallo, M.E.: *Defining Agile Patterns* IN: [DMM+06], pp.373-390, 2006.

[BGK+07] Broy, M.; Geisberger, E.; Kazmeier, J.; Rudorfer, A.; Beetz, K.: *Ein Requirement-Engineering Referenzmodell.* Informatik Spektrum Band 30 Heft 3; Juni 2007.

[BGP06] Bilda, Z.; Gero, J.S.; Purcell, T.: *To sketch or not to sketch? That is the question.* Design Studies Volume 27, Issue 5, pp.587-613, Sept. 2006.

[BGT+04] Bozorgzadeh, E.; Ghiasi, S.; Takahashi A.; Sarrafzadeh, M.: *Incremental Timing Budget Management in Programmable Systems.* International Conference on Embedded and Reconfigurable Systems and Architecture, pp.240-246, July 2004.

[BHJ+10] Birk, A.; Heller, G.; Janzen, D.; Reiser, M.-O.: *Wo steht das Requirements-Engineering? – Bewertung und Gegenüberstellung von RE-Frameworks.* Softwaretechnik-Trends 30:1, pp.6-7, Feb. 2010.

[BHM01] Benediktsson, O.; Hunter, R.; McGettrick, A.D.: *Processes for Software in Safety Critical Systems.* Software Process: Improvement and Practice, vol. 6 issue 1, pp.47-62, 2001.

[BHS07] Buschmann, F.; Henney, K.; Schmidt, D.C.: *Pattern-oriented software architecture: On patterns and pattern languages.* Vol. 5; John Wiley & Sons Ltd, England, 2007.

[BHV09] Bella, F.; Hörmann, K.; Vanamali, B.: *From CMMI to SPICE – Experiences on How to Survive a SPICE Assessment Having Already Implemented CMMI.* Lecture Notes in Computer Science Volume 5089, Springer Berlin / Heidelberg, pp.133-142, 2009.

[BJ91] Boerstler, J.; Janning, T.: *Bridging the gap between Requirements Engineering and Design.* In: Proc. 15th International Computer Software & Application Conference, 1991.

[BJ92] Boerstler, J.; Janning, T.: *Traceability between Requirements and Design: A Transformational Approach.* In: Proc. 16th International Computer Software & Application Conference, 1992.

[BJL98] Booch, G.; Jacobson, I.; Rumbaugh, J.: *The Unified Modeling Language User Guide.* Addison-Wesley, 1998.

[BK06] Boehm, B.; Kitapci, H.: *The WinWin Approach: Using a Requirements Negotiation Tool for Rationale Capture and Use.* In: [DMM+06]; pp.173-190, 2006.

[Blo95] Bloch, P.: *Seeking the ideal form: Product design and Consumer Response.* Journal of Marketing 59, pp.16-29, 1995.

[BLO+06] Briand, L.C.; Labiche, Y.; O'Sullivan, L.; Sówka, M.M.: *Automated impact analysis of UML models.* Journal of Systems and Software 79, pp.339-352, 2006.

[BMH+98] Brown, W.H.; Malveau, R. C.; McCormick, H.W.; Mowbray, T.J.: *AntiPatterns – Refactoring Software, Architectures, and Projects in Crisis.* New York, John Wiley & Sons, Inc., 1998.

[BMR+00] Buschmann, F.; Meunier, R.; Rohnert, H.; Sommerlad, P.; Stal, M.: *Patternori entierte Softwarearchitektur. Ein Pattern-System.* Addison-Wesley, München, 2000.

[Bo82] Boehm, B.: *Software Engineering Economics.* Prentice-Hall 1982.

[Bo91] Bohner, S. A.: *Software Change Impact Analysis for Design Evolution.* In: Proc. 8th International Conference on Software Maintenance and Reengineering, 1991.

[Bo94] Booch, G.: *Objektorientierte Analyse und Design: Mit praktischen Anwendungsbeispielen.* Addison-Wesley, 1994.

[Bo00a] Boehm, B.: *Requirements that Handle IKIWISI, COTS, and Rapid Change.* IEEE Computer, Vol. 33, No. 7, pp.99-102, July 2000.

[Bo00b] Bosch, J.: *Design and Use of Software Architectures – Adopting and evolving a product-line approach.* Pearson Education Limited, Harlow, 2000.

[Bo05] Boehm B.: *The Future of Software and Systems Engineering Processes.* (Online version: http://sunset.usc.edu/publications/TECHRPTS/2005/usccse2005-507/usccse 2005-507.pdf (Access: 2006/10)), 2005.

[Bo01] Borchers, J.O.: *A Pattern Approach to Interaction Design.* John Wiley & Sons LTD. Chichester, England, 2001.

[BP06] Brcina, R.; Prechtel, M.: *Feature-orientierte Plattformentwicklung und Verfolgbarkeit.* Softwaretechnik-Trends, Band 26 Heft 4, pp.3-8, 2006.

[Br87] Brooks, F. P.: *No Silver Bullet: Essence and Accidents of Software Engineering.* IEEE Computer Vol. 20(4), pp.10-19, 1987.

[Br95] Brooks F. P.: *The Mythical Man-Month – 20th Anniversary Edition.* Addison Wesley, Reading MA, 1995.

[BR00] Bennett, K.H.; Rajlich, V.T.: *Software maintenance and evolution: A roadmap.* IN: ICSE '00: Proceedings of the International Conference on The Future of Software Engineering, Limerick, Ireland, ACM,New York, USA, pp.73-87, 2000.

[Br06] Broy, M.: *Challenges in Automotive Software Engineering.* Proceeding of the 28th international conference on Software engineering, Shanghai, pp.33-42, 2006.

[Br07a] Brcina, R.: *Arbeiten zur Verfolgbarkeit und Aspekte des Verfolgbarkeitsprozesses.* Softwaretechnik-Trends 27:1, pp.3-8, Feb. 2007.

[BR07b] Broy, M.; Rumpe B.: *Modulare hierarchische Modellierung als Grundlage der Software- und Systementwicklung.* InformatikSpektrum Band 30 Heft 1, pp.3-18, Feb. 2007.

[BRS05] Bauer, A.; Romberg, J.; Schätz, B.: *Integrierte Entwicklung von Automotive-Software mit AutoFOCUS.* Informatik Forschung und Entwicklung Band 19; Heft 4, pp.194-205, July 2005.

[BSA07] Blaauboer, F.; Sikkel, K.; Aydin, M.N.: *Deciding to adopt requirements traceability in practice.* Lecture Notes in Computer Science Volume 4495, pp.294-308, 2007.

[BSS+06] Buckingham Shum, S.J.; Selvin, A.M.; Sierhuis, M.; Conklin, J.; Haley, C.B.; Nuseibeh, B.: *Hypermedia Support for Argumentation-Based Rationale: 15 Years on from gIBIS and QOC.* In: [DMM+06], pp.111-132, 2006.

[BT04] Boehm, B.; Turner, R.: *Balancing Agility and Discipline – A guide for the perplexed.* Addison Wesley, Pearson Education, Boston MA, 2004.

[Bu96] Buchanan, R.: *Wicked Problems in Design Thinking.* In: Margolin, V.; Buchanan, R. (Eds): The Idea of Design, The MIT Press, pp.3-20, Feb. 1996.

[CBB+03] Clements, P.; Bachmann, F.; Bass, L.; Garlan, D.; Ivers, J. Little, R.; Nord, R.; Stafford, J.: *Documenting Software Architectures: Views and Beyond.* Addison-Wesley, Pearson Education, Boston MA, 2003.

[CCL00] Canfora, G.; Casazza, G.; Lucia, A.d.: *A Design Rationale Based Environment for Cooperative Maintenance.* International Journal of Software Engineering and Knowledge Engineering (IJSEKE), Vol 10, Issue 5, pp.627-645, 2000.

[Co90] Coggins, J: *Design and Management of C+ Libraries.* Chapel Hill, North Carolina: University of North Carolina, 1990.

[CB88] Conklin, J; Begeman, M: *gIBIS: A hypertext tool for exploratory policy discussion.* ACM Transactions On Information Systems. Vol. 6, Issue 4, pp.303-331, 1988.

[CB96] Conklin, E.J.; Burgess-Yakemovic, K.C.: *A process-oriented approach to design rationale.* In: [MC96], pp.393-427, 1996.

[CBS+02] Chen, C.; Bozorgzadeh, E.; Srivastava, A.; Sarrafzadeh, M.: *Budget Management with Applications.* Algorithmica 34, pp.261-275, 2002.

[CBV07] Conklin, J.; Basadur, M.; Van Patter, G.K.: *Rethinking Wicked Problems.* NextD Journal Issue TEN, Conversation 10.1, (Online version: http://www.nextd.org/pdf_− download/NextD_10_1.pdf, (Access: 2009/05)), 2007.

[CCC03] Cleland-Huang, J.; Chang, C.K.; Christensen, M.: *Event-Based Traceability for Managing Evolutionary Change.* IEEE Transactions on Software Engineering vol. 29(9), pp.796–810, 2003

[CFG+05] Conrad, M.; Fey, I.; Grochtmann, M.; Klein, T.: *Modellbasierte Entwicklung eingebetteter Fahrzeugsoftware bei DaimlerChrysler.* Informatik Forschung und Entwicklung Band 20 Heft 1-2, pp.3-10, Oct. 2005.

[Ch67] Churchman., C.W.: *Wicked Problems. Guest Editorial, Management Science,* vol. 4 no. 14, pp.141-142, 1967.

[CKK02] Clements, P.; Kazman, R.; Klein, M.: *Evaluating Software Architectures − Methods and case studies.* Addison-Wesley, 2002.

[CKS+09] Chanda, J.; Kanjilal, A.; Sengupta, S.; Bhattacharya, S.: *Traceability of requirements and consistency verification of UML use case, activity and Class diagram: a formal approach.* International Conference on Methods and Models in Computer Science (ICM2CS), pp.1-4, Piscataway, NJ, USA, 2009.

[Cl05] Cleland-Huang, J.: *Toward improved traceability of non-functional requirements.* In: Proceedings of the 3rd international Workshop on *Traceability* in Emerging Forms of Software Engineering (TEFSE '05), Long Beach, California, Nov. 2005.

[Cl06] Cleland-Huang J: *Just enough requirements traceability.* 30th Annual International Computer Software and Applications Conference COMPSAC 2006 (IEEE Cat. No. 06P2655), pp.2-3, Piscataway, NJ, USA, 2006.

[CL09] Chang, H.-F.; Lu, S. C-Y.: *Decomposition and Traceability in Software Design.* 33rd Annual IEEE International Computer Software and Applications Conference, pp.13-18, 2009.

[CNY+00] Chung, L.; Nixon, B.A.; Yu, E.; Mylopoulos, J.: *Non-Functional Requirements in Software Engineering.* Kluwer Academic, Dordrecht, 2000.

[Co68] Conway, M.E.: *How do committees invent?* Datamation, 14,4, pp.28-31, April 1968.

[Co89] Conklin, J.: *Design Rationale and maintainability.* In: Proceedings 22nd annual Hawaii international conference on system science, Vol. 2, Los Alamitos, CA, USA. IEEE Computer Society, pp.533-539, 1989.

[Co95] Coplien, J. O.: *A generative development-process pattern language.* In: [CS95], pp.183-237, 1995.

[Co00] Cockburn, A.: *Writing Effective Use Cases.* Addison-Wesley Professional 2000.

[Compendium] Compendium Institute: Homepage of the Rationale Management Tool Compendium: http://compendium.open.ac.uk/institute/index.htm (Access: 2009/05).

[Co05] R. Coyne: *Wicked problems revisited.* Design Studies Volume 26, Issue 1, pp.5-17, January 2005.

[Co06] Conklin, J.: *Dialogue Mapping: Building Shared Understanding of Wicked Problems.* John Wiley and Sons, Ltd., Jan. 2006.

[CR92] Carroll, J.M.; Rosson, M.B.: *Getting around the task-artifact cycle: how to make claims and design by scenario.* ACM Transactions for Information Systems Vol. 10(2); pp.181-212, 1992.

[CR98] Carroll, J.M.; Rosson,M.B.; Chin, G. Jr.; Koenemann, J.: *Requirements development in scenario-based design.* IEEE Transactions of Software Engineering 24(12), pp.1156-1170, 1998.

[CRF+06] Cuesta, C. E.; Romay, M.P.; Fuente, P.d.l.; Barrio-Solórzano, M.: *Coordination as an Architectural Aspect.* In: Electronic Notes in Theoretical Computer Science 154, pp.25–41, 2006.

[Cs90] Csikszentmihalyi, M.: Flow: *The Psychology of Optimal Experience.* Harper Perennial, New York, 1990.

[CS95] Coplien, J. O.; Schmidt, D. C. (Eds.): *Pattern languages of program design.* ACM Press/Addison-Wesley Professional, New York, 1995.

[CSL+01] Carlshamre, P.; Sandahl, K.; Lindvall, M.; Regnell, B.; Natt och Dag, J.: *An Industrial Survey of Requirements Interdependencies in Software Product Release Planning.* Fifth IEEE International Symposium on Requirements Engineering (RE'01), 2001.

[CS03] Cleland-Huang, J.; Schmelzer, D.: *Dynamically Tracing Non-Functional Requirements through Design Pattern Invariants.* In: Proceedings of the Second International Workshop on *Traceability* in Emerging Forms of Software Engineering (TEFSE'03), 2003.

[CSB+05] Cleland-Huang, J.; Settimi, R.; BenKhadra, O.; Berezhanskaya, E.; Christina, S.: *Goal-centric Traceability for Managing Non-functional Requirements.* In: Proceedings of the 27th International Conference on Software Engineering (ICSE'05), pp.: 362–371, 2005.

[CSD+05] Cleland-Huang, J., Settimi, R., Duan, C., Zou, X.: *Utilizing Supporting Evidence to Improve Dynamic Requirements Traceability.* In: Proceedings of the 13th IEEE International Requirements Engineering Conference (RE 2005), pp.135–144, 2005.

[CKI88] Curtis, B.; Krasner, H.; Iscoe, N.: *A field study of the software design process for large systems.* Communications of the ACM 31, 11, 1988.

[CNY+99] Chung, L.; Nixon, B. A.; Yu, E.; Mylopoulos, J.: *Non-functional requirements in software engineering.* Kluwer Academic Publishers International Series in Software Engineering, Vol. 5, Springer October, 1999.

[Cu90] Curtis, B.: *Empirical studies of the Software Design Process.* In: Proc. Human Computer Interaction Interact '90. Amsterdam, 1990.

[Cu92] Curtis, B.: *Insights from empirical studies of the software design process.* Future Generation Computing Systems, 7 (2-3), pp.139-149, 1992.

[CY04] Cysneiros, L.M.; Yu, E.: *Non-Functional Requirements Elicitation.* In: [PD04], pp.115-138, 2004.

[DAU01] Defense Acquisition University (Eds.): *Systems Engineering Fundamentals.* Defense Acquisition University Press, Jan. 2001.

[DC04] Dick; J.; Chard, J.: *The Systems Engineering Sandwich: Combining Requirements, Models and Design.* (Online version: http://www.telelogic.com/corp/download/index.cfm?–id=3640; (Access: 2006/06)), 2004.

[De78] DeMarco, T.: *Structured Analysis and Systems Specifications*, Yourdon Press Computing Series, 1978.

[De99] Dellen, B.: *Change Impact Analysis Support for Software Development Processes.* Phd thesis. Department of Computer Science, University of Kaiserslautern, Germany, 1999.

[De04] DeMarco, T.: *Was man nicht messen kann, kann man nicht kontrollieren.* Mitp-Verlag, Bonn, 2004.

[DH03] Dunkel, J.; Holitschke, A.: *Softwarearchitektur für die Praxis.* Springer-Verlag Berlin Heidelberg, 2003.

[DHM98] Dröschel, W.; Heuser, W.; Midderhoff, R. (Eds.): *Inkrementelle und objektorientierte Vorgehensweisen mit dem V-Modell 97.* Oldenbourg, München, 1998.

[DGN+00] Do, E.Yi-L., Gross, M.D., Neiman, B.; Zimring, C: *Intentions in and relations among design drawings.* Design Studies Vol 21 No 5 pp 483-503, 2000.

[DIN69905] DIN 69905: *Projektabwicklung, Begriffe.* May 1997.

[Di04a] Diederichs, H.: *Komplexitätsreduktion in der Softwareentwicklung – Ein systemtheoretischer Ansatz.* Books on Demand Gmbh, Norderstedt, 2004.

[Di04b] Dittert, K.: *Softwarearchitektur: Mythen und Legenden.* OBJEKTspektrum 3/2004, pp.34-39, 2004.

[DK96] Domeshek, E.; Kolodner, J.L.: *The Desiners' Muse: Providing Experience to Aid Conceptual Design of Complex Artifacts*. In: Maher, M.L.; Pu, p.(eds.): Issues and Applications of Case-Based Reasoning to Design, Lawrence Erlbaum Associates, Mahway, NJ, pp.11-38, 1996.

[DKM96] Dellen, B.; Kohler, K.; Maurer, F.: *Integrating Software Process Models and Design Rationales*. In. Proceedings of 11th Knowledge-Based Software Engineering Conference (KBSE '96), Syracuse, NY, pp.84-93, 1996.

[DLL09] Dong, L.; Li, Y.; Li, J.: *Improved method of dynamic requirement traceability based on code comments*. Computer Engineering and Design, Vol. 30, No.1, 16 Jan. 2009, pp.113-115, 221, 2009.

[DMM+06] Dutoit, A.; McCall, R.; Mistrik, I.; Paech, B (Eds.): *Rationale Management in Software Engineering*. Springer, Berlin 2006.

[DMM+06a] Dutoit, A.; McCall, R.; Mistrik, I.; Paech, B.: *Rationale Management in Software Engineering: Concepts and Techniques*. In: [DMM+06], Springer, Berlin 2006.

[Do03] Douglass, B.P.: *Real-Time Design Patterns: Robust Scalable Architecture for Real-Time Systems*. Addison Wesley, Pearson Education, Boston, 2003.

[Do04] Douglass, B.P.: *Real Time UML Third Edition – Advances in the UML for Real-Time Systems*. Addison Wesley, Pearson Education, Boston, 2004.

[Do05] Douglas, I.: *Capturing and managing decision making rationale*. IEEE International Conference on Information Reuse and Integration, pp.172 – 176, Aug. 2005.

[DP98] Dömges, R.; Pohl, K.: *Adapting Traceability Environments to Project-Specific Needs*. Communications of the ACM, Vol. 41, No. 12, pp.54-62, 1998.

[DP02] Dutoit A, Paech B.: *Rationale-Based Use Case Specification*. Requirements Engineering Journal. vol. 7, no 1, pp.3-19, 2002.

[Eb98] Ebert, C.: *Putting requirements management into praxis: dealing with nonfunctional requirements*. Information and Software Technology 40, pp.175-185, 1998.

[Eb05] Ebert, C.: *Systematisches Requirements Management Anforderungen ermitteln, spezifizieren, analysieren und verfolgen*. dpunkt Verlag GmbH, Heidelberg, 2005.

[Eb08] Ebert, C.: *Systematisches Requirements Engineering und Management – Anforderungen ermitteln, spezifizieren, analysieren und verwalten*. 2. aktualisierte und erweiterte Auflage. dpunkt Verlag GmbH, Heidelberg, 2008.

[Ec03] Eckel, B.; Allison, C.: *Thinking in Java*. 3rd Edition, Prentice Hall, New Jersey, 2003.

[Ec04] Eckstein, J.: *Agile Softwareentwicklung im Grossen – Ein Eintauchen in die Untiefen erfolgreicher Projekte*. dpunkt Verlag GmbH, Heidelberg 2004.

[EDG+06] Espinoza, H.; Dubois, H.; Gérard, S.; Medina, J.; Petriu, D.; Woodside, M.: *Annotating UML Models with Non-Functional Properties for quantitative analysis*. In: Lecture Notes in Computer Science; Volume 3844, Heidelberg, pp.79-90, 2006.

[Ee05] Eeles, P.: *Capturing Architectural Requirements*. DeveloperWorks, July 2005, (Online version: http://www-128.ibm.com/developerworks/rational/library/4706.html; Access 2008/11), 2005.

[EFS98] Ebeling, W.; Freund, J.; Schweitzer, F.: *Komplexe Strukturen: Entropie und Information*. Teuber, Leipzig, 1998.

[Eg03] Egyed, A: *A Scenario-driven approach to trace dependency analysis*. IEEE Transactions on Software Engineering, 29(2), pp.116-132, February 2003.

[EG04] Egyed, A.; Grünbacher, P.: *Indentifying Requirements Conflicts and Cooperation: How Quality Attributes and Automated Traceability Can Help*. IEEE SW, Nov./Dec. 2004.

[EGH+07] Egyed, A.; Grünbacher, P.; Heindl, M.; Biffl, S.: *Value-Based Requirements Traceability: Lessons Learned*. 15th IEEE International Requirements Engineering Conference 2007.

[Eh88] Ehn, P.: *Playing the language-games of design and use-on skill and participation*. IN: Proceedings of the ACM SIGOIS and IEEECS TC-OA 1988 conference on Office information systems, Palo Alto, California, pp.142—157, 1988.

[Eh89] Ehn, P.: *Work-oriented design of computer artifacts*. Hillsdale, NJ: Lawrence Erlbaum Associates, 1989.

[Em10] Emmanuel, T.: *Planguage – Spezifikation nichtfunktionaler Anforderungen*. Informatik Spektrum 33 (3), pp.292-295, 2010.

[ER03] Endres, A.; Rombach, D.: *A Handbook of Software and Systems Engineering – Empirical Observations, Laws and Theory*. Addison Wesley 2003.

[ESS02] El-Ramly, M.; Stroulia, E.; Sorenson, P.: *Mining System-User Interaction Traces for Use Case Models*. In: Proceedings of the 10th international Workshop on Program Comprehension (IWPC'02), IEEE Computer Society, Washington, DC, pp.21-29, 2002.

[Fa95] Faulk, S.R.: *Software requirements: A tutorial.* NRL report 7775, Naval Research Laboratory, Washington DC, 1995.

[Fe86] Feyerabend, P.: *Wider den Methodenzwang.* Taschenbuch Wissenschaft 597, Erste Auflage, Suhrkamp Verlag Frankfurt am Main, 1986.

[FGH+94] Finkelstein, A.C.W.; Gabbay, D.; Hunter, A.; Kramer, J., Nuseibeh, B.: *Inconsistency handling in multiperspective specifications.* IEEE Transactions on Software Engineering, Vol.20, No.8, pp.569-578, 1994.

[FGS+01] Fornarciary, W.; Gubian, P.; Sciuto, D.; Silvano, Ch.: *Power estimation of embedded systems: A Hardware/Software codesign approach.* In: Micheli, G; Ernst, R.: Readings in Hardware/Software Co-Design. Morgan Kaufmann 2001, pp.249-258, 2001.

[Fi91] Finkelstein, A. C. W.: *Tracing back from requirements.* In: Tools and Techniques for Maintaining Traceability During Design IEE Colloquium, Computing and Control Division, Professional Group C1 (Software Engineering), Digest Number: 1991/180, December 2, pp.7/1-7/2, 1991.

[Fi98] Filman, R.E.: *Achieving ilities.* In: Proceedings of the Workshop on Compositional Software Architectures, Monterey, CA, 1998.

[FK07] Fritzsche, M.; Keil, P.: *Agilität und Prozessreife: Erfüllbarkeit der CMMI – Prozessgebiete durch agile Methoden am Beispiel von XP.* IN: Software Engineering 2007 (SE 2007). Bonn: Köllen Verlag [= Lecture Notes in Informatics, Vol. 105]. pp.95-106, 2007.

[FL02] Fettke, P.; Loos, P.: *Methoden zur Wiederverwendung von Referenzmodellen – Übersicht und Taxonomie.* In: Becker, J.;Knackstedt, R. (Eds.): Referenzmodellierung 2002. Methoden – Modelle – Erfahrungen, Münster, pp.9-33, 2002.

[FLM+96] Fischer, G.; Lemke, A.C.; McCall, R.; Morch, A.I.: *Making argumentation serve design.* In: [MC96], pp.267–293, 1996.

[FMM89] Fischer, G.; McCall, R.; Morch, A.I.: *JANUS: Integrating hypertext with a knowledge-based design.* Proceedings of the second annual ACM conference on Hypertext, pp.105-117, 1989.

[Fo97] Fowler, M.: *Analysis Patterns – Reusable Object Models.* Addison Wesley Pearson Education, Indianapolis, 1997.

[Fo99] Fowler, M.: *Refactoring: Improving the Design of Existing Code.* Addison Wesley Longman Inc., New York, 1999.

[Fo02] Fowler, M.: *Patterns of Enterprise Application Architecture.* Addison-Wesley Longman Publishing Co., Inc., Boston, MA, USA, 2002.

[Fo03] Fowler, M.: *Design – Who needs an Architect?* IEEE SW Volume 20, Issue 5, pp.11-13, Sept.-Oct. 2003.

[Ga86] Gall, J.: Systemantics: *How systems really work and how they fail.* Second Edition. Ann Arbor, MI: The General Systemantics Press, 1986.

[GB08] Gallagher, K.; Binkley, D.: *Program Slicing.* Frontiers of Software Maintenance, Beijing, China, October 1-4, 2008.

[GC87] *Grady, R.; Caswell, D.: Software Metrics: Establishing a Company-wide Program. Prentice Hall, 1987.*

[GDM+10] Groß, A.; Dörr, J.; Menzel, I.; Müller, M.: *Experimenteller Vergleich zweier Techniken zur Anforderungsspezifikation. Use Cases vs. Funktionale Spezifikation.* Softwaretechnik-Trends 30:1, pp.14-15, Feb 2010.

[GEM01] Gruenbacher, P.; Egyed, A.; Medvidovic, N.: *Reconciling software requirements and architectures: The CBSP Approach.* Proceedings Fifth IEEE International Symposium on Requirements Engineering, pp.202-221, 2001.

[GEM03] Gruenbacher, P.; Egyed, A.; Medvidovic, N.: *Reconciling software requirements and architectures with intermediate models.* Software and Systems Modeling 3, August 01, pp.235-253, 2004.

[Ge05] Geisberger, E.: *Requirement Engineering eingebetteter Systeme.* Dissertation Shaker 2005.

[GF94] Gotel, O.C.Z.; Finkelstein, A.C.W.: *An analysis of the requirements traceability problem.* Proceedings of ICRE94, 1st International Conference on Requirements Engineering 1994, Colorado Springs, Co; IEEE CS Press, pp.94-101, 1994.

[GF95] Gotel, O.C.Z.; Finkelstein, A.C.W.: *Contribution Structures.* Proceedings of the Second IEEE International Symposium on Requirements Engineering (RE '95), 1995.

[GF96] Gotel, O.C.Z.; Finkelstein, A.C.W.: *Extended Requirements Traceability: Results of an Industrial Case Study*. In: Proc. 3Th International Symposium on Requirements Engineering, pp.169-178. 1996.

[GGJ+00] Gunter, C. A.; Gunter, E. L.; Jackson, M.; Zave, P.: *A Reference Model for Requirements and Specifications*. IEEE Software Vol. 17, Issue 3, pp.37-43, May 2000.

[GG03] Goldenson, D.; Gibson, D.: *Demonstrating the Impact and Benefits of CMMI: An Update and Preliminary Results*. Special Report CMU/SEI-2003-SR-003, Software Engineering Institute, Carnegie Mellon University, 2003.

[GG05] Gerlich, R.; Gerlich, R.: *111 Thesen zur erfolgreichen Softwareentwicklung – Argumente und Entscheidungshilfen für Manager, Konzepte und Anleitungen für Praktiker*. Springer, Berlin, Heidelberg, New York, 2005.

[GG07] Galvao, I.; Goknil, A.: *Survey of Traceability Approaches in Model-Driven Engineering*. IN: EDOC '07: Proceedings of the 11th IEEE International Enterprise Distributed Object Computing Conference, pp.313-324, 2007.

[GHJ+95] Gamma, E.; Helm, R.; Johnson, R.; Vlissides, J.: *Design Patterns: Elements of Reusable Object-Oriented Software*. Addison-Wesley, Reading, MA, 1995.

[Gi05] Gilb, T.: *Competitive Engineering*, 1. Edition, Elsevier Butterworth Heinemann, Amsterdam, 2005.

[GM57] Goode, H.; Machol R.: *Systems Engineering: An Introduction to the Design of Large-Scale Systems*. McGraw-Hill, New York 1957.

[GK07] Gross, T.; Koch, M.: *Computer-Supported Cooperative Work*. Oldenbourg, München, 2007.

[GL91] Gallagher, K.B.; Lyle, J.R.: *Using Program Slicing in Software Maintenance*. IEEE Transactions on Software Engineering, Vol. 17, No. 8, pp.751-761, 1991.

[Gl02] Glass, R.L.: *Sorting Out Software Complexity*. Communications of the ACM Vol. 45, No. 11, Nov. 2002.

[Go95] Goel, V.: *Sketches of Thought*. MIT Press, Cambridge, MA, 1995.

[Go96] Goguen, J.A.: *Formality and informality in requirements engineering*. Proceedings of ICRE 96, 2nd International Conference on Requirements Engineering, 1996, April 15-18, Colorado Springs, Colorado, IEEE Computer Society Press, 1996.

[Go99] Goel, V.: *Cognitive roles of ill-structured representations in preliminary design*. In: J.S. Gero and B. Tversky (eds.) Visual and spacial reasoning in design, MIT, Cambridge, KCDCC, University of Sydney, Australia, (Online version: http://wwwfaculty.arch.usyd.edu.au/kcdc/books/VR99/goel.html; Access: 2009/05), pp.131-144, 1999.

[GP04] Gerdom, M.; Posch, T.: *Pragmatische Software-Architektur für Automotive Systeme*. OBJEKTspektrum 05/2004; (Online version: http://www.sigs.de/publications/os/2004/05/gerdom_posch_OS_05_04.pdf   (Access 2005/11)), pp.64-66, 2004.

[Gr87] Grudin, J.: *Social evaluation of the user interface: Who does the work and who gets the benefit*. In: INTERACT'87. IFIP Conference on Human and Computer Interaction. Stuttgart, Germany, pp.805-811, 1987.

[Gr88] Grudin, J.: *Why CSCW applications fail: problems in the design and evaluation of organization of organizational interfaces*. In: Proceedings of the ACM Conference on Computer-supported Cooperative Work 1988, ACM, New York, pp.85-93, 1988.

[Gr92] Grady, R.B.: *Practical Software Metrics for Project Management and Process Improvement*. Prentice Hall, 1992.

[GR96a] Gruber, T.R.; Russell, D.M.: *Generative design rationale: Beyond the record and replay paradigm*. In: [MC96], pp.323–349, 1996.

[Gr96b] Grudin, J.: *Evaluating opportunities for design capture*. In: [MC96], 1996.

[Gr03] Graham, B.: *Requirements Traceability for Embedded Systems*. Embedded Systems Conference Class 323, April 22-26, 2003.

[Gr05] Grimm, K.: *Software-Technologie im Automobil*. In: [LR05], pp.407–430, 2005.

[GSC+04] Greenfield, J.; Short, K.; Cook, S.; Kent, S.: *Software Factories – Assembling Applications with Patterns, Models, Frameworks and Tools*. Wiley & Sons Publishing Inc, Indianapolis, 2004.

[Gu03] Gullapalli, V.: *Best practices improve hierarchical design constraints*. Tech Online, Nov. 2003, (Online version: http://www.eetimes.com/news/design/showArticle.jhtml;jsessionid=O4YQ3DC1YP CQKQSNDLRSKHSCJUNN2JVN?articleID=16502497&printable=true   (Access 2007/12)), 2003.

[Ha72] Haney, F.M.: *Module connection analysis – A tool for scheduling software debugging analysis*. Proceedings of AFIPS Joint Computer Conference, pp.173-179, 1972.

[Ha87] Harel, D.: *State Charts: A visual formalism for complex systems.* Science of computer programming, pp.231-274. 1987.

[Ha99] Hause, M.: *Successfully Managing An Incremental Real-Time Project; Part Three: Requirements Management.* Whitepaper at Artisan Software (Online version: http://www.artisansw.com (Access 2005/10)), 1999.

[Ha00] Han, J.: *Experience with Designing a Requirements and Architecture Management Tool.* Proceedings of the International Conference on software Methods and Tools (SMT'00), pp.179-188, 2000.

[Ha01a] Hahsler, M.: *Analyse Patterns im Softwareentwicklungsprozess.* Dissertation, Abteilung für Informationswissenschaft, Wirtschaftsuniversität Wien, 2001.

[Ha01b] Han, J.: *TRAM: A Tool for Requirements and Architecture Management.* Australasian Computer Science Conference (ACSC '01), pp.60-68, 2001.

[Ha02] Hazzan, O.: *The reflective practitioner perspective in software engineering education.* Journal of Systems and Software Volume 63, Issue 3, pp.161–171, Sept. 2002.

[HA06a] Horner, J.; Atwood, M.E.: *Effective Design Rationale: Understanding the Barriers.* In [DMM+06], pp.72-90, 2006.

[Ha06b] Haynes, S.R.: *Three Studies of Design Rationale as Explanation.* In: [DMM+06], p.53-71, 2006.

[HAZ07] Harrison, N.B.; Avgerion, P.; Zdun, U.: *Using Patterns to Capture Architectural Decisions.* IEEE Software, pp.38-45, July/August 2007.

[HB91] Hamilton, V.L.; Beeby, M.L.: *Issues of Traceability in Integrating Tools.* Proceedings of IEE Colloquium on Tools and Techniques for Maintaining *Traceability* during Design, Dec.1991.

[HDH+06] Hörmann, K.; Dittmann, L.; Hindel, B.; Müller, M.: *SPICE in der Praxis, Interpretationshilfe für Anwender und Assessoren.* dpunkt Verlag GmbH, Heidelberg, 2006.

[HGK+09] Hove, D.; Goknil, A.; Kurtev, I.; Berg, K.v.d.; Goede, K.d.: *Change Impact Analysis for SysML Requirements Models based on Semantics of Trace Relations.* ECMDA Traceability Workshop, ECMDA-TW, Enschede NL, pp.17-28, 2009.

[HH04] Heumesser, N.; Houdek, F.: *Experiences in Managing an Automotive Requirements Engineering Process.* 12th IEEE International Requirements Engineering Conference, pp.322-327, 2004.

[HHL+06] Hagge, L.; Houdek, F.; Lappe, K.; Paech, B: *Using Patterns for Sharing Requirements Engineering Process Rationales.* In: [DMM+06], pp.409-427, 2006.

[HHP03] Hatley, D.; Hruschka, P.; Pirbhai, I.: *Komplexe Software-Systeme beherrschen.* MITP Verlag, 1. Auflage, Bonn, 2003.

[HHS64] Heiser, H.; Holzer, H.; Sommer, W.: *Budgetierung. Grundsätze und Praxis der betriebswirtschaftlichen Planung,* De Gruyter & Co., Berlin, 1964.

[HJD02] Hull, M. E. C.; Jackson, K.; Dick, A. J. J.: *Requirements Engineering.* Springer, London Berlin Heidelberg, 2002.

[HJL96] Heitmeyer, C.L.; Jeffords, R.D.; Labaw, B.G.: *Automated Consistency Checking of Requirements Specifications.* ACM Transactions on Software Engineering and Methodology Vol. 5 (3), pp.231–261, 1996.

[HKL09] Hsueh, N.-L.; Kuo, J-Y.; Lin, Ch.-Ch.: *Object-oriented design: A goal-driven and pattern-based approach.* Software and Systems Modeling, Volume 8, Issue 1, pp.67-84, Feb. 2009.

[HMC+07] Hood, C.; Mühlbauer, S.; Rupp Ch.; Versteegen, G.: *iX Studie 01/2007 Anforderungsmanagement.* 2. erweiterte Auflage, Heise Zeitschriften Verlag, Hannover, April 2007.

[HNS00] Hofmeister, C.; Nord, R.; Soni, D.: *Applied Software Architecture.* Addison-Wesley, 2000.

[HR02] Hruschka, P.; Rupp, Ch.: *Agile Softwareentwicklung für Embedded Real-Time Systems mit der UML.* Carl Hanser Verlag, München, 2002.

[HPW+99] Haumer, P.; Pohl, K.; Weidenhaupt, K.; Jarke, M.: *Improving reviews by extended traceability.* In: Proceedings 32nd Hawaii International Conference on System Sciences, 1999.

[HS06] Hruschka, P.; Starke, G.: *Praktische Architekturdokumentation: Wie wenig ist genau richtig?* OBJEKTspektrum, 01.2006, pp.53-57, 2006.

[HT03] Hunt, A.; Thomas, D.: *Der Pragmatische Programmierer.* Carl Hanser Verlag, München, 2003.

[HWA+07] Habli, I,; Weihang, W.; Attwood, K.; Kelly, T.: *Extending argumentation to goal-oriented requirements engineering.* Advances in Conceptual Modeling – Foundations and Applications. ER 2007 Workshops CMLSA, FP-UML, ONISW, QoIS, RIGiM, SeCoGIS. Springer-Verlag, Berlin, Germany, pp.306-316, 2007.

[HWF+08] Hood, C.; Wiedemann, S.; Fichtinger, S.; Pautz, U.: *Requirements Management – The interface Between Requirements Development and All Other Systems Engineering Processes.* Springer Verlag, Berlin Heidelberg, 2008.

[IBR+01] In, H.; Boehm, B.W.; Rodgers, T.; Deutsch, W.: *Applying WinWin to Quality Requirements: A Case Study.* ICSE, pp.555-564, 2001.

[IEC61508] IEC 61508: *Functional safety of electrical / electronic / programmable electronic safety-related systems (E/E/PES).* International Electrotechnical Commission, 1999-2005[273].

[IEEE1016] IEEE 1016-2009: *IEEE Recommended Practice for Software Design Descriptions.* Institute of Electrical and Electronics Engineers, 2009.

[IEEE1074] IEEE 1074-2006: *IEEE Standard for Developing Software Life Cycle Processes.* Institute of Electrical and Electronics Engineers, 2006.

[IEEE1220] IEEE 1220-1994[274]: *IEEE Standard for Application and Management of the Systems Engineering Process.* Institute of Electrical and Electronics Engineers, 1994.

[IEEE1220-2005] IEEE 1220-2005: *IEEE Standard for Application and Management of the Systems Engineering Process.* Institute of Electrical and Electronics Engineers, 2005.

[IEEE12207] IEEE/EIA 12207-2008: *Systems and Software Engineering – Software Life Cycle Processes (ISO/IEC 12207:2008(E)).* IEEE/EIA Standard for Industry Implementation of International Standard ISO/IEC 12207 [ISO12207], Standard for Information Technology-Software life cycle processes, International Electrotechnical Commission, 2008.

[IEEE1471] IEEE 1471-2000: *Recommended Practice for Architectural Description of Software-Intensive Systems.* Institute of Electrical and Electronics Engineers, 2000.

[IEEE610] IEEE 610: *IEEE Standard Glossary of Software Engineering Terminology.* Institute of Electrical and Electronics Engineers, 1990 (reaffirmed 2002), 2002.

[IEEE830-84] IEEE 830-1984: *IEEE Recommended Practice for Software Requirements Specifications.* Institute of Electrical and Electronics Engineers, 1984.

---

[273] Different parts have different release dates.
[274] Now replaced by [IEEE1220-2005].

[IEEE830-98] IEEE 830-1998: *Recommended Practice for Software Requirements Specifications*. Institute of Electrical and Electronics Engineers, 1998.

[IR97] Isenmann, S.; Reuter, W.D.: *IBIS – a Convincing Concept ... But a Lousy Instrument?* Symposium on Designing Interactive Systems, pp.163-172, 1997.

[ISO12207] ISO/IEC 12207: *Information Technology-Software Life-Cycle Processes*. International Standards Organization, International Electrotechnical Commission, 1995.

[ISO15504] ISO/IEC 15504: *Information Technology — Process Assessment*. International Standards Organization, International Electrotechnical Commission, 2003-2006.

[ISO15288] ISO/IEC 15288: *Systems and software engineering – System life cycle processes*. International Standards Organization, International Electrotechnical Commission, 2008.

[ISO26262] ISO/IEC 26262: *Road vehicles – Functional safety*. International Standards Organization, International Electrotechnical Commission, Draft 2009.

[ISO9126] ISO/IEC 9126: *Software engineering – Product quality*. International Standards Organization. International Standards Organization, International Electrotechnical Commission, 2001-2004.

[ISO25000] ISO/IEC 25000: *Software Engineering – Software product Quality Requirements and Evaluation (SQuaRE) – Guide to SQuaRE*. International Standards Organization, International Electrotechnical Commission, 2005.

[Ja72] Janis, I.L.: Victims of Group Think: *A Psychological Study of Foreign Policy Decisions and Fiascos*. Houghton-Mifflin, Boston, MA, 1972.

[Ja04] Jäälinoja, J.: *Requirements implementation in embedded software development*. VTT publications 526 (Online version: http://www.vtt.fi/inf/pdf/publications/2004/P526.pdf (Access: 2009/09)), VTT Technical Research Centre, Finland, 2004.

[Ja08] Jackson, M.: *The Name and Nature of Software Engineering*. In: Börger, E.; Cisternino, A. (Eds.): Advances in Software Engineering, Lipari Summer School, LNCS 5316, Springer Berlin Heidelberg, pp.1-38, 2008.

[Ja09] Jamshidi, M. (Eds.): *Systems of Systems Engineering: Principles and Applications*. CRC Press Tayöpr & Framcox Group, LLC, Boca Raton, 2009

[JB05] Jansen, A.; Bosch, J.: *Software Architecture as a Set of Architectural Design Decisions*. Proceedings of the 5th Working IEEE/IFIP Conference on Software Architecture (WICSA), pp.109-120, 2005.

[JL05] Jönsson, P.; Lindvall, M.: *Impact Analysis*. In: Aurum, A.; Wohlin, C. (Eds.): Engineering and Managing Software Requirements. Springer Verlag Berlin Heidelberg, pp.117-142, 2005.

[Jo02] Jones, C.: *Estimating Software Requirements*. CROSSTALK – The Journal of Defense Software Engineering, June 2002, (Online version: http://www.stsc.hill.af.mil/crosstalk/2002/06/jones.pdf (Access: 2010/09)), 2002.

[JPD+94] Jarke, M.; Pohl, K.; Dömges, R.; Jacobs, S.; Nissen, H.W.: *Requirements Information Management: The NATURE Approach*. Engineering of Information Systems 2, 6, (Online version: http://citeseerx.ist.psu.edu/viewdoc/summary?doi=10.1.1.45.4846; Access: 2009/09)), 1994.

[JP94] Jarke, M.; Pohl, K.: *Requirements Engineering in the Year 2001 – (Virtually) Managing a Changing Reality*. Software Engineering, Vol. 9, Nr. 6, p.257-266, 1994.

[JRZ04] Jeckle, M.; Rupp, Ch.; Zengler, B.: *UML 2.0 Neue Möglichkeiten und alte Probleme*. Informatik Spektrum Band 27, Heft 4, pp.323-331, Aug. 2004.

[Ka96] Karsenty, L.: *An empirical evaluation of design rationale documents*. In: Proceedings of the SIGCHI Conference on Human Factors In Computing Systems, ACM, New York, pp.150-155, 1996.

[KCF+04] Klein, T.; Conrad, M.; Fey, I.; Grochtmann, M.: *Modellbasierte Entwicklung eingebetteter Fahrzeugsoftware bei DaimlerChrysler*. Proc. Modellierung, Marburg 2004 (Online version: www.immos-projekt.de/site_immos/download/p3_KCF+04.pdf (Access 2005/11)), pp.31-41, 2004.

[Ke90] Kelley, C.: *Does it fit the bill?* International Journal of General Systems, 18(6), pp.32–34, 1990.

[Ke05] Kelleher, J.: *A Reusable Traceability Framework using Patterns*. In: Proceedings of the 3rd international Workshop on Traceability in Emerging Forms of Software Engineering. TEFSE '05. ACM, New York, NY, pp.50-55, 2005.

[KF09] Kindel, O.; Friedrich, M.: *Softwareentwicklung mit AUTOSAR: Grundlagen, Engineering, Management in der Praxis*. dpunkt.verlag GmbH, Heidelberg, 1. Edition, 2009.

[Ki98] Kirkman, D.P.: Requirement Decomposition and *Traceability*. Journal Requirement Engineering. Vol. 3, No.2, pp.107-114, 1998.

[Kl97] Klein, M.: *An Exception Handling Approach to Enhancing Consistency, Completeness, and Correctness in Collaborative Requirements Capture*. Concurrent Engineering Research and Applications, vol. 5, no. 1, pp.37-46, 1997.

[KM00] Knethen, A.v.; Münch, J.: *Entwicklung eingebetteter Software mit UML: Der Do-It-Prozess V1.0*. SFB-Report No. 05/2000, Sonderforschungsbereich 501, Dept. Of Computer Science, University of Kaiserslautern, 2000.

[KM05] Kempa, M.; Mann, Z.A.: *Model Driven Architecture*. Informatik Spektrum Band 28 Heft 4, pp.298-302, Aug. 2005.

[KM06] Kucera, M.; Mauser, H.: *Semi-Automatic Reliability Assessment of Safety Related Embedded Systems*. Proceedings of the 18th IASTED International Conference on Parallel and Distributed Computing and Systems, Dallas, USA, Nov. 2006.

[Kn74] Knuth, D. E.: *Computer Programming as an Art*. Communications of the ACM Volume 17 Number 12, Dec. 1974.

[Kn01a] Knethen, A.v.: *A Trace Model for System Requirements Changes on Embedded Systems*. Proc. of 4th International Workshop on Principles of SW Evolution; Sept. 2001.

[Kn01b] Knethen, A.v.: *Change-Oriented Requirements Traceability*. Support for Evolution of Embedded Systems; Fraunhofer IRB Verlag, Stuttgart, 2001.

[Kn02] Knethen, A.v.: *Change-Oriented Requirements Traceability. Support for Evolution of Embedded Systems*. Proc. of International Conference on Software Maintenance, Oct 2002, pages 482-485.

[Kn06] Kneuper, R.: *CMMI. Verbesserung von Softwareprozessen mit Capability Maturity Model Integration*. Volume 2, dpunkt Verlag GmbH, Heidelberg, 2006.

[Ko93] Kolodner, J.: *Case-based reasoning*. Morgan Kaufmann, San Mateo, CA, 1993.

[KP02] Knethen, A.v.; Paech, B.: *A Survey on Tracing Approaches in Practice and Research*. IESE Report No. 095.01/E (Online version: http://publica.fraunhofer.de/–eprints/urn:nbn:de:0011-n-91973.pdf; (Access 2008/10)), 2002.

[KR70] Kunz, W.; Rittel, H.W.J.: *Issues as Elements of Information Systems*. Working Paper, No.131, July 1970.

[Kr95] Kruchten, P.: *Architectural Blueprints – The "4+1" View Model of Software Architecture.* IEEE SW 12 (6), pp.42-50, Nov. 1995.

[KR98] Korel, B.; Rilling, J.: *Dynamic Program Slicing Methods.* Information and Software Technology Special Issue on Program Slicing, 40 (11-12), pp.647-659, Dec. 1998.

[Kr99] Kruchten, P.: *Der Rational Unified Process: Eine Einführung.* Addison Wesley, 1999.

[Kr03] Kruchten, P.: *The Rational Unified Process: An Introduction,* Third Edition. Addison-Wesley Professional 2003.

[Kr04] Kruchten, P.: *An Ontology of Architectural Design Decisions in Software-Intensive Systems.* In: 2nd Groningen Workshop Software Variability, pp.54-61, Oct. 2004.

[Kr08] Kruchten, P.: *What do software architects really do?* Journal of Systems and Software. Vol. 81, No. 12, pp.2413-2416, Dec. 2008.

[KRP+93] Klein, M. H.; Ralya, T.; Pollak, B.; Obenza, R.; Harbour, M. G.: *A practitioner's handbook for real-time analysis: Guide to Rate Monotonic Analysis for Real-Time Systems.* Kluwer Academic Publishers, Norwell, MA, USA, 1993.

[KS98] Kotony, G; Sommerville, I.: *Requirements Engineering – Processes and Techniques.* Wiley and Sons, UK 1998.

[KS03] Kossiakoff, A.; Sweet, W.: *Systems Engineering-Principle and Practice.* Jon Wiley and Sons, Inc., 2003.

[KS06] Kelleher, J.; Simonsson, M.: *Utilizing use case classes for requirement and traceability modeling.* Proceedings of the 17th IASTED International Conference on Modeling and Simulation. ACTA Press, pp.617-625, Anaheim, CA, USA, 2006.

[LD01] Lang, M.; Duggan, J.: *A Tool to Support Collaborative Software Requirements Management.* Requirements Engineering. Vol. 6. No. 3, pp.161-172; 2001.

[LDL98] Lamsweerde, A.v.; Darmont, R.; Letier, E.: *Managing Conflicts in Goal-Driven Requirements Engineering.* IEEE Transactions on Software Engineering, Vol. 24, No. 11, pp.908-926, Nov. 1998.

[Le89] Lehman, M.M.: *Uncertainty in computer application and its control through the engineering of software.* Journal of Software Maintenance: Research and Practice, 1(1); Pages 3-27.

[Le90a] Lee, J.: *A Qualitative Decision Management System.* In: Winston, P.H.; Shellard, S. (eds.): Artificial Intelligence at MIT: Expanding Frontiers, Vol.1, MIT Press, Cambridge, MA, pp.104-133, 1990.

[Le90b] Lee, J.: *SIBYL: a Tool for Managing Group Design Rationale.* In Proceedings of the 1990 ACM Conference on Computer-Supported Cooperative Work (CSCW '90). ACM Press, New York, NY, pp.79-92, Oct. 1990.

[Le96] Lehman, M.M.: *Laws of Software Evolution revisited.* In: Montangero, C. (Eds.): Lecture Notes in Computer Science, Vol. 1149. Springer Verlag, London, pp.108-124, 1996.

[Le97] Lee, J.: *Design Rationale Systems: Understanding the Issues.* IEEE Expert 12(3), pp.78-85, 1997.

[Le02] Letelier, P.A.: *A framework for requirements traceability in UML-based projects.* Proceedings of 1st International Workshop on *Traceability* in Emerging Forms of Software Engineering, Edinburgh, UK. September, 2002.

[LF06] Lehman, M.M.; Fernández-Ramil, J.: *The Role and Impact of Assumptions in Software Engineering and its Products.* In: [DMM+06], pp.313-328, 2006.

[Li94] Lindvall; M.: *A study of traceability in object-oriented systems development.* Licenciate thesis, Linköping University, Institute of Technology, Sweden, 1994.

[LK08] Lee, L.; Kruchten, P.: *Visualizing Software Architectural Design Decisions.* ECSA, pp.359-362, 2008.

[LL91] Lee, J.; Lai, K.Y.: *What's in Design Rationale?* Human-Computer Interaction, Vol.6, pp.251-208, 1991.

[LL96] Lee, J.; Lai, K.Y.: *What's in Design Rationale?* In: [MC96], pp.21-51, 1996.

[LL00] Louridas, P.; Loucopoulos, P.: *A Generic Model for Reflective Design.* ACM Transactions on Software Engineering and Methodology, Vol. 9, No. 2, pp.199–237, April 2000.

[LL07] Ludewig, J.; Lichter, H.: *Software Engineering – Grundlage, Menschen, Prozesse, Techniken.* 1. Auflage, dpunkt Verlag GmbH, Heidelberg, 2007.

[LLY+08] Li, Y.; Li, J.; Yang, Y.; Li, M.: *Requirement-Centric Traceability for Change Impact Analysis: A Case Study,* Lecture Notes in Computer Science, Vol. 5007, Springer, pp.100-111, 2008.

[LO95] Leite, J.C.S.P.; Oliveira, A.P.: *A client oriented requirements baseline. Requirements Engineering*. IEEE International Conference on Second IEEE International Symposium on Requirements Engineering (RE'95), pp.108-115, 1995.

[LPP10] Löw, P.; Pabst, R.; Petry, E.: *Funktionale Sicherheit in der Praxis: Anwendung von DIN EN 61508 und ISO/DIS 26262 bei der Entwicklung von Serienprodukten.* 1. Edition, dpunkt Verlag GmbH, Heidelberg, 2010.

[LRB96] Lewis, C.; Rieman, J.; Bells, B.: *Problem-centered design for expressiveness.* In: [MC96], pp.147-184, 1996.

[LR05] Liggesmeyer, P.; Rombach D. (Eds.): *Software Engineering eingebetteter Systeme Grundlagen – Methodik – Anwendungen.* 1. Auflage, Elsevier, 2005.

[LRW¹97] Lehman, M.M.; Ramil, J.F.; Wernick, P.D.; Perry, D.E.; Turski, W.M.: *Metrics and laws of software evolution – The nineties view.* In: Proceedings of the 4th International Software Metrics Symposium. November 5-7, Albuquerque, USA, pp.20-32, 1997.

[LS80] Lientz, B.P.; Swanson, E.B.: *Software Maintenance Management.* Addison-Wesley Longman Publishing Co. Inc., Boston, MA, 1980

[LS98] Lindvall, M.; Sandahl, K.: *How well do experienced software developers predict software change?* Journal of Systems and Software 43 (1), pp.19-27, 1998.

[LW99] Leffingwell, D.; Widrig, D.: *Managing software requirements – A unified approach.* Addison Wesley, Longman, Amsterdam, Nov. 1999.

[Ma08a] Marwedel, P.: *Eingebettete Systeme.* Springer, Berlin Heidelberg, 2008.

[Ma08b] Mader, S.: *Wikipatterns.* Wiley Publishing Inc., Indianapolis 2008.

[Matlab] Mathworks Inc.: Homepage of the Design Tools Matlab Simulink and Matlab Stateflow: http://www.mathworks.de/ (Access: 2010/09).

[MB05] Madachy, R.; Boehm, B.: *Software Dependability Applications In Process Modeling.* In: Acuna, S.T.; Juristo, N. (Eds.): Software Process Modeling, Springer Science+Business Media, Inc., New York, pp.65-86, 2005.

[MBO+92] Mc Call, R.; Benett, P.; d'Oronzio, P; Oswald, J.; Shipman, F.M. III; Wallace, N.: *PHIDIAS: Integrating CAD graphics into dynamic hypertext.* In: Streitz, N.; Rizk, A.; André, J. (eds.): Hypertext: Concepts, Systems and Applications. Cambridge University Press, New York, NY, pp.152-165, 1992.

[MBP+04] Moll, K.; Broy, M.; Pizka, M.; Seifer, T.; Berger, K.; Rausch, A.: *Erfolgreiches Management von Software-Projekten*. Informatik Spektrum Band 27 Heft 5; pp.419-432, Oct. 2004.

[Mc78] McCall, R.: *On the structure and use of issue systems in design*. Doctoral Disseration, University of California, Berkeley 1978.

[Mc79] McCall, R.: *Final Report for Project STIEC (Scientific and Technical Information in the European Community)*. Studiengruppe für Systemforschung, Heidelberg 1979.

[MC96] Moran, T.; Carroll, J. (eds.): *Design Rationale Concepts, Techniques, and Use*. Lawrence Erlbaum Associates, Mahwah NJ, 1996.

[Mc01] McBreen, P.: *Software Craftsmanship: The New Imperative*. First Edition, Addison-Wesley Professional, 2001.

[ME01] Micheli, G.; Ernst, R. (Eds.): *Readings in Hardware/Software Co-Design*. Morgan Kaufmann, 2001.

[MEK03] Müller, G.; Eymann,T.; Kreutzer, M.: *Telematik- und Kommunikationssysteme in der vernetzten Wirtschaft*. Oldenbourg, München, 2003.

[MGE+03] Medvidovic, N.; Gruenbacher, P.; Egyed, A.; Boehm B.W.: *Bridging models across the software lifecycle*. The Journal of Systems and Software 68, pp.199–215, 2003.

[MHD+07] Müller, M.; Hörmann, K.; Dittmann, L.; Zimmer, J.: *Automotive SPICE in der Praxis – Interpretationshilfe für Anwender und Assessoren*. dpunkt Heidelberg, 2007.

[Mi56] Miller, G.: *The Magical Number Seven, Plus or Minus Two*. Psychological Review 63, pp.81-97, 1956.

[MISRA2004] Motor Industry Software Reliability Association: *MISRA-C: Guidelines for the use of the C language in critical systems*, 2004.

[MKS] Homepage of the Application Lifecycle Management Tool Suite MKS: http://www.mks.com/products/requirements (Access: 2010/09).

[MMM+03] Maletic, J.I.; Munson, E.V.; Marcus, A.; Nguyen,T.N.: *Using a Hypertext Model for Traceability Link Conformance Analysis*. Proceedings on *Traceability* in emerging forms of software engineering (TEFSE'03), pp.47-54, 2003.

[Mo04] Moro, M.: *Modellbasierte Qualitätsbewertung von Softwaresystemen.* Doktorarbeit 2004. Books on Demand GmbH; 1. Ed., Dec. 2004.

[MR07] Mohan, K.; Ramesh, B.: *Traceability-Based Knowledge Integration in Group Decision and Negotiation Activities.* Decision Support Systems Vol. 43, Issue 3, pp.968-989, April 2007.

[MSC94] Marshall, C.C.; Shipman, F.M. III; Coombs, J.H.: VIKI: *Spatial Hypertext Supporting Emergent Structure.* Proceedings of the 1994 ACM European conference on Hypermedia technology (ECHT'94) Edinburgh, Scotland, ACM, 1994.

[Mu00] Müller, J.-A.: *Systems Engineering.* Manz-Verlag Schulbuch (Fortis), Wien , 2000.

[Mu04] Muller, G.: *CAFCR: A Multi-View Method for Embedded Systems Architecting; Balancing Genericity and Specificity* Doctors Thesis Technische Universiteit Delft, 2004, (Online version: http://citeseer.ist.psu.edu/muller04cafcr.html (Access: 2007/12).

[Mu06a] Müller, F.: *Das weiche Moment – Der Faktor Mensch in der Softwareentwicklung.* iX 02/06, pp.46-50, 2006.

[Mu06b] Mühlbauer, S.: *Werkzeuge im Anforderungsmanagement.* OBJEKTspektrum RE/2006, (Online version: http://www.sigs-datacom.de/fileadmin/user_upload/ zeitschriften/os/2006/RE/muehlbauer_OS_RE_06.pdf (Access 2010/08)), 2006.

[MW03] McManus, J.J.; Wood-Harper, T.: *Information systems project management: methods, tools and techniques.* Pearson Education, 2003.

[MWS+07] Meng, X.; Wang, Y.; Shi, L.; Wang, F.: *A Process Pattern Language for Agile Methods.* Software Engineering Conference, 2007. APSEC 2007. 14th Asia-Pacific Volume , Issue , 4-7, pp.374-381, Dec. 2007.

[MXP05] Marcus, A.; Xie, X.; Poshyvanyk, D.: *When and how to visualize traceability links?* In: Proceedings of the 3rd International Workshop on Traceability in Emerging Forms of Software Engineering (TEFSE '05). ACM, New York, NY, pp.56-61, 2005.

[MYB+91] Mac Lean, A.; Young, R.M.; Bellotti, V.; Moran, T.: *Question, Option, and Criteria: Elements of Design Space Analysis.* Human-Computer Interaction. Vol. 6, pp.201-250, 1991.

[MZG99] Myers, K.L.; Zumer, N.B.; Garcia, P.E.: *Automated Capture of Rationale for the Detailed Design Process.* In Proceedings of the Eleventh National Conference on Innovative Applications of Artificial Intelligence (IAAI-99), AAAI, Menlo Park, CA, pp.876-883, 1999.

[NBA08] Noppen, J.; Broek, p.v. d.; Aksit, M.: *Software Development with Imperfect Information.* Soft Computing 12; pp.3–28, 2008.

[Ne90] Nelsen, E.D.: *System Engineering and Requirement Allocation.* In: Thayer, R. H.; Dorfman, M., (eds): System and Software Requirements Engineering, Los Alamitos, CA, USA. IEEE Computer Society Press, pp.60–76, 1990.

[NER00] Nuseibeh, B.; Easterbrook, S.; Russo, A.: *Leveraging Inconsistency in Software Development.* IEEE Computer April 2000.

[Ni04] Nierstrasz, O.: *Software Evolution as the Key to Productivity.* In A. Knapp, M. Wirsing and S. Balsamo (Eds.) Radical Innovations of Software and Systems Engineering in the Future, LNCS, vol. 2941, Springer Verlag, pp.274-282, 2004.

[NJJ+96] Nissen, H.W.; Jeusfeld, M.A.; Jarke, M.: *Managing Multiple Requirements Perspectives with Metamodels.* IEEE Software, Vol. 13, No. 2, pp.37-48, 1996.

[NS06] Nguyen, L.; Swatman, P.A.: *Promoting and Supporting Requirements Engineering Creativity.* In: [DMM+06], pp.207-230, 2006.

[Nu01] Nuseibeh, B.: *Weaving together requirements and architectures.* IEEE Computer 34 (3), pp.115-117, 2001.

[OKK+02] Obbink, H., Kruchten, P., Kozaczynski, W., Hilliard, R., Ran, A., Postema, H., Lutz, D., Kazman, R., Tracz, W., Kahane, E.: *Report on Software Architecture Review and Assessment (SARA), Version 1.0.* (Online version: http://philippe.kruchten. com/architecture/SARAv1.pdf (Access: 2010/05)), 2002.

[OM07] Ocampo, A.; Münch, J.: *The REMIS Approach for Rationale-Driven Process Model Evolution.* Lecture Notes in Computer Science, Volume 4470, Springer Berlin / Heidelberg, pp.12-24, 2007.

[OMG] Official Web-Site of the Object Management Group: http://www.omg.org; (Access 2010/09).

[Pa1897] Pareto, V.: *Cours d'économie politique.* Lausanne: Rouge 1897.

[Pa72] Parnas, D.L.: *On the criteria to be used in decomposing systems into models.* Communications of the ACM 15(12), pp.1053-1058, 1972.

[Pa85] Parnas, D.L.: *Software Aspects of Strategic Defense Systems.* Communications of the ACM 28(12), 1326–1335, 1985.

[Pa97] Palmer, J.D.: *Traceability.* In: Thayer, R.H.; Dorfman, M. (Eds.): Software Requirements Engineering, pp.364-374, 1997.

[Pa01] Paulk, M.C.: *Extreme Programming from a CMM Perspective.* IEEE Software, pp.1-8, Nov. Dec. 2001.

[PB88] Potts, C.; Bruns, G.: *Recording the Reasons for Design Decisions.* In: Proceedings of the 10th International Conference on Software Engineering , Singapore, pp.418-427, 1988.

[PBG04] Posch, T.; Birken, K.; Gerdom, M.: *Basiswissen Softwarearchitektur – Verstehen, entwerfen, bewerten und dokumentieren.* dpunkt-Verlag, 2004.

[PCC+93] Paulk, M.; Curtis, B.; Chrissis, M.; Weber, C.: *Capability Maturity Model for Software, Version 1.1,* Technical Report CMU/SEI-93-TR-024, Software Engineering Institute, Carnegie Mellon University, 1993.

[PDJ94] Pohl, K.; Dömges, R.; Jarke, M.: *PRO-ART: PROcess based Approach for Requirements Traceability.* Nature Report Nature-94-07, RWTH Aachen, Informatik V, Germany, 1994.

[PD04] Prado Leite, J.C.S.d.; Doorn, J.H. (Eds.): *Perspectives on Software Requirements,* Kluwer Academic Publishers 2004.

[Pe86] Peter, L.J.: *The Peter Pyramid.* William Morrow,. New York, 1986.

[Pe04] Pettit, R.C. IV: *Lessons Learned Applying UML in Embedded Software Systems Design.* Second IEEE Workshop on Software Technologies for Future Embedded and Ubiquitous Systems 2004

[PG96] Pinheiro, F.A.C.; Goguen, J.A.: *An Object-Oriented Tool for Tracing Requirements.* IEEE Software, Vol. 13, No. 2, pp.52-64, 1996.

[Pi96] Pinheiro, F.A.C.: *Design of a Hyper-Environment for Tracing Object-Oriented Requirements.* Wolfson Collage, Dissertation, University of Oxford, 1996.

[Pi00] Pinheiro, F.A.C.: *Formal and Informal Aspects of Requirements Tracing.* Workshop em Engenharia de Requisitos (WER2000), Rio de Janeiro 2000, (Online version: www.inf.puc-rio.br/~wer00/zip/pinheiro.ps *(Access: 2010/09)),* 2000.

[Pi04] Pinheiro F.A.C.: *Requirements traceability.* IN: [PD04], pp.91-113, 2004.

[PDK+02]. Paech, B. Dutoit, A.H.; Kerkow, D.; Knethen, A.v.: *Functional requirements, non-functional requirements, and architecture should not be separated – A position paper.* International Workshop on Requirements Engineering: Foundation for Software Quality (REFSQ'2002), Essen, Germany, 2002.

[PKD+03] Paech, B.; Knethen, A.v.; Doerr, J.; Bayer, J.; Kerkow, D.; Kolb, R.; Trendowicz, A.; Punter, T.; Dutoit, A.H.: *An Experience-Based Approach for Integrating Architecture and Requirement Engineering.* International Conference on Software Engineering (ICSE 03), Portland, Oregon, pp.142-149, 2003.

[Po58] Polanyi, M.: *Personal Knowledge.* University of Chicago Press, Chicago 1958.

[Po66] Polanyi, M.: *The Tacit Dimension.* Doubleday, New York 1966.

[Po93] Pohl, K.: *The Three Dimensions of Requirements Engineering.* CAiSE '93: Proceedings of Advanced Information Systems Engineering, Springer-Verlag, London, UK, pp.275-292, 1993.

[Po96] Pohl, K.: *Process-Centered Requirements Engineering.* 2nd Edition, John Wiley & Sons, NY, 1996.

[Po99] Pohl, K.: *PRO-ART: A Process Centered Requirements Engineering Environment.* IN: Jarke, M.; Roland, C.; Sutcliffe, A.; Dömges, R. (Eds.)): The NATURE of Requirements Engineering, Shaker Verlag, pp.255-278, 1999.

[Po08] Pohl, K.: *Requirements Engineering – Grundlagen, Prinzipien, Techniken.* 2. korrigierte Auflage, dpunkt Verlag GmbH, Heidelberg, 2008.

[PR09] Pohl, K.; Rupp, Ch.: *Basiswissen Requirements Engineering – Aus- und Weiterbildung zum 'Certified Professional for Requirements Engineering'.* dPunkt Verlag, Heidelberg, 2009.

[PS05] Pohl, K.; Sikora, E.: *Requirements Engineering für eingebettete Systeme.* In [LR05], pp.101-140, 2005.

[PSS04] Paech, B.; Santen, T.; Schlingloff, H.: *Abschlussbericht QUASAR: Integrierte Qualitätssicherung und Anforderungsanalyse zur Softwareentwicklung im Umfeld Fahrzeug,* IESE-Report, 063.04/D, Kaiserslautern, (Online version: http://publica. fraunhofer.de/eprints/urn:nbn:de:0011-n-215843.pdf (Access: 2010/04)), 2004.

[PT93] Potts, C.; Takahashi, K.: *An Active Hypertext Model for System Requirements.* In: Proceedings of the 7th International Workshop on Software Specification and Design (Redondo Beach, California, December 06-07, 1993). IEEE Computer Society Press, Los Alamitos, CA, pp.62-68, 1993.

[PU99] Prechelt, L.; Unger, B.: *Methodik und Ergebnisse einer Experimentreihe ueber Entwurfsmuster*. In: Informatik Spektrum 14 Nr. 3, March 1999.

[PV96] Pena-Mora, F.; Vadhavkar, S.: *Augmenting Design Patterns with Design Rationale*. Artificial Intelligence for Engineering Design, Analysis, and Manufacturing, Vol. 11, pp.93-108, 1996.

[PWG+93] Paulk, M.; Weber, C.; Garcia, S.; Chrissis, M.; Bush, M.: *Key practices of the Capability Maturity Model, Version 1.1*. Technical Report CMU/SEI-93-TR-025, Software Engineering Institute, Carnegie Mellon University, 1993.

[Py78] Pye, D.: *The Nature and Aesthetics of Design*. The Herbert Press, London 1978.

[Ra98] Ramesh, B.: *Factors influencing requirements traceability practice*. Communications of the ACM, 41(12), pp.37-44, 1998.

[RD92] Ramesh. B.; Dhar, V.: *Supporting Systems Development by Capturing Deliberations During Requirements Engineering*. IEEE Transactions on Software Engineering. Vol. 18, No. 6, June 1992.

[RD98] Reichert, M.; Dadam, P.: *ADEPTflex – Supporting Dynamic Changes of Workflows Without Losing Control*. Journal of Intelligent Information Systems Vol. 10, pp.93-129, 1998.

[RE93] Ramesh, B.; Edwards, M.: *Issues in the Development of a Requirements Model*. In: Proceedings of IEEE International Symposium on Requirements Engineering, IEEE Computer Society Press, Los Alamitos, CA, USA, pp.256-259, 1993.

[Re97] Reenskaug, T.: *Why Programmers don't use Methods and what we can do about it.* ObjectEXPERT Jan. 1997, (Online version: http://heim.ifi.uio.no/~trygver/1997/Why/970329why.pdf (Access: 2006/11)), 1997.

[Re02] Reißing, R.: *Bewertung der Qualität objektorientierter Entwürfe*. Göttingen: CuvillierVerlag, 2002.

[REQTIFY] Homepage of the Traceability Tool Reqtify: http://www.geensoft.com/en/article/reqtify/ (Access: 2010/09).

[RHAPSODY] Homepage of the UML Desgin Tool IBM Rational Rhapsody Architect for Software: http://www-142.ibm.com/software/products/de/de/ratirhaparchforsoft/ (Access: 2010/09).

[Ri72] Rittel, H.W.J.: *On the planning crisis: Systems analysis of the first and second generations*. Bedriftsokonomen, Norway, 8, pp.390-396, 1972.

[Ri06] Riebisch, M.: *Prozess der Architektur- und Komponentenentwicklung.* In: Reusser, R.; Hasselbring, W. (Eds.): Handbuch der Software-Architektur. dpunkt, Heidelberg, pp.65-88, 2006.

[RJ01] Ramesh, B.; Jarke, M.: *Towards Reference Models for Requirements Traceability.* IEEE Transactions on Software Engineering, Vol.27, No.1, January, pp.58-93, 2001.

[RLV06] Roeller, R.; Lago, P.; Vliet, H.v.: *Recovering architectural assumptions.* Journal of Systems and Software 79, pp.552-573, 2006.

[Ro01] Rothlauf, J.: *Total Quality Management in Theorie und Praxis.* R. Oldenbourg Verlag München Wien, 2001.

[RPP04] Riebisch, M.; Philippow, I.; Pashov, I.: *Integration von Feature Modellen in die evolutionäre Weiterentwicklung von Software Produktlinien Architekturen.* Technische Universität Ilmenau, 2004.

[RR99] Robertson, S.; Robertson, J.: *Mastering the Requirements Process.* Addison Wesley Professional, Reading MA, 1999.

[RS92] Reeves, B.; Shipman, F.M. III: *Supporting Communication between Designers with Artifact-Centered Evolving Information Spaces.* In: Proceedings of the 1992 ACM Conference on Computer-Supported Cooperative Work, Nov. 1-4, Toronto, Ontario, Canada, pp.394-401, 1992.

[RS02] Rupp, C.; Sophist Group: *Requirements-Engineering und Management.* Carl Hanser Verlag München, 2002.

[RS07] Rupp, C.; die Sophisten: *Requirements-Engineering und Management – Professionelle, Iterative Anforderungsanalyse für die Praxis.* Carl Hanser Verlag München 2007.

[RTM02] Ramesh, B.; Tiwana, A.; Mohan, K.: *Supporting Information Product and Service Families with Traceability.* In: Proceedings of 4th Workshop on Product Family Engineering (PFE-4), pp.353-363, 2002.

[Ru02] Rupp, C.: *Requirements and Psychology.* IEEE Software May/June, pp.16-18, 2002.

[RW73] Rittel, H.J.; Webber, M.M.: *Dilemmas in a General Theory of Planning.* Policy Sciences Vol. 4, Elsevier Scientific Publishing Company Inc., Amsterdam, pp.155-169, 1973.

[RW84] Rittel, H.J.; Webber, M.M.: *Planning Problems are Wicked Problems*. In: Cross, N. (ed.): Developments in Design Methodology, Chichester,. Wiley, New York, pp.135-144, 1984.

[RWA07] Rochimah, S.; Wan Kadir, W.; Abdullah, A.: *An Evaluation of Traceability Approaches to Support Software Evolution*. International Conference on Software Engineering Advances (ICSEA), 2007.

[RUP+90] Ramamoorthy, C.V.; Usuda, Y.; Prakash, A.; Tsai, W.T.: *The Evolution Support Environment System*. IEEE Transactions on Software Engineering, 16(11), pp.1225-1234, 1990.

[Sa92] Sage, A.: *Systems Engineering*. John Wiley & Sons, Oct. 1992.

[SA96] Sharrock, W.; Anderson, R.: *Organizational Innovation and the Articulation of the Design Space*. In: [MC96], pp.429-452, 1996.

[Sa05] Santen, T.: *Formale Entwicklungsmethoden und Analysetechniken*. In: [LR05], pp.249-280, 2005.

[Sa06] Salem, A.M.: *Improving Software Quality through Requirements Traceability Models*. In: IEEE International Conference on Computer Systems and Applications, 2006, pp.1159-1162, 2006.

[SBJ+98] Stevens, R.; Brook, P.; Jackson, K.; Arnold, St.: *Systems Engineering: Coping with Complexity*. Prentice Hall, May 1998.

[SC04] Sousa, G.; Castro, J.: *Improving the Separation of Non-Functional Concerns in Requirement Artifacts*. 12th IEEE International Requirements Engineering Conference (RE'04), pp.350-351, 2004.

[SCB+04] Settimi, R.; Cleland-Huang, J.; Ben Khadra, O.; Mody, J.; Lukasik, W.; DePalma, C.: *Supporting Software Evolution through Dynamically Retrieving Traces to UML Artifacts*. Proceedings of the 7th International Workshop on Principles of Software Evolution (IWPSE'04), pp.49-54, 2004.

[Sch83] Schön, D.A.: *The Reflective Practitioner: How Professionals Think in Action*. Temple Smith, London, 1983.

[Sch85] Schön, D.A.: *The Design Studio: An Exploration of its Traditions and Potentials*. London: RIBA Publications Limited, 1985.

[Sch87] Schön, D.A.: *Educating the Reflective Practitioner: Toward a New Design for Teaching and Learning in the Professions*. Jossey-Bass, San Francisco, 1987.

[Sch99] Schefe, P.: *Softwaretechnik und Erkenntnistheorie.* In: Informatik Spektrum 22, pp.122–135, 1999.

[Sch00] Schmidt, M.: *Implementing the IEEE Software Engineering Standards.* Sams Publishing, 2000.

[Sch02] Schienmann, B.: *Kontinuierliches Anforderungsmanagement: Prozesse – Techniken – Werkzeuge.* Addison-Wesley, München, 2002.

[Sch05] Scholz, P.: *Softwareentwicklung eingebetteter Systeme.* Springer 1st Edition, April 2005.

[Sch06] Schneider, K.: *Rationale as a By-Product.* In: [DMM+06], pp.91-109, 2006.

[Sch07] Schulmeister, R.: *Grundlagen hypermedialer Lernsysteme.* 4. Auflage, Oldenbourg, München, 2007.

[SE96] Stienen, H.; Engelmann, F.: *Die BOOTSTRAP-Methode zur Bewertung und Verbesserung der Software-Entwicklung.* Wirtschaftsinformatik, Heft 6, pp.609-624, 1996.

[SG96] Shaw, M.; Garlan, D.: *Software Architecture: Perspectives on an Emerging Discipline.* Prentice Hall, 1996.

[Sh03] Shamonsky, D. J.: *Tactile, Spatial Interfaces for Computer-Aided Design – Superimposing physical media and computation.* Massachusetts Institute of Technology (Online version: http://dorthee.com/thesis.html (Access: 2009/05)), 2003.

[SHB91] Steigerwald, R.; Hughes, G.; Berzins, V.: *CAPS as a Requirements Engineering Tool.* In Proceedings of the Conference on Tri-Ada '91: Today's Accomplishments; Tomorrow's Expectations (TRI-Ada '91). ACM, NY, pp.75-83, 1991.

[SHT89] Streitz, N.A.; Hannemann, J.; Thüring, M.: *From Ideas and Arguments to Hyperdocuments: Travelling through Activity Spaces.* In: Proceedings of the 2nd ACM Conference on Hypertext (Hypertext'89), pp.343-364, 1989.

[SHH+92] Streitz, N.; Haake, J.; Hannemann, J. Lemke, A.; Schuler, W.; Schütt, H.; Thüring, M.: *SEPIA: A Cooperative Hypermedia Authoring Environment.* Proceedings of ACM Conference on Hypertext (ECHT'92), Milano, pp.11–22, 1992.

[Si96] Simon, H.: *The Sciences of the Artificial.* MIT Press, Third Edition, 1996.

[Si98] Silva, A.: *Across Version/Variant Requirement Traceability in Avionics Software Development and Testing.* Proceedings DASIA 98. – Data Systems In Aerospace – (SP-422). ESA. 1998, pp.215-221. Paris, France, 1998

[Si06] Simon, F.: *Einführung in Systemtheorie und Konstruktivismus.* Carl-Auer-Systeme, Heidelberg, 2006.

[SM99a] Shipman, F.M. III; Marshall, C.: *Formality Considered Harmful: Experiences, Emerging Themes, and Directions on the Use of Formal Representations in Interactive Systems.* Computer Supported Cooperation Work (CSCW) Vol. 8, No.4, pp.333-352, 1999.

[SM99b] Shipman, F.M. III; McCall, R.: *Incremental Formalization with the Hyper-Object Substrate.* ACM Transactions on Information Systems 17, pp.199-227, 1999.

[Sm99c] Smith, D. D.: *Designing Maintainable Software.* Springer-Verlag, 1999.

[So01] Sommerville, I.: *Software Engineering.* 6. Auflage; Addison Wesley, München, 2001.

[So07] Sommerville, I.: *Software Engineering.* 8. aktualisierte Auflage; Addison Wesley, München, 2007.

[Sp02] Spanoudakis, G.: *Plausible and Adaptive Requirement Traceability Structures.* In: Proc. 14th International Conference on Software Engineering and Knowledge Engineering, 2002.

[SR09] Sage, A. P.; Rouse, W. B.: *Handbook of Systems Engineering and Management.* Jon Wiley & Sons, Inc. New Jersey, 2009.

[SS97] Sommerville, I.; Sawyer, P.: *Requirements Engineering: A Good Practice Guide.* John Wiley & Sons, 1997.

[SS07] Schneider, K.; Stapel, K.: *Informationsflussanalyse für angemessene dokumentation und verbesserte Kommunikation.* In Software Engineering 2007 (SE 2007), Lecture Notes in Informatics, Vol. 105, pp.263-264, 2007.

[St73] Stachowiak, H.: *Allgemeine Modelltheorie.* Springer-Verlag, Wien, 1973.

[St95] Standish Group: *Chaos Report 1995.* (Online version: http://www.projectsmart.co.uk/docs/chaos_report.pdf (Access: 2009/08)), 1995.

[St01] Standish International Group: *Extreme Chaos.* (Online version: http://www.standish group.com/sample_research/PDFpages/q3-spotlight.pdf (Access: 2008/06)), 2001.

[St04] Stein, S.: *Emergenz in der Softwareentwicklung – bereits verwirklicht oder Chance?* Diplomarbeit 2004 (Online version: http://emergenz.hpfsc.de/da_sstein.pdf (Access: 2008/10)), 2004.

[St05] Starke, G.: *Effektive Software-Architekturen – Ein praktischer Leitfaden.* 2. aktualisierte und erweiterte Auflage, Carl Hanser Verlag, München, 2005.

[Su01] Suh, N.P.: *Axiomatic Design: Advances and Applications.* Oxford University Press, 2001.

[SV08] Santos Soares, M.d.; Vrancken, J.: Model-driven user requirements specification using SysML. Journal of Software, Vol.3, No.6, June 2008, pp.57-68, 2008.

[SWG+08] Schmied, J.; Wenzel, P.-R.; Gerdom, M.; Hehn, U.: *Mit CMMI Prozesse verbessern! – Umsetzungsstrategien am Beispiel Requirements Engineering.* 1. Auflage, dpunkt Verlag GmbH, Heidelberg, 2008.

[SYSML] *Systems Modeling Language v.1.2, 2010.* OMG adopted specification, June 2010, (Online version: http://www.sysml.org/docs/specs/OMGSysML-v1.2-10-06-02.pdf, (Access 2010/09)), 2010.

[SZP04] Spanoudakis, G.; Zisman, A.; Perez-Minana, E.; Krause, P.: *Rule-Based Generation of Requirements Traceability Relations.* Journal of Systems and Software, Vol. 72(2), pp.105-127, 2004.

[SZ06] Schäuffele, J.; Zurawka, T.: *Automotive Software Engineering: Grundlagen, Prozesse, Methoden und Werkzeuge effizient einsetzen.* 3. Auflage; Vieweg Friedrich & Sohn Verlag, 2006.

[TAU] Homepage of the Design Tool IBM Rational Tau: http://www-01.ibm.com/software/awdtools/tau/ (Access: 2010/09).

[TA05] Tyree, J.; Akerman, A.: *Architecture Decisions: Demystifying Architecture.* IEEE SW, Vol. 22(2), pp.19-27, 2005.

[TAG+05] Tang, A.; Ali Babar, M.; Gorton, I.; Han, J.: *A Survey of the Use and Documentation of Architecture Design Rationale.* In: Proc. of 5th Working IEEE/IFIP Conference on Software Architecture (WICSA'05), 2005.

[TBI04] Technical Board International Council on Systems Engineering (INCOSE): *Systems Engineering Handbook.* Version 2a, June 2004.

[TCS98] Thurner, E.; Cin, M.D; Schneeweiß, W.: *Verlaeßlichkeitsbewertung komplexer Systeme.* In: Informatik Spektrum 21, Nr. 6, June, 1998.

[Te96] Tenner, E.: *Why things bite back: technology and the revenge of unintended consequences.* Vintage, New York, 1996.

[Te01] Tewari, A.: *Modern Control Design with MATLAB and SIMULINK.* John Wiley and Sons Ltd. 2001.

[Ti89] Tilbury, A.J.M.: *Enabling software traceability.* In IEE Colloquium on 'The Application of Computer Aided Software Engineering Tools', pages 7/1–7/4, London, UK. IEE, 1989.

[TJH07] Tang, A.; Jin, Y.; Han, J.: *A rationale-based architecture model for design traceability and reasoning.* Journals of Systems and Software Vol. 80 (6), pp.918-934, June 2007.

[TKT+07] Turban, B.; Kucera, M.; Tsakpinis, A.; Wolff, C.: *An Integrated Decision Model for Efficient Requirement Traceability In SPICE Compliant Development.* Paper presented at the WISES 2007. Fifth Workshop on Intelligent Solutions in Embedded Systems, pp.273-286, 2007.

[TKT+08] Turban, B.; Kucera, M; Tsakpinis, A.; Wolff, Ch.: *Erweiterte Traceability zwischen Anforderungen und Design.* Embedded Software Engineering Kongress, Sindelfingen, Dec. 2008.

[TKT+09] Turban, B., Kucera, M., Tsakpinis, A., Wolff, C.: *Bridging The Requirements To Design Traceability Gap.* In: M., Natividad; R. Seepold (Eds.): Intelligent Technical Systems. Series: Lecture Notes in Electrical Engineering, Vol. 38, 2009.

[TM00] Tsumaki, T.; Morisawa, Y.: *A framework of requirements tracing using UML.* Proceedings of 7th Asia-Pacific Software Engineering Conference, Singapore (APSEC'00), Dec. 2000.

[TN97] Tryggeseth, E.; Nytrø, Ø.: *Dynamic Traceability Links Supported by a System Architecture Description.* Proceedings of the International Conference on Software Maintenance (ICSM 97), pp.180-187, 1997.

[To58] Toulmin, S.: *The Uses of Argument.* Cambridge: University Press, 1958.

[TTW07] Turban, B.; Tsakpinis, A.; Wolff, C.: *Ein Entscheidungsmodell für das Tracing von Anforderungen.* In: Software Engineering 2007 (SE 2007), Bonn: Köllen Verlag [Lecture Notes in Informatics, Vol. 105], 2007.

[Tv99] Tvete, B.: *Introducing Efficient Requirements Management. Database and Expert Systems Applications.* International Workshop on 10th International Workshop on Database & Expert Systems Applications, 1999.

[TWT+08] Turban, B.; Wolff, C.; Tsakpinis, A.; Kucera, M.: *A Decision Model for Managing and Communicating Resource Restrictions in Embedded Systems Design.* In: Proc. Sixth IEEE Workshop on Intelligent Solutions in Embedded Systems (WISES 2008), Regensburg, pp.163-174, July 2008.

[UML] Official Web-Site of the UML-Project: http://www.uml.org (Access 2010/05).

[VM02] Veer, G.C.v.d.; Melguizo, M.C.: Mental Models. In: Jacok, J.A.; Sears, A. (Eds.): *The Human-Computer Interaction Handbook: Fundamentals, Evolving Technologies and Emerging Applications.* Lawrence Erlbaum & Associates, pp.52-80, 2002.

[VJN+06] Ven, J.S.v.d.; Jansen, A.G.J.; Nijhus, J.A.G.; Bosch, J.: *Design Decisions: The Bridge between Rationale and Architecture.* In: [DMM+06], pp.329-348, 2006.

[VSH01] Versteegen, G.; Salomon, K.; Heinold, R.: *Change Management bei Software-Projekten.* Springer-Verlag Berlin Heidelberg, 2001.

[WBM94] Witt, B.I.; Baker, F.T.; Merritt, E.W.: *Software Architecture and Design – Principles, Models, and Methods.* Van Nostrand Reinhold, New-York, 1994.

[WC01] Wassenaar, H.J.; Chen, W.: *An Approach to Decision-Based Design.* Proceedings of DETC'01 ASME 2001 Design Engineering Technological Conference, Pittsburgh, PA, Paper No. DETC2001/DTM-21683, 2001.

[We76] Weizenbaum, J.: *Die Macht der Computer und die Ohnmacht der Vernunft.* Suhrkamp, 1976.

[We79] Weiser, M.: *Program Slicing: Formal, Psychological and Practical Investigations of an Automatic Program Abstraction Method.* PhD thesis, The University of Michigan, Ann Arbor, Michigan, 1979.

[We82] Weiser, M.: *Programmers use slices when debugging.* CACM, 25(7), pp.446-452, July 1982.

[We84] Weiser, M..: Program slicing. IEEE Transactions on Software Engineering, 10, pp.352-357, July 1984.

[We06] Weilkiens, T.: *Systems Engineering mit SysML/UML.* dpunkt GmbH, Heidelberg, 2006.

[We07] Weilkiens, T.: *Systems Engineering with SysML/UML: Modeling, Analysis, Design.* Morgan Kaufmann Publishers, Burlington, MA, 2007.

[WH02] Wu, J.; Han, J.: *xmlTRAM+: using XML technology to manage software requirements and architectures.* Proceedings of the 8th Australian World Wide Web Conference (AUSWEB 02), Sunshine Coast, Queensland, Australia, July 2002, pp.237-245, 2002.

[WinWin] Homepage of the Win Win Spiral Model and Tool. Center for Software Engineering University of Southern California: http://sunset.usc.edu/research/WINWIN/winwinspiral.html (Access 2010/08).

[Wi73] Wilson, P.: *Situational relevance. Information Storage Retrieval.* Vol. 9, Issue 8, pp.457-471, 1973.

[Wi95] Wieringa, R.J.: *An introduction to requirements traceability.* Technical Report IR-389, Faculty of Mathematics and Computer Science, University of Vrije, Amsterdam, Sept. 1995.

[Wi98] Wieringa, R.J.: *Traceability and Modularity in Software Design.* Proceedings of 9th International Workshop of Software Specification and Design; Ise-Shina (Isobe), Japan 1998.

[Wi03] Wiegers, K.E.: *Software Requirements.* Microsoft Press, 2003.

[Wi05] Wiegers, K.E.: *Software Requirements.* Microsoft Press, German Translation of [Wi03], 2005.

[Wi06] Wirfs-Brock, R.J.: *Refreshing Patterns.* IEEE SOFTWARE Vol. 23, No. 3 May/June 2006, pp.45-47, 2006.

[WN94] Watkins, R.; Neal, M.: *Why and how of requirements tracing.* IEEE Software July 1994, pp.104-106, 1994.

[Wo79] Woodfield, S.N.: *An experiment on unit increase in problem complexity.* IEEE Transactions on Software Engineering, Mar. 1979.

[WRW+05] Weber, B.; Rinderle, S.; Wild, W.; Reichert, M.: *CCBR–Driven Business Process Evolution.* International Conference on Case-Based Reasoning (ICCBR'05), pp.610-624, Chicago, Aug. 2005.

[WS09] Welsh, K.; Sawyer, P.: *Requirements Tracing to Support Change in Dynamically Adaptive Systems.* Lecture Notes In Computer Science (LNCS), Vol. 5512, Springer, pp.59-73, 2009.

[WV03] Welie, M.v.; Veer, G.C.v.d.: *Pattern Languages in Interaction Design: Structure and Organization: Structure and Organization.* In: Rauterberg, M.; Menozzi, M.; Wesson, J. (Eds.): Proceedings of Interact '03, September, Zürich. IOS Press, pp.527-534, 2003.

[WW02] Weber, M.; Weisbrod, J.: *Requirements Engineering in Automotive Development – Experiences and Challenges.* Proceedings of IEEE Joint International Conference on Requirements Engineering, pp.331-340, 2002.

[WW03] Weber, M.; Weisbrod, J.: *Requirements Engineering in Automotive Development – Experiences and Challenges.* IEEE Software Jan./Feb. 2003, pp.16-24, 2003.

[WWB04] Weber, B.; Wild, W.; Breu, R.: CBRFlow: *Enabling Adaptive Workflow Management Through Conversational Case-Based Reasoning.* Lecture Notes in Computer Science (LNCS), Vol. 3155/2004, pp.89-101, 2004.

[Yo03] Young, R. R.: *Requirements Engineering Handbook.* Artech House Publishers, Boston 2003.

[Yu94] Yu, W.D.: *Verifying software requirements – a requirement tracing methodology and its software tool – RADIX.* IEEE Journal of Selected Areas in Communications, Vol. 12(2), pp.234-240, 1994.

[Zh98] Zhao, J.: *Applying Slicing Technique to Software Architectures.* Fourth IEEE International Conference on Engineering Complex Computer Systems (ICECCS'98), Monterey California, 1998.

Index

abstraction hierarchies 272
aesthetics 15, 69, 71
analysis
  analysis models 44, 195, 214, 219
  software analysis 195, 213
  systems analysis 195, 213
application life-cycle management 214, 237, 241
arbitrary complexity 80, 95, 294
architecture
  4+1 View Model 82, 317, 379
  architectural decision 191, 316
  architectural skeleton 208
  architecture description language 105
  architecture documentation 82, 107, 189, 271, 380, 383
  architecture evaluation 339
  decision model 191
  SW architecture 39, 67, 107, 134
  system architecture 49, 67, 130, 131
  three layer architecture 97, 102, 371
artificial intelligence 175
Automotive SPICE 59, 61, 118, 148
AutoSAR 111, 330
bad smells 71, 89
base practice 145
baseline 125, 136, 269, 288, 368
baselining 239
benefit problem 138, 227
bounded rationality 76, 91, 294, 319
CAN matrix 282

change control board 125, 130, 315
change management 52, 53, 199, 241, 334
CMMI 61, 117, 151, 186
code generation 17, 92, 106, 114, 155, 194, 209, 246, 255
cognitive dissonance 262, 295, 304
complexity 2, 19, 52, 76, 83, 95, 102
complication 77, 247, 262
conceptual integrity 74, 83, 102, 139, 178
configuration management 121, 251
consistency checking 387
consistency maintenance 240
Conway's law 203
crosscutting concerns 97, 299, 381
  design decisions 321
decision trees 192
design
  abstraction 80
  bottom-up design 84
  design theory 79
  detailed design 39, 67, 70, 134, 214
  encapsulation 81
  four variable model 213, 246
  hierarchy 81
  modularization 80
  preliminary design (sketching) 92, 285, 384
  structure 80
  system design 67
  top-down design 83, 94
  view partitioning 81

views 73, 80, 104, 109, 111, 145, 157, 210, 272, 380
design constraint 48, 214
dominoes effect 200, 354
DRY-principle 69, 107, 133, 145
eXtreme Programming 140
flow 91
formal 15, 114, 162, 194
formal methods 194
formality 182
formalization 165, 183
group-think 89, 179, 183
Grudin's principle 181, 244, 258, 263, 319
hierarchic decomposition 73, 77, 111, 212, 272, 380
ilities 35
impact analysis 56, 135, 161, 194, 197
    actual impact set 199
    estimated impact set 199
    starting impact set 199, 324, 355
influence factors assessment 189, 328
informal 72, 163
information retrieval 164, 234, 246, 255
intermediate model 205, 248, 336
intrusiveness 164, 181, 193
knowing-in-action 90, 102, 181, 263, 295, 304, 381
Lastenheft 128
linear 83, 84, 105, 252, 317
model
    abundant properties 13, 139, 255
    descriptive model 14, 45, 105
    essential properties 13, 140
    prescriptive model 14, 105
    preterated properties 13
    pretreated properties 139, 255

model driven development 194, 196, 246
model simulation 112
neuralgic point 262
nonlinear 105, 260, 317
pareto principle 54, 74, 115, 190, 209
patterns 173
    analysis patterns 97
    anti-patterns 69, 99, 103
    architectural patterns 97
    architectural styles 97
    design patterns 98, 102
    formalization 101
    idioms 98
    means 99
    model-view-controller pattern 98
    pattern catalog 101, 173
    pattern language 98, 101
    pattern mining 234
    pattern template 99
    process patterns 98
    requirement patterns 38, 97
    usability patterns 99
permanent work product 205
Pflichtenheft 128, 145
primary change 200, 354
principle of SW uncertainty 316
problem space 26, 92, 104, 142, 313
process model 31, 49, 118, 120, 121
    descriptive process models 139
    prescriptive process models 139
process standard 54
product line 213
product line management 240, 257
R2A
    abstraction hierarchy tree 380
    abstraction layer 272, 381

abstraction node 272, 305, 380
abstraction nodes hierarchy 272, 354
architecture documentation 311
architecture evaluation 339
bottom-up design 309
budgeted resource constraint 310, 336, 340, 343
change effort factor 390
complexity 277
configuration management 382
consistency checking 377
decision model 147, 223, 310, 317, 337, 351, 383
design constraint 310, 315, 340, 343
dribble-down 302, 305, 381, 387
dribble-up 302, 306, 381, 387
impact analysis 136, 189, 353, 384
impact set 356
interactive tracing 353, 357
life-cycle of requiremental item 361
linking 310
meta-data 357
meta-model 371, 374
metric for measuring complexity 340
non-guided tracing 353, 358
patterns 338
prescriptive elements in decision model 323
product line 281, 335
rationale as a by-product 320, 382
requirement 315
requirement dribble process 284, 295, 301, 304, 381

requirement influence scope 220, 299, 305, 382
requiremental item 315, 343, 381
requiremental items taxonomy 383
requirements source document 290
rule engine 377
scaffold (i.e. skeleton) 278, 310
selective tracing 353
semi-formal decision model 320, 323
semi-formal skeleton 223, 327, 383
supplier management 359, 363, 385
top-down design 309
traceability as a by-product 295, 304, 307, 382
variation point 281, 335, 371, 374, 380
views 274, 311, 348, 380, 385
rationale
argumentation schema 173
capture limitations 178
cognitive limitations 178
Compendium 170
descriptive approaches 162
DRL 171
formal representation 163
formalization 163
IBIS 166, 176
informal representation 162
intrusiveness 162
PHI 167
prescriptive approaches 162, 172
QOC 168, 320
rationale as a by-product 180, 184

rationale bearer 163, 181, 185, 262
rationale capture 165
rationale capture problem 179, 185
rationale management system 165
rationale paradox 184
rationale schema 165
rationale seeker 181, 185, 321
RATSpeak 171
retrieval limitations 178
semi-formal representation 162
tame problems 192
usage limitations 178
views 190
RE framework 41, 49, 60, 210, 212, 214
refactoring 52, 66, 294, 297
reflection-in-action 90, 168
requirement influence scope 222
requirement interchange format 240
requirements
    functional requirements 35, 39, 46, 49, 80, 114, 145, 222, 301, 316
    nonfunctional requirements 35, 61, 97, 102, 145, 222, 299
    non-functional requirements 49
requirements specification 217, 271, 290, 336
    views 210
ripple effects 200, 354
safety engineering 151, 185
safety-critical 18, 22, 61, 63, 162, 242
scaffold 162, 277, 278
secondary change 200, 355

semantic gap 104, 213, 220, 248, 252
skeleton 99, 162, 264
software uncertainty principle 54
solution space 26, 83, 104, 127, 130, 142, 213, 313
SPICE 21, 61, 118, 124, 176, 186, 324, 366
    maturity level 119, 137
stable intermediate forms 77, 79, 82, 103, 188, 298, 305
state chart 106, 113, 114, 156
state machine 106, 113, 114
structured analysis 82, 212, 218, 272, 275, 379
structured design 212
supplier management 21, 116
SysML 218, 228, 252, 293, 350
tacit knowledge 50, 79, 90, 102, 104, 181, 182, 188, 295
tame problems 84, 87
temporary work product 205
thinking-in-action 263
total quality management 117
traceability
    automated approaches 219
    backward traceability 207, 215
    benefit problem 242, 304, 382
    bidirectional traceability 150, 215, 238
    conceptual trace model 201, 204, 372, 383
    dependency analysis 198, 211, 217, 253, 389
    evolutionary traceability 60, 214, 239, 251
    explicit relationships 216
    forward traceability 207, 215
    functional traces 221
    horizontal traceability 59, 151

implicit relationships 216
interactive tracing 232
intrusiveness 244
linking 105, 142, 145, 213, 218, 221, 239, 252
name mapping 107, 138, 217, 219, 255, 287
nonfunctional traces 204, 221, 227
non-guided tracing 232
refinement 211
requirements fan-out 254, 269, 305, 389
satisfy-link 228, 252, 294, 323, 344
selective tracing 232
surrogate module 250
tool couplings 232, 249
trace definition 193, 204, 230
trace extraction 193, 232, 353
trace production 193, 216, 231
traceability analysis 198
traceability as a by-product 216, 232, 245, 263
traceability environment
circularity problem 233

traceability matrix 207, 218, 221, 239, 256
traceability patterns 229
traceability process 229
traceability reference model 201, 223, 372
vertical traceability 59, 151
UML 66, 111, 349
adoption in practice 154
MARTE profile 351
meta-model 112, 210
object constraint language 210, 373
semi-formal semantics 252
UML Profile for Schedulability Performance and Time 349
UML Profile for Schedulability, Performance, and Time 223
use case 45, 252
views 82, 210, 275
use case 214, 239
validation 114
V-cycle process model 151
verification 115
wicked problems 84, 86, 90, 95, 167, 299